The Founding Fathers

ALSO BY CHARLES W. MEISTER
AND FROM MCFARLAND

Chekhov Criticism, 1880 Through 1986 (1988)

Chekhov Bibliography: Works in English by and about Anton Chekhov; American, British and Canadian Performances (1985)

Dramatic Criticism: A History (1985)

Year of the Lord (1983)

The Founding Fathers

Charles W. Meister

McFarland & Company, Inc., Publishers
Jefferson, North Carolina, and London

The present work is a reprint of the library bound edition of
The Founding Fathers, first published in 1987 by McFarland.

LIBRARY OF CONGRESS CATALOGUING-IN-PUBLICATION DATA

Meister, Charles W., 1917–
 The founding fathers / Charles W. Meister.
  p. cm.
 Includes bibliographical references and index.

 ISBN 978-0-7864-6759-4
 softcover : acid free paper

 1. United States—Constitution—Signers. 2. United States.
Constitutional Convention (1787) 3. United States—Politics
and government—1783–1789. I. Title.
E302.5.M45 2012
973.3'092'2   87-42514

BRITISH LIBRARY CATALOGUING DATA ARE AVAILABLE

© 1987 Charles W. Meister. All rights reserved

*No part of this book may be reproduced or transmitted in any form
or by any means, electronic or mechanical, including photocopying
or recording, or by any information storage and retrieval system,
without permission in writing from the publisher.*

On the cover: Howard Chandler Christy, *Signing of the Constitution*, oil on canvas, 20' × 30', 1940; located in the United States Capitol, House wing, east stairway; background image is Article 1 of the United States Constitution

Manufactured in the United States of America

McFarland & Company, Inc., Publishers
 Box 611, Jefferson, North Carolina 28640
 www.mcfarlandpub.com

To the Reader

It is fitting, in the bicentennial year of 1987, not only to recall the main events of the Constitutional Convention of 1787 but also to recount the highlights of the lives of the leading framers of that great document.

Of the 55 delegates who attended the Convention, a mere handful stand out as having made the chief contributions to the new charter of government. This book shows precisely which ideas came from these leaders. Benjamin Franklin, Alexander Hamilton, and George Washington are included not so much for their work at the Convention as for their great influence in shaping the ideals and institutions of the new nation. Other great Americans, like John Adams, John Hancock, Patrick Henry, Thomas Jefferson, and Thomas Paine, are not included because they had no direct hand in the shaping of the Constitution.

Biographical details for the selected framers generally illuminate matters bearing directly or indirectly upon their contributions to the Constitution and their activity in or ideas about government.

Here we will see how one framer drew up the American federal court system, and how another, as president of Congress, invited a German prince to come to the United States to be the king of the nation. We shall find out which framer's portraits were popular in England during the Revolutionary War, and which one had a five-year love affair with a woman who came to his office seeking financial aid. One framer told Jefferson that they should not prescribe textbooks for students at the University of Virginia, and another, as president, told a Moslem country that the United States was not a Christian nation. One man, after making some of the most important contributions, refused to sign the Constitution, and another, between the years 1791 and 1795, turned down positions as commander of the army, Supreme Court justice, secretary of war, and secretary of state.

A wooden-legged man was the greatest lover among the framers, and another, who believed in a world federation of nations, was a fugitive from justice at the time of his death. One framer, invited to be the chief speaker at a bridge dedication, gave a one-sentence address and then went home. Another was fired as secretary of state by Washington in what was that great man's gravest political error. Still another, given dictatorial powers by his state under one-man rule, disciplined himself to act solely in the interests of his constituents.

Clearly, then, here are men who were human but whose aggregate contribution achieved what was probably the world's greatest political document. The federal Constitution has served as the foundation for the rise of the United States and has been copied as a model by many other nations. The men who achieved what Washington called "the miracle at Philadelphia" are the substance of this book.

Table of Contents

To the Reader	v
1. The Miracle at Philadelphia	1
2. The Great Compromise	27
3. Oliver Ellsworth: The Education of a Connecticut Yankee	47
4. Benjamin Franklin: The World Recognizes an American	68
5. Nathaniel Gorham: The Voice of Business	95
6. Alexander Hamilton: A Portrait in Paradox	112
7. James Madison: Political Theorist Turned Pragmatist	141
8. George Mason: Champion of Human Rights	173
9. Gouverneur Morris: Witty and Aristocratic Lothario	191
10. Charles Cotesworth Pinckney: The Soldier and Patriot	212
11. Edmund Randolph: The Conscientious Moderate	240
12. John Rutledge: The Benevolent Dictator	269
13. Roger Sherman: The Awkward Clear-Headed Yankee	292
14. George Washington: The One Indispensable Man	312
15. James Wilson: The Capitalist and World Citizen	348
16. The Founding Fathers Today	374
References	395
Bibliography	407
Index	411

1. The Miracle at Philadelphia

It was July 4, 1787. George Washington was troubled. It looked as if there could be no united nation after all. Following a number of painful compromises, the Constitutional Convention had come, in the words of one delegate, to a full stop.

As president of the Convention, Washington wondered what he could do. Try as he might to unify the group, he found built-in discord among the members. Large state versus small state, North versus South, free versus slave, manufacturing versus agricultural—the cleavages seemed too numerous and too profound.

He wrote to a friend that he despaired of any favorable solution and regretted having ever come to Philadelphia.

It was a hot summer day. Despite the closed windows (so that no news would be released prematurely), flies buzzed incessantly and bit calves exposed by knee breeches. The long harangue by Luther Martin a few days previously had exhausted everyone's patience. Apparently Martin believed that the new government should be framed for states rather than for individuals, but it took him nearly two sessions to say so.

White-haired Benjamin Franklin had moved on June 28 that sessions open with a prayer. The small progress made in a month of meetings, he said, was "proof of the imperfection of the human understanding." We had sought through ancient history for models of government, he said, and had looked in vain at the constitutions of modern European nations. But why, he asked, have we "not once thought of humbly applying to the Father of lights to illuminate our understanding? God governs in the affairs of men. Without his concurring aid we shall succeed in this political building no better than the builders of Babel. What is worse, mankind may hereafter from this unfortunate instance despair of establishing governments by human wisdom and leave it to chance, war, and conquest."[1]

Devoid both of spirit and funds to pay a chaplain, the delegates ignored Franklin's suggestion. The Convention seemed about to dissolve. Alexander Hamilton went home to New York. One delegate, Gouverneur Morris, said that "the fate of America was suspended by a hair."

Despite the holiday, Washington found little to celebrate. He reviewed the events of the past year in his mind. Are we, he felt, going to continue to be thirteen quarrelsome sovereignties, or can we find a way to pull together? Thinking of his army's lack of equipment and clothing, thinking of the near outbreaks of rioting in Philadelphia and Massachusetts, he wondered whether the political sense of America would ever realize that a strong national government must be erected.

"No morn ever dawned more favorably than ours did," he had written to James Madison in 1786, "and no day was ever more clouded than the present! Wisdom and good examples are necessary at this time to rescue the political machine from the impending storm."[2]

His nearest friends had advised him not to go to Philadelphia. David Humphreys said he would be wise not to be associated with the coming failure. His fellow general, Henry Knox, said it was good judgment to avoid "political operations of which there are such various opinions." John Jay called the Convention illegal, since it was not observing the amendment process as prescribed by the existing Articles of Confederation. Even Madison, fearful of signs of shipwreck, thought it might be best for Washington to hold back until there were definite signs that the Convention could succeed. Had he been too rash, ignoring the cautionary signs of his closest confidants?

The crucial issue was whether, in the Senate, the states would have equal votes. That arrangement under the Articles of Confederation had been unsatisfactory. The vote on July 2 broke down to a tie, and so an 11-member committee had been elected to try to resolve the issue. When he saw who had been elected by the delegates, Washington found little reason for optimism. Writing to Hamilton in early July, he said that he could find "but little ground on which the hope of a good establishment can be formed."[3]

Universal Acclaim

Out of this cloud of pessimism came the bright sun of political genius. The Constitution of the United States of America is not only the greatest ever penned, but one of the most significant political documents of all time. Writing in December 1787, John Adams said that "the deliberate union of so great and various a people in such a place is, if not the greatest exertion of human understanding, the greatest single effort of a national deliberation that the world has ever seen."[4] British prime minister William Gladstone called it "the most wonderful work ever struck off at a given time by the brain and purpose of man."[5]

When Holland in 1795 and Switzerland in 1798 set up new governments the United States Constitution was used as a model. Countless nations since then have done likewise, including Australia, Belgium, Brazil, Canada, and the Soviet Union.

Andrew Jackson, putting aside South Carolina's attempt at secession in 1832, reminded that state that "the Constitution forms a government, not a league." Thirty years later Abraham Lincoln's response to the same state was, "As President, I have no eyes but constitutional eyes."

An Englishman called the Constitution "the American royal family," serving the nation as symbols both of union and of national cooperation. Alexis de Tocqueville marvelled at the invisibility of government in the United States: "The administrative power presents nothing either centralized or hierarchical in its Constitution."[6] James Bryce said that the stability of the American government derived from universal acceptance of the Constitution as the supreme law of the land. But despite the power of the national government, Bryce added, this is government by law instead of by personality, the authority of the government being wisely limited so that demagogues cannot use charisma to usurp people's rights.

Walter Bagehot said that the men of Massachusetts could make any government work. But scarcely so — Massachusetts government was extremely ineffective under the Articles of Confederation.

It is hard to exaggerate the importance of that summer's work in Philadelphia. "If," said Clinton Rossiter, "it is admirable for a people to seek independence, fight for survival, or commit itself to the care and feeding of many countries, it is uncommon for a people to resolve to be a nation unlike any other that has ever existed and, in the course of a single season, to lay an almost complete political foundation for its unique form of nationhood."[7]

Later Washington, and then Madison, referred to the Constitutional Conventional as "the miracle at Philadelphia." How had this miracle occurred? A partial answer was given by Douglas Southall Freeman: "The level of leaders' arguments had been so high in the Convention that only the most obtuse of men of small ability had taken the floor often. Nothing had been so inspiring, so mysterious, as the rearing of a constitutional structure, stone by stone, while the eyes of masons had been intent on the course they were laying today, not on the larger design."[8]

America Before 1776

The colonies had much experience in government in colonial times, varying from 167 years in Virginia to 41 years in Georgia. Colonial legislatures reflected their British background. The bicameral legislature, used in 11 colonies, came from English models that originated in the Middle Ages. Immunity of arrest for governmental representatives, except for serious crimes, dates back to the Anglo-Saxon period. Freedom of speech for representatives had been confirmed in the English Bill of Rights in 1689. Colonial laws, charters, and constitutions granted these immunities.

Geographical isolation made colonial governments both detached from England and independent of one another. "From South Carolina it was as easy to go to England as to Boston. Newspapers from London reached Savannah faster than mail sent overland from Massachusetts or Connecticut."[9] John Adams referred to Massachusetts as "our country." John Rutledge, who had been educated in England, said that his first visit to a foreign country came when he arrived in New York. A few years later troops under Washington refused to swear allegiance to the United States, insisting that "New Jersey is our country!" At the time nine infant states still had their own navies.

If colonial legislatures passed questionable laws, colonial courts could declare them unconstitutional by showing a violation of charter. Appeals would go to a Committee for Appeals in the Privy Council, which functioned as a final court, somewhat like the modern Supreme Court.

Following the practice of the mother country, 11 colonies (all but Pennsylvania and Rhode Island) had established churches, meaning that they received taxes for their support. Church vestries assessed tithes, which varied according to the needs of the poor and the demands of building committees. Vestrymen assigned poor children to apprenticeships. Churchwardens brought civil suit against those who missed church, worked on the sabbath, or were drunk or cursed. Masters could not fire pregnant mothers. When Jane Morrison, an indentured servant, had a mulatto child, the court empowered the churchwardens to collect £15 from her, and indenture her for another five years if she refused to pay.

In New England, where non-Anglican churches prevailed, clergymen in their sermons popularized the doctrines of natural rights, the social contract, and resistance to government for the sake of conscience. They also stressed the fundamental principle of American constitutional law, namely, that government, like its citizens, is bound by law, and that when it transcends its authority it breaks the social contract and destroys the government.

Federalism in America was a transplant of British imperialism. Just as the empire, under the crown, united all colonies, so did the new Constitution ultimately come to be the federating mechanism. But the idea was hard learned. As imperialism seemed an unwanted outside authority, so did the new national concept seem to colonies used to governing themselves. Zealous of state prerogatives, they preferred confederation to national union. From the New England Confederation onward, the confederacy had strictly limited authority.

In an effort to placate Indians upon conclusion of the war with France in 1763, Britain sought to guarantee the Indians' rights to land between the Allegheny Mountains and the Mississippi River. This inevitably led to land disputes as the colonists pushed westward. The crown now got involved in land policy, entering an area that, for the most part, colonial assemblies had previously handled.

To help pay for the war that Britain had fought in defense of the colonies, Parliament passed the Stamp Act in 1765. Stamps had to be used on legal papers, college diplomas, packs of cards, newspapers, books, advertisements, and liquor licenses. So incensed were the colonists that even before the law went into effect, the stamp officers had all been forced to resign. Few people bought stamps.

The Stamp Act Congress in New York in 1765 advocated boycott of English goods. By the end of 1765 deliveries of £700,000 worth of British goods had been cancelled by colonial firms, and ultimately some £4,000,000 worth of goods were involved. Since the Stamp Act had been calculated to raise £60,000, it had been a total failure. By early 1766 businesses in 25 British cities (including London, Bristol, and Glasgow) were petitioning Parliament for repeal of the act.

Although the act was repealed in March 1766, Parliament at the same time passed the Declaratory Act, asserting the right of King and Parliament to lay whatever tax they wished upon the colonies. To ensure Parliament's support in his oppressive measures, George III used "gold pills," plain envelopes containing from £50 to £1000, depending upon the member's importance in the anti-American vote.

By 1773 the issues had become clear-cut. Governor Thomas Hutchinson of Massachusetts, loyal to the crown, insisted that "it is impossible there should be two independent legislatures in one and the same state."[10]

The colonists had a ready reply: there are many legislatures in an empire. Each colony has two legislatures: the provincial assembly for internal government, and the imperial assembly, Parliament, for external government. Recent problems, they pointed out, stemmed from the external government interfering in the sphere of the internal government.

That same year intercolonial committees of correspondence were set up to strengthen opposition to the recently passed tea tax. The East India Company wanted the tax repealed, but George III had enough of American impudence. Tea ships were sent to America's four leading ports.

At Charlestown, tea was unloaded to mold in a damp basement. At Philadelphia, citizens persuaded the captain to return his cargo to England. At Boston, a group of patriots disguised as Indians dumped 342 chests of tea into the harbor on the night of December 16, 1773. At New York a gale kept the ships from landing, but later, in April 1774, a mob dumped 18 cases of tea into New York Harbor.

Gouverneur Morris, like Benjamin Franklin, resented destruction of British property, and felt that Parliament had the right to regulate American trade. The crowd might roar out such words as liberty and religion, Morris said, but could not begin to comprehend their meaning.

But even conservatives like Morris had to admit that American merchants must be allowed to make a profit, and that it was getting increasingly difficult to do so. Thus, when New York sent delegates to the First Continental Congress in Philadelphia in September 1774, even Morris's associates, John Jay and James Duane, signed the Continental Association, a pledge to boycott British goods.

England's strategy in 1774 was to punish Massachusetts as an example of what would happen to recalcitrant colonies. The Boston Port Bill closed the harbor except for military supplies. The Quebec Act extended Canada's frontier to the Ohio River. The Massachusetts Government Act suspended the charter of the colony; henceforth Council members would be appointed by the King. The Quartering Act was extended, and the Administration of Justice Act provided that serious crimes would no longer be tried in Massachusetts, but in another colony or in England.

George III could have scarcely devised a better way to unite the colonies. Seeing what was in store for them unless they gave in to what they considered economic exploitation, they were ready for the spark that would ignite the separation movement.

The Articles of Confederation

That spark was provided on April 19, 1775, when British troops fired on American militia at Lexington and Concord. By nightfall there were 49 Americans and 73 British dead. Settlement of differences would no longer be by word but by armament.

When the Continental Congress, in June 1776, appointed a committee to draw up a declaration of independence, it also appointed a committee to draft a "form of confederation." It took five laborious years for the Articles of Confederation to be finally ratified. Meanwhile government had to go on, and so the disunited states acted under the Articles as if they had been approved.

The Articles replaced the king's imperialism as the unifying cement, but lacked the two of his powers which were in greatest dispute: taxation and regulation of trade. Resentful of the king's misuse of these powers, the colonists were reluctant to grant them to the new government. It took 11 years of hardship to demonstrate that when the central government lacks these powers, the nation falls into either anarchic disunity or vast commercial exploitation.

The 13 colonies quickly transformed themselves into states. Eight states composed new constitutions in 1776, and Connecticut and Rhode Island revised their charters to serve as constitutions. In 1777 Georgia and New York adopted constitutions, as did Massachusetts in 1780.

Although the Declaration of Independence posited sovereignty in the people, in practice the new nation followed the mother country in looking to the legislature as the spokesman for the people. "The Americans," in other words, "became almost instant devotees of republicanism in 1776."[11]

The Articles of Confederation thus provided for no executive other than a president of the Congress. The only national courts were those for trial of piracy and felony on the high seas, and for hearing appeals in cases of captured prizes.

Even the powers of the legislature were limited under the Articles. There was no method of compelling a state to carry out the laws of the Continental Congress. The more important powers of Congress required approval by nine states. Amendments required unanimous approval of the 13 states. To raise funds, such as to support Washington's army, Congress issued a requisition upon each state in proportion to the value of its privately held land, as well as that figure could be determined. Many states soon were in arrears in paying their requisitions, and Congress could do nothing to ensure payment.

In 1781 a veto by Rhode Island blocked an amendment calling for a 5 percent duty upon imports and prizes. In 1786 New York vetoed an amendment granting Congress permission to levy certain duties and to raise an annual sum of $1,500,000 based on the population of the states.

During the Revolutionary War the British closed their West Indian ports to American trade. After the War Britain excluded this trade through heavy duties, but entered its products into America duty free. It was impossible to get the 13 new states to agree on a navigation act which would keep English merchants from underselling American businessmen.

To make matters worse, states with good ports taxed goods to be shipped to neighbors lacking a good port. Madison said that "New Jersey, placed between Philadelphia and New York, was likened to a cask tapped at both ends, and North Carolina, between Virginia and South Carolina, to a patient bleeding at both arms."[12]

British economic warfare had two effects: it quickly depleted American specie (gold and silver used to pay for foreign goods), and it forced the new Congress to look at national methods of dealing with common commercial problems of the states.

To finance the War, Congress used the following methods (in descending order of importance): bills of credit (loans which circulated as paper money), domestic loans in the form of government bonds, requisitions upon the states, and foreign loans. By 1781 all of these methods had been exhausted. In Congress Gouverneur Morris wrote up the draft of a plan to establish a national bank, the Bank of North America. The purpose of the bank was "to secure private resources to bolster public credit and cement the interest of private business to public finance."[13] This bank, organized by Robert Morris (no relation to Gouverneur Morris) provided valuable financial help to Congress during the closing months of the War.

Separation from England also provided religious problems to the new states. Many Anglican priests fled to England at the outbreak of hostilities. In some states, such as North Carolina, only Anglican clergy could perform marriages and baptisms. "Dissenters, such as Baptists and Presbyterians, whose ranks were rapidly expanding, were refused admission to corporations, were prevented from holding civil and military offices, and were excluded from the universities."[14]

Nearly every church group in America found it necessary to reorganize as a result of the separation. The new state constitutions continued to call for professions of Christian faith in order to hold office and in some cases to vote. Georgia, North Carolina, and South Carolina called for profession of Protestant faith in order to hold public office. Some state constitutions, such as those of Delaware and Massachusetts, empowered the legislature to enforce church attendance. Maryland, Massachusetts, and Rhode Island provided tax funds for churches, but most states forbade the establishment of any one church in the state.

Jean de Crèvecoeur, whose *Letters from an American Farmer* helped interpret the new nation to Europeans, praised American religious tolerance: "Persecution, religious pride, the love of contradiction, are the food of what the world commonly calls religion. These motives have ceased here. Zeal in Europe is confined; here it evaporates in the great distance it has to travel; there it is a grain of powder inclosed."[15]

As America's prospects for a military victory improved, Britain offered to cancel its restrictive legislation. In October 1777 General John Burgoyne surrendered his army at Saratoga. In February 1778 France signed a military treaty with the United States. That same month Lord North got Parliament to pass legislation repealing virtually all acts to which the Americans had objected. The next month America was offered home rule government, the equivalent of dominion status.

But Henry Laurens of South Carolina, president of Congress, said that the United States would settle for no less than independence, and the War continued.

In a mutual assistance pact with France, Spain joined the War on America's side in June 1779. In 1780 Catherine the Great invited European nations to join Russia in an armed neutrality pact. Fearing that Holland might use its West Indian port, St. Eustatius, as a supply base for the United States, Britain captured the island in 1780, and now was fighting France, Holland, Spain, and the United States.

With crucial aid from French land and naval forces, the American army forced the surrender of Lord Cornwallis at Yorktown in September 1781, and the war was virtually over. But the new nation's problems continued. In June 1783 a group of veteran soldiers, disgruntled at not having been paid, marched on the Congress in Philadelphia and drove it to Princeton. Under constant criticism, Congress then moved to Annapolis, then to Trenton, then to New York City.

In 1784 four states sent no delegates to Congress, and three more states, disgusted, withdrew theirs and so Congress, lacking a quorum, disbanded. Virginia separately ratified the peace treaty with England. New Jersey ran its own customs service. Richard Henry Lee, president of Congress in 1785, was a states-rights man who opposed a strong central government.

From October 1785 to May 1786 Congress met on only three days, lacking a quorum on the other days. "By 1785 the government of the United States was a wheedling beggar. The total income of this government in 1786 was less than one-third of the charges for annual interest on the national debt."[16]

The dictionary maker Noah Webster wrote in 1785 that "so long as any individual state has power to defeat the measures of the other twelve, our pretended union is but a name, and our confederation a cobweb."[17] George Washington told Henry Knox in 1785 that "contracted ideas, local pursuits, and absurd jealousy are continually leading us from those great and fundamental principles which are characteristic of wise and powerful nations, and without which we are no more than a rope of sand, and shall as easily be broken."[18]

For all their weaknesses, however, the Articles of Confederation had at least kept the nation alive in its infancy. They had served several functions. They had kept alive the idea of national unity and they had shown that certain important functions of government, such as conducting a war and pursuing foreign relations, were clearly national in character, to be carried out by a central government with adequate powers. The Ordinances of 1784, 1785, and 1787, passed by Congress for the development of the Northwest Territory, showed that a republican form of government could exercise vision, discipline, and fairness in expanding into new lands.

Above all, perhaps, the very failures of the Articles of Confederation made it easy for the framers of the new Constitution to identify areas that needed to be bolstered if the nation were to be secure from enemies, prosperous in its commerce, and fair to its citizens in protecting their civil rights.

Preparation for the Constitutional Convention

From time to time the Continental Congress appointed committees to suggest amendments to the Articles of Confederation, but nothing came of the recommendations. Thomas Paine's pamphlets had spoken of the rights of man, and in 1780 in "Public Good" he said that "our strength and happiness are continental, not provincial."

By 1780 Alexander Hamilton had already outlined a plan of government with a strong central authority. Signing himself "The Continentalist," Hamilton wrote six articles in 1781 and 1782 in which he spelled out his suggestions. On July 4, 1782, he wrote that "there is something diminutive and contemptible in the prospect of a number of petty states, with the appearance only of union, jarring, jealous, and perverse, without any determined direction, weak and insignificant by their dissensions in the eyes of other nations."[19]

A Philadelphia merchant, Pelatiah Webster, printed a pamphlet in 1783 called *A Dissertation on the Political Union and Constitution of the Thirteen United States of America*. Several of Webster's ideas came to be embodied in the Constitution.

Noah Webster, a cousin of Pelatiah's, seeking a federal government strong enough to give him copyright protection for his famous *Blue-Backed Speller*, published in 1785 *A Plan of Policy for Improving the Union of the American States*, in which he asked for the creation of a new national constitution.

River navigation was a problem to the disunited states. Can Maryland, owner of the Potomac River, charge Virginia for the use of it? But careful — since Virginia owned the entrance to the Chesapeake Bay, would she exclude Maryland from access to the Potomac? Representatives from both states met at Mount Vernon in March 1785 and agreed to grant each other reciprocal rights. They also agreed to levy identical import duties against foreign nations.

But other states used the Potomac too, so in November 1785 Maryland called for Delaware and Pennsylvania to join in a four-state meeting. Madison saw his chance and got John Tyler, speaker of the Virginia House and father of the subsequent president, to issue an invitation to all 13 states to attend the meeting at Annapolis, for the purpose of discussing uniform trade regulations.

On September 11, 1786, delegates from Delaware, New Jersey, New York, Pennsylvania, and Virginia met, and decided that there were important defects in the system of federal government "of a nature so serious as to render the situation of the United States delicate and critical, calling for an exertion of the united virtues and wisdom of all the members of the Confederacy."[20]

Although the Annapolis meeting was supposed to confine itself to commercial matters, Hamilton cleverly seized on a phrase in the New Jersey instructions to their delegates: "and other important matters," and got the recommendation to Congress worded that a convention of all thirteen states be held at Philadelphia "on the second Monday of May next, to take in consideration the situation of the United States, to devise such further provisions as shall appear to them necessary to render the Constitution of the federal government adequate to the exigencies of the Union."[21] Congress on February 21, 1787, approved the meeting, and all states except Rhode Island agreed to send delegates. "Rogue Island," said a Boston newspaper in disgust, "should be dropped out of the Union or apportioned to the states which surround her."

Daniel Shays, a War veteran from western Massachusetts, led a revolt of small property owners against foreclosures for overdue debts. When they attempted to seize weapons from the Springfield arsenal in January 1787 they were repulsed, but fear spread that the government would soon succumb to rioting mobs. Washington commiserated: "What a triumph for our enemies, to verify their predictions! What a triumph for the advocates of despotism, to find that we are incapable of governing ourselves, and that systems founded on the basis of equal liberty are merely ideal and fallacious."[22]

That same month Dr. Benjamin Rush wrote that although the American War had ended, the American revolution was just beginning. "Nothing but the first act of the great drama is closed," he said. "It remains yet to establish and perfect our new forms of government, and to prepare the morals and manners of our citizens for these forms of government."[23]

John Adams had been doing just that. In *Thoughts on Government* in 1776 Adams gave a lucid statement of the American Whig philosophy of ordered liberty. His efforts to help produce the Massachusetts constitution had resulted in what was probably the best state document of its kind. In 1787 Adams published the first volume of *A Defence of the Constitutions of Government of the United States of America*. John Dickinson stated that this book "has diffused such excellent principles among us that there is little doubt of our adopting a vigorous and compounded federal legislature."[24]

There was unrest as well as expectation in America in May 1787. Martial law had been declared in Georgia, where the Creek Indians, incited by the Spanish, were preparing to attack Savannah. A rumor said that a seditious group in New York was communicating with the Viceroy of Canada. Massachusetts had just put down the Shays Rebellion. Rhode Island, said Francis Hopkinson, designer of a U.S. flag, was "governed by miscreants." Hopkinson also reported a serious storm brewing in the Southwest about navigation on the Mississippi.

In a letter to a friend, Henry Knox said, "We are verging fast to anarchy. The present Convention is the only means of avoiding the most flagitious evils that ever inflicted three million people."[25]

On the second Sunday in May, the 14th, the only states having delegates present were Pennsylvania and Virginia. There were other conventions that month in Philadelphia, including one of Baptists and another of Presbyterians. The Society of the Cincinnati were meeting, presenting a problem for their president, George Washington, who had told them that he could not attend because of pressing business at Mount Vernon. Other groups meeting were the American Philosophical Society, the Pennsylvania Society for the Abolition of Slavery, and the Society for Political Enquiries, an organization to discuss current issues. The latter three groups, all sponsored by Benjamin Franklin, often met in his home.

Up until May 25, Madison used the time to have the Virginia delegation get familiar with the plan to be presented by Edmund Randolph and to be known as the Virginia Plan. Finally on May 25 there were seven states represented, and so the Convention could begin. The seven states were Delaware, New Jersey, New York, North Carolina, Pennsylvania, South Carolina, and Virginia.

The Delegates to the Constitutional Convention

So rich was America in political leaders that a second convention might have been called of those not in attendance, and the quality would have suffered little. Included in the second group would have been John and Samuel Adams, John Hancock, Patrick Henry, John Jay, Thomas Jefferson, Richard Henry Lee, John Marshall, James Monroe, Thomas Pinckney, and Edward Rutledge.

The delegates who did serve provided all kinds of talents. Connecticut nominated three able lawyers: Oliver Ellsworth, William Samuel Johnson, and Roger Sherman. From Delaware came ex-Congressman Gunning Bedford, Jr.; John Dickinson, chairman of the Congressional committee that had framed the Articles of Confederation, and past president of both Delaware and Pennsylvania; lawyer George Read, signer of the Declaration of Independence; future governor Richard Bassett; and legislator Jacob Broom.

Two of Georgia's delegation, Nathaniel Pendleton and George Walton, never attended the Convention; William Pierce was a businessman; and the other two, both ex-congressmen, were Abraham Baldwin and William Few. Maryland provided its attorney-general, Luther Martin; Dr. James McHenry, who had served as secretary to George Washington; and three ex-congressmen, Daniel Carroll, Daniel of St. Thomas Jenifer, and John Francis Mercer.

The Massachusetts delegation was less distinguished than it might have been. Francis Dana was selected but did not attend. Caleb Strong represented rural interests; Rufus King later became a Congressional leader; Elbridge Gerry, merchant and political leader, had signed both the Declaration of Independence and the Articles of Confederation; and Judge Nathaniel Gorham was the recent president of Congress.

The New Hampshire delegates, ex-Congressman Nicholas Gilman and ex-President John Langdon, arrived very late at the Convention. Their colleagues John Pickering and Benjamin West did not attend. The New Jersey delegation consisted of Chief Justice David Brearley; war hero Captain Jonathan Dayton; William Houston, Princeton mathematics professor; Governor William Livingston; Attorney-General William Paterson; and Abraham Clark, who did not attend.

New York provided Alexander Hamilton; John Lansing, ex-congressman and mayor of Albany; and Judge Robert Yates, who had helped frame the New York constitution. From North Carolina came ex-Congressman William Blount; lawyer William Davie; ex-Governor Alexander Martin; state legislator Richard Spaight; and Dr. Hugh Williamson. South Carolina sent ex-Congressman Pierce Butler; lawyer Charles Pinckney and his cousin, General Charles Cotesworth Pinckney; and ex-Governor John Rutledge. Henry Laurens, former president of Congress, was chosen but did not attend.

The most illustrious delegations came from Pennsylvania and Virginia. Pennsylvania sent George Clymer, signer of the Declaration of Independence; merchant Thomas Fitzsimons; lawyers Jared Ingersoll, Gouverneur Morris, and James Wilson; financier Robert Morris; and president (of Pennsylvania) Benjamin Franklin.

Even with Patrick Henry, Richard Henry Lee, and Thomas Nelson declining to serve, Virginia still had the outstanding delegation. It included Judge John Blair, lawyers George Mason, Edmund Randolph, and George Wythe; Dr. James McClurg; James Madison; and George Washington.

Three-fourths of the delegates had served in the Continental Congress, and 30 of the 55 had seen military service. Their average age, despite Franklin's 81, was 43. Forty had served in state governments, 34 had practiced law, and 20 had helped write state constitutions.

Geographically, they represented every area of the United States except the back country. Because of their mobility, their views were far from provincial. Franklin had lived in Boston, Philadelphia, London, and Paris. Hamilton was 15 when he came from the Leeward Islands to New York. Many Southerners went to college in the North. Charles Cotesworth Pinckney and John Rutledge attended college in England. One-third had studied, worked, or traveled abroad. James Wilson lived in Scotland for his first 23 years. Washington, seldom in Virginia from 1776 to 1783, called himself "a citizen of the great republic of humanity at large."[26]

"The Framers knew that they were special men,"[27] and thus a special *esprit de corps* quickly arose among them. Looking around the room, Washington saw half a dozen men who had voted him into command in 1775, a dozen who had served through campaigns under him, and another dozen who had supported him during the lean years of the Congress.

Dickinson, Johnson, and Rutledge had worked closely together in the Stamp Act Congress. "Yates had studied law with Livingston, Livingston had been a partner of Hamilton, Hamilton had brightened the life of Madison, Madison had swapped books with Williamson, Williamson had done experiments with Franklin, Franklin had been amused by Sherman, Sherman had sold books to Baldwin, Baldwin had talked of the ancients with Johnson, Johnson was an old friend of Gouverneur Morris, and Gouverneur Morris had worked closely with Yates in New York's dark days of 1776–77."[28] Financier Robert Morris had associated closely with at least ten delegates in the early days of Congress, and with another ten in private and public financial transactions. They were quite familiar with one another's strengths, weaknesses, and idiosyncrasies long before the Convention started.

The poor were not represented in the Convention any more than they are in today's Senate. Most delegates were from comfortable to well-off, and a few were wealthy. Even the wealthy, however, like Washington, were land poor, having considerable acreage but little ready cash. The chief land speculators were Gorham, Mason, Robert Morris, Washington, and Wilson.

Small states had few western land holdings. Virginia at one time had all of the Northwest Territory, plus what is now West Virginia and Kentucky. When well-known land speculators argued for large-state power, delegates from Delaware, Maryland, and New Jersey wondered if they had their pocketbooks in mind. Nevertheless, even Charles Beard agreed that delegates represented the economic interests of their constituents rather than their personal interests.[29]

The founding fathers did not believe in "rugged American individualism," nor in the laissez-faire doctrines of Adam Smith. They believed it incumbent upon the government to foster trade and commerce; to build roads, bridges, and canals; and to be alert to the needs and the services required by the people.

At the same time the framers had no blind faith in government by the people. "Democracy" to most delegates meant rule by an ignorant mob. Paterson observed that "the democratic spirit beats high," meaning trouble. Randolph said they needed to "restrain the fury of democracy," and he regretted "the democratic licentiousness of state legislatures."[30]

When they referred to the people, the framers were far from laudatory. Madison said they "are subject to transient impressions." Sherman said that they lacked information and were easily misled. Gouverneur Morris called them "dupes of those who have more knowledge." Hamilton agreed, stating that "the people seldom judge or determine right." Gerry concluded that "our evils flow from the excess of democracy."[31]

Despite these comments, they often showed faith in the people's ability to govern themselves. Madison insisted that the executive should be elected by the people. Gerry and Sherman liked annual elections to the House of Representatives, to give the people a chance to check up on them. Dr. Benjamin Rush probably expressed the views of most framers as he differentiated a republic from a democracy in 1787: "All power is derived from the people. They possess it only on election days. After this, it is the property of their rulers, nor can they exercise it or resume it, unless it is abused."[32]

Although many were rationalists and deists, few were relativistic concerning moral standards. Martin Diamond asserts that "unlike modern 'value-free' social scientists, the Founding Fathers believed that true knowledge of the good and bad in human conduct was possible, and that they themselves possessed sufficient knowledge to discern the really grave defects of popular government and their proper remedies."[33]

The intellectual background of the framers was Whig, going back ultimately to Cicero's ideas on republican government. John Locke in his second treatise, *Of Civil Government* (1690), had expressed the doctrine of the social compact and the natural rights of man. The Swiss jurist Jean Jacques Burlamaqui defended natural law by tracing its origins to God's law as expressed through human reason and moral instincts. French jurist Baron de Montesquieu in *The Spirit of Laws* (1750) gave convincing proof of the requirement that the branches of government in a republic should be separated and balanced.

This Whig consensus postulated certain beliefs: Natural law provides moral standards for individuals and nations. A good society protects man's natural rights to life, liberty, property, and freedom of conscience. The basis of all government is the consent of the governed. The best government is the republican form, since it is chosen by the people, and is representative, responsible, and nonhereditary. The basis of all human society, including government, is private morality.

Although well versed in Roman and English history, the framers were not doctrinaire. "They adapted their principles to the character of the American people while seeking to elevate that people by the persuasion of those principles. They well understood America's unique conditions and potentialities, the enduring needs and aspirations of its people. Finally, they were not the spokesmen of parties. They enjoyed the spirit of detachment which parties cannot suffer to exist."[34]

The framers were conscious of the importance of their mission. Franklin warned that if the Convention "does not do good, it must do harm, as it will show that we have not wisdom enough among us to govern ourselves, and will strengthen the opinion that popular governments cannot long support themselves."[35] Madison agreed, stating that the plan now being studied would "decide forever the fate of republican government." Wilson cautioned that they were providing a Constitution for future generations, and Rutledge said, "We are laying the foundations for a great empire." Mason felt that the Revolution itself was insignificant compared to the influence the document being framed had upon "the happiness or misery of millions yet unborn."[36]

Clinton Rossiter believes it fair to call them "heroes," for they bravely embarked on an uncertain enterprise for purposes larger than the gratification of their own desires: "The Framers shaped history as no other group of Americans has ever done, exactly because they forced a choice that did not have to be made—certainly not then, perhaps not ever."[37]

"In spite of their human shortcomings," says Howard Swiggett, "the leaders were unpurchasable men and as a result possessed of an easy assurance. It was a simple matter for any of them to go anywhere as the equal of any personage in the world. If, after all they had achieved, they were a little more competent than anyone else, it was not to be wondered at."[38]

Thomas Jefferson, the American envoy in Paris, took one look at the list and said it was "an assembly of demi-gods." The French *chargé d'affaires* in Philadelphia, G.W. Otto, justly summarized that "if all the delegates named for this convention are present, we will never have seen, even in Europe, an assembly more respectable for the talents, knowledge, disinterestedness, and patriotism of those who compose it."[39]

The Virginia Plan

On May 25, 1787, delegates from seven states opened the Constitutional Convention in the room above Independence Hall in the Philadelphia State House. To cut down on noise interference, the cobblestone streets were covered with earth. The weather being stormy, Franklin stayed home and thus could not nominate Washington to be president of the Convention. The pleasant task was thus assumed by Robert Morris, seconded by Rutledge, and passed unanimously.

After being ushered to the chair by Robert Morris and Rutledge, Washington modestly accepted, asked indulgence for his unconscious errors, and gave this advice: "If to please the people, we offer what we ourselves disapprove, how can we afterwards defend our work? Let us raise a standard to which the wise and honest can repair. The event is in the hand of God."[40]

Major William Jackson was elected secretary of the Convention. Madison positioned himself strategically in front of Washington and facing the group, so as to take down in his journals the most accurate account of what went on at the Convention.

There were usually no more than 30 of the delegates present at any one time, and never were there more than 11 states represented at once. Of the 55 delegates, 29 attended most sessions, 10 missed several weeks, 12 missed long critical portions, and 4 were absent from most of the convention.

Rhode Island was missed. Thirteen leading Providence merchants wrote to the Convention, regretting their absence and hoping that Rhode Island would suffer no commercial loss from "sister states" on that account. Several weeks later Washington wrote that "Rhode Island still perseveres in that impolitic, unjust, and one might add scandalous conduct which seems to have marked all her public councils of late."[41]

As the Convention began, George Wythe presented the recommendations of the Rules Committee, which were adopted. Only one person could speak at a time. The speaker would address the chair. Members would listen, not read or speak to neighbors. Each state would have one vote. A quorum would be seven states. An item could be reconsidered at a later time, to give delegates a chance to change their votes. Later, the rules were amended to permit a second vote the day after a vote was taken, to give delegates a chance to reflect upon their decisions. Thus progress was slow, but improvements could be added when thought up.

The Convention adopted a rule of secrecy, to protect delegates from criticism, to free them from public pressures, and to permit them to save face in case they wished to change their votes. Madison later said that there would have been no Constitution if the debates had been public. Jefferson, in Paris, was furious that "they began their deliberations by so abominable a precedent as that of tying up the tongues of their members. Nothing can justify this example but the innocence of their intentions, and ignorance of the value of public discussion."[42] Johnson, Mason, and other delegates agreed with Madison's view that "had the members committed themselves publicly at first, they would have afterwards supposed consistency required them to maintain their ground, whereas by secret discussion no man felt himself obliged to retain his opinions any longer than he was satisfied of their propriety and truth, and was open to the force of argument."[43]

Sentries were posted at the doors to prevent entry by nondelegates. Windows were closed in the hot Philadelphia summer to frustrate eavesdroppers. When one anonymous delegate lost his papers one day, Washington angrily chided members to be more careful, and it did not happen again.

The Convention used the familiar parliamentary practice of sitting as a Committee of the Whole. This permitted informal discussion with probing and frequent change of position. Nathaniel Gorham, as chairman of the Committee of the Whole, actually presided over much of the Convention while Washington sat as a Virginia delegate. This practice provided an additional review of the committee's actions when they were formally presented to the Convention for adoption, with Washington presiding.

Fifteen years of public discussion of most of the issues had winnowed out most faulty positions. Thus there were unanimous votes, without much discussion, on such important issues as regulating commerce with foreign nations, the exclusive rights of Congress to coin money, the surrender of fugitive slaves, and the right of Congress to levy taxes for the general welfare and to pass such laws as were "necessary and proper" to carry out its specified powers.

On May 29 Randolph presented the Virginia Plan to the Convention. He summarized the weakness of the nation under the Articles of Confederation: There was insufficient protection from enemies without and from harmful competition within the Union. States violated international treaties. The national government did little to facilitate internal improvements for agriculture, manufacturing, and transportation. Courts of justice were at the mercy of state legislatures.

Randolph's 15 points, most of which had been drawn up by Madison, were as follows:
1. The Articles of Confederation should be amended and enlarged.
2. Representation should be based on population or on contributions.
3. The legislature should have two houses.
4. The first house should be elected by the people.
5. The second house should be elected by the first house, out of persons nominated by state legislatures.
6. The national legislature should be empowered to pass laws wherein "separate states are incompetent," with power of enforcement.
7. An executive should be elected by the legislature, and be ineligible for re-election.
8. A council of revision, consisting of the executive and judges, should have a qualified veto over legislative acts.
9. The judiciary should have one or more supreme tribunals, as well as inferior courts of national scope.
10. New states need not have unanimous approval of the legislature.
11. All state and territory governments should be republican in form.
12. Present Congress should be continued until new articles of union are adopted.
13. The Constitution may be amended without assent of the legislature.
14. All state officers should be bound by oath to support the new Constitution.
15. Ratification of the Constitution, after approval by Congress, should be by state conventions "expressly chosen by the people."

On May 30 Gouverneur Morris moved the consideration of three substitute resolutions:
1. A merely federal union will not achieve the goals of the Articles of Confederation: common defense, security of liberty, and general welfare.
2. No treaties among the states could achieve these goals.
3. Thus, a national government should be established, consisting of a supreme legislature, executive, and judiciary.

Since point 3 subsumed points 1 and 2, attention was given to point 3. After some discussion it passed 6–1, with Connecticut voting against it. The very first vote of the Constitutional Convention violated the call approved by Congress — instead of trying to amend the Articles of Confederation, the Convention would endeavor to draw up a new Constitution calling for a three-part government.

Who Should Elect the Legislature?

Benjamin Franklin, president of the Supreme Executive Council of Pennsylvania (in effect, governor), preferred the unicameral legislature such as Pennsylvania had, but most delegates favored the two-house system that they were accustomed to under the British and in their colonial assemblies, so that part of the Virginia Plan drew little argument.

But who should elect the legislators? Not the people, said Sherman on May 31, for they are too easily misled by demagogues. Gerry agreed with Sherman, but Mason said that the people should elect the representatives to the lower house, "the grand depository of the democratic principle." Wilson agreed with Mason, saying that since the people are the base of a government pyramid, there could not be much structure unless the base was broad. Madison concurred, stating that so much depends upon this house that the whole government is unrepresentative unless the people elect their delegates to it. So the Committee of the Whole voted 6-2-2 for election by the people (New Jersey and South Carolina opposed, Connecticut and Delaware divided).

The Committee reconsidered the issue on June 6. Charles Pinckney opted for state legislatures to select lower-house members, since people seem less fit judges. Gerry reported that the Massachusetts electorate had sometimes chosen criminals and lazy louts. Sherman said that to keep harmony between state and national governments, the choice should be left to state legislatures. Charles Cotesworth Pinckney said that if state legislatures were left out, they would never approve the new Constitution. In places where the population is widely scattered, as in South Carolina, he said, it is impracticable to call for the vote by the people.

But once again the people had their champions. Dickinson said that one branch must be elected by the people, and it should be the lower house. Wilson pointed out that state governments are always preserved in federations, even though the people elect the national representatives. Mason opined that state legislatures were more inept than the people, printing paper money when asked not to by the citizens. Madison felt that the best way to safeguard against the tyranny of the majority was to enlarge the electorate, thereby dividing the national community into so many different interests that no one special interest group could lord it over the others. The motion for election by state legislatures to the lower federal house lost that day by a vote of 3-8.

A final effort by those favoring state legislatures came on June 21. Charles Cotesworth Pinckney said that this method permitted local sovereignty, since the precise method could vary from state to state.

Rutledge agreed, saying that had the present delegates to this Convention been elected by the people, they would have been a far less distinguished group. Sherman said he still preferred to have representatives of the lower house chosen by state legislatures, but if it was the sense of the Convention to give the election to the people, he would accept the Convention's decision.

Hamilton preferred election by the people, lest the states gain too much power. Mason said that this method was the only security for the people's rights. Wilson added that state officials frequently block what is best for the nation. King concurred, fearing that states would be zealous to keep down federal taxes in order to raise taxes for state purposes. Pinckney's motion was defeated 4–6.

On the length of terms for lower-house representatives, Ellsworth, Sherman, and Wilson favored annual elections, and Dickinson, Hamilton, and Madison wanted three-year terms. On June 21 the Convention adopted Randolph's motion for two-year terms by a vote of 7–3–1.

A more spirited debate occurred over who should elect the Senate. On May 31 Randolph said that the Senate was a check upon "the turbulence and follies of democracy." It should thus be a small body, chosen by the national lower house out of persons nominated by state legislatures. Sherman said that each state legislature should elect one member to the national Senate. Wilson said that the people should elect the Senate, perhaps, as in New York, by combining several House districts to form one Senate district. Randolph's motion was voted down in the Committee of the Whole by a vote of 3–7.

Perhaps because of the progress being made to elect the lower house by the people, a big change took place in the next discussion on June 7. Dickinson said that state legislatures were more likely to select distinguished representatives than were the people. Gerry preferred this method as a way to give commercial interests protection from landed interests. Mason said that giving power to state legislatures would protect states from national encroachment. Only Wilson held out for election by the people, stating that if the two houses had different methods of election, there would be dissension between them. The vote in the Committee of the Whole, to have state legislatures choose the Senate, now was approved 10–0.

The final discussion of the issue began on June 25. Charles Pinckney said that state legislatures should select senators. Ellsworth agreed that this would be the best way to insure wisdom in the Senate. Wilson said that the people's interests would best be preserved by giving them the right to select their senators, but a chorus of states'-rights voices—led by Dickinson, Johnson, Mason, and Williamson—overwhelmed him in a

Convention vote of 9-2, with only Pennsylvania and Virginia voting against having state legislatures select senators. And so it remained until Amendment 17 to the Constitution was ratified on May 31, 1913, providing for the election of senators by the people.

How long should be the term of senators? Madison favored nine-year terms, feeling that as America's population grew, "republican principles" had to be protected from the levelling tendency of the vote by the poor. Gorham, however, proposed six-year terms, and the vote carried 7-4.

The Convention in Uproar

The question of proportional representation in the national legislature almost undid the Convention. David Brearley on June 9 said that if Virginia had 16 votes to Georgia's 1, that would be unfair to Georgia but that if Virginia and Georgia each had 1 vote, that would be unfair to Virginia. The remedy he proposed was to take the present map of the United States, erase the existing boundaries, and divide the whole into thirteen equal parts.

William Paterson, also from New Jersey, said that the Convention should stick to its charge and amend the articles for a confederation, not a nation, of sovereign and equal states. If large states contribute more, it is because they have more property to protect. Rather than see New Jersey swallowed up under the proposed national plan, New Jersey would leave the Union.

Wilson, riled, responded that equal numbers of voters should have equal numbers of representatives. One vote per state had not worked under the Articles of Confederation. Unless New Jersey, or any state, is willing to part with some of its sovereignty in order to have a sufficiently strong national government, there is no point to the present Convention.

When the discussion resumed on June 11, Sherman made his proposal for the Great Compromise: the House should be apportioned according to the number of free inhabitants, but in the Senate the states should have equal votes. Pandemonium ensued. Everyone tried to speak at once. Amendments were offered on every side.

Rutledge said that the House should be apportioned on the basis of the amount of money each state paid into the national treasury. Butler, also of South Carolina, made a similar recommendation: states should be represented according to their total wealth. Gerry wanted to know why, if the South was going to count slaves as property, should not the North count horses and cattle?

Peacemaker Franklin rose to his feet. Until now, he said, our debates have been cool and productive. Now, as one side warms up, so does the other. If we are to promote the common good, we must regain our spirit of harmony. We need some type of proportional representation, and with patience we shall determine the proper type. I am reminded, Franklin continued, of how Scotland had feared being swallowed up by England at the Act of Union in 1707. Later, when Lord Bute became prime minister and brought many Scotsmen into the government, it looked as if Jonah had swallowed the whale! States should remember the experience of Scotland: more shall be gained than lost through union. Franklin's wit cooled many rising tempers, but the hard decisions still lay before them.

The New Jersey Plan

On June 14 Paterson asked for time to submit another plan, "a purely federal one," and so the Convention adjourned until the next day. On June 15 Paterson presented the so-called New Jersey Plan. It amended the Articles of Confederation by granting Congress powers to raise money through import duties and a stamp tax, to regulate commerce, and to compel delinquent states to honor requisitions. It had a plural executive elected by Congress, and a supreme court appointed by the executive. The executive were authorized to enforce laws and treaties in the face of state opposition.

Opponents to the New Jersey Plan formed a waiting line. C.C. Pinckney noted that New Jersey had not opposed the previous plan until it thought it would lose an equal vote in the Senate, so perhaps the Virginia Plan was not so bad after all. Wilson wanted to know if a citizen of Delaware would be downgraded to be known as a citizen of the United States of America. In listing the faults of the New Jersey Plan, Wilson said that it had a unicameral legislature, a plural executive, no national lower-court system, and control through a small minority of the legislature.

Randolph showed how his plan was government for individuals rather than for states. Innocent people in uncomplying states need have no coercive action against them. In a financial crisis like the present, he said, when we owe the army, we owe France, and we owe bond-holders, we dare not continue a government that proved that it could not get the job done. Only a national government would have the strength to do what was necessary. "The present is the last moment for establishing one," he felt, adding that if they failed, "the people will yield to despair."[44]

At this point, on June 18, Hamilton rose and instead of discussing either major plan, proposed one of his own in an all-day speech. Feeling that no good executive could ever be selected on republican principles, he advocated a single executive chosen for life, and a Senate chosen for life, during good behavior. The Senate, he said, would be "a permanent barrier against every pernicious innovation, whether attempted on the part of the Crown or of the Commons."[45] No one supported Hamilton's plan and so it was not even discussed by the Convention. Some felt that he had possibly made egregious suggestions intentionally in order to make the Virginia Plan seem more attractive.

On June 19 Madison proposed, point by point, to tear down the New Jersey Plan. How would it prevent states from trespassing upon each other? How would it prevent internal riots and turmoils? How would it protect the nation against foreign powers? When the vote was taken that day the Virginia Plan was preferred over the New Jersey Plan 7-3, with Delaware, New Jersey, and New York voting for the New Jersey Plan.

State vs. National Sovereignty

By now the Convention was taking the form of a debate between proponents and opponents of a strong central government. One delegate who joined proponents like Hamilton and Madison was Rufus King. King showed how limited was the sovereignty of individual states: they could not make war or peace, conclude treaties or alliances, or by themselves raise an army or navy of sufficient size to defend themselves. Since they could not do the first thing demanded of a nation, namely defend their inhabitants, they needed to create a national sovereignty adequate for their defense, and limit themselves to certain stated internal matters.

The opponents replied on June 20. John Lansing of New York asked if someone from Georgia could rule on what is best for someone in New Hampshire. With so many state laws to review, how could the national government ever do a good job of it? Mason asked how the American people, ever zealous of their liberties, could surrender them to Congress? And how would taxes be gathered: would the national army march from state to state to collect delinquent taxes? Luther Martin gave a lengthy diatribe against a bicameral legislature. Also, a national judiciary with authority over the states, he felt, would be both resented and ineffectual. Congress, in his opinion, should represent not the people but the state legislatures.

Representation in the legislature was next discussed on June 28. Madison said that small states need not fear a coalition of large states, which each had different economies; they would be much more likely to compete against one another. Wilson said that equal votes for each state could lead to the "rotten borough" system of Parliament, where Old Sarum sent representatives for a rock!

Sherman declared that if a rich man had more votes than a poor man, the rights of the poor would be forfeited. Johnson asked, why not represent the people in one branch of the legislature and the states in the other branch? Gorham told the small states that they had more to gain through union than the large states, since large states could more readily sustain themselves if there were no union.

Hamilton predicted that if there were no union, small states would soon ally themselves with European powers, thereby losing their liberty. William Pierce of Georgia said that equal votes for states had not worked under the Articles of Confederation. Although he was from a small state, Pierce said that he considered himself a citizen of the United States. Gerry added that we have never had independent states, for none could survive alone. Instead of behaving like brothers, which we are, Gerry said, we are beginning to act like political negotiators.

A vote favoring proportional representation in the lower house then passed by a margin of 9-1 on June 29.

Ellsworth then said, Since we want a government that is partly national and partly federal, now that the lower house exhibits the national part, let us have equal votes in the Senate for the federal part. Baldwin thought that the Senate ought to be apportioned according to property.

The following day Wilson said that just as there was proportional representation in the lower house, so should there be in the Senate, and for the same reasons. Ellsworth disagreed, saying that to act as a check upon the House, it would be better to keep the Senate small, say one member per state.

Growing impatient, Madison wondered why Connecticut had not paid the requisitions asked of it by Congress. We pay what we can afford to pay, Ellsworth replied angrily. What is more, the muster rolls will show that Connecticut provided more troops than Virginia in the past war! Sherman, seeking to calm tempers, said that perhaps the problem was not that Congress had passed the wrong laws but that it had lacked the power to carry them out.

William Davie of North Carolina said that proportional representation would make the Senate unduly large. Embarrassed, Wilson reluctantly agreed.

Once again it was the peacemaker's time to speak. When a table plank doesn't fit, Franklin said, the carpenter takes a little off each side. Franklin then suggested a compromise: Have equal votes in the Senate but have all appropriations apportioned according to sums contributed to the national treasury.

King argued that equal votes in the Senate implied that states were more important than individuals, a position he could not support. What is more, added Jonathan Dayton of New Jersey, why go back to the equal-vote system which has proved itself ineffective?

Gunning Bedford of Delaware was ready with an answer. All things run by self-interest. Small states are struggling to keep from being squeezed out by large states. If that happens, they will align themselves with some foreign power. King was adamant: Let us never hear talk of allying ourselves with foreign powers. We can define the rights of states so clearly that the national government will never be able to invade them.

The ballot for equal votes in the Senate on July 2 showed a deadlock, 5–5–1 (with Georgia divided). C.C. Pinckney suggested that a compromise committee be selected. He said that now he felt that there should be equal votes in the Senate, in order to fairly represent smaller states. In the ensuing discussion, Gouverneur Morris stated that the clash between the House (biased for the poor) and the Senate (biased for the rich) produced the necessary check-and-balance system.

Madison strenuously opposed the appointment of a committee, saying that it would delay proceedings. But a committee was elected by ballot, one from each state, and the 4th of July holiday was spent in recess. The committee members elected were Baldwin, Bedford, Davie, Ellsworth, Franklin, Gerry, Martin, Mason, Paterson, and Yates.

2. The Great Compromise

George Washington had reason to be troubled. In his room at the home of Robert Morris, Washington picked up the list of delegates elected to the compromise committee. Except for Franklin, virtually all on the list represented not only the views of the smaller states but also a concept of government in which the national sovereignty would be so limited that the same old problems would continue: weak defenses, interstate rivalry, insufficient funds for needed roads and canals.

Brandywine, Germantown, Monmouth—was America going to have to go through all this once again? To Washington, the discouraging fact was that the Convention seemed to be switching back to the strong-state, weak-national government framework. Was even the Virginia Plan, so carefully orchestrated by Madison but supported by almost all of the nationalist delegates, going to be reconsidered and defeated? How many lessons would America have to learn before realizing that there could not be one strong state without a strong Union?

Although the committee worked on July 4, the Convention was in recess. The Indian Queen Tavern, on 4th Street near Chestnut, buzzed with excitement. It had become an informal headquarters for the delegates. Here Mason and Madison dined with Rutledge and Charles Pinckney. Gorham and Caleb Strong of Massachusetts discussed issues with Hugh Williamson of North Carolina and Richard Bassett of Delaware. The dinner table became an extension of the Convention floor.

The committee gave its report on July 5. The House was to have one representative for each 40,000 inhabitants; all appropriation measures would originate in the House, not to be altered by the Senate; each state would have an equal vote in the Senate.

The nationalists attacked ferociously. Wilson said that the committee had exceeded its powers. Madison asked, who cares where money bills originate? Either we shall be unjust, he said, in order to please small states, or we shall be just, and displease them. Butler stated that the Senate should represent the states in proportion to property owned by the state.

Gouverneur Morris accused committee members of taking a parochial view. We are here, he said, as representatives of America—in fact, of the whole human race! If we achieve no Union, small states will inevitably be unable to resist being absorbed either by neighboring states or by a foreign power.

Bedford now apologized for his previous threat for small states to align themselves with foreign powers. He meant to state that these states would have to seek some sort of protection. Siding with Bedford, Paterson stated that he felt that Madison and Gouverneur Morris had shown little concern for the problems of the small states.

On July 14 the debate over representation in the Senate resumed. King said that he could not support equal votes in the Senate, that it was better to do nothing than to do what was unjust. Caleb Strong retorted that the small states had conceded on the issue of where money bills could originate; now it was time for the larger states to concede.

Madison gave a host of reasons why, in his opinion, equality of votes in the Senate was wrong: the minority could not only overrule the majority, but could extort for its own measures or obtrude progress in the Congress, because of the Senate's peculiar powers. Moreover, the evil increases as each new state gets an equal vote. Finally, this provision would greatly enhance the North (where there were many small states) at the expense of the South. Wilson once again reminded the Convention to avoid repeating the error of the Articles of Confederation in giving each state one vote.

Ellsworth said that in his experience in Congress, no good measure had ever failed because of the lack of a majority of states supporting it. Is a veto by a majority of states, even granting they are the smallest ones, less democratic than the veto of a single executive, who comes from only one state?

Now the peacemaker was Johnson. The two approaches were, Johnson said, not contradictory but complementary. They were two halves of a unique whole, combined so that "in one branch the people ought to be represented, in the other the states."

Madison was the last of the nationalists to be placated. He felt that here was a principle that could not be compromised.

The vote, so crucial to subsequent American history, was by the narrowest of margins, 5-4-1. Voting for the committee recommendation were Connecticut, Delaware, Maryland, New Jersey, and North Carolina. Opposed were Georgia, Pennsylvania, South Carolina, and Virginia. Massachusetts had a divided vote, and the New York delegates had gone home.

The next nine working days of the Convention were the most harmonious of all. Later Madison told Martin Van Buren that "the threatening contest in the Convention of 1787 did not turn on the degree of power to be granted to the federal government but on the rule by which the states should be represented and vote in the government."[1] Madison told historian George Bancroft that "from the day when every doubt of the right of the smaller states to an equal vote in the Senate was quieted, they exceeded all others in zeal for granting powers to the general government."[2]

There were, nevertheless, sticky topics left to discuss. Does government exist to protect property? Should property-holding be a qualification for voting, or for holding a public office?

Property is the main object of society. So said Gouverneur Morris and Rutledge on July 5, and Butler and King on July 6. Most state constitutions required voters to own property, ranging from £20 in New York to £60 in Massachusetts, but Delaware, New Hampshire, and Pennsylvania had no property requirements for voters.

Franklin resolved this issue quickly. He saw no reason why the voter need own property. He expressed his dislike for everything that, in his words, "tended to debase the spirit of the common people." Some of the greatest rogues he had ever met, he confessed, were the richest rogues. He reminded the delegates of the Scriptural injunction to rulers, that they should hate covetousness. His position was adopted without even a call for a vote.

The only states not requiring that office holders own property were Connecticut and Pennsylvania. In South Carolina the governor needed to own at least £10,000 of property.

In those days poverty very likely meant sloth. Even a poor immigrant, through hard work, could readily acquire land at a reasonable price. The idle rich were virtually nonexistent. America began as a middle-class nation. Jefferson said that here "every one may have land to labor for himself, if he chooses. Everyone, by his property, is interested in law and order. Such men may safely reserve to themselves a wholesome control over their public affairs, and a degree of freedom which in the hands of the *canaille* of the cities of Europe would be instantly perverted to the destruction of everything public and private."[3]

On July 6 Gouverneur Morris restated his view that property, as well as the number of inhabitants, should be the basis for apportioning the Senate. Rutledge so moved. The vote lost, 1-9, with only South Carolina supporting the motion. Remarkably, the Convention went on to not require that public office holders own property.

Slavery

Not so readily solved was the issue concerning slavery. The Confederation Congress in 1783 had established a contribution ratio of five slaves equal to three free inhabitants in setting requisitions to be paid by the states to the federal government. By their contributions, eleven states had already accepted this ratio.

To secure more representation in the House, Butler and C.C. Pinckney argued on July 11 that slaves should count as equals to free citizens. Gerry and Gorham preferred the three-to-five ratio established by Congress. Butler said that since this government is being instituted primarily to protect property, slaves should count equally with free inhabitants.

Wilson raised some embarrassing questions. If blacks are citizens, why not count them one-to-one in assessing requisitions? If they are property, why isn't other property used in computing the number of representatives? Furthermore, there has been some blending of blacks and whites—how should these people be counted? Further discussion was postponed.

On August 21 Luther Martin suggested a tax on imported slaves as a way to discourage a practice inconsistent with the principles of the Revolutionary War. Rutledge replied that religion and humanity have nothing to do with slavery: "Interest alone is the governing principle with nations."[4] The slave trade helps the North as well as the South, Rutledge said. He would make it a state responsibility to subdue slave insurrections.

Compromise was in the air. Ellsworth said that "the morality and wisdom of slavery are considerations belonging to the states themselves."[5] The next day Sherman said that although he himself opposed slavery, he felt that the quickest way to get rid of the evil was to leave it to the involved states.

Mason was not so sanguine. "This infernal traffic," he declared, "originated in the avarice of British merchants. The British government constantly checked the attempts of Virginia to put a stop to it. Slavery discourages arts and manufactures. The poor despise labor when performed by slaves. They produce the most pernicious effects upon manners. Every master of slaves is born a petty tyrant. They bring the judgment of Heaven upon a country."[6]

Ellsworth drily commented, referring to Mason's own slaves, that as he had never owned a slave, he could not judge the effects of slavery upon character. "Let us not intermeddle," he counseled. "As population increases, poor laborers will be so plenty as to render slaves useless. Slavery, in time, will not be a speck in our country."[7]

C.C. Pinckney said that South Carolina and Georgia could not do without slaves. Charles Pinckney remarked that left alone, South Carolina would eventually abolish slavery, but if compelled by the federal government, would pull out of the Union.

Dickinson considered it inadmissible for the Constitution to authorize further importation of slaves. King observed that the topic should be discussed only in a political light, not as a moral issue. Gouverneur Morris suggested appointment of a committee to discuss this matter, as well as the concern of some northern states over a navigation act.

A committee of 11 members reported a compromise on August 24: Congress would do nothing about the slave trade before 1800; Congress could tax imported slaves at average import duty rates; a simple majority (no longer a two-thirds majority) would be sufficient to pass a navigation act. On August 29 this recommendation was adopted, except that the year 1808 was substituted for 1800. Finally, on September 12 a tax limit of $10 was set on each imported slave. An important precedent was being set in that matters affecting the common good, such as slavery, were now the proper realm of the national government.

The Congress

How much pay should legislators get? Not a cent, said Franklin. Nothing for senators, declared C.C. Pinckney—after all, they are expected to be wealthy. Wilson said that Congress should set their own salaries. By no means, said Madison; set the amount in the Constitution. Wilson's view prevailed.

Should congressmen be permitted to hold other offices at the same time? Of course, said Wilson, why discourage merit? Yes, agreed Gorham, for we need not fear corruption, as in England. But the noes carried the day, led by Butler, Gerry, and Mason, with Gerry stating that otherwise there might be an undesirable intermingling of the legislative and executive branches.

How many years of residence in America should be required of congressmen? Gouverneur Morris said that if it takes seven years to learn to be a shoemaker, it ought to take at least 14 years to learn to be a legislator. Butler, a former major in the British army, also wanted a long period of residence, since foreigners might bring ideas dangerous to the American form of government. Mason supported Morris, but Ellsworth and Madison felt it would discourage capable newcomers to America. No residence requirement at all is needed, Franklin and Wilson felt. Franklin said we should be flattered to have immigrants choose America, and should place no impediment in their way. Wilson reminded the delegates that many of Washington's generals had been foreigners, but no one had complained of their loyalty or service. The years of residence were finally set at nine for senators and seven for representatives.

Should Congress have the power to tax? Not articles exported from any state—those taxes should be within the power of the states, said

Mason and John Francis Mercer of Maryland. Madison disagreed, pointing to the current economic warfare between the states. Congress was given the power to tax, but all levies must be uniform throughout the nation.

On August 17 the Convention debated whether Congress or the president should have the power to declare war. Butler thought it should be the president's prerogative. Gerry, shocked, wondered then how they could call themselves a republic. Ellsworth said that there was a big difference between declaring war and concluding peace—it should be easier to get out of war than into it. On the vote to give Congress the power to declare war the result was 8-1 in the affirmative.

The bogie of a large standing army as a threat to the republic colored the debate over the militia. C.C. Pinckney cited an example from the recent war in which dissimilarity among the states' militia had led to disastrous consequences. But common rules will not work, Ellsworth observed; a four shilling fine in New England will get better results than forty lashes elsewhere. Charles Pinckney expressed little faith in a militia, since it could not prevent outbreaks of anarchy. Sherman said that without it, states could not keep law and order.

John Langdon of New Hampshire now served as a peacemaker. The national and state governments are not enemies, he declared on August 23, but are complementary ways of serving the good of the people: "In transferring power from one to the other, I only take out of my left hand what it cannot so well use and put it into my right hand where it can be better used."[8] Congress was then given the authority to call out the militia to suppress insurrections and invasions, reserving to the states the authority to select officers and train the militia according to the manner prescribed by Congress.

The Executive Branch

When the Convention turned its consideration to the nature of the executive, one overpowering fact made the discussion quite objective: the presence of George Washington. "In immediate terms, the problem was non-existent; in other words, everybody knew that under any system devised, George Washington would be President."[9]

Imagine the stature of such a leader, that in this pantheon of political giants, they were unanimous in recognizing their superior! Thus, the immediate pressure of politicking to elect one's local hero was not there, and delegates were free to actually discuss the principle of how best should the executive department be set up.

On June 2 Madison suggested that if the powers of the executive were defined, it would be easier to know whether a single or a plural executive would be best. Those powers he saw as executing the national laws, making appointments, and executing such other powers as prescribed by Congress.

Rutledge stated that to pinpoint responsibility and to gain efficiency, a single executive would be best. Wilson agreed, pointing out that no state had a plural executive. Butler added that if three were appointed, they might become sectional representatives, and so there would be a more unified administration under one executive.

Only Randolph held out for a plural executive, saying they would provide greater coverage, both geographically and in terms of special interests, and that they would be a safeguard against a monarchy. On that topic Wilson quickly retorted that "plurality in the executive would probably produce a tyranny as bad as the thirty tyrants of Athens or the Decemvirs of Rome."[10] On June 4 the Convention voted 7-3 for a single executive, and this recommendation was never changed.

A great speech by Franklin, moving that the executive should not be paid, proved to be a dead end. Since people are moved greatly by ambition and avarice, Franklin said, some persons "will move heaven and earth" to get this job. But the kind of leaders we seek — wise, kind, and lovers of peace and order — do not seek a post for the salary involved. "Have we not seen our general," with a wave at the chair, "a patriot whom I will not now offend by any other praise," serve without pay "through fatigues and distresses, with the common anxieties peculiar to his station?"[11] Franklin felt that America would surely always have at least three or four men with both ability and public spirit.

Hamilton seconded Franklin's motion. Madison's notes record that "no debate ensued. The proposition was treated with great respect but rather for the author of it than from any apparent conviction of its expediency or practicability."[12]

The biggest problem lay in deciding on how the president was to be chosen. Again and again the Convention reconsidered its actions, until a total of 60 ballots had been taken. Five times they voted to have the president appointed by Congress, and once against that method. Once they voted for the president to be selected by electors chosen by the state legislators, and twice they voted against that method.

Should the people elect the president? Even Mason said that would be "as unnatural as to refer a trial of colors to a blind man." Certainly we should educate the people into how to govern themselves, Mason admitted, but too much hangs on the presidency to make it a means of public education. If the outcome of that election depended, said Mason, "upon public debate and discussion of national issues, not reason so much as passion, not candor so much as deception, not statesmanship so much as demagoguery would too often prevail over the public mind. Far from educating the people, such elections would lead to their corruption."[13] It is hard to realize that Mason had not witnessed a television debate between presidential candidates.

On July 25 Madison summarized the findings of the Convention to date on this issue. The judiciary cannot select the president, since they are appointed by a president. The legislature should not select him, for it would split the legislature badly, it would lead to intrigue with candidates, and it would encourage foreign powers to try to control American elections. Selection by state legislatures or state executives would lead to the above weaknesses, and more. Since the Convention had recently decisively rejected the elector system, it seemed that the only method left was direct election by the people.

Ignoring Madison, Charles Pinckney moved election by Congress. Gouverneur Morris guaranteed Pinckney that the resulting intrigue would be unbearable; the best method was election by the people. Not so, declared Gerry. Election by the people simply means election by the best organized special interest group, he said, the group best able to manipulate the people.

The electoral college, as described in Article II, Section 1 of the Constitution, is thus not a Rube Goldberg invention, as John P. Roche has recently named it, but an effort to inoculate this important selective process from the frailties of human nature. Each state has as many electors as congressmen. State legislatures direct how these electors are to be selected. The electors vote, in their states, by ballot for two persons, at least one of whom shall not be a resident of their state. The president of the Senate opens the ballots in the presence of Congress. If there is no majority, the House of Representatives selects the president. (Amendment 12 to the Constitution, approved September 25, 1804, provided for separate ballots for president and vice-president.)

Impeachment of the president drew much consideration. Madison declared that a whole legislature is not likely to be inept or traitorous, but one person could well be. True, said Mason. After all, what man is above justice? Franklin said that in the past, an inept executive was assassinated, depriving him of a chance for vindication. Orderly procedures needed to be set up to protect both the nation and the accused.

On July 20 Gouverneur Morris said he had been swayed by the debate, and he now favored the impeachment process. History shows that even kings can be bribed. Our president is not our king, but the prime minister. The people, he said, are the king.

On September 8 Madison moved that the Supreme Court, rather than the Senate, be the impeachment tribunal. Gouverneur Morris demurred, saying that was too small a tribunal. Sherman said that since the president appoints the justices, he should not be tried by the Supreme Court. Madison's motion died, 2-9.

The Senate was empowered to try all impeachments, with the chief justice of the United States presiding when the president is tried. A two-thirds majority is required for removal from office. (This saved Andrew Johnson in 1868 by one vote.)

One of Madison's favorite ideas was a council of revision, consisting of the executive plus members of the judiciary, acting with the power to negate legislation. Mason liked the idea of giving judges a chance to rule on the constitutionality of an act before it became a law. But the majority of the delegates resented this interference with the executive's prerogatives by giving the judiciary a double check on legislation, so the idea was defeated.

The Judicial Branch

The Virginia Plan called for a national judiciary consisting of one or more supreme tribunals and a series of national inferior courts. Judges were to be chosen by Congress, "to hold their offices during good behavior," with jurisdiction involving foreigners, maritime questions, or concerning "the collection of the national revenue, impeachments of any national officers, and questions which may involve the national peace and harmony."

The biggest question involved the jurisdiction of the national inferior courts. Many delegates felt that the state courts could handle anything not subject to the jurisdiction of the Supreme Court. After heated discussion, a typical compromise was achieved: inferior courts were not required, but Congress was permitted to establish them if they proved to be necessary.

There was some argument over who should appoint federal judges. Gorham suggested a system that had worked well in Massachusetts: appointment by the executive with the advice and consent of the Senate. Mason objected, saying that the president would have too limited a range of knowledge of possible qualified candidates. Gorham replied that legislatures were no more responsible than the executive, for they are full of intrigue and cabal. Sherman preferred appointment by the Senate, for in more men there is more wisdom. Randolph and Bedford agreed with Sherman.

Gorham insisted that responsibility would be focused more clearly on one person, so on July 18 he moved that the president appoint the judiciary with the advice and consent of the Senate. The vote was 4-4.

The issue returned to the agenda on July 21. Gouverneur Morris said that if we can trust the president to be commander-in-chief of the army, we should think him able to appoint judges. I disagree, said Mason; if he can appoint judges, the president will have undue influence over the judiciary. Madison felt that the people's will was better reflected by the president, who was elected by them, than by the Senate, who were selected by state legislatures. So he moved appointment by the president with at least one-third concurrence by the Senate. His motion was voted down, 3–6. Further action had to await a later date.

Separation of Powers

The delegates realized that judges, who were not elected, would be on shaky ground overruling an act passed by the legislature, who were elected. The aim was for a clear enough statement of each principle in the Constitution so that judges who were fair-minded and intelligent could see whether the act was constitutional.

Hamilton, in *The Federalist* No. 81, later clarified this issue. In a difference of opinion as to the constitutionality of a particular case, the Supreme Court had the final say. Although Congress could not overrule that decision, it could pass a law affecting future cases.

As students of Montesquieu and Burlamaqui, the Founding Fathers felt that a "mixed regime" was best, that is, a government with separate branches for making laws, enforcing them, and interpreting them. This regime also represented different classes of people — rich and poor, propertied and unpropertied. One aspect of the mixture was a bicameral legislature, mixing the democracy of the House with the aristocracy of the Senate. Madison stated that where the legislative and executive branches were combined there could be no liberty.

When Sherman listed only a few functions for the national government, Madison quickly added the security of private rights and the uniform dispensation of justice. Many states were doing poorly in these areas, he felt. Some state legislatures were overruling courts, and others were blocking effective executive action. Part of the effectiveness of the new Constitution, he said, would be in making sure that states, in overhauling their constitutions, would be sure to safeguard the rights of their citizens.

As governor of Virginia, Jefferson knew that legislatures can be tyrannical, saying that "173 despots would surely be as oppressive as one."[14] Intrusion of one branch into the prerogative of another undermined the republic, he said.

The check-and-balance system had many applications. Part of this lay in a distrust of democracy, a feeling that if the people really had their way, it might work to their disadvantage. So "cooling off" spots were added between the people and the law. The Senate could check the House of Representatives, and the president could veto acts of Congress, as could the Supreme Court.

Madison saw this system as a protection against government by factions or special interest groups. The process would prevent any one party or view from taking total control of the government. Pluralism in government was a further safeguard — there would be so many factions that no one could long dominate the others.

The unwritten British "Constitution" referred to the division of powers in the English government, checks and balances that, along with common law, existed to preserve the people's liberty.

When the colonial Englishmen became Americans in 1776, the term Constitution came to mean a written, formalized statement of the division of powers, so that there could be no encroachment of one sovereignty upon another, the blend of sovereignties being necessary for safeguarding the people's liberty.

The Constitutional Convention was merely an extension of the English system. James I had postulated the divine right of the king, Charles I the divine right of the lords, and the American Constitution the divine right of the people. When John Adams put the phrase "We, the people" into the Massachusetts constitution in 1780, he said that "it is Locke, Sidney, Rousseau, and de Mably reduced to practice."[15]

Special Committees

On July 26 the Convention elected by ballot an important committee called the Committee of Detail. Elected were Ellsworth, Gorham, Randolph, Rutledge, and Wilson. Their job was to go over all agreed-upon material, systematize it, and return it to the Convention as a preliminary Constitution by August 6. The Convention then recessed until that date.

Washington had few worries now. The elected delegates all had a sense of the need for an adequate central government. True, Ellsworth had spoken for the small states and Rutledge had shown a sectional bias. But all of them had made significant contributions, and the geographical distribution could not have been better: Rutledge came from the deep South, Randolph from the upper South, Wilson from the Middle States, Ellsworth from lower New England, and Gorham from upper New England.

Quite likely Washington relaxed with some of the other delegates at the boarding house of Mrs. Mary House on the corner of 5th and Market streets. Around her dinner table were found such boarders as Madison, Mason, Charles Pinckney, Randolph, and George Read. On the second floor the rooms of Madison and Pinckney adjoined. Read had told fellow Delaware delegate John Dickinson of Pinckney's early draft of a constitution before Dickinson had arrived at the Convention.

On August 6 the Committee of Detail gave its report to the Convention. Starting with the amended Virginia Plan, they had added elements from both the New Jersey Plan and Pinckney's plan. They had also borrowed material from the Articles of Confederation and from various state consitutions, particularly that of New York. Finally, they drew on their familiarity with such earlier works as colonial charters, the Massachusetts Body of Liberties, Connecticut's Fundamental Orders, and Franklin's Plan of Union of 1754.

The result was much of the present form of the Constitution. The report listed 18 specific powers of Congress, plus the authority to make all laws necessary to execute the prescribed powers. State governments were prohibited from such acts as coining money, making treaties, and printing money without the consent of Congress. There would be no export tax by Congress, nor could Congress interfere with the rights of a state to import "such persons" as it considered proper to admit. Criminal trial was to be by jury, and habeas corpus rules maintained except where rebellion or invasion required protection of the public safety.

The Committee of Detail gave the Constitution such key words as president, Senate, House of Representatives, and Supreme Court. Its work, ably chaired by Rutledge and mostly written by Wilson, was accepted by the Convention with few changes.

On August 31 a Committee on Postponed Matters, consisting of 11 delegates, was set up. This committee's work also proved to be very fruitful. They established that the president would be re-electable for four-year terms, and they spelled out the workings of the electoral college. They said that the president, with the advice and consent of the Senate, had the power to make appointments and treaties. The only change that the Convention made in their recommendations was to substitute the House of Representatives in place of the Senate as the body to elect the president when no candidate had a majority of the electoral votes.

The final major committee appointed by the Convention was the Committee of Style and Arrangement, selected on September 8 for the purpose of putting all material under the proper headings and in the language appropriate for a constitution. Once again the five delegates had been felicitously chosen. Johnson made an excellent chairman, having diplomatic manners and a quiet approach that commanded respect. Hamilton and Gouverneur Morris were known to be talented writers.

King was an eloquent orator who, coming to the Convention with misgivings about the national government, had been converted by the force of the logic he had heard. Madison, the fifth member, was universally acknowledged to be the most knowledgable delegate on matters of constitutions and governments.

In this committee chief credit must be given to Gouverneur Morris. Madison said that "the finish given to the style and arrangement fairly belongs to the pen of Mr. Morris."[16] The chief addition made by this committee was the preamble. The famous phrase "We, the people" came, of course from John Adams, but it became a *cause célèbre* as Patrick Henry used it in the Virginia ratification convention as an example of the violation of states' rights, and European democrats began borrowing the phrase as a rallying point in their effort to depose absolutist monarchs.

The language of the Constitution was at once simple and dignified. Caleb Strong in the Massachusetts ratification convention said, "For my part, I think the whole of it is expressed in the plain common language of mankind."[17] On September 12 the draft was adopted by the Convention with few changes.

End of the Convention

Knowing that their work needed flexibility, the delegates provided for ways to amend the Constitution. Madison and Mason felt that Congress need not be the cause of the need for amendment. Nevertheless the Convention approved, on a motion by Gouverneur Morris on August 30, that Congress be empowered to call a convention to consider an amendment, at its own discretion.

Following discussion, the Convention on September 17 approved two methods of amendment: two-thirds of both houses of Congress can propose an amendment, or two-thirds of the state legislatures can ask Congress to call a convention to propose an amendment. In each case, the amendment required ratification by three-quarters of the state legislatures or three-quarters of state ratification conventions.

Madison, in *The Federalist* No. 49, recommended that amendments be rare, for in constant revisions, emotions rather than reason would rule the government, he said, and the process, if overdone, would tend to destroy respect for law.

Methods of Ratification

How should the Constitution be approved by the people? Ellsworth recommended referring it to the state legislatures. By no means, replied Gorham and Randolph, who agreed that local demagogues might oppose it because of the fear of surrendering some of their power to the national authority. Madison said that the people, who were in fact "the fountain of all powers," were the proper ones to approve the document in their state conventions. Mason agreed with Madison, stating that "legislators are the mere creatures of the state constitutions and cannot be greater than their creators. Whither then must we resort? To the people. It is of great moment that this doctrine should be cherished as the basis of free government."[18]

Still suffering from the fact that the Articles of Confederation required unanimous ratification, the delegates adopted the statement that approval by nine states would be sufficient to ratify the Constitution.

Toward the end of the Convention, public curiosity about the document was hard to control. On August 29 the *Pennsylvania Gazette* said that states were neglecting roads and canals, waiting to see whether the national government would take over these responsibilities, and businesses were eager to see if there would be encouragement for them in the new government.

About to adjourn, the Convention received a proposal for a bill of rights from Mason. Submitted too late, it was defeated 10-0. Gorham offered a last-minute change in the figure for apportioning the House of Representatives, from 40,000 to 30,000. Washington deviated from his usual practice and spoke on behalf of the motion, which passed unanimously.

Franklin's final speech was a classic. The older he grew, he confessed, the more he doubted his infallibility, and so he now paid more respect to the opinions of others. He was therefore willing to accept parts of the Constitution which were not of his original preference. He doubted whether any other convention could produce better results, since in every group of persons there is a pooling of not only their wisdom but also their prejudices, errors, and selfish views as a part of their human nature. If we delegates return to our constituents, Franklin said, and merely report what we conceive to be its flaws, the Constitution cannot be accepted, or if accepted, be effective as the basis of our government. He then pleaded for unanimous approval of the Constitution by all of the delegates.

But it was not to be. Randolph, who had wanted a second convention to consider suggestions from the state ratifying conventions, refused to sign, and predicted that the necessary nine states would not ratify the document. Mason abstained on the ground that it should have included a bill of rights. Martin refused to sign, feeling that insufficient concern had been shown for the rights of the states. Gerry said that Massachusetts might well break out in a civil war between democracy, "the worst of all political evils," and its opposition, equally extreme. He would not sign the Constitution, for had it been more conciliatory it might have dampened rather than fed the coming conflagration.

Although the Constitution itself had been approved by all of the state delegations, a total of 16 of the 55 delegates did not sign it. No one delegate got everything he wanted, which was one of the reasons the document was as good as it was. Better to agree on what we can get, knowing that this is an improvement over the Articles of Confederation, most felt, rather than expect some day to produce a perfect document. In Carl Van Doren's words, "it might be possible to give the future world a safe foundation for its house, and leave it to posterity, if it would, to model that house with justice and adorn it with wisdom and goodness."[19]

In his letter to the president of Congress transmitting the Constitution, Washington said that "individuals entering into society must give up a share of liberty to preserve the rest. It is at all times difficult to draw with precision the line between those rights which must be surrendered and those which may be reserved. In all our deliberations on this subject, we kept steadily in our view that which appears to us the greatest interest of every true American, the consolidation of our Union, in which is involved our prosperity, felicity, safety, perhaps our national existence. This led each state to be less rigid on points of inferior magnitude than might have been otherwise expected. And thus the Constitution which we now present is the result of a spirit of amity, and of that mutual concession which the peculiarity of our political situation rendered indispensable."[20]

While the delegates were signing the Constitution, Franklin made his famous comment that he now knew that the sun painted on the back of the Convention president's chair was a rising, not a setting, sun.

When the signing was finished on September 17, many of the delegates went from the State House to the City Tavern for a round of celebratory drinks. There they took leave of each other in the spirit of veteran soldiers who had mutually endured an arduous campaign. Truth to say, the battle was far from over.

Ratification Conventions

Probably the two leading factors in getting the Constitution ratified were Washington and Franklin. Many of the delegates were not known nationally, but in work places, taverns, and churches—the places where public opinion is molded—mention that these two giants favored the new document was probably enough to persuade the vote.

American voters have always been apathetic. Because of indifference, three-quarters of the adult white males in the United States failed to vote in elections held to select delegates to state ratification conventions. Of those who voted, three out of five favored ratification. There was far from a groundswell of approval for the work done that hot summer in Philadelphia.

The chief arguments used against ratification were these: (1) This is an untested and unpredictable form of government. (2) The delegates violated their mandate (to amend the Articles of Confederation). (3) There is no bill of rights guaranteeing individual liberties. (4) This violates the rights of states and threatens their existence. (5) This is a step towards monarchy or aristocracy.

Judging by action taken at state ratifying conventions, the most serious charge was the lack of a bill of rights. Going back to Magna Carta in 1215, Englishmen have zealously protected their rights. Parliament had from time to time passed laws for this purpose, as had colonial assemblies in America. Eight state constitutions contained bills of rights, so Americans had come to expect them as a part of any constitution.

Thomas Jefferson sent Madison his two main objections to the new Constitution in December 1787. Jefferson feared that re-election of the president might make him a lifetime officer, and there was no bill of rights, "what the people are entitled to against every government on earth, and what no just government should refuse or rest on inference."[21]

Speaking on the lack of a bill of rights, Wilson in October 1787 said that "it would have been superfluous and absurd to have stipulated in a federal body of our own creation that we should enjoy those privileges of which we have not been divested."[22] Hamilton, in *The Federalist* No. 84, dated May 28, 1788, said that to single out specific rights would by implication undercut protection for countless other unstated ones. Since a constitution cannot list all rights, why mention some? Bills of rights are needed against monarchs, but people do not need to safeguard themselves against themselves.

Nevertheless, five state ratification conventions passed favorably on the Constitution with the understanding that a bill of rights would be quickly added. Madison made it his first order of business in the new Congress, and Amendments 1–10 became a part of the Constitution on December 15, 1791, when Virginia became the 11th state to ratify them.

The most important part of the ratification process was the appearance of *The Federalist*, written by Hamilton, John Jay, and Madison. Jefferson called this work "the best commentary on the principles of government ever written," and along with many others said that it was the best work for determining the intent of the framers and the ratifiers of the Constitution.

Jay wrote five of the papers, chiefly on foreign relations. Madison wrote 29, specializing in the working of Congress and the relationship between the state and national governments. Hamilton composed the vast majority of them, 51, confining himself largely to the roles of the executive and the judicial branches of the government.

Trying to allay fears of novelty, Madison said in *The Federalist* that "if the new Constitution be examined with accuracy and candor, it will be found that the change which it proposes consists of much less in the addition of new powers to the Union than in the invigoration of its original powers."[23]

The goal of government, Madison said in *The Federalist* No. 51, is justice, which must be pursued constantly in any government founded on the principles of liberty. Sometimes, he continued, people need protection from government itself: "In framing a government which is to be administered by men over men, the great difference lies in this: you must first enable the government to control the governed, and in the next place oblige it to control itself."[24]

The Federalist essays appeared in New York newspapers from October 1787 until May 1788. "All three of the writers might have been irritable under Antifederalist abuse. But they avoided personalities and picayune contentions, raised the whole argument to the highest level of political theory and practice, and followed an order that gave their discussions a cumulative effect."[25] These essays soon took their place as almost a part of the Constitution, since most of them were written by two prominent delegates.

In some states the essays did not appear until after ratification. But their chief influence, in the short run, was upon state ratifiers.

States that had struggled under the Articles of Confederation quickly ratified the Constitution by large margins. Delaware by a vote of 30-0, New Jersey by 38-0, and Georgia by 26-0 were the first states to ratify, along with Pennsylvania, where a steamroller convention produced a 46-23 margin. Other states with comfortable margins were Connecticut at 128-40, Maryland at 63-11, North Carolina at 194-77, and South Carolina at 149-73.

States that were reasonably prosperous felt less reason for a change, as reflected in the closeness of the votes favoring adoption. In Massachusetts the vote was 187-168, in New Hampshire 57-47, New York 30-27, and Virginia 89-79.

In some states the battle for ratification was vicious. Opponents to the Constitution in Virginia were former governor Benjamin Harrison, Patrick Henry, Richard Henry Lee, and future president James Monroe. Henry linked "the tyranny of Philadelphia" to "the tyranny of George III. I believe this similitude will be incontestably proved."[26] Richard Henry Lee said that the Constitution would undoubtedly produce either a monarchy or an aristocracy: "To say that a bad government must be established for fear of anarchy is really saying that we must kill ourselves for fear of dying."[27]

New York ratified only after New York City threatened to secede from the state. In North Carolina rednecked Protestants predicted that the Pope would be elected President, and that Jews, Moslems, and pagans would be encouraged to come to America to seek public office. After rejecting the Constitution at a state convention, North Carolina ratified on November 21, 1789, by which time 12 amendments had already been proposed.

Seven times Rhode Island refused to call a convention, then refused to ratify when the convention finally met, and then eventually ratified on May 29, 1790, when the leading town in the state had seceded and other towns had threatened to follow suit.

Nevertheless, by July 4, 1788, a grand procession was held in Philadelphia, celebrating the ratification of the Constitution. At the end of the parade toasts were drunk, starting with one "to the people of the United States" and ending 13 rounds later with a toast "to the whole family of mankind."

The Achievement

Jean de Crèvecoeur, who had named his daughter America-Frances and had early defined the nation in his classic "What, Then, Is an American?" told Jefferson that upon reading the new Constitution in November 1787, he would be willing to fight for it, or to return to Europe should it fail.

It was, of course, far from perfect. Little attention had been paid to the judicial system, the electoral method of selecting the president was complicated and undemocratic, and there should have been a bill of rights in the original draft. Probably Arthur T. Prescott was right in saying that "they failed to foresee the necessity of a party system, and to guard against its evils. The result was perennial party organizations maintained as ends in themselves by parasitic practices, and producing biennially and quadrennially a crop of candidates who rely more on political jugglery than on the enlightenment of the public. This lack of prophetic insight has made America a stronghold for bosses and spoilsmen."[28]

Clinton Rossiter said that "Virginia, Pennsylvania, Connecticut, South Carolina, and Massachusetts, in that order, produced 95 percent of the thoughts, decisions, and inventive moments that went into the document, and the others were largely along for the ride."[29] Maybe so, but good leadership does not exist without good followership, and there were a mutual stimulation and a cross-pollination of ideas among the entire group that command admiration and respect across the centuries.

For one thing, many states rewrote their constitutions in the aftermath of 1787, often calling on the framers for assistance. Many of the framers had positions of leadership in the new government — who better to put into practice theories hammered out through countless hours of debate?

There were a new optimism and a feeling of confidence under the new Constitution. New York merchants raised $32,000 to refurbish the old City Hall for the inaugural ceremony. American ships began sailing even to India and China. Shipbuilding yards flourished. Southern planters again found world markets for their cotton, rice, and tobacco. In the Middle and Northern states, factories began turning out goods.

Jefferson gave main credit for the economic upturn to the Constitution and the loyalty it inspired in Americans. Former foes of the Constitution were now converted: Samuel Adams, Patrick Henry, the Clintons in New York. Richard Henry Lee became one of Virginia's first senators.

America's finances also improved. By taxing imports, the Treasury raised funds to start paying off debts incurred during the War. United States bonds began to sell above par. New bond issues were readily marketed in London and Amsterdam. Currency began to be stabilized; clipped Spanish doubloons and pieces of eight grew ever more rare.

The Constitution, says Rossiter, "was designed to be the last formal act of the Revolution, and it put the stamp of irrevocable legitimacy on the three great legacies of 1776: independence, republicanism, and union."[30]

How can we account for the great success of the Constitutional Convention? The country was in bad shape — everyone admitted that. Drastic action was needed, and the country was ready to accept it. The things that bound the delegates together were greater than the things that separated them. They were all patriots, Whigs, republicans, with a Lockean view of property.

Respect for Washington was a key factor. Under his watchful eye, "they behaved for the most part in a manner that encouraged frankness, dampened suspicion, soothed hurt feelings, and made compromise a virtue rather than a weakness. The Convention, for all its innate dignity and regard for form, operated as a large committee rather than a small assembly, and it was able to move with a minimum of posing and pouting toward a goal only dimly perceived in the opening days."[31]

One contribution to its success was the rule of secrecy, which kept delegates from the usual stupid and ludicrous and unnecessary efforts to save face. The Convention had good leaders, and most of them had a lot of experience in government. There was scarcely (save for Madison, and possibly Mason and Wilson) a brilliant political theorist in the group. These were people used to making things work. When they reached an impasse, they made excellent use of representative study committees. Despite their justifiable self-assurance, they had the innate modesty to admit that they could learn from their fellows.

As Rossiter summarizes it, they had "a sense of the limits of their wisdom, a consensus of purpose that made it possible for them to keep talking across barricades even in their most gladiatorial moments. Since neither the existence of a religion nor the fortune of a party was at issue, the Framers could afford to set their sights on something less than total victory for the states, sections, and interests they represented."[32]

Alexis de Tocqueville found it refreshing to see a great people turn "a calm and scrutinizing eye" upon a government that had ceased functioning, "carefully examine the extent of the evil," and patiently wait two years for a remedy, "to which it voluntarily submitted without its costing a tear or a drop of blood from mankind."[33]

3. Oliver Ellsworth: The Education of a Connecticut Yankee

A farmer now practicing law, Oliver Ellsworth walked the ten miles from his farm to Hartford when court was in session. From such a simple beginning came the man who would grow into a major Connecticut statesman, a leading framer of the Constitution, Chief Justice of the United States, and the father of the American judicial system. How did he develop from a zealous defender of the sovereignty of his state into the Federalist leader in the Senate, called by John Adams "the finest pillar of Washington's whole administration"?[1]

Ellsworth's great-grandfather had been among the first settlers of Connecticut. His grandfather had been a storekeeper, and his father, a farmer, served as captain in the state militia. The family had always lived in Windsor, just north of Hartford.

On April 29, 1745, Oliver was born, the second son of David and Jemima Ellsworth. Living conditions were primitive in Windsor. There was only one carriage in town. People ate off wooden trenchers. Oliver developed a capacity for hard work by toiling on his father's farm.

An enterprising young man, Oliver rented a farm from his father, and found that he could make more money that way. The Congregational Church was the established church of Connecticut, and father wanted Oliver to become a minister. Thus the young man was schooled by the Reverend Joseph Bellamy, a friend of Jonathan Edwards.

In 1762 Ellsworth entered Yale, where he was more of a mischief maker than a student. The previous year Yale students had rioted and beaten their tutor, Mr. Boardman, with clubs. Students complained that the administration of President Thomas Clap was too strict, and that the food was poor: breakfast for four was a loaf of bread, and supper for four an apple pie and a quart of beer. The classical curriculum also had little appeal for most students.

Ellsworth was frequently disciplined for misconduct. In July 1763 he and ten other students had to "scrape and clean the college yard," perhaps for "having a treat or entertainment last winter." Later, Ellsworth and three classmates, "after evening prayers ran and hallooed in the college yard,"[2] and each was fined one shilling. In 1764 Ellsworth was fined four shillings for having "a general treat or compotation of wine, both common and spiced."[3]

On July 27, 1764, at the request of his parents, Ellsworth was dismissed from Yale. Rumors said that he had filled the inverted college bell with water, and it froze. Further rumors described a college official's coming to Ellsworth's room in search of signs stolen from New Haven merchants, whereupon Ellsworth, knowing that students could not be interrupted while praying, began to pray Matthew 12:39 — "He said unto them, An evil and adulterous generation seeketh after a sign, and there shall be no sign given to it."[4]

Despite what must have seemed like Oliver's unpromising aptitude for the profession, his father insisted that he continue to prepare for the ministry. Princeton, which Ellsworth attended in 1765, had about 100 students, half of whom were students of theology. The curriculum thus had much emphasis on oratory and composition, excellent training for Ellsworth and his classmates fated to serve crucial roles in the Continental Congress and the Constitutional Convention.

Fellow students at Princeton included Gunning Bedford, Hugh Henry Brackenridge, Aaron Burr, Philip Freneau, Henry Lee, James Madison, Luther Martin, William Paterson, and Benjamin Rush. Here Ellsworth made lifelong friendships that paid dividends in subsequent American political history.

Now he was a better student, holding office in both literary and debating societies. Along with Martin and Paterson, he helped found the Well Meaning Club, a debating society that argued the Stamp Act against Madison and Samuel Stanhope Smith of the American Whig Society. Another debate concerned the relations between the colonies and the mother country. He had finally found a relevant college curriculum!

His impishness now had legal ramifications. Called on the carpet for wearing a hat in the college yard, he escaped disciplinary action by showing that since his headgear lacked a brim, it could not technically be classified as a hat.

Still obedient to his father's wish for him to be a clergyman, Ellsworth, upon graduation from Princeton in 1766, spent a year studying theology under Dr. John Smalley of New Britain. Ellsworth's first sermon had a ten-page introduction defining religious terms. Papa and Dr. Smalley agreed — this man is cut out to be a lawyer.

Ellsworth studied law under future governor Roger Griswold, and under Jesse Root of Coventry, with whom he later served in Congress.

Since Blackstone's *Commentaries* were not yet available, the textbooks were Jacob's *Law Dictionary* and Bacon's *Abridgement*, which was 150 years old and had little on the law of contracts and other branches of common law. At the time common law was little used in Connecticut courts, but it grew more popular as there came to be more professionally trained lawyers and judges. Ellsworth had little training in constitutional law, and he had never read much political theory.

But he did attend court sessions, and there is where he learned most of his law. To support himself, he would chop wood at his Windsor farm and haul it for sale to Hartford. He was admitted to the bar in 1771.

Taking stock of his abilities, he realized that he had little knowledge and less imagination. So, like Franklin, he embarked on a course of self-improvement: he decided to concentrate on a subject so intently that he would not even hear a cannon if it went off. As a result, in later years he was accused of being absent-minded, for he would gaze out of a window and mumble to himself about his thoughts. Snuff helped him concentrate, and in time he became noted for his inordinate use of that form of tobacco.

Love now entered Ellsworth's life. He called on the daughter of a leading family of East Windsor, the Wolcotts. But when he saw the dark eyes of her 16-year-old sister Abigail, "demurely carding tow in the chimney corner," his next visit was to see her. They speedily married in 1772. Although she showed little evidence of the great intellectual growth that he evinced throughout life, she was "an uncommonly loving and lovable woman,"[5] and their long life together was filled with domestic felicity.

The Lawyer

By looking at him you could tell that Ellsworth had chopped a lot of wood. At 6'2" he was slim and sinewy, with broad shoulders and erect carriage. He had a large head, with blue eyes and a high forehead. Though perhaps not handsome, "he had the strong jaws, the long chin, the firm lips, the steady eyes, which indicate the man of purpose and persistency."[6]

If he did not seem to offer brilliance, he at least was fully in command of his talents: good work habits, a logical mind, and oratorical eloquence. He was quiet almost to the point of introversion, and secretive in his private life, particularly concerning finances. A typical Yankee, he was both deeply religious and also practical and shrewd.

The farm bought from his father supported the newlyweds better than did his law practice. His law earnings during his first three years totaled £9.[7] He cut and split the rails for a fence around his farm.

Lacking a horse, he walked ten miles to Hartford when court was in session. People made fun of a college graduate who had to chop wood to support himself.

As if in a fairy tale, fame and fortune came fast. By winning a big case in 1773 involving an important legal principle, Ellsworth suddenly had all sorts of clients. He was elected to the Connecticut Assembly in fall 1773, and continued to serve until May 1775. In May 1774 he became justice of the peace for Hartford County, and in 1775 he sold his farm and moved to Hartford, where he could no longer represent Windsor in the Assembly.

But then he was elected to the Assembly from Hartford. Developing a reputation for thrift and financial shrewdness, he served on the Committee of the Pay Table, which managed the state's military finances. He was also a member of the Council of Safety, which shared with the governor the responsibility for all military decisions. When the war broke, he served briefly in the militia but saw no combat.

In February 1776 Ellsworth was sent to the camp of George Washington, to request repayment of money advanced by Connecticut to pay her own troops. Laying siege to Boston, Washington said he had no funds. Ellsworth paid a similarly futile visit to see General Philip Schuyler to recover funds paid to Connecticut troops stationed in Canada. During the first New Jersey campaign, Ellsworth helped recruit troops for General Charles Lee. Later, in 1779, Ellsworth urged Governor Jonathan Trumbull to secure artillery for the militia in preparation against a coming British invasion.

A good businessman, Ellsworth built houses in Hartford for rental income. Many of his law cases were commercial ones, chiefly Connecticut farmers suing merchants in New York or Rhode Island. In 1779, when Noah Webster was studying law under him, Webster estimated that Ellsworth's firm handled between 1000 and 1500 cases each year. Webster said that there was scarcely a Hartford case that did not use Ellsworth as an attorney, especially in *nisi prius* trials.

No Connecticut lawyer had ever risen so fast, considering the number of cases and the money earned. Ellsworth was now the highest paid lawyer in the state. In addition to buying real estate he was soon lending money at interest. He built a big home, and was a stockholder in the Hartford Bank and the Hartford Broadcloth Mill. He served as state's attorney for Hartford County from 1777 until 1785.

Despite his great success as a lawyer, there was no sign of deceit, trickery or unethical conduct in his practice. He excelled in oratory that was unadorned but convincing. Describing Ellsworth's manner, Timothy Dwight called "his reasoning invincible; his images glowing; his sentiments noble; his phraseology remarkable for its clearness and precision;

his style concise and strong; and his utterance vehement and overwhelming."⁸ He was a modern Demosthenes, Dwight said.

Ellsworth, continued Dwight, "was formed to be a great man. His presence was tall, dignified, and commanding." One was overawed in his company. "When Washington was not present," Dwight said, "there was probably no man who would be more readily acknowledged to hold the first character."⁹

The historian G.H. Hollister said that Ellsworth used logical argument, "and used a peculiar style of condensed statement, through which there ran like a magnetic current the most delicate train of analytical reasoning. His eloquence was wonderfully persuasive and his manners solemn and impressive. He had the best judicial powers in that elder age of our republic."¹⁰

The Congressman

Although elected to the Continental Congress in 1777, Ellsworth did not attend until October 1778. Like many other delegates, he kept busy at home rather than go to Philadelphia to serve. He was re-elected each year until the fall of 1783, when he declined to run.

In December 1777 he was a member of a committee inquiring into the failure of a military expedition into Rhode Island. Although only 32 congressmen responded to the roll call when Ellsworth first attended, the list included illustrious names like Samuel Adams, Elbridge Gerry, John Jay, Henry Laurens, Richard Henry Lee, Gouverneur Morris, Robert Morris, and Roger Sherman. Ellsworth said that he had made Sherman his model in life, and John Adams remarked that was praise enough for both. Through their many years of working together there was no evidence of jealousy or antagonism between these two Connecticut luminaries.

One of Ellsworth's first acts in the Congress was to support a resolution blaming the country's ills on low morality, as seen in playgoing, gambling, and horse racing. His first impulse as a member of financial committees was to blame the crisis on too much spending, but experience soon revealed that the real problem was a shortage of funds.

He served on three committees that were embryonic structures for the present government: the Marine Committee later became the Navy Department; the Board of Treasury ultimately turned into the Treasury Department; and the Committee of Appeals was a forerunner of the Supreme Court.

Ellsworth was also appointed to special committees. One investigated seizures of property when the British evacuated Philadelphia.

Another found Robert Morris not guilty of improperly selling goods to the army. Still another tried to discover whether Benedict Arnold was unpatriotically consorting with Tories. A committee conferred with Washington concerning the office of the inspector general. Another reviewed foreign policy, in an effort to cut down on disputes between America's overseas diplomats.

Ellsworth's private letters were terse and unemotional. He wrote to his brother David, asking him to look after his family. Once his entire letter to his wife Abigail was:
"One week and then
Oliver Ellsworth."[11]

One of the functions of a congressman was to keep his state informed about the actions of Congress. Ellsworth told Governor Jonathan Trumbull that the delay in ratifying the Articles of Confederation was one of the biggest problems facing the confederation. States lacking western land holdings, such as Delaware, Maryland, and New Jersey, said they would not ratify until the states with land holdings, such as Connecticut, Pennsylvania, and Virginia, would cede their holdings to the federal government for distribution to soldiers at the close of the War. Ellsworth and Sherman suggested that Connecticut cede some of its western holdings for this purpose, but their state took no action at this time.

When Connecticut received its requisition of $1,700,000 to be paid to the federal treasury, Ellsworth and Sherman recommended speedy payment with inflated currency, confident that the money would buy more in the years ahead. Poor prophets did they seem several years later when the currency was "not worth a Continental"!

The hard realities facing the central government helped bring Ellsworth out of his provincialism. As a member of the Committee of Appeals, he sat in judgment on an interesting case.

Gideon Olmstead and some other Connecticut men, while prisoners of war, had mutinied, captured the British sloop *Active*, and headed for port. But then the United States brig *Convention* seized the *Active* as an enemy vessel. Olmstead and his crew claimed the *Active* and its cargo as a prize. The jury in the Pennsylvania Court of Admiralty gave Olmstead's party one-fourth of the prize, with the other three-fourths going to the crew of the *Convention*. Ellsworth's committee reversed that decision, granting Olmstead's party the full prize.

Although 38 previous maritime prize cases had not been contested, in this case the Pennsylvania court refused to obey the Congressional committee, and gave the money to the crew of the *Convention*. Thirty years later John Marshall and his Supreme Court overturned the Pennsylvania court decision.

Meanwhile, Congress did two things: passed a series of resolutions stating that states should obey the authority of Congress, and established a national court of appeals to handle all maritime appellate cases. Ellsworth's part in helping set up this national court was a preparation for his work both on the Constitution and in framing the Judiciary Act of 1789.

Since Congress was experiencing such difficulty in getting states to meet their requisition quotas, it turned to assessing quotas in goods (such as beef or wheat), and the states were more willing to respond to this system. Ellsworth was put on the committee to supervise this work.

In January 1780 Ellsworth wrote Governor Trumbull that in the army vicinity meal was selling at $8 per quart and corn at 50 cents per ear. Ellsworth tried to get a law passed freezing prices, but the states would not agree. He wrote to his brother David in March 1780 that it would be more profitable for him to be at home, "but you know when a soldier goes forth in public service he must stay until he is discharged and though the weather be stormy and his allowance small, still he must stand to his post."[12]

In 1780 Ellsworth made the suggestion, adopted on March 18, that the old currency be redeemed at 1/40. The states were to accept the old bills as taxes, and then turn them in for new money at the ratio of 40 to 1. Even this effort at deflation failed, however, and soon the old money was at 1/150 or higher.[13]

In June of that year Robert Morris came up with the idea that the army would pay for supplies by subscriptions, promises by Congress to repay the loaner at a later date. These notes were negotiable, and thus served as a form of currency. By this means the army received more of its badly needed supplies. Ellsworth was made chairman of the committee in Congress to supervise the process.

Becoming more interested in foreign affairs, Ellsworth rejoiced in the help America was getting from Spain, as Bernardo de Gálvez attacked the British holdings in West Florida. Ellsworth was happy to see that most of Europe was lining up opposed to Britain, and he would have drawn even more comfort had he realized how many Englishmen sympathized with the revolting colonists. Ere long, said Ellsworth in 1780, Britain will cease bothering us. She now carried a pretense of self-sufficiency, "much perhaps as a merchant on the eve of bankruptcy makes an uncommon parade of wealth and business, in order to keep up the delusion till chance achieve something in his favor."[14]

While in the Congress, Ellsworth continued to serve as a member of the Connecticut government. He was still on the Committee of the Pay Table, and he served on the Governor's Council until 1785. The Council constituted the upper house of the state legislature, and had duties that were at times legislative and at other times executive or judicial.

Someone accused Governor Trumbull of conniving to trade with England. Ellsworth was made chairman of the investigating committee, which cleared Trumbull of any wrongdoing.

With the end of the War nearing, Congress wondered how it would pay all of its debts. In January 1783 Robert Morris described his plight to Benjamin Franklin: "Imagine the situation of a man who is to direct the finances of a country almost without revenue surrounded by creditors, a government whose sole authority consists in the power of framing recommendations."[15]

Ellsworth found himself in a strange alliance with John Rutledge, agreeing that the national government should make a special effort to help South Carolina, the only state to pay all of its requisitions, and a state which had suffered much from war destruction and looting.

By now Ellsworth was recognized as one of the leaders of Congress, with Hamilton, Madison, Rutledge, and James Wilson. Along with Hamilton and Madison, he was on the committee to recommend to the states adoption of a law assessing a 5 percent impost on imported goods, plus specific duties on other items.

Hamilton had been pushing for a general convention to amend the Articles of Confederation. Congress appointed Ellsworth chairman of a committee to consider Hamilton's proposal. Although no specific action was taken, probably because conditions had not yet become acute, still this was a sign that sometime in the future this important assignment would have to be faced.

With Hamilton, Ellsworth served on a committee denying Rhode Island delegates the right to send information concerning foreign negotiations to the Rhode Island governor, and also on another committee to ask states to carry out treaty recommendations about Tories and for Americans to meet their financial obligations to Englishmen. Despite the bitterness of the War, Ellsworth sought no revenge on Great Britain, but wanted good relations with her and with all nations.

With Hamilton and Madison, Ellsworth reported favorably on a treaty of amity and commerce with Holland. With Hamilton and Rutledge, he approved the work of John Adams in setting up a similar treaty with Great Britain on May 1, 1783.

Ellsworth, Hamilton, Madison, and Wilson approved a report directing Washington to occupy frontier forts as soon as the British departed. With Hamilton and Madison, he served on the committee in charge of neutrality agreements with England. These three men were also given the responsibility in April 1783 of drafting a whole plan of administration for the Union, covering foreign affairs, military and naval establishments, weights and measures, and "other articles of the Confederation not attended to during the war."[16]

When army troops marched on Congress in 1783, Ellsworth served as go-between in trying to get Pennsylvania officials to quell the disorder. From Princeton, Ellsworth's committee sent an order for General Robert Howe to march on Philadelphia but, by now, mortified Washington had already taken steps to quash the protest.

As he left Congress in July 1783, Ellsworth summarized his views in a letter to Governor Trumbull from Princeton: "How long Congress will remain here is uncertain. But it will soon be of very little consequence where Congress goes, if they are not made respectable as well as responsible, which can never be done without giving them a power to perform engagements, as well as to make them. It was intended to have given them this power in the Confederation, by declaring their requisitions for the common defense sacredly binding on the states, but in practice it amounts to nothing." People think danger is past, but disunion or anarchy rapidly approaches. "There must, Sir, be a revenue somehow established that can be relied on for national purposes as exigencies arise, or it will be impossible to support national existence. The power of Congress must be adequate to the purpose of their constitution."[17]

To get the states to cooperate, Ellsworth now realized, coercion would have to be used. But he favored coercion by law and not by arms. This called for, he said, a government "partly national, partly federal."[18]

In 1785 Ellsworth resigned as state attorney for Hartford County and as a member of the Governor's Council in order to take a seat, along with Sherman, on the Connecticut Superior Court. He grew greatly in this post. His chief influence was to mitigate the severity of certain state laws. For example, sentenced for polygamy, Judah Benjamin received ten lashes, had the letter "A" branded on his forehead, and had to wear a halter on his neck as long as he lived in the state.

Historians of the state judicial system rank Ellsworth as one of its ablest judges. Like most people in Connecticut, however, he seems to have been silent on the big national issues. In fact, the state's delegates to the Constitutional Convention were elected on May 12, two days before the Convention was slated to begin in Philadelphia.

The Framer

When Connecticut finally got around to selecting delegates, it did an excellent job. It was the only state not to send a dud to the Convention. Ellsworth and Sherman proved to be two of the strongest members of the Convention, and Dr. William Samuel Johnson, president of Columbia College, had the quiet dignity that earned him the respect of everyone.

Fellow delegate William Pierce of Georgia wrote vignettes of each delegate. He praised Ellsworth as "a gentleman of clear, deep, and copious understanding; eloquent; attentive to duty." He was excellent in reply, Pierce said, for he takes the strong points of an adversary and "takes off the force of them, so as to admit the power of his own. Much respected for his integrity and venerated for his abilities."[19]

Faithfully representing his constituents, Ellsworth wanted to preserve as much state sovereignty as possible, consistent with getting a national government that worked. He said, "My happiness depends as much on the existence of my state government as a new-born infant depends upon its mother for nourishment."[20]

Ellsworth's love for Connecticut may have influenced the name of the new nation. On June 20 the Convention unanimously approved to substitute "the government of the United States" for the phrase "a national government" in the opening resolution of the Constitution, upon Ellsworth's motion. The word "national" was dropped from every other usage in the Constitution. As the process evolved, Ellsworth's wish of a government partly national and partly federal came true: the House of Representatives, catering to the large states, supplied the national principle and the Senate, serving the small states, demonstrated the federal principle.

When James Wilson asked Ellsworth if it was fair for one-fourth of the population to rule the other three-fourths (as could happen in the Senate), Ellsworth replied that "the power is given to the few to save them from the many. No instance of a confederacy has existed in which an equality of voices has not been exercised by the members."[21] We are going too far in overhauling the Articles of Confederation, Ellsworth said. We are razing the foundations when we need only repair the roof!

On June 29 Ellsworth gave a very influential talk that helped set up the Great Compromise. He argued that only cooperation between large states and small states could achieve the mutual respect and tranquility sought for in the new government. If proportional representation was used in both houses, he said, the Union would be severed in two at the Delaware River.

Since he believed that "the only chance we have to support a general government is to graft it on the state governments,"[22] he favored such things as state pay for national legislators, state legislatures to select senators, states to fix their own suffrage qualifications, state control of their militia, and ratification of the Constitution by state legislatures.

Although he favored annual elections to the House of Representatives, he preferred that the president be chosen by electors rather than by the people directly. He believed in a six-year term for the president.

Ellsworth was one delegate who worked hard to achieve compromises off the Convention floor. His friendship with Rutledge undoubtedly helped achieve the compromise in which Connecticut agreed not to limit the importation of slaves, in return for which South Carolina agreed to permit Congress to pass a navigation act by a simple majority. Ellsworth and Sherman were both attacked by abolitionists for their soft stand on slavery, but their response was twofold: there will be no Union if we try to get the South to abandon slavery, and time will do away with this infamous institution.

Ellsworth's biographer, William G. Brown, says that "there were probably few important things done in the convention after the great compromise that Ellsworth did not have a hand in. He had stamped forever with the imprint of his mind his country's fundamental law."[23]

As a mark of Ellsworth's leadership, he was one of the five delegates elected by ballot to go over the entire draft of the Constitution to date, and put it into a suggested final form. For ten days the entire nascent form of government was in the hands of Ellsworth, Gorham, Randolph, Rutledge, and Wilson in this Committee of Detail.

When Rossiter says that Ellsworth "may have done more in Philadelphia for the Union than Hamilton, Wilson, and the two Pinckneys together,"[24] the only exception would have to be Wilson, who ranked among the top in important contributors.

In 1847 John C. Calhoun listed the names of the persons responsible for the fact that the government was a federal rather than a national one: "Their names ought to be written on brass, and live forever. They were Chief Justice Ellsworth and Roger Sherman, and Judge Paterson of New Jersey. The states further south did not see the future. But to the coolness and sagacity of these three men, aided by others not so prominent, do we owe our present constitution."[25]

The Ratifier

Ellsworth played a leading role in getting Connecticut to ratify the Constitution. From November 1787 to March 1788 he wrote 13 letters, signed "A Landowner," to the Hartford *Connecticut Courant* and the Litchfield *American Mercury*.[26] He listed four types of opponents of ratification[27]: (1) former friends of England; (2) small-minded politicians who spread jealousies; (3) state officeholders determined to keep their jobs; (4) debtors who are neither honest nor industrious.

In December Ellsworth blasted the nonsigners. Mason, he said, must have wanted a ban on slave importation so that he could breed slaves to sell to South Carolina and Georgia. Gerry's main concern, he felt, was to try to redeem Continental currency. Luther Martin he castigated as an obstructionist and as a falsifier of what had really happened in the Convention.[28]

At the ratifying convention in Hartford in January 1788 Ellsworth was a main speaker. In his opening talk he said that a stronger union was needed for defense, the economy, peace among the states, and justice to individuals and small states. Let Connecticut stop paying tribute to Massachusetts and New York, he pleaded. Also, Europe is waiting for our nation to fall apart, so as to gobble up the small states. And why should we let Rhode Island block what is good for us? Why be governed by a minority?

Later in the convention, answering objections to the new government, especially the power of Congress to tax, he drew upon his experience in the Continental Congress to remind listeners of how flimsy the old government had been. His logic and rhetoric proved to be too much for the opposition.

In 1833 in a debate over nullification, Daniel Webster read to the Senate extracts from Ellsworth's speeches at this convention. Webster referred to Ellsworth as "a gentleman of the clearest intelligence, and of the utmost purity and integrity of character."[29] On another occasion when Ellsworth's son William, then a congressman, thanked Webster for his stirring defense of the Union and the Constitution, Webster said that Ellsworth's two speeches at the Connecticut ratification convention were among his most important sources of knowledge on those subjects. So Webster and Calhoun, with nearly contrary views on the Constitution, agreed on the greatness of the contributions to it made by Ellsworth.

The Senator

Connecticut's first two senators under the new Constitution were Ellsworth and William Samuel Johnson. The first Senate framed rules for the national legislature and for conduct of the departments of the national government. Ellsworth knew most of his 21 colleagues from the Continental Congress or the Constitutional Convention. It was a chummy group — on cold days they left their seats and gathered around the fireplace. No senator was more active those days than Ellsworth.

As chairman of the committee on the federal judiciary, it was he who drafted the bill that became the Judiciary Act of 1789, the one establishing the federal court system. Burton Hendrick, for this work, calls Ellsworth "the chief agent in establishing the American judicial system."[30] One of his colleagues called the bill his child, saying that Ellsworth defended it "with the care of a parent, even with wrath and anger."[31]

The act used language that in places was intentionally broad and vague, so that experience and Congress could fill in details as they became clear and necessary. The act set up a unique system of courts, federal and regional. Because he had seen state courts ignore or overrule decisions of Congress, Ellsworth was determined to see the nation have a strong system of regional federal courts, to try cases within the federal domain.

The Supreme Court was established with six justices holding two annual sessions. Each state had a federal district court, with jurisdiction in admiralty cases, as well as specified small offenses. There were then three United States Circuit Courts, consisting of two Supreme Court justices and the district court judge. This court would hear appeals from the district court, try high crimes, and have original jurisdiction in cases between foreigners and United States citizens, and between citizens of different states.

Drafting this bill was difficult, because provisions had to be made for ten classes of cases, for delineation among jurisdictions of the Supreme, district, and Circuit courts, and for distinction between jurisdictions of state courts and federal courts.

Perhaps Ellsworth's biggest error came in connection with this act, which gave the Supreme Court the power to issue writs of mandamus, that is, writs commanding persons to perform an action. Only courts of original jurisdiction have this authority, and the Constitution declared that the Supreme Court was such a court only in cases affecting diplomats, and cases in which a state is a party.

On this distinction Chief Justice John Marshall declared that part of the Judiciary Act of 1789 unconstitutional, and said that Secretary of State James Madison need not obey the mandamus writ to deliver to John Marbury a commission as justice of the peace in the District of Columbia. This famous case established the point that the Supreme Court can declare an act of Congress unconstitutional, and thus, in its sphere is superior to Congress. Nevertheless, Ellsworth's pioneer legislation in setting up the American judicial system has, on the whole, stood up well through the changing forces of history.

Ellsworth was the leader of the federalist forces in the Senate. In this role, he effectively carried out policies developed by Washington, Hamilton, and Jefferson. Kenneth Umbreit says that his was a secondary type of leadership, "which carries out the decisions of others intelligently and effectively with labor, patience, and skill."[32]

There is no doubt that Ellsworth's greatest skill came in working with people to secure common goals. Nevertheless he at times showed a primary type of leadership.

For example, in addition to his work on the Judiciary Act he was chairman of the committee to adopt Senate rules as well as rules for joint conferences with the House of Representatives. He also chaired the committee which divided the Senate into three groups, with one-third being elected each biennium. He wrote the first act concerning consular services, and he helped make the first plans concerning the census, the postal service, and the military forces. In addition, he served on committees to develop titles and salaries for the president and the vice-president.

Because of his experience in financial matters, Ellsworth worked closely with Hamilton in getting the new commercial acts adopted. This meant that Ellsworth supported legislation for the national bank, the first tariff, and the plan for funding the national debt, including federal assumption of state war debts. His watchful eye over public spending earned him the title of "the Cerberus of the Treasury."[33] As one of Hamilton's chief helpers, he deserves credit for helping reestablish the financial credit of the young nation.

When Rhode Island continued to refuse to ratify the Constitution, Ellsworth led what he admitted as "a pretty bold measure" of getting a nonintercourse act passed concerning the small state. In a short time Rhode Island became the final original state to ratify the Constitution.

For better or worse, Ellsworth had a hand in the origin of Jay's Treaty with England. In March 1794 a group of Senators led by Ellsworth decided that action was needed. England was disregarding our status as neutral in its war against France. Republicans, led by Jefferson and Madison, were pushing for support of France and for possible war against England. Federalist leaders in the Senate chose Ellsworth as their spokesman.

Ellsworth recommended that an envoy, preferably Hamilton or John Jay, be sent to England to negotiate a treaty of commerce, with a pledge from England to stop interfering with American shipping. Initially surprised, Washington acceded, and the controversial treaty that resulted may have helped avert war with England. Although the treaty was vigorously opposed in the House, Ellsworth and his friends made sure that it was approved in the Senate.

The Chief Justice

When Jay resigned as the first chief justice in order to go to England to negotiate, Washington appointed John Rutledge to the position. Rutledge openly opposed Jay's Treaty, however, disappointing not only Washington but also most Federalists in Congress. As a result, the Senate in December 1795 refused to confirm the appointment of Rutledge.

Washington then suggested the post to Hamilton, and then to Patrick Henry, but both declined. The post was then offered to Associate Justice William Cushing, who considered for a week before declining. Washington could not nominate the very gifted Associate Justice James Wilson, since Wilson already had a bad reputation for not paying debts.

By now Ellsworth was the logical choice for chief justice, being not only a Federalist but also a respected legal authority. There was no problem getting him confirmed by the Senate, and so Ellsworth served as chief justice of the United States from March 1796 until November 1800.

Since many appeals cases involved admiralty law, Ellsworth now devoted much of his time to a study of that field. Some of the associate justices resented his appointment, feeling that his training and experience in common law were insufficient.

Ellsworth seems not to have consulted his colleagues much. Once, on the circuit in Philadelphia, Associate Justice Samuel Chase kept telling attorney Jared Ingersoll to stop talking, for the court did not want to hear the point argued. After several such incidents, Ingersoll sat down. Ellsworth tapped his snuff box, took a pinch, and said, "The court has expressed no opinion, sir, upon these points, and when it does you will hear it from the proper organ of the court. You will proceed, sir."[34]

In many ways Ellsworth found his new position less attractive than his Senate role. He now was with his family less frequently. The constant traveling for circuit court duty was hard on his health. Although he had an outstanding record as a trial attorney, he lacked the background in common law and international law that some of his colleagues had.

In place of legal theory, he tended to use precedent in deciding cases. Thus when Isaac Williams, born in Connecticut, tried to become a French citizen, Ellsworth said that it was impossible because of the common law doctrine of perpetual allegiance, and the common law, Ellsworth judged, is a part of the law of the land. In a similar case Jay had pointed out the fundamental difference between a feudal sovereignty and republican sovereignty.

A later Supreme Court, in Wheaten v. Peters, overruled Ellsworth's decision, stating that "there can be no common law of the United States. When a common law right is asserted, one must look to the state in which the controversy originated."[35]

In his opening charge to a grand jury in Savannah in 1796 Ellsworth enunciated his philosophy of law: "Laws violated with impunity are, to a republic, the symptoms of death. National laws are national ligatures. They are the means by which it pleases Heaven to make, of weak and discordant parts, one great people. Let there be vigilance for the execution of laws, laws made by all and having for their object the good of all. So let us rear an empire sacred to the rights of man."[36]

In a case in which North Carolina was confiscating debts due to Englishmen, Ellsworth ruled that a treaty bears the force of law, and being of national scope, cannot be gainsaid by a state law, as in this case. Since courts had not yet clearly established their boundaries, early Supreme Court decisions were helpful in getting this important job done.

At times Ellsworth showed admirable modesty. Once when his coach broke down, Ellsworth got underneath and fixed it. A bystander wanted to know who was the skillful mechanic. "The chief justice of the United States," replied Ellsworth, with a twinkle in his eye.

There were many maritime cases to consider, for France and England were at war and both nations were violating American neutrality. Early in his tenure came the case of the *Mary Ford*, an English ship which had been captured by the French, relieved of crew and cargo, and left for destroyed. An American vessel found her and brought her to Boston for salvage. The British consul intervened for the original owner, and the French consul for the captors.

The district court gave the original owners two-thirds of the sale money, with one-third to the American salvors. The French captors appealed to the Circuit Court, who gave the two-thirds to them. Now the original owners appealed to the Supreme Court, questioning the jurisdiction of the district court. Solomon-like the Supreme Court affirmed the district court's original jurisdiction but sustained the Circuit Court's decree of settlement.

In the case of Wiscart v. Dauchy, Ellsworth and Wilson clashed. Wilson argued that the Constitution gave the Supreme Court the right to re-examine evidence in all maritime cases. Ellsworth, referring both to the Constitution and the Judiciary Act of 1789, distinguished writs of error from appeals—the former re-examine merely the law, the latter both the law and the facts. "It is of more importance, for a judicial determination, to ascertain what the law is," said Ellsworth, "than to speculate what it ought to be."[37]

Ellsworth kept politics out of his judicial role. When England protested that its ship *Phoebe Ann*, taken by a French privateer into port at Charleston for repairs, should be returned as a violation of international law, evidence indicated that the repairs had not amounted to an increase of her gunpower and thus was justified. Setting aside his preference of England over France, Ellsworth said that "suggestions of policy and conveniency cannot be considered in the judicial determination of right; the treaty with France, whatever that is, must have its effect."[38]

Considering the fact that Ellsworth was not simply a judge but a person who made significant contributions as a legislator and a framer, his short stint as chief justice was not lacking in merit. American colleges must have thought so, for in 1797 both Dartmouth and Princeton awarded him honorary LL. D. degrees. Yale had already done so in 1790, forgiving the lad who had "hallooed through the court yard, after evening prayers," 27 years previously.

The Diplomat

In February 1799 President Adams nominated three special envoys to France: Ellsworth, William Vans Murray, and Patrick Henry. When Henry declined to serve, he was replaced by William Davie.

Ellsworth had an excruciating decision. Should he accept this difficult but important mission, probably meaning he would have to resign as chief justice? A number of Ellsworth's friends, most of them partial to England, wanted him to stay home. Hamilton did not want reconciliation with France, against whom the United States had been in an undeclared war for over a year. Others advising Ellsworth to turn down the appointment included Rufus King, Timothy Pickering, and Oliver Wolcott.

Adams selected Ellsworth as the only New England Federalist temperate enough to make an effort to really understand France. On November 3, 1799, Ellsworth and Davie sailed for France. Their stormy trip presaged a turbulent round of negotiations.

At Lisbon they learned that Napoleon had overthrown the Directorate and seized control of the government. They set sail for France, but a great storm drove them back to Arras in Spain. The overland trip to Paris ruined Ellsworth's health—he was never really well again.

Napoleon had decided to court the United States as a possible ally against England. Thus the Americans were treated well, which had not been the case with previous envoys Gouverneur Morris and Charles Cotesworth Pinckney. Ellsworth found it hard to keep up with Napoleon's quick mind. The complaint was returned. Tradition says that when Napoleon saw Ellsworth's grave, firm face, he said, "We must make a treaty with this man."[39]

A quite different version of Ellsworth and his colleagues was given by Thomas Paine, who complained that the group had snubbed such Republicans as Joel Barlow and United States consul Fulwar Skipworth. In October 1800 Paine wrote to Jefferson that "three more useless mortals never came upon public business." They were, he said, "rather an injury than a benefit. They set themselves up as a faction as soon as they arrived."[40]

Paine visited Ellsworth, attacking the two Federalist moves: Jay's Treaty, and the recall of James Monroe. Paine recommended that the United States treat France and England equally, for "the principle that neutral ships make neutral property must be general or not at all."[41]

One day Ellsworth had a long discussion with Charles de Talleyrand, French foreign minister, on how France might establish a republic like the American one. Ellsworth recommended setting up a supreme tribunal, with wise and well paid judges, who would guarantee that all citizens have equal rights. Good advice, replied Talleyrand, but alas—his countrymen, he said, would never wait for so slow a process.

When the ultimate philosopher Comte de Volney asked Ellsworth for his appraisal of a utopian plan of government he had devised, Ellsworth responded that "there is only one thing for which you have made no provision: the selfishness of man."[42]

Ellsworth served as head of the American delegation. He toned down the belligerent attitude of Secretary of State Pickering, stating American objectives clearly but courteously, so that France could revise its previous policy and still save face. Adams told Pickering that "Mr. Ellsworth is so great a master of business, and his colleagues are so intelligent, that I should not be afraid to allow them a greater latitude of discretion, if it were not unfair to lay upon them alone the burden of the dangerous response that may accompany this business."[43]

Napoleon's brother Joseph headed the French delegation, whose main contention was that American neutrality and Jay's Treaty both broke the agreements of the 1778 treaty with France. Ellsworth's response was that that treaty covered only defensive wars, not aggressive ones, and that both Ambassador Genet and Talleyrand had told America that she was not expected to take part in France's war against England. Ellsworth also complained that France had violated United States neutrality by impressing American sailors and seizing American cargo. Its agents had further failed to pay for many supplies bought in the United States. After Jay's Treaty had been signed, the Directorate had become more bold, treating as a pirate any ship lacking a bill of lading, and justifying the search and seizure of any ship carrying anything made in England. American policy, Ellsworth explained, was to ask for reparations for all these seizures.

France's position, as Napoleon returned from the Battle of Marengo, was to offer the United States one of two options: Either consider the old treaty in force (in which case France will pay reparations), or draw up a new treaty (with no indemnity payments) in which France is placed on an equal footing with England.

Unable to arrive at a treaty agreement, the two nations instead signed what Napoleon called a convention. Its main terms called for no indemnities; postpone decision concerning past treaties; ships seized but not yet condemned would be returned to the United States; all debts would be guaranteed between the two nations; only military supplies and equipment would henceforth be considered contraband.

Even with no treaty Napoleon remained charming. He gave Ellsworth a costly piece of Gobelin tapestry, "and with a truly French cognizance of his one vice presented him also with a gold snuff-box."[44] Joseph Bonaparte treated the American envoys to a splendid farewell party.

Reaction to this treaty was much milder than that to Jay's Treaty. Republicans generally were satisfied with it. Northern Federalists felt it conceded too much but Southern Federalists felt it was all that was possible under the circumstances. President Adams was satisfied, especially after Rufus King, minister to Great Britain, reported that the British had no particular complaint about it. It was generally agreed that at a time when major leaders like Hamilton and Jefferson were engaging in personal vendettas, Ellsworth had served his country well, rising above the temptations of party factionalism and personal ambition.

Ellsworth still had his sense of humor. He sent this poem to his eight-year-old twin sons:

> The men in France are lazy creatures,
> And work the women and great dogs;
> The ladies are enormous eaters,
> And like the best toadstools and frogs.[45]

In a letter to his son he described a harrowing experience: "Robbers came round the house where Daddy lives the other night, and the gardener shot off his two-barrel gun and killed two of them. Daddy believes, if the robbers come into his room, they will get killed, for he keeps a gun and two pistols charged all the time."[46]

When Ellsworth learned of Timothy Pickering's resignation as secretary of state, he wrote to Oliver Wolcott, Jr., secretary of the treasury, begging him not to resign: "Though our country pays badly, it is the only one in the world worth working for. The happiness it enjoys is so much superior to what the nations of Europe enjoy that no one who is able to preserve and increase that happiness ought to quit her service while he can remain in it with bread and honor."[47]

In 1800 Ellsworth visited England. At Westminster Hall, he was invited to sit beside Lord Kenyon, the British chief justice. He visited a small town called Ellsworth, near Cambridge, where he found many persons of his name, and learned that the name came from "Eelsworth," place of eels, for a nearby stream rich with eels. Ellsworth liked England, even its climate, so well that he gave up a planned vacation in southern France for a trip to the spas at Bath.

His reaction, as a Federalist, to the Republican victory in 1800 was surprisingly mild. "So the anti-Feds are now to support their own administration, and take a turn at rolling stones uphill," he wrote Rufus King. Speaking of Jefferson, he continued: "His party also must support the government while he administers it; and if others are consistent and do the same, the government may even be consolidated and acquire new confidence."[48]

Final Years

Having resigned as chief justice, Ellsworth retired to Elmwood, his large frame house near Windsor, in 1801. Here his chief concern was his family, and his hobbies the study of theology and agriculture.

Of his children, seven lived long and successful lives. Only Oliver, Jr., died young, in 1805, and Ellsworth grieved deeply his loss. One son, Harry, became the first commissioner of patents, and another, William, became a congressman, governor, and judge.

Apparently being a Federalist was enough to draw Tom Paine's wrath. In 1803, while visiting friends in Connecticut, Paine met with Republicans, "advising them of ways to deprive Ellsworth of his influence."[49] In a fiery letter to the Hartford *American Mercury*, Paine called Ellsworth a monarchist who was trying to sabotage the Constitution and install a hereditary form of government in the United States. Since he offered no evidence, Paine's attack was soon forgotten.

Once again a farmer, Ellsworth wore plain clothes in town. He walked the mile to church. When someone suggested that he buy a new sleigh, he replied that if he did, his neighbor would too, and then his neighbor's neighbor—soon everyone would want a new sleigh just because he could not stand his old pung.

He bought a store for two of his sons, and then worked as clerk in the store. One could not tell by his appearance that he was probably the wealthiest, and certainly the most distinguished, man in Windsor.

From time to time he still served on the Governor's Council, which also acted as a court of appeals. One time when the younger Jonathan Trumbull, now governor, called for a vote, the Council were unanimous for a decision until the vote reached Ellsworth. When he gave reasons for differing, in a few short sentences, the Council reversed itself and voted with Ellsworth.

Another time Ellsworth befriended a young lawyer arguing a case before the Council. The young man seemed to be ignored by his senior associate, even though it had been his reasoning that won the case. A few days later Ellsworth visited the young man in his office, saw his meager collection of law books, and offered to lend him the money to buy more books. The young man became Ellsworth's son-in-law, and later the chief justice of Connecticut.

Ellsworth also befriended college students, especially law students. Ironically, as a member of the Council, he was automatically a Yale governor. Hopefully he was not too strict concerning student discipline. All of his sons who lived to manhood attended Yale.

Religion played a cardinal role in his life. It came first, then patriotism, then duty towards one's job. All of his decisions were checked by reference to a hard-and-fast Christian moral standard.

He attended church regularly and had daily family devotions. He prayed to a personal God, and believed in an afterlife. Over half of the books in his library were on religion. He managed to get the split First Congregational Church of Windsor re-united, and then helped to raise funds for a new church building.

Although he was not sectarian, Ellsworth did believe in an established church, saying that "the primary objects of government are the peace, order, and prosperity of society. To promote these objects, good morals are essential. Institutions for the promotion of good morals are therefore objects of legislative support."[50]

In his final year he was appointed the chief justice of Connecticut, but before he could take office he suffered a serious seizure, so he withdrew his acceptance. In his last days he had extreme pain from gout and kidney stones.

Ellsworth died at Elmwood on November 26, 1807, and was buried in Windsor. Save for John Adams, he was at the time New England's most distinguished surviving patriot. Unlike many Federalists, he refrained from negative criticism of the Jefferson administration, always feeling that one should place loyalty to one's country ahead of party loyalty.

And so the Connecticut Yankee had grown from a zealous defender of states' rights into a person who realized that without a strong Union there can be no strong states. By his actions Ellsworth demonstrated that one need not surrender love of one's locality as one develops an ever expanding concept of governmental sovereignty.

Perhaps Ellsworth's chief asset was his common sense—"he knew when to be cautious and when to be bold." He had a modest awareness of his limits and a quiet confidence in his strong values. Above all, he never once questioned the destiny of America. His reputation, in Brown's words, is secure: "It rests on the same foundations that uphold the strength and greatness of his country."[51]

4. Benjamin Franklin: The World Recognizes an American

The official peacemaker at the Constitutional Convention was a man universally accepted as one of the great men of the century. Benjamin Franklin already had achieved success as a printer, publisher, scientist, inventor, writer, philosopher, diplomat, and statesman before he was elected as a delegate from Pennsylvania at the age of 81.

Franklin's father, Josiah, emigrated from Ecton, England, in 1683. As a nonconformist Congregationalist he, like so many others, sought a religious haven in the new world. Benjamin described his father as a strong and talented person, one often consulted for advice or as an arbitrator between contending parties.

Josiah's first wife, Anne, died bearing their seventh child. Josiah then married 22-year-old Abiah Folger, who bore him 10 children. Benjamin was the 15th child of the 17, and the youngest son of a youngest son for five generations. He was born January 17, 1706, in Boston.

Franklin's maternal grandfather, Peter Folger, was a Nantucket merchant. He bought Mary Morrils as an indentured servant for £20 and later married her. Their daughter Abiah was "a discreet and virtuous woman," Franklin wrote on his mother's tombstone.

Unable to make a living as a dyer, Josiah became a candlemaker. At the age of 10 Benjamin dropped out of grammar school, where he had failed arithmetic, in order to help his father. "Ben boiled the noxious animal fat, skimmed, mixed, and dipped, turning out candles for the town watch, and fragrant cakes of soap."[1]

From the start Benjamin was the most promising of Josiah's children. His Uncle Benjamin encouraged the young lad as a poet, so Benjamin wrote several ballads, had brother James print them, and sold them on the streets of Boston. But Papa told Benjamin to stop it, thereby saving us from what appeared to be a pretty bad poet.

Papa wanted Benjamin to be a preacher. But one day, after the winter's provisions had been salted, Benjamin said, "Father, if you were to say 'Grace' over the whole cask — once and for all — it would be a vast saving of time." About this time Josiah took his son out of Boston's Latin School, and gave him to George Brownell, who ran a school for writing and arithmetic.

The Printer

At the age of 12 Benjamin was apprenticed to his brother James, a printer who was nine years older. Benjamin liked to read, preferring Plutarch, Bunyan, Defoe, and Cotton Mather's *Essays to Do Good*. Later he tried to model his writing style on *The Spectator*.

Working on James's paper, the *New England Courant*, gave Franklin the chance to publish his first prose. Under the pseudonym Silence Dogood, he pretended to be a widow who commented on current affairs.

As a vegetarian, Franklin asked James for half the money normally paid an apprentice for board. With this money he not only fed himself but bought books with the money he saved. He stopped being a vegetarian, he said, when he noticed that large fish ate smaller fish. "Then, thought I, if you eat one another, I don't see why we mayn't eat you. So convenient a thing it is to be a reasonable creature, since it enables one to find or make a reason for everything one has a mind to do."[2]

As he grew, Franklin developed an athletic build. He was such a good swimmer he gave lessons. He was about five foot ten, with a large head, light brown hair, and grey eyes. Inventive, he devised a kite to pull him downwind while swimming. Printers marveled that he could carry a large form of type in each hand, reducing in half the time required to do the job.

When James was jailed for printing a fictitious story about pirates off the coast of Maine, Franklin ran the paper by himself for a month. Then when James was forbidden from printing the paper for having attacked religious hypocrisy, Franklin's name appeared as a coverup on the masthead. Franklin's apprentice indentures were returned to him, for use in future employment. A new set of secret indentures was drawn up, but Franklin felt he need not honor them, since James could not make them public without revealing the ruse. Franklin seized the opportunity, and sailed to New York City in 1723.

The only printer in New York City needed no help but referred Franklin to his son, Andrew Bradford, a printer in Philadelphia. When Franklin arrived there, his first stop was at a Quaker meeting house, where, fatigued, he fell asleep during the silent service.

Andrew Bradford also needed no help, but referred Franklin to his rival, Samuel Keimer, who gave Franklin a job and found lodging for him with John Read, Franklin's future father-in-law.

Governor Sir William Keith, at odds with the proprietors of Pennsylvania, was seeking a vehicle for voicing his views. He offered to set up Franklin as a printer but asked him to see if his father would help provide funds. Josiah Franklin refused to do so, promising Franklin he would help him later, if he stopped writing satire.

On a visit to Cotton Mather, Franklin was warned about a low overhead beam: "Stoop!" Not hearing the warning, Franklin bumped his head on the beam. "You are young," philosophized Mather, "and have the world before you. Stoop as you go through it, and you will miss many hard bumps."[3] Franklin said that he had learned early the danger of carrying one's head too high in life.

Returning to Philadelphia, Franklin stopped off in New York to visit his brother John. Governor William Burnett, hearing that Franklin had many books, invited him to see his library, and they talked about books and authors. Franklin considered it fortunate that a poor boy like him had already become friendly with two governors.

Still thinking he might set up a print shop for Governor Keith, Franklin sailed in November 1724 for London, where he hoped to purchase printing equipment. When he received no promised letters from Keith, however, he began work for two London printers, Samuel Palmer and James Watts.

While printing a book by William Wollaston on religion, Franklin found that he opposed the ideas in the book, so he wrote and printed *A Dissertation on Liberty and Necessity, Pleasure and Pain* in 1725. In this work he denied free will, and said that all people have equal amounts of pleasure and pain.

Thomas Denham, a friendly Quaker merchant, offered Franklin a job as a clerk in his Philadelphia store, so Franklin returned home in October 1726. When Denham died several months later Franklin felt free to return to his first love, printing.

He once again worked for Keimer, quit after a quarrel, and then returned to Keimer's shop. To print paper money for New Jersey, Franklin contrived the first copperplate press in America.

In 1727 Franklin organized the Junto, a social club that lasted thirty years. Following Cotton Mather, the group responded to a list of questions at each Friday's meeting: What of interest have you read lately? Has any business failed, and why? Have you heard of any good cures for illness? Does any one of our members need help?

A friend, Hugh Meredith, got his father to set them up in printing business. Franklin wrote an anonymous pamphlet defending the use of paper currency. Then he got the contract to print currency for Pennsylvania and this led to other printing jobs for the state.

In 1728 Franklin drew up a set of "Articles of Belief and Acts of Religion." Here he expressed belief in one Supreme Being, the Father of many lesser gods. Since there can be no happiness without virtue, Franklin said, the Father delights in seeing me virtuous. He asked God to save him from atheism, to keep him loyal to his prince and his country, and to help him be sincere, humble, friendly, just, honest, and grateful to God for all of His blessings.

In later years he was a deist and freethinker, but he felt that the majority of mankind needed "the motives of religion to restrain them from vice."[4] He contributed, at various times in his life, to the support of several Protestant churches and a Jewish synagogue in Philadelphia. Later he helped his friend John Carroll become the first American bishop of the Roman Catholic Church. He said that he was ready to accept the first Moslem missionary to America.[5]

Determined to concentrate on character building, Franklin described in his autobiography how he focused on one virtue at a time, ending with the admonition "Imitate Jesus and Socrates." In arriving at an important decision, he used what he called "moral algebra." This meant listing all reasons for and against the measure, reflecting on the list, and finally seeing which side outweighed the other. A judicious temperament and a fair mind were lifelong attributes of Franklin's.

In the keen competition between the newspapers of Keimer and Bradford, Keimer's was winning until Franklin wrote a popular series of articles, criticizing everyday foibles, under the pen name of Busy-Body. No longer able to compete, Keimer sold his paper to Franklin in October 1729.

Knowing how much people judge by appearances, Franklin dressed simply, paid his bills on time, and never idled or went fishing. His paper succeeded because he used more local material, increased the advertisements, and wrote much of the material himself. Sometimes he wrote letters to himself as editor, and answered them. He liked to use humorous squibs and hoaxes. But, learning from his Boston experience, he avoided slander. In religion he was neither scoffing nor partisan. He defended freedom of the press, saying that truth is always an overmatch for error. By 1730 he succeeded Bradford as the official printer for the state of Pennsylvania.

Now that his finances were improving Franklin began to look for a wife. His friend, Mrs. Thomas Godfrey, suggested one of her relatives. Franklin asked for a dowry of £100 to pay off his print-shop debt. Mrs. Godfrey said that they had no such funds. Franklin suggested that they could mortgage their home! Mrs. Godfrey said that his printing business would probably fail anyway, and so the match was off.

He did better the next time. Deborah Read's husband had deserted her, and Franklin felt somewhat guilty over having left her when he went to London. They were wed on September 1, 1730, and the marriage was long and harmonious.

An illegitimate child, William, was born in 1731 to Franklin. The mother, unknown, could have been Deborah. At any rate, she reared the child as if her own. A son, Francis, was born in 1732 but died of smallpox in 1736. Their daughter, Sarah, born in 1743, became a favorite of her father. Other relatives on both sides of the family often lived with them, and so the Franklin household teemed with life.

The Civic Improver

Franklin had the knack of turning a private need into a public blessing. Craving companionship, he formed the Junto, many of whose members became leaders in their fields. Since they loved to read, Junto members pooled their books into a common library in Franklin's home. When this system failed because of lack of care of borrowed books, Franklin got the members to set up a subscription library in 1731. Dues paid for books bought in London. Nonsubscribers could borrow books by paying a rental fee. A library building was rented, which had not only books but also fossils, Indian robes, globes, and telescopes.

Fearful that criminals would outwit the volunteer watch in the city Franklin got Philadelphia to initiate a regular force of paid watchmen who made nightly rounds. Chilly at night, he invented the Franklin stove, which was designed to resemble (with its doors open) an open fireplace but was set out in the middle of a room. He refused to patent his stove, saying that just as we benefit from the inventions of others, so should we share with them our inventions.

Franklin might well have patented his method of securing civic improvements. Locating a need, the Junto members would discuss the best solution to the problem. Franklin would then write about it in his newspaper, and finally call a public meeting for action.

In this way Philadelphia set up a fire department in 1736. Next came a street department, with suggestions for paving, repairing, cleaning, draining, and de-icing streets. After that came a plan for street lighting. Philadelphia could almost say that it became the leading city of the colonies because of this industrious and ingenious printer.

In 1743 Franklin organized the American Philosophical Society as a kind of intercolonial Junto to permit America's learned men to meet and discuss common interests. Most members were scientists who reported on the most recent developments in their fields. Franklin volunteered to be secretary. Of the first ten members from Philadelphia, five had also been Junto members.

Also in 1743 Franklin drew up a proposal for an academy. At the time all American colleges were church-related. When peace came to England in 1748 Franklin published a pamphlet, *Proposals Relating to the Education of Youth in Pennsylvania*. In it he pointed out that the original settlers had been well educated in Europe, but now education had been neglected. He recommended that students eat "temperately and frugally" and "be frequently exercised in running, leaping, wrestling, and swimming." Students should learn drawing, mathematics, history, science, and commerce. There should be much attention to public speaking, and they should learn to write in a clear and concise style.

In November 1749 Franklin was elected president of the academy, a position he held until 1756. For a building, the academy took over a large structure formerly used by the great preacher George Whitefield. Saving themselves the cost of erecting a building, the trustees of the academy agreed to assume the mortgage, keep a large hall open for occasional preachers, and maintain a free school for poor children.

Franklin supervised the remodeling of the building and drew up the curriculum for the English school. The richest and best educated subscribers insisted on a Latin school, with the head of it being the overall rector, with a salary twice that of the English master.

The academy opened on January 7, 1751, and was incorporated in 1753. Franklin remained a lifelong trustee of this forerunner of the University of Pennsylvania.

The Publisher

Since he had the presses for his newspapers, it was natural for Franklin to start publishing books. He printed the first German hymnal in America, and in 1732 the first German-American newspaper. Other books he printed included the *Psalms* of Isaac Watts, the *New England Psalter*, and books by Daniel Defoe, Jonathan Edwards, Increase Mather, and Samuel Richardson. He also imported books to sell, such as those by Alexander Pope and James Thomson, whose poem *The Seasons* "brought more tears of pleasure into my eyes than all I ever read before,"[6] he said.

When he printed *The Constitution of the Free Masons* in 1734 it was the first Masonic book published in America. That year he became Grand Master of St. Johns Lodge of Free Masons.

In 1741 he printed an early medical treatise, Cadwallader Colden's *Essay on the Iliac Passion*. In 1744 he printed the first novel in America, Richardson's *Pamela*. He also published the first detailed account of Niagara Falls, written by the Swedish traveler Peter Kalm.

Andrew Bradford published America's first magazine, the *American Magazine*, on February 13, 1741. Franklin followed it with the *General Magazine* on February 16, 1741. They were monthlies. Bradford's ran for three months and Franklin's for six months. In his magazine Franklin published America's first magazine advertisement, publicizing a ferry over the Potomac on May 10, 1741.

No doubt Franklin's biggest success as a publisher came with *Poor Richard's Almanac*, begun in December 1732. The name came from an actual Richard Saunders, an English almanac compiler. Franklin professed to have a running encounter between Richard and his wife Bridget, a "battle of the sexes" that has always sold well. By 1748 the almanac sold 10,000 copies each year. It used many stereotypes of unattractive women: gossips, shrews, and constant talkers. Franklin knew that men would buy such books in order to have a good laugh.

Almanacs were popular because they predicted the weather for the farmer, and contained statistical data useful to the merchant. Franklin loved to use proverbs as filler material. His quotation from "Father Abraham" is well known: True, government taxes are heavy, but "we are taxed twice as much by our idleness, three times as much by our pride, and four times as much by our folly; and from these taxes the commissioners cannot deliver us."[7]

As a source for his proverbs, Franklin drew upon a number of current English anthologies. But his ear for memorableness stamps him as one of the greatest proverb artists in the English language. He used parallelism, balance, alliteration, and metaphor to chisel the proverb into its lasting form. For example, he took John Ray's bland "Fresh fish and new come guests smell, by that they are three days old" to the laconic "Fish and visitors smell in three days." Also, he turned Thomas Fuller's "The maintaining of one vice costeth more than ten virtues" into "What maintains one vice would bring up two children."[8] In nearly each case it was Franklin's form of the proverb that has been kept alive in the folklore of our society.

A versatile genius, Franklin found that his successes fed one another. By 1734 he was the public printer for not only Pennsylvania but also Delaware and New Jersey (and later for Maryland). His appointment as clerk of the Pennsylvania Assembly, which ran from 1736 to 1751, virtually assured that he would have the state's printing contracts. After he became postmaster at Philadelphia in 1737, he could use the riders to deliver his own newspapers.

As a printer, Franklin manufactured more of his own supplies than has any other American commercial printer. "He cast type, made paper molds, mixed inks, made contributions to press building, did engraving, forwarded experiments in stereotyping, and worked at logotypy."[9]

As a master printer, he set up many printers in many colonies. These were usually men he trained and then gave the capital to set up a printing business. Usually he received one-third of their profits. When brother James died in 1735, Franklin trained his brother's son and sent him back to run his brother's former business in Newport, Rhode Island.

A merchant, Franklin now owned a store selling commodities: cheese, coffee, soap, pencils, maps, lumber, horses. He also offered for sale the unexpired time of indentured servants. He frequently offered slaves for sale, and sometimes bought slaves as an investment.[10]

A tribute to the preaching of the Methodist missionary George Whitefield was his ability to get frugal Ben to contribute to an orphanage Whitefield was building in Georgia. At the start of the sermon Ben had decided to give nothing. After a short while, he thought he could spare a few coppers. As Whitefield waxed hot, Ben re-examined his pocket for three or four silver dollars — later, for five gold pistoles. By the time the offering plate came, he emptied his whole pocket into the plate.

He and Whitefield became unlikely good friends. Franklin printed his sermons, and invited him to lodge in the crowded quarters above his print shop.

Of a quite different note were a series of bagatelles that Franklin wrote at this time. In 1745 came "Advice to a Young Man on the Choice of a Mistress," in which Franklin recommended an older woman: you will not be corrupting a young person, and anyway the older woman is more grateful. In "Reflections on Courtship and Marriage" the following year Franklin made an early plea for women's equality. Then in 1747 came "The Speech of Polly Baker," a prostitute's plea for compassion. Polly, being prosecuted for having her fifth illegitimate child, asks what is to be done to the fathers — one is a magistrate, another a prominent merchant, and so on.

As a publisher, Franklin's printing was neat and legible but not fancy. In fact, some of his protégés became better printers than he. Later in life he admired specimens of fine printing he found in England and France. When it came time for him to write his will, this many-sided genius began it thus: "I, Benjamin Franklin, Printer . . ."

The Scientist

Dr. Archibald Spence of Edinburgh lectured in America between 1743 and 1751. In 1746 Franklin heard him lecture on electricity, and started to conduct his own experiments. One of them showed that many objects had positive and negative charges. Franklin's clear writing helped other scientists duplicate his experiments, such as those demonstrating that an electric spark makes a hole in paper, kills small animals, passes instantaneously through many people, and can discharge a battery of eleven guns.

Twice Franklin was nearly killed by electric shocks. In one experiment he placed spirits in a spoon on one side of a river, induced a spark on the other side, and thus ignited the spirits, showing that water conducted electricity. Paralytics came to him for treatment, and he would place a charge in the numb arm or leg. Some of them were moderately improved in the capacity to move the member.

The turning point in Franklin's life came in 1750 when Edward Cave in London published *Experiments and Observations on Electricity, Made at Philadelphia by Mr. Benjamin Franklin*. The book came from letters Franklin had sent to Peter Collinson, a member of the Royal Society. The book was constantly republished throughout Europe, and made Franklin famous. It went through ten editions, including revisions, in four languages by 1776.

Louis XV in France had the lightning rod experiment repeated successfully, and sent Franklin his thanks for preserving Paris and other French cities from lightning damage. Immanuel Kant called Franklin a new Prometheus who had stolen fire from heaven.

What were Franklin's contributions to the study of electricity? He drew lightning from a cloud by a kite, thus showing that lightning is electricity. He invented the lightning rod, and made the first electrical battery. His conception of electricity as a flow of positive and negative forces advanced study in this field. He was the first to use in English many electrical terms: armature, battery, brush, charge, conductor, electrician, minus, negative, plus, positive.[11]

In the 1753 issue of *Poor Richard's Almanac* Franklin gave simple, practical instructions on how to install a lightning rod on a building. He gave "God in his Goodness" credit for the invention. Up to now, he said, lightning was seen as evidence of divine wrath — now it could be seen as a method of sharing divine energy, or at least avoiding damage caused by a so-called "act of God." A Boston clergyman attacked lightning rods as a means of avoiding God's punishment for sin. Others said that too much electricity sent into the earth would cause earthquakes.

But Franklin's fame was secure. In 1753 he received honorary M.A.

degrees from Harvard and Yale, and a gold medal from the Royal Society. In 1756 he was elected as a member of the Royal Society, and received an honorary M.A. degree from William and Mary College. Honors continued to follow him the rest of his life.

His inquisitive mind led Franklin to make other discoveries. He was the first to study the Gulf Stream; on each crossing of the Atlantic he would make soundings with bottles. He explained why boats move slower in shallow water: the displaced water cannot go deep, so retards the sides of the boat. He figured out why northeast storms start in the southwest (because the hot air there rises, and air from the northeast rushes southwest to fill the gap).

Franklin pioneered in the diagnosis of lead poisoning, and the study of heat absorption by different colors. As a botanist, he sent the first kohlrabi, Chinese rhubarb, and Scotch cabbage seed to America. He played a leading role in the first American voyage of Arctic exploration, sending Captain Charles Swaine in 1753 on a search for the Northwest Passage.

Yankee ingenuity showed up in his many inventions. He devised a smokeless chimney, and the first flexible catheter used in America. He invented bifocal glasses, and a musical instrument, which he called the armonica, from partially filled water glasses. He invented a duplicating machine, and a glass contraption for showing blood circulation.

His domestic gadgets provided comfort. His study chair had a foot-operated fan. In his bathtub he had a bookrest so that he could read while soaking. He had a chair, the seat of which inverted to become a ladder. He had a long extension arm for taking things down from high shelves. His pressing machine, George Washington testified, produced better results than merely ironing clothes.

In addition to the many civic improvements he provided for Philadelphia, he came up with America's first idea of crop insurance for farmers. Impatient with spelling inconsistencies in English, he devised a phonetic alphabet and pushed for spelling reform.

It is easy to see why one might go as far back as Leonardo da Vinci to find another example of such many-sided genius. It is also easy to see why he qualified as the leading citizen in his world. In one step America had demonstrated that its culture could produce as well rounded a figure as could any country in the world.

The Statesman

It was inevitable that Franklin would eventually turn his attention to politics. In his early forties Franklin was financially independent and could spare time to once again work on public projects.

In 1747 England was at war with France over the Austrian succession. A French raiding party on the Delaware River came within twenty miles of Philadelphia. Franklin wrote a pamphlet, *Plain Truth*, admonishing city residents to arm themselves for protection. Some citizens asked why they should bear arms if the Quakers would not. That is like the man, said Franklin, "who refused to pump in a sinking ship, because one on board whom he hated would be saved as well as himself."[12]

Franklin called a meeting and asked the people to form a defense association. Soon there were 10,000 members of this volunteer militia. They outfitted themselves, elected officers, and met every other week for drill. Franklin was elected colonel, but he declined the honor, and instead took his turn as a common soldier. He helped organize a lottery to raise funds to build a fort and buy cannons for it.

Public recognition for Franklin now came fast. In 1748 he was elected to the Philadelphia city council. The next year he was selected as grand master of the Free Masons of Pennsylvania. The governor of Pennsylvania appointed him a peace commissioner that year, and again in 1752. In 1751 he was elected as a burgess in the Pennsylvania Assembly. Vacating the position as clerk of the Assembly, he got his son William appointed in his place.

The chief problems facing the Assembly were Indian affairs, the paper currency, and taxation of proprietary land. Franklin early saw the need for united colonial action for defense against Indian attacks. In 1751 he asked for united action for this purpose: "A voluntary union would be preferable to one imposed by Parliament, for it would be more easy to alter and improve as circumstances should require."[13]

Franklin was on the commission that negotiated a treaty with the Six Nations at Carlisle in 1753. It would be strange, he opined, if tribes of Indians speaking different languages could form a permanent union, but a dozen English colonies could not.

The first hospital in Pennsylvania was suggested by Dr. Thomas Bond, one of the first members of the American Philosophical Society. Franklin became a subscriber and a promoter, and was on the first board of managers. When a new building was occupied in 1755, he became president of the hospital board.

When Parliament passed a law restricting the production of iron, Franklin pointed out that "in another century the greatest number of Englishmen will be on this side of the water." Restricting American growth restricted the market for British goods. "A wise and good mother will not do it. Weakening the children weakens the whole family."[14]

In 1753 Franklin, along with William Hunter of Williamsburg, was appointed deputy postmaster-general of the colonies. He named his son William postmaster of Philadelphia, and the following year made him controller of the postal service for the colonies. Postal riders were now required to carry all posted newpapers, not at all hurting Franklin who was "publisher or partner of 7 or 8 newspapers, a chain stretching from New York to Antigua."[15]

Postal service improved rapidly. It was now possible to write from Philadelphia to Boston and get a return letter within three weeks. By 1761 the postal service returned to London its first operating profit. Part of the reason for the success was improved bookkeeping, and part was due to the faster service, which increased the volume of mail. Just as important, in Carl Van Doren's opinion, was the fact that "no man had ever done so much to draw the scattered colonies together."[16]

In 1754 Franklin was a member of the Pennsylvania delegation to Albany to draw up an intercolonial treaty with the Six Nations. He proposed a plan of union in which there would be a grand council chosen every three years by the colonial assemblies, and a president appointed by the king. "In the current state of colonial jealousy and separation," said Van Doren, "none was willing to yield so much power to a general council."[17]

Had it been adopted, Franklin's plan of union might have saved the colonies for the crown. By now Franklin had made valuable friendships with American leaders throughout the colonies, and he was being accepted by them as one of their number.

When Governor William Shirley of Massachusetts asked Franklin for his reaction to Shirley's alternate plan, Franklin's letters of criticism contained the seeds of the whole Revolutionary argument: "Excluding the people of the colonies from all share in the choice of a grand council would probably give extreme dissatisfaction, as well as taxing them by act of Parliament, where they have no representative." British frontiers in America, like their frontiers everywhere, deserve support from the total empire, Franklin said. Americans were already paying heavy taxes, direct and indirect, to England. Restraint upon American commerce benefited British merchants out of American pockets, he argued. Imposing new direct taxes would seem "hard measure" to Englishmen who risked their lives and fortune to extend the dominion of the mother nation only to find that "they have forfeited the native rights of Britons."[18]

In 1755 Franklin met Catherine Ray in Rhode Island. They exchanged letters and became lifelong friends. In one letter he told her to practice multiplication: "I would gladly have taught you that myself, but you wouldn't learn."[19] But learn she did, for after marrying William Greene in 1758 she bore him six children.

Also in 1755 Franklin and his son William assembled 150 wagons with four horses each, plus 259 pack horses, for General Edward Braddock's ill-fated campaign to recapture Fort Duquesne. When a war party of Shawnee massacred the Moravian mission village of Gnaddenhuetten, Franklin was sent by the Assembly to organize the frontier defenses. Fat and fifty, he took to rough outdoor living as naturally as to printing or inventing. Though he had no rank, the Moravians called him General Franklin.

Franklin insisted that proprietary lands should be taxed, but the governor, a spokesman for Thomas Penn, disapproved. Finally Penn contributed £5,000 to help defend the colony, to be raised from uncollected quitrents, which the Assembly was empowered to collect. When the Quakers heard that bounties were to be offered for Indian scalps, they left the Assembly.

The Colonial Agent

The Assembly chose Franklin to ask Penn in London for more defense funds. Since England was now at war with France, the voyage was especially long as Franklin's ship took a devious course to avoid French privateers. With time on his hands, Franklin wrote an especially long introduction to the next year's almanac, and called it "The Way to Wealth." This work proved to be exceptionally popular. It has had 70 editions in English, 56 in French, 11 in German, 9 in Spanish, plus editions in many other languages, including Chinese, Greek, and Russian.[20]

There were delays as Franklin tried to get action from Penn and the Parliament, so Franklin visited with British scientists. In February 1759 he received an honorary LL. D. degree from the University of St. Andrews. Lord Kames, the Edinburgh judge, became his friend, telling him that "the foundations of the future grandeur of the British empire lie in America, foundations strong enough to support the greatest political structure human wisdom has yet erected."[21]

Franklin eventually got the Privy Council to approve a compromise in which the unsurveyed lands of the proprietor would not be taxed but the surveyed ones would. He proved to be a poor investor of funds, however, investing some of Pennsylvania's reimbursement for war expenses in British government stock which declined in value.

Franklin's illegitimate son William had an illegitimate son, called William Temple Franklin, born in London in 1760. Then in 1785 William Temple returned the favor by having an illegitimate son in Passy, France.

As France and England discussed peace conditions, many Englishmen preferred to let France have the "hopeless wilderness" of Canada and instead receive Guadaloupe, a rich sugar island in the West

Indies. Franklin saw a rich future for Canada, especially in conjunction with America. England need never fear America's secession, he said — the colonies could not even unite at Albany to oppose the French and the Indians. That is, unless they suffer grievous tyranny and oppression.

The philosopher David Hume praised Franklin. "America," Hume said, "has sent us many good things — gold, silver, sugar, tobacco, etc. — but you are the first philosopher, and indeed the first great man of letters for whom we are beholden to her."[22] In 1762 Oxford gave Franklin an honorary degree of doctor of civil laws, and his son William received an honorary M.A.

Lord Bute then got William appointed governor of New Jersey, feeling that Franklin would be more cooperative if his son had a royal appointment. William made friends easily and started out as a popular governor.

In fall 1762 Franklin and his son arrived back in Philadelphia. Some members of the Assembly grumbled at William's appointment. Have we paid £3,000 in living expenses these past five years to Franklin, they asked, just to get a royal appointment for his son?

At the conclusion of the war with France, Indians on the frontier exploded. Feeling hemmed in on all sides, they attacked frontier settlements in western Pennsylvania. White posses were organized to massacre Indians, using tactics some Indians had used. Franklin spoke on behalf of sanity and understanding, showing how the Indians had been mistreated. During a time of high emotions, he became very unpopular with zealots.

When the Paxton Boys, a group of fanatic Presbyterians, began to slaughter peaceful Indians, Franklin wrote a pamphlet attacking them for inhumanity. The Paxton Boys responded with a lawless march towards the capital. Franklin, at the head of a force of his own, intercepted them at Germantown. He warned them that they would suffer unless they disbanded, and so they went back home. "For about 48 hours I was a very great man,"[23] Franklin chuckled.

Franklin eventually concluded that Thomas Penn would permit little self-government, and so, as speaker of the Assembly, he wrote the draft of a petition to George III asking that Pennsylvania be made a royal colony. This action cost him his seat in the Assembly, for John Dickinson beat him by campaigning against royal status.

Although beaten in his race for the legislature, Franklin was elected by the Assembly to present this petition to the King. Little did Franklin realize, when he sailed in November 1765, that he would remain in London for the next ten years!

The big issue now was the Stamp Act. Initially Franklin counseled obeying the law while striving to have it repealed. At this time he still held out hope for a reconciliation with England. He was amazed how well the colonists' boycott worked. He then shifted positions and lobbied hard to get the Stamp Act repealed, showing British merchants what it was costing them in lost business.

The House of Commons asked Franklin to testify concerning the Stamp Act in February 1766. Edmund Burke said that this was like a schoolmaster being examined by a group of schoolboys. Franklin cleverly kept the emphasis on how much England, not America, was losing because of the act.

First, Parliament members friendly to Franklin asked leading questions: What taxes are paid in Pennsylvania? Are the Indians a problem? Would it cost more to collect the tax than the tax would bring in?

Then came the questions from unfriendly members: Should America be protected at no expense to itself? Does Parliament have a right to tax all Englishmen? If we repeal this law, how many others will Americans want repealed?

The final questions (again from friends) were: "What used to be the pride of the Americans?" Franklin replied: "To indulge in the manufactures of Great Britain." And now what is their pride, he was asked, and responded, "To wear their old clothes over again till they can make new ones."[24] His questioning ended on February 13 and the repeal was approved on February 21.

Once again Franklin was a hero throughout the colonies, for the examination, including his clever answers, was published widely, not only in America but in England and on the continent. Now, with the boycott lifted, I will send you a fine new gown of Pompadour satin, Franklin told his wife.

In 1767 Franklin traveled to Hanover, where he met the fabulous Baron Münchhausen. Hanover was also ruled at that time by George III. The baron gave Franklin letters to scholars at the University of Göttingen. He was now elected as a member of the Royal Society of Sciences in Hanover.

At Versailles Franklin found the splendid palace "a prodigious mixture of magnificence and negligence," with fallen walls, broken windows, and "water-works out of repair."[25] On his visit to France he found scientists who called themselves *franklinistes*, which amused him. He met the Physiocrat leader François Quesnay. He himself sounded like a Physiocrat when he said, in 1768, that a nation acquired wealth in three ways: first, plunder like the Romans; "the second, commerce, which is generally cheating; the third, by agriculture, is the only honest way."[26]

Besides representing Pennsylvania, he became the agent for Georgia in 1768, New Jersey in 1769, and Massachusetts in 1770. He was becoming the general agent, or spokesman, for the colonies in England.

He described the "Causes of the American Discontents" in the *London Chronicle* in 1768. He meant to be conciliatory, saying that Americans were grateful for repeal of the Stamp Act, and that they would accept the Quartering Act, provided it was temporary. But they found the Townshend Acts offensive, he said, for now they cannot even manufacture their own hats, nails, or steel, nor import wine or fruit from Portugal without paying a commission to a British merchant. We are loyal to the king, Franklin said, but the Parliament wants us to surrender our properties. "This unhappy new system of politics," he said, "tends to dissolve those bonds of union and to sever us forever."[27]

Franklin suffered the invariable fate of peacemakers: England felt that he was too pro-American, and many Americans accused him of being pro-British. A private letter to his son in March 1768 revealed that his effort to maintain a middle ground was losing way: One was forced to admit either that Parliament can make all of our laws or that she can make none, "and I think the arguments for the latter more numerous and weighty than those for the former."[28]

Franklin became a land speculator in 1766, when he bought 20,000 acres in Nova Scotia. In 1769 he and William joined the Grand Ohio Company, that planned to set up a new colony beyond the Alleghenies. Franklin mentioned to George Whitefield that "you and I" could establish a Christian settlement there which would give the heathen Indians an example of pure religion. Confused land titles and other complications led to the failure of the Grand Ohio Company. Contrary to the charges of Charles Beard at a later date, Franklin would have benefited more, as a land speculator, had Britain won the War, because then the land would have stayed in the hands of the Grand Ohio Company, since it had the support of some influential British leaders. As it was, the land reverted to the federal government when the United States won.

In 1771 Franklin began his autobiography in the form of a letter to his son William. It was so revelatory of his personality that it became a classic in the field. Often he spoofs himself, chiding himself for pretending to a virtue that was compromised. Sometimes he seems to be suggesting that "his counsels of thrift and prudence should not be taken seriously. Franklin, moreover, often failed to live down to his principles, and generosity and kindliness then overwhelmed his business instincts."[29]

On a visit to Ireland that year, he was invited to sit in the Irish Parliament in Dublin. Ireland was watching America sympathetically. Franklin advised his colonial clients to keep up trade with Ireland, even when there was a boycott of English goods.

He then toured Scotland and was charmed by Scottish tunes, which he felt exceeded all others in uniting melody and harmony. He was, naturally, something of a musician. He liked to sing, and he wrote lyrics for familiar tunes. He learned to play the violin, harp, guitar, and armonica. Both Mozart and Beethoven composed music for the armonica.

When his son-in-law Richard Bache came to England with £1,000 to purchase a government post (as was the custom), Franklin advised him to return home and open a store in the house Franklin owned. He also gave Bache £200 sterling to pay for his trip to England and back.

His playfulness was revealed in 1772 at Lord Shelburne's home at Wycombe. Franklin told the group that he could quiet the waves on a nearby stream. He walked several hundred paces upstream, made some magic passes, and waved his bamboo cane three times. Amazingly, the waves subsided. He then explained that he carried oil in a hollow joint in his cane, and a few drops of oil had calmed the water.

Toward the end of 1772 Franklin got hold of ten letters, six written by Thomas Hutchinson before he became governor of Massachusetts and four written by Andrew Oliver before he became lieutenant-governor. These native Americans decried Boston mob action; their homes had been destroyed by mobs in the Stamp Act protest. They recommended to Parliament an abridgment of colonial liberties.

Franklin believed that Hutchinson and Oliver had presented a one-sided view, and were more responsible than Parliament for the oppressive laws that had been passed. Possibly violating the privacy of these men, Franklin sent the letters to Thomas Cushing in America, advising Cushing to show the letters to the Committee of Correspondence.

Franklin warned Cushing not to make the letters public. But Samuel Adams read them to the Massachusetts Assembly in secret session. Somebody printed them, and the Massachusetts Assembly petitioned George III to remove Hutchinson and Oliver from office.

William Whately, brother of the man who had received the letters, sued Franklin for printing private letters without permission. News of the Boston Tea Party had just arrived in England, and although Franklin condemned the destruction of the tea, the British wanted revenge. As a colonial agent Franklin was available, and so he was called before the Privy Council and humiliated.

Alexander Wedderburn, the solicitor-general who conducted the questioning of Franklin, had been dismissed from the Scottish bar for insulting the president of the court. Wedderburn attacked Franklin in what Lord Shelburne called "scurrilous invective." Is it a sign of English liberty, Wedderburn asked, to attack British ships, plunder her goods, or destroy their homes? Is a government bad to protest such action?

Franklin took the abuse in silence, knowing that to speak would be an error. The Privy Council rejected the petition of Massachusetts to unseat Hutchinson and Oliver, and fired Franklin as deputy postmaster-general. Whately's suit was pending in chancery court.

Philosophical about the abuse, Franklin blamed it on rising tempers: "The populace, who are used to it, love to have a good character cut up now and then for their entertainment. Having been long engaged in public business, this treatment is not new to me."[30]

Wedderburn's attack made Franklin a hero in America. Horace Walpole wrote a poem about it[31]:

> Sarcastic Sawney, swollen with spite and prate
> On silent Franklin poured his venal hate.
> The calm philosopher, without reply
> Withdrew, and gave his country liberty.

Franklin got revenge in 1773 in two great pieces of political rhetoric. In "Edict by the King of Prussia," he published a hoax in a London newspaper, claiming Prussia's right to tax all Englishmen because of their Anglo-Saxon origin. Franklin cleverly put many of the American complaints about Britain into the English objections to the German rule. This tract was made more pointed by the German background of George III.

The other essay, "Rules by Which a Great Empire May Be Reduced to a Small One," contains seemingly serious advice towards an obviously ridiculous goal. Like a great cake, says Franklin, an empire is easiest diminished around the edges. Thus, ignore remote colonies, send castoffs as their governors and judges, and harass them with novel taxes. If they petition for redress, ignore it. Say that your taxing power has no limits. Deprive them of their constitutional liberties, and if they protest, call it treason. In this way you will soon be rid of the burden of governing them.

The ironic fact of British history has been that these absurd "rules" have all too often been followed, with dire consequences for the empire.

The British ministry now tried to use Franklin as a peacemaker. Lord Richard Howe's sister played some chess games with Franklin, and asked him to intervene with the colonies on behalf of the crown. Rebuffed, Lord Howe then offered him a bribe if he would be loyal to the king, but of course Franklin turned it down.

Dr. John Fothergill and David Barclay, a wealthy London Quaker, asked Franklin to draw up a plan of reconciliation, and so he did. In the plan, Boston would pay for the destroyed tea, and the tea tax would be dropped. No British troops would be stationed in America without the colonists' consent, and Parliament would disavow any authority over internal legislation in the colonies. The plan was passed along to the British ministry, where it was of course rejected.

A group of British leaders, including Lords Camden, Chatham, and Shelburne, plus Edmund Burke and Charles James Fox, agreed with Franklin that the crown should make concessions to America, but their bill was defeated in Parliament.

In December 1774 Franklin's wife Deborah died of a stroke. In London, Franklin had to miss the funeral.

His great patience turned to rage when Franklin heard General Alured Clarke say that "with a thousand British grenadiers he would go from one end of America to the other and geld all the males, partly by force and partly by a little coaxing."[32] Furious, Franklin drew up an insolent response, but then followed the advice of his friend Thomas Walpole and did not send it.

Sensing that his mission to England was at an end, he sailed for America in March 1775. Aboard ship he lamented that "so glorious a fabric as the present British empire was to be demolished by these blunders." Broken, he said, was "that fine and noble China vase, the British empire."[33]

The Patriot and Diplomat

He arrived in Philadelphia on May 5. The following day he was chosen by the Pennsylvania Assembly as a delegate to the Second Continental Congress, to meet in Philadelphia on May 10. At 69 he was the oldest man in Congress.

On May 13 an order for his arrest was issued in London, to answer charges in the Whately case. Franklin collected the money due him as a Massachusetts agent. He also gave Massachusetts authorities £100 raised by Englishmen for the benefit of Americans wounded at Lexington and Concord.

When his son William rejoiced at still being governor of New Jersey, Franklin admonished him: "I don't understand it as any favor to me or to you, the being continued in office. I think independence more honorable than any service. You will find yourself in no comfortable situation, and perhaps wish you had disengaged yourself."[34]

Franklin was right. William remained a loyalist and served a prison term as a Tory, after which he became president of the Associated Loyalists in New York City.

Although he was one of the boldest members of Congress, Franklin was usually silent. James Madison said that Franklin's method was to avoid argument by listening to an adversary and then "overthrow him with an anecdote."

Thomas Jefferson, who served with Washington in the Virginia legislature and with Franklin in the Continental Congress, said of them: "I never heard either of them speak ten minutes at a time, nor to any but the main point. They laid their shoulders to great points, knowing that the little ones would follow of themselves."[35]

Franklin was appointed to most of the major committees of Congress. Since he had been through these arguments many times, he listened patiently as the younger delegates got educated. When Congress voted another petition to the king, Franklin said that it was useless. And so it was, for Lord Dartmouth did not bother to show it to George III.

Franklin drafted few state papers, leaving that chore to more oratorical members. He was active on the saltpeter committee, and was chairman of the committee to establish a new postal system. Elected postmaster-general, he gave his annual salary of $1,000 for the relief of wounded soldiers.

A master at printing money, he made sketches for the new currency. In order to frustrate counterfeiters, he worked out elaborate leaf designs.

The Pennsylvania Assembly elected him president of the Committee on Safety, which ran the government while the Assembly was not in session. Because of the tense military situation, he worked chiefly on defense preparations. In September 1775 he presided for the first time as president of the American Philosophical Society. Although he had been president for the past seven years, he could not preside while living in London.

His contributions as a member of the committee to draft the Declaration of Independence were few. He changed "truths to be sacred and undeniable" to "truths to be self-evident." He added to the king's acts "abolishing our most valuable laws." He also changed the accusation that foreign mercenaries were being sent to "deluge us in blood" to "destroy us."[36]

England asked that a peace mission meet with Lord Richard Howe, so Congress sent Franklin, John Adams, and Edward Rutledge to meet with Howe. Howe said that he could not recognize them as delegates of Congress, but he would speak to them as gentlemen of great ability and influence. Both sides were adamant, however, at this meeting on Long Island, and so negotiations were dropped.

Lord Howe by sea and his brother General William Howe by land then drove Washington's army out of Manhattan, first to Harlem Heights and then to White Plains. New York City was burned and one-third destroyed, for which loyalists blamed retreating patriots.

In September 1776 Congress appointed Franklin, Jefferson, and Silas Deane as commissioners to France, in an effort to get French support against the British. Since Jefferson's wife was ill, he was replaced by

Arthur Lee. Franklin took his two grandsons to Paris, William Temple, now nearly 17, and Benjamin Franklin Bache, who was 7.

In 1775 France had set up Caron de Beaumarchais, author of *The Marriage of Figaro* and *The Barber of Seville*, in what looked like a private company to sell arms and supplies to America in return for staple goods. It was unclear whether this was to be a gift or to be paid in kind. Arthur Lee told Congress about the plan, and Congress appointed Silas Deane as the agent to secure the arms and supplies.

Franklin was an instant hit in Paris. The French, seeking revenge for the treaty of 1763, admired the Americans for talking back to the British. Franklin was not only a spokesman for freedom but a man admired as a philosopher, scientist, and citizen of the world. He combined the primitive virtues of a Rousseau with the wit and wisdom of a Voltaire. He wore his fur hat, practical on the sea voyage, but now a symbol of the common man in Paris.

Richard Morris may have felt that Franklin's affected Quaker garb was a "subtle form of reverse ostentation that ill accorded with his preachments about humility,"[37] but the French loved it. Within a few weeks, everyone in Paris had to have a Franklin image: bracelet, ring, medallion, snuffbox, or a miniature for the fireplace mantel. In Nantes, women began wearing wigs shaped like a fur cap, a fashion called hair à la Franklin.

There were paintings and busts, statuettes, drawings, and prints of America's philosopher. Soon Franklin's face appeared on clocks, watches, dishes, vases, handkerchiefs, and pocket knives. "Probably no man before Franklin had ever had his likeness so widely current in so many forms."[38] Franklin was surely America's secret weapon on the continent of Europe.

The Franklin fad even spread to England, war or not. In 1777 the Wedgwood pottery works could scarcely turn out enough Franklin medallions and busts to meet the great demand!

Franklin's French caused natives to smile. At one meeting of the French Academy of Sciences he could not keep up with the speedy dialogue so he hit upon the idea of applauding whenever his Passy neighbor applauded. He later discovered that he was applauding the loudest whenever he himself was being praised.

A trusting soul, Franklin used lax security in his work. As a result, British spies like Paul Wentworth and Dr. Edward Bancroft had an easy time intercepting his dispatches and relaying the information to London.

In 1777 the American emissaries received a secret subsidy of two million livres from the French. This enabled them to outfit Captain Lambert Wickes in his ship *Reprisal*, and in a month he brought back as prizes five British ships, which were sold at Lorient.

Unlike the British nobility, the French nobility sought out Franklin and honored him. Even his bad French amused them. "He bore himself always as the wise and simple philosopher they desired him to be."[39]

Helped by the news of Burgoyne's surrender at Saratoga, the Americans and French signed a treaty of alliance against Great Britain in 1778. The treaty pledged French assistance in the American struggle for independence, in return for American aid to France should she ever engage Britain in war. Their ports would be open to each other, and they would be the most-favored nations towards each other in trade.

Hearing of the treaty stirred the British to seek to end hostilities. Their commission of envoys promised home rule within the empire, with repeal of all objectionable acts passed since 1763. But Congress held out for independence, as did Franklin when he was approached by the British several times and asked to serve as a peace negotiator.

Franklin assisted American privateers in their campaign against British shipping. By early 1778 London estimated that privateers had cost Britain £1,800,633. A total of 559 British ships had been captured and converted to American use. *The Black Prince* alone captured 75 British ships in one year.[40]

Franklin also worked to improve conditions in British POW prisons. He wrote to Edmund Burke that "since the foolish part of mankind will make wars, not having sense enough otherwise to settle their differences, it certainly becomes the wise part, who cannot prevent these wars, to alleviate as much as possible the calamities attending them."[41]

He was such a persona non grata with George III in 1778 that the king had Franklin's sharp-pointed lightning conductors replaced with blunt-ended ones. Sir John Pringle, pointing out that "the laws of nature were not changeable at Royal pleasure," was forced to resign as Queen's physician and as president of the Royal Society. Popular rhymes in London lampooned George III for his stupidity.

In 1778 Franklin and Voltaire met at the French Academy of Sciences and embraced each other. How charming, went the cry through Europe, that Solon and Socrates should embrace! Houdon executed a marble bust of Franklin that year. Turgot devised a Latin epigram for Franklin which said that "he snatched lightning from the sky and the sceptre from tyrants."[42]

A quarrel broke out among the envoys. Deane was suspected of getting payments for alleged gifts to the United States. Arthur Lee suspected Deane, and accused Franklin of being secretive. So John Adams was sent by Congress to check up on the envoys.

Adams felt that the envoys were living extravagantly. Franklin's landlord at Passy, however, took no rent, saying it was enough reward that his house was immortalized by Franklin and his entourage.

Adams said that Franklin was admired above Leibnitz, Newton, and Voltaire. "There was scarcely a peasant or footman," he said, "who was not familiar with Franklin's name and who did not consider him a friend to humankind."[43] They felt that he would abolish monarchy and hierarchy throughout the world, and restore the golden age.

But Adams disliked Franklin, finding him noncommittal and indirect. "He loves his ease, hates to offend, and seldom gives any opinion till obliged to do it,"[44] said Adams, who felt that Franklin was too frivolous, and too ready to flatter and be flattered.

Was Franklin a lecher in Paris? Folklore would have it so, but Van Doren says that "there is no support for the tradition which insists that the philosopher was a lively lecher in France."[45]

Madame Brillon, wife of a much older treasury official, flirted with Franklin for years. Yet he knew her mother and grandmother, and was on friendly terms with M. Brillon. He wrote for her two of his famous bagatelles, "The Ephemera" and "The Whistle."

Madame Helvetius was the widow of a rich farmer-general. She entertained countless famous people at her estate in Auteuil. Abigail Adams was shocked to see her kiss Franklin's cheeks and forehead when she greeted him. He proposed to her but was rejected, and then wrote a famous bagatelle about a dream in which he saw Mrs. Franklin in the Elysian Fields with M. Helvetius. Commenting on this bagatelle the critic Charles Sainte-Beuve said that Franklin "never allowed himself to be carried away by feeling, in youth or in age, in love or in religion. His romantic posture was almost ritualistic. He almost seemed relieved at the chance to convert an emotional rebuff into a literary exericse."[46]

At Versailles, Marie Antoinette called Franklin *l'ambassador électrique*. He returned the compliment saying that her eyes "do more mischief in a week than I have done in all my experiments."[47]

Franklin wrote constantly to Catherine Greene, Polly Stevenson Hewson, and Georgiana Shipley when he by no means could have been expecting sexual favors from them.

He joined the Masonic lodge of the Nine Sisters in 1777, and the following year took part in an elaborate Masonic memorial service for Voltaire. In 1779 he was chosen grand master of the lodge, which was useful to him in his diplomatic mission. He made friends there with influential Frenchmen who were seeking liberty for France and the United States. Opposed to absolutism, the lodge had men who played an important part in French history, such as the Marquis de Condorcet, Georges Danton, and Brissot de Warville.

Franklin was also famous in Italy. Giovanni Beccaria had made him known there as early as 1756. He was made a foreign member of the Padua Academy of Sciences in 1782, and of that of Turin in 1783.

In August 1781 Franklin, John Adams, and John Jay were appointed peace commissioners to negotiate with the British. Franklin wrote to Adams: "I have never known a peace made, even the most advantageous, that was not censured as inadequate. 'Blessed be the peacemakers' is, I suppose, to be understood in the other world, for in this they are frequently cursed."[48] But he gladly accepted the role.

For the first three months of their assignment, Franklin negotiated alone with the British. He was tough on loyalists. He also wanted England to cede Canada to the United States in payment for raids and depredations during the War. When the treaty was signed in September 1783, Franklin wrote to Josiah Quincy, "May we never see another war! For in my opinion there never was a good war or a bad peace."[49]

Franklin also warned against British retaliation, saying that "Britain will be long watching for advantages to recover what she has lost. Let us, therefore, beware of being lulled into a dangerous security."[50]

Now that the United States was an independent nation, many European countries sought trade treaties. Franklin was involved in negotiating many of them.

John Adams continued to have ambivalent feelings about Franklin. On the one hand he doubted that Franklin's international reputation could be explained without doing a complete history of 18th century philosophy and politics. Adams lacked Franklin's grace and charm in dealing with the French. Adams cited Franklin's Polly Baker hoax as one of his many "outrages to morality and decorum." Adams not only questioned Franklin's liberal sexual morality but wondered if he would ever grow up, even in old age.

Mesmerism became a great fad in Paris in 1784. Franklin was put on a committee of the French Academy of Sciences to investigate it. Although they located no universal magnetic fluid, Franklin said that perhaps the treatment aided rich people who otherwise are never in good health because they are always taking medicine.

Possibly Franklin received the first airmail letter. In 1785 Dr. John Jeffries delivered a letter to him, sent from London to Paris, with a balloon crossing the Channel from Dover to a point near Calais.

Thomas Jefferson, newly arriving in Paris to replace him, said that he found "more respect and veneration attached to the character of Dr. Franklin in France than to that of any other person, foreign or native."[51] Jefferson considered Franklin to be the greatest American of all. It was, he said, a school of humility to succeed him as minister to France.

As he left Paris in 1785, Franklin received from Louis XVI a parting gift consisting of a miniature of the king set with 408 diamonds. Franklin's goods for shipment filled 128 boxes. At Rouen, townspeople would not let him go, insisting upon giving him every manner of recognition. After more than eight years in France, he was returning as "the most famous private citizen in the world."[52]

The Framer

Within a month after returning to the United States Franklin was elected first to the state Council and then as president of Pennsylvania. As president he abolished the oath of allegiance for office holders, revised the penal code so that only murder and treason would be capital offenses, and restored the charter of the Bank of North America. He kept none of his annual salary of £1500. He was re-elected in 1786 and 1787.

His biggest problem was to try to settle the tug of war over the Wyoming district land in western Pennsylvania between Connecticut and Pennsylvania. A decision in 1787 gave the land to the original Connecticut settlers, and compensated Pennsylvania claimants with land in another district.

Despite the fact that at 81 he was the oldest delegate to the Constitutional Convention, Franklin would arrive early enough to attend prior sessions of the Pennsylvania Council. Like Washington at the Convention, he was largely a presence—a conciliator with wisdom, good humor, and common sense.

At the Convention, he opposed giving the executive an absolute veto over the legislature, having seen the proprietary governor abuse this prerogative. His biggest single contribution was the suggestion that money bills should originate in the House of Representatives, and thus he played a key role in the Great Compromise.

His sympathies were thoroughly democratic. He wanted all male citizens to vote, not just freeholders. He wanted no property qualifications for office holders. He did not see why immigrants should have to wait for years before being eligible to hold office. He wanted a council to be set up to act as a check upon the executive.

Whenever a situation grew tense or the debate reached a stalemate, the delegates turned to Franklin for a word of calm assurance, or a plea for mutual forbearance. He and Washington worked together perfectly as a strong, silent, and healing duo.

At the conclusion of the Convention he made his great speech of reconciliation, asking delegates to put aside narrow interests so that a Constitution could be adopted that would not only answer a host of current needs but more importantly serve as the cornerstone for a great nation. The rising sun he noticed on the back of Washington's chair was partly the refulgence of a citizen of the world who loved his native country above all others.

Final Years

When he first heard of the French Revolution, Franklin said: "God grant that not only the love of liberty but a thorough knowledge of the rights of man may pervade all the nations of the earth, so that a philosopher may set his foot anywhere on its surface and say, 'This is my country.'"[53]

The older he grew, the more he opposed slavery. He wrote a few antislavery tracts in his early years, generally showing that the cost of keeping slaves made it dearer than hiring day laborers. In 1764 he said that blacks had a "strong sense of justice and honor." In 1772 he grew angry at that "detestable commerce," the slave trade, and the following year he aided a movement to abolish slavery.

In 1787 he became president of the Pennsylvania Abolition Society, the oldest one in the world. He proposed a program to educate free blacks for employment. His last public act was to send Congress a petition to end "the traffic in the persons of our fellowmen." When some Southerners denounced the petition, he wrote a fictitious account of an official in Algiers involved in enslaving Christians: "Plundering and enslaving Christians is unjust, but it is in the interest of this state to continue the practice; therefore, let the petition be rejected."[54]

Franklin's will granted £1000 each to the cities of Boston and Philadelphia, for loans to "young married artificers" at 5 percent interest, to be repaid one-tenth of the principal each year. In 100 years, Franklin said, the sum would be £131,000 and in 200 years it would be about £4,000,000. This sum is still maintained and is expected in 1991 to be about $4,000,000. This is considered to be the largest money gift ever made by a philosopher.[55]

Franklin had long suffered from gout and kidney stones. As he aged, he grew hard of hearing. In 1791 he had two severe attacks of pleurisy, and finally a fatal empyema in his left lung. He died on April 17, 1791.

Philadelphia had a huge funeral in his honor. On a motion by James Madison, the House of Representatives unanimously approved the wearing of mourning for a month. In Paris the French National Assembly wore mourning for three days.

Franklin, in proving that common people could produce a giant, at the same time demonstrated that this new nation need be second to none in turning out a person at once frivolous and wise — a philosopher, scientist, and political leader of international repute. By becoming a premier citizen of the world, Franklin made his country eminently acceptable to all reasonable people.

Let Carl Van Doren write his eulogy: "In any age, in any place,

Franklin would have been great. Mind and will, talent and art, strength and ease, wit and grace met in him as if nature had been lavish and happy when he was shaped. Even his genius could not specialize him. He moved through his world in a humorous mastery of it. Sometimes, with his marvelous range, in spite of his personal tang, he seems to have been more than any single man: a harmonious human multitude."[56]

5. Nathaniel Gorham: The Voice of Business

The man who presided over most of the Constitutional Convention was Nathaniel Gorham, a delegate from Massachusetts. On May 30 Gorham was elected chairman of the Committee of the Whole. Since most matters of Convention business, especially important ones, were first discussed in the Committee of the Whole, where debate was informal and votes frequently reversed, Gorham presided over a great deal of the Convention. Only when the Convention was nearing a consensus on an issue would the topic be returned to the floor of the Convention, with Washington in the chair.

Gorham also served on the Committee of Detail and several other important committees. Who was this rather obscure Yankee who played a significant role in the framing of America's most basic governmental document?

Gorham was born in Charlestown, Massachusetts, on May 21, 1738. He was the oldest of five children of Nathaniel and Mary Soley Gorham. One of his ancestors was Desire Howland, the daughter of John Howland of the *Mayflower*.

After receiving a public school education, Gorham was apprenticed at the age of 15 to Nathaniel Coffin, a merchant in New London, Connecticut. He worked for Coffin until 1759, when he returned to Charlestown to open up his own business.

As a merchant, Gorham was very successful. Within a few years he was one of the most prosperous businessmen in Massachusetts. He married Rebecca Call in 1763, and ultimately they had nine children. A handsome man, he was described by William Pierce as "rather lusty, with an agreeable and pleasing manner."[1]

He was a member of the Ancient Fire Company, which included the bluebloods of Boston, and he was one of the incorporators of the Charles River Bridge. He was very active in his state's public life. He served in the colonial legislature from 1771 to 1775, as a delegate to the Provincial Congress in 1774–75, and as a member of the state Board of War from 1778 to 1781.

He held many other positions in Massachusetts. He was a delegate to the state constitutional convention in 1779–80, a state senator in 1780, and a member of the state house of representatives from 1781–87, being speaker in 1781, 1782, and 1785. In July 1785 he was appointed judge of the Middlesex County court of common pleas. He was also a member of the governor's council in 1788–89.

As might be expected, Gorham was a spokesman for business interests in the legislature. Van Beck Hall says that "he had the reputation of being a political trimmer,"[2] that is, one who has no set position but pragmatically switches sides whenever he deems it necessary. He could usually be counted on, however, to look at a problem from the standpoint of a businessman.

Unrest in Massachusetts

There was great unrest in western Massachusetts in the 1780s. Coteries of dissatisfied farm workers, yeomen, and husbandmen were led into expressing their protest at economic conditions — unemployment, inflation, and high interest rates — by lower-grade militia officers, unpaid former Revolutionary War officers, a few justices of the peace, and a judge.

Samuel Ely, a former Congregational minister, early in 1782 traveled through Hampshire County telling listeners to revoke the 1780 constitution, for he had a better one in his pocket. On April 12, 1782, a mob of his followers interfered with court hearings.

Ely was jailed for six months and fined £250. On June 12 an armed mob broke into the Springfield jail and freed Ely. Local police took three rioters as hostages, in an effort to get Ely back. Rioters marched from Hatfield to Northampton to free the hostages. The disturbance was finally quelled.

On June 27 the General Court suspended habeas corpus for six months and authorized Governor John Hancock to jail "any person whose being at large may be judged by His Excellency and the Council to be dangerous to the people and well-being of this or any of the United States."[3] The people of western Massachusetts had learned that they could attract the attention of the authorities by mob action.

In August 1782 the General Court appointed a committee, consisting of Gorham, Samuel Adams, and Artemas Ward, to travel to Hampshire County to investigate the causes of the dissatisfaction and to explain the state's financial status to the citizens.

The committee met with a large delegation at Hatfield from August 7 to August 10. This meeting recommended tax reductions, lower state salaries, and pardon of all but Ely for those who had engaged in riots that year. The General Court adopted the recommendations from the meeting, and even pardoned Ely in 1783 on condition that he leave Massachusetts.

In addition to his role in state politics, Gorham was a member of the Confederation Congress in 1782, 1783, and 1785-87. A fellow Congressman, Jacob Read of South Carolina, gave his impressions of Gorham and Elbridge Gerry to Charles Thomson, secretary of Congress, in a letter in October 1784: "In Boston I saw Honest Gorham who pressed me very much to spend a day with him in Charlestown where he lives. I met Gerry in the street — he is a malignant white-livered rascal."[4]

By serving in both legislatures at once, Gorham could use one role to support the other. For example, in 1785 he voted to grant supplemental state funds to Congress. Also, as unrest grew in Massachusetts, he began to favor a stronger central government with power to use the militia to put down disturbances. He also supported governor James Bowdoin's efforts to keep the peace. He opposed efforts to cut Bowdoin's salary and he also opposed an effort in the state legislature to override the governor's veto of the salary-cut bill.

The President of Congress

The year 1786 was a big one for Gorham. Serving in the Confederation Congress, he feared the outbreak of violence between New Jersey and New York. In a letter to James Warren on March 6 he wrote that "there is no reason that Rhode Island, Delaware, and Georgia should have equal weight in the federal councils with Massachusetts, Pennsylvania, and Virginia. As unanimity is now necessary upon the most trivial questions, we feel all the inconveniences of the liberum veto of a Polish Diet. The assembly of New Jersey have lately entered into a resolution that they will not comply with any requisition of Congress until New York gives up their impost or applies it for the general purposes of the Union.

"Indeed, there is nothing but the restraining hand of Congress (weak as it is) that prevents New Jersey and Connecticut from entering the lists very seriously with New York, and bloodshed would very quickly be the consequence. However New Jersey may suffer by her paying taxes to New York, her refusal to comply with the requisition is unjustifiable, and unless she rescinds her resolution must work the end of all federal government."[5]

The next day Gorham was put on a Congressional committee, along with Charles Pinckney and William Grayson, to visit New Jersey to attempt to persuade the legislature to rescind the resolution. Grayson warned the legislature that now New Jersey had an equal vote with the large states, but continued resistance to the federal government would bring in a new constitution in which small states would have a subordinate role to large states.

Gorham and Pinckney also addressed the legislature and four days later the resolution was rescinded. A New Jersey newspaper said that the speeches of Grayson and Gorham proved "by a variety of arguments" and "in a very able and pointed manner" the inappropriateness of New Jersey's refusal to pay the requisition.[6]

In April Gorham wrote a letter to Governor Bowdoin describing the problems of the Confederation Congress. Rarely, he said, were more than nine states represented, and yet it took unanimous decisions on all important matters. A treaty with the Barbary Powers was concluded without sending a representative there, an action that would have improved the treaty. "The delegates," he said, "have no powers relative to the formation of the court necessary to bring to issue the cause between Massachusetts and New York."[7]

On May 15 Gorham became temporary president of Congress, replacing David Ramsay who had been filling in for the ill president, John Hancock. He must have done a good job because on June 6 he was elected to the position.

On July 4 President Gorham had a public levee recognizing the anniversary of the Declaration of Independence. The secretary of Congress wrote letters to high government officials inviting them and their guests to attend. To John Jay, secretary for foreign affairs, the invitation was extended to "the foreign ministers and others in public characters from foreign courts within your department, and to such strangers of distinction as you may judge proper."[8]

There was a ringing of bells and a discharge of cannon on July 4. At noon there was a grand procession to the governor's house, then to the house of President Gorham, where the governor and the mayor of New York City extended the compliments of the day to the Confederation Congress. Afterwards everyone adjourned for collation at Carre's Tavern.

Shays' Rebellion

Meanwhile economic conditions were growing increasingly worse, especially in western Massachusetts. Many small farmers were losing their land through seizure for overdue debts and delinquent taxes. Town meetings and county conventions called for a moratorium on taxes, and for the issuance of paper money.

The malcontents, many of them disfranchised by the loss of their property, gathered in a mob at Northampton on August 29 to intimidate the court to cease action against debtors. Daniel Shays, a local officeholder of Pelham, led the group when they appeared in uniform at the supreme court in Springfield in September.

There were varying degrees of action involved in the protests. The more conservative persons recommended conventions—meetings to draw up lists of grievances to be sent to the governor. Regulators wanted postponement of court action but generally tried to avoid violence. Many neutral citizens were so disgusted with conditions that they stood aside and let the more radical ones interfere with the courts and impede other governmental functions. Sometimes court sessions had to be abandoned because the required number of grand jurors could not be impaneled.

In October "Regulators attempted to steal cannon from Dorchester Neck, freed a prisoner from the Worcester jail, almost mobbed Theodore Sedgwick in Berkshire County, and about 130 turned out to block the Bristol County Court of Common Pleas."[9] When conservatives called for military action against the Regulators, Governor Bowdoin stiffened and called out the militia to keep the courts open.

Gorham promised Bowdoin federal help if he needed it. In a letter of October 22 Gorham said that "the affairs of the western country are in such a state as to induce Congress to propose an augmentation of troops—a considerable number of which are assigned to Massachusetts, if the General Court should agree to raise them."[10]

An abortive effort by the rebels to seize arms from the Springfield arsenal was quashed in January 1787, and the uprising was basically at an end. There were, however, some positive results. "The protest moved to the ballot box: the conservative power, which had been so indifferent to the plight of the poor farmers was overthrown; many of the reforms the Shaysites had desired were enacted into law, and all the rebels were amnestied."[11]

To a conservative like Gorham the rebellion turned him into a nationalist. He could see that economic problems needed national solutions, and that armed outbreaks were more than state militia could handle. But before he was ready for a national convention to amend the Articles of Confederation, he tried a weird scheme.

The story is found in volume six of the *Life and Correspondence of Rufus King*. Under the dateline of May 10, 1824, President James Monroe charged that some of the Federalist supporters of Washington were believers in monarchy. King's memorandum reads as follows: "Colonel Miller this evening said to me, speaking of President Monroe, that he had told him that Mr. Gorham, formerly President of Congress, had written a letter to Prince Henry, brother of the great Frederick, desiring him to come to the United States to be their king, and that the Prince had declined by informing Mr. Gorham that the Americans had shown so much determination against their old King that they would not readily submit to a new one. Mr. Monroe added that General Armstrong had given him this information and that the papers or correspondence was in the hands of General Hull.[12]

In his article in the *American Historical Review*, Richard Krauel argues that this event actually took place, and that Gorham was acting on behalf of a party of associates.[13] What makes it all the more incredible is the fact that at the time he wrote the letter Gorham, as president of Congress, was the highest ranking official in America!

Had this information been more generally known in 1787, Gorham not only might not have been elected chairman of the Committee of the Whole but he also might have not been selected as a delegate to the Constitutional Convention. This information would also have given greater credence to the charge of Jefferson and fellow Republicans that there was a Federalist monarchical plot at work. So little attention was given to this offer, on both sides of the Atlantic, that it can only be seen as a desperate last-ditch effort to shore up a society that looked to Gorham as if it was crumbling on all sides.

The Framer

The Massachusetts delegation to the Constitutional Convention consisted of Francis Dana, Elbridge Gerry, Gorham, Rufus King, and Caleb Strong. Dana did not attend the Convention. Gerry, a merchant and a signer of the Declaration of Independence, was known to be erratic and inconsistent. Rufus King was handsome and charming, and was slowly won over to a Federalist position. Caleb Strong was a spokesman for rural Massachusetts. Like its state, the delegation had a strong mercantile interest.

William Pierce called Gorham "a man of good sense rather than great ability." Pierce saw him as a Boston merchant "high in reputation and much in the esteem of his countrymen." Pierce said that Gorham was "a good clear communicator, but not much improved in education."[14]

Since Gorham roomed at the Indian Queen tavern, he would have had easy access to others who stayed there, such as Hamilton, Madison, Mason, Charles Pinckney, John Rutledge, and Caleb Strong. No doubt the delegates had long hours of discussion of issues at the close of the day.

As chairman of the Committee of the Whole, Gorham shared the gavel with Washington. Each morning Washington would take the chair for the necessary preliminaries and then turn the gavel over to Gorham. Most of the day would be spent in the Committee of the Whole. When matters were ready for formal action, Gorham would return the gavel to Washington.

Gorham was undecided on whether the Convention could save the federal government. He advised Massachusetts Representative Theophilus Parsons on June 18 not to pay the requisition, except for the cash part, since six or seven states had not yet paid their 1785 requisitions. "In short," he said, "the present Federal Government seems near its exit, and whether we shall in the Convention be able to agree upon mending it, or forming and recommending a new one, is not certain."[15]

The spring elections in Massachusetts had brought out many rural voters who defeated Bowdoin and many incumbent senators. Gorham concluded that the nation needed a new Constitution since "the present phantom of a government must soon expire."[16] The news that the delegates received from back home was not reassuring, as "the court extended the law suspending debt suits, struck down anti-Regulator legislation, refused to provide for the state's bond holders, and Hancock and his council refused to hang any of the convicted Regulators."[17] Thus, step by step the Massachusetts delegates were working their way into the position favoring a strong central government.

The Massachusetts delegation was badly split on whether to support the Great Compromise. Gerry became a member of the committee working on the Compromise and supported it as well as states' rights in general. King and Gorham took a much more nationalistic position. They "opposed any state interference in the election of either branch of the national Congress, supported national control over the militia, and hoped that placeholders, government contractors, and other directly interested men would be allowed to sit in Congress."[18]

Gorham reminded the delegates that Massachusetts had once been three colonies: Massachusetts Bay, Plymouth, and Maine; that present Connecticut had included both the former Connecticut and New Haven; and that New Jersey was a combination of East Jersey with West Jersey. Each time, Gorham said, union was feared and opposed but each time it had worked out well. Gorham went so far as to say that perhaps Delaware should be annexed to Pennsylvania, and New Jersey divided between New York and Pennsylvania.[19] Gorham said that he was prepared to stay in the Convention as long as it would take to prepare a plan for national union that could conscientiously be recommended to the people.[20]

On June 25 Gorham spoke on behalf of a Senate based upon the relative population of the states. King had earlier favored this method, and Gerry opposed it. On June 29 and 30 all three defended their positions.

On July 5 and July 6 Gerry defended the Great Compromise, and Gorham and King opposed it. When the final vote on the Compromise was taken on July 16, Gerry and Caleb Strong favored it, and Gorham and King opposed it. The split in the Massachusetts delegation permitted the measure to pass by a 5-4-1 vote.

Gorham was identified with a monarchist position, possibly because of his letter to Prince Henry of Prussia. On a visit to Philadelphia to testify before Congress, the Reverend Manasseh Cutler is described by Theodore C. Pease as sitting up "till half after one that morning of July 13 in deep speech with Nathaniel Gorham, the brains of the monarchical party in the United States."[21]

Gorham served on a committee to determine the apportionment of the House of Representatives. He frankly confessed that a part of the committee's report was designed to give the original states the power of "dealing out the right of representation in safe proportions to the Western states."[22] At first this part of the committee report was accepted by the Convention, but later a new method of apportionment was adopted.

On July 16 Pierce Butler objected to the vague term "incompetent" in granting Congress power "to legislate in all cases to which the separate states are incompetent." Gorham replied that "the vagueness of the terms constitutes the propriety of them. We are now establishing general principles, to be extended hereafter into details which will be precise and explicit."[23] Rutledge agreed with Butler, and moved that the clause be referred to a committee to specify the powers involved, but the motion lost by a vote of 5-5.

How should Supreme Court justices be appointed? Appointment by the Senate was better than appointment by the whole Congress, Gorham said on July 18, but even the Senate was too large a body and "too little personally responsible" to ensure a good choice. He cited the successful Massachusetts practice where judges were appointed by the executive with the advice and consent of the Senate. In defense of his position, Gorham said that the national executive would be responsible to look carefully through all of the states for qualified judges. Senators, he declared, might be indifferent toward candidates from other states, for "public bodies feel no personal responsibility and give full play to intrigue and cabal." The Senate, he felt, could have no better information than the executive, who would be more answerable for a good appointment, "as the whole blame for a bad one would fall on him alone."[24]

Should the Congress be empowered to establish federal courts other than the Supreme Court? Certainly, said Gorham on July 18, pointing to existing maritime courts as examples that seemed to be working well. "Inferior tribunals," he stated, "are essential to render the authority of the national legislature effectual."[25]

Gorham scarcely sounded like a monarchist that day, as he asked for the federal government to have the authority to help a state subdue a rebellion "known to exist in the empire." Without this power, an enterprising citizen could arouse partisans in favor of a monarchy, "threaten to establish a tyranny," and the general government would be "compelled to remain an inactive witness of its own destruction."

As to internal disputes within the states, as long as they are confined to words, they are harmless and should be tolerated, he judged. "If they appeal to the sword," he added, "it will then be necessary for the general government, however difficult it may be to decide on the merits of their contest, to interpose and put an end to it."[26]

Madison and Wilson wanted the Supreme Court justices and the President to constitute a council of revision, with the power to veto laws they considered unwise. Gorham said on July 21 that this would be very wrong, for "as judges they are not presumed to possess any peculiar knowledge of the mere policy of public measures." Nor was it necessary to safeguard their rights under the Constitution. "It would be best," Gorham said, "to let the executive alone be responsible, and at most to authorize him to call on judges for their opinions."

Gorham granted that a check upon the legislature was needed but that there were two reasons why the Supreme Court should not be a part of that check: "Judges ought to carry into the exposition of the laws no prepossessions with regard to them." Also, "as judges will outnumber the executive, the revisionary check would be thrown entirely out of the executive hands, and instead of enabling him to defend himself, would enable the judges to sacrifice him."[27]

When Gouverneur Morris recommended that each state have three Senators, Gorham on July 23 said that a smaller number would be preferable. A large Senate would make it hard to decide on such important matters as war and peace, he said, and as the number of states increased, the Senate could easily grow into being too large to be efficient.

That same day he stated that he doubted whether oaths taken by the executive and the judiciary to support the Constitution would be of much value. When Wilson declared that such oaths might interfere with the amending process, Gorham saw no such danger as long as the amending process was carried out in the prescribed manner.

Having served many years in a state legislature, Gorham felt it would be very wrong to have state legislatures ratify the federal Constitution. He gave his reasons on July 23. State legislators would be afraid they might lose their jobs under the new document. Since most state legislatures are bicameral, it would be hard to get approval through both houses. Artful legislators would find technical ways to delay a vote on the issue for years. Further, many of the best men in a state, such as the clergy, were not legislators—why should they be excluded? The clergy, Gorham added, had been very valuable during the framing of the Massachusetts constitution.

Gorham opposed requiring unanimous approval by the states in the ratification of the new Constitution. He reminded the delegates of how little Rhode Island impeded the present Congress, and predicted that New York would probably oppose the new document because it would take away the state's ability to tax its neighbors. On August 31 Gorham advocated state conventions for the ratification process, and on September 10 he voiced the fear that the differing ratification plans desired by the states would result in the defeat of the new Constitution.

On July 24 Gorham was elected by ballot to be one of the five members of the important Committee of Detail. Although he seems to have contributed less to the committee's recommendations than did Rutledge or Wilson, his work here may have been the basis for the statement by another committee member, Ellsworth, who in later years asserted that the Constitution had been drawn up by Gorham, Hamilton, Madison, Rutledge, Wilson, and himself.[28]

Gorham on July 26 expressed the opinion that Congress should draw up the qualifications for its members. Persons having debts need not be disqualified as Congressmen, he said, since that would be unfair to businessmen who necessarily borrow funds in the course of their daily business.

On August 13 he saw no need for years of residence in America in order to be eligible to run for Congress. "When foreigners are naturalized," he said, "it would seem as if they stand on an equal footing with natives."[29]

When the report of the Committee of Detail was ready to be given to the Convention on August 7, Gorham suggested that it bypass the Committee of the Whole and go straight to the floor of the Convention, and his suggestion was adopted. On that day Gorham also said that the Constitution should establish the meeting dates of Congress, to save future confusion and squabbling by members of Congress. Congress, he stated, should meet at least once a year as a check upon the executive.

Concerning the election of the executive, Gorham on August 7 recommended a joint ballot for president and vice-president. If separate ballots were used, he felt, each branch of Congress might support its favorite, resulting in undue delay and contention. On September 4 he agreed that the vice-president should be the person having the second highest total of electoral votes, unless his vote total is less than a majority of the votes cast, in which case the decision should go to the Senate, lest "a very obscure man with very few votes" be elected vice-president.[30]

When Gouverneur Morris recommended that persons eligible to vote for congressmen be restricted to property owners, Gorham on August 8 vigorously protested. In cities like Boston, New York, and Philadelphia, where mechanics and merchants are permitted to vote, he declared, the results were at least as good as where only freeholders are eligible to vote. Again sounding like anything but a monarchist, he said that "the people have long been accustomed to this right in various parts of America, and will never allow it to be abridged. We must consult their rooted prejudices if we expect their concurrence in our propositions."[31]

Also on August 8 Gorham raised doubts about how long the Union might last. Madison pointed out that "if the Union should be permanent," the ratio of one Representative for 40,000 inhabitants might have to be changed, lest the House become unduly large. Gorham replied that "it is not to be supposed that the government will last as long as to produce this effect. Can it be supposed that this vast country, including the western territory, will 150 years hence remain one nation?"[32] Ellsworth then made the consoling observation that if the country lasted that long, amendments to the Constitution could keep it a workable document.

How many members should it take to constitute a quorum in Congress? On August 10 Gorham said that less than a majority should be sufficient, probably recalling the sparse days in the Confederation Congress. As the House of Representatives grows larger, he believed, there will be many delays if the quorum requirement is set too high.

On August 14 John Dickinson moved equal pay for members of the two houses. Gorham answered that "this would be unreasonable. The Senate will be detained longer from home, will be obliged to remove their families, and in time of war perhaps to sit constantly. Their allowance should certainly be higher. The members of the Senates in the states are allowed more than those of the other house."[33] Dickinson withdrew his motion, and the Convention stated that compensation was "to be ascertained by law."

Gorham was less sanguine about the Senate's possible desire for power. On August 15 he agreed that the Senate could amend money bills but by no means should originate them, since if that power were granted to the Senate, it would soon demand exclusive right to do so, an intolerable condition.

Gorham looked like "a political trimmer" on the issue of paper money. On August 16 he agreed that Congress needed to have the right to borrow money but that it should avoid the dangerous practice of issuing paper money. On August 28 he stated that it would be permissible for states to issue bills of credit "with the consent of the United States Congress," so that there would be some control. To absolutely prohibit paper money, he now felt, perhaps thinking of the people of western Massachusetts, "would rouse the most desperate opposition from its partisans."[34]

On August 17 Gorham and King spoke unsuccessfully in favor of having the national treasurer appointed by the Congress. The Convention saw no reason to make a distinction between the treasurer and other national officers. Gorham said that the people were accustomed to having the treasurer appointed by the legislature, and not to do so would "multiply objections to the system."[35]

The following day, when Gorham added the phrase "and support" to the powers of Congress "to raise armies," Washington must have smiled in relief.

On one issue the Massachusetts delegation was in total accord: national support for commerce. Gorham opposed the two-thirds vote needed to pass a navigation act. He said that the only motive for New England in the Union was a commercial one, since the Eastern states could protect themselves. He "bluntly warned that Massachusetts would have little reason to join a union that would not assist her commerce."[36] He hoped that the new government would not levy duties on the coastal trade, and that states would not be permitted to levy inspection and packing charges on their exports.

On August 29 Gorham promised that the Northern and Middle states would not combine in opposition to the Southern states, since they had such widely differing interests.

Treaty making proved to be a thorny issue at the Convention. If all treaties must be ratified before being effective, Gorham said on August 23, envoys would be at a loss on how to proceed, for they would be given instructions by the making body (the executive) which might differ from the expectations of the ratifying body (the Senate).

Later, on September 7, when Madison proposed that the Senate alone, by a two-thirds vote, be authorized to conclude treaties of peace (since the president, having wartime powers, might be slow to agree to peace terms), "Gorham thought the precaution unnecessary, as the means of carrying on the war would not be in the hands of the President but of the legislature."[37]

When Gorham supported the tax on slaves that were being imported, he was careful to point out that he did not want his action interpreted as a belief that slaves were property, but rather to discourage the further importation of slaves.

When a committee was appointed by ballot on August 25 to define the power of Congress to regulate commerce, Gorham was chosen to represent Massachusetts. He probably surprised committee members when he agreed that it might be proper to have all incoming vessels stop at Norfolk, "on account of the better collection of the revenue."[38]

On August 29 Gorham was appointed, along with Johnson, Randolph, Rutledge, and Wilson, on a committee to develop recommendations on interstate comity. Gorham on September 3 upheld the right of congressmen to hold federal office. Otherwise, he reasoned, the federal government would be stricter than the states or than all other nations. Eligibility to hold office, he believed, "was among the inducements for fit men to enter into the legislative service."[39]

On September 12 Elbridge Gerry, skeptical of too powerful a national government, made a strong plea for a bill of rights to be included in the Constitution. Included in his proposal was trial by jury, freedom of the press, no *ex post facto* laws, and publication of the House journals and of all governmental expenditures. Gorham and King joined the majority in opposing a bill of rights. Later, when Gerry refused to sign the Constitution, he cited this as one of his key reasons.

Gorham and King also disagreed with Gerry's view that ratification should require approval of all 13 states, since all of them had ratified the Articles of Confederation. But even Gerry agreed that ratification could by no means be entrusted to a direct popular vote. "Gerry opposed submission to the people since 'the people of Massachusetts have at this time the wildest idea of government in the world' and proved his point by stating that they had tried to abolish the state senate. At last the Convention decided to submit the document to specially elected conventions where it would be be bottled up by legislative maneuvering and for which the people, according to Gorham, would choose 'better men' who would naturally favor the new charter."[40] In Massachusetts, at least, Gorham's prediction seemed accurate, for the large number of state officeholders elected to the ratification convention helped carry a favorable vote.

At the last minute, Gorham moved that the Convention change the basis for apportioning House membership from 1/40,000 to 1/30,000. Washington broke his long silence to support Gorham's motion and it carried unanimously. Gorham and King were the only Massachusetts delegates who signed the Constitution, since Caleb Strong was absent and Gerry had mental reservations against it.

Gorham continued as a member of Congress from September 20 to October 12, 1787. He then ran for the position of lieutenant-governor of Massachusetts. "The House, controlled by the moderates, nominated Thomas Cushing and Gorham, and the Senate elected Cushing by a unanimous vote."[41] Gorham ran well in the rural areas but was overwhelmed by the eastern metropolitan vote.

Gorham knew that ratification of the Constitution would not be easy in Massachusetts. The first chore was to convince the General Court to hold a ratification convention. Over 55 percent of the members of the

General Court came from towns opposed to the Constitution. To make matters worse, Gerry supplied abundant copies of his list of reasons for opposing the document.

Rufus King tried to influence his former cronies in Maine to vote for ratification. Congregational ministers urged their parishioners to support the Constitution, and the federalists got leading Baptists, such as Isaac Backus and Samuel Stillman, to do likewise. The federalists were effective in getting anti-Constitution people voted down as convention delegates. Gerry, for example, was defeated at Cambridge.

The biggest worry concerned western delegates. Gorham felt that they would automatically oppose what Boston favored, and Boston was moving toward adoption.

Gorham admitted that "we cannot gain the question without some amendments,"[42] so the federalists asked John Hancock to propose them, in order to win Hancock and his supporters to their side. Hancock had been flattered into believing that he would be nominated for President if Virginia voted against ratification.

Hancock thus supported the Constitution, presenting a list of nine amendments, on such matters as limiting the federal power to tax and to control elections, and making sure that Congress could not benefit any one company of merchants through the commerce clause."[43] By the addition of the amendments, the support of Samuel Adams and others was obtained. Gorham now felt that the biggest battle for ratification had been won.

The convention was held in late January 1788. Gorham borrowed a copy of Franklin's final speech at the Constitutional Convention, to be used to show that even if the document was imperfect, it deserved America's support as a great improvement over the Articles of Confederation.

In his speeches at the convention, Gorham specialized in responding to the critics of the document. The chief criticism was that the people were surrendering their liberties to the national government. Also, why had there been no stand against slavery? One critic "shuddered at the idea that Roman Catholics, papists, and pagans might be introduced into office, and that popery and the Inquisition may be established in America."[44]

Gorham reviewed the safeguards to American liberties achieved through the separation of powers and the check-and-balance relationship among the branches of government. To a critic who wanted all governmental proceedings published, Gorham stated that this could hinder the effectiveness of the government. "In case of treaties with foreign nations," he said, "would it be policy to inform the world of the extent of the powers to be vested in our ambassador, and thus give our enemies opportunity to defeat our negotiations?"[45]

Gorham denied the assertion that the new government could pass a poll tax. He said that giving the federal government the power to regulate commerce would enable America to compete favorably against the products of Nova Scotia, which had been protected for a long time by British laws.

Gorham then spoke on behalf of the impost and excise taxes. "By impost and excise," he said, "the man of luxury will pay, and the middling and the poor parts of the community, who live by their industry, will go clear; and as this would be the easiest mode of raising a revenue, it was the most natural to suppose it would be resorted to."[46]

After Amos Singletary, an old farmer from Worcester County, had decried the smooth lawyers who had stolen away their liberties, a younger farmer, Jonathan Smith from Lanesborough in the Berkshire Hills, replied that the black cloud of rebellion had recently spread over Massachusetts because of problems unanswered by the Articles of Confederation. "We have no lawyer in our town," Smith said, "and we do well enough without." But if someone disputed title to your 50-acre farm, you would do well to go in with your neighbor, a lawyer owning a 5000-acre farm, who also had a disputed title. "Some gentlemen say, don't be in a hurry," Smith continued. "Take time to consider. There is a time to sow and a time to reap. We sowed our seed when we sent men to the federal Convention. Now is the harvest, the time to reap the fruit of our labor. If we don't do it now, I am afraid we shall never have another opportunity."[47]

The debate continued for seven days. Finally on February 5 the Constitution was approved, 187-168. By giving the opposition a full opportunity to state their position, proponents had built a following from among even those who had originally opposed the Constitution.

One of them, Major Benjamin Swain of Marlborough, voiced the opinions of many when he said that "the Constitution has had a fair trial. There had not, to his knowledge, been any undue influence exercised to obtain the vote in its favor. Many doubts which lay on his mind had been removed. Although he was in the minority, he should support the Constitution as cheerfully and as heartily as though he had voted on the other side of the question."[48] With citizens like Jonathan Smith and Benjamin Swain, it is hard to have a Constitution that does not work!

The Speculator

In June 1788 Gorham was once again elected to Congress. The following month he received a letter from George Washington, which said: "Although I shall not live to see but a small portion of the happy effects which this system will produce for my country, yet the precious idea of its prosperity will be a consolation amidst the increasing infirmities of nature and the growing love of retirement."[49]

To settle a boundary dispute, New York had ceded to Massachusetts a vast tract of land called the Genesee Country. To raise revenue, Massachusetts in April 1788 sold the 6-million-acre tract to Gorham and Oliver Phelps of Windsor, Connecticut, who had formed a partnership rather than bid against each other. The purchase price was $1,000,000, payable in three annual installments in the scrip of Massachusetts, called the "consolidated securities," which were selling far below par. Even rural legislators supported the transaction, showing that they did not oppose speculation as long as it did not hurt their pocketbooks.

In July 1788 Gorham and Phelps managed to clear the eastern part of the land, some 2,600,000 acres, of Indian title claims. During the next two years they sold large amounts of the land to settlers, sometimes as much as a whole township at a single sale.

Gorham was again a candidate for Congress in 1789. In the December primary in Middlesex County he led the field with 37 percent of the vote, compared to 26 percent for Gerry, the second highest candidate. Perhaps because of his business obligations, Gorham withdrew from the January election, and Gerry won handily.

In April 1790 Henry Knox asked Gorham for a reaction to the defeat in a House committee of Hamilton's plan for the federal assumption of state war debts. Gorham said that "the adverse vote was attributable in some measure to the bitter feeling aroused by the debate on the Quakers' memorial for the suppression of the slave trade."[50] In this letter Gorham also warned that unless Congress made more progress in doing its business, "they would sink in the estimation of the people."[51]

By the 1790s Gorham was in financial difficulty. Among other things, an unexpected rise in the value of the scrip made the purchase price much higher than Gorham and Phelps had anticipated. To help raise funds, they sold a million acres of the land to Robert Morris. Unable to meet their payments on the remainder, they returned the land to Massachusetts, although title to the western section was still in Indian hands. Gorham had never visited the vast domain but his son Nathaniel had been a pioneer settler there.

When Robert Morris tried to buy the rest of the property, he found that the Senecas were disgruntled because they felt that they had not received what Gorham and Phelps had promised them. Not realizing that Gorham was now insolvent, Morris recommended that Gorham and Phelps pay the Senecas what they demanded, although not until the current Indian war was over, when one could determine which tribe would be in charge of the disputed lands.[52]

Despondent over his financial losses, Gorham suffered a breakdown of health, from which he never recovered. At the age of 58 he died, of apoplexy, at Charlestown, on June 11, 1796. One of his sons, Benjamin, after serving in the state legislature, served in the national Congress in the years 1820–1821, 1827–1831, and 1833–1835. Then the Gorham name sank into obscurity, perhaps because of the distaste relating to Gorham's land speculation.

6. Alexander Hamilton: A Portrait in Paradox

Saint or demon? George Washington swore by him, saying that even his weaknesses bore social good. Thomas Jefferson and James Madison connived to undermine his program, feeling that he was destroying the Constitution. "No one did more for all Americans than Alexander Hamilton,"[1] said a recent biographer. He was two-faced and untrustworthy, replied another one. Supremely able and yet astonishingly inept, it is little wonder that a third biographer, John C. Miller, called him "a portrait in paradox."

What was there about Alexander Hamilton that caused people to react so strongly toward him? Was it a condition built into his very personality?

His grandmother, Mary Faucett, lived in the British West Indies. She was a beautiful and intelligent woman who had separated from her husband. Her daughter Rachel, who inherited her beauty and wit, married John Michael Levine, a German Jew, in 1745. Levine mistreated Rachel, but when she left him in 1750, she was jailed.

Rachel was trilingual (English, French, Spanish). Her family had been aristocratic leaders in the West Indies for a century. She was haughty and imperious, traits she bequeathed to her son. It is alleged that he also got from her his good looks, skill at conversation, and fastidiousness in dress.

Out of jail, Rachel abandoned her four-year-old son Peter, left St. Croix for Nevis, and began a relationship with James Hamilton, young son of the Lord of Cambuskeith. They never married. Their two sons were James, Jr., and Alexander, who was born in Nevis on January 11, 1755. In later years Alexander alleged that he had been born in 1757.

In 1759 Levine divorced Rachel for desertion. Bankrupt, James Hamilton abandoned Rachel and their two sons. For his education, Rachel tutored Alexander. Rachel operated a general store in St. Croix, and she taught him how to keep accounts.

When Alexander was ten, the worst hurricane in a century hit the island of Nevis, where he lived. While others took cover, Alexander ran against the wind and the rain to the home of his aged aunt. He barricaded the windows and set up protection against the storm. His heroism saved his aunt's home from damage, and helped save her life. Overcoming difficulties was a trait he learned early.

Rachel sent Alexander to a school run by a Jewish woman. She would have the short boy stand on a table, so as to be seen, as he recited the Ten Commandments in Hebrew.

As a boy he liked to read Plutarch's lives of the great Greeks and Romans, and the poetry of Alexander Pope.

He learned rapidly. As a clerk to the merchant Nicholas Cruger, he showed precocity in business management. At the age of 14 he told his friend Ned Stevens that ambition was brimming over in him. In fact, he wished for a war, he said, so that he could demonstrate his prowess. He felt that in times of emergency, military solutions were preferable to political ones. His *beau ideal* was Julius Caesar.

In 1768 Rachel died, leaving a small estate to James, Jr., and Alexander. But Levine showed up and seized control of Rachel's estate for their son Peter. The Hamilton brothers were left penniless.

Alexander never forgave the Levines, father and son, nor his mother, but he showed at least outward respect for his absent father, James Hamilton. It was later observed that he trusted no one. There were few persons in his youth, especially in his family, who behaved in a way designed to bolster his faith in human nature.

From his youth he was an overachiever, trying to compensate for his feelings of inadequacy and nonacceptance. He was always unduly concerned over his reputation. His ambition led him to become audacious and highly competitive.

When he was 16 Hamilton was put in charge of the store while Cruger was in New York. He did a masterful job of running the store. By lowering the price on worm-eaten flour and water-logged mahogany, he saved some poor merchandise. He sent some skinny mules out to pasture, fattening them up in order to get a better sales price. He ordered ship captains around so as to receive the best shipment terms. Upon his return, Cruger found that the store showed greater profits than when he ran it.

On August 31, 1772, a terrible hurricane hit St. Croix. Hamilton's vivid writeup of the storm impressed Cruger and Hugh Knox, a Presbyterian minister. They raised funds in order to send him to America for further schooling. The plan was for him to study medicine on the mainland, and then come to St. Croix as a doctor.

In October 1772 Hamilton sailed for Boston. En route, his ship caught fire and was saved only by the heroic actions of the passengers and crew.

The Student

Boston in winter did not appeal to him, and so Hamilton moved to New York City, where he was befriended by Hercules Mulligan. Two Presbyterian ministers, John Mason and John Rodgers, took an interest in him. They sent him to a preparatory school in Elizabethtown, New Jersey, that was run by the patriot Francis Barber. Hamilton stayed for a while at the home of the Whig leader William Livingston, who was also to be a delegate to the Constitutional Convention. Here too Hamilton met John Jay, who at the time was courting Livingston's daughter Sarah.

Hamilton studied hard, often being up past midnight. In summer he arose at dawn in order to study in a cemetery. His notebooks show extensive study of the book of Genesis. He also had detailed material on the geography of North and South America.

He came to be a good friend of Elias Boudinot, perhaps because both had Huguenot forebears, Hamilton through Rachel's side.

Since both Livingston and Boudinot were trustees of Princeton, Hamilton applied there for admission. Dr. John Witherspoon, president of Princeton, examined Hamilton at his home. Hamilton's academic background seemed satisfactory, but when he asked to be able to accelerate at his own rate (being older than the average entering student), Witherspoon checked with the trustees and Hamilton was turned down.

When he entered King's College (Columbia) in 1774, however, he was enrolled as a sophomore. He began the study of medicine but soon had to drop it, for he lacked the premedical courses.

His roommate, Robert Troup, said that Hamilton was very religious, praying aloud morning and evening. A zealous believer, Hamilton tried to make converts to Christianity.

He switched to the mathematics curriculum, but possibly due to the rising political temperature, he read some classics in the field of political theory. This included Blackstone, Burlamaqui, Grotius, Hobbes, Locke, Montesquieu, Pufendorf, and above all David Hume, whose skeptical rationalism influenced him throughout his life. Sometimes he would join other students going down the Hudson River to hear some Liberty Boys orate in favor of the Association and its boycott.

On July 6, 1774, Hamilton attacked British policy at a meeting celebrating the release of patriot Alexander McDougall from prison. Hamilton helped persuade the audience to send delegates to the First Continental Congress.

Samuel Seabury, first Episcopal bishop in America, admonished Americans to obey the crown. In an anonymous letter Hamilton asked

Seabury, "How would you like to pay four shillings out of every pound to be squandered upon court sycophants? Would you not think it very hard to pay ten shillings per annum for every wheel of your carriages, and two or three shillings for every one of your hearths?"[2]

In December 1774 Hamilton published "A Full Vindication of the Measures of Congress," in which he denied the authority of Parliament over the colonies, saying that the only connection to Britain was through the king. Quoting Blackstone, he said that the law of nature, "dictated by God himself, is superior to any other. It is binding over all the globe. No human laws are of any validity if contrary to this."[3]

The natural rights of mankind, said Hamilton, derive from this law of nature. "Hence," he continued, "the origin of all civil government must be in a voluntary compact between the rulers and the ruled," so as to secure the "absolute rights" of the ruled.[4]

Quoting Blackstone again, he said that "it follows that the first and primary end of human laws is to maintain these absolute rights of individuals."[5] Hamilton concluded that "it is the unalienable birthright of every Englishman who can be considered a free agent to participate in framing the laws which are to bind him."[6]

In February 1775 Hamilton again replied to Seabury in "The Farmer Refuted." Here he quotes Blackstone to justify revolution by a resort to first principles: Human rights are given by God, and thus no mortal power can lawfully curtail them. When these rights are denied, society is dissolved and revolution is permitted. Hamilton still saw the king as the connecting principle to the colonies. He quoted Hume as saying that "every man must be supposed a knave," and that government needs to protect people from the evil of their own passions.

On May 10, 1775, a group of 400 students tried to tar and feather the college president, Myles Cooper, for alleged Tory activity. Hamilton and Robert Troup awoke Cooper and stalled off the crowd while Cooper escaped.

Later, in October, Hamilton tried unsuccessfully to keep a mob from destroying the press of Tory printer James Rivington. He then wrote an angry letter to John Jay, protesting the behavior of "the unthinking populace," whose actions could easily "run into anarchy." He suggested that Congress station troops in New York City to keep law and order.

It is not so much that Hamilton liked Tories, but he felt that many of them were not beyond redemption, and that tenderness might convert them faster than severity. Hamilton had a high regard not only for law and order but for due process, civil liberties, and a nation's treaty obligations. His deep respect for the sanctity of property tended to force him closer to the Tory position, as high-tempered patriots began to harass loyalists and their property.

In appearance, Hamilton was a remarkable man. He was short and erect, with a very graceful carriage. His face was handsome. He had a fair complexion, rosy cheeks, and penetrating deep-blue eyes. His hair was reddish-brown, powdered, and gathered in a clump behind. Whenever he spoke, people listened attentively.

The paradox of his character was now apparent. Beneath the veneer of the popular political epithets against the crown there were surfacing the deep currents of his native aristocratic beliefs. West Indian society had no middle class, just planters and slaves. He was an aristocrat both by heritage and by preference. In his endless quest for recognition, self-acceptance was his first hard step. His immaculate grooming was a part of his campaign to convince the world that he really was a man of quality. Legitimacy was his lifelong quest.

One of the Intolerable Acts was the Quebec Act passed by Parliament in June 1774. Designed to placate French Canadians, it granted recognition to the Roman Catholic Church and extended the boundaries of Quebec to the Ohio on the south and the Mississippi on the west.

Americans could justly protest the boundary shift, but Hamilton's "Remarks on the Quebec Bill" asserted that Canada would soon be a country full of Papists conducting a new Inquisition. Here his inflated rhetoric backfired, for neutral Canadians were unfavorably impressed by this sort of Protestant bigotry.

He now regularly wrote to John Jay, who was in the New York Assembly. Impressed by Hamilton's letters, Jay encouraged him to keep him posted on the news about New York City. Later, when the state constitution was being written, Hamilton agreed with Jay that voters should be property owners. Jay had said that "those who own the country ought to govern it."[7] Even as late as 1790 only about one-tenth of New York City's male residents were eligible to vote.

The Soldier

In 1776 Hamilton became a captain of artillery in the New York militia. Knowing math well, he easily passed a cram course in artillery science. After recruiting his own company of 68 officers and men, he used his personal credit to clothe and equip them.

In August that year he led a disorderly withdrawal to Harlem Heights. But at New Brunswick his guns covered Washington's army crossing the Delaware, and prevented Cornwallis from crossing. Washington's troops were thereby enabled to hit Princeton.

Just as when he was a mere lad, Hamilton kept trying to get fighting commands, but he could not. In March 1777 he received an appointment as a lieutenant-colonel, being assigned as aide-de-camp to Washington. This was the turning point in his career. From now on leaders, especially those in New York, followed his career very closely.

In the fall of 1777 Washington sent Hamilton north to get reinforcements from General Horatio Gates, recent victor at Saratoga. Gates wanted to contribute only an inferior brigade, but Hamilton's persuasiveness got Gates to add in addition the brigade of General John Glover.

Many of America's best leaders were in military or diplomatic work by 1778. Some were now in state government posts. The quality of representation in the Congress has thus atrophied. In a letter to Governor George Clinton in February 1778, Hamilton asked for better representatives from the states: "You should not beggar the councils of the United States to enrich the administration of the several members. How can we hope for success in our European negotiations if the nations of Europe have no confidence in the wisdom and vigor of the great continental government?"[8]

Hamilton was a major witness against General Charles Lee in his court-martial in July 1778, following the Battle of Monmouth. Instead of attacking, as ordered, Lee kept changing the positions of his troops until they were thoroughly confused and ran. Washington immediately regrouped the forces and repulsed the British, who had over 1,000 casualties.

After being found guilty and being suspended from command for one year, Lee was angry at Hamilton for testifying against him. When Lee made a derogatory remark about Washington, John Laurens challenged Lee to a duel. When they fought on December 24, 1778, Hamilton was Laurens's second. Slightly wounded, Lee wanted a second exchange of shots. The good sense of the seconds prevailed, however, and the duel ended.

Laurens wanted to raise several battalions of black troops. Hamilton supported the idea, stating that "their natural faculties are as good as ours."[9] In his letter to Jay advocating the plan, Hamilton said that he felt that the blacks should be given their freedom as a reward.

Knowing that the French fleet needed staple food products, Congressman Samuel Chase of Maryland attempted to secure a flour monopoly. When he heard of this, Hamilton wrote three letters signed "Publius" to the *New York Journal* in the fall of 1778, exposing Chase's project. He said that the price of flour had already doubled because of Chase's greed. All through his life Hamilton opposed those who tried to derive big profits from their governmental posts.

In 1780 Hamilton married Elizabeth, daughter of General Philip Schuyler. The wedding not only brought him a loving and faithful wife but it also gave him entree into New York's aristocracy. The upward climb towards full respectability was making progress.

Only 25, Hamilton wrote a letter to James Duane, a member of Congress, in 1780, calling for a convention to set up a strong national government. Many of his statements were prophetic. He showed Duane the weaknesses of the present system, in which Congress could control the army but not finance it. Also, government by committees will not work — Congress should set up executives in each of the main areas of government. Army enlistments should be raised to three years, or the duration of the War.

Congress, said Hamilton, should be given the power to levy taxes, both internal and external; to make appropriations; to regulate interstate and foreign commerce; to control foreign affairs; to make war and peace; to establish courts; to coin money; and to charter banks.

Hamilton described why a national bank was needed. Paper credit will not last long, he said, unless it has both public and private support: "The only certain manner to obtain a permanent paper credit is to engage the moneyed interest in it, by making them contribute the whole or part of the stock, and giving them the whole or part of the profits." So it had been, he said, with all successful banks, such as those in Amsterdam, London, and Venice. "And why can we not have an American bank?" he asked. "Are our moneyed men less enlightened to their own interest?"[10]

The fall of 1780 proved to be a bad season for Hamilton. First he interceded unsuccessfully on behalf of Major John Andre, who had been captured when Benedict Arnold tried to turn West Point over to the British. Since he had operated in plain clothes, Andre was sentenced to be hanged as a spy. Hamilton wrote to General George Clinton, suggesting that Andre be exchanged for Arnold. Denied, Hamilton requested that Andre be shot by a firing squad, but Washington supported the sentence of the Board of General Officers, and so Andre was hanged.

Hamilton then asked Washington to intercede for Captain Charles Asgill, a captured British officer chosen by lot to be killed in retaliation of the British execution of Captain Joshua Huddy. Washington refused, but Congress granted Asgill a reprieve upon a request from the King of France.

The Reverend William Gordon then asserted that he had heard Hamilton say in a Philadelphia coffee house that "it was high time for people to rise, join General Washington, and turn Congress out of doors."[11] Hamilton denied this, calling Gordon a liar. Gordon asked Washington to court-martial Hamilton, but Washington told Gordon that no court-martial would be held unless more substantial evidence could be produced.

Perhaps in a fit of deep depression, Hamilton confided to John Laurens: "I hate Congress. I hate the army. I hate the world. I hate myself. The whole is a mass of fools and knaves."[12]

In February 1781 came the big break with Washington. Washington told Hamilton that he wanted to see him, but Hamilton was delayed twice by business with other officers. When he arrived, Washington bawled him out: "Colonel Hamilton, you have kept me waiting for ten minutes. You treat me with disrespect." Hamilton replied, "I am not conscious of it, Sir, but since you have thought it necessary to tell me so, we must part." "Very well, Sir, if it be your choice," answered Washington.

Washington tried to heal the breach but Hamilton would not permit it. He told his father-in-law, General Schuyler, that he disliked being aide-de-camp, for it was "a kind of personal dependence." He had supported Washington because he was an honest leader who was needed for the American cause to win. But, he said, "for three years past I have felt no friendship for him and have professed none. The truth is our dispositions are the opposites of each other, and the pride of my temper would not suffer me to profess what I did not feel."[13]

Schuyler advised Hamilton to regain his former position, since his knowledge of French was needed for communication with the French officers serving with Washington. Hamilton's pride won out, however, and the breach remained.

After resigning as Washington's aide, he applied for an army commission. While awaiting action by the army, he wrote six articles that showed his growing nationalism. "As too much power leads to despotism, too little leads to anarchy, and both, eventually, to the ruin of the people," he said. There may have been some excuse for setting up a weak Confederation, but there is no excuse for continuing it.

Who suffers most when the federal government cannot regulate trade, he asked, and then replied: workers, landowners, federal coffers, the federal army, and merchants. Since it is impossible to devise a tax that will be equal to all, "the rich must be made to pay for their luxuries, which is the only proper way of taxing their superior wealth."[14]

Hamilton received his commission as colonel in time to lead an attack at the crucial battle of Yorktown. When Lt. Col. John Joseph Gimat was assigned command of the American troops attacking redoubt number 10, Hamilton protested to his commanding officer, Lafayette, that he, being Gimat's superior, deserved the command. Lafayette consulted Washington and they came up with a compromise: the attack would be by Gimat's troops led by Hamilton.

On October 14, 1781, Hamilton led his men over the parapets, in the face of heavy British fire, and the redoubt fell. Cornwallis admitted that with the loss of redoubts 9 and 10, his situation was critical. In a few days he asked for surrender terms, and the last major battle of the War was over.

The Legislator

Writing as "The Continentalist," Hamilton on July 4, 1782, said that in government, "the great art is to distribute the public burdens well." America's uniqueness, he said, made it "as ridiculous to seek for models in the small ages of Greece or Rome as it would be to go in quest of them among the Hottentots."[15]

Robert Morris, New York superintendent of finance, gave Hamilton a job as receiver of taxes for the state. In this capacity he met with the state legislature, and on August 15, 1782, drew up a resolution to Congress asking for a convention to be called to amend the Articles of Confederation.

After a three-month crash course as a law clerk in Albany, he was admitted to the bar in October 1782. He started to specialize in cases defending Tories and their property rights. For this he grew unpopular among some patriots.

He nevertheless was elected as a delegate to Congress for the year starting in November 1782. Washington commended him to General John Sullivan, a congressman from New Hampshire: "Few men have a more general knowledge than he possesses, and none whose soul is more firmly engaged in the cause, or who exceeds him in probity or in sterling virtue."[16]

President of the 30-member Congress was his old friend Elias Boudinot. Other members included Oliver Ellsworth, Nathaniel Gorham, James Madison, John Rutledge, and James Wilson. Since both wanted a strong central government, Hamilton and Madison became close friends.

To help pay off war debts, Congress proposed a 5 percent impost on foreign goods, but Rhode Island opposed it and so it was defeated.

When the army at Newburgh threatened mutiny over nonpayment of their wages, Hamilton notified Washington, who mollified them with an emotional appeal for loyalty and patience. He and Washington were once again friends.

What parent has not agreed with Hamilton's description of his seven-month-old son Philip: "he is a truly fine young gentleman, the most agreeable in his conversation and manners of any I ever knew"?[17]

Hamilton knew that with the peace would come the herculean task of uniting the country, "to effect which mountains of prejudice must be leveled," he said in a letter to Washington. He continued: "The centrifugal is much stronger than the centripetal force in these States—the seeds of disunion more numerous than those of union."[18]

In April 1783 Congressman Hamilton wrote a draft of the ratification of the preliminary peace treaty with England.

In mid-June of that year about 500 soldiers, many of them drunk, marched on Congress to demand their back pay. Most of the 15 Congressman on duty had fought hard to try to raise funds for just such purposes. Hamilton walked out through the ranks of the revolting soldiers. It was said justly that he hated mobs, but his actions showed that he certainly did not fear them. He proposed that Congress leave Philadelphia. At Princeton, he prepared for Congress a long list of weaknesses that needed to be changed in the Articles of Confederation.

As a lawyer, he benefited from having married Elizabeth Schuyler. The Schuylers were related to four other leading Dutch families. Also, Hamilton's brother-in-law, John B. Church, was one of the richest men in America. Other rich friends of his were Gouverneur and Robert Morris.

His good looks attracted the attention of women, with whom he liked to flirt. Elizabeth's sister, Angelica Church, was a beautiful woman with whom he carried on a flirtation. His first daughter, born in 1784, was named Angelica.

In December 1783 Hamilton defended a Tory client, asserting that under international law, the client need not pay rent for the time his building was occupied by British troops. Hamilton was asserting that the peace treaty with England took precedence over New York state law.

Hamilton and Aaron Burr were legal rivals. Both were good lawyers who were short, trim, handsome, well-dressed, and liked by women. Burr generally handled cases for radical Whigs, while Hamilton specialized in defending conservative Tories. Burr admitted that his rival was more eloquent, being "a man of strong and fertile imagination, of political genius—a powerful declaimer."[19]

In 1784 Hamilton helped found the Bank of New York. He wrote the bank's constitution and charter, and served as a director. Burr, however, held twice as many shares of bank stock as he. Since Governor George Clinton refused to approve the charter, the bank operated without one until 1791, by which time Hamilton, as Secretary of the Treasury, was pushing for a charter for a national bank.

Although he owned slaves all of his life, Hamilton was active in the New York Manumission Society. As chairman of the committee on what members should do with their own slaves, Hamilton recommended freeing them, but the Society denied the motion.

Burr was more active than Hamilton in the Society. Burr suggested that blacks should be given permission not only to hold office but also to intermarry with whites. Both suggestions were rejected. By 1808, when the importation of slaves was banned, New York had a slave population of 15,000. The last vestiges of slavery in the state disappeared in 1841.[20]

By 1787 the Hamiltons had three children: Philip, Angelica, and Alexander. That year they adopted a little girl, the daughter of Colonel Edward Antil, who had asked for help from the Society of the Cincinnati, and then died. Years later the girl married the successful merchant Arthur Tappan.

Hamilton was making a good living by defending Tories. Partly as a result of his efforts, by now the former loyalists had been restored to their full rights as citizens.

The Framer

As previously mentioned, Hamilton had an important hand at the Annapolis Convention in getting Congress to call a convention to work on "important matters" relating to the Articles of Confederation. His own contributions to the Constitutional Convention, however, were not nearly so significant.

Delegate William Pierce said that Hamilton was deservedly famous for his talents, which were a clear and strong judgment and the ability to get to the root of a matter. His voice was not strong, making him "a convincing speaker rather than a blazing orator." His language was sometimes didactic and sometimes light and tripping. He had stiff manners, Pierce said, "sometimes with a degree of vanity that is highly disagreeable."[21]

Hamilton's attendance at the Convention was confined virtually to the opening and closing days. He was there from May 25 to June 29 and from September 6 to September 17. The only other day he attended was August 13.

The other New York delegates, John Lansing and Robert Yates, opposed Hamilton in his advocacy of a strong central government. Feeling that the Convention was exceeding its authority in drawing up a new constitution, Lansing and Yates withdrew from the Convention on July 5.

Hamilton's biggest contribution was his controversial speech on June 18. He said that the British government was the best in the world, and that the vast expanses of the United States meant that eventually the nation would have to be under a system resembling monarchy. John Adams had reached a similar conclusion in his *Defense of the Constitution of the United States* published that year.

The one democratic feature in Hamilton's plan, rare at that date, was election of House members by the people. Senators and the executive would be elected by electors chosen by the people, and would serve for life during good behavior. The executive would have a complete veto on all laws passed. All militia, including those of the states, would be under federal control. The state governors, appointed by the central government, would have the power to veto all state legislation.

Hamilton's aristocratic preferences stuck out. "The people," he said, "are gradually ripening in their opinion of government. They begin to be tired of an excess of democracy." The voice of the people was by no means the voice of God. "The people are turbulent and changing; they seldom judge or determine right." The rich should thus have "a distinct permanent share in the government" to "check the imprudence of democracy."[22] Hamilton later said that he intended for the powers of government to be divided between the few and the many, so that each could check on the other.

William Samuel Johnson expressed some of the Convention's reaction to Hamilton's speech in declaring that although "the gentleman from New York has been praised by everybody, he has been supported by none."[23] The Convention did not bother to discuss Hamilton's plan, but returned to the debate between the advocates of the Virginia and New Jersey Plans.

Although some people thought that Hamilton intentionally chose an extreme position in order to make the Virginia Plan seem more moderate, in fact Hamilton had also attacked the Virginia Plan in his speech.

Madison reports Hamilton as saying on June 26 that "he acknowledged himself not to think favorably of republican government, but addressed his remarks to those who did think favorably of it, to prevail on them to tone their government as high as possible. He professed himself to be as zealous an advocate for liberty as any man whatever."[24]

When the small states blocked the movement towards a strong central government, fearing that they might lose their autonomy, Hamilton had a ready answer: "The more close the union of the states, and the more complete the authority of the whole, the less opportunity will be allowed the stronger states to injure the weaker."[25]

Toward the end of the Convention Hamilton changed hats, and from the needler he became the appeaser. Seeing that his views were not going to be adopted, and realizing that the new Constitution, by strengthening the central authority, was a vast improvement over the Articles of Confederation, he stopped being an idealist, turned pragmatist, and worked ceaselessly to get the new document approved. He now saw the wisdom of sending it to both Congress and the state legislatures for approval.

The final day he made a plea for all delegates to sign the document. A few prominent nonsigners, he said, would do infinite mischief by abetting those who were ready to attack the Constitution. "No man's ideas were more remote from the plan than his own were known to be,"[26] he confessed, but is not anarchy far worse than the chance of good that might come from the plan?

Nevertheless, his final act at the Convention was to give Madison a copy of a separate constitution that he had worked on during the Convention. It differed somewhat from the version of his June 18 speech.

The Ratifier

Hamilton's fame as a framer rests largely on the incredible work he did in getting the Constitution ratified. *The Federalist*, of which he was the chief author, not only cogently answered almost any criticism that could possibly have been raised concerning the new structure of government, but also constituted a valuable contribution to the history of political theory.

Equally important was his work in getting New York to ratify the Constitution. The majority of the people, and their leaders, were opposed to it. In no other state was one man so crucially influential in swaying a hostile group to switch sides to support the new document.

Madison said that *The Federalist* was Hamilton's response to the strong opposition movements they discerned in New York and Virginia. All three writers — Hamilton, Jay, and Madison — used the pseudonym "Publius," after Publius Valerius, founder of the Roman republic.

In *The Federalist* No. 15 Hamilton argued that the authority of the union must extend to "the persons of the citizens — the only proper objects of government." He also saw that authority strong enough to enter into international alliances: "There is nothing absurd or impracticable in the idea of a league or alliance between independent nations for certain defined purposes precisely stated in a treaty regulating all the details of time, place, and circumstance."[27]

The selfishness of human nature, Hamilton believed, brings about dissension and aggression between individuals and among nations. To avoid domestic strife and foreign conquest, a government with adequate powers is necessary. These powers, he said in *The Federalist* No. 23, "ought to exist without limitation, because it is impossible to foresee the extent and variety of national exigencies."[28]

In *The Federalist* No. 35 Hamilton said that it was visionary to suppose that any form of government could represent all classes of people. Mechanics and laborers, he said, tended to select merchants to represent them, for they know that "their habits have not been such as to give them those acquired endowments without which in deliberative assembly the greatest natural abilities are for the most part useless."[29]

Hamilton did not favor the wealthy, as such. Rather he favored those with merit, who, he felt, were more numerous among the wealthy. Moreover, although both the rich and the poor have virtues, the vices of the poor are worse than those of the rich. The chief vice of the poor, envy, leads to resentment and eventual destruction of property. The chief vice of the rich, ambition, leads to the desire for political power, which in meritorious persons can foster society's benefit. The learned professions, said Hamilton, have no distinctly separate interest in society, and thus are important political arbiters between the rich and the poor, since their neutrality permits them to select the public good.

Being a gifted rhetorician, Hamilton knew the nature of his audience. Hence, although he agreed that "our prevailing passions are ambition and interest, and it ever will be the duty of a wise government to avail itself of the passions, in order to make them subservient to the public good,"[30] here he showed a more benevolent view of human nature. "The supposition of universal venality in human nature," he wrote in *The Federalist* No. 76, "is little less an error in political reasoning than the supposition of universal rectitude."[31]

In *The Federalist* No. 78 Hamilton averred that the Supreme Court could be trusted because it lacked direct access to material power. The executive commands the army and the legislature commands the purse, but the judiciary must rely on wisdom, judgment, and righteousness. They cannot gain control over the community by manipulating the people.

The Supreme Court, he felt, needs to be independent of the executive and the legislature, and should have the final authority on the constitutionality of laws passed by Congress. It acts as "intermediate body between the people and the legislature, to keep the latter within the limits assigned by their authority,"[32] and to save society from democratic tyranny, for "the many, aroused by demagogues, may pressure their representatives in Congress to enact laws which would not only oppress the few, but also be destructive of those institutions of government designed to protect the few."[33]

In this essay Hamilton said that the Constitution is binding upon the American people "collectively as well as individually," apparently intending for it to be also binding upon their descendants. Unlike Jefferson, Hamilton did not think that each generation comprised a distinctly new nation. Jefferson said that "no constitution, no law, no contract, is binding beyond the span of nineteen years."[34]

In response to the complaint that the Constitution lacked a bill of rights, Hamilton said that none was needed, since the document itself was a bill of rights, providing habeas corpus and trial by jury, and protecting against bills of attainder and *ex post facto* laws. When the people themselves are sovereign, he said, a bill of rights is superfluous, for "the people surrender nothing and they retain everything."[35] Enumeration of some rights might accidentally omit others, he felt.

At the New York ratification convention in June 1788, Hamilton was one of the staunchest defenders of the Constitution. When Gilbert Livingston protested that the Senate had too much power, Hamilton replied that a strong Senate was needed to protect the people from their own weaknesses. "Frequently led into the grossest errors by misinformation and passion," he said, "they do not possess the discernment and stability necessary for systematic government."[36]

Carl Van Doren says of Hamilton that "with brilliant precision he analyzed the defects of the Confederation, explained the advantages of the proposed new government, defended the powers of Congress and particularly the Senate, and insisted that the states still had all the rights they could need in the union."[37]

Ratification in New York was made easier by the fact that when the vote was taken on July 26, 1788, ten states had already approved the Constitution, meaning that without approval, New York would have been an island in the new nation. Nevertheless, the narrowness of the margin of victory, 30-27, shows that without Hamilton's yeoman services, New York would have had the embarrassment of at least a second ratification convention.

When the necessary nine states had ratified, a big celebration was held in New York City on July 23. Over 5,000 people paraded, and there was a public feast for 6,000 persons. The most imposing float in the parade was a Federal ship *Hamilton* mounted on a wooden trailer and pulled by ten draft horses. It was completely rigged with 32 guns, 30 sailors, and a full complement of officers. It was an apt tribute to a man who by now deserved to be called a Founding Father.

The Secretary of the Treasury

Reviewing several recent biographies of Hamilton, Geoffrey C. Ward called him "our first and greatest Secretary of the Treasury, and, second perhaps only to Washington, the man most responsible for creating a nation out of 13 mutually antagonistic states."[38] Hamilton's deep influence upon the political economy of the nation in its first decade remains with us to this day. Jefferson's agrarian democracy has gradually been replaced by a manufacturing technocracy that was prepared for by Hamilton's wide-sweeping measures.

The many-sided program that Hamilton launched to rescue the nation's finances from the doldrums of the Confederacy constitutes, in Rossiter's words, "the brightest pages in a record of achievement in the field of public finance that no other American has ever come close to in matching."[39]

Appointed by Washington on September 11, 1789, Hamilton was confirmed that same day by the Senate. Robert Morris, the only other possible candidate for the position, had recommended Hamilton. What others saw as unbridled ambition, Washington took to be a commendable perfectionism. After years of working closely with Hamilton, Washington said that his ambition was of "that laudable kind that prompts a man to excel in whatever he takes in hand."[40] The burning coal in Hamilton's heart would yet prove that he was legitimate, he was recognized, he was admired.

As a cabinet officer he was, like his boss, scrupulously honest. To accept a cabinet post at $3,000 a year he gave up a law practice that brought him three times as much. In fact, his personal finances never recovered from his sacrifice, and despite the fact that he had once again had a lucrative law practice, he died in debt.

In taking the cabinet post Hamilton made another sacrifice — his friendship with James Madison. For a decade this duo had prepared the nation for a charter of greatness, working together in mutual harmony. The climax of the relationship had been reached in their joint authorship of *The Federalist* papers.

But now things were changing. Madison, who had been Washington's closest political adviser, found his place usurped by Hamilton. Moreover, the issues that Washington was deciding in Hamilton's favor were those that Madison, on grounds of principle, could not support. The federal train was headed for a collision.

Hamilton believed that the first thing the national government had to do was to establish its financial credibility. Such problems as paper currency, inflation, and the lack of faith in redemption of government loans had caused investors, at home and abroad, to regard federal obligations with a chary eye.

In January 1790 Hamilton presented his plan to fund the national debt. Not only would foreign loans be paid off as soon as possible (thus reducing interest charges), but the federal government should also honor all domestic loans at face value, and in addition assume the debts contracted by the states during the War. To pay for all this, Hamilton suggested that Congress levy import duties and an excise tax on alcoholic beverages.

Madison provided Hamilton's chief opposition, insisting that a difference should be made between original holders of federal obligations, whose investments had helped provide badly needed funds in wartime, and subsequent speculators who had bought up large numbers of federal obligations below par, gambling that they would make a big profit if the federal government redeemed them at face value.

Hamilton admitted the desirability of the goal but said that it would be impossible to check the train of ownership so as to establish two separate and distinct groups. Madison's motion was thus voted down in the House of Representatives by a margin of 36–13.

On the assumption of the state war debts, Madison made a telling point. Some states had undergone major sacrifices to eliminate these debts on their own, he said. Were they to be penalized simply because other states had been laggards in meeting their obligations?

Again Hamilton answered brilliantly. It is one thing to talk about state funds provided to help conduct the War, he said, but what about those states that had provided the highest proportion of manpower — how were they to be compensated? And what about the states where most of the battles had been fought, and thus had suffered the most destruction and looting — were they to receive some sort of federal compensation?

It was not only Hamilton's persuasive logic that carried the day, however. At a historical luncheon at Jefferson's house in June 1790, Madison and Jefferson agreed to get some Virginia support for the bill assuming state debts, in return for which Hamilton would throw his support behind the decision to locate the permanent national capitol on the Potomac. True to his word, Madison got Representatives Richard Lee and Alexander White to switch their votes, and the assumption bill squeaked through the House, 31–29.

This is not the whole story, however. A more crucial vote on the issue occurred in the Senate, where the famous "luncheon swap" cut no muster. Here traditional logrolling and vote swapping, including the designation of Philadelphia as the national capitol until 1800, was probably the most critical factor in the decision.

The next big issue, the controversy over a national bank, once again had Hamilton and Madison at odds. Hamilton recalled how Britain, after its revolution of 1688, had chartered the Bank of England in order to solve its financial problems and at the same time solidify the merchant class Whigs in support of the government. Hamilton had long stated that "the only plan that can preserve the currency is one that will make it the immediate interest of the monied men to cooperate with the government in its support."[41]

In December 1790 Hamilton defended his plan for the national bank before the House of Representatives. Since credit provides far more purchasing power than currency, he said, a national bank would greatly augment the nation's productive capital. Capital was the factor of production most needed now when there was an abundance of raw materials and an adequate labor supply. The bank would provide a source for governmental loans, especially in emergencies. It would also facilitate payment of taxes, for there would be more credit sources for taxpayers, as well as a facility for making loans to those needing them.

All of this made little impression upon Madison, the leader of the House. He saw the plan as a scheme to line the pockets of the few, and as an unconstitutional abuse of the power of the national government. Since the Constitution did not specifically state that Congress could establish a bank, Madison argued that such a power did not exist. It is interesting that within a few years after writing the document, the Founding Fathers had fundamental differences about what the Constitution meant.

Hamilton stressed a broad interpretation, saying that certain powers are implied in such broad phrases as "to promote the general welfare." Hamilton once more had his way. By a vote of nearly two-to-one in the House and three-to-one in the Senate, the Bank of the United States was approved. What must have hurt Madison was that Hamilton had beat him decisively even in his own bailiwick.

Hamilton gave his "Report on Manufactures" to Congress in December 1791. In it he advocated federal aid to infant industries, so as to provide profit to owners, jobs to workers, and self-sufficiency for the national economy. In the event of war, he said, it is important to have a strong manufacturing nation. He envisioned the United States one day being an industrial giant.

Hamilton was no believer in the laissez-faire capitalism of Adam Smith. He felt that the national government should have the power to both aid and regulate business. He can be called a mercantilist, since he favored governmental intervention so as to strengthen the economy. Business, and the nation, he felt, deserved national assistance and protection through bounties, tariffs, roads, canals, and public improvements. Since he knew that private enterprise could result in abuse, he favored public banks that would put "public utility" ahead of private profit.

Believing that workers had an important role to play in the economy, he favored high wages for them, feeling that American employers could afford to pay higher wages than European ones. To bolster the labor force, he encouraged immigration. He wanted governmental assistance to skilled foreign craftsmen who were in short supply in America. He saw the need for women and child labor as industry expanded faster than the population increased.

It was relatively easy for Hamilton to adopt a national view. A product of the West Indies, he identified with no one state or section as his native home. Little wonder that he was scarcely ever accused of partiality.

His "Report on Manufactures" stated that the federal government's authority to raise money was "plenary and indefinite" except for three restrictions in the Constitution: (1) all taxes shall be uniform throughout the United States, (2) there can be no tax on articles exported from a state, and (3) all direct taxes shall be levied in proportion to the numbers involved.

"The general welfare," he said, is a phrase "as comprehensive as any that could have been used," and it is up to Congress to construe the term. "And," he added, "there seems to be no room for a doubt that whatever concerns the general interests of learning, agriculture, manufactures, and commerce are within the sphere of the national councils, as far as regards an application of money."[42] The only qualification is that the object for which the appropriation is made would have general, and not merely local, applicability.

The theory proved to be easier than the practice. In 1789 Hamilton had helped John Fenno establish a newspaper, *Gazette of the United States*, to help support federalist views. Hamilton wrote for the paper, contributed some personal funds, and helped Fenno get some government printing jobs.

In retaliation Jefferson and Madison set up Philip Freneau's *National Gazette* as an organ for expression of their views. Freneau was made a translator at the State Department, and he too received assistance in getting government jobs. Each side in the newspaper war accused the other of using government funds to serve personal ambition and party goals, rather than for what was best for the nation.

A major bone of contention between Jefferson and Hamilton was foreign policy. Hamilton wanted to court Britain, America's chief trading partner. Jefferson wanted to court France, out of gratitude for help during the War and in hope that the French Revolution would genuinely serve the cause of liberty.

Jefferson got Madison to introduce a bill calling for England to abandon her Northwest forts and to remove trade restrictions. Fearing that England would retaliate with even harsher measures, Hamilton managed to get the bill defeated.

Perhaps because Washington leaned so heavily on him for advice, Hamilton began to act as if he were a prime minister, first among equals. While Washington and Jefferson were out of town, Hamilton arranged for repayment of $40,000 of an American loan to France, to help put down a slave insurrection in Haiti. Feeling that Hamilton was invading his area of responsibility, Jefferson described him as "a singular character of acute understanding, disinterested, honest, and honorable in all private transactions, yet so bewitched by the British example as to be under conviction that corruption was essential to the government of the nation."[43]

Jefferson prepared a strong statement to England, telling her to abandon the Northwest forts. Washington approved Jefferson's stand. Hamilton met secretly with British minister George Hammond and told him that the paper was due to Jefferson's "intemperate violence" and did not express the view of the administration. "One would have to search far in American history," wrote Dumas Malone, "to find a more flagrant example of interference by one high officer with the policy of another which was clearly official policy."[44]

It is quite true, however, that Madison, sometimes spurred on by Jefferson, had become Hamilton's chief adversary in getting the new financial and economic policies adopted. Writing to a friend in 1792 Hamilton described the split between the former close friends. I cannot fathom why he constantly opposes my actions, Hamilton said. "The opinion I once entertained of the candor and fairness of Mr. Madison's character has given way to a dedicated opinion that it is one of a peculiarly artificial kind."[45]

Where he once firmly believed that America needed a strong central government, Hamilton continued, now Madison is the chief enemy of that position: "The attachment to the government of the United States has given way to something very like dislike in Mr. Madison's mind."[46] Hamilton went on to give his views on republican government. "I have strong hopes of the success of the republican theory, but I am far from being without doubts. It is yet to be determined by any experience whether it be consistent with that stability and order in government which are essential to public strength and private security and happiness."[47]

Years later, in 1831, Madison wrote more kindly of Hamilton, saying he had "intellectual powers of the first order" and "integrity and honor in a captivating degree." Although his theory of government was not republican, Madison said, he had the "candor to avow it" and "the greater merit of cooperating faithfully."[48]

Madison's biographer, Ralph Ketcham, also finds Hamilton's motives to have been pure. "Self-interest, sectional hostility, and opposition to republican government seems not, as the Secretary's critics, beginning with Jefferson, have sometimes charged, to have been among Hamilton's motives for the plans" to fund the national debt and assume state debts.[49]

Washington, of course, was caught in the middle. He knew that both sides meant well, but highhanded conduct by both factions gave him many a sleepless night. In an effort to reduce tension, he asked Jefferson to present him with a written reason for his numerous disagreements with Hamilton's policies.

When Washington showed Jefferson's views to Hamilton, he said that "here and there some severity appears. I have not fortitude enough always to hear with calmness, calumnies which include me."[50] He told Washington that it would be hard enough to extinguish the public debt if all officials worked together toward the goal. But when persons of high reputation exert every energy to defeat national laws, public opinion is confused and public support is lacking, "and thus those who clamor are likely to be the principal causes of protracting the existence of the debt."[51]

Although Hamilton did view a national debt as a kind of blessing, in that it united the nation, he also insisted that "the creation of debt should always be accompanied with the means of extinguishment."[52]

Much as he disliked New York Governor George Clinton as a candidate for Vice-President in 1792, Hamilton disliked Burr even more, accusing him of being unprincipled and overly ambitious. "I feel it a religious duty to oppose his career," Hamilton stated that year, later naming him "an embryo Caesar."[53] When New York and Pennsylvania Republicans unanimously agreed to support Clinton, Burr withdrew from the race.

In early 1793, as the war between France and England heated up, differences once again flared. Hamilton, in a series of articles signed "Pacificus," advocated neutrality. Individuals may behave benevolently towards one another, he said, but nations never do, and hence the United States should avoid getting caught up in a European war. This fit into Washington's philosophy, and so he issued a neutrality proclamation.

Jefferson was irate. He felt that America should honor its treaty of 1778 with France, when the United States promised to assist France in wartime. He also felt that only Congress, not the president, had the power to declare neutrality, since only Congress could declare war. Detecting Hamilton's style beneath "Pacificus," he admonished Madison: "For God's sake, take up your pen. Select the most striking heresies and cut him to pieces in the face of the public."[54] Disappointed by Hamilton's incursions into his sphere of authority, Jefferson resigned as Secretary of State at the end of the year.

As England continued to interfere with American shipping and refused to abandon forts on the western frontier, a prewar philosophy gripped the nation. Looking for new sources of revenue, Hamilton suggested excise taxes on carriages, snuff, sugar, and auction sales. Madison immediately protested that these were aimed at the South. When a tax on public securities and bank stock was considered, financial interests in the North complained.

The excise law of 1791 taxing whiskey had long been opposed in the back country. In 1794 rebellious distillers refused to pay the tax, and violence threatened. Hamilton headed a military force to put down the insurrection. The most sacred duty of a citizen, he said, is to respect the Constitution and its laws. How can society exist unless lawbreakers are forced to conform to the law?

The success of Hamilton's system of economic reform depended to a great extent upon trade with England. Duty on British imports constituted the largest annual source of income into the national treasury. Almost 90 percent of all United States imports came from England, with over half of these being carried in American ships. England was also the chief source of foreign credit. A war against England would cripple America's finances.

For these reasons, among others, Hamilton supported Jay's Treaty in 1795 with a series of letters signed "Camillus." He quoted Grotius as saying that when wars cease, "a free course shall be given to the recovery of private debts on both sides."[55]

Hamilton showed why the United States should observe international law. We had done so as a part of the British empire, he said, and had not rebelled against that aspect of the empire. Common law, used in state laws, is based on the law of nations. In our revolt against England, we had appealed to the international conscience of mankind. Our treaties are made and observed in the framework of international law, he observed.

Jay's Treaty, he continued, observed the law of nations. It adjusted controversies with England without surrendering anything vital to America. It got for the United States advantages from England that no other nation had, and above all, it avoided costly and fruitless war.

Jefferson again goaded Madison to respond: "Hamilton is really a colossus to the anti-Republican party. Without numbers, he is a host within himself. For God's sake, take up your pen, and give a fundamental reply to Camillus."[56] Perhaps wondering why Jefferson, now a private citizen, did not reply himself, Madison remained silent.

Hamilton's meddling continued, however, to work a disservice to the national interest. He met secretly with Hammond again, and told him that England need fear no American alliance with France. Hammond told Lord Grenville, the British prime minister, and thus Jay's ability to gain further concessions ceased. Later, Hamilton condemned Edmund Randolph for revealing confidential information concerning Jay's Treaty to the French foreign minister.

Richard B. Morris felt that Hamilton was a two-faced person. Morris cites not only this example but a similar one when Hamilton undermined the efforts of Gouverneur Morris to get a favorable trade treaty with England by disclosing confidential information to British agent George Beckwith.[57]

In January 1795 Hamilton, feeling the pressure of personal financial problems, resigned. As he left government service, he gave Washington a plan to reduce the national debt, to prevent "that progressive accumulation of debt which must ultimately endanger all government."[58]

In charge of Hamilton's finances, Robert Troup said that now all that he owned was his household furniture. Troup tried to interest him in western land speculation, but Hamilton felt that as a former high official he should abstain. "This may be too great refinement," he said. "I know it is pride. But this pride makes it part of my plan to appear truly what I am."[59]

He remained friendly with Washington, and helped him frame a farewell address. He collaborated with Washington on paragraphs 7 through 17 of the speech given four years later, just as Madison had previously collaborated on the other paragraphs.

Writing in "Defense of the Funding System," Hamilton revealed his philosophy of government. The gifted leader, he said, takes human nature as he finds it, with good and evil qualities, and favors those institutions which follow mankind's natural bent so as to maximize human happiness.

In February 1796 Hamilton defended a carriage tax in the first case in which the Supreme Court passed on the constitutionality of an act of Congress (*Hylton v. United States*). Arguing that since the tax was uniform it was legal, Hamilton got the Court to support the statute.

The Politician

Determined to keep Jefferson out of the presidency, Hamilton persuaded New England voters to support not only John Adams but also Thomas Pinckney. Hamilton knew that the South would split its vote between Jefferson and Pinckney. As a result Adams beat Jefferson in the electoral college by a vote of 71–68.

But his maneuvering backfired on Hamilton. Adams, accusing Hamilton of trying to get Pinckney elected president, called Hamilton "proud-spirited, conceited, a hypocrite, with as debauched morals as Franklin."[60] Jefferson had helped drive the wedge between Adams and Hamilton by telling Adams: "You may be cheated of your just succession by a trick worthy of the subtlety of your arch-friend of New York, who has been able to make of your real friends tools to defeat their and your just wishes."[61]

A whispering campaign regarding Hamilton's sex life now surfaced.

In 1791 Maria Reynolds, 23, appealed to Hamilton for financial aid. When he brought it to her house that night he was received in her bedroom. "Some conversation ensued from which it was quickly apparent that other than pecuniary consolation would be acceptable,"[62] Hamilton wrote later. The affair continued for five years, while Betsey and the children lived in Albany.

Eventually, of course, came the blackmail, which Hamilton paid to Maria's husband. James Monroe, as an investigator for Congress, got familiar with all the details and passed them on to Jefferson. Several times a duel almost broke out between Hamilton and Monroe.

In August 1797 Hamilton confessed the liaison in a pamphlet he published. He was adamant that he had not shown any favoritism to Treasury Department employees, thus refuting another charge against him. Of Maria, "the variety of shapes which this woman could assume were endless," he said. He felt that he had "nothing to lose" in this public disclosure concerning his "reputation for chastity concerning which the world had fixed a previous opinion." He would not speculate on that opinion, nor on how well founded it was. But, he said, "there is a wide difference between vague rumors and the evidence of a positive fact."[63] There is no evidence that Betsey or the Schuylers ever held this indiscreet amour against him.

When he wrote in opposition to the French Revolution in 1798, one of his charges was that the lax divorce laws would undermine the French family. He also stated that the attacks upon the church might "pervert a whole nation to atheism."

Despite America's enmity towards France at the time, Hamilton did not recommend an alliance with England. He advocated continued neutrality, until President Adams asked him to assist Washington in arming for a possible war against France. Hamilton's efficiency at organization helped the nation quickly outfit a 50,000 man army. Excelling at details, he could soon report that the personnel, arsenals, forts, and supplies were in a good state of readiness.

Francisco de Miranda, a Venezuelan revolutionist, was working on a scheme to free the Spanish-American colonies from Spain. Hamilton tried to coordinate a plan to use the British fleet, the American army, and Miranda's men to overthrow the Spanish. When the campaign failed, Hamilton philosophized: "You see I am in a humor to laugh. Should you get the plague, if you are a true philosopher you will consider this only a laughing matter."[64]

Since Washington no longer went into the field, Hamilton was the most active of the generals. He even made most of the decisions for Secretary of War James McHenry. He said that since soldiers are motivated by vanity, they should wear loops, cockades, and cocked hats.

When some troops rebelled, he advocated using more troops than necessary, impressing the rebels with the show of strength.

He was shocked at Jefferson's Kentucky Resolutions and Madison's Virginia Resolutions, which stated that state legislatures could overrule federal law. He called these resolutions "signs of progressive gangrene." It was time, he said, "to surround the Constitution with more ramparts and to disconcert the schemes of its enemies."[65] This was to be done by enforcing the Constitution through courts and, if need be, military power, and to push through a program of internal improvements, such as roads, communication, and grants for inventions and discoveries in agriculture and the arts, that would more effectively unite the states.

The presidential election of 1800 was an especially nasty one. Hamilton said that he would not support Adams for re-election, "even though the consequences should be the election of Jefferson. If we must have an enemy at the head of the government, let it be one whom we can oppose, who will not involve our party in the disgrace of his foolish measures."[66] Thus, as he swung through the nation disbanding military units, Hamilton supported the candidacy of Charles Cotesworth Pinckney.

When Adams learned that Hamilton was working to defeat him, he fired Hamilton's friends in the cabinet: James McHenry as secretary of war and Timothy Pickering as secretary of state. Adams told McHenry that Hamilton was "an intriguant, a man devoid of every moral principle. Mr. Jefferson is an infinitely better man, a wiser one. I would rather be Vice-President under him than indebted to such a being as Hamilton for the Presidency."[67]

McHenry showed this to Hamilton, who wrote a sarcastic and provocative public letter attacking Adams. "There are great defects in his character," Hamilton said, "which unfit him for the office of Chief Magistrate."[68] This letter harmed Hamilton more than Adams, split Federalist ranks asunder, and made probable the loss of the election.

The electoral college vote ended in a tie between Burr and Jefferson. Hating Burr more than Jefferson, Hamilton made clear his preference. But what really decided the election was the solidarity of the Republicans behind Jefferson. On the 36th ballot the House of Representatives finally elected Jefferson when Maryland, South Carolina, and Vermont cast blank ballots.

Many years later Hamilton's son James served briefly as secretary of state. He described a conversation with Albert Gallatin, secretary of the treasury under Jefferson. Gallatin, it was alleged, was told to scrutinize carefully the records of Hamilton to see what "blunders and frauds" he could uncover. Gallatin's report to Jefferson was: "I have found the most perfect system ever formed. Any change would injure it. Hamilton did nothing wrong."[69]

In a letter to James Bayard in January 1801, Hamilton gave his opinion of Jefferson: "His politics are tinctured with fanaticism; he is much too earnest in his democracy; he has been a mischievous enemy to the principal measures of our past administration; he is crafty and persevering in his objects; he is not scrupulous about the means of success, nor very mindful of the truth, and he is a contemptible hypocrite."[70]

His spleen vented, Hamilton had to admit that Jefferson was incorruptible, and that he did not favor the House (as was charged) but believed in a strong Senate and a strong executive as well.

The Lawyer

Hamilton now returned to private law practice, and devoted a lot of time to gardening and family life. He was now an exemplary family man, utterly absorbed in his wife and children.

A twin tragedy hit the family in 1801. Hearing his father's name insulted, Hamilton's son Philip challenged George Eacker to a duel, and was killed. Angelica, Philip's 17-year-old sister, lost her mind over the tragedy. Hamilton and Betsey never really recovered from the double loss.

In May 1802 Betsey delivered a baby son, whom they also named Philip. They now lived in Harlem Heights, on what is now a 35-acre plot from 140th to 147th Streets and from Edgecombe Avenue to Hamilton Place.

Hamilton, despondent, wrote to Gouverneur Morris in February 1802: "Mine is an odd destiny. Perhaps no man in the United States has sacrificed or done more for the present Constitution than myself. I am still laboring to prop the frail and worthless fabric. Every day proves more and more that this American world was not made for me. The time may arrive when the minds of men will be prepared to make an effort to recover the Constitution."[71]

Hamilton now proposed the formation of an organization to support the Constitution and the Christian religion. It would disseminate information about these two causes, and would assist charitable institutions that helped immigrants and scientific workers. James Bayard told Hamilton that although his plan showed "great ingenuity," the times were not right for its reception.

Chancellor James Kent called Hamilton the best lawyer in the state, for his "courteous manner, clear style, power of analysis, innate dignity, and melodious voice."[72] Kent was particularly impressed by his work in the case of Harry Croswell, who in 1802 had been convicted of libeling Jefferson. Croswell said that Jefferson had paid James Callender, a printer, to grossly slander Washington and John Adams.

Hamilton handled Croswell's appeal before the New York Court of Errors in February 1804. Hamilton made two points: "the truth published with good intent should not be subject to action for libel; in such actions questions of fact should be submitted to a jury."[73]

Although the appeal was denied, the next state legislature passed a bill permitting the truth to be sufficient defense in a charge of libel, and the new state constitution also contained this provision.

Final Years

Hamilton did not conceal his contempt for Aaron Burr. His letter to James Bayard in 1801 had said that Burr was "a man of extreme ambition, selfish, and decidedly profligate. His understanding is much overrated. He is far more cunning than wise."[74]

When Burr ran for governor of New York in 1804, Hamilton supported his opponent Morgan Lewis. Even though he was vice president at the time, Burr was working with Samuel Hunt and Timothy Pickering on a plan for the northernmost seven states to secede from the Union, so Hamilton had more than personal motives to oppose Burr. Lewis easily beat Burr, 30,000 votes to 22,000.

Burr's final charge against Hamilton grew out of a letter sent by Dr. Charles Cooper to General Philip Schuyler on April 23, 1804. It said that Hamilton, at a private dinner party, had said that Burr was "a dangerous man, not to be trusted." Cooper added, "I could detail to you a still more despicable opinion which General Hamilton has expressed of Mr. Burr."[75]

The latter phrase led Burr to write to Hamilton on June 18, 1804, demanding an explanation. "More despicable," replied Hamilton, admits of many shades of meaning. The charge is too vague to be answered, he said. After all, what opinion is admissible between political opponents?

Still angry at Hamilton's part in his defeat for governor, Burr persisted in having an apology. He found Hamilton's reply lacking in "sincerity and delicacy." The meaning of "more despicable" he found to be derogatory to his honor, which required a more definite reply.

Hamilton knew that Burr wanted a duel. Hamilton's deliberate evasiveness almost seemed suicidal, particularly considering his plan not to return fire. Hamilton said that Burr's position showed "nothing short of predetermined hostility."

After getting his affairs in order, Hamilton wrote to Betsey: "This letter, my dear Eliza, will not be delivered to you unless I shall have first terminated my earthly career to begin, I hope, a happy immortality. If it had been possible for me to have avoided the interview, my love for you and my precious children would have been alone a decisive motive. But it was not possible without sacrifices which would have rendered me unworthy of your esteem. The consolations of religion, my beloved, can alone support you. I cherish the sweet hope of meeting you in a better world."[76]

At a 4th of July dinner given by the Society of the Cincinnati, Hamilton seemed cheerful and gregarious while Burr appeared to be glum. When Hamilton sang pleasantly, Burr cocked his head to listen.

John B. Church, Hamilton's brother-in-law, furnished the pistols. Church had earlier dueled Burr in a dispute over the Holland Land Company. Although neither man had been hit, Burr's coat had been ripped by Church's bullet.

Hamilton exonerated Burr from blame, saying that he had probably heard remarks that were "enlarged by falsehoods." Hamilton's last letter was a plea to Theodore Sedgwick to help save the Union from being dissolved by secession. Dissolution, he said, would not relieve "our real disease, which is democracy, the poison of which by a subdivision will only be more concentrated and consequently more virulent."[77]

A few days before July 11, Samuel Bradhurst, a follower of Hamilton and a relative of Burr by marriage, tried to stop the duel. He and Burr got into an argument, and they dueled. Burr was unhurt but Bradhurst was wounded in the shoulder.

Weehawken was a popular dueling spot because of its privacy and easy accessibility. Early on the morning of July 11 they arrived at the spot. Hamilton and Burr greeted each other formally. Hamilton had decided to throw away the first shot and perhaps the second.

Both men fired. Hamilton fell, and Burr left quickly. Seeing Dr. David Hosack, Hamilton said, "This is a mortal wound, Doctor," and then fainted. As Hosack worked on him, Hamilton said, "My vision is indistinct," then "Take care of that pistol; it may go off and do harm."[78]

Doctors agreed that the case was hopeless. Episcopal Bishop Benjamin Moore, president of Columbia College, administered the last communion only after Hamilton promised to disavow dueling should he recover. He was carried to his home.

When all seven of his children came to his bedside, he could not speak, being overcome with grief. He said several times to Betsey, "Remember, my Eliza, you are a Christian."[79] He died at 2 p.m. on July 12, 1804. Autopsy revealed that a bullet had hit a rib, then passed through the liver and diaphragm, and lodged in a lumbar vertebra.

Burr was hounded out of New York City and forced to travel south.

Months later the Vice President resumed his role as president of the Senate.

At the impressive funeral held in New York City, Gouverneur Morris gave the funeral oration. His message was, "I charge you to protect his fame." With the crews wearing mourning, a British warship and two French frigates joined American naval vessels in salvos lasting 48 minutes. Hamilton's memory needed no longer relate to being illegitimate, nor unwanted, nor unrecognized.

Many tributes were paid him. Talleyrand, who knew all the famous men of his time, said that his only equals were Napoleon and Charles James Fox. François Guizot said that in the American Constitution, "there is no element of order, or durability, which he did not powerfully contribute to introduce and give efficacy to."[80]

Nicholas Murray Butler called him "the greatest and most commanding intellect that the new world has produced. Only Jonathan Edwards and Ralph Waldo Emerson can approach him."[81]

Leonard D. White praised Hamilton's influence on government: "The moral standards of the Federalist public service were extraordinarily high. The sale of office was unknown. Fraud in the financial transactions of the general government could not be discovered even in repeated investigations by Hamilton's opponents. Probably never in the history of the United States has the standard of integrity of the federal civil service been at a higher level."[82]

It is no wonder that Hamilton's fame has endured. A quasicynical modern age that no longer believes in man's perfectibility finds in Hamilton a realist who, not seeing human nature in a rosy hue, can still work hard to make human life more rewarding. Businessmen and bankers warm up to his doctrines naturally. The poor, for all of Hamilton's disinterest in them, benefit from his broad interpretation of the Constitution, granting the national government extended powers, so that there might be a Tennessee Valley Authority, a social security program, and many other types of social legislation in "the general welfare."

Finally, without realizing it, Hamilton became the philosopher of a technological society. The idyllic agrarian democracy of Jefferson never came to be. Factories and cities and expanded credit became the wave of America's future. Hamilton had prepared the way.

7. James Madison: Political Theorist Turned Pragmatist

The best read of the Founding Fathers, James Madison was the expert on political structures to whom the delegates to the Constitutional Convention deferred on questions relating to forms of government. He retained a lifelong capacity for growth. As experience indicated his political theories were inadequate, he changed them. Many of the policies he opposed in Washington's administration he pragmatically adopted under the stress of turbulent conditions in his own presidency. His own life was the record of a man struggling between politics as it should be and politics as it is.

The first of 12 children, he was born in Port Conway, Virginia, on March 16, 1751. His father, James Madison, Sr., was a wealthy planter who served as a justice of the peace. A strong-minded grandmother, Frances Madison, played an important role in rearing young James. Five of his siblings died in infancy or of childhood diseases. One brother, Ambrose, helped manage his private affairs and later his estate Montpelier.

As a child he was overly protected, living in the shadow of his father's prestige. He was short and frail with a feeble voice. He had light hair and hazel eyes. Books, not people, were his interest. Because of his introverted personality, his social maturity came late; at the age of 11 he had read all of the books in his father's library.

The Student

His tutor Donald Robertson taught James to read Latin and Greek. Forty years later James could correct translations from the Latin. He also studied geography, literature, and mathematics, borrowing books from Robertson's library. "All that I have been in life," said Madison, "I owe largely to that man."[1]

At 16 Madison studied at home under the Rev. Thomas Martin, rector of the Brick Church attended by the Madison family. Martin's brother

Alexander later became a senator, governor, and a delegate to the Constitutional Convention. Since William and Mary College was in the doldrums, Madison took the advice of Martin and attended Princeton.

The Latin and Greek part of the Princeton entrance examination gave Madison no trouble. Because of his reading background he was able to complete the three-year curriculum in two years.

The Princeton curriculum was a blend of classical and modern studies. It included ethics, geography, history, logic, mathematics, rhetoric, and science. The intellectual atmosphere had two influential currents: New Light Presbyterianism tended to challenge all orthodox religion, and political dissent fit into the prevailing pattern of rising hostility towards England.

Although the atmosphere was religious and the school day long, students were taught "to cherish the spirit of liberty and free enquiry." One of Madison's teachers, William Houston, later served as a Constitutional Convention delegate.

At Princeton Madison was one of the organizers of the American Whig Society. Among his friends were the future governors: Henry Lee of Virginia; Morgan Lewis of New York; and Aaron Ogden of New Jersey. Other friends were Gunning Bedford, Hugh Henry Brackenridge, William Bradford (attorney-general in Washington's cabinet), Aaron Burr, Philip Freneau, and Samuel S. Smith, future Princeton president.

Writers studied by Madison included Addison, Francis Bacon, and Montaigne. In his senior year he studied Aristotle's *Politics* under President Witherspoon. Here Madison learned that any form of government can be perverted, and that religious persecution greatly harmed society. Witherspoon had his students read the standard political writers, including Burlamaqui, Hobbes, Locke, Montesquieu, and Pufendorf.

Witherspoon, a signer of the Declaration of Independence, said that he never knew Madison to do or say an improper thing. Apparently he was unaware of the scatological poems Madison wrote at the time of his graduation. Or if he knew, that may have been the reason why Madison was the only one of the 12 graduates who did not speak at commencement.

Upon graduating, Madison suffered a breakdown in his health, brought on by too much studying and remorse over the death of a classmate. He had nervous indigestion and dizzy spells, and he thought he had epilepsy because he was subject to attacks that kept him from thinking. Like many a hypochondriac, he lived to a ripe old age of 84.

Too ill to travel home, Madison stayed on another year at Princeton to study Hebrew and law. Although he seemed apolitical, he was aroused by the Boston Tea Party, and by the arrest of six Baptist preachers in Virginia.

Back home, he tutored his siblings. We must frame our economy, he wrote William Bradford, "according to the precepts of wisdom and religion." He recommended that Bradford read "history and the science of morals, seasoned with a little divinity."[2] At the time Madison was taking notes on the Four Gospels and the Acts of the Apostles.

He did not believe in an established church. "Ecclesiastical establishments tend to great ignorance and corruption,"[3] he wrote Bradford. Unfortunately, he added, among established clergy one often finds luxury, pride, and knavery. To keep their support, they often propped up governments that were oppressive, he felt. "Religious bondage shackles and debilitates the mind and unfits it for every noble enterprise,"[4] Madison said. Had the Church of England been established in the middle and northern colonies, he opined, there would have been slavery there too.

Unfriendly as he was to the church, Madison had deep faith in God. In fact, his belief that all people were God's children affected his political tenet that the individual had an importance that no government should invade. "The Christian affirmation that each human soul has infinite worth," says Ralph Ketcham, "and the emphasis in the Protestant tradition that the essence of this worth is the relationship of each individual to the Almighty, were of vast significance. There were, therefore, limits to the claim the state could make upon the individual."[5]

Most of the Founding Fathers were committed to the same moral standards, even heterodox Franklin and Jefferson. "To them all, the Ten Commandments, the Sermon on the Mount, and the twelfth chapter of Romans were canonical."[6]

Although he lived on into the age of Keats and Byron, Madison remained at heart a child of the Enlightenment. He was perfectly at home with the neoclassical literary outlook of Addison, Pope, and Swift, and he was himself, as Ketcham has observed, a model Augustan gentleman. Politically he subscribed to the views of John Locke, feeling that when man enters society he gains certain protections in exchange for surrendering certain privacies.

He loved to "breathe the free air" of Philadelphia, as he attended a Presbyterian synod meeting there in May 1774. Streets paved and lighted, rows of three-story brick buildings, and churches of eight different denominations within several blocks all appealed to him.

Effigies were being burned of Alexander Wedderburn for abusing Franklin, and of Governor Thomas Hutchinson for closing the port of Boston. Madison may have attended the meeting at City Tavern on May 20, 1774, calling for a "Congress of deputies of all the colonies" to confront Lord North and his policies.

The Patriot

A plague of dysentery hit Virginia hard in 1775, killing Madison's seven-year-old sister Elizabeth in May and his four-year-old brother Reuben in June. His father, as chairman of the Committee of Public Safety, appointed James as a member, and he took his job seriously. He recommended tar and feathers for Tory pamphleteers, and was gleeful when a clergyman's "seditious" documents were seized and burned.

He joined his father in signing a letter of praise to Patrick Henry for asking for compensation for gunpowder which Governor John Dunmore had removed from the county magazine. The letter ended: "We give as our opinion that the blow struck in the Massachusetts government is a hostile attack on this and every other colony, and a sufficient warrant to use violence and reprisal in all cases where it may be expedient for our security and welfare."[7]

As a colonel in the Orange County militia in October 1775 he began to read the writings of radical English Whigs. In *Essay on Toleration* by Philip Furneaux he found the doctrine of religious liberty carried to its ultimate limit, stating that government had no right to interfere with freedom of conscience. Joseph Priestley, in *Essay on First Principles of Government*, emphasized that taxes could be levied justly only with the consent of the governed, and that the administration of laws must be uniform and predictable, two standards that Madison always used in evaluating laws.

In April 1776 he was elected to represent Orange County in the Virginia constitutional convention. He amended the phrase "fullest toleration in the exercise of religion" to read "free exercise of religion" in George Mason's Virginia Declaration of Rights. Madison's change implies an inherent personal right rather than a limit upon state action.

Madison collaborated with Jefferson in getting the Anglican church disestablished in Virginia. Over the objections of Edmund Pendleton, they got the remuneration to Anglican clergy suspended for one year, and it was never resumed.

On May 15 the constitutional convention instructed the Virginia delegates to Congress "to declare the United Colonies free and independent states." Richard Henry Lee on June 7 so moved, in Congress. Following approval of the Declaration of Independence, the phrase "God save the King" came out of Anglican prayers, being replaced by prayers for the magistrates of the commonwealth.

Madison lost the election to the Assembly in 1777, because he refused to buy the rounds of drinks traditionally asked of candidates. He liked to stand up for principles against the standards of the crowd.

The Assembly selected him to the Virginia State Council, where he served from November 1777 until December 1779. The eight-member Council had revisionary powers over the House of Delegates. Housing was short during the legislative session in Williamsburg, so he stayed with his second cousin, the Rev. James Madison, president of William and Mary College. To partially compensate for his room and board, Madison had his father send dried fruit and a large amount of flour to the Rev. Madison.

On the Council he served under two governors, Patrick Henry and Thomas Jefferson. Here he gained valuable administrative experience, dealing with such questions as the War needs, hostile Indians, tax levies, and liaison with Congress. Here too began a lifelong friendship with Jefferson.

In 1779 Madison opposed Henry's efforts to establish the Protestant Episcopal Church (the successor to the Anglican Church). The Presbyterians now supported the measure, feeling that they too would soon derive support from the state. Madison said that such an establishment would be a violation of the Virginia Declaration of Rights. The bill passed, but was repealed in 1787, when the Episcopalian laity saw how the measure limited their control of the church.

The Continental Congressman

When the Virginia Assembly selected Madison as a delegate to the Continental Congress in 1779, he wondered if he had received a demotion. There was more prestige in serving as a state legislator at that time. Such leaders as Henry, Jefferson, Richard Henry Lee, and George Wythe had left the Congress to accept state offices.

Congressional salaries were not only low but also were usually in arrears. Jefferson told Madison that congressmen's horses were often turned loose in the street for nonpayment of livery bills. Madison and other congressmen often borrowed money from a patriotic Jew, Haym Salomon, who loaned money to them at no interest charge. "Madison always remembered the Jewish broker fondly and used his patriotic conduct to defend Jews generally against slanderous charges of selfish profiteering during the Revolution."[8]

The youngest congressman, Madison quickly learned of the problems of the central government. He readily realized that the federal government must have the power to tax and to control the currency.

Because of his personality, he was given assignments concerning diplomacy. As chairman of a committee, he kept Congress from censuring Benjamin Franklin for having defended Silas Deane when Deane was accused of charging for supplies which were supposedly a gift from

France. In May 1781 he wrote a letter on behalf of the Congress praising John Jay for renegotiating Mississippi River rights with Spain.

Madison waas never an isolationist. He did not believe that the United States could stand without allies. Above all, he favored France because of its traditional opposition to Britain. Fluent in French, he sometimes translated French documents. He enjoyed the sumptuous dinners at the French legation in John Dickinson's large mansion on Chestnut Street. The French minister, the Chevalier de la Luzerne, said that Madison was regarded as "the man of soundest judgment in Congress. He speaks nearly always with fairness and wins the approval of his colleagues."[9]

In the fall of 1782 Madison drew up a list of 500 books for a library of Congress to use for consultation purposes. He attacked the Virginia legislature in early 1783 for paying so little of its requisition, and for refusing to vote to approve a permanent funding plan for the federal government. Sounding like Hamilton, he took out after Patrick Henry, Arthur Lee, and Richard Henry Lee. He regretted that Edmund Randolph's replacement in Congress, John Francis Mercer, no longer pressed Virginia to meet its federal obligations. "His frustration and piddling success more than anything else pointed toward the Constitution of 1787."[10]

Again sounding like Hamilton, Madison in March 1783 introduced a financial plan in Congress which called for federal assumption of the states' war debts. Then, to satisfy the southern states, which objected to having slaves included in their requisition quotas, he introduced into Congress the three-fifths rule which the United States Constitution later adopted, that five slaves would count as three free inhabitants.

He drafted instructions to John Jay concerning western lands in the Treaty of Paris. Since the crown had asserted title to those lands, Madison said, that title now passed to the federal government rather than to individual states. He was trying to curtail land speculation. On the whole he practiced what he preached: "Never to deal in public property, lands, debts or money whilst a member of the body whose proceedings might affect these transactions."[11]

Working with George Mason and Joseph Jones, Madison got the Virginia legislature to approve to cede its claims in the Northwest Territory, subject to these conditions: (1) Congress would create new states there, (2) Virginia would be repaid for the expedition by George Rogers Clark, (3) Virginia's land bounties to its soldiers would be honored, and (4) the ceded lands would be for the benefit of the United States.

As with so many things in the realm of social life, Cupid worked more slowly with Madison than with most swains. At 32 he fell in love with Kitty Floyd, daughter of William Floyd, a signer of the Declaration of Independence. Floyd tabbed Madison as a comer. But Kitty preferred another suitor, 19-year-old William Clarkson, who was given to "hanging around her at the harpsichord." Madison's form of courtship was to discuss with Papa the latest news from Congress, such as the dreadful need for an impost. Kitty wrote Madison that she no longer considered him to be her suitor.

Madison was no traveler. He had no yen to see Europe, the western frontier, or the states south of Virginia. Jefferson tried in vain to get him to move to a place two miles from Monticello.

At 34 he still had no profession. He began to read law in December 1783 but it did not appeal to him. His father gave him 560 acres in August 1784 but he did not want to be a planter.

He wrote to Edmund Randolph that "another of my wishes is to depend as little as possible on the labor of slaves."[12] Tilling the soil with his own hands never dawned on a man of his social class and physical condition. He finally got interested in land speculation, and in March 1786 bought 900 acres, jointly with James Monroe, in the fertile Mohawk Valley. He also bought land in Kentucky, and tried unsuccessfully to persuade Jefferson to borrow money from French bankers so that he, Jefferson, and Monroe could go into a joint land venture.

Madison was elected to the Virginia legislature in 1784. Earlier, when Jefferson was governor, Madison had played a leadership role in getting the state's Assembly to adopt Jefferson's Statute for Religious Liberty. Now he made such a powerful argument against a tax to support religion that the issue never even was presented. A tax to go to a church violated someone's freedom of conscience, he said, and thus should not be allowed. If it is permitted, the next step is for the legislature to pass a law requiring everyone to subscribe to the doctrines of that church.

Madison pushed through the Virginia Assembly a modernization of 117 statutes, required in converting Virginia from a colony to a state. He had less success in his effort to revise Virginia's antiquated court system. Here the opponents of change won out.

He and Jefferson often discussed science. Madison was elected a member of the American Philosophical Society in January 1785.

By now economic depression was breeding turmoil. Specie flowed to England to buy goods, farm prices fell and farmers were unable to pay their debts, so they asked for paper money (bills of credit), or payment in kind, or postponed payments.

Britain closed West Indian ports to American ships, maintained troops on the western frontier, and failed to return the slaves they had taken when they retreated during the War. Spain closed the lower Mississippi to American traffic, and both Spain and Britain incited Indians to attack American frontiersmen.

It took no genius to see that the Virginia legislature could not solve these problems by itself. The reason that Madison and other Virginia legislators were developing a national perspective was that Virginia's problems (and hopes for solutions) were national in scope.

Unlike Hamilton, Madison was no early proponent for a federal constitutional convention. He had supported specific amendments to the Articles of Confederation: to give Congress power to tax imports, fix state apportionments, enact navigation acts, and regulate commerce. But when the New York and the Massachusetts legislatures called for a special convention to revise the Articles, he was lukewarm.

The decline of the economy helped him change his mind. At the Annapolis Convention in August 1786 he said he hoped to see a broad consideration of revision of the Articles there, but he doubted that it would occur. In fact, he did not think that even a commercial agreement could be reached there. By October that year he felt that conditions were so bad that state legislatures throughout the colonies would now support a convention to revise the Articles of Confederation.

As he faced 1787, Madison feared that most state legislatures were ignoring minority interests, who in turn were using violence to make their presence known. He feared that convention delegates might think only of outbreaks like Shays' Rebellion and show no faith in the people's ability to govern themselves. His fear was that republican government might not be given a fair chance, and monarchical structures would be erected in desperation.

At the same time, he realized that a corrupt democracy would also lead to despotism. He wrote to Jefferson that "wherever the real power in a government lies, there is the danger of oppression. In our government the real power lies in the majority of the community, and the invasion of private rights is chiefly to be apprehended from acts in which the government is the mere instrument of the major number of the constituents."[13] By now Madison went beyond the traditional Whig belief that political freedom meant freedom from government to feel that true political freedom meant defined use of the government in the public interest.

The Framer

Madison prepared for the Constitutional Convention by reading many books on history and government. He compiled a 41-page booklet called *Of Ancient and Modern Confederacies*. He referred to this pocket-sized work during the Convention, and he drew heavily from it in papers 18, 19, and 20 of *The Federalist*. Using problem areas from the American government, he listed various plans for financial support, diplomatic representation, cooperation in time of war, regulation of commerce, and coercion of disobedient members. He also listed the causes for the failure of each confederacy.

In the spring of 1787 Madison wrote a paper listing the weaknesses of the Articles of Confederation. The chief evil was that state governments had lost sight of the general welfare. "A sanction is essential to the idea of law," he wrote, "as coercion is to that of government. The federal system, being destitute of both, wants the great vital principles of a political constitution."[14]

In David Hume's "Idea of a Perfect Commonwealth," Madison found the idea that the larger the democracy, the more varied the viewpoints and hence the greater the protection against monolithic autocracy. He told Jefferson in March 1787 that he now approved a veto by Congress over state laws.

He wrote letters to George Washington and Edmund Randolph outlining the plan of government he favored. He called it a "mixed government," since it observed Randolph's concern for local autonomy along with Washington's desire for a stronger central government. He told Washington that surely no national legislature would be as foolish as the state legislatures that had approved paper currency.

In his letter to Randolph in April 1787 Madison said that he felt that the Virginia delegation should introduce into the Convention some "leading propositions," such as a national executive, a national judiciary, Congressional veto over state laws, and a bicameral national legislature selected on the basis of proportional representation.

William Pierce described Madison at the Convention as "a man of great modesty, with a remarkable sweet temper." On every great question, Madison took the lead, Pierce said, for he was the best informed person on every point that was debated. To Pierce he was the perfect blend of the profound politician with the scholar.

Jefferson criticized the delegates for adopting the rule of secrecy, but "many years later Madison believed that no constitution would have been adopted if the debates had been publicized."[15] He also felt that there had never been an assembly of men more pure in their motives or more exclusively dedicated to their goals than were these delegates.

As the Virginia Plan was being discussed, Madison kept his eye on his major goals. Most important of all was to establish a strong federal government, one having a republican structure. Stability in the government was to be achieved by granting long terms of office.

Perhaps his most important speech came on June 6. Gerry, C.C. Pinckney, Rutledge, and Sherman had all questioned whether the people should elect the lower house of the legislature. Wilson wanted to give the vote to the people. Madison was eloquent in support of Wilson's position. A major weakness of the current government was, he said, that the people were underrepresented. Get them involved in their government, Madison advocated, and they will not riot. Riots occur when their rights are denied, or when their society is so small that it is easily controlled by demagogues. Giving more authority to the central government will help alleviate the conditions that lead to riots.

The day after Hamilton's long speech, Madison pointed out the defects of the New Jersey Plan. It left states free to violate laws and treaties, as well as to encroach on the authority of the central government, he said. States could continue to prey on one another, through trade wars and the printing of paper money. With no central authority to keep them in line, large states would continue to exploit small states. When the vote approved the Virginia Plan 7-3, the Articles of Confederation were basically dead. Madison could already feel that great improvement had been made in the structure of American government.

Madison persistently opposed the Great Compromise, for he felt it was wrong for the states to have equal votes in the Senate. His reasons: this denied proportional representation, it might have the minority governing the majority, and Virginia (with one-fifth of the American population) had more to lose than any other state.

After the Great Compromise was adopted, his strategy was to transfer power away from the Senate, to the executive, the judiciary, or the people. For example, on June 13 he had supported appointment of judges by the Senate; now, on July 18 he said that the executive should appoint judges with the concurrence of the Senate.

He refuted the idea that the smaller the political unit, the greater the freedom. He said that "a citizen of Delaware was not more free than a citizen of Virginia, nor would either be more free than a citizen of America."[16] For him the crucial question was not the size of the governing unit but rather its structure.

Should the Constitution be ratified by the people or by their legislature? It would be a dangerous doctrine, said Madison, to give a legislature the power to change the Constitution which created it, so ratification should be by the people, in state conventions. The Confederation Congress could not possibly draw up a constitution as good as the one being drafted here, Madison insisted. The difference between a system founded merely on legislatures and one founded on the people is the difference between a league (or a treaty) and the new Constitution.

As the Convention neared its end, Madison could feel proud that many of the most important features of the new government had been either suggested or supported by him. His greatest disapointments were the equal state votes in the Senate, the election of senators by state legislatures (rather than by the people), the elimination of the council of revision, and the limitation of the federal veto over state laws.

He sounded disappointed when he broke the rule of secrecy on September 6 to give Jefferson a summary of the suggested new document. He concluded by saying that "the plan should it be adopted will neither effectually answer its national object nor prevent the local mischiefs which everywhere excite disgusts against the state governments."[17]

Was he "The Father of the Constitution," as some claimed? Edmund Burke said that it is not too hard to set aside one government and draw up another on paper. "But to form a free government, that is, to temper together the opposite elements of liberty and restraint in one conscious work, requires much thought, deep reflection, a sagacious, powerful, and combining mind."[18] Burke felt that by performing this task at the Convention, Madison deserved to be called the father of the document.

In the final years of his life, Madison told William Cogswell: "You give me credit to which I have no claim, in calling me 'the writer of the Constitution of the United States.' This was not the offspring of a single brain. It ought to be regarded as the work of many heads and many hands."[19]

Despite his modesty, his contributions to the Constitution can be thought of as unique. He was the chief contributor to the Virginia Plan, the one adopted with modifications. He was the leading expert on government and political theory, the one that the delegates looked to as the expert in these fields. With Hamilton, he made crucial contributions to the ratification of the document. He played the key role in the adoption of the first ten amendments, and his voice was important as the first Congress filled out the new governmental structures as described by the Constitution. Capping his contributions, he kept a lengthy, accurate account of the proceedings of the Convention for posterity. No one else came even close to having had the influence that he had upon the new blueprint for government.

The Ratifier

Madison was moved by the failure of his fellow Virginians, Mason and Randolph, to sign the document. He focused his attention upon whether the Convention erred in not including a bill of rights in the Constitution. A chance meeting with an old friend, Baptist preacher John Leland, may have swung his decision. Leland agreed to support ratification at the Virginia convention if Madison would introduce a bill of rights afterward. Leland wanted a bill of rights as protection against an established church or any kind of religious persecution.

Madison later virtually authored the First Amendment. To him separation of church and state formed "the great barrier against usurpations on the roots of conscience." If this separation breaks down, it will leave "crevices through which bigotry may introduce persecution."[20] For his work on this amendment Richard B. Morris ranks Madison among America's foremost libertarians.

Madison's role in writing *The Federalist* papers was second only to Hamilton's. In No. 10 Madison showed that factions are better controlled in a larger society. He predicted that as time passed, the gap between the rich and the poor in America would grow ever greater. In No. 14 he pointed out that in a large society like America, only a republic (not a democracy) is possible. In Nos. 18–20 he listed the weaknesses of previous confederacies. In 37–41 he showed how the new government was a mixed one, partly federal and partly national, and that the Convention had not been an illegal body but reflected the ideals of the Declaration of Independence.

In Nos. 45–51 he dealt with the separation and balance of powers in the new government. In No. 51 he wrote that "in framing a government which is to be administered by men over men, the great difficulty lies in this: you must first enable the government to control the governed, and in the next place oblige it to control itself."[21] In Nos. 52–58 Madison answered specific questions regarding the House of Representatives, and he did the same thing for the Senate in Nos. 62–63.

At the Virginia ratification convention Patrick Henry was the leading opponent of the Constitution. He spoke against it on 18 of the 23 days that the convention met. Several days he made three speeches, one day five, and one day eight. In one speech alone he was on his feet for seven hours.

Henry made two points: the Constitution contained insufficient safeguards to individual liberties, and the central government was so strong that it was bound to lead to tyranny.

Madison answered Henry's high-flown rhetoric with facts. Was it democracy for one state, Rhode Island, to block 12 others? Was it desirable for the national government to be as weak as it currently was? Which clause would lead to tyranny? Which single state acting alone can preserve the Mississippi River from Spanish domination?

Clutching at any straw, Henry had quoted Jefferson as being opposed to the Constitution. Madison's retort was a classic. With all due respect to Jefferson, he had been in Paris and was not very familiar with the new document. Anyhow, why bring up views of persons outside the convention—Virginians can think for themselves. If you must quote a great Virginian's view on the Constitution, quote George Washington; he was there and he presided. Finally, said Madison quoting from his correspondence with Jefferson, I have reason to know that he does indeed favor this Constitution! As John P. Roche summarized, "to devise an assault route into this rhetorical fortress was literally impossible."[22]

When George Mason said that the new Constitution should have outlawed slave trade immediately, Madison replied that would have kept South Carolina and Georgia out of the Union. Furthermore, had slave importation ceased, those two states would have bought slaves in Virginia at higher prices than current ones. Is this what Henry and Mason wanted?

Thinking that Virginia would be the ninth state to ratify, Madison asked if Virginia would rather destroy the Union than surrender any of its position. What state had not sacrificed in order to achieve an adequate central government? If Virginia were to ratify, it might be "one of the most fortunate events that ever happened for human nature."[23]

Defeated at the ratifying convention, Henry threw his support behind Richard Henry Lee and William Grayson as Virginia's first senators, thus keeping Madison out of the Senate. Henry wanted Congress to call for a second Constitutional Convention, a move that he knew Madison would oppose. On June 26, 1788, Virginia ratified the Constitution by a vote of 89-79.

The Republican Opposition Leader

In late 1788 Congress selected New York as the temporary national capitol. Madison, who always liked Philadelphia, disliked seeing the capitol move still farther north from the geographical center of the states.

In early February 1789 Madison defeated his friend James Monroe by 336 votes in the race for House of Representatives. Madison and Washington were now close friends. He visited Mount Vernon frequently, and wrote the draft of Washington's first acceptance speech, changed but little by Washington.

Since Washington considered him to be the wisest and best informed political leader in the country, Madison was the leading adviser as the new president looked for persons to fill federal posts. Hamilton was his choice, as well as Washington's, to be secretary of the treasury.

Washington wanted Madison to be secretary of state, but he was ineligible because of a law he had fostered: a member of Congress cannot serve in an office created during his tenure, until after a lapse of a year after his departure from Congress. Madison then recommended Jefferson for the role, and Washington gladly assented.

Madison was still applying Witherspoon's lectures on Aristotle. "A state exists for the sake of the good life," Aristotle had said, and thus education in virtue is indispensable if republican government is to succeed. That government is best, Madison quoted Aristotle as saying, which enables its citizens "to act virtuously and live happily."[24]

Madison felt that no matter how carefully structured the form of government, unless it leads to the good life it is mere opportunism. His great admiration of the new president rested upon Washington's embodiment of the Aristotelian virtues.

Madison was still a good friend of Hamilton in October 1789 when Hamilton asked him for ideas on how to fund the national debt. Madison suggested an excise tax on home distilleries, a higher duty on imported liquors, and a land tax, thereby pre-empting the states from that important source of revenue. Hamilton appealed to "your friendship"; Madison concluded with "affection and regards."

Both men must have known that they were in a temporary truce, for they had had ample opportunity to search out each other's philosophy to the naked root, and the differences could not have been more extreme. Underlying Madison's vision was the heavenly city as conceived by the thinkers of the Enlightenment, built upon the perfectibility of man as a child of God. Hamilton's framework, resting on Hume and Hobbes, based itself upon human self-concern, with the government as a vehicle for converting individual greed into social gain.

The chasm was widened by Madison's preference for agrarian simplicity contrasted with Hamilton's preference for urban manufactures. The news of the day drove them further apart. Madison applauded the French Revolution whereas Hamilton feared its consequences. Hamilton wished to befriend America's best trading partner, England, but Madison deplored England's intervention in France's social reform. When Washington accepted his new job with some reluctance, he too must have wondered how long it would take for the differences to erupt.

The first Congress started tamely enough. Madison, in the House of Representatives, moved for measures to raise federal funds: high import duties on luxuries, tonnage rates favoring American ships, and a lowering of certain import duties so as to encourage trade.

What term of address should be used in speaking to the president? Madison successfully fought off highfalutin titles in favor of simply "Mr. President." Chastened by his experience in the Virginia ratifying convention, Madison led the move to get the first 12 amendments to the Constitution approved, and by September 1789 Congress had passed favorably on them.

In the second Congress the ideological differences appeared. Madison had no trouble supporting Hamilton's suggestion to pay off the

$12,000,000 in foreign loans. But he could not agree to pay off all governmental obligations at face value when speculators had bought them at well below par. His motion to give speculators only the highest market value plus interest was defeated by Congress as impracticable.

On the assumption of state war debts by the federal government, Madison opposed Hamilton as a matter of principle. It seemed unfair to Madison to help states like Massachusetts and South Carolina, which had made little effort to pay off their debts, in the same way as states like Virginia, which on their own had already retired a great deal of that debt. Madison was unimpressed by Hamilton's rebuttal that those states had provided many soldiers or the terrain for fighting the war.

For the most part, Madison's opposition to the national bank was also based on grounds of principle. The Constitution, Madison said, was "a grant of particular powers only," and the Convention had specifically rejected the proposal to give the federal government the power to charter corporations like the national bank. Madison said that arguments voiced in state ratification conventions against the bank were proper sources to refer to in interpreting the Constitution. The doctrine of implied powers advanced by Hamilton, he said, struck at the very heart of a government of limited and enumerated powers.

Madison was on shakier ground when he said that the "necessary and proper" clause in the Constitution refers only to the authority needed to carry out the enumerated powers. In *The Federalist* No. 44 he had explained this clause differently, saying that "whenever a general power to do a thing is given, every particular power necessary for doing it is included."[25] He was beginning to adjust his ideology to fit into more current concerns.

Frustrated at seeing Hamilton's access to the public in John Fenno's *Gazette of the United States*, Madison set up Philip Freneau's *National Gazette* as an opposition paper. In a letter to Edmund Randolph he said he did this because he wanted "a free paper edited by a man of republican principles and a friend to the Constitution, some antidote to the doctrines circulated in favor of monarchy and aristocracy."[26] In 1791-92 Madison contributed 17 articles to the *National Gazette*.

Speaking on war in February 1792, Madison said it would be eliminated only when the people really wanted peace. He also wrote that each generation should be required to pay for the cost of its wars.

The following month Madison defined Locke's statement that property was the goal of government to include not only man's material possessions but also his freedom of expression, liberty of conscience, and safety of person. "As a man is said to have a right to his property," he wrote, "he may be equally said to have a property in his rights."[27] Government exists, then, to protect all these types of property.

In *The Federalist* No. 10 Madison stated that a large number of small groups would keep down the danger of factions, that is, vested interests that look out only for themselves. But his experience in Congress was teaching him that a large number of neutral groups is no necessary safeguard to democracy. The reason is that neutrals may be indifferent, or uninformed, or make errors of judgment, or logroll to support a bill they do not care for in order to gain support for a bill they want.

Abandoning his earlier position, Madison said that the only protection for liberty, federalism, republicanism, and legislative justice would come from an informed public opinion that cherished these values. There was no healthy equilibrium to result from the clash of freely competing political forces. Since political education and organization were needed to safeguard these goals, a political party is the most convenient organ for getting these jobs done. Madison thus played a key role in the origin of political parties in the United States.

Washington's decision to remain neutral in the war between France and England had shifting support. The beheading of Louis XVI in January 1793 made Washington's policy of not supporting France look very attractive. But then Britain stepped up its policy of interfering with American shipping, and some people clamored for war. Madison wanted to respond by an embargo against British goods.

When Jefferson called for him to respond to Hamilton's defense of neutrality, Madison replied reluctantly. He wanted no battle with Hamilton. He called these five essays the "most grating" task he had ever performed. At every step, he said, he felt "the want of counsel on some points of delicacy as well as of information to sundry matters of fact."[28] His general position was that the making of war and peace should rest in the hands of the legislature rather than the executive.

Washington was more than Madison could handle. In a letter to Jefferson he wrote that "the influence of the Executive on events, the use made of them, and the public confidence in the President are an overmatch for all the effort Republicanism can make. The party of that sentiment in the Senate is completely wrecked, and in the House in a much worse condition than at an earlier period."[29] Later he complained that the popularity of Washington's "great and venerable name" was often used to get support for "unpalatable measures."

In the summer of 1793 Madison and his brother Ambrose bought 7000 acres of land in Kentucky to supplement earlier family purchases there. Discovery of an error in the survey and deed reduced the value of the land, which finally sold for $3,000. In 1796 Madison sold his 900 acres in the Mohawk Valley for $5,250.

He did not like the use of violence, even when he was sympathetic with its users. He felt that "peasant revolts" like the Whiskey Rebellion played into the hands of the opposition by making it popular to use force to put down the uprising. In his personal life, he was preparing to show tenderness to a widow who had caught his eye.

Dolley Payne, a Quaker girl, married lawyer John Todd in 1790. They had three children, sons Payne and Temple, and a daughter Anna. On October 24, 1793, Dolley lost both her husband and Temple to yellow fever. She had a good income from her husband's estate. Now, as a most eligible widow, she was in great demand. Financially well off, vivacious, well educated, full bosomed, she had many suitors in the spring of 1794.

She wrote a note to her best friend, Eliza Collins: "Aaron Burr says that the great little Madison has asked to be brought to see me this evening."[30] She abandoned her Quaker grey for a gown the color of crushed mulberries.

Soon Madison asked Dolley to marry him. Advice from the Quakers was negative—mourn your dead husband and raise young Payne and Anna. But Martha Washington, her sister Lucy's aunt by marriage, told her not to worry about the age differential but accept the proposal: "He'll make a husband all the better for those 17 extra years. Between him and the General there's great esteem and friendship."[31]

Their wedding took place on September 15, 1794, at Harewood, the estate of George Steptoe Washington, the president's nephew and ward. As a wedding gift Madison gave Dolley a necklace and earrings of carved gems showing scenes from Roman history.

She was precisely what he needed. She was all heart, he was all mind. She was a natural homemaker—as eldest girl in her family, she was used to keeping house, cooking, and caring for children. She loved to entertain, and so now the bookworm was forced out of his library and into the drawing room. Friends noticed a livelier warmth in him now.

Perhaps her Quaker background gave her the strength to bear tragedy. Just after Christmas in 1794 she learned of the loss of two brothers: Temple had died of an illness, and Isaac was killed in a duel. She stoically fought off grief so as not to dishearten "the great little Madison."

Religion became a bond of unity between them. He liked the Quaker stress on sincere inner probing leading to social action. Since she was too convivial to be a "straight" Quaker, they met halfway: each took what he or she thought was the best of the faith, and lo, it was one and the same! Scarcely has any American president been so fortunate in the choice of a mate.

His domestic happiness strengthened him for countless political hard knocks. Federalists called him a turncoat for opposing in Hamilton's program many ideas he had formerly favored. Congressman Theodore

Sedgwick said that he was "an apostate from all his former principles." Vice President John Adams said that he was "a studious scholar, but some of the most stupid motions stand on record to his infamy."[32]

Madison had little use for Adams, and castigated him with uncharacteristic choler. He found Adams to be the opposite of Washington: Washington, a hero in the field, was properly cautious in making political decisions. Adams, with no military experience, was "a perfect Quixote as a statesman,"[33] jumping in with solutions before he had even defined the problems.

The Alien and Sedition Acts of 1798 were the result of a war-fever hysteria, designed to cut down on the activity of alien Frenchmen who were assisting the Republican opposition to the administration of President Adams, as well as to quiet Republican newspaper opposition.

Madison and Jefferson sprang into action. In the Kentucky Resolutions Jefferson said that a state legislature could declare a federal law null and void. Madison did not go quite as far in the Virginia Resolutions. He said that if a state considers a federal law to be unconstitutional, it has the right to ask other states to join her in setting up a convention to consider whether the law was constitutional or not. Madison said that the Sedition Act eliminated the freedom of the press guaranteed by the First Amendment.

Vice President Jefferson contemplated secession from the Union. In August 1799 he wrote to Madison that it might be necessary "to sever ourselves from that Union we so much value rather than give up the rights of self-government."[34] Madison replied, no disunion.

In September 1799 Jefferson said in a letter to Wilson Cary Nicholas that "Mr. M. does not concur in the reservation proposed above, and from this I recede readily, not only in deference to his judgment but because, as we should never think of separation but for repeated and enormous violations, so these, when they occur, will be cause enough of themselves."[35]

Extremism was forcing both sides into errors, the Federalists passing the Alien and Sedition Acts, and the Republicans responding with the Kentucky and Virginia Resolutions. To help keep the federal government "within the just limits of the Constitution" by "wise and firm state measures," Madison returned to the Virginia legislature in 1799. He sponsored a bill to put all presidential electors on a statewide ticket, eliminating selection by district. Although this had the effect of depriving the minority party of representation, it was preparation for Virginia to cast all of its electoral ballots for Jefferson in 1800.

The Secretary of State

Foreign diplomats were surprised to see how jovial the new secretary of state could be on those rare occasions when he let himself go. Partly because of his plain, black, old-fashioned dress, he tended to impress people as being gloomy.

At first Madison admired Napoleon as one who had curbed the grim excesses under Danton and Murat. But now the French Revolution had replaced a king's tyranny with a general's, and Madison could see little improvement in the change.

Madison instructed American Minister James Monroe to try to buy the Louisiana Territory, and if he failed, to establish closer relations with Great Britain. France, needing money to finance its war against England, sold the vast territory for about four cents an acre. Some Federalists say that the land was not worth that much, and others predicted that the land might be lost because of faulty land titles.

Was the Louisiana Purchase illegal? Napoleon had reacquired the territory from Spain in 1800, promising Spain never to cede Louisiana to a third power. The French constitution forbade the sale of French territory except by a vote of the French legislature, which Napoleon had not bothered to consult. And where in the United States Constitution was Jefferson's authorization to make the purchase?

Madison confessed to John Quincy Adams that the Constitution did not provide for such a purchase, but now shifted to the broad interpretation of the Constitution, saying that circumstances surrounding particular actions must guide the degree to which a strict construction of the Constitution should obtain. Hamilton no doubt thought back to Madison's reasoning on the national bank issue.

This great action by President Jefferson ironically buried once and for all his (and Madison's) theory that a broad construction of the Constitution was necessarily a dangerous approach.

At the huge celebration at the White House over the purchase, Dolley presided as usual as the hostess. Long a widower, Jefferson was pleased to have such a gracious lady in charge of social arrangements. He was not even ruffled when stately dames chided Dolley for not wearing a handkerchief in her ample bosom, or for dipping frequently into a convenient snuff box.

As if orchestrated by Tisiphone, the avenging Fury, the Republicans seemed destined to be frustrated by obstacles similar to the ones the Federalists had encountered. Madison wanted the Floridas so badly for the United States that he overplayed his hand. He told Spain that if she did not cede West Florida to the United States or sell it at a reasonable price, Britain would take it away from her. As a matter of fact, both

France and Britain stood by Spain, and Madison's boldness nearly precipitated the kind of unnecessary war that he had accused Adams of in 1798.

British interference with American vessels and seizure of American seamen increased, despite Madison's learned pamphlet in 1805, called *An Examination of the British Doctrine*, which quoted international law to show there was no basis for the British action. But using the war against Napoleon as their basis, British ships continued to exclude American ships from West Indian ports. Ironically, as the hated Jay's Treaty expired, English depredations mounted. Perhaps Madison and Jefferson would have liked to replay their stands in the year 1795!

This was particularly true in 1806 when William Pinkney and James Monroe negotiated a new treaty with Britain, which after granting some concessions in the West Indies, "made no reference to impressment, failed to provide indemnifications for past spoilations, and was less favorable than Jay's Treaty in its provisions for trade with the British East Indies."[36]

The Republicans by now had suffered an ideological holocaust. Many of their former theories had to be abandoned, and many of the policies they adopted were Federalist ones. For the sake of efficiency they retained many Federalist officeholders. They passed no amendments limiting federal borrowing or spending. In the Yazoo Case, they approved the action of federal commissioners overruling a state legislature.

"The Jeffersonians discovered that many Federalist measures, including even the much-reviled national bank, were more useful than they had supposed."[37] The intensity of their "opposition rhetoric" had obscured the fact that Jefferson and Madison had advocated forceful governmental action for legitimate republican ends.

Since 1776 these two great Americans had been national builders. "If this meant that they accommodated themselves, admittedly or otherwise, to programs and achievements of their political foes, this was to them less harmful than betraying national interests."[38] As Jefferson had phrased it in his First Inaugural: "We are all Republicans; we are all Federalists."

A diplomatic visit by Mellimelli, the Bey of Tunis, in late 1805 provided Moslem pomp and American humor. "According to Eastern custom," the American government bore the expenses of Mellimelli's retinue, including providing concubines which Madison adroitly entered into State Department cashbooks as "appropriations to foreign intercourse."

At President Jefferson's New Year's reception, Mellimelli admitted that American women looked angelic but somehow did not seem to be his type. "Then he spied a large black woman in the kitchen and embraced her enthusiastically, shouting that she reminded him of his best and most expensive wife, 'a load for a camel.'"[39]

On June 22, 1807, the British vessel *Leonard* attacked the United States warship *Chesapeake* a few miles from Hampton Roads, killing three, wounding eighteen, and impressing four crewmen. The *Chesapeake* had refused search orders for deserting English sailors, only one of whom was aboard the *Chesapeake*. Madison told American diplomats in Europe to prepare for war with England.

But war did not come. Jefferson's policy of harsh talk but little armament had failed. The Navy was so ill-prepared that it could not even protect key ports like New Orleans, New York, and Norfolk. The militia was in a deplorable state throughout the Union. The secretary of war found, for example, "seven cannon in all Pennsylvania, and one musket for each five men."[40]

Jefferson and Madison, who had pushed for war against England in 1795, were finding that there was much difference between criticizing the administration and being it.

Madison had long recommended an economic boycott as a better alternative to war. When Jefferson announced the embargo on all American trade with Europe in December 1807, he was closely following Madison's draft.

The Embargo Act hurt American commerce more than it hurt England and France, at whom it was aimed. It did not even achieve another one of its purposes: force those two nations to stop seizing American ships. Little was now done, since Jefferson's second term was running out, and Madison, seeking the presidency, did not want to further alienate New England by harsh talk of war.

The President

As secretary of state, Madison had taken no part in the elections of 1802, 1804, and 1806. Here his conduct could have been a lesson to Hamilton. Even as a presidential candidate, Madison scarcely breathed a word about the election.

Many slanders were thrown at him during the campaign. John Randolph of Roanoke, a Congressional leader, called him an unprincipled visionary who would drag the United States into war. Serene, Madison refused to defend himself, as if he remembered the quotation from the Abbé du Bos he had copied into his notebook while in college: "People who are too tender of their reputations and too deeply piqued by slander are conscious of some inward infirmity."[41]

The model of a Stoic, he never seemed to lose his temper or his self-control. Charles Jared Ingersoll said that "victory never elated, disasters never depressed him." He was "true to friends, patient with adversaries, resolute but forbearing even with public enemies."[42]

Dolley bore many crosses in the 1808 campaign. Hardest to bear was the abuse poured upon her husband, who was certainly a good man. That year death took her mother, her sister Polly, and two nieces. Her uncle's mansion Auburn burned down, and she not only suffered from inflammatory rheumatism but also had a tumor on her knee. Even the news of Madison's nomination, by a caucus of Republican members of Congress, scarcely cheered her.

Entering the presidency, Madison's grief matched Jefferson's feeling of relief. Jefferson said that "never did a prisoner, released from his chains, feel such relief as I shall in shaking off the shackles of power."[43] Madison was at his wit's end over what to do about England. The embargo was nearly killing the New England economy, and there was talk of secession. Would England help New England secede? Leaders in Boston had declared all who enforced the embargo to be "enemies to the Constitution and hostile to the liberties of his people."[44]

Madison's first cabinet, chosen for sectional balance and political necessity, was a mediocre one. Unable to get the Senate to confirm Gallatin as secretary of state, he left him as secretary of the treasury and put indolent Robert Smith in at state. Attorney General Caesar Rodney gave his main attention to his private law practice. Dr. William Eustis became secretary of war, with no qualifications except his congeniality and good connections in New England. Secretary of the navy was Paul Hamilton, chosen because he had been governor of South Carolina. The only capable administrator was Gallatin, and he was unpopular because he was determined to have the national government live within its budget.

Madison had two choices in foreign policy: adhere to French and British shipping restrictions, in which case the economy would suffer; or support American shippers and help the economy flourish, but run the risk of war. He chose the latter alternative.

In June 1809 Madison lifted the embargo on trade with England, and 600 American ships sailed there. Madison had mistakenly believed that the British had cancelled the Orders in Council which had cut off American trade with Europe. George III would not give in to Madison, refusing to accept "anything in which he was so personally insulted," referring to Madison's insistence upon punishment of Admiral Berkeley for the attack upon the *Chesapeake*.

Insolent British Minister Francis Jackson made American citizens angry at the English, and thereby helped the Republicans in the 1810 elections. Jackson made fun of Nathaniel Macon's Bill No. 1, which barred all French and British vessels from American harbors. He lampooned a Congress where, as he said, one member "had been horsewhipped by the President's secretary and another had been severely wounded in a duel."[45] The whip wielder had been Dolley's handsome cousin Isaac Coles. The wounded limb belonged to Dolley's brother-in-law John Jackson, who had spoken against a slur cast on the Republican leadership.

Financial problems limited military options. In 1810 Congress refused to recharter the Bank of the United States, which for twenty years had served the republic well. Gone now were Madison's qualms about its constitutionality. When Congress refused to raise duties, as requested by Gallatin, European nations knew that the United States lacked the finances to conduct a war, and so Madison's foreign policy was cramped.

By now Madison had become a convert to the broad interpretation of the Constitution that had been advocated by Hamilton. Madison supported the Erie Canal project, not because he had found authorization for it in the Constitution but because it clearly served the national interest, and could conceivably even enhance national security.

Macon's Bill No. 2 in May 1810 "legalized trade with all countries but permitted severance of trade with the enemy of whichever belligerent was the first to accept American terms."[46] In this bold effort Madison dangled an agreement with either France or Britain that would give it a trade advantage over its rival. After that, however, Madison planned to dangle the imbalance before the second power, hoping it would come to terms in order to remove its disadvantage.

In 1810 about 80 percent of the inhabitants of West Florida were Americans. Spanish authority was crumbling there as first France and then Britain looked longingly at it. In the fall of 1810 Madison ordered Governor William Claiborne of Orleans Territory to occupy West Florida. When criticized for acting by executive fiat, and thus forgetting the Republican proscription against the "implied powers" of the Constitution, Madison defended his move by saying that in an emergency situation, the government must act quickly.

Like all presidents before him, Madison proposed the establishment of a national university. Its goals would be to enlighten public opinion, expand patriotism, reduce sources of jealousy and prejudice, and extend social harmony among the citizens.

One day in Washington Madison and his secretary Edward Coles saw a group of blacks in chains on their way to a slave market. Coles said it was fortunate that no foreign minister was with them, thus saving Madison "the deep mortification of witnessing such a revolting sight in the presence of the representative of a nation less boastful of its regard for the rights of man but more observant of them."[47] Coles had freed his slaves, and chided Madison for not freeing his. Madison did have, however, the reputation for being humane and kindly toward his slaves.

Based upon a flimsy promise that France would repeal its decrees against American shipping, Madison got Congress in March 1811 to pass a law forbidding entry of British ships and goods into the United States. Napoleon did not live up to the French promise. France continued to seize American cargoes, and Napoleon got what he wanted: war between the United States and England.

Robert Smith had proved worthless as secretary of state. In befriending his brother Senator Samuel Smith of Maryland, he often opposed Madison's policies. Perhaps Robert Smith was making a play for the presidency in 1812. Now Madison had in Smith what Washington had in Jefferson — a recalcitrant secretary of state. When Smith told British chargé John Morier in 1811 that England had a right to complain about American diplomacy, Madison fired him and replaced him with James Monroe.

During this crisis with England, Madison was so patient and conciliatory that the British could not believe that he was contemplating war. Partly it was his theory that it should be Congress that declares war. Also, he was reluctant to surrender his long-held faith in the effectiveness of economic sanctions.

The coming election, however, sealed his decision: he must not appear to be a wishy-washy president. As early as December 1811 Dolley predicted that war was coming.

On June 17, 1812, Madison, with the support of Congress, declared war on England for not repealing the Orders in Council. That very day Parliament repealed those Orders, but since it took at least a month to get the news across the Atlantic, war came. Madison had conferred with Jefferson, and the two agreed that there were grounds for war against both France and England, but chose England for practical reasons.

Despite years of hostility towards England, Madison was sad to be at war against her. He felt that war indicated a failure of diplomacy, and he knew how ill-prepared the nation was to go to war. "Jeffersonian republicanism simply was not a vehicle designed for effective travel down the road to war."[48]

Madison expected Napoleon to show his appreciation for America's entrance into the war against England by ceasing to interfere with American shipping. When that did not happen, Madison and Monroe wrote a series of anti-French editorials for the *National Intelligencer*. Once again Madison sounded like Hamilton in 1793: "Our government will not, under any circumstances, form a political connection with

France," and would in fact shift to befriend England if "England acts with wisdom and France perseveres in her career of injustice and folly."[49]

As unpopular as the war was, Madison was re-elected, beating Federalist candidate DeWitt Clinton 128–89 in the electoral college. Clinton never found a platform: if he would favor the war, he would lose Northern votes, and if he opposed it, he would lose Southern ones.

In his new cabinet Madison replaced ineffectual Dr. Eustis as secretary of war with scarcely better General John Armstrong, recent minister to France. But as secretary of the navy Madison found a good replacement for alcoholic Paul Hamilton in a Philadelphia sea captain, William Jones.

This war almost drove New England into secession. John Lowell, in a pamphlet called *Mr. Madison's War*, urged the militia not to fight in this unjust and unconstitutional war. One clergyman said that "if at the present no symptoms of civil war appear, they certainly will soon." Another stated that "as Mr. Madison has declared war, let Mr. Madison carry it on. The Union has long since virtually dissolved." Former Secretary of State Timothy Pickering wrote that "to my ears there is no magic in the sound of Union. If the great objects of union are utterly abandoned, let the Union be severed."[50]

Madison and Jefferson must have had a few conscience qualms, as they recalled what they had said in the Kentucky and Virginia resolutions.

New England courts ruled that the state governors, rather than federal officials, would declare the emergency warranting the call of the militia. The governors of Connecticut and Massachusetts refused to furnish the militia quotas set by Madison. One trick was to arrest potential recruits for alleged debts, book them and bail them, saying that they were not subject to military service while under "court orders."

When the British burned the White House in 1814, they said that it was in retaliation for American burnings of Canadian towns. In early 1813 a fire of unknown (but probably not American) origin had destroyed Canada's small frame Parliament building in York (later called Toronto). An American general, against orders, had burned the Canadian village of Newark. The British had avenged themselves by conducting burnings in Black Rock, Buffalo, Lewiston, and Manchester. The American officers who ordered the burning of Dover in Canada had been court-martialed.

In July 1814 the British were winning the battle over Lake Champlain, the first step in their plan to isolate New England. To counteract a large warship the British were building on Lake Champlain, Madison overruled Secretary of the Navy Jones and had a 20-gun brig built there. Within a month it was ready for action.

The tides of war were turning. In September came victory in the battle at Baltimore. Then the new brig led to an American victory on Lake Champlain. The Americans captured two sloops, a frigate, and a brig, and sent General George Prevost's army of 14,000 back to Canada — and now New England was safe.

Madison was one of the few American leaders who saw the seriousness of the British invasion of Washington. He asked governors for more militia, and appointed General William Winder as commander of the Baltimore-Washington area. But Winder called up only one-fifth of Maryland's militia, and not many of those had responded.

Secretary of War Armstrong placed militia, rather than regulars, in the defense of Washington. Armstrong still had not established the supply depots that Madison had asked for three months before. They won't strike here, Armstrong said, but will hit Baltimore!

General Robert Ross unloaded 4,000 British soldiers from 50 ships on August 17 at the mouth of the Patuxent River, 35 miles southeast of Washington. Madison overruled Armstrong and transferred militia from Alexandria to Washington, but the militia arrived unarmed. It's too late to open the armory tonight, said Armstrong — come back tomorrow! The 100 soldiers guarding the White House had vanished into thin air.

Dolley wrote frantically to her sister on August 23: "Our kind friend, Mr. Carroll, has come to hasten my departure, and is in a very bad humor with me, because I insist on waiting until the large picture of General Washington is secured. I have ordered the frame to be broken and the canvas taken out — it is done. And now, dear sister, I must leave this house, or the retreating army will make me a prisoner in it, by filling up the road I am directed to take."[51]

As the British advanced into the outskirts of town, Secretary of the Navy Jones ordered the burning of the Navy Yard, and of a sloop and a frigate that might otherwise be captured.

Although American forces were twice as many as the British, they were ill trained and poorly positioned, and the city fell. General Ross and Admiral Sir George Cockburn ordered the Capitol burned. At the White House Cockburn sat down to a meal still on the table and drank a toast "to Jemmy's health." He took as mementos Madison's old hat and a cushion from Dolley's chair. Other structures burned, besides the Capitol and the White House, were private homes which sheltered snipers, a number of public buildings, and the printing office of the *National Intelligencer*, "so the rascals cannot longer abuse my name,"[52] said Cockburn.

Dolley was uncharacteristically bitter over the burning. Seeing passing American troops, she wished they had "10,000 such men to sink our enemy to the bottomless pit."[53] Monroe agreed with Dolley, saying that the British from the highest to the lowest were "all damned rascals!" Madison, meanwhile, was unperturbed. He channeled his anger into ways to bring the war to a successful conclusion.

He replaced Armstrong with Monroe as acting secretary of war. Troubled as he was with England, Madison now admitted that his biggest worry was New England. The Hartford Convention was calling for a new convention to revise the Constitution, and Pickering was openly advocating secession.

As he sat in the Octagon House in Georgetown, the White House a charred ruin, Madison must have wondered how frequently the New England secessionists were quoting the Virginia Resolutions he had written in 1798.

Although their long war against France had ended successfully, and despite their successful raids along the eastern coast of the United States, the British were ready to talk peace with the commissioners appointed by Madison. The long contest with France had drained Britain's economic and military strength. The British knew that another long war faced them if they tried to conquer America, and that if they succeeded the Americans would once again be ungovernable pests. Finally, they needed their troops back in Europe during the postwar settlement period. Napoleon's conqueror, the Duke of Wellington, clinched matters when he declared the United States unconquerable.

The year 1815 finally brought good news to Madison and to America. The Hartford Convention, perhaps hearing of the peace negotiations, adjourned on January 5 without calling for forceful resistance to the federal government. The battle of New Orleans ended with a great American victory on January 8 (although the news did not reach Madison until February 5). In a half-hour battle, the British had lost over 2,000 men, of whom 289 were killed. American casualties were 71, including 13 killed. Superior military strategy by General Andrew Jackson had been the decisive factor in the battle.

On February 15 Madison learned that the Treaty of Ghent, concluding the war against England, had been signed on December 24. Great victory that it was, the battle of New Orleans had been wholly unnecessary.

Reviewing his part in the war, Madison could now identify the administration's errors. Worst of all was the lack of popular support for the war, and the dreadful chasm with New England. There had been poor planning of the Canadian campaign, and slow communications with military commanders. The nation had suffered from a lack of military preparation and especially from a lack of naval power.

But Dolley's "great little Madison" could also point to his achievements. Although he was not a military man, he had almost singlehandedly severed Britain's final chance for political and military hegemony over the United States. He had set high standards for preserving civil liberties during wartime. He did not try to censor critics, as Adams had done in 1798. There was no tarring and feathering of dissidents, as in the Revolutionary War. He had not suspended habeas corpus, as Lincoln felt obliged to do in the Civil War. There was no spying on neighbors (as in World War I) nor any forced evacuation of citizens (as in World War II). Madison had as much provocation as Lincoln, Wilson, and Franklin D. Roosevelt, but, true to his deepest values, he gave the widest possible latitude to those who had views opposed to his own.

This is not to say that he had not suffered an enormous reversal in his political practices. He now asked Congress for a standing army in peacetime — anathema in the old days. Once he had opposed navigation laws — now he saw them as necessary for American trade to prosper. So too with the second Bank of the United States — perhaps Hamilton had some good ideas after all. Now Madison advocated tariffs and tonnage duties that favored American shippers. He wanted to help American manufacturers by making sure that foreign competition did not escape taxation. "He had become a Hamiltonian in a way that he had never been in the 1780's."[54]

In his final message to Congress in 1817, Madison praised the American people and the Constitution, "the offspring of their undisturbed deliberations and of their free choice. They have found it to contain in its combination of federative and elective principles a reconcilement of public strength with individual liberty, of national power for the defense of national rights with a security against wars of injustice."[55] Madison took pride in the fact that the Constitution, in whose making he had played a major role, had "without losing its vital energies" expanded into service over a vast territory with a rapidly growing population.

Final Years

Like Washington and Jefferson, Madison felt greatly relieved upon leaving the presidency. As they returned to Montpelier in the spring of 1817, he and Dolley felt like Adam and Eve being expelled not out of but into an earthly paradise. Also like Washington and Jefferson, he had not saved a cent of his $25,000 annual salary. He was rich in land and slaves but poor in money.

Jefferson considered Madison to be an expert in farming. Madison served as president of the Albemarle Agricultural Society. Like Hamilton, he wanted to free his slaves to permit them to fight in the Revolutionary War, but the Virginia Assembly had disapproved. In the Congress he had been mute on the slavery issue, knowing that his constituents would not support abolition.

He believed that the federal government should use money obtained for the sale of western lands for the resettlement of the black people in Africa. This was the policy of the American Colonization Society, of which he became president in 1833. This Society transported 3,000 black people to Liberia from 1820 to 1834.

Payne Todd, Dolley's son, gave Dolley many anxious moments. He had accompanied Gallatin on a futile trip to Russia, and had fallen in love with a Russian countess. Her parents considered Payne far below her station, and so the affair ended. Disconsolate, Payne took to drinking, gambling, and visiting prostitutes. In two years he spent $10,000 (the equivalent of $200,000 today). Madison mortgaged some of his property to pay Payne's debts, but eventually Payne landed in a debtor's prison.

Madison joined a huge committee established by Jedidiah Morse, the commissioner of Indian affairs, for the purpose of improving policy towards the Indians. Although Madison felt that this problem was second only to the slave question, the committee never got into operation.

As chairman of the Board of Visitors of the University of Virginia, Jefferson asked Madison to prepare a list of books on religion for the university library. Madison's list ranged from the early Church Fathers to Boston Unitarians, after he had finished the "extremely tedious" task of separating "the moral and metaphysical part" of the list from the nonrecommended "doctrinal and controversial part."

Jefferson and Madison differed on how to teach government to university students. In this field, Jefferson said, we are the experts, not the professors, so to avoid "heresies which may be taught," such as the views of states'-rights extremists or of "that school of quondam federalism," the textbooks should be the Declaration of Independence, *The Federalist*, and 1798 and 1800 Virginia Resolutions, and works by John Locke and Algernon Sidney.

Madison objected to Jefferson's list. The Declaration of Independence, he said, did little to combat the "constructive violations" of existing constitutions. *The Federalist* failed to anticipate many misconceptions and was not accepted as authoritative by either political party. The Virginia Resolutions were even more objectionable, said their author, because they were so partisan.

Madison proposed Washington's Farewell Address as an addition to Jefferson's list. The best safeguard against heresy, he said, was an able professor. "Madison's letter persuaded Jefferson that prescribing textbooks to guard against 'poisonous opinions' was inadmissible in a university dedicated to free inquiry."[56]

At Jefferson's death in 1826 Madison took over as rector of the university until 1834. Upon his death, he left the bulk of his large library to the university.

When South Carolina fought the "Tariff of Abominations" as unconstitutional, Madison assured Henry Clay that setting tariffs came under the Constitution's clause authorizing Congress to regulate commerce in the national interest.

As a delegate to the convention to revise the Virginia constitution in 1829, Madison was the only survivor from the original Virginia convention of 1776. He recommended extending the suffrage to all householders and all heads of family who paid taxes. When the convention got hung up over whether slaves should count in apportioning the legislature, he made a plea for unity that sounded like Franklin's in 1787.

Both Daniel Webster and Robert Hayne quoted Madison in their famous debate over nullification in 1830. Webster referred to Madison's support of the Union and of tariffs. Hayne quoted Madison's statement in the Virginia Resolutions that states had the right to object to federal laws.

Asked his present opinion, Madison said that there is a difference between objecting to a law, and dissolving the Union over it. He thus tended to side with Webster.

Madison wrote a lengthy reply to Hayne in the *North American Review* in October 1830. Madison said that the American government, under the Constitution, was partly national and partly federal. The federal government was supreme in its realm of authority. In cases of disputed authority, the Supreme Court was the final arbiter. The Constitution had built-in safeguards against federal usurpation of individual or states' rights. Nullification would lead to the demise of the union, for it left the federal government no means to defend itself against a state's usurpation of its authority.

Madison was now acclaimed by President Andrew Jackson, as well as by John Quincy Adams, Henry Clay, and Daniel Webster, as a nonpartisan elder statesman, the undeclared "honorary chairman" of an informal and unformed national committee to save the Union.

Claiming he "adhered to the doctrines of that ablest, wisest, and purest of American statemen, James Madison," Clay in 1833 wrote a compromise tariff that led to the repeal of South Carolina's nullification ordinance. "What madness in the South," remarked Madison, "to look for greater safety in disunion."[57]

In his writing, Dolley now had to be his fingers, for arthritis had made his own into brittle sticks. In 1831 his doctor told him that he had several potentially fatal ailments: heart trouble, a nervous affliction, and liver disease.

When Jefferson's Kentucky Resolutions were quoted in 1832 in defense of nullification and secession, Madison replied that "allowances ought to be made for a habit in Mr. Jefferson, as in others of great genius, of expressing in strong and round terms impressions of the moment. The idea that a Constitution which has been so fruitful of blessings, and a Union admitted to be the only guardian of the peace, liberty, and happiness of the people, should be broken up without greater than any existing cause, is more painful than words can express."[58]

Madison approved of Jackson's forthright stand against nullification and secession, but he did not like his stand on the national bank. He considered Jacksonian democracy to be dangerously close to mobocracy. By using the spoils system rather than the merit system, and by leaning to the irrational and opportunistic feelings of the moment, it was lowering the quality of American government, he felt.

When Jonathan Elliot published the debates of the state ratification conventions of 1788, Madison assisted him by giving him copies of the debates of North Carolina and Pennsylvania. Madison did not alter historical records in line with hindsight judgment.

He edited a three-volume edition of the *Madison Papers*, for which Dolley received $30,000 in 1840. Dolley sold his remaining papers to the federal government in 1848 for $25,000.

In 1834 Madison sent to the English princess Victoria the autograph she requested from him. That year Harriet Martineau visited him, and was most impressed by his morality and his heart, as she was by the intellectual companionship that Dolley had given him through the years.

They had now come full circle — when they had met, it had been his intellect and her heart. Growing together in their thoughts, they had reinforced each other as do all couples united in love.

Also in 1834 Madison wrote "Advice to My Country," a plea that the Union be cherished and perpetuated. As Ketcham summarizes, Madison "cherished the Union because only the cooperative power it released could bring the social justice necessary to fulfill the moral equality of man. He cherished liberty because only it could open to man the opportunities due his limitless potential."[59]

When John Marshall died in 1835, Madison replaced him as president of the Washington National Monument Association. How correct, said Madison, to raise a noble shaft to that great man! Major Thomas McKenney, writing to Dolley about monuments, said correctly: "Mr. Madison will leave monuments behind him, go when he may, as lasting as time."[60]

Near the end of his life, Madison observed that "our country, if it does justice to itself, will be the workshop of liberty to the civilized world, and do more than any other for the uncivilized."[61]

He used his last strength to read the manuscript of George Tucker's life of Jefferson. He rejected the idea of taking stimulants so as to die on July 4, as had Jefferson, John Adams, and Monroe in their respective years.

As his life ebbed, his spirits rose. He believed that the root of everything lay in a primal world—why then should he fight it? All there was to the trip was a change of consciousness.

On June 28, 1836, his niece Nelly Willis noticed that he was not swallowing his food. "What's the matter, Uncle James?" she asked. Smiling he replied, "Nothing, my dear, but a change of mind,"[62] and his head dropped for the final time.

It was easy to eulogize a man who was not only great but also good. The three congressmen who spoke to his memory three days after his death agreed in calling Madison "the Father of the Constitution." Daniel Webster, calling him "the wisest of our Presidents, except Washington," said that "he had as much to do as any man in framing the Constitution and administering it."[63]

John Quincy Adams worked two months on a two-and-a-half-hour eulogy of Madison that he gave in Boston in September. Among other things, he praised Madison's mind as the equal of Jefferson's, "tempered with a calmer sensibility and a cooler judgment." Henry Clay voiced the feelings of many in calling Madison America's "first political writer," and after Washington, the "greatest statesman."

And so the studious little man had applied his learning to the very real problems of a Titan of a nation, struggling in its infancy to strike out on a bold new political venture. Fortunately for his country, Madison's mind remained flexible, so that he could learn not only from his experience (including his errors) but from his opponents and their errors.

In his mind he turned over forms of government as an auditor balances accounts, looking for assets and liabilities in a judicious weighing and evaluating. As a political theorist, his greatest strength was his refusal to be doctrinaire. As a political leader, the best thing he had to offer was his character. As a framer, there was no one to equal him.

8. George Mason: Champion of Human Rights

If Madison was a political theorist who became a pragmatist, George Mason was a political theorist who remained an idealist. Mason was an enigma: "a gentleman who trusted the voice of the people."[1] These contradictions made him a most reluctant statesman but one who still was, in Jefferson's words, "of the first order of greatness."

No one, not even Madison, knew more about republican government than he, and no one, not even Jefferson or Paine, made such a contribution as he to the constitutional rhetoric of the 1770s. His thoughts are indelibly stamped into some of America's most fundamental political documents. Perhaps it is enough to say that "Madison and Jefferson always deferred to him as their mentor in matters of political theory."[2]

George Mason was the fourth person in America to bear that name in a direct line. He was born in Virginia on December 11, 1725. Aside from some private tutoring, he was self-educated.

His father drowned in the Potomac in 1735. His mother, Ann Thomson Mason, was left with three children of whom the oldest was George. She proved to be a remarkable woman, fully capable of running the family estates with efficiency and profit.

George did not go to college or pass the bar, but he was widely read. His uncle, John Mercer, was a lawyer who had an excellent library at his nearby estate, Marlborough. Here Mason got familiar with the classics as well as with every important legal work, from Edward Coke's commentaries on Thomas Littleton to Mercer's own abridgment of the laws of Virginia. One book especially caught his attention: *Every Man His Own Lawyer*. Through his reading he became an acknowledged authority on colonial charters.

The Planter

At the age of 21 he inherited his father's large estate. He now owned thousands of acres of choice farm land in Maryland and Virginia, as well as additional thousands of uncleared acres in the western country.

In appearance, he had a sturdy frame and brown hair, hazel eyes, and bushy eyebrows. He was by nature an introvert, preferring the company of books to people.

Mason was fastidious over details. When his mansion Gunston Hall was built on Dogue's Neck on the Potomac, he insisted that only sand from wells or the river shore be used in the mortar, since clay or loam might contain cockroaches. In the main hallway he had the architect carve a pineapple, the ancient symbol of hospitality. The dining room had Chinese decorative motifs of the sort found in fashionable 18th century manor houses.

Like many plantations, Mason's was nearly self-sufficient. Besides the mansion it had schoolhouse, smokehouse, spinning and weaving house, laundry, blacksmith shop, and quarters for ninety slaves, whose jobs varied from household servant to carpenter to distiller to field hand.

The plantation of nearly 5000 acres included a deer park. Corn and wheat provided food; tobacco provided cash income. From England came fine furniture, damask draperies, printed silks, calf-bound books, silverware, jewelry, tools, and toys.

Across the Potomac in Maryland, Mason found Ann Eilbeck "elegantly shaped" and "her complexion remarkably fair and fresh."[3] He was 24 and she 16 when they were wed on April 4, 1750. They had nine children who survived the rigors of infancy, before she died in March 1773 of "a slow fever."

Before he was 30 Mason was a justice of the peace in Fairfax County. Besides trying a wide variety of cases, the position also involved joining other J.P.'s in monthly "court days." Then they not only tried all sorts of civil and criminal cases but also "approved road building and other public works, levied taxes, called elections, and made the county's laws. Orphans, bastards, and slaves fell under their charge."[4]

Washington's Neighbor

His neighbor, George Washington, often sat with Mason on court day. In addition to the above duties, they also licensed inns and set the prices for room, board, and wine. Mason received £2,000 annually from the court for running the Occoquan ferry. Once the names of both Mason and Washington were presented to the court by the grand jury for having omitted their fine carriages from the property lists for tax returns.[5]

When Washington was at Mount Vernon, he and Mason were together constantly. In spring they surveyed the boundaries of their adjacent lands. In summer they swapped prize produce from their farms, and in fall they hunted together. Often they jointly arbitrated disputes between merchants. On court days in Alexandria Mason often stopped at Mount Vernon on his way to or fro. When vestry meetings took them to Pohick Church, Washington usually stopped off at Gunston Hall.

As vestryman Mason supervised indentured servants, placed apprentices, and provided for the destitute. In 1754 he became a trustee for Alexandria, a town he had a hand in founding.

The Lords of Trade had granted 500,000 acres of Virginia's western territory to the Ohio Company. Lawrence Washington had been chairman of the Ohio Company, Mason was treasurer, and Uncle John Mercer was secretary. The land was a rough triangle, with present Pittsburgh at the apex, the western leg being the Ohio River, and the eastern leg the headwaters of the Potomac and James Rivers. This land was also claimed by Pennsylvania, the French, and the tribes of the Six Nations, who used the territory as their hunting ground.

In his thirties Mason suffered from the gout and erysipelas. The gout was so painful that it crippled him, and it provided him with a convenient excuse to avoid the bumpy five-day carriage ride to Williamsburg.

His illness, plus his natural reserve, made him a taciturn person. When in pain he was crabby and short tempered. Even his humor tended to be sarcastic rather than whimsical.

Although he was a genial host, he was far too open and honest to be a back-slapping candidate for public office. Neighbors "gradually came to realize that if George Mason said something was so it probably was; and if he said it was not a good thing to support then they had better leave it alone."[6]

Mason served in the colonial militia, and in 1759 he and Washington were elected to the House of Burgesses. Practical politics was not Mason's forte. Pompous speeches bored him, and log-rolling filled him with disgust. To make matters worse, "the extensive stupidity of human nature in committee irritated his quick intelligence almost beyond endurance."[7]

After this experience Mason conveniently used ill health as a reason to avoid public office. Upon the death of his wife he said that he needed to be with his children. On the rare occasions when he left Gunston Hall he left them in the care of his nearest neighbors, Martin and Anne Cockburn of Springfield. Even in his will Mason warned his sons to guard against the shams of political life.

As the years passed, Mason confined himself to his plantation and business concerns, with an occasional fling at a leadership role in his community. There was little to indicate that a magnificent political outlook was gestating.

The Patriot

As was true with many other patriots, the Stamp Act brought forth a protest from Mason. He joined Patrick Henry and Richard Henry Lee in helping draft a plan to enable certain landlords and debtors to avoid using stamped paper.

To his embarrassment his cousin George Mercer appeared as the stamp agent for Virginia. The colonists made it hot for Mercer, who returned to England with the news that they would boycott British goods unless the Act were repealed.

Signing himself "A Virginia Planter," Mason sent an open letter to the London *Public-Ledger* in the spring of 1766. Mason said that Americans were tired of being treated as if they were unruly schoolboys. Now that the Stamp Act had been repealed, why not similar action for the Navigation Acts, which force Americans to do business with England, and which provide for trial across the sea by a judge whose income may depend upon a conviction? Compulsion was no way, he said, to develop a favorable trade relationship. Another law like the Stamp Act, he warned, "would produce a general revolt in America." These words, he said, came from no hothead but from a semiretired farmer "who adores the wisdom of the British Constitution."[8]

In April 1769 Washington wrote Mason that since armed revolt against England should be only a last resort, should Virginia draw up a boycott, something like the enclosed one from Maryland? Washington did not know that Mason had drafted Maryland's plan for a boycott. Mason revised the draft and returned it to Washington, who introduced it into the House of Burgesses.

The plan called upon Virginians to refrain from buying a long list of imported taxed articles. Mason also wanted a nonexportation ban on such goods as furs, timber, and tobacco. "We owe to our Mother country the duty of subjects," Mason said, "but will not pay her the submission of slaves."[9]

Governor Norborne Botetourt dissolved the session, so the burgesses moved to the Raleigh Tavern, where they approved the nonimportation resolutions. The boycott was partially carried out. At one of the balls given by Governor Botetourt, over a hundred ladies appeared dressed in homespun. William Nelson, president of the Virginia Council, told a friend in London that virtually all of his clothes had been made in America.

When he noticed people secretly importing British goods, Mason suggested that each county appoint a committee to watch incoming ships and reship contraband to its port of origin. He realized that to be effective, the boycott would have to be colony-wide. The Continental Congress later drew up its Association boycott based partly on Mason's statement.

In creating a sense of continental unity in opposition to the crown, "no one was more important than Mason."[10] Gunston Hall, just off the main road from Philadelphia, offered refuge to many patriots at work on the rising opposition. Edmund Randolph said of Mason that "he was behind none of the sons of Virginia in knowledge of her history and interest. At a glance he saw to the bottom of every proposition which affected her."[11]

In 1773, when the Grand Company of Pennsylvania, whose promoters included Benjamin Franklin, tried to secure the title to the land claimed by the Ohio Company, Mason answered with "Extracts from the Virginia Charters." Mason refuted Franklin's contention that the crown could dispose of lands ceded by the Indians, by showing that this land had been included in Virginia's charter, which preceded the date of the cession by the Indians.

In 1774 Mason petitioned the Virginia Council for grants of western lands for the Ohio Company. "That very day Parliament passed the Quebec Act, extending the boundary of Quebec down to the Ohio River and thus preventing the Ohio Company's western expansion."[12] As Parliament struck not only at their liberties but also at their wallets, the public outcry became more general.

The Fairfax Resolves

In Fairfax County Washington and Mason opened a subscription to aid Boston, whose harbour had been closed because of the Tea Party. Wheat, flour, and money were collected, and imports violating the boycott were impounded, to be sold for the benefit of this fund.

On July 18, 1774, Washington chaired a county committee at which Mason read 24 resolutions, afterward called the Fairfax Resolves. They formed the basis for action not only by the Virginia Assembly but also by the Continental Congress.

In the Fairfax Resolves Mason stated that the most important part of the British constitution was the principle that the people were to be governed only by laws to which they had given their consent, or else they would lose their freedom. At first Parliament passed laws of mutual benefit, Mason said, but recently revenue measures have been instituted.

"Taxation and representation are in their nature inseparable; the right of withholding or granting of their own money is the only effective security of a free people against the encroachments of despotism and tyranny."[13]

The British government, Mason continued, seemed determined to dissolve "the original compacts by which our ancestors bound themselves and their posterity,"[14] by doing such things as abolishing trial by jury, abrogating the charter of Massachusetts, giving accused Americans trial in England, and raising revenue without the colonies' consent.

Mason called for a boycott on imports from England, especially on slaves: "We take this opportunity of declaring our most earnest wishes to see an entire stop forever put to such a wicked, cruel, and unnatural trade."[15] Mason asked for a colony-wide boycott of imports from and exports to England until the port of Boston would be opened.

The Resolves also called for a general Congress: "A Congress should be appointed, to consist of deputies from all of the colonies, to concert a general and uniform plan for the defense and preservation of our common rights, and continuing the connection and dependence upon Great Britain under a just, lenient, permanent, and constitutional form of government."[16]

Mason was now warming up to his purpose. In January 1775 he proposed to Fairfax County that it organize a militia, "to relieve our mother country from any expense in our protection, and render it unnecessary to keep any standing army (ever dangerous to liberty)."[17]

Washington presided that June when Mason gave his famous address to the militia, speaking in favor of annual rotation of officers. "All men are by nature born equally free and independent," he said. In entering into society, they give up no more of their rights than are necessary. Government exists for the good and the safety of the people. Whenever its power extends further than those goals, it is not government but oppression. The most effective means of preventing this oppression is by frequent votes of the people. "Let us never lose sight of this fundamental maxim," Mason warned, "that all power is derived from the people."[18]

Ironically, although a motion in favor of rotation in office carried, it was immediately amended to exclude "the gentleman who by the unanimous voice of the company now commands it," and Mason called Washington's exclusion "a very proper one, justly due to his public merit and experience."[19]

When Washington was elected as a delegate to the Second Continental Congress, Mason reluctantly replaced him in the Virginia Convention, the extralegal body governing the colony from Richmond. Governor Dunmore had removed the gunpowder from the magazine at Williamsburg, and fled.

The Convention was badly split between patriots and loyalists. Mason rejected an offer from the Convention to be a delegate to the Continental Congress. Since war was expected, Mason helped plan the defenses, serving on the Virginia Committee of Safety and the Fairfax Committee of Correspondence.

Action now quickened. Boston was placed under martial law. Patrick Henry was talking rebellion. Now Mason was glad to return to the Virginia Convention, and was barely voted in. There was a growing spirit of unity not only in the Convention but throughout the colonies. On May 15, 1776, the Virginia Convention informed their delegates in the Continental Congress to support a declaration of freedom from England.

The Virginia Declaration of Rights

The Virginia Convention, engaged in writing a new state constitution, appointed a committee to draw up a bill of rights to be used as a preamble to that constitution. Although Mason was not chairman of the committee, most of the wording of the Virginia Declaration of Rights was his. R. Carter Pittman called Mason's draft "the most influential constitutional document in American history."[20]

One factor that made this work so impressive was that it rested upon a long tradition of English statements of freedom. Forerunners included the Magna Carta, the Petition of Rights of 1628, the Habeas Corpus Act of 1679, the Bill of Rights of 1689, and the Act of Settlement of 1701.

Experience in colonial government had produced such kindred works as the Laws and Liberties of Massachusetts in 1648 and Pennsylvania's Frame of Government in 1682. By Mason's day it was common to expect basic statements on government to include such things as annual elections, three branches of government, a ban on standing armies, and due process in court procedure.

Mason followed a standard school of political theory that stemmed from John Locke and Algernon Sidney. The first part of his treatise closely follows Locke's second "Treatise of Civil Government." Mason "had become convinced that there was a mystical kind of *natural* law at work in this world that, if made a matter of practice, would surely put an end to the bondage of ignorance."[21]

More immediately, sections of Mason's treatise can be traced to his previous utterances, especially to the Fairfax Resolves and to his address to the Fairfax militia summarized above. Despite all of the forerunners, Mason deserves credit for the particular unity he gave the work, as well as to many of the inspiring phrases. The summary of the Virginia

Declaration of Rights given below is an abridgment in the words of the original[22]:

1. All men are by nature free and independent, and have certain inherent rights, namely, the enjoyment of life and liberty, and pursuing happiness and safety.
2. All power is vested in the people; magistrates are their trustees and servants, at all times amenable to them.
3. Government is instituted for the common benefit of the people. That government is best which is capable of producing the greatest degree of happiness and safety, and is most effectually secured against the danger of maladministration. Whenever any government shall be found contrary to these purposes, a majority of the community hath an unalienable right to alter or abolish it.
4. The offices of the magistrate, legislator, and judge ought not to be hereditary.
5. The legislative and executive powers of the state should be separate and distinct from the judiciary. Members of the first two should, at fixed periods, be reduced to a private station, and the vacancies be supplied by frequent and regular elections.
6. All men have the right of suffrage, and cannot be taxed without their own consent, nor bound by any law which they have not assented for public good.
7. All power of suspending laws without consent of the representatives of the people is injurious to their rights and ought not to be exercised.
8. In all capital or criminal prosecutions a man hath a right to demand the nature of his accusation, to be confronted with the accusers and witnesses, to call for evidence in his favor, and to a speedy trial by an impartial jury of his vicinage, without whose unanimous consent he cannot be found guilty, nor can he be compelled to give evidence against himself.
9. Excessive bail ought not to be required, nor excessive fines imposed, nor cruel and unusual punishments inflicted.
10. General warrants to search or to seize any person not named are grievous and oppressive, and ought not to be granted.
11. In controversies respecting property, and in suits between man and man, the ancient trial by jury is preferable.
12. Freedom of the press is one of the great bulwarks of liberty, and can never be restrained but by despotic governments.
13. A well regulated militia is the proper defense of a free state. Standing armies, in time of peace, should be avoided, as dangerous to liberty. In all cases, the military should be governed by the civic power.

14. People have a right to uniform government.
15. No free government, or the blessings of liberty, can be preserved but by a firm adherence to justice, moderation, termperance, frugality, and virtue.
16. Religion can be directed only by reason and conviction, not by force, and therefore all men are equally entitled to the free exercise according to the dictates of conscience. It is the mutual duty of all to practice Christian forbearance, love, and charity towards each other.

After this tour de force, says Josephine F. Pacheco, "no constitution-making body could ignore the principles that Mason had proclaimed."[23] Jefferson drew heavily upon it in the Declaration of Independence and in the Virginia Statute for Religious Freedom. Mason was the most important influence upon young Jefferson. They were frequent collaborators and constant correspondents. Among values they shared were the love of rural life, states' rights, religious freedom, and a bill of rights. Samuel Adams said that Mason's treatise was "a feast to our little circle,"[24] drawing up the Declaration of Independence at Philadelphia.

States drawing up new constitutions borrowed heavily from Mason. In 1776 alone four states besides Virginia embodied his ideas in their new constitutions. Delaware copied Virginia's constitution, adding a section forbidding the importation of slaves, an addition Mason would have applauded. Maryland also copied it, forbidding any future legislature from tampering with the bill of rights "on any pretense whatever." In dealing with the rights of man, North Carolina's constitution guaranteed the hunting rights of certain Indian tribes. In Pennsylvania, 14 of the 16 articles in its constitution resembled Mason's statements. By 1783 all 13 colonies had constitutions with material taken from Mason.

Nor was America the only nation influenced by this seminal thinker. Lafayette and other French leaders saw to it that one of the first actions of their revolution was to phrase a Declaration of the Rights of Man, which had many parallels to the Virginia statement. Other nations have included concepts similar to Mason's in their constitutions and other statements of rights. Possibly even the Universal Declaration of Human Rights sponsored by the United Nations can be seen as a latter-day offspring of Mason's mighty pen.

Having approved of the Virginia Declaration of Rights, the Virginia Convention turned its attention to its main task of writing a state constitution. Again Mason had a major role to play. The practical articles of the constitution were somewhat less lofty than the preamble's ideals. The House of Delegates and the Senate consisted of property owners, and voters too were confined to white male property holders. There were annual elections to the House, and four-year terms for senators. The governor and the state council were elected by the two legislative assemblies. All laws originated in the House of Delegates. No ratification convention was called to approve the new constitution.

Although the constitution watered down many of Mason's idealistic phrases as contained in the preamble, here at least was a beginning in the direction of a greater Constitution to come. And "in one sense the history of the United States is the effort of excluded groups to claim the Declaration of Rights for themselves, to expand the significance of the ideals that Mason set forth in 1776."[25]

Having sired pregnant political phrases that shall ring for all time, Mason, the tender father, headed home, filling his traveling trunk with buckles, buttons, ribbons, and other necessaries for his children, as well as a few toys to brighten their days.

The Legislator

Impatient as he was in working with groups, Mason neverthless now felt a call to serve in the Virginia House of Delegates. Some of the legislation on which he worked in 1776 included bills for a new court system, for a revision of state laws, for a boundary settlement with Pennsylvania, and for a plan to grant the governor and the council emergency powers because of the war conditions.

In November the House of Delegates was presented with a petition of nearly 10,000 signatures alleging religious discrimination: why were Anglicans still on the tax rolls? Jefferson resigned from the Continental Congress to help Mason support the petition. Jefferson called the battle "the severest contest in which I have ever been engaged."[26]

Mason finally drew up a compromise, repudiating the old heresy acts of Parliament and freeing dissenters from taxes levied in support of the established Church. But there were still some Anglican prerogatives, for example, only Anglican clergy could perform legal marriages. Complete disestablishment came in 1785 as a result of the efforts of Mason and Madison.

In 1777 Washington impressed Mason with the problems of inflation, telling him that "a rat in the shape of a horse is not to be bought at this time for less than £200."[27] Mason agreed to return to the House of Delegates.

Mason's plan to stabilize the currency was to set aside Virginia's western lands as a sinking fund to retire state debts. His hope was that other states would do likewise.

A group of Virginians, including Jefferson, Mason, George Wythe, and Governor Patrick Henry, developed a plan to assist the war effort by having George Rogers Clark lead a raiding party against British outposts north of the Ohio River. This action would also serve to tighten Virginia's claim to ownership of the entire Northwest Territory.

This expedition was to be easily financed, since Clark and his men were to receive some of the land as their compensation. When Clark captured Kaskaskia, things looked promising. But a rival group in the Virginia legislature had its own claims, and the two groups fought to a standstill.

In early 1780 Mason married Sarah Brent of nearby Dumfries. She was 50 and he was 54. Terms of the marriage were very businesslike: She had a lifetime tenure at Gunston Hall if she survived him and had no children by him (an unlikely prospect at her age!). If she did have children by Mason, she would share fully in the estate.

In the summer of 1781 British raids on the Potomac nearly captured Gunston Hall. Each time Mason heard rumors of the approach of British soldiers he would pack his family and head inland. Where are our allies, the French? he would cry in desperation.

When the French did arrive later that year, at Yorktown, Cornwallis surrendered and the War was virtually at an end. But the economic problems continued. By now the Continental Congress had issued $240,000,000 of paper money, and the individual states a total of $200,000,000 more. Mason said of a debt due him in 1782 that repayment in paper money was scarcely better than repayment in a bundle of last year's newspapers!

Compounding American problems was the fact that peace ended the emergency unity brought about by wartime threats. Mason attacked those who refused to pay debts owed to English merchants, saying that the War had not been fought "to avoid our just debts or to cheat our creditors."[28]

In addition to the nearly worthless paper currency, many states had run up big debts due to the War. Mason demanded fiscal soundness for Virginia, but when the Continental Congress tried to levy taxes in order to balance the national budget, Mason demurred. In his mind this was not inconsistent, for he foresaw one tax leading to another until finally there would be a standing national army, and then liberty would be lost.

Late in 1783 Madison tried to get Mason to support a national tax, saying it was necessary to save the Confederacy from bankruptcy. Mason showed little interest. He simply lacked the national vision of Jefferson and Madison.

In 1785 again the question was raised, Should the state support "teachers of the Christian religion?" Jefferson was now minister to France, but it was his Statute for Religious Freedom, turned down by the legislature in 1779, that was now being reconsidered. Mason, Madison, and other supporters of the statute maneuvered Patrick Henry out of the Assembly and into the governor's chair, where he could no longer block the bill, and so it finally passed. It became the prototype to that part of the First Amendment to the Constitution dealing with religion.

At the Mount Vernon Convention concerning Potomac River rights in 1785, Washington was chairman and Mason was secretary. By now Washington must have been making a determined effort to convince his learned neighbor of the need for interstate collaboration toward solving interstate problems.

The education, however, seemed not to take. When Mason was appointed by the House of Delegates as a Virginia representative to the Annapolis Convention in 1786, he stayed home.

Perhaps he was following Voltaire's advice in *Candide* to "cultivate one's garden." For he did return to the Virginia Assembly in 1786, for the express purpose of opposing the state's issuance of paper money. Herein he was successful, getting the Assembly to adopt his four resolutions that stated that only gold and silver coins were tender in discharge of debts.

Mason's brilliant florescence of political rhetoric in the mid-1770s, rather than his more recent stands against the national government, led to his inclusion into the distinguished group of Virginia delegates to the Constitutional Convention.

The Framer

Because he did not sign the Constitution, Mason is often remembered as if he were a negative influence on the Convention. As a matter of fact, he was one of the most active framers, and many of his contributions were adopted in the final document. His attitude was generally positive, up until the concluding days of the Convention.

At the outset Mason felt that American public opinion was settled on two points: "In an attachment to republican government and in an attachment to more than one branch in the legislature."[29]

Mason was one of the few spokesmen for the poor. In debating how the legislature should be chosen, he said that there was a good selfish reason why the rich should provide for the poor: they or their posterity could one day be poor. "Therefore," said Mason, "every selfish motive, every family attachment, ought to recommend such a system of policy as would provide no less carefully for the rights and happiness of the lowest than of the highest order of citizens."[30]

When Gouverneur Morris tried to insert a provision that the original Atlantic states could never be outvoted by new states, Mason said that the new western states must be treated equally. "They will have the same pride and other passions which we have," he believed, "and either will not unite with, or will speedily revolt from, the Union if they are not in all respects placed on an equal footing with their brethren."[31]

Mason and Madison quarreled over whether it was necessary to have a year's ineligibility to serve at the end of each congressman's term. Mason thought it would be a good way to keep down corruption. Madison disagreed, saying that one reason that Virginia had a poor legislature was that well qualified persons often refused to run. This was, perhaps, a dig at Mason, as was Madison's further comment that the defects of the Virginia constitution were "evident to every person."

On August 8 Mason's sympathy for the poor reappeared, as he explained why all appropriation measures must originate in the House. The Senate, he said, tends to be the few representing the few, and thus the purse strings should never be put into its hands. A quaint figure of speech served his purpose: "An aristocratic body, like the screw in mechanics, working its way by slow degrees and holding fast whatever it gains, should never be suspected of an encroaching tendency."[32]

When the electoral college was discussed, most delegates assumed that, after Washington's day, no candidate would have an electoral majority and thus most presidential elections would be decided by the Senate. This meant, in effect, that the large states would nominate and the small states would elect. Mason said that 19 times out of 20 this would happen: "those who think there is no danger of there not being a majority for the same person in the first instance ought to give up the point to those who think otherwise,"[33] and apparently many did.

Protectors of the rights of large states hastened to change the legislative body to decide such elections from the Senate to the House, where large states would have greater representation, and so it was approved.

In speaking against continuance of the slave trade on August 22, Mason said that this "infernal traffic" had originated in "the avarice of British merchants." Because of the "pernicious effects on manners" of a country by slavery, "the general government should have the power to prevent the increase of slavery."[34]

Philip Mazzei earlier stated that although Mason wanted freedom for slaves, "he convinced us that if they were not educated before being freed, the first use they would make of their liberty would be loafing, and hence they would become thieves out of necessity."[35]

In the Convention, Mason was pushing not for emancipation but for an immediate stop to the slave trade. The postponement of the abolition of the slave trade until the year 1808 was one of the factors leading to his decision not to sign.

When Nathaniel Gorham on September 12 pointed out the difficulty of specifying which cases should have jury trials, Mason agreed, and said that the best way to handle this and other omissions would be by a bill of rights. "He wished the plan had been prefaced with a bill of rights. It would give great quiet to the people, and with the aid of the state declarations, a bill might be prepared in a few hours."[36] But nearing the end of their long Convention, the delegates unanimously rejected the motion.

On the following day the Committee of Style and Revision was ready with its report. Before the report could be discussed, Mason, "after descanting on the extravagance of our manners, the excessive consumption of foreign superfluities, and the necessity of restricting it, moved that a committee be appointed for encouraging, by the advice, influence, and example of the members of the Convention, economy, frugality, and American manufacturers."[37] Perhaps out of courtesy to Mason the committee was appointed, but it never reported back.

On September 14 Mason moved for a clause requiring "that an account of the public expenditures should be annually published." When some delegates protested that this might be impracticable on occasion, it was amended to read "shall be published from time to time."[38]

The following day, just before the vote was to be taken on the final form of the Constitution, Mason, Gerry, and Randolph insisted that they could not sign the document unless there would be a second convention to act upon amendments that might be suggested at the state ratification conventions. Randolph so moved, but his motion was defeated unanimously. The nonsigners were now called upon by the public to state their positions.

The Virginia Ratification Convention

Mason, like all delegates, had seen some of his proposals voted down. He wanted a simpler amending process, and he had hoped to see a president's advisory council established. He would like to have seen a provision against a standing army in peacetime, and a warning that the national government might not redeem depreciated governmental obligations at par. He preferred that it take a two-thirds vote by Congress (rather than a simple majority) to approve navigation acts.

Before leaving Philadelphia Mason met with a group of local politicians who agreed with him that the Constitutional Convention had added to, rather than solved, America's problems. He showed them his list of objections: (1) there was no bill of rights, (2) there was poor control over the executive, who might easily become a tool of the Senate or of his cabinet, (3) the federal judiciary would destroy the state constitutions, (4) the North would have commercial monopolies, and (5) under this Constitution, government would soon degenerate into either a corrupt aristocracy or a tyrannical monarchy. These objections were put into pamphlet form and distributed by the antifederalists.

Leaving town, Mason and James McHenry of Maryland, who had signed the Constitution, rode away in a carriage, debating their positions. Near Baltimore the argument ended when the driver overturned the carriage, slightly injuring both men.

No doubt one objection loomed over all the rest. The author of the Virginia Declaration of Rights could not see why a similar statement should not have been a part of the Constitution. To him it was not a matter of personal pride but of political principle.

He knew that there had been good monarchies (such as those of Solomon, Hadrian, and Henry of Navarre), just as there had been bad democracies, that is, those manipulated by demagogues to become mobs, or ignorant enough to elect legislators sunk in bribery and corruption. There was, therefore, no ultimate safeguard based upon the form of the government.

How, then, could government based upon the consent of the people be made to be also wise and good government that would protect the natural rights of the people? To Mason the answer was obvious: the governmental structure must give the power to the people, but prevent the misuse of that power through a bill of rights that no kind of power could transcend.

Madison, by the way, saw this necessary protection in the check-and-balance system of the new government, and Jefferson, also zealous to protect individual rights, combined the viewpoints of Mason and Madison to ask for both types of safeguards.

Mason had learned that a strong central government was needed in order to protect the nation externally and umpire disputes internally. But when Congress got the power to overrule state laws, that meant that Virginians, for example, no longer had the protection of a bill of rights. Unless such a statement existed in the federal document, Virginians were surrendering their guaranteed rights for a few commercial advantages and assurances. To Mason, the trade was a poor one.

In the fall of 1787 Mason and Patrick Henry got the Virginia Assembly to pass a bill setting up a ratification convention, but with an explicit recommendation for a second federal convention to consider amendments proposed by the states. They delayed the date of the Virginia convention until June 1788, not wanting smaller states to be influenced by Virginia's action, in the event that Virginia ratified the Constitution.

Campaigning for a seat in the Virginia convention, Mason's opponent said that it was well known that Mason's mind was failing. Mason replied, "Sir, when yours fails, nobody will ever discover it."[39]

At the Virginia convention Patrick Henry led the opposition to the Constitution, and Madison led its defense. In his speech at the convention, Mason pulled out all the stops.

Since the Constitution gave the national government the power to levy direct taxes, Mason said, this would totally destroy state government. The proper method of national fund raising, he said, was for the states to be asked to contribute to the federal coffers, and only if they refused should Congress tax the people directly.

The ten-square-mile federal district, he predicted, would become a sanctuary for every kind of criminal, since it would lack local law enforcement agencies. Slave importation must cease now, he demanded. Much as I value union, he said, "I would not admit the Southern states (South Carolina and Georgia) into the union unless they agree to the discontinuance of this disgraceful trade."[40]

Mason warned that the Constitution was so vague in its assurance of liberty that it might drive the people into rebellion against it. Henry Lee replied that such talk incited rebellious feelings in people, so that if rebellion should come, the audience should remember who started such talk.

Crushed when Virginia voted 89–79 to ratify the Constitution, Mason and Patrick Henry considered running another convention of their own, to see in what ways the Constitution might be made more palatable. Unknown to them, New Hampshire on June 21 had become the needed ninth state to ratify, and so Virginia would have found itself outside the Union had it not voted for the Constitution.

Final Years

Mason was pleased when Congressman Madison, in drafting Amendments 1–10 as a Bill of Rights, drew heavily upon the Virginia Declaration of Rights. Mason, like Jefferson, felt that Amendment 10 was the most important one, for it granted to the states or to the people "all powers not delegated to the United States by the Constitution, nor prohibited by it to the states." To them this was the guarantee that would keep the central government from ever getting so powerful as to destroy either state government or individual liberties.

As might be expected, Mason's opposition cost him some friendships. Madison tangled with him more than once in the Constitutional Convention. Washington referred to Mason as "my quondam friend." When

Edmund Randolph swung back to support the Constitution, Mason referred to him as "young Arnold," feeling that Randolph's treason resembled that of Benedict Arnold. But it is interesting to note that when Senator William Grayson died in 1790, Governor Edmund Randolph appointed Mason to the Senate, with no evidence of hard feeling. Mason declined the seat, pleading "a severe fit of gout."

Mason believed that in the new government Hamilton's measures favored northern business at the expense of the rural south. He told Jefferson that Hamilton had "done us more injury than Great Britain and all her fleets and armies."[41] As Madison switched from support of Washington's administration to opposition to it, Mason applauded the change.

On the French Revolution, Mason wrote in May 1790 to his son John: "I heartily wish the French nation success in establishing their new government upon the principles of liberty and the sacred rights of human nature, but I dread the consequences of their affairs remaining so long in an unsettled state."[42]

When President Washington approved the boundaries for the District of Columbia, Mason was one of the 19 owners of the land. His plot consisted of 2,000 acres of land just above Little Falls.

Unlike Franklin, Mason had no use for nepotism. When both his son John and Joseph Fenwick, John's senior partner in a law firm, applied for Mason's recommendations for the position as American consul at Bordeaux, Mason recommended Fenwick because he thought that he was better qualified than John.

On Sunday, September 30, 1792, Mason and Jefferson had a long discussion on political matters, of which Jefferson had left detailed notes. A week later, on October 7, at Gunston Hall, Mason died of a severe fit of colic, and was buried alongside his wife Ann.

Jefferson properly eulogized him as "a man of the first order of wisdom among those who acted on the theatre of the Revolution — of expansive mind, profound judgment, cogent in argument, and earnest for the republican change on democratic principles."[43]

Perhaps because his ending was less distinguished than his beginning, George Mason tends to be underrated by posterity. But his achievements were so solid and his contributions so immense that one need never fear that his name will be forgotten. As Alfred North Whitehead has said, the clash of doctrines that occurred in the Constitutional Convention was not a disaster but an opportunity, since it gave eloquent expression to the opposition between liberty and authority. It is well for us that Mason threw his weight onto the side of liberty, both when the crown was the oppressor and when he detected a like possibility in the new structure of federal government.

Had all the delegates been like Mason, the new central government might have been as weak as the nation under the Articles of Confederation. But had there been no Mason and no Virginia Declaration of Rights, the Declaration of Independence and the Constitution, the two basic political documents of the United States, would have been incomparably weaker.

9. Gouverneur Morris: Witty and Aristocratic Lothario

On May 12, 1780, while attempting to drive a pair of wild horses pulling his phaeton, Gouverneur Morris was thrown from the carriage. His left leg, caught in a wheel, was shattered and had to be amputated. A huge man who posed as a stand-in for Washington in Houdon's statue of the first president, Morris bore his loss of limb with "becoming fortitude." His close friend John Jay alleged that the accident occurred as Morris was making a hasty getaway from a rendezvous with Eliza Plater, wife of Colonel George Plater. Whether true or not, it was generally accepted that "the amputation did not diminish his prowess with the ladies."[1]

Who was this aristocratic lover, whose phrasing lasts to the present in the sonorous articles of the Constitution? How did he come to throw in his lot with the common man, alienating him from his family and friends?

His grandfather Lewis Morris was the first native-born chief justice of the New York Supreme Court, serving from 1715 until 1733. When he denied Governor William Cosby's suit for salary arrears, Cosby fired him. Lewis Morris's attacks on Cosby were printed by John Peter Zenger, resulting in Zenger's famous trial and acquittal on the charge of seditious libel.

Lewis Morris, Jr., his son, was a member of the New York council, an assemblyman, and a judge of the court of vice-admiralty at New York City. His second wife, Sarah Gouverneur, gave birth to the son Gouverneur on January 30, 1752. Lewis, Jr., had six children by his first wife and four by Sarah.

Gouverneur did not like his half-brothers, the youngest of whom was 32 years older than he. He took a paternal interest in his three sisters, particularly after his father died when Gouverneur was only ten years old. His father's will provided that Gouverneur have "the best education to be had in Europe or America," but not in Connecticut, "lest he should imbibe that low craft and cunning so incident to the people of that country, disguised under the sanctified garb of religion."[2] All three of Lewis's sons had withdrawn from Yale in 1746 after a running dispute with the college.

Gouverneur showed the maturity and quickness of intellect often found in the children of older parents. He also showed a spirit of independence and eccentricity, as a part of his family inheritance. Throughout this area, tall tales came to be called "Morrisanias," after the family estate Morrisania, located ten miles north of New York City in what is now the Bronx. The 1920-acre manor was across the Hudson River from Manhattan, slightly south of the current junction of 132nd Street and Cypress Avenue.

The Student

After home tutoring, Gouverneur was sent to a Huguenot preparatory school at New Rochelle, where he learned to speak excellent if somewhat provincial French.

At the age of 12 he entered King's College, easily passing the entrance examinations that included material on Latin and Greek. His first chore was to make a copy of the college statutes.

In 1764 the college had two professors: President Myles Cooper, who taught history, Greek, Latin, literature, and philosophy, and Robert Harpur, professor of mathematics and natural philosophy (science). In 1765 Samuel Clossy was added to teach natural philosophy, and then Harpur taught only mathematics.

Gouverneur's class had nine students, of whom six completed the four-year curriculum. His favorite subjects were Latin, mathematics, and Shakespeare. The school day began and ended with a religious service. The curriculum was classical, modeled after Oxford's. In history Morris studied the social compact theory and the natural law ideas of Hugo Grotius and Samuel von Pufendorf—the very men whom John Locke had studied before writing his famous treatises on government.

In August 1766 Morris was badly scalded when boiling water from an overturned kettle fell on his right arm and side. He had to convalesce at home for over a year until the wound healed. In fact, the flesh never grew back properly, so that he bore scar tissue all of his life.

Because he was a rapid learner he was able to rejoin his class, and he received the B.A. degree in May 1768. He gave a student commencement address on "Wit and Beauty," two qualities that engaged his attention throughout his life.

He now entered the law office of William Smith, a leading Whig and friend of William Livingston. The patroon Robert R. Livingston lived at Clermont on the Hudson. Morris began by making the right social connections, such as a friendship with the Livingstons. Smith was noted for the history of New York that he had written.

As a law student, Morris read Bossuet's *Discourse on Universal History*, which stated that government was a necessary restraint upon mankind's evil passions, and that the best form of government was an absolute monarchy tempered by justice and reason. Morris also read many works on common law, especially Sir William Blackstone's *Commentaries*, which had become a classic during the past few years.

On constitutions, Morris read Sir Thomas Smith's *De Republica Anglorum* (1565), which saw courts as a defense against the supreme authority of the king, with Parliament as the highest tribunal. He read such writers on civil and natural law as Matthew Bacon's *Abridgement* and Thomas Wood's *Institutes*. Pufendorf was studied for his reconciliation of Christianity with rationalism. Although Pufendorf stressed private property, he also emphasized the moral responsibility of property owners, and the great need for peace among nations.

In May 1771 Morris received the M.A. degree from King's College. Although the degree was largely honorary, it recognized his law studies. At the commencement he spoke on "Love" as a universal force, explaining its religious, familial, and patriotic aspects. On the latter theme he said that "a Briton's love of country is firmly fixed on the solid base of freedom. What then must be his love who lives under a Constitution dispensing the joys of freedom!"[3]

Morris was tall, well built, with light brown hair, blue eyes, and an appealing ring to his voice. He was an outdoorsman: farmer, fisherman, horse breeder, hiker. He did not smoke but had a fine taste for wine.

He had a good mind, a ready wit, and the drive of a young aristocrat with a modest inheritance to outdo his half-brothers. With innate high spirits, he had a charming levity and an indifference to public opinion. He fell in love with Catherine Livingston but when she showed no interest in him, he was not bothered in the least. Why should he worry, he asked, for he was "constitutionally one of the happiest among men."[4]

It was not long before he had the reputation of a gallant. Normally his affairs were with women of rank, beauty, and high intellect. He may at times have been wrongheaded or immoral, but he was virtually never filled with hatred, malice, or envy.

The Legislator

In 1772 came his first publication, a pamphlet attacking the use of paper money. The proper way to pay off recent war debts, he averred, was through a program of taxation.

At the age of 23 he entered the New York legislature. "His ability to think in national terms, to persuade by debate, and to write were as a whole exceeded by none of the patriot leaders."[5] Like Hamilton, he came to political maturity overnight. Both seemed to have at their fingertips almost everything written on government, particularly the financial end of it.

His pamphlet on paper currency was adopted as policy by the Continental Congress, and from then on he was considered to be an expert on governmental finances. A gifted writer, he was chosen as chairman of the Committee on Correspondence by the New York legislature in 1775.

As the revolutionary fervor mounted, there was confusion over how to treat loyalists. Some of Morris's friends, like William Smith and Peter Van Schaack, were allowed to pass peaceably into British territory but some prominent loyalist leaders were publicly hanged. Morris protested the use of violence, and came to the rescue of loyalist editor James Rivington, whose press in New York City had been destroyed by the Sons of Liberty. Like John Adams, who defended the British officers and soldiers accused in the Boston Massacre, Morris was a fair-minded patriot. He disliked American border raids into Canada, saying that they caused unnecessary ill will.

"I plead the cause of humanity to a gentleman,"[6] he explained. Later this absence of decent humanity horrified him as he witnessed the French Revolution. He believed in the brotherhood of man under the Fatherhood of God.

Objecting to the harassment of Quakers in Pennsylvania, Morris wrote to Robert R. Livingston that he knew their religious views were a matter of indifference to people like themselves, who "consider mankind from their relation to us by the same common Parent and not from the similitude of their ecclesiastical tenets."[7] Morris may have been an aristocrat by birth and breeding, but his instinctive feeling for man's spiritual equality made him a ready convert to a movement to assert human dignity and freedom.

After a term out of Congress, Morris re-entered in May 1776. Now in tune with the national sentiment, he saw the British government as tyrannical, and he was ready for separation. Instead of openly declaring independence, however, Morris favored secret treaties with European governments in which they would recognize America's independence. He moved for the New York legislature to set up a convention to adopt a new state constitution. When he noticed that New Yorkers were enlisting in New England militias because of higher salaries there, he got the Continental Congress to grant New York soldiers equal pay.

Civil wars split families. Remaining loyal to England were his mother, two brothers-in-law, and his half-brother Staats Long Morris, who became a major-general in the British army. Joining Morris in the patriot cause were his brother-in-law Samuel Ogden, and his half-brother Lewis Morris, last Lord of the Manor at Morrisania and a signer of the Declaration of Independence.

Morris persuaded the New York legislature to retreat to White Plains in July 1776, as the British army advanced. John Jay protested the move, saying it would retard the prosecution of Governor William Tryon and other Tories accused of helping the British capture New York City. Washington's further retreat, however, solved the problem, for now the legislature had to move farther inland to escape the British.

The New York legislature appointed a committee of Morris, Jay, and Robert R. Livingston to write a state constitution. Although Jay was the principal author of the new document, Morris had considerable input. He favored a strong executive, one with a qualified veto power over the legislature, and with exclusive appointive powers. Morris lost on both scores—the veto was vested in a council of revision, and appointments were to be made by a special council. New Yorkers had had too many problems with autocratic royal governors to accept a strong executive of their own design.

Reflecting his stand on private property, property qualifications for voters were raised from a simple freehold to a freehold of at least £20. Morris believed that since property was the foundation of society, government should protect it and should enforce all contracts.

Slaves were human beings, not property, in his opinion. Morris tried to get a motion passed freeing all slaves as soon as the War was over. "A regard to the rights of human nature and the principles of our holy religion," he said, "call upon us to dispense the blessings of freedom to all mankind."[8] Livingston got the motion beat by a vote of 31–5.

Morris fought Jay's religious prejudice. A descendant of Huguenots, Jay said he wanted "to erect a wall of brass around the country for the exclusion of Catholics." Since he believed in religious liberty, Morris got Jay's motion amended to protect the liberty of conscience generally. Jay then pushed through an amendment requiring new citizens to "abjure allegiance to every foreign king and potentate, in all matters ecclesiastical as well as civil."[9] Although Morris could not defeat the amendment, it was superseded a decade later when the federal Constitution reserved naturalization to the central government.

Morris was confident that, despite current setbacks, America's eventual victory over Britain was assured. He pointed out that to England, "an American war is tedious, expensive, uncertain, and ruinous. Three thousand miles of boisterous ocean are to be passed over, and the vengeful tempests which whirl along our coasts are daily encountered. At least three months' expense must be incurred before one gun can be fired against an American village. A hardy, brave people, or else a destructive climate, must be subdued, while the troops, exhausted by fatigue, find at every step that desertion and happiness are synonymous terms."[10]

The fact that two of his sisters married Tories embarrassed Morris, especially when a letter from a brother-in-law described him as loyal to the king. Morris quickly quelled suspicion by pointing out that the letter in question had been written in 1775, while he was in the process of a change of allegiance.

In a letter to Hamilton in May 1777 Morris said that the new state constitution was acceptable, although "there are faults in it not to be wondered at." One of the faults, he felt, was that "a simple legislature soon possesses itself of too much power for the safety of its subjects."[11]

Now in the Continental Congress, Morris showed military insight as a member of the army committee. A visit to Valley Forge convinced him that Lafayette was here not only to help America but to advance the cause of France. Morris could see that Washington's failures in the field were due basically to a lack of supplies rather than a want of military competence.

Morris and Washington became good friends. Washington, Morris said, was the one great American he had known. The support by Morris carried Washington through a great crisis of public support when his army was bogged down. Washington considered Morris to be a forceful and gifted man with purely human faults. Washington permitted persons with dissimilar moral values to be his colleagues in the common cause for national liberty.

Sent by Congress to find out why the Battle of Ticonderoga had been lost, Morris reported correctly that Schuyler's troops had been outnumbered. Morris predicted that the best battle strategy would be to retreat through the woods, tiring out the pursuing British troops.

The New York legislature asked Morris to get more military assistance for the state. At first, Washington said that he could spare only the two brigades previously committed. At Philadelphia, however, the Congress replaced Schuyler with Horatio Gates, and told Washington to give New York more help. Washington supplied a crack regiment, and Gates went on to defeat Burgoyne in the crucial battle of Saratoga.

Morris became the mouthpiece of Congress in the war of words against Great Britain. Stinging from the defeat at Saratoga, and wanting to use Burgoyne's "frozen" army against the French in Europe, the British sent negotiators to Philadelphia, promising forgiveness if the Americans laid down their arms. Morris replied, on behalf of Congress, sometimes in formal papers and sometimes in newspaper articles. The French minister, Conrad Gérard, praised Morris for his adamant but graceful stand.

In his longest response, *Observations on the American Revolution*, Morris catalogued British oppression and then concluded that "the portals of the temple we have raised to freedom shall be thrown wide as an asylum to mankind. America shall receive and comfort the oppressed and the poor of every nation and every clime."[12]

When the British army withdrew from Philadelphia in 1778, the British commander, Lord Carlisle, published an appeal to Americans for conciliation. "Oh, my Lord," commented Morris, "you have fleets and armies and proclamations, and you now threaten us with newspapers!"[13]

The cabal in Congress to replace Washington with Gates failed by a single vote. Once again character was revealed. Morris stood staunchly by Washington's side, and as the smoke cleared, Washington brushed the whole matter aside with magnanimity.

Washington, aged 46, knew how to be tactful in rejecting rash advice from his 26-year-old friend in the Congress. In May 1778 Morris advised Washington to requisition the goods needed by his army in Philadelphia, and levy a charge of £100,000 on the city. A quick reply from the commander said: "Your idea of levying contributions on Philadelphia widely differs from mine. It would be looked upon as an arbitrary stretch of military power. It would inflame the country and lay the foundation for much evil."[14]

Congress kept the talented pen of Morris busy. In summer 1778 Morris wrote an address "On the Present Situation" to be read in every pulpit. It closed with "If you exert the means of defense which God and nature have given you, the time will soon arrive when every man shall sit under his own vine."[15] In July he wrote up a report, adopted by Congress, for a treasury board to be set up, consisting of an auditor, a comptroller, and a treasurer.

In August his committee report called for a poll tax to pay internal debts, and an import tariff to eliminate foreign debts. He also recommended that western lands be ceded to the federal government and used as security for European loans. Unready to move towards a strong central government, Congress turned down these proposals.

As a member of the Commissary and Quartermaster Committee, Morris helped push through a new plan in which suppliers had to deliver goods directly to the troops, thereby saving much government expense. Together with Congressmen Nathaniel Scudder and William Whipple, Morris sent orders to the 13 governors, asking for an inventory of food, the raising of state taxes, the depression of whiskey distilling, and demanding harsh penalties against bribery and corruption.

Morris was also asked by Congress to draw up a manifesto on British cruelty toward prisoners. He was also the chairman of the committee which drew up instructions to Benjamin Franklin as the first American minister to France.

Had Governor George Clinton of New York heeded the advice of Morris, he would have better served his state. Morris recommended not pushing the matter of Vermont statehood, but letting time solve the issue. He advised the governor to levy taxes rather than print paper money, and he thought that loyalty tests should be made more reasonable, so that it would take more than the testimony of one witness to confiscate the property of alleged loyalists.

Clinton Rossiter accurately summarized the position of Morris now: "If his morals were too relaxed, his wit too sportive, his temper too sophisticated, and his manner too cynical for some solemn people, he was nevertheless widely regarded as one of the brightest young men in a country full of bright young men."[16]

In February 1779 Morris was appointed to chair a Congressional committee seeking to get Spain to enter the French-American alliance against England. Two goals were to reinforce American fishing rights off Newfoundland and to secure free navigation on the lower Mississippi. Spain was, however, unready to act at this time.

Thomas Paine, secretary to the Committee on Foreign Affairs, charged Silas Deane with pocketing French money intended as a gift to the United States. Morris, feeling that Paine was acting beyond his authority and at the same time violating the secrecy of his office, got Paine fired, and the two were never again friends.

Paine now led an attack upon the character of Morris. He got hold of an old letter in which Morris had said that "we of New York hold the keys of the 13 states in our hands and in our power to give them up to the King of England."[17] Morris explained that the out-of-context statement was made long before he had served either in the state legislature or in Congress.

Governor Joseph Reed of Pennsylvania continued the attack upon Morris, alleging that as a member of Congress he had not only infringed upon Pennsylvania's prerogative but had acted as a lawyer against the best interests of Pennsylvania. Morris replied that he did what Reed himself, or any good lawyer, would do, namely represent the best interests of his clients. Morris showed that perhaps the most damaging letter had been written at Reed's own request. Ultimately Reed apologized to Morris, but the charges left a taint upon Morris's name.

The Patriot

Probably the leading factor in Morris's defeat for Congress in 1779 was the fact that he had been doing business with William Constable, who had been doing business with the British. Morris now remained in Philadelphia in order to engage in private law practice and to write articles favoring the patriot cause.

In February 1780 he wrote a series of letters to the *Pennsylvania Packet*, in which he demonstrated the futility of trying to enact laws to declare depreciated currency to be legal tender. "Money is of too subtle and spiritual a nature to be caught by the rude hand of the law,"[18] he said. Taxation, in his opinion, would not only raise the necessary revenues but would also fight the constantly rising inflation.

Immobilized for six months by the loss of his leg, he had to turn down the job offered him as Franklin's secretary in Paris.

The loss of the leg did not mean the loss of amour. In November 1780 Robert R. Livingston wrote him: "I congratulate the Beau Monde on your restoration to them. I am told you are Master of the Ceremonies to La Belle Madame Bingham." Mrs. Bingham was the wife of their friend William Bingham. Morris replied, "My restoration to the Beau Monde is like a resurrection from the grave."[19]

After the defection of Benedict Arnold in the fall of 1780 there were rumors of many other setbacks. One rumor that Morris heard was that 12,000 Russian troops had landed in New York City to augment the British forces. That was not true, but in fact Catherine the Great refused to recognize the new nation that year, fearing that the American revolutionary ardor might spread to her country.

In March 1781, when Robert Morris became superintendent of finance, he appointed Gouverneur Morris as his assistant. The two men were not related. Robert had been born on the same date as Gouverneur, but 18 years earlier. Gouverneur was at this time his protégé, learning of the intricacies of finance from him. One of the men they worked with was Haym Salomon, a commercial paper broker who had come from Poland in 1772 and who was very helpful to the patriot cause.

In later years Gouverneur came to the rescue of Robert Morris when his financial deals started to backfire. Gouverneur always disapproved of Robert's tendency to mingle his private interests in with those of the infant nation.

Gouverneur tried to get a permit to go through British lines to visit his ill mother at Morrisania, where the British were quartered. The request was denied on the ground that it was improper to give such a permit to a person who had held high offices in the American government.

In June 1783, when Morrisania was liberated, Morris visited the estate for the first time in seven years. Even though his mother had remained loyal to the crown, the estate was a mess. For two years a British regiment had camped there in a settlement of 70 huts. They had used 45 cattle and 94 sheep, and had deforested 470 acres of timberland.

Morris helped his mother present a claim of £8,000 to the British government for the use of her property. Mrs. Morris died in 1786, and General Staats Long Morris eventually received £1,341 for the lost timber. Gouverneur bought the estate from his half-brother, who remained in England after the War.

In February 1783 Morris suggested to northern commander General Henry Knox and southern commander General Nathaniel Greene that the unpaid soldiers should pressure Congress for payment. Knox's reply was that "as the present constitution is so defective, why do not you great men call the people together and tell them so? That is, have a convention of the states to form a better constitution. This appears to us, who have a superficial view only, to be the most efficacious remedy."[20]

When a group of rebellious soldiers picketed Congress later that year, Congress finally promised to pay the soldiers a lump sum amounting to five years' pay. The creation of war debts, these and others, constituted national obligations, and Morris realized that this meant that sometime soon a national government would have to be created strong enough to at least meet its financial obligations.

Foreign visitors evaluated Morris realistically. In 1782 a Frenchman, Prince de Broglie, stated that although Morris had great spirit and nerve and was well educated, he was very sarcastic, and "his superiority, which he has taken no pains to conceal, will prevent his ever occupying an important place." The Dutch visitor Gijsbert van Hogendorp in 1784 was slightly more considerate. After conceding that Morris was pedantic and callous, with a vain air of superiority, he added, "but his brilliant qualities cover all these defects."[21]

In the spring of 1785 Morris addressed the Pennsylvania Assembly concerning their resolution to abolish the Bank of North America. In a long talk full of wit and wisdom, Morris explained how money and credit are used to build a new nation's industry. To attack a bank for making available financial resources that might be misspent, he said, would be like keeping people from using water because a few might drown themselves.

In 1785 Morris and John Jay founded the New York Manumission Society, for the abolition of slavery. It was more than a propaganda group, for it performed many services for black people.

The Framer

Morris was surprised to be selected as a delegate to the Constitutional Convention from Pennsylvania, because he had fewer friends there than in New York. He had doubts that the common man could govern himself well, but he had faith that the new national government would be a good one.

He looked forward to the adventure, saying afterward that "it shows the boldness of the experiment in which we were engaged that we were forced to take all other nations, whether dead or living, as warnings not examples."[22]

New Englanders thought of him as a playboy. William Pierce described Morris as "fickle and inconstant, but no man has more wit." Morris, said Pierce, had read a lot and "knows all the sciences." His mastery of rhetoric charmed all who heard him, said Pierce, for Morris was "one of those geniuses in whom every species of talents combines to render him conspicuous in public debate."[23]

The Convention aroused his deepest feelings. He gave 173 speeches in the Convention to Madison's 161. Like Madison and Hamilton, Morris felt that the whole world was looking to them for light. "The whole human race," said Morris, "will be affected by the proceedings of this Convention."[24]

In the deliberations Morris tended to represent the viewpoint of the commercial and propertied interests. He believed that property, as well as the number of people, should be considered in apportioning the numbers of legislators in both houses. He was made chairman of the first committee to recommend methods of apportionment.

On July 2 Morris recommended that senators be appointed by the executive, and that they serve for life without pay. His goal was to have an aristocratic body that would balance the popularly elected House. His motion drew no support.

Morris unknowingly prepared the way for the Great Compromise when he said on July 12 that "direct taxation ought to be proportional to representation."[25] This statement helped persuade large states to swing over to accept the Compromise.

Fearful lest new western states some day wrest control from the Atlantic states, Morris spoke against granting them equal status in the Union. Most delegates admired Madison's wry response: "Apparently the gentleman determines the human character by the points of the compass."[26] Nevertheless, Morris spoke against slavery so eloquently at the Convention that Abraham Lincoln quoted him 73 years later in his speech at Cooper Union.

In terms of substance, Morris's greatest contribution to the Convention came on the discussion of the executive. He said that the poorest method of selecting the president would be by having the Congress appoint him. Within bounds Congress worked fine, he said, but "when a strong personal interest happens to be opposed to the general interest, the legislature cannot be too much distrusted."[27] Intrigues and factions, in his opinion, vitiated the effectiveness of a legislature unless there was a good way to guard against its special interests.

Originally Morris felt that the president should not be impeachable. Either he will be impeachable or he will be assassinated, Franklin remarked. Morris reluctantly changed his mind.

On granting each house the authority to discipline absent or wayward members, Morris took quite a different stance. Madison had moved for a two-thirds vote, feeling that a bare majority might not be enough to protect members from actions based on personal bias.

Morris disagreed, saying that this power could be safety trusted to a majority. To ask for more could produce abuses by the minority, in which case "a few men from factious motives may keep in a member who ought to be expelled."[28]

On August 31 a Committee on Unfinished Business was elected by ballot. Morris represented Pennsylvania on this committee, on the recommendations for the executive. He seems to have played an important role in making many of the provisions that still govern the presidency.

The term was to be for four years, and the incumbent could be reelected. Each state was to choose, in its own fashion, a number of electors equal to its Congressional delegation. Meeting in their own states, electors would send in sealed votes for two candidates. If there was no majority, the Senate would choose the president from among the five highest candidates. The Convention later changed the choice from the Senate to the House of Representatives, to give more adequate representation to the larger states.

When the draft of the Constitution was ready for its final form, it was given to the Committee on Style, on which Morris excelled. It was his felicitous phrase that started the Constitution: "We, the people of the United States, in order to form a more perfect union...." Morris and the committee had accomplished the near impossible: "Out of what was almost a hodge-podge of resolutions they had made a presentable document."[29]

Shortly before his death, Madison wrote to Jared Sparks that "the finish fairly belongs to the pen of Mr. Morris. A better choice could not have been made, as the performance of the task proved. It is true that the state of the materials was a good preparation, but there was sufficient room for the talents and taste stamped by the author on the face of it."[30]

Morris was also entrusted with the responsibility of writing the letter of transmittal for Washington to sign and send to Congress.

Morris had carefully chiseled his literary style, based on a wide reading background. His diary and letters are full of quotations from Chesterfield, Sterne, Swift, and especially Shakespeare. His mind was amply supplied with a storehouse of cadences and figures of speech appropriate for virtually any occasion.

A rare instance of his religious faith emerged when Hamilton wrote him in June 1788 of the dim prospects for Virginia ratification. "Be of good cheer," Morris counseled. "My religious belief prevails where my understanding falters and I feel faith as I lose confidence. Things will yet go right."[31] His faith did not include churchgoing, however, for in ten years of diary entries he mentions going to church only once.

He wrote 12 volumes of diaries from 1789 to 1816. He apparently designed them as a record of an active man in high place, as a chronicle of his times. Since he was constantly busy with more important matters, entries are terse and objective.

The Diplomat

Gouverneur Morris arrived in France in January 1789, on business for Robert Morris and William Constable. His specific mission was to try to sell large blocks of land in the Genesee River valley and in the St. Lawrence River area. He was well received in Paris, because of his affable nature, his knowledge of French, and his reputation as an American leader.

He had a low opinion, however, of the French people. They have, he said, "no religion but their priests, no law but their superiors, no morals but their interests."[32] Because he felt that they were not ready for self-government, he recommended moderation on the eve of a revolution! Lafayette bluntly accused him of harming the cause of democracy. Morris just as bluntly replied that he was "opposed to democracy from regard to liberty."

When Jefferson returned to America in October 1789, Morris remained as the most conspicuous American leader in Paris. No minister was designated at this time, since the Revolution had opened chasms in French society, and Washington wished to wait to see the outcome before committing the new nation to a step which might backfire.

With deep sympathy for Louis XVI, Morris felt that the king should use French troops, rather than the Swiss Guard, in the palace defense. Jefferson thought it would make no difference, but when the violence came, the Swiss Guard were among the first defense troops to be massacred.

In March 1789 began the long love liaison between Morris and Adelaide de Flahaut, 28-year-old wife of the 63-year-old Count de Flahaut. She spoke English, unlike her husband, who was director of the Gardens of the King, and hence the Flahauts lived in rooms at the Louvre.

Adelaide's child was by another lover, Charles Maurice de Talleyrand-Perigord, bishop of Autun and future prime minister. Although she accepted Morris as her lover, she refused to have a child by him, feeling that she could not commit an infidelity to Talleyrand! Both her lovers were crippled, since Talleyrand had a club foot.

Adelaide and Morris remained lovers for three years, during which time Morris was absent from Paris for about a year. Morris said that they had had intercourse several hundred times, but insisted that they had never slept together all night or even lain naked in each other's arms. At first they protected appearances, but later, as the Revolution made conditions more hectic, he was often seen emerging from her boudoir.

In June 1789 the French sculptor Jean Antoine Houdun used Morris as a model for a sculpture of George Washington. Morris felt flattered that, wooden leg or not, he still had a regal bearing that could represent his friend, the president.

A member of the States-General, the French legislative body, asked Morris to put together his recommendations for a French constitution. Morris did this, suggesting that the National Assembly be dismissed until the constitution was completed. Morris seems to have forgotten that 11 years had elapsed in the United States between the outbreak of the Revolution and the call for a Constitutional Convention.

Jefferson also gave Lafayette a Charter of Rights calling for "annihilations of distinctions of order." Morris did not believe that France would accept such a change. The American experience would not work in France, Morris said, where there was illiteracy at the bottom and inexperience and corruption at the top of French society. The outcome would more likely be butchery and terror, Morris predicted. He wrote to William Carmichael that the French "want an American Constitution without reflecting that they have not American citizens to support it."[33]

When Lafayette admonished Morris for failure to support the revolutionary movement in France, Morris told Lafayette that his party was leading France straight towards destruction. "He tells me he is sensible his party are mad," Morris reported, "but is not the less determined to die with them."[34] Better to bring the party to their senses, said Morris, and then live for France rather than die for her.

In July 1789 Spain seized three British ships and the British post at Nootka Sound off Vancouver Island. Spain and France were then allies. Morris recommended that France declare war on England, as a means of keeping the empire united. Morris was also interested in reducing England's presence along the Pacific coast, where boundaries were in dispute. This hardline approach towards England continued when Jefferson became secretary of state.

On Bastille Day (July 14, 1789) Morris, with a green bow in his hat honoring the Third Estate, went to the Louvre to comfort his lover Adelaide. When the mob passed carrying the governor's head on a pole, Morris called it "the Liberty Pole of France." Several days later, however, when he saw a mob carrying a man's head on a pike for having accepted a ministry post, he exclaimed, "Gracious God, what a people! We cannot parade the heads of our fellow citizens and drag the mangled carcasses through the streets."[35]

France declared war on her traditional ally Austria for making plans to restore the French monarchy. Morris considered the war a harsh move, for it would automatically unite Austria, England, and Spain against France. As he witnessed the mounting violence, he felt that a monarchy was France's only hope for law and order. But his heart of hearts told him that this monarchy was doomed.

Morris advised Talleyrand on methods of setting up the new government. He appreciated Talleyrand's sophistication, meaning that he did not have to make "dreadfully tiresome" explanations "for one of those half-way minds which see just far enough to bewilder themselves."[36]

Morris was now so absorbed in his love affair with Adelaide that he failed to warn his London business partner, William Constable, of the precarious financial status of their friend Robert Morris. As a result Constable lost a goodly sum of money to Gouverneur's neglience, for which the latter felt much remorse.

In January 1792 the Senate voted 16–11 to confirm Washington's appointment of Morris as minister to France. Voting against him were such luminaries as Aaron Burr, Gunning Bedford, James Monroe, and Roger Sherman. Jefferson persuaded Washington to tone down a critical letter to Morris informing him of the appointment. Even so, Washington mentioned that some senators had complained about his imprudent conduct, his levity and hauteur, his support of monarchy, and a quick-triggered imagination which allowed too little time for deliberation.

"I have the fullest confidence," wrote Washington with crossed fingers, "that you would find no difficulty, considering yourself as a representative of this country, to effect a change and thereby silence your political opponents."[37] Lafayette was less sanguine. Morris is my friend, he told Washington, but he is not only an aristocrat but also a counterrevolutionary, and thus poorly fits in with the present French effort to install a representative democracy.

Morris developed a plan for Louis XVI to flee France. The king, still technically in power, turned it down. Morris then gave him this advice: (1) Do not try to bribe the Assembly "because they have too little consistency or fidelity to be worth corrupting." (2) Win the poor over by giving them bread; they are more important than the Assembly. (3) I (Morris) can arrange for you to have 12 million pounds of flour in five months. Issue a daily ration of 200,000 pounds to the people. "It is a great affair of state and I want no profit from it,"[38] Morris said.

Later, on July 24, 1792, Louis XVI asked Morris to accept custody of his papers and money, and Morris received 547,000 francs which he distributed among the king's followers. Later Morris received more money, which he turned over to the king's daughter in Vienna in December 1796.

Also that July Morris was called to the deathbed of John Paul Jones and drew up his will for him. Morris discreetly departed to allow Jones a private farewell with his lover, Aimée de Tellison. Later when Morris took the Queen's doctor to the bedside of Jones, he had already expired.

Morris was the only diplomat who remained in Paris through the Reign of Terror. Others had been ordered out by their governments, but it took longer for the news to get to America. When the mob insisted on searching the American legation for guns, Morris turned them away. The next morning he was given an official apology.

Robert Morris had written to Gouverneur, advising him to leave Paris. Not until he received orders from Washington, Gouverneur replied. "It is not permitted to abandon a post in the hour of difficulty,"[39] he added. He then related to Robert Morris the numerous advantages to the United States in keeping the legation open.

"No one at Paris," said one biographer, "could have represented the United States better than Morris did in the stormy years, 1792-94. He weathered the Terror with dignity and courage."[40]

A victim of the Terror (almost as Morris had predicted), Lafayette was now a prisoner of the Austrians at Magdeburg. Although he did not like Lafayette, Morris asked American bankers in Amsterdam to extend a loan of 10,000 florins to be given to Magdeburg officials for comfortable sustenance to an old American ally. Morris declared that he was not intriguing for Lafayette's escape, "for I cannot enter into intrigues of that sort directly or indirectly, because it is not becoming the dignity of the United States to act in an underhand manner."[41]

When Lafayette's wife asked for the United States to underwrite his debts, Morris said that it could not be done, but he gave her his personal loan of 100,000 francs. He later declined a request for an additional 150,000 francs, but he assured Lafayette's children that the United States would take care of them.

Another victim of the Terror, Thomas Paine, asked Morris to get him out of Luxembourg Prison. Morris tried, but was turned down with the explanation that Paine, upon accepting French citizenship, was subject to the jurisdiction of French laws.

Paine continued to blame Morris, and then Washington, for not freeing him from the clutches of the French radicals. But there was little factual basis for Paine's complaint. When he said that Morris was largely responsible for his imprisonment, even Paine's biographer said that "by the standards of reasonable men Paine's charges were outrageous."[42]

When Washington asked France to recall Citizen Edmond Genêt for his willful violation of American laws, the French government insisted that Morris be replaced, so in 1794 James Monroe replaced Morris in Paris. Morris traveled through Europe and England before returning to the United States on December 23, 1798.

Final Years

At first Monroe seemed to be successful at making friends with the French. He got caught in the backwash of Jay's Treaty, however, when France considered the United States as a virtual ally to England. Recalled in 1796, Monroe wrote a long attack on Washington and Morris in his *View of the Conduct of the Executive*.

Normally mild-mannered Washington, in a 44-page reply to Monroe, defended Morris, "known to be a man of first rate ability, and his integrity and honor had never been impeached. He pursued steadily the interests of his country with zest and ability. Had Mr. Monroe done the same we should not be in the situation we are now."[43]

In April 1799 Morris visited Robert Morris in debtors' prison. Robert still owed Gouverneur $24,000, exclusive of the amounts Gouverneur had supplied to cover Robert's European debts. Like several other Founding Fathers, Robert's financial empire had collapsed when his extensive land speculation went sour. When Robert was discharged from jail in 1802, Gouverneur took him in to his home, and gave him a sizable amount of money for a fresh start.

Disappointed in John Adams as president, Morris tried to get Washington to run again. In a letter dated December 9, 1799, Morris warned that unless Washington agreed to run, he would see the office held by an unqualified person. Washington probably never read the letter, for he took sick on December 13 and died the next day.

Morris gave the funeral oration for Washington at St. Paul's Church in New York City on December 31. Though eulogizing "the one man in whom his critical mind found no fault," he seems to have been coldly biographical. "Pronounced my oration badly,"[44] he wrote in his diary.

Could Morris have been president in 1800? Robert R. Livingston thought so. When Jefferson was finally selected on the 36th ballot in the House of Representatives, Livingston wrote Morris: "Had you run with Jefferson you would beyond all question have been chosen by the House of Representatives to fill the first office of the Union."[45]

In 1800 Morris was appointed to fill out the unexpired term of James Watson in the Senate. At first he showed a conciliatory attitude towards the Republicans, saying that no matter who gets elected, "the opposition will act as an outward conscience and prevent the abuse of power."[46] When Jefferson's administration tried to repeal Adams's Judiciary Bill, Morris unsuccessfully led the opposition, saying that the repeal would be unconstitutional. He chided Hamilton for not opposing the repeal, saying that "it will enable your personal enemies to say that you wished the repeal to take effect, so as to overturn the Constitution."[47]

In 1802 Adelaide married the Portuguese minister to France. Count de Flahaut had been killed during the French Revolution.

Morris supported a Senate resolution of war against France in 1803. He wanted the United States to occupy New Orleans, and he resented Napoleon's interference with American shipping. Although nothing came of the resolution, it may have strengthened Jefferson's hand as he negotiated for the Louisiana Purchase.

When Federalists attacked the purchase as too costly or as imperialism, Morris showed true national colors: "I should indeed have lost all shame as well as pretence to understanding if I did not approve. A few millions more or less in the price is a fit subject for democracy to bawl about, but unworthy of notice."[48]

His private Federalist bias stuck out, however, in a letter he wrote to Henry W. Livingston. Morris alleged that the intent of the framers was to disallow new states from entering the Union. "I always thought," he said, "that when we should acquire Canada and Louisiana it would be proper to govern them as provinces, and allow them no voice in our councils."[49] Here Morris sounds gullible enough to repeat the errors of Great Britain, errors he had vigorously opposed at an earlier date.

Hearing of Hamilton's being shot in the duel with Burr, Morris hurried to his side and stayed until Hamilton died. In his funeral oration he carefully avoided reference to Hamilton's abundant faults. He also had to stem the emotional storm demanding Burr's scalp in revenge.

Then, would not a public subscription for Betsey Hamilton and the children be demeaning? So Morris suggested that twenty wealthy men pay off Hamilton's debts of about $100,000, and that is what was done.

Trustees of Columbia College elected Morris to fill Hamilton's place on their board. Need the college president always be an Episcopalian, as stated in the college charter? Morris and fellow trustee Rufus King found a way around the dilemma. They saw to it that the new vice-president was not an Episcopalian, and by the time he was ready for the presidency, the charter had been altered unobtrusively.

At the age of 55 the bon vivant with a wooden leg shot the rapids of the St. Lawrence River in a canoe. After a long trip down that river he predicted that "the proudest empire in Europe is but a bubble compared to what America will be in the course of two centuries."[50]

Enter the mysterious Anne Randolph. Anne had delivered a stillborn infant, whose father had been her brother-in-law Richard Randolph. At the trial over whether she had killed the baby, Anne was acquitted largely on her sister Judith's testimony that there was no love intrigue between Anne and Richard.

But the Randolph family had ostracized Anne, treating her like a harlot or a mentally defective person. A friend of her parents, Morris felt sorry for her. In April 1809 he brought her to Morrisania to be his housekeeper.

John Randolph of Roanoke, Richard's frenetic brother, wrote to Anne that "the idea of his marrying you never entered my head, another course did. You are a vampire that, after seeking the best blood of my race, has flitted off to the North and struck your fangs into an infirm old man."[51]

At Christmas dinner that year Morris surprised his nine guests with the news that this was their wedding day. Anne was not at the table for dinner, but later came down the stairs wearing an old brown dress patched at the elbows. He was 57 and she was 35.

Furious, and probably dejected over a lesser inheritance, his nieces and nephews protested the matrimony of this odd couple. When niece Gertrude Meredith complained to him, Morris blithely retorted: "If I had married a rich woman of 70 the world might think it wiser than to take one half that age without a farthing. If the world were to live with my wife, I should certainly have consulted its taste, but as that happens not to be the case, I thought I might endeavor to suit myself."[52]

The mates were entirely pleased with each other. But her relatives were determined to persecute her. When her sister Judith's son Tudor grew ill with tuberculosis, Anne and Morris invited Tudor to live with them at Morrisania. Tudor's idea of gratitude was to tell his uncle John Randolph of rumors that Anne was engaging in "lewd amours" and that she had poisoned his father.

John Randolph of Roanoke thereupon wrote Morris a letter, warning him about Anne and describing vivid details of how she had allegedly murdered her baby. Morris's nephew, David B. Ogden, then sent Morris an anonymous letter, repeating these charges and adding a few more. It seemed as if there was a conspiracy against Anne.

Morris received all these charges with equanimity. He who had been in many a woman's bedroom remained true to his much-maligned wife. It was as if through their mutual suffering they were undergoing a purgatorial cleansing of whatever imperfections of which they had been guilty. As scapegoats were they also performing a cleansing of the projected sins of their accusers?

He and Anne attended a Shaker service at Lebanon Springs in 1810. He listened to the preaching, full of "the superstition which duped our ignorant forefathers seven centuries ago," he said. He was incredulous at the urging of the "poor creatures to abandon conjugal pleasures for that pure felicity which attends celibacy."[53] Morris listening to a sermon on celibacy could have attracted an audience.

In 1812 George Clinton, longtime governor of New York and political foe of Morris, died, and he was asked to deliver the funeral eulogy. A gifted speaker, Morris extolled Clinton's virtues and overlooked his prejudice and ill will.

Morris saw one of his dreams come true that year. As chairman of the Erie Canal Commission, he had long lobbied in Washington for appropriations to construct the canal. On June 17 the Erie Canal bill passed, and the following day Congress declared war against England.

Like most Federalists and those favoring the commercial interests, Morris felt that President Madison was rash in prosecuting the war. He felt that Napoleon was a far greater threat to American interests than was Britain, and he believed that Madison's real goal was to conquer Canada.

Morris went so far as to advocate that Congress not honor the president's war loans. Shades of his support of Washington's army during the Revolution!

In his intemperance Morris now considered that the secessionist demands of the Hartford Convention were too timid. That Convention demanded that unless seven new amendments were added to the Constitution, there would be a peaceable dissolution of the Union. The major requests fit in with Morris's aristocratic preferences: abolish representation of slave population; only native-born men would be eligible for federal office; and admission of new states only upon two-thirds approval by both houses of Congress. The genial give-and-take atmosphere of the Constitutional Convention was abandoned for the type of doctrinaire provinciality he had once opposed.

A similar vein of jingoism was apparent in his opposition to the tariff of 1816. Why tax farmers, he asked, to support "the scum of England and

Ireland, who come to live in ease and idleness as mechanics," who "put to work many poor children with a spinning jenny, till they are old enough to become drunkards and prostitutes?"[54] Morris, from a somewhat professional perspective, might surely have spared a kindlier word for prostitutes!

That year a stricture developed in his urinary canal. When he tried to relieve the stricture by forcing a whalebone through it, the results were lacerations and great pain. He had long suffered from gout in his right leg. He died of influenza on November 6, 1816, at the age of 64. Four months previously he said that he still felt "the gaiety of inexperience and the frolic of youth."[55]

His generous consideration of Anne in his will is a model for husbands who love their wives. Anne received Morrisania with all furnishings and maintenance costs for life, plus $2600 per year. And then, in a deft Morris touch, were she to remarry the allowance would be increased by $600 per year, to cover her increased expenses. Anne died in 1837 at the age of 63.

Morris was one of a kind. He scarcely seemed to belong to the company of the framers of the Constitution, and yet had he not been there, something vital would have been lacking. He was a big man, with a large heart and great faults. He did not know how to operate on a petty scale. He never apologized for being an aristocrat.

It was easy to condemn him, but difficult to keep up with his good works. Born at the wrong time and place, he was never cut out to be a revolutionary. But he had a serenity and a magnanimity that put new force into the term *noblesse oblige*. His zest for life would be refreshing in any historical period and in any society. And his heritage in the sterling phrases of the Constitution has extended to every generation of Americans in all classes and conditions — yes, even to "mechanics" and "drunkards."

10.
Charles Cotesworth Pinckney: The Soldier and Patriot

Which framer of the Constitution, between the years 1791 and 1795, declined to serve as commander of the American army, as Supreme Court justice, as secretary of war, and as secretary of state? Which framer was the only one of the group to be a three-time candidate for president? If your answer to these questions is Charles Cotesworth Pinckney, you are correct.

His grandfather Thomas Pinckney arrived in South Carolina in 1692. By his second wife, Mary Cotesworth, Thomas had two sons, William and Charles. A successful merchant, Thomas sent Charles to England for a law education.

Charles Pinckney, father of Charles Cotesworth Pinckney, soon became affluent as a result of his law practice and good real estate investments. He established the Pinckneys in South Carolina, financially and socially. A devout Anglican, he donated generously to his church.

He was known for his broad-mindedness. He defended the right of dissenters to be seated in the state legislature without swearing an oath to uphold the New Testament. He supported education for blacks, contributing to the building of a school to teach them to read and write.

In 1735 he defended the right of the state legislature to draft money bills without approval from Parliament. He said that the South Carolina Commons House had powers as great as those of Parliament. He served as Speaker of the House from 1736 to 1740.

King George II in 1750 appointed him to be a member of the royal council of the state. This automatically made him a legislator, an advisor to the governor, and a judge in the Court of Chancery. Governor James Glen appointed him interim chief justice in 1752, but the royal confirmation never came. Instead, Peter Leigh, accused of a voting fraud, received the appointment. South Carolinians felt rebuffed, for if Charles Pinckney could not get a royal appointment, who among them could?

Charles Pinckney's second wife, Elizabeth Lucas, was the daughter of a British army officer who had been governor of Antigua. Eliza, as she was called, ran her father's plantation in South Carolina, and with his help pioneered in introducing a new crop, indigo. Before long indigo became one of the leading crops in the state. Belmont, the Pinckney plantation, was located five miles north of Charlestown.

Charles Cotesworth Pinckney was born on February 14, 1745. His toys taught him the alphabet; he could spell before he was two. In a few years he could play with his sister Harriott, born in 1748, and his brother Thomas, born in 1750.

The family had daily religious services. Young Charles quickly developed a love of Christ and the church. The parents took the children to England for schooling. There his father died in 1758, leaving Charles Cotesworth as the masculine head of the family. A good businesswoman, Eliza ran the plantation and kept her sons in school in England. She wrote to Charles: "God make you worthy of such a father as yours. What I fear most for you is heat of temper."[1]

Pinckney's schooling was at an academy at Camberwell, and then at another private school at Kensington Borough in London. From there he went on to the "public" preparatory school, Westminster. The headmaster, Dr. William Markham, trusted Pinckney's character completely. Once Markham reputedly said to him: "Speak, Pinckney. My decision shall be guided by your sentiment."[2]

The curriculum at Westminster was religion and the classics. An excellent Latin scholar, Pinckney had a penchant for jokes and pranks, and showed a quick temper upon being aroused.

Pinckney entered Oxford in January 1764. Christ Church College was a hotbed of Whig protest against the ruling House of Hanover. Students paraded against George III. When the Stamp Act was passed, Pinckney had a portrait of himself painted showing him vigorously declaiming against it.

American students were looked down upon in English schools as cultural inferiors to the island British. Pinckney resented the discrimination, even though several English students befriended him.

By terms of his father's will, Pinckney inherited two plantations and other land in South Carolina, plus some property in England. He perhaps unconsciously picked up the common distrust that the landed gentry showed towards persons engaged in commerce.

While at Oxford he began his study of law at the Middle Temple. He listened to Sir William Blackstone lecture on the slow accumulation of British rights and liberties, and how the law protected man's freedoms in society.

In November 1766 he left Oxford prematurely to study law full time at the Middle Temple. The curriculum was desultory and disorganized—

a student could escape legal exercise and residence requirements by the payment of adequate fees. The final examination was to swear an oath against popery and go through the form of a legal argument.

Conscientious Pinckney used his time well, reading law books and attending court trials and sessions of Parliament. He was impelled by a strong sense of family pride and loyalty to make a success of his life. His character was impeccable: "Not many parents can say of a youth of 22 that he has never once offended them."[3]

In 1768 he spent some time at the Royal Military Academy across the Channel at Caen, studying military science. In 1769 he finished his schooling in London and was admitted to the bar.

The Patriot

Pinckney was elected to the Commons House in South Carolina in September 1769. In his first session the Commons House voted to send £10,500 to England to help pay the election costs of the radical John Wilkes. The followers of Wilkes kept electing him but the House of Commons refused to seat him because of his opposition to the crown.

Pinckney voted in support of the Wilkes fund. When the governor of South Carolina refused to forward the money to Wilkes, the Commons House responded by denying approval of all money bills asked for by the governor or his council. This was nothing new—for decades Southern legislatures had refused to carry out instructions from the crown.

The obnoxious British laws, plus the harassment of the prominent merchant Henry Laurens, led Charlestown to adopt an agreement concerning nonimportation of British goods in June 1769. Angry South Carolinians also set up a Committee of Correspondence to make protests to the British ministry. Pinckney tried to get through a bill establishing public schools in the colony, but the governor prorogued the Commons House before the bill could be passed.

In 1770 George III denied that the Commons House had power equal to that of Parliament, and said that the royal council had the authority to pass or amend money bills. Pinckney and other leaders called this "seditious doctrine," for it interposed "some power to raise money upon the inhabitants of this province other than their own representatives."[4]

Pinckney was admitted to the South Carolina bar in January 1770. In a spectacular case the next year Pinckney and his associates got their client Dr. John Haley off with a manslaughter charge, after Haley had killed Peter DeLancey in a duel.

Pinckney was now a community leader. He served as church warden and vestryman. He supported the public library and helped found the Charlestown Museum. He encouraged music and theater, playing the violoncello at the annual St. Cecilia Society Ball. He was an amateur botanist, and an ensign in the Charlestown militia regiment.

He was not handsome, but his broad shoulders gave him a commanding appearance. He had dark eyes, a Roman nose, and a wide mouth poised to laugh. His personality was outgoing. A good conversationalist, he loved to tell stories. He liked dancing, music, good food, fine wine, and the company of attractive women.

In 1772 he was put on the important Committee on Grievances, which protested Governor Charles Montague's effort to unseat obstreperous Commons House members by holding elections in distant Beaufort.

In 1773 Pinckney became one of the first museum curators in South Carolina. In March of that year he showed Josiah Quincy, Jr., around town. Quincy, who was testing South Carolina's commitment to the patriot cause, came away impressed by Pinckney as "a man of brilliant powers."[5] Pinckney became acting attorney-general for three districts that year, and was promoted to be infantry lieutenant in the militia.

In September 1773 he married Sarah (Sally) Middleton, whose father Henry owned twenty plantations and 800 slaves. Middleton later served as President of the Continental Congress. Edward Rutledge married Sally's sister Henrietta, and Charles Drayton married Sally's other sister Hester. The intermarriage among these families built up an aristocracy of South Carolina power and authority.

The Soldier

Since duty, honor, and service were his bywords, Pinckney took well to army life. He believed in discipline and in loyalty to one's country, and so he progressed rapidly through the officers' ranks.

Each year the governor would prorogue the legislature because of protest actions it had taken. In 1774 the General Meeting was the popular body for expressing protest. In 1775 Pinckney became a member of the General Provincial Congress which started meeting in Charlestown.

In April 1775 Pinckney and three other men staged a raid on the royal arsenal, leaving the government without arms. That month he was put on a Committee of Intelligence, whose main job was to unite upcountry leaders with those in low-country Charlestown.

Rumors ran that the royal government was arming Indians and blacks for an attack upon Charlestown. Pinckney was selected to serve on a Special Committee to prepare the town's defense. Two Tories were tarred and feathered by Committee members. Working with Georgians, the Special Committee seized a British schooner in the Savannah harbor, capturing nearly 17,000 pounds of gunpowder. In July they sent nearly 5,000 pounds of it to Washington and the Continental Army.

Pinckney was elected as top captain in the South Carolina regiments that year. Assigned to recruit in New Bern, North Carolina, he captured two British spies. As an officer he took good care of his men. Because he was strict on discipline, few loved him but most of them respected him.

In September a force under Colonel William Moultrie seized Fort Johnson, which guarded Charlestown Harbor. Captain Pinckney's grenadiers were scheduled to play a key role in the attack, but the British had pulled out after first dismounting the cannons. In November Pinckney was promoted to major.

On December 19 Major Pinckney, with a force of four captains, 200 soldiers, and a number of mechanics and laborers, remounted the gun battery at Haddrell's Point at night. By morning their 18-pounders were firing about a mile at British ships, driving them back towards Sullivan's Island. When the Americans built a fort on Sullivan's Island, the British fleet withdrew, taking with them the last royal governor of South Carolina, Lord William Campbell.

In February 1776 Pinckney was appointed lieutenant colonel of the First Infantry Regiment of South Carolina. That month he was also made chairman of a committee to draw up a plan of government for the state. He was considered neutral enough to lead the committee which had seven conservative members, led by John Rutledge, and three extremists who wanted immediate separation from Britain, led by Christopher Gadsden.

Pinckney served as a bridge between the two groups. "From conviction he favored radical measures, while by temperament he wanted to use moderate means to achieve them."[6] John Rutledge made the final report for the committee on March 24, and two days later it was adopted.

Pinckney had little to gain by opposing the crown, and much to lose. He acted according to principle. He was probably influenced toward independence by his brother Tom, his brother-in-law Arthur Middleton, and his friend the firebrand William Henry Drayton. By now he was also animated, to use his own words, by a "love of military glory, which should swell the soldier's breast and lead him to renown."[7]

In June Pinckney and his forces eagerly awaited the British attack upon Fort Johnson, since the British fleet was anchored within a few miles of Charlestown. Instead, the British attacked Fort Sullivan. Fortunately Governor John Rutledge and Colonel Moultrie had ignored the command of General Charles Lee of the Continental Army, and not abandoned Fort Sullivan.

On June 28 the attack was repulsed, aided by unfavorable winds, unskillful pilots in the narrow channel, and several rows of stubborn palmetto trees. While Charlestown was still celebrating their military independence from British forces, word arrived of the signing of a political Declaration of Independence in Philadelphia.

In October he became Colonel Pinckney, in command of the First South Carolina Continental Regiment. He and Captain Thomas Pinckney were now officers in the regular army, serving under Washington. Pinckney became restive for action, as the fighting was now taking place in the North.

In June 1777 Lafayette and Baron de Kalb visited Charlestown. Knowing French, Pinckney readily conversed with them, and found out that Washington's major campaigns would continue to be in the North. Pinckney asked for and received permission to join Washington's army in the field.

He served as Washington's aide-de-camp in the battles around Philadelphia. At the battle of Brandywine Creek on September 11 he helped stem a retreat of troops under General John Sullivan. He remained cool in combat and was especially useful at the height of battle, when actions must be instinctive. As he watched Washington at work, he learned how quickly commanders must make decisions as battle conditions change. He also learned that poor reconnaissance and lack of knowledge of terrain can easily lead to defeat.

Here and at the battle of Germantown on October 4 Pinckney won Washington's confidence by his intelligence, zeal, and courage. When asked by Washington about Charlestown's ability to withstand attack, Pinckney said that he feared that his native city had been lulled into a false security by the relative absence of fighting.

At Washington's suggestion he returned to Charlestown to command his regiment in December 1777. The regiment was moved from Fort Moultrie to Charlestown to bolster the town's defense. Pinckney found out that in his absence he had been re-elected to the state General Assembly.

The big issue in the adoption of the new state constitution in 1778 was the disestablishment of the Anglican church, a move which Pinckney favored and John Rutledge opposed. The church tax, in Pinckney's opinion, was taxation without representation for dissenters. His father would have been proud of him. Why fight for political independence, he asked, and then deny religious liberty? Even under the new constitution, Protestantism was the official religion, for only Protestants were eligible to hold public office.

In April 1778 Pinckney was sent south to help repel British forces raiding Georgia from Florida. The British were receiving assistance from loyalists and from Creek Indians. Pinckney's troops experienced great discomfort in Georgia. The sultry weather caused great sickness, and supplies were in short order. Worst of all was the conflict in top leadership between state and Continental forces. Governor John Houston of Georgia refused to cede command to General Robert Howe, commander of the southern forces of the Continental Army.

Christopher Gadsden resigned as brigadier-general rather than serve under Howe, and then wrote a public letter condemning Howe. A duel ensued. Pinckney, as Howe's second, insisted that Howe, as the insulted one, shoot first. Pinckney stepped off the eight paces. Howe's bullet grazed Gadsden's ear — Gadsden fired into the air. Shoot again, said Howe, but Gadsden refused, apologized, and the duel was over.

The British captured Savannah in December 1778 and kept control of Georgia for the remainder of the War. By May 1779 their forces under General Augustine Prévost were in the outskirts of Charlestown. Tom Pinckney's plantation was burned and his slaves carried away. Belmont's furniture was destroyed. Pinckney generously offered to divide his estate with his mother and Tom.

Pinckney's portly figure was a testimony to his love of food. He was on good enough terms with his commanding officer, General Benjamin Lincoln, to josh about the trouble he was having gathering food in preparation for the siege of Charlestown. Pinckney told Lincoln that perhaps generals should fast, for philosophers tell us that fasting quickens mental ability, but doctors state that animal energy in man is best helped by good wholesome food. Thus, said Pinckney, "I hold it to be an undeniable maxim in war that soldiers should have their bellies full."[8]

Resolute action under the leadership of Brigadier-General William Moultrie and Governor John Rutledge repulsed the British siege of 1779. In October 1779 Pinckney joined forces with other American and French troops in an effort to recapture Savannah, but the effort failed, and the British were able to bolster their supplies in preparation for another attack on Charlestown the following year.

As the British advanced upon Charlestown in the spring of 1780, Lincoln wanted Pinckney to withdraw from Fort Moultrie in order to help defend Charlestown. Pinckney demurred, stating that he could inflict more damage upon the British from Fort Moultrie.

At first Pinckney's decision seemed sound. In April his battery fired upon the British, inflicting 29 casualties without the loss of a man. When the British stores ship *Acteus* grounded near Haddrell's Point, Pinckney sent a detachment with two field pieces which destroyed *Acteus* so badly that the crew set fire to it and retreated to the safety of other ships.

But Lincoln had unwisely massed several thousand men on the Charlestown neck. British land forces gradually blocked every route of retreat out of Charlestown. On April 19 Lincoln called for a Council of War to see whether further resistance was sensible. "Let's fight!"[9] said Pinckney, accusing the French engineer, Colonel DeLaumoy, of not wanting to continue the battle. DeLaumoy said that it was hopeless to fight against such superior numbers. But the decision that night was to continue the battle. Pinckney now withdrew his forces from Fort Moultrie in order to bolster the town garrison.

It was, however, only a matter of time. When Lincoln called a final Council of War on May 8, only 11 of the 60 officers voted to continue the fight. Pinckney, of course, was one who did not wish to surrender.

During the siege, 20 Americans deserted to the British side, and just prior to the surrender, several British went over to the American side! On May 11 General Lincoln surrendered Charlestown to the British forces under Sir Henry Clinton.

The captured officers, including Pinckney, were incarcerated at Haddrell's Point (near present Mount Pleasant). Nearby was cousin Charles Pinckney's home, where Pinckney was allowed to stay. Friends and family could visit him, and he had a black servant. But he longed to be in Charlestown with his family. When the British tried to get him to switch sides, he protested so vigorously that they confiscated most of his property.

In August 1780 British troops seized 33 leading Americans, including Pinckney's two brothers-in-law, Edward Rutledge and Arthur Middleton, and took them to confinement at St. Augustine.

In November Pinckney contracted malaria. The following month his baby son, named after him, died of malaria in Charlestown, but he was not even permitted to attend his own son's funeral.

To save their properties, many American leaders switched to the British side. These included his cousin Charles Pinckney, his brother-in-law Daniel Horry, and his father-in-law Henry Middleton. They refused to face "sequestration by the British of town property, plantations, and slaves, or penury, hardship, and physical labor or hanging or imprisonment."[10]

Charles Pinckney joined 163 other "loyal inhabitants" of Charlestown who congratulated Lord Cornwallis on his victory at Camden, and denounced "the contemptible remains of that expiring faction" which had opposed "that government under which they formerly enjoyed the highest degree of civil and political liberty."[11]

Tom Pinckney's mother-in-law, Rebecca Motte, supplied Lieutenant Colonel Harry Lee with combustible arrows to burn down her own house, where British troops were entrenched. Fortunately for her, the

British surrendered quickly, and the Americans rushed in and saved the mansion from destruction.

British treatment of civilians and captured American soldiers was so intolerable that many volunteered to serve in the partisan forces led by Francis Marion and Thomas Sumter. In June 1780 Sir Henry Clinton ordered all South Carolina men to serve in the British army against American troops. House burnings and other acts of cruelty by British forces under Major James Wemyss and Colonel Banastre Tarleton further swelled the ranks of partisan volunteers.

When asked by Edward Rutledge what he would do when the British asked him to switch sides, Pinckney replied: "If I had a vein that did not beat with love for my country, I myself would open it. When asked the question you mention, I will give it such an answer as is becoming an American officer, a man of honor, and a devotee to the freedom and independence of his country."[12]

In the summer of 1781 a prisoner exchange was in the offing, so Pinckney, his brother Tom, Edward Rutledge, and their families were sent to Philadelphia. In March 1782 Pinckney and William Moultrie were exchanged for General John Burgoyne. Pinckney joined the forces of General Nathaniel Greene near Dorchester, about 55 miles northwest of Charlestown. But hostilities were nearly over. In December 1782 the British forces left Charlestown, and Pinckney and his family finally returned home.

During the War Pinckney had loaned South Carolina at least £21,500. Generals Robert Howe and Benjamin Lincoln both praised Pinckney as an officer and as a leader of men, but he had never taken part in a major winning battle. On November 3, 1783, the day that Washington ordered the Continental Army disbanded, Pinckney became a brigadier-general by brevet. He had given eight and a half years of loyal service to his country.

The Lawyer

Post-war South Carolina was a turbulent place. Many estates had been burned or plundered, with the slaves stolen. Interest rates on loans ran as high as 50 percent. In heavy debt, the state government had to choose between high taxes and repudiation of the debt. Rabble-rousers like Dr. James Fallon led mobs in raids against wealthy landowners. In one such raid, Major Thomas Pinckney and the militia had to quell the mob by using sabers.

Rumors said that Fallon would lead a mob to seize the chief officials, the Pinckneys and the Rutledges, take their estates, and give them to the poor. Like many others, Pinckney was land poor—he owned property but had borrowed money to rebuild his estates, and so for the next decade he lived on the brink of financial ruin.

Edward Rutledge wanted harsh treatment of British sympathizers, but his business partner Pinckney recommended that they be reaccepted as citizens without penalty. General Greene wanted to auction off horses captured from the British. Not when owners can identify them as their property, said Pinckney, for under the doctrine of the right of postliminium, an army must return property to the original owners after recovery from the enemy. When a council of officers supported Greene's decision, South Carolinians interpreted the action as an invasion of their rights by the Continental government.

The unsettled conditions were good for lawyers, and Pinckney, who returned to his law practice, began to make good money at it. Once on circuit he made fifty guineas before breakfast. Even though he never charged fees to widows or orphans, he still averaged £4,000 sterling per year. Although he lacked oratorical skills, he could rely upon a clear logical mind and a wide reading background.

Judge Aedanus Burke considered Pinckney to be long-winded. Once, while Pinckney was presenting his case, Burke tucked up his robe and headed for the door. "Go on, General Pinckney," Burke said. "You love to hear yourself talk. Meanwhile, I'll go out and look at the camel."[13] A camel was part of a traveling show at the moment.

Pinckney's wife Sally died of tuberculosis on May 8, 1784. Several days later her father, Henry Middleton, added a codicil to his will: "It is my desire that my son-in-law Charles Cotesworth Pinckney do receive every benefit and advantage to which his wife would have been entitled had she survived me."[14]

At the age of 38 a widower with three daughters, Pinckney gave them to the care of his mother, Eliza, who was living with his sister, Harriott Pinckney Horry at Hampton, the Horry estate, for Eliza's mansion had been destroyed during the War.

As business partners Edward Rutledge and Pinckney bought two plantations on credit, a trading sloop, and 1000 acres of plantable swamp. Pinckney also bought shares in a canal company which never brought him any profit. He and Rutledge agreed on negotiating the boundary dispute with Georgia, and on ways to make it easier for new lawyers to practice. Pinckney opposed amercement, a heavy tax on former Tories, but Rutledge favored it. Rutledge opposed continued importation of slaves, which Pinckney favored, not on moral but on economic grounds.

Pinckney helped found the Charleston (the name had been changed in 1783) chapter of Mount Zion Society in 1785. The purpose of this society was to establish a college at Winnsboro. After helping push a bill through the state legislature for this purpose, he served as an officer of the society, as a fund raiser, and later as a college trustee. In 1786 he became president of the Charleston Library Society, and served off and on as an officer and a friend of the library for the next forty years.

Throughout the 1780s Pinckney and his brother Tom were active in the state legislature. Pinckney served on many legislative committees. By the year 1788 each Pinckney received 510 votes and Edward Rutledge 506 votes, the most cast that year.

In 1786 Pinckney married Mary Stead, who brought him not only charm and intelligence but also £14,000. He now spent so much time handling their business affairs that he had little time left to concern himself about national matters.

Although the issuance of paper money looked like a quick solution to state financial problems, especially from the standpoint of a planter, Pinckney opposed it, for he knew it brought on inflation. Instead, he favored strengthening the national government by giving it the power to tax.

In 1786 Pinckney, Edward and John Rutledge, and three other members of the state House of Representatives brought in a committee report urging that states cede control of all foreign trade to the Confederation for a 15-year period. Pinckney now felt that the only way to strengthen South Carolina was to strengthen the national government.

The Framer

It was a belated honeymoon, the trip to Philadelphia, for Pinckney and his bride of ten months. Although he got seasick, Pinckney quickly recovered and appreciated Washington's warm greeting to the Convention.

Pinckney was ambivalent. He knew that the nation required a stronger government, and yet "the great art of government is not to govern too much."[15] No doubt the central government must control trade, but does this mean that Massachusetts will control South Carolina? Does control of trade mean control of slavery? Surely the central government should assume the states' war debts. At first his native conservatism led him to believe that the Convention should confine itself to revising the Articles of Confederation. As the concept of a new kind of government naturally unfolded, his vision gradually enlarged to encompass that government and its fundamental document.

He had no new plan to present to the Convention, as did his cousin Charles Pinckney. Brilliant but superficial, Charles revealed to his colleagues a plan for a constitution, but it was never discussed on the floor of the Convention. Some of its contents seem to have been drawn upon by the Committee of Detail as it did its important work of consolidating and systematizing Convention contributions.

With nothing of his cousin's ebullience, Charles Cotesworth Pinckney was an unobtrusive but a solid force in the Convention. "When he spoke it was with conviction, and what he said was listened to with respect."[16] Like Franklin, he kept his cool and when tempers flared, he would suggest a method of compromise that would be fair to both sides. For example, when the great impasse developed between large and small states, it was his suggestion to set up a committee, one member per state, to see if a recommendation could come out of a smaller group. Wilson and Madison, as representatives of large states, opposed Pinckney's motion, but the Convention adopted it and the outcome was the Great Compromise.

Whatever his private feelings may have been, Pinckney never forgot the viewpoints of his constituents. In apportioning members of the House of Representatives, he felt that the superior wealth of the southern states should entitle them to increased representation. Not to do so would be, in his opinion, a form of taxation without representation. In one year, he pointed out, South Carolina had exported goods worth £600,000, "all the fruit of the labor of her blacks."[17] If the national government had authority to tax exports, northerners could run the government on southern revenues. If representation is not on the basis of exports, he argued, then exports should not be the basis for raising revenues.

He opposed Gerry's motion to have all money bills originate in the lower house. His experience in the South Carolina legislature told him that this resulted in either conflicts between the two houses or evasion by the upper house giving informal amendments to the lower house before the fact. State legislatures, not the people, should elect the Congress, he felt, since the people are easily swayed by demagogues into accepting stupid actions like the issuance of paper money.

Tired of boarding-house meals at the Convention, he asked his sister Harriott to have plenty of vegetables planted in the garden of his town house for his return home.

Two motions he favored were adopted: that the Senate, as well as the House, could originate bills, and that members of both houses should be eligible to hold state offices concurrently. He wanted Senators' terms to be shortened to four years, to keep them more responsive to the public. He advocated no pay for Senators, feeling that only public-spirited persons should serve. Franklin seconded Pinckney's motion on this point. If they must be paid, Pinckney said, let the states pay them — this will make them more responsive to the states' needs. He recommended full federal control over the militia, having seen the ineffectiveness of an army fighting under divided commands.

Unfortunate from the modern perspective, he resisted the efforts of people like Mason and Wilson to get slavery abolished. "He contended that the importation of slaves would be for the interest of the whole Union. The more slaves, the more produce to employ the carrying trade; the more consumption also, and the more of this, the more of revenue for the common treasury."[18] On August 22 he said that "he did not think South Carolina would stop her importation of slaves in any short time, but only stop them occasionally as she now does."[19] He agreed to make slaves liable to a tax equal with other imports.

Several months later, when members of the state legislature objected to the year 1808 as the final year for slave importation, Pinckney explained how the compromise over slavery had been worked out. "'Show some period,' said the members from the Eastern states, 'when it may be in our power to put a stop, if we please, to the importation of this weakness, and we will endeavor, for your convenience, to restrain the religious and political prejudices of our people on this subject.'"[20]

When Charles Pinckney moved that Congress should have no power to pass an act regulating commerce (including navigation acts) except by a two-thirds vote, his cousin disagreed. Because the New England delegates had been so "liberal" on the importation of slaves, said Charles Cotesworth Pinckney, he felt that a simple majority vote in Congress on commerce acts would be satisfactory. Before coming here, he said, he had prejudices against the Eastern states, but here he had found their delegates to be "as liberal and candid as any men whatever." Following this talk, "a spirit of amity for a moment pervaded the whole Convention."[21]

By the close of the Convention Pinckney felt that a good balance had been achieved between state and federal power. When Gerry announced that he could not sign the document, Pinckney quickly replied that he would not only sign it but support it with all his influence.

He had made fewer specific contributions than the leaders in the Convention but he was, like Washington and Franklin, one of the main stabilizing factors in the deliberations of the delegates. Compromises between North and South, between large and small states, between commercial and rural interests — in these matters his actions played a decisive role. Going home by coach he and his wife stayed overnight at Mount Vernon, where he promised Washington that he would work hard for ratification in South Carolina.

The Ratifier

In the South Carolina legislature, Charles Pinckney reported on what the Convention had achieved. Rawlins Lowndes, former governor, spoke against the Constitution, saying that the Convention had exceeded its powers. The executive was too powerful, he said, and South Carolina would be forced to surrender its sovereignty. He closed with what he hoped would be his epitaph: "Here lies the man that opposed the Constitution because it was ruinous to the liberty of America."[22]

Charles Cotesworth Pinckney gave the rebuttal to Lowndes. Pinckney cited international law to show the origin of the articles dealing with foreign affairs. He quoted specific cases in the Convention to illustrate the process at work—how compromise is necessary in order to achieve progress. In a speech twice as long as any other, he showed a mastery of the issues of concern to his audience. When he finished, Lowndes admitted that he was "almost willing to give up his post."[23]

The vote in the legislature was 76-75 in favor of Charleston as the site of the ratification convention. The rural up-country people were bound to oppose the new Constitution, and so the balance lay with the eight middle-country parishes.

People in Charleston treated the delegates to the ratification convention courteously, courting their vote. News that Maryland had just ratified helped swing undecided delegates.

In his speech at the convention Pinckney pointed out that the Articles of Confederation had brought the nation neither tranquility at home nor respect abroad. He emphasized that the northern states had come to the rescue of the South when middle states led a fight to forbid further slave importation. A bill of rights, he declared, would have ill come from a state where slavery was widespread.

The vote for ratification, 149-73, on May 23, 1788, was due largely to the fact that 88 percent of the delegates from the Charleston area voted for the new Constitution. The influence of the Pinckneys and the Rutledges was too much for the up-country people to counteract.

Pinckney quickly sent the good news to Washington. Bells rang, cannons boomed, citizens paraded, and a victory dinner was served at the "Federal Green."

How thoroughly Pinckney now supported the new federal government can be seen by what he wrote in 1788: "Separate independence and individual sovereignty of the several states were never thought of by the enlightened band of patriots who framed the Declaration of Independence. Let us then consider all attempts to weaken this union, by maintaining that each state is separately independent, as a species of political heresy which can never benefit us but may bring on us the most serious distresses."[24] Prophetic that a South Carolinian should voice such warnings to his state, in view of what happened there in 1828, 1832, and 1861!

The Diplomat

Since the Pinckneys and the Rutledges had done so much in support of the federal union, and since they were his close friends, President Washington turned to them for advice concerning federal appointments, particularly in the South. Pinckney and Edward Rutledge were so involved in their business and law interests that they wanted no national post. They tended to recommend to Washington friends of theirs whom they trusted, those who had sacrificed most during the War, and those who believed in and supported the new federal government.

Both families now saw that the best way to safeguard the interests of South Carolina was to establish an effective but not monolithic national government. "The Pinckneys and the Rutledges were the flower of the southern oligarchy, and it is difficult to deny that they were worthy of their heroic pretensions to leadership in South Carolina and the nation."[25]

South Carolina was changing. The 1790 census showed that 80 percent of the white population lived in the up-country. The state capital was moved to Columbia. A convention was set up to draft a new state constitution. Pinckney and Edward Rutledge were prime forces in the convention. Pinckney was on the two most important committees: the Committee on Elections and the Committee on Detail and Arrangement. Many state officials had offices in both Charleston and Columbia. The low-country around Charleston managed to maintain control of both houses, but in the state senate by only one vote.

Pinckney lost his motion to have no pay for state legislators. He was elected to the state senate, where he served until 1796. He had seats on nearly every important senate committee, and was much more influential there than he had been in the lower house.

To strengthen support for the federal government, Washington toured the South in 1791. To fill the position on the Supreme Court left vacant when John Rutledge resigned to become chief justice of South Carolina, Washington sent joint letters to Pinckney and Edward Rutledge asking "Will either of you accept the office, and if so, which?"[26] Both declined for business reasons.

When Washington saw how well things were run in South Carolina, he told Hamilton to consult the Pinckneys and Rutledges on future appointments. Hamilton assured Pinckney that the federal government relied upon his "zeal for the support of the national laws."

When Tom Pinckney was appointed minister to Great Britain, his brother gave him a reading list on international law. He also looked after Tom's business affairs, and reminded him to send frequent letters to Secretary of State Jefferson.

Seeking supporters, Hamilton courted Pinckney and Edward Rutledge. In 1792 he wrote Pinckney that although he once "very much esteemed" Jefferson, he had since found him to be "a man of sublimated and paradoxical imagination, propagating opinions inconsistent with dignified and orderly government." John Adams, on the other hand, was in Hamilton's opinion "a firm, honest, and independent politician."[27]

Pinckney had some differences, however, with Hamilton. He did not like Hamilton's failure to differentiate between original holders and subsequent purchasers of government securities. Pinckney also praised the French Revolution as a movement towards republican government, saying that the violence which was the consequence of all revolutions would gradually subside.

When Citizen Genêt arrived in Charleston, Pinckney joined the city in giving him a grandiose welcome. Later, when Genêt attacked Washington, Pinckney withdrew his support of Genêt. South Carolina tended to be pro-French because it still remembered the depredations by the British troops during the American Revolution.

In May 1793 Eliza Pinckney died in Philadelphia, where she had gone for treatment for breast cancer. Washington requested, and was granted, permission to be one of her pallbearers, apparently out of a desire to honor the Pinckney brothers. In 1794 Washington offered Pinckney the position of secretary of war, but he declined because of business and family demands upon his time.

In 1794 war against England appeared imminent over British interference with American shipping. The South Carolina legislature appointed Pinckney as major-general in charge of one of its two divisions. He enthusiastically plunged into raising and training his troops. When John Jay went to England to negotiate his treaty, Tom Pinckney was made envoy to Spain, where he negotiated the Treaty of San Lorenzo, which gave the United States unrestricted use of the Mississippi and a favorable boundary settlement in the Southwest on land adjacent to that held by Spain.

Although he privately disliked Jay's Treaty for being too favorable to England, Pinckney did not publicly speak against it, as did John Rutledge. When Edmund Randolph was removed as secretary of state, Washington offered the position to Pinckney in August 1795. Pinckney declined, alleging business reasons, but he did not want to support an unpopular and perhaps an unwise treaty. He also felt that he should not accept this post while his brother Tom was envoy to Spain.

To oppose both John Adams and Jefferson for the presidency in 1796, Hamilton, helped by Edward Rutledge, got Tom Pinckney to be a candidate. The plan was for Tom Pinckney to split the votes of the North with Adams and the votes of the South with Jefferson, and thus acquire more electoral votes than Adams and Jefferson.

Hearing of Hamilton's intrigue, Adams got many electors to vote for minor candidates. The electoral college count ended Adams 71, Jefferson 68, and Tom Pinckney 59. Ironically, by favoring Tom Pinckney, Hamilton helped elect his adversary Jefferson as vice president.

Angry at Citizen Genêt's dismissal and at the provisions of Jay's Treaty, France insisted that James Monroe be replaced as American minister. Washington offered the job to John Marshall, but he turned it down. Washington then asked Charles Cotesworth Pinckney to take the post.

In his letter to Pinckney, Washington said that the United States was torn by factions "more disposed to promote the views of another power than to establish a national character of their own." He warned that unless "virtuous and independent men of this country" were to serve their government in this crisis, it would "not be difficult to predict the consequences." Pinckney was the ideal man for the job, Washington said, because of his abilities and character, and because he was "acceptable to all parties."[28]

Edward Rutledge advised Pinckney to accept the position, and so he did. Pinckney had the necessary qualifications: he loved his country, and had served it on the battlefield and at the Constitutional Convention. As a successful lawyer, he knew international law. He was fluent in French, and had supported the French Revolution. He was, moreover, beyond the pale of petty party politics, which was tearing the nation asunder, partly to gratify personal egos and ambitions.

His mission had a stormy beginning. In a heavy Atlantic gale, Pinckney told the mate of their ship that he would support him in a mutiny against a rough and abusive captain. The mate led a successful mutiny and directed the remainder of the journey.

Pierre Adet, French minister to the United States, denounced Pinckney from the beginning as a tool of Hamilton and an enemy of France. To avenge Jay's Treaty, the French announced that they would treat American ships as Britain did — the alliance of 1778 was dead. Adet told Pinckney that unless he was replaced by a Jeffersonian, France would expand its policy of virtual warfare against American merchant ships.

Pinckney liked Jefferson, and Hamilton — in fact, anyone who would support a strong Union. He wrote in a letter to Secretary of State Timothy Pickering that "I ardently wish that we would banish all party distinctions and foreign influence, and think and act only as Americans."[29]

In December 1796 the French Directory told Pinckney that "it will no longer recognize nor receive a minister from the United States until after a reparation of the grievances demanded of the American government, which the French republic has a right to expect."[30] The chief grievances were the failure to support France in its war with England, and the pro-British aspects of Jay's Treaty.

In January 1797 Pinckney was ordered by the French government to leave France. His patience was finally exhausted. He not only felt personally insulted but he believed that this was an affront to his nation. His wife, Mary, was glad to leave Paris. They had been socially ostracized, there had been threats of arrest, and the cold, smoky apartments did not appeal to her.

In February they traveled by carriage to Amsterdam, waiting five months to learn what the United States government wanted done.

The XYZ Affair

Word finally arrived. President Adams had appointed Pinckney as chairman of a three-man mission to negotiate with France. The other members were Elbridge Gerry and John Marshall. Adams knew that commissioners do not negotiate well, being indecisive and disunited. But he had good sectional representation (with one each from the North, Middle, and South) and he felt that the two Federalists could handle Gerry, the Jeffersonian.

Jefferson wrote a letter to Gerry expressing pleasure at his appointment, saying that he was the only one of the three who could help preserve the peace. Earlier Jefferson had told Tom Pinckney that his brother's conduct "has met with universal approbation. It is marked with that coolness, dignity, and good sense we expected of him."[31]

Thomas Paine, as a foe of the Federalists, had urged that the Directory not recognize Pinckney. Although the Directory had their own reasons for their actions, "Paine, of course, claimed complete credit for Pinckney's difficulties."[32]

With not much to do in Amsterdam, Pinckney and Mary went to dinners and dances. They loved the waltz, the current rage, although they had some reservations about its decency. Pinckney would not permit their daughter Eliza to be waltzed, "unless occasionally in a country dance." Social life was greatly restricted for the Pinckneys, because the Dutch did not dare offend the ebullient French.

Reading untrue accounts in a French newspaper that he had been replaced by Madison, Pinckney wrote to Pickering that "if it is thought the service I was sent to perform can be better executed by Mr. Madison or any other gentleman, I earnestly request that no idea of delicacy with regard to me may prevent the nomination from immediately taking place. Act therefore in this case as the honor and interest of our country requires."[33]

Marshall wrote Washington that Pinckney worked ceaselessly to defend America's interests. Washington told Pinckney that his conduct was "universally approved" and "deserves to be so."

Unfortunately, Pinckney saw few grounds for compromise with France. The envoys had no leeway to make concessions, and the French were not in a conciliatory mood. Moderate legislators had been jailed or banished. Freedom of religion and of the press were curtailed by a ruling clique of ex-terrorists who had called upon Napoleon to help restore them to power. Firmness against the United States, as well as all foreign powers, was a sign they were using to keep themselves acceptable to the French populace.

When Gerry finally arrived at The Hague, Pinckney sent him advice on the best roads and inns, the proper bribe to be paid to get through French customs, and to wear a French cockade in his hat to prevent being stopped constantly by French authorities.

As he traveled towards Paris, Pinckney mused on how his attitude towards France had changed. France was now bullying many small European nations. Paris was rife with violence and disorder. If laws were not obeyed, would it pay to sign a treaty? Corrupt and power-mad men had betrayed the high ideals of the French Republic. Wondering whether Jefferson would preach "Love France!" if he saw what was happening, Pinckney came closer to the position of President Adams, who said that the French were "no more capable of a republican government than a snowball can exist in Philadelphia a whole week under a burning sun in August."[34]

Thomas Paine cautioned Talleyrand not to concede anything to the American envoys at their first meeting. Then he wrote a letter to the envoys, advising the United States to accept the status of an unarmed neutral. Marshall wanted to ignore the letter but Gerry wanted to give it serious consideration. Caught in the middle, Pinckney wrote a cautious and noncommittal reply to Paine.

On October 18, 1797, the envoys heard of the famous bribe offer. Jean Hottinguer, Talleyrand's agent, told them that the French would stop attacking American ships if four conditions were met: (1) President Adams should explain his remarks about France in his May 16 message to Congress, (2) the United States should reimburse its citizens for any

French debts due them, (3) the United States should assume financial responsibility for French spoliations of American commerce, and (4) the United States should give a loan to France and a bribe to the Directory, both of unspecified amounts.

The envoys asked for the specific amounts of the loan and the bribe. The next day Hottinguer gave them the terms in writing. The bribe was to be 1,200,000 livres, or about $250,000.

Pinckney and Marshall flatly refused the offer, but Gerry, feeling that preserving the peace would cost the United States some price, wanted to keep negotiating the demands. From here on the mission was divided, two to one. Adams admonished Gerry that he was doing precisely what he had been told not to do — split the mission.

After a great French victory in Austria, Hottinguer told the envoys that the Directory was "becoming impatient and would take a decided course with regard to America"[35] unless the demands were met. Pinckney said that a bribe was out of the question. Hottinguer replied that now that France was the supreme military power in the world, there was no more neutrality — a nation was either for or against France.

Gerry answered that if war comes, the whole world would know that France caused it. Pinckney observed that no American wanted war, but it would be preferable to permitting one's commerce to be destroyed by another power. Hottinguer warned that America should not align itself with Britain. Pinckney answered that America would do whatever was in her best interest.

Hottinguer returned to the bribe. Angry, Pinckney said that was a dead issue. Not in our opinion, said Hottinguer; what is your final answer?

"Not a sixpence!" shouted Pinckney defiantly. It is perhaps too bad that he really did not say what Robert G. Harper later attributed to him: "Millions for defense but not one penny for tribute."

Undiscouraged, Hottinguer said that the bribe money would be wisely spent. The wheels of French diplomacy, he explained, rarely moved without the driving force of money. He reminded the envoys of French assistance during the American Revolution. Pinckney and Marshall downplayed that contribution, stating that France was acting in its self-interest in opposing Great Britain.

With no permission to do so, Gerry negotiated privately with Talleyrand and his agent, Lucien Hauteval. Talleyrand said that the loan was the most important part of the demands. He reminded Gerry that since he and his colleagues were envoys extraordinary and ministers plenipotentiary, they were empowered to commit the American government at their discretion.

As time passed, Marshall weakened slightly and said that perhaps the bribe could be considered if the French would stop seizing American ships. An American banker, Mr. Bellamy, then represented Talleyrand and warned the envoys not to make public these demands.

The envoys, of course, kept Adams informed of the negotiations. When Adams submitted the correspondence of the envoys to Congress, he shielded the names by calling Hottinguer, Bellamy, and Hauteval simply X, Y, and Z. Hence the name, the XYZ Affair.

Adams was cheered when he told Congress that he would "never send another minister to France without assurances that he will be received, respected, and honored as the representative of a great, free, powerful, and independent nation."[36]

As a diplomat, Pinckney's strength was his loyalty to his country. His weakness was that, as a frank man of honor, he could not bend in his position. He would rather fight a war than be devious, or than sacrifice a principle. When Gerry continued to meet privately with Talleyrand and Bellamy, Pinckney and Marshall told him to stop the secret dealings, and finally Gerry did.

A niece of Voltaire, Madame de Villette, ran the boarding house where Gerry and Marshall lived. Marshall told his wife that Madame de Villette "generally sits with us two or three hours in the afternoon."[37] According to Mary Pinckney, she made the situation "very agreeable" for Gerry and Marshall, who did not know that she, too, was Talleyrand's agent.

She asked Pinckney to agree to the loan and when he refused, she said that she would use the Republican party in the United States to discredit the envoys. Talleyrand completely misread Pinckney, for threats only drove him further from the French position. A few days later Gerry was informed by the Directory that they wanted Pinckney sent home but the other two envoys were welcome to stay.

In January 1798 Marshall wrote a long paper defending America's neutrality. Later that month the envoys asked that their negotiations be placed on an official basis or else discontinued.

In a meeting with Talleyrand, Marshall learned that he and Pinckney were considered by the Directory to be lackeys of the pro-British Adams administration, and that they were no longer welcome as envoys. Pinckney chastised Gerry for ignoring Adams's directions in splitting the mission.

Desiring to have Pinckney and Marshall voluntarily return to America, Talleyrand sent the noted playwright, Pierre Beaumarchais, to tell them that they would find many powerful enemies at home if they did not accept the Directory's terms.

On March 21 Gerry said that he too would leave if his colleagues were expelled. On March 26 Gerry told Pinckney that he had decided to remain in Paris in order to work for peace. Gerry said that unless the United States accommodated France, Napoleon would do to New England what he had done throughout Europe.

Pinckney told Gerry that by remaining in Paris he would embarrass his country and add to the danger of war. Gerry accused Pinckney and Marshall of "not candidly communicating" with him. Pinckney's temper flared. If anyone has been secretive, it has been you, he charged. Gerry replied that Talleyrand had asked that their talks be kept secret. That is precisely the point, fumed Pinckney. Do you represent Adams or Talleyrand?

When tempers cooled, Gerry admitted that only his respect and fondness for Pinckney had convinced him to accept this appointment. Pinckney later wrote to Rufus King that he had "never met a man of less candor and so much duplicity as Mr. Gerry."[38]

Back in America, the Republicans, who controlled the House of Representatives, called Adams a warmonger for his preparedness attitude. Vice President Jefferson called his message of March 19 "insane." When the Republicans demanded to see the letters from the envoys, Adams not only gave them to Congress but had 10,000 copies of them printed and distributed to the public.

When the readers saw the French corruption and duplicity, Adams, Pinckney, and Marshall became heroes, and Gerry was lucky he stayed behind in Paris. In April Pinckney received passports and permission to remain in southern France while Mary convalesced from illness.

The General

In the war preparations Adams got Washington to once again serve as commander-in-chief. Washington recommended Pinckney as second in command, since he had a good military record, he was from the South (where the French would probably attack), and he would not want to serve under Hamilton. Later, when Hamilton protested, Washington recommended that the three top generals under him should be, in order, Hamilton, Pinckney, and Henry Knox. From Washington's letter to Hamilton, it appears that he wanted Hamilton to cede second place to Pinckney, for he made a long list of Pinckney's military achievements.

Hamilton's response was to point out his own many qualifications for the position. Hamilton ignored Washington's point that many political supporters would be lost to the Federalist cause if Pinckney were listed under Hamilton.

Knox was furious, refusing to serve under Hamilton, and predicting that Pinckney would do likewise.

Both Washington and Knox had misread Pinckney. He not only agreed to serve under Hamilton but said that he would serve under Knox too if Knox would accept. It was typical of Pinckney to put the cause of America ahead of his own ego gratification. In 1778, during the Georgia campaign, he was the only top officer who was not rank-conscious. In 1794 he had not complained when Andrew Pickens was chosen over him to command the troops of South Carolina. He acquiesced readily when he thought Madison had been appointed to replace him in Paris. He was the kind of American leader who put his personal glory second to what seemed best, in the opinion of others, for the betterment of his country. As a patriot, his only match was Washington.

In August 1798 Pinckney returned to America, to find that he had been commissioned a major-general on July 25. He met with Washington, Hamilton, and Secretary of War James McHenry to discuss overall war plans. Pinckney was to command all troops in Virginia, North and South Carolina, Georgia, Kentucky, and Tennessee.

Everywhere he was feted as a hero of the XYZ Affair, but Charleston outdid all other towns. A small fort near Charleston was named "Fort Pinckney, as a tribute of respect for Major-General Pinckney, our late envoy to the Republic of France."[39] A new musical composition appeared: "General Pinckney's March."

Edward Rutledge, who had supported Jefferson for president in 1796, now switched over to the Federalist camp. Now all of the Rutledges and Pinckneys were Federalists except Charles Pinckney, who continued to be his cousin's chief adversary.

The undeclared war against France lasted two years. There were no land battles, but the Navy's 45 ships and 365 privateers captured 84 French vessels, in retaliation for French interference with American shipping.[40] The overthrow of the Directory by Napoleon and two other consuls in November 1799 ended the threat of an all-out war. The peace treaty was signed on October 1, 1800.

Clutching at straws, the Republicans decided to attack Federalist Pinckney with rumors and innuendo. When five French citizens were found aboard the Danish ship *Minerva* in Charleston Harbor, Republicans implied that one of the women was Madame de Villette, that Pinckney had got her pregnant in Paris, and that she was pursuing the errant father. The rumor mongers failed to observe that this woman was a mulatto, and that all five French people were on their way to join a slave insurrection in Santo Domingo against the French government there.

As might be predicted, Pinckney opposed both the Alien and Sedition Acts of Adams and the Kentucky and Virginia Resolutions of Jefferson and Madison. William Vans Murray, the new minister to France, "was puzzled because both Pinckney and Marshall opposed the Alien and Sedition Acts, despite their harrowing experiences in France. It evidently did not occur to Murray that their experiences in France made both generals more determined than ever to preserve free men's rights in the United States."[41]

The deaths of Washington in 1799 and of Edward Rutledge in 1800 robbed Pinckney of two of his best friends. With his partnership with Rutledge dissolved, some of Pinckney's prestige dwindled in South Carolina.

The Presidential Candidate

Who would be the Federalist candidate for president in 1800? Adams was unpopular because of the Alien and Sedition Acts, his troubled foreign policy, and his alienation of certain Federalist leaders. Secretary of State Pickering felt that a ticket of Pinckney and Oliver Ellsworth would draw support from all over the country. Hamilton wanted the nomination, but dared not campaign openly against Adams.

Doubtful that he could get the nomination for himself, Hamilton plotted to defeat both Adams and Jefferson. He urged the Federalist caucus in Philadelphia in May 1800 to pledge every elector to support Adams and Pinckney equally. This, he felt, would elect Pinckney, since many southerners would vote for Jefferson over Adams.

To discredit Adams, Hamilton prepared a letter of his faults and gave it to faithful Federalists. But Aaron Burr managed to get a copy of the letter and made it public. Adams and his supporters fought fire with fire. First of all, Adams fired Hamilton's two friends, Pickering and Secretary of War McHenry. Then, he disavowed Pinckney as a running mate, which had the effect of bolstering Jefferson's candidacy. In those days it would have been possible for the president and vice president to merely switch jobs.

Hearing of the intrigue, Pinckney lost faith in Adams. He knew of Hamilton's plan to get him elected, "but he was unwilling to be elected on the basis of deceit in the North and broken promises in the South."[42]

To discredit both Adams and Pinckney, the Republicans dredged up a letter Adams had written in 1792 to Tench Coxe, later commissioner of revenue, in which Adams alleged that both Pinckney and his brother Tom had plotted to have Tom replace Adams as minister to England in the 1780s. This letter hurt both Adams and Pinckney in the election, even though Tom Pinckney wrote to show that the letter was either a forgery or else referred to Charles Pinckney.

To keep the Federalist party united during all of this civil war, Pinckney publicly asked every Federalist who voted for him to also vote for Adams. Secretary of the Navy Benjamin Stoddert predicted that if Pinckney "should defeat himself, he will gain by the defeat. It will be the noblest revenge for the imprudent letter of Mr. Adams."[43] In effect, Pinckney was squelching Hamilton's plan, for if South Carolina gave Adams as many votes as Pinckney, Adams would be elected.

Tom Pinckney got Charles Pinckney to admit that he had seen the letter in 1792, but had failed to show it to his cousins. Under attack, Adams said that he knew no Pinckneys in 1792, but that since Charles Pinckney was in Congress at that time, he must have been the Pinckney referred to in the letter. The public was so thoroughly confused by now that the Republican strategy worked effectively in helping get Jefferson elected.

In all of this mudslinging, only Pinckney remained aloof. He was so universally respected that the Republicans offered to run him for vice president on their ticket (which might have got him elected president!). Pinckney refused, saying it would be disloyal to Adams to be a vice presidential candidate on both tickets.

Actually, in South Carolina Pinckney had such a strong following that there the Republicans settled for a Jefferson-Pinckney ticket. Had 13 more South Carolina legislators consistently supported the Federalist ticket, it would have carried the state. According to Henry De Saussure, later chancellor of South Carolina, the South Carolina legislative committee offered Pinckney "enough electoral votes to give him the presidency. Pinckney replied that he did not want the presidency as a result of intrigue."[44] He said that if people could not vote jointly for Adams and him, they should vote their convictions. He found it hard to recommend Jefferson after seeing the party fervor that Jefferson had fomented against Washington.

On the eve of the election, too late to affect the outcome, Adams finally supported Pinckney. His letter, published on October 29, said: "It is but justice and duty in me to declare that I have not the smallest reason to suspect you or your brother ever solicited any appointment under the government — that the whole conduct of both has shown minds able and independent, wholly free of any kind of influence from Britain or any other country, and both have rendered with honor and dignity great and important services to our country. I will add in the sincerity of my heart that I know of no two gentlemen whose characters and conduct are more deserving of confidence."[45]

In South Carolina Charles Pinckney led the attack against his cousin. A military man would not make a good president, he said in blitheful disregard of Washington. His anti-French stand would hurt

America, it was alleged, and furthermore he was a stooge for Hamilton who was trying to win South Carolina away from its Republican roots. The Federalists, who nicknamed him "Blackguard Charley," suspected him of getting Tench Coxe to publish the letter by Adams that allegedly attacked his cousins.

Despite his diffidence towards campaigning, Pinckney did well in the election. The electoral votes in 1800 were Burr 73, Jefferson 73, Adams 65, and Pinckney 64. It is likely that had he employed modern campaign ethics, he would have been elected president.

To test his strength in South Carolina, as well as to attract voters onto his ticket, he also ran for the state legislature in 1800. He won in Charleston 623–387, and was also elected by two other parishes, safety insurance in case he lost in Charleston. No party man, he refused to head the Federalist party in his state, and so party leadership went to his nephew, John Rutledge, Jr.

Pinckney was still a wealthy man. In 1801 his taxable property was three homes, 89 slaves, and 6524 acres of land. Jointly with the estate of Edward Rutledge he owned 230 slaves and 5720 acres of land.

As a state senator, Pinckney sponsored legislation to establish a state college, and a court of inferior jurisdiction in Charleston. He was chairman of the military committee and of the committee to revise the state's gambling laws.

As time passed, his influence waned. In 1803, over his protest, the state was redistricted so as to benefit Republicans. When his senate term expired in October 1804, his public career in South Carolina was at an end.

He and Mary spent the summer of 1803 in New England, to benefit Mary's health. Pinckney renewed friendships with many New Englanders. He consoled Hamilton over his son's death in a duel. He received an honorary doctor of laws degree from Harvard. Like any fair-minded Federalist, he supported the Louisiana Purchase, and agreed that the world had not ended with Jefferson's election.

In February 1804 he was selected as the Federalist candidate for president, with Rufus King for vice president. Amendment 12 to the Constitution, then in the process of being ratified, required that votes for the two offices be separate.

He was selected, not because the Federalists felt they could beat Jefferson, but because his choice offended no one and thus kept the party unified for a future election. He was a perfect "caretaker" candidate, uniting the South with the North. Moreover, his sturdy patriotism helped counteract the charge that some Federalists in New England were hatching a secessionist plot.

Pinckney was probably the least publicized candidate in the history of presidential elections. Most people did not know that he was running. All they knew of him, at the moment, was that he was conducting a crusade against dueling. This was an outgrowth of not only the two Hamilton duels but also the fact that he had dueled Daniel Huger in 1785, and had twice served as a second at other duels. The electoral vote in 1804 was 162-14 for Jefferson.

In 1808 Pinckney did no campaigning at all. Governor Charles Pinckney got a friend of his to attack his cousin in a series of newspaper articles in Charleston in October. There were some old and some new charges. His military background was still used against him, and he was said to be too old and out of touch with current national issues. He was described as a good lawyer but an incapable statesman. Madison, who did little campaigning in his own right, beat Pinckney 122-47 in the electoral college.

Final Years

As usual Pinckney took his defeat gracefully. He took part in no more elections. When the War of 1812 broke out, he offered to do everything he could to help, and admonished fellow Federalists who failed to support what he called "America's War" — not Madison's. Tom Pinckney accepted the position as major-general in command of the southern forces.

Pinckney found time in his final years for community activities. Although he did not gamble, he served two years as president of the local jockey club. He had a term as president-general of the Society of the Cincinnati. He remained active in the local library, museum, and agricultural society. He supported deep-sea fishing to give variety to his slaves' diet.

In 1810 he was a leader in establishing the Bible Society of Charleston, which became affiliated with the American Bible Society in 1817. With his close friend, Baptist minister Richard Furman (after whom Furman University is named), he worked to eliminate dueling and to bring religion to the slaves. In his will he set aside ten guineas each year so that a minister could be hired to preach a sermon each May and October on "The Greatness and Goodness of God."

A lavish host, Pinckney specialized in entertaining sick friends who were convalescing. He engaged in philanthropy, and gave many gifts to Tom's sons. Since he lived so long, in his final years he gave information about the nation's formative years to many historians.

When Lafayette visited Charleston in March 1825, he and Tom rode in the parade honoring the illustrious Frenchman. He suggested that perhaps his nephew Daniel Horry might marry Lafayette's niece Elenore. He died on August 16, 1825, at the age of 80.

Christopher Gadsden, who knew him well, said that "his private life was exemplary as the head of a family, the kindest of brothers, a sincere and constant and generous friend, a good citizen, fulfilling alike his duties to the government and to the community, and placing his great influence firmly on the side of law, order, morality, and religion."[46]

His mother, had she lived, would have seen that indeed he had been "worthy of such a father" as his. He is best seen as a reflection of his ideal, Washington. Like Washington, he was a good, if not a great, military leader. Both men had courage and undying love for their country. Neither had time to engage in petty politics or personal ego trips, for a country had to be founded and there was work, and honor, enough for all. Had Pinckney not been such a good man, perhaps he would have been what the world vulgarly calls a great man. Inscribed in his epitaph are the words: "Maintained the principles of the Constitution."

11. Edmund Randolph: The Conscientious Moderate

Edmund Randolph, the man who presented the Virginia Plan which after much alteration became the United States Constitution, refused to sign the historic document. Washington, after getting Randolph to be secretary of state, did his best to get Randolph to resign. All of his life Randolph was accused of being indecisive, of being a mugwump who was never deeply committed to any one position. Was Randolph conscientious as he threaded the maze of Revolutionary controversy, or was he wishy-washy, a straw easily tossed about on the waves of circumstance?

His uncle, Peyton Randolph, has been called "probably the most intimate friend Washington ever had."[1] Peyton Randolph was an early Revolutionary leader. In 1754 he was appointed by the Virginia House of Burgesses to argue against the levying of a pistole fee on every land-patent, and won the case. He helped drive the Indians back to Fort Duquesne. He wrote the protest for the Burgesses against the Stamp Act, but he voted against Patrick Henry's violent resolution for separation. He became speaker of the House of Burgesses in 1766. In 1773 he was named chairman of the Colonial Correspondence Committee, and the following year of the Virginia Convention. He was elected unanimously to serve as president of the Continental Congress in 1774.

When Peyton resigned as king's attorney in 1766, he was replaced by his brother John, who had married Ariana Jennings, daughter of the king's attorney in Maryland. John's mansion, Tazewell Hall, had the largest library in Virginia. John, who played the violin with Jefferson, had made a curious compact with him: If John survived Jefferson, he was to have £800 worth of volumes from Jefferson's library, but if Jefferson survived John, he was to have John's violin, plus all the music that John had composed for the violin. An able lawyer with courtly manners, John was on the Williamsburg city council and was clerk of the House of Burgesses.

Edmund, the son of John and Ariana, was born on August 10, 1753. Popular and good-looking, Edmund was fond of his two pretty sisters.

They had an idyllic childhood, like the charmed children in a fairy tale. They were loved by not only their parents and Uncle Peyton and Aunt Elizabeth but also by the constant stream of distinguished visitors to Tazewell Hall, which included Washington and Jefferson, among many others. They lived 100 steps from the House of Burgesses and the General Court, so they often visited there.

At the age of ten, Edmund attended the grammar school run by William and Mary College. The classes, dealing chiefly with the classics, ran from 7 a.m. until 6 p.m., with a brief midday break. Edmund took music and dancing lessons, and played such boyhood games as trap ball, pall-mall, and foot races. As a boy of 15, Edmund wondered why his father refused to sign the Virginia Association, a pledge to boycott English goods, when Uncle Peyton had been one of its sponsors.

At the age of 16 Edmund enrolled in the school of philosophy at William and Mary College. Six months later he won one of the two student scholarships. It carried a stipend of £30, plus free board and tuition for a year. The following year he won it again, and gave a student oration honoring the founders King William and Queen Mary.

In the fall of 1772 Randolph resigned his scholarship and left college, never to return. Instead, he began the study of law under his father. He entered the Williamsburg Masonic lodge in March 1774, and was qualified to practice law that summer.

As a lawyer he soon had many cases, for he had a reputation for legal accuracy and exact thinking. When Jefferson was elected to the Virginia Convention, he transferred his pending cases to Randolph.

The Patriot

Randolph's tranquil youth was disturbed by the drums of war. In April 1775 Governor Dunmore removed the gunpowder from the public magazine in Williamsburg. In May the Continental Congress assumed the responsibilities for military operations throughout the colonies. On August 15 Randolph was appointed aide-de-camp to Washington, with the assignment of copying Washington's important correspondence. Later he was given the job of writing rough drafts of letters for his commander.

Feeling that his oath as king's attorney was binding, John Randolph sailed with his family for England in September. Edmund remained in Washington's camp. John told Peyton to sell his property, pay his debts, and send the remaining money to England. Slightly more than a month later, Peyton died of an apoplectic stroke, and Edmund came home to help Aunt Elizabeth settle the estate.

In appearance, Randolph had a noble stature, dark eyes, and a handsome face. His voice was pleasant, and his facial expression indicated a kindly heart. His elegant language indicated a wide reading background. In later years he tended to be portly.

The Continental Congress appointed him mustermaster for the Williamsburg district in early 1776. Elected to the Virginia Convention in April, he was the youngest member. Here he served on many committees and also on the Admiralty Court. In May, when the Convention instructed the Virginia delegates in Congress to propose a declaration that "the United States are free and independent states," Randolph was put on the committee to draft a declaration of rights.

He was also appointed attorney-general (the job his father had held under the title of king's attorney), but the position carried few responsibilities. His chief function was to provide legal advice to state officials, so he now had time to resume his private law practice. Although he was a personal friend of Patrick Henry, he often opposed him at the bar.

In August 1776 he married Betsy Nicholas, daughter of Virginia Treasurer Robert Carter Nicholas. Born within 12 hours of him, she had attended his elementary school. Although their families were rivals, her "cheerfulness, good sense, and benevolence" won Randolph over to her.

In November he was elected mayor of Williamsburg, and the town also appointed him to decide questions concerning Tories' properties.

At the age of 24 Randolph was named the rector of William and Mary, meaning that he was now the presiding officer of the college from which he had dropped out. When he was appointed by the Virginia Assembly as a delegate to the Continental Congress in June 1779, he retained his job as attorney-general but relinquished his role as clerk of the House of Delegates.

Randolph was present at the battle of Stony Point, which he described in a letter to Jefferson on July 27, 1779. In that letter he asked Jefferson for his ideas on the conditions for peace with England. Since he knew French, letters from France to Congress were often given to him to translate. He resigned from Congress in 1779 in order to return to his Virginia law practice.

Because the British navy threatened Williamsburg, the capital was moved to Richmond in 1780. The Randolphs moved there in January 1780, but had to leave before General Benedict Arnold and his British troops burned Richmond on December 30, 1780.

The Randolphs returned to Richmond, where Betsy bore their first child, a son Peyton, in February 1781. When Lord Cornwallis moved his troops toward Richmond, the legislature moved west to Charlottesville. There a raiding party of Cornwallis's men nearly captured the Virginia

Assembly in June 1781. Another westward move for the legislature put it in Staunton. The Virginia troops under Lafayette fought a purely guerrilla war against the British, avoiding a direct confrontation because of inferior numbers.

The Legislator

On June 13, 1781, Randolph was elected to the Continental Congress by the Virginia Assembly. He disliked leaving Betsy and the baby in so dangerous a place as Virginia at that time.

Arriving in Philadelphia, Randolph noted the decline in the quality of current congressmen. On the whole, he felt, they were a sincere but ineffectual lot. He became a close friend of James Madison, and tried to get the Congress to pay Madison, for it was greatly in arrears in paying delegates.

Congress was carefully scrutinizing the Articles of Confederation, seeking for ways to get more authority for doing its job. Because of his experience on the Admiralty Court, Randolph was placed on a committee to set up a national court of appeals to handle admiralty cases. He drafted an ordinance to determine "what captures on water shall be legal."[2]

Randolph was appointed to a committee to see how to strengthen the federal government by getting better support from the states. Among the 21 recommendations were to levy an embargo, to appoint tax collectors, and to seize state property when states fell behind in meeting requisitions. Congress did little with these recommendations except to suggest that states impose separate taxes to meet requisition quotas. Randolph wrote this final resolution.

His fortunes improved that fall. In September he was cheered by the arrival of Betsy and the baby in Philadelphia. On October 24 news arrived of the surrender of Cornwallis at Yorktown. Randolph moved that Congress go in procession to the Dutch Lutheran Church and thank God for the success of the allied arms of the United States and France.

Randolph was a close friend and relative of Jefferson, who, being ten years older than he, had been a good friend of his father. They fought for similar values during the Revolutionary period. When Jefferson was accused of cowardice for fleeing the governor's mansion under Arnold's attack, Randolph sprang forward as his champion.

In October 1781 Randolph wrote to Jefferson, begging him not to sequester himself from public life. Later he urged Jefferson to accept a mission to France. Randolph bought the Collé estate near Monticello, and the families often visited each other. When Jefferson's wife's death hit him hard, Randolph consoled him and encouraged him to re-enter the public arena.

In December Randolph wrote, on behalf of Congress, a circular letter to the states, urging compliance with requests for men and money. Also that month he wrote, for Superintendent of Finance Robert Morris, the ordinance incorporating the Bank of North America. Morris was doing what Congress could not do—harnessing private credit to help finance the nation.

In January 1782 Randolph chaired a committee which authorized the American minister in Paris to sign a consular treaty with France. He worked several months on a ponderous report on fisheries off the Newfoundland coast, but Congress took no action on it.

He took his family in March 1782 back to Virginia, where he was still attorney-general. By now a nationalist, he found the state absorbed in solving local problems. Washington's letter for funding was interpreted by many Virginians as an unsolicited intrusion.

Since the last stages of the War had been fought in the state, there was much property destruction. Virginians began venting their spleen upon loyalists. Some people attacked British sympathizers, others stole their property. As attorney-general, Randolph had little use for lawbreakers on either side.

In October 1782 the Virginia Assembly repealed a law granting a 5 percent duty on imports, as requested by Congress. Randolph was angry to see Virginia's parochial outlook. He realized, however, that the state was struggling to meet its requisition quotas, pay its war debts, and deal with its currency problems.

When Aunt Elizabeth died in late 1782, her estate was supposed to go to John Randolph in London. Edmund used estate money to pay his father's remaining debts, but he refused to break up slave families by selling them. Rather than do this he paid out of his pocket the equivalent money to his family in London.

That year he won a case, as attorney-general, that he wished he had lost on constitutional grounds. In line with the Virginia constitution, the House of Delegates had pardoned three men found guilty of treason. The Virginia Court of Appeals voided the pardon on the basis of a state treason law. Randolph would have preferred having the Court of Appeals declare the law unconstitutional, for he felt it was a faulty precedent for a legislative act to overrule a constitution.

In order to complete a report on Virginia's western lands, he resigned his seat in Congress in December 1782. He now was kept busy with a wide variety of law cases: writing wills, collecting bills, advising businessmen, defending criminals, among others. "His practice was said to be the largest in Virginia,"[3] and his law income second only to that of the famous Henry Tazewell. Overwork, however, left him subject to colds and other respiratory ailments.

When John Randolph died in London in early 1784, Randolph became heir to Peyton Randolph's three farms. But he also inherited the debts of his father and his uncle, including the obligations due his sisters under Peyton's will. Betsy urged him to sell Peyton's slaves to meet these obligations, but once again he refused to have a hand in breaking up black families. He thus derived little benefit from his uncle's will, for the income from the farms barely paid for the cost of maintaining the slaves.

In a letter to Jefferson in April 1784, Randolph cast doubt upon the value of the Society of the Cincinnati. He also decried the use of violence against British subjects, one of whom had been tarred and feathered despite the fact that he carried a permit signed by the governor of Virginia.

Patrick Henry, noting a decline in morality in Virginia, made an effort to get the Assembly to once again establish a state church. This time Henry was helped by the Presbyterians, who felt that they might share income with the Anglicans. Religious fervor brought tempers to a boil in 1785.

Like his father and Uncle Peyton, Randolph was a deist, who believed not in the personal God of Christianity but in God as a First Cause and the Prime Mover of the universe. At the time of the Revolution, chief Virginia towns like Williamsburg and Fredericksburg were the colonial centers of freethinking.[4] Jefferson and George Wythe played chess on Sunday at Tazewell Hall until Betsy put a stop to it.

Outwardly an Anglican, Randolph recognized that the Church of England had grown affluent and lazy, but that "the Presbyterian clergy were indefatigable. They understood the mechanism of haranguing, and have often been whetted in dispute on religious liberty."[5]

Randolph liked to kid Madison about his being a Methodist. Together the two decided to set as their goal the adoption by the Virginia Assembly of Jefferson's Statute on Religious Freedom. Madison concentrated on changing the Presbyterian position, and Randolph worked on the Anglicans. Thus, instead of Patrick Henry getting an established church for Virginia, he saw the legislature adopt a far-sighted protection of freedom of worship according to one's conscience.

George Washington's business affairs in Virginia were entirely entrusted to Randolph. Much as he needed money, Randolph refused to accept payment from Washington for legal or administrative services. Through Randolph's efforts Washington received important additions to his estates, but when he tried to pay Randolph he was told: "Excuse me from accepting fees for any business which I may execute for you in the line of my profession. It is indeed a poor mode of acknowledging the repeated acts of friendship which I have experienced from your hands."[6]

The two men worked together on speculation concerning the development of waterways. Washington kept Randolph informed about the Potomac River Company, and Randolph did the same for Washington concerning the James River Company. In August 1785 Randolph wrote to Washington asking him to serve as president of the James River Company.

In January 1786 Randolph was chosen by the Virginia Assembly to head the eight-man delegation to the Annapolis Convention. The purpose of the Convention was to consult concerning uniform commercial regulations throughout the nation. Between March and May he worked hard to organize the delegation.

That summer the death of one-year-old John brought great grief to Randolph and Betsy. As an attorney, Randolph won an important case against John Marshall, who represented Lord Fairfax. Randolph won a decision for his client Isaac Hite, who had settled 54 families on land acquired from Fairfax.

When the Annapolis Convention opened on September 11, only 12 delegates from five states were present. Only three states (Delaware, New Jersey, and Virginia) had enough members present to meet the quorum requirements.

Randolph submitted a preliminary draft, which set forth the major conclusion of the Convention—that this group was too small to accomplish its purpose, and therefore the states should send delegates to another convention, where they would have the broad powers granted to the New Jersey delegates at this Convention, to consider "how far a uniform system of commercial regulations and other important matters might be necessary to the common interest and permanent harmony of the several states."[7] On his way home, Randolph stopped at Mount Vernon to tell Washington what had happened at Annapolis.

The Governor

On November 7, 1786, the joint houses of the Virginia legislature elected Randolph governor. He resigned as attorney-general and turned his large law practice over to John Marshall.

Washington sent Randolph his congratulations, adding that "our affairs seem to be drawing to an awful crisis. It is necessary, therefore, that the abilities of every man should be drawn into action in a public line to rescue them if possible from impending ruin."[8]

Randolph's salary as governor was £800 a year. He knew that the governor had little power. The state constitution said that the governor, with the advice of a state council, would execute the laws of the commonwealth, and "shall not, under any pretense, exercise any power or prerogative by virtue of any law, statute, or custom of England."[9]

Unlike Jefferson, Randolph was a vigorous governor. He inspected shipyards, checked on the preparedness of the militia, and gave meticulous orders on the conduct of the various government departments. He informed the House of Delegates that the militia would continue to be weak if the legislature insisted on selecting popular men rather than experienced ones as officers.

General George Rogers Clark had been high-handed in seizing Spanish property in Kentucky. When landowners there protested, Randolph and the council chastised Clark. This action helped prepare for later negotiations with the Spanish.

America, it seems, was having trouble in the Middle East. Randolph gave the good news to friends of James Mercier that he had found out that Mercier was not dead, as had been reported, but had been a slave in Arabia, and "lately redeemed by the American Consul."[10] A daughter, Edmonia, was born to the Randolphs in April 1787.

In 1787 Randolph wrote to an Indian leader, promising to punish white men who had killed some Indians: "Brother, why should we go to war? In the year 1781 we threw an axe into the pit, covered it with earth, and stood hard upon it. If I had chosen to dig up the earth, I might have demanded satisfaction for the burning of the women who were prisoners in the Chickamogga towns. But I thought it better to believe that these monstrous cruelties were hated by you because you are brave. I will cut up all thorns which grow in the path between us, and make it easy and safe for us to travel it together as brothers."[11]

In selecting delegates to the Constitutional Convention, Randolph and the Assembly chose some men who had an antifederal outlook, for they wanted to fairly represent the views of the people. They also felt that attending the Convention would be an educational experience for some of those whose views did not extend beyond Virginia.

There was always a great question of whether Washington would attend the Convention. In November 1786 he told Randolph he could not go to Philadelphia because he had already told the Society of the Cincinnati that he would be busy the next May. Washington admitted the urgency of the assignment: "However delicate the revision of the federal system may appear, it is a work of indispensable necessity. The present Constitution is inadequate. The superstructure totters to its foundations, and without help will bury us in its ruins."[12]

In his return letter Randolph pleaded with Washington to reconsider his decision. "What our enemies have foretold seems to be hastening to its accomplishment," Randolph said, "and cannot be frustrated but by an instantaneous union among the friends of federal government. The gloomy prospect still admits one ray of hope that those who carried on the revolution can yet rescue America from the impending ruin."[13]

In December Washington repeated that he declined the great honor, because of "other measures I had previously adopted." Randolph would not be put off, but wrote on January 4 that the council concurred with him in "entreating you not to decide on a refusal immediately."[14]

In March Randolph resumed his persuasion. "I must call upon your friendship," he said, "to excuse me for again mentioning the convention at Philadelphia. Every day brings forth some new crisis, and the Confederation is, I fear, the last anchor of our hope. I doubt whether the existence of that body through the year may not be questionable under the present circumstances."[15]

Finally the great man changed his mind. On March 18 Washington wrote to Randolph that "I have come to a resolution to go, if my health will permit, provided the Executive may not have turned its thoughts to some other character. I have of late been so much afflicted with a rheumatic complaint in my shoulder that at times I am hardly able to raise my hand to my head, or turn myself in bed. I hope your Excellency will be found among the attending delegates."[16]

Found among the papers of George Mason was Randolph's draft of a national constitution, somewhat different from the Virginia Plan which he introduced to the Constitutional Convention. Many of its features, however, were found in existing state constitutions.

This draft mentioned that the constitution should state essential principles only, lest the government be bound by inflexible details that ought to change as society changes. A preamble should show how the ineffectiveness of the present government made this Convention necessary.

The first resolution, stated the draft, should establish the national legislative, executive, and judicial departments, each independent except as specified. The legislature should be bicameral, with the House originating the money bills and the Senate approving treaties and appointing the judiciary. The Supreme Court would have jurisdiction over all cases affecting national peace and harmony.

In addition to its usual duties, the legislature elects the executive, the draft continued, which would consist of several persons. The House, elected by the people, would be the base of the government. It would elect the Senate, from persons nominated by the state legislatures. Judges would serve for life, on good behavior.

This draft is useful as an insight into many of the positions that Randolph took when these issues were debated in the Convention.

The Framer

On Sunday, May 20 the Virginia delegation attended mass at a Philadelphia Catholic church, "more out of compliment than religion," said Mason, "and more out of curiosity than compliment."[17]

Perhaps because he was governor of the state, Randolph was given the honor of presenting the Virginia Plan to the Convention, and sometimes it was referred to as the Randolph Plan. Although all of the Virginia delegates had a chance for input into the plan, it was believed that Madison was its chief architect.

Randolph's initial presentation of the plan was good. "If Madison's ideas fell on fertile ground," says a modern commentator, "Randolph did a convincing job of sowing them in his opening speech."[18]

Randolph had to assure the delegates constantly that this plan did not destroy the authority of the states. When Charles Pinckney moved that the national legislature be empowered to veto any state laws it considered to be improper, Randolph and Mason voted against the motion.

Unlike most delegates, Randolph favored an executive consisting of three or more persons, since a single executive smacked to him of monarchy.[19] On the other hand, because of his fear of "democratic licentiousness," he supported the move for a strong upper house.

By June 13 Gorham, for the Committee of the Whole, could report that already 19 resolutions had been agreed upon, most of them from the Virginia Plan. Randolph stuck to principles, even when they appeared to oppose his own interest. Appointed by ballot on July 6 to a committee to recommend the ratio of representatives to population in the House, Randolph challenged the committee as being unrepresentative, since all five elected members came from large states.[20]

Later, he opposed giving the legislature the power to decide how the House would increase in size as the population grew, for he felt that the legislature would not wish to dilute its power through expansion. As an alternative, he said that increase in size should be tied to the census figure, the method ultimately adopted.

Hearing complaints from small states that their views were being ignored, Randolph tried to concoct ways to protect their interests. One suggestion he had was that when cases affected them, the lower house would have only one vote per state. Another was that if a state or an individual felt harmed by a law, both would have appeal to the national judiciary.

Before he could introduce these proposals, however, the Great Compromise of July 16 had been reached, and Randolph was unhappy, for he said that all previous agreements had been based upon the idea that both houses would have proportional representation. He felt that the Great Compromise initiated such wholesale change that there should be a period of recess to allow both large and small states to reconsider their positions.[21]

On July 23 Randolph told why he believed that the Constitution should be ratified by the people in state conventions. It is their document, he argued, and therefore they should have direct input. Ratification by state legislatures opens up the process to local demagogues who would fear losing their jobs if the Constitution were adopted.[22]

Elected to the Committee of Detail on July 24, Randolph was assigned the enormous task of drawing up a preliminary draft of a constitution from all the Convention's work up to this point. He adhered closely to the resolutions that had been approved. Perhaps he had been chosen to write the preliminary draft because it was he who had initially introduced the Virginia Plan.[23] After Rutledge revised Randolph's draft, James Wilson had a major hand in drawing up the final version as reported back to the Convention.

Writing to Jefferson in Paris, Randolph said that he hoped that the Convention would do something about forcing states to pay their obligations to the federal government, since a "delinquent state makes itself a party against the rest of the Confederacy."[24]

When some delegates argued against having money bills originate in the House, Randolph strenuously opposed them, saying that the Senate was aristocratic and the executive monarchical — the people controlled the House, and thus should control their own purse strings.

In the contest between northern and southern states, Randolph, and the Convention, found a dilemma: unless South Carolina and Georgia could continue to import slaves, they would leave the Union; if they were given this right, "it would revolt the Quakers, the Methodists, and many others in the states having no slaves."[25] Randolph recommended referral of the dilemma to a committee to see if a compromise could be reached, and it was so done.

Increasingly Randolph came to feel that the smaller states were gaining too much influence for the good of the federal government. By August 29 he said that there were now features of the Constitution so odious to him that he doubted whether he could support it. On August 31 he expressed the hope that in the ratification process, states could propose amendments.

From this point on, Randolph was moody and uncooperative. On September 10 he listed his objections to the present form of the document[26]: (1) the Senate was now the court of impeachment of the executive, (2) the small size of the House of Representatives, (3) no limits to a standing army or to navigation acts, (4) poor delineation between federal and state legislatures and judiciaries, (5) Congress can tax exports and can fix their own salaries, and (6) the president's unqualified power to pardon treason.

To remedy these defects, Randolph recommended that the Constitution be sent to the state legislatures and then to state conventions having the power to accept, reject, or amend it. After that, there would be a final constitutional convention empowered to adopt or reject the suggested changes. When the Convention voted on Randolph's recommendations, it turned them down.

At the end of the Convention he said that he could not sign the Constitution unless there would be a second national convention. Was he expected, he asked, "to promote the establishment of a plan which he verily believed would end in tyranny?"[27] Randolph announced that he considered himself free to either support it or not, as his future judgment directed. He predicted that the required nine states to ratify would never be achieved, and the result would be confusion and unrest.

Most delegates thought that Randolph was simply covering his options in case the people opposed the plan. As he traveled homeward, Randolph was surprised to find that most of the people he talked to seemed to favor the new Constitution.

Whatever his motivation in refusing to sign the Constitution, there is no doubt that he was acting according to his principles. He knew that he was taking an unpopular step, one that would draw upon him much criticism. But he risked this disapproval knowingly, apparently because he had serious reservations about the final form of the document.

The Ratifier

By October Randolph was already beginning to change his mind. In a letter written in Richmond to Madison he said that "the opinions of Mr. Henry gain ground. He and I have had several animated discussions, but he recedes so far from me that we must diverge. The bar are generally against it, so are the judges of the General Court. I am persuaded that there must be strong exertions made to carry it through. The people of this town are still in rage for the Constitution."[28]

Richard Whately said that "the smaller the mind, the sooner it is made up."[29] It took a long time for Randolph to deliberate on this issue. The change came not when he thought that his complaints had been answered but when he thought of what would happen if the Constitution were to be turned down. Sensing that it was either this imperfect document or chaos, out of patriotism he surrendered his private preferences in the interest of national unity. George Mason, Patrick Henry, and other opponents of the Constitution now considered him to be a turncoat, a lost leader.

Randolph attached to his approval a request for a second national convention, something that made Madison and Washington uneasy. Madison pointed out that no two states agreed on the amendments they wanted. Randolph had to admit that the amendments requested by Massachusetts were dreadful, having the effect of either weakening the Union or harming the South.

In a letter to Madison in February 1788 Randolph showed that to say "no religious test shall ever be required for a national office" implied that Congress had power over religion. Randolph preferred the wording "Congress shall make no law respecting an establishment of religion, or prohibiting the free exercise thereof," as found in the Virginia amendments. Ultimately this statement became the First Amendment.[30]

The Virginia ratification convention opened on June 2, 1788. It was primarily a battle between Randolph and Patrick Henry. A letter was read from Jefferson in France, stating that he hoped nine states would ratify the Constitution and the other four refuse to do so until a Bill of Rights and certain other amendments were added. Had the convention followed Jefferson's advice it would not have ratified the Constitution, for, unknown to the convention, New Hampshire had become the ninth state to ratify, four days previously.

Henry attacked Randolph as inconsistent. Angry, Randolph said that he now believed that the preservation of the Union could depend upon Virginia's vote. Privately Randolph said of Henry that "his asperity is warranted by no principle of parliamentary decency, nor compatible with the least shadow of friendship, and if our friendship must, let it fall, like Lucifer, never to rise again."[31]

Henry then suggested that under this Constitution, the federal government might abolish slavery through the use of military force. Randolph again became angry. That, he replied, was an objection dishonorable to Virginia, that while securing its citizens' rights it should resent the fact that some day "those unfortunate men now held in bondage may, by the operation of the general government, be made free."[32]

Henry hinted that Randolph had switched sides from some hidden, and thus probably selfish, reason. Before Randolph could respond, "the convention compelled Henry to ask Randolph's pardon."[33] Randolph replied that "were it not for the concession of the gentleman, he would have made some men's hair stand on end, by the disclosure of certain facts."[34]

Now it was Henry's turn to get angry. Eyes flashing, he demanded either an explanation or a retraction. Ignoring him, Randolph produced his letter of October 10, 1787, for "the curious and malicious," which explained why he had previously opposed the Constitution. Pointing out a number of inconsistencies in Henry's remarks, Randolph called him "discourteous and malicious."[35]

Would there be a duel between the governor and the ex-governor? Henry's second called on Randolph that night, but fortunately tempers cooled down and there was nothing more violent than the verbal attacks. Before the convention voted, Randolph raised his arm and said, "I will assent to the lopping off of this limb before I assent to the dissolution of the Union."[36]

After the convention ratified the Constitution by a vote of 89-79, George Wythe, chairman of a committee on amendments, presented a list of 40 proposed amendments, 20 corresponding to the Virginia Bill of Rights and 20 apparently written by Henry and his colleagues. All 40 were approved and recommended to the Congress.

Governor Again

Ever so slowly, Randolph was learning that a judicious, thoughtful position of weighing pros and cons is unpopular during a time of crisis. Most people do not like to think. Blacks and whites are more easily grasped than greys. Randolph regretted the either-or dichotomy that was already beginning to dominate American political life.

By now Randolph had more principles than supporters. By not signing the Constitution, he had offended the federalists. By working for ratification, he had alienated the states' rights proponents. By standing up to Patrick Henry, he was no longer the friend of the old-line conservative patriots. The miracle was that, despite all this opposition, he served as governor of Virginia from October 1787 until November 1788.

Despite incomplete records, Randolph found that Virginia could substantiate proof to Congress on all but 8 out of 130 categories of reimbursable wartime expenses. Also, in ceding its western lands to the federal government, Virginia had reserved certain lands north of the Ohio River as grants to its wartime veterans. Randolph got the president of Congress to agree to live up to the original agreement.

When white settlers began moving into Cherokee lands in violation of the Treaty of Hopewell, Randolph asked Secretary of War Henry Knox to move the white settlers out. Knox promised to do so, but instead the Treaty of Hopewell was "adjusted" to accommodate the white settlers. The Cherokees were learning that some white folks spoke with a forked tongue and others were honest.

George Clinton, president of the New York ratification convention, sent a circular letter to Randolph asking if he would support a second Constitutional Convention. Unbelievably, Randolph said he would, and asked Madison for advice. Madison was solidly opposed to the idea and wondered whether Randolph would ever learn to stop championing lost causes. Randolph reminded Madison that many framers of the Constitution were anything but virtuous statesmen: "The management of some stages of the Convention created disgustful apprehension of the views of some particular characters. I reverence Hamilton because he was honest and open in his views."[37]

The Attorney-General

To support a second federal convention, as well as to have a hand in revising Virginia's state statutes, Randolph resigned as governor on November 12, 1788, and was immediately elected by the Assembly to fill a vacant seat. By the time he was seated, however, the Assembly had already approved Clinton's suggestion, and so Randolph could have stayed on as governor. Once more Randolph was favoring a lost cause, for Clinton's proposed second convention never met.

The chief legislation sponsored by Randolph affected the courts. He drafted bills re-establishing district courts, restructuring the High Court of Chancery, and separating the Court of Appeals from other state courts.

A baby girl, Lucy, became the fifth child of the Randolphs in 1789. The joy over the new arrival was dimmed by the revelation that Betsy had sores in her mouth that seemed cancerous, and no medical treatment seemed available.

On October 8, 1789, Randolph wrote Washington, thanking him for the appointment as Attorney-General. He hoped that perhaps Betsy could get medical attention in New York City. He asked Washington for a delay until March, to finish work in the Virginia Assembly on codifying state laws, and to get his plantations "on a proper footing" after he had made "two injudicious purchases of land made after the decline of its price."[38]

Most southern landowners were land poor. Between the ages of 22 and 42 Randolph had never been out of public office, and this was costly to him, for public salaries were low and private income largely unavailable. Randolph managed the business affairs of Washington and Madison with no compensation.

To get money, Randolph mortgaged his farm in Charlotte County to William and Mary College for £1200. As attorney-general his salary, set at $2000 annually by the Senate, had been reduced to $1500 by the House. Randolph asked Madison to rent a house for him in New York at $166 per year, but all Madison could find was one renting for $250 per year.

In March 1790 Randolph arrived home in Williamsburg to find Betsy carrying a 7-month-old dead fetus. Betsy feared she would die, so Randolph could not return to New York. On May 19 the premature birth of the dead fetus ended the crisis over Betsy's health. In August Betsy and the children joined him in New York, but the capitol was being moved to Philadelphia, and so Randolph went on ahead to arrange housing for them. During Randolph's frequent absences due to Betsy's ill health, Washington was remarkable for his patient concern and understanding. Once feeling he had missed too much time from his position, Randolph offered to resign, but Washington would not hear of it.

In March 1791 Congress raised his salary $400 per year. Randolph spent the money on better care of his slaves, after sending some of the money to his mother in England.

As an expert lawyer, Randolph occasionally had law students studying under him. Lawrence Washington, nephew of the President, soon showed more interest in a beautiful heiress than in the study of law, and so he left Randolph's tutelage. John Randolph of Roanoke (no relation to Edmund) already showed signs of mental instability as a law student. He nevertheless was eventually admitted to the bar, and years later when he was a leader in Congress he admitted that he had learned much about the English constitution from Randolph.

The House of Representatives, displeased with some portions of the Judiciary Act of 1789, asked Randolph to revise it. He came up with three suggestions: Federal circuit judges should be set up to relieve Supreme Court justices from serving there; and Congress should draw up a code of law for federal courts.

As attorney-general, Randolph ruled that a sheriff could not deliver election ballots after his term of office had expired. He also issued a mandamus to circuit judges in New York and Pennsylvania, telling them to hear pension cases, as requested by the President. In 1791 he aided Jefferson in trying to get Thomas Paine appointed postmaster-general.

Caught in a political crossfire, Washington asked his cabinet members for their opinions as to the constitutionality of a national bank. Randolph said it was constitutional but inexpedient. Jefferson called it unconstitutional because Amendment 10 stated that powers not specified were reserved to the states or to the people. Hamilton wrote a masterful refutation of both of these opinions and so two days later Washington signed the bill creating the national bank.

As Washington's personal legal adviser, Randolph recommended that he break his slaves' period of residency in Philadelphia before a six-month period expired, for at that time state laws gave slaves their freedom if they had residency for six months. Washington depended on Randolph so often for advice that Jefferson wrote to Madison that "the government is now solely directed by Randolph."[39]

As the animosity between Hamilton and Jefferson surfaced, Washington used Randolph as a neutral adviser to try to deal with issues on objective, rather than partisan, grounds. In March 1792 there was a question about whether a bill adjusting membership in the House of Representatives in accordance with the 1790 census was constitutional. Hamilton said it was, Jefferson said it was not, and Randolph agreed with Jefferson. Washington took their advice, and thus came the first bill ever vetoed by a president of the United States.

The case of *Chisholm v. Georgia* in 1792 brought out some interesting interpretations of the new Constitution. The state of Georgia issued an injunction to stop payment of money awarded a British subject by a federal circuit court. Randolph carefully defended his opinion that a state cannot overrule a federal court decision. Are states superior to individuals, he asked, and then replied, "The framers of the Constitution could never have thought thus. They had seen that legislators were not so far sublimer than other men as to soar beyond the region of passion. Individuals had been victims of the oppression of states. The present Constitution produced a new order. It derives its origin immediately from the people. If a state shall injure an individual of another state, the latter must protect himself by a remonstrance."[40]

The Supreme Court agreed with Randolph. James Wilson said that the people are sovereign, not the state of Georgia. Shall a state, he asked, "when summoned to answer a fair demand of its creditor, be permitted Proteus-like to assume a new appearance, and to insult him and justice by declaring, 'I am a sovereign state?' The sovereign when traced to his source must be found in the man."[41]

Justice William Cushing said that "the rights of individuals and the justice due to them are as precious as those of states. Indeed, the latter are founded on the former, and the great end of them must be to secure and support the rights of individuals, or else government is vain."[42] Chief Justice John Jay concurred, pointing out that in that very court Georgia was suing two citizens of South Carolina, and there was a correlation between the right to sue and the liability to be sued.

In 1793 Jefferson suggested switching Gouverneur Morris, minister to France, with Thomas Pinckney, minister to England, because of French complaints that Morris was befriending the deposed Louis XVI. When Washington asked Randolph for his advice, Randolph counseled waiting for the arrival of the new French minister, Genêt. Find out from

Genêt what specific charges the French have against Morris, Randolph suggested, and then give Morris a chance to respond to those charges.

Following Randolph's advice, Washington appointed William Paterson to fill the Supreme Court vacancy caused by the resignation of Thomas Johnson. Randolph was the first lawyer approved to practice before the Supreme Court.

Because Randolph seemed less partisan than Hamilton and Jefferson, Washington had Randolph draw up the Neutrality Proclamation of 1793. Should Genêt be received with no strings attached, even though France was at war with England, Holland, and Spain? Randolph agreed with Jefferson that he should, in accordance with the 1778 treaty with France. Secretary of War Henry Knox supported Hamilton's position that this would violate the Neutrality Proclamation.

To keep Hamilton and Jefferson from clashing, Washington followed Randolph's advice on enforcing the Proclamation through district attorneys, who reported to Randolph, rather than through customs officials, who reported to Hamilton.

In June 1793 two French privateers captured an English vessel, the *Little Sarah*, in American waters off the Virginia capes. Hamilton and Knox said that the vessel should be returned to England, in accordance with the Neutrality Proclamation. Before agreeing with Jefferson that the vessel need not be returned, Randolph gave Washington a detailed explanation of the conflicting precedents from international law. Since there was such a confusing labyrinth of conflicting laws, Randolph said, "nothing can lead through the labyrinth but an adherence to sound principle, which is always uniform. Upon principle, restitution ought not to be attempted."[43]

Making too much of a good thing, Genêt then outfitted the *Little Sarah* in an American port as a privateer, and sent it out to prey upon British shipping. Since this action clearly violated the Neutrality Proclamation, the question was, Should the United States ask France to recall Genêt for the violation? Jefferson was silent, Hamilton said that Genêt should be recalled, and Washington tended to agree with Hamilton.

Washington sent Randolph on a trip to feel the public pulse about the war between France and England. How do Philadelphia merchants feel about English vessels seized as French prizes in their harbor? How do Virginia people react to the Neutrality Proclamation?

Randolph reported that the public reacted according to the way it affected their pocketbooks. Wanting trade with England, Philadelphia merchants were pro-British. Virginia planters, on the other hand, seeking French markets, were pro-French. Washington was grateful for having an unbiased cabinet officer upon whom he could rely.

In Maryland Randolph found support for the federal policies. In Virginia many spoke against Hamilton, said Randolph, attacking him not so much for his policies as his personality. "The best administration upon the face of the earth," Randolph declared, "may be vilified and almost ruined unless they be protected by frequent and candid publications."[44]

The newspaper war, with Freneau supporting Jefferson and Fenno supporting Hamilton, was scarcely a "candid publication that protected the administration." Partly out of his friendship with Jefferson and Madison, and partly out of his conviction for freedom of the press, Randolph tended to support the right of a State Department employee (Freneau) to attack governmental policies.

In August 1793 John Jay and Rufus King published a statement in the New York *Diary* that Genêt had threatened to appeal his dismissal directly to the American people. Genêt asked the federal government to sue Jay and King for libel. Defending freedom of the press, Randolph refused to sue, feeling that there were no grounds.

Jefferson's pro-French proclivities now caused him to attack Randolph. In a letter to Madison on August 11, 1793, Jefferson said that "Randolph is the poorest chameleon I ever saw. With me he is a Whig, with Hamilton a Tory, and with the President he is what he thinks will please him. The last is his strongest hue, though the second tinges him very strongly. I have kept on terms of strict friendship with him, that I might have some good out of him, and because he has really some good private qualities."[45]

Jefferson also attacked Randolph in letters to James Monroe and W.B. Giles, leader of the Senate Republicans. In a letter to Giles in 1795 Jefferson said that Randolph was two-faced: he pretended to favor the people, but really did not; he pretended to favor a French treaty, but really did not; he pretended to favor an English treaty, but objected to the men chosen to achieve it.

Jefferson objected to those men (first Hamilton, and then Jay) even more vociferously than did Randolph. Jefferson was interpreting facts in his own way, in order to make Randolph look bad.

Of the 19 important issues that occurred while Jefferson was secretary of state, Randolph voted with Jefferson on 16. Of the other three, only one affected foreign policy, which was Jefferson's area. This one case involved striking out four words in Jefferson's letter asking for Genêt's recall. Randolph remained a true friend to Jefferson all of his life, apparently unaware that Jefferson was undermining him.

Was Randolph a chameleon or a mugwump? His contortions at the end of the Constitutional Convention and during ratification are hard to understand. Although he was decisive as a governor, as a counselor he sometimes seemed diffident. How can one understand such paradoxical behavior?

Elbridge Gerry described Randolph as daring "to think for himself and to speak his opinion without pouring libations on the altar of popularity."[46] Letters of Washington, Hamilton, John Adams, and Timothy Pickering indicate that Randolph took clear and decisive stands on many issues.

Hamilton suggested Randolph as minister to France at a time when it took the utmost courage to serve there. Although Randolph's vote had favored Jefferson far more often than Hamilton, the latter respected the independence of Randolph's opinion even when he did not agree with the specific stand.

Randolph's major flaw was that he lacked common sense. He was capable of repeating errors that a more sensible person could have easily avoided. But there was little bitterness or venom in his make-up.

Committed to government under principles of law based upon the Constitution, he was firm almost to the point of being obstinate. It would, however, be virtually impossible to impeach his motives. Beneath his complex personality lay a character grounded in solid values. Few of his legal opinions have been challenged as faulty, and none as shallow. With the mind of a judge he weighed and considered alternate equities. If his decisions were often slow, they were nearly always sound.

Yellow fever raged in Philadelphia in 1793. When Hamilton and his wife caught it, Randolph removed his family to Germantown, and then to Lancaster, sixty miles west of Philadelphia. On October 24 Randolph recommended to Washington that Congress move to Lancaster. He arranged for Washington's board, minus dinner, at $10 per week with a German clergyman near Lancaster.

The plague was so bad that courts were at a standstill. Needing money, Randolph considered returning to Virginia to practice law. To move to Lancaster, he had borrowed $150 from a Philadelphia merchant. He received a loan from Hamilton and was turned down on another from Jefferson. His credit was so poor that he could not act as guarantor for a loan for his brother-in-law Wilson Nicholas.

The Secretary of State

When Jefferson resigned as secretary of state he recommended Randolph as his replacement. Washington considered other possible candidates but either they did not want the position, like Madison, or were not good choices, like John Jay and Robert R. Livingston.

After being sworn in on January 2, 1794, by Justice James Wilson,

Randolph assured Washington that no party considerations would influence him in "this perilous office." He then wrote to Hamilton and Knox, promising cooperation with them and asking for their cooperation in return.

The Senate, considering Gouverneur Morris to be antirepublican in France, asked to see his correspondence. Washington followed Randolph's advice and gave the Senate that part of the correspondence germane to its legislative capacity, but withheld the part addressed to the executive which might have harmed the government by exposure.

In the ideological struggle concerning France and Britain, Randolph maintained a neutral stand, trying to do what was best for the nation. He was therefore of great value to Washington, whose goal was the same. Not coveting the presidency, Randolph could act more impartially than some of his more ambitious friends.

Randolph risked Washington's displeasure in opposing Hamilton as a special envoy to England. Hamilton declined Washington's offer, probably realizing that the Senate would not confirm his appointment.

Hamilton got into trouble for using funds for a purpose other than for which they were intended. Reminded of the problem, Washington remembered that he had sanctioned the use in a letter to Hamilton. Randolph was helpful in clearing the names of both leaders from any indication of wrongdoing. When Washington thanked Randolph, Randolph replied that "your character is an object of real affection to me. There is no judgment in which I ever had equal confidence. The people venerate you," because your unbiased mind is grounded in their welfare.[47]

The new French minister, Joseph Fauchet, brought orders from Robespierre's government to arrest Genêt. But Fauchet let Genêt escape, and he settled in the United States rather than risk an appointment with the guillotine. Seeing Fauchet's more moderate approach made Randolph feel that perhaps relations with France would improve.

Genêt, however, was still a problem. He organized a move to take Florida from the Spanish, with George Rogers Clark seizing Louisiana from the French. Washington prepared to send Anthony Wayne to block Clark from the lower Mississippi. Randolph advised caution rather than gunpowder, and fortunately both projects dissolved.

Randolph opposed Jay as a special envoy to England. The chief justice, he thought, should not look for "executive honors." If he accepts, Randolph said, he should first resign as chief justice so that there would be no intermingling of branches of government.

Tom Pinckney would make an excellent envoy to England, Randolph felt. When the power to negotiate a trade treaty was added to the role, Randolph was convinced that Jay would be so polite as to concede too much to the British. Randolph's judgment proved to be prophetic.

Kentuckians were arming themselves for possible conflict with Spain, which controlled the lower Mississippi. Seeking dialogue, the Spanish Commissioner Josef de Jaudenes asked for an envoy with "character, conduct, and splendor." Randolph recommended Jefferson, and tried to lure him out of temporary retirement with the offer. Jefferson, however, declined to serve, as did Patrick Henry when offered the job.

During the turmoil over the Whiskey Rebellion, Randolph kept Washington informed on both domestic and foreign affairs. Hamilton persuaded Washington to make a show of military force in order to discourage the rebels. Randolph felt that military might was warranted only after every legal and peaceful avenue of reconciliation had been exhausted. Eventually Randolph got representatives from both sides to settle their differences amicably.

To answer the attacks by pro-French Republicans upon Jay's Treaty, Randolph wrote a series of letters signed "Germanicus" in which he distinguished between French and American liberty. In France, laws were passed to muzzle the opposition. In the United States, the opposition was granted its voice. Randolph believed that in a republic, "unrepublican organizations could be effectually met by appeals to the reason and the heart of the people."[48]

In a letter written before Jay's Treaty was signed, Randolph had assured France that the United States would always be interested in the plight of countries pursuing liberty, such as France. Now Randolph was criticized from two sides: the pro-British thought he should not have called France a country pursuing liberty, and the pro-French accused him of a false friendship, since his country had agreed to a treaty that favored the British.

When Hamilton recommended Randolph as the minister to France to replace Gouverneur Morris, Randolph declined to serve. Some people wanted Aaron Burr, but Randolph vigorously opposed him. When Randolph suggested James Monroe, Monroe declined out of deference to Burr. When, however, Monroe learned that the position would probably go to William Paca of Maryland, Monroe accepted the assignment.

As Hamilton and Knox resigned in 1795, Randolph became the senior cabinet officer. But ironically a good deal of his function was now gone: there were no longer warring factions between which Washington needed a peacemaker.

Because he had no concealed depths, it must have been hard for Randolph to disguise his dislike of Jay's Treaty. Jay, he felt, had deviated from his instructions, giving up too much and getting too little in return. Specifically, Randolph felt that public opinion would oppose the treaty, and the pro-French Republicans, who scarcely needed it, would be given additional fuel to feed the fires of discontent.

In a letter to Washington in July 1795, Randolph mentioned retirement. He said that he would not serve under any other President, and he knew that Washington would not consider a third term. His wife was ill, Randolph added, and he needed to raise funds through a private law practice. If the enemies of your administration succeed in splitting the country in two, Randolph said, he would practice law in Philadelphia, for then "Virginia will not be, for me or my family, a proper country to dwell in."[49]

The Fauchet Affair

Joseph Fauchet, the French minister, realized that he would be fired because of the pro–British aspects of Jay's Treaty. In desperation he tried to get the Senate not to approve the treaty. Randolph warned Fauchet that he was invading American sovereignty by entering into public debate on current issues facing the President and Congress.

Randolph recommended to Washington that he not sign Jay's Treaty until the British order banning American trade to the West Indies was lifted. The British lifted the order, Washington signed the treaty, and the British reinstated the order.

The British now conspired to get Randolph fired as secretary of state. Foreign Office archives in London list the complaints of Lord Grenville's government against Randolph: (1) he falsely accused the British of stirring up Indian opposition, (2) his style "breathes a spirit of hostility" towards England, (3) his statement of friendship with France exceeds the intent of Congress, and (4) his list of American vessels supposedly taken by the British is "highly improper and inflammatory."[50] George Hammond, the English minister to the United States, told Jay that England wanted Randolph fired.

In March 1795 the British warship *Cerberus* captured the French corvette *Jean Bart*. A packet of papers thrown overboard from the *Jean Bart* was picked up by a boat from the *Cerberus*. Among other things, it contained dispatches from Fauchet to the French government.

The dispatches quoted Randolph as saying that Washington was the friend of France and the mortal foe of England. Hammond gave a copy of these letters to Oliver Wolcott, secretary of the treasury, and Wolcott shared them with Secretary of State Pickering and Attorney-General William Bradford. They showed the letters to Washington.

Two of Fauchet's dispatches seemed to be especially damaging to Randolph. In the sixth dispatch Fauchet quoted Randolph as asking Fauchet if he would make loans to four American flour merchants who were in debt to English merchants. These men, Randolph allegedly said, could pick up the information necessary to save the United States from a civil war, by showing that England had stirred up trouble in the American West in order to disunify the country.

In the tenth dispatch Fauchet sermonized on the ethics of the loans that were supposedly requested: "Thus with some thousands of dollars the French Republic could have decided on civil war or peace! Thus the consciences of the pretended patriots of America have already their prices! What will be the old age of this government if it is thus early decrepit? Such is the evident consequence of the system of finances conceived by Mr. Hamilton. He has made of a whole nation a stock-jobbing, speculating, selfish people."[51]

These intercepted letters were also a part of Lord Grenville's reason for wanting to have Randolph fired.

Washington had been away at Mount Vernon. When he returned he was distressed because Randolph had not written a memorial to England and shown it to the other cabinet officers. As a matter of fact, Randolph had written the memorial, given it to Pickering, and asked him to show it to Wolcott and Bradford. Pickering, or perhaps all three men, made it look as if Randolph had not carried out Washington's request.

On August 19, 1795, in the presence of Pickering and Wolcott, Washington asked Randolph to explain the references to him in the two dispatches. Before Randolph could respond, Washington asked him to leave the room while he consulted with Pickering and Wolcott. By the time he returned to the room, Randolph, furious, said to Washington: "Your confidence in me, sir, has been unlimited. When I find that confidence so immediately withdrawn without a distant hint being dropped to me, I hereby resign."[52]

In what may have been the gravest error of his career, Washington had completely misread Randolph's character, conduct, and intent. His belligerent attitude toward Randolph must have been based on the belief that Randolph had either passed confidential information to Fauchet, asked for a bribe for some American merchants, or both.

Washington is one of the few great men of history who were also good men. Had he committed many blunders like this mishandling of a trusted colleague he would not now be also considered a good man.

In his letter to Charles Cotesworth Pinckney inviting him to be secretary of state, Washington, said that the nation was in a "violent paroxysm," and he urged Pinckney to accept the position vacated by the disgraced Randolph.[53]

This blow ended Randolph's career, and cast a shadow upon his integrity. He spent the rest of his life vindicating his name and trying to recover from the shock administered to him by his close friend and idol.

To clear his name, Randolph asked Pickering for copies of letters from Washington to Randolph that were in the State Department files. Pickering gave him the copies, but a crucial one in which Randolph said he would delay signing Jay's Treaty until the British lifted the trade order was missing. When Randolph asked for the missing letter, Pickering refused to grant it, saying that his resignation was occasioned "solely by the evidence of his criminal conduct exhibited in Mr. Fauchet's letter."[54]

Randolph felt like a Greek protagonist whom the gods had decided to level. First, forced to resign for no good reason. Then, refused access to material that would help vindicate him. Now, being called a criminal by a former colleague! Two years later, himself now secretary of state and war with France imminent, Pickering said that Randolph's work had been flawless in handling diplomacy with France.[55] But of course it was too late—the damage had been done.

Determined to clear his name, Randolph chased Fauchet to Newport, Rhode Island, where Fauchet was embarking for France. Fauchet's ship left prematurely, to escape a British patrol boat. Randolph hired the swiftest sailing vessel in port and chased Fauchet's ship, but to no avail—the ship was too far at sea.

The next day the man who had piloted Fauchet's ship out of the harbor gave Randolph the letter that Fauchet had promised him. Randolph had asked if the phrase "pretended patriots" referred to him. Fauchet's letter declared, "I was mistaken in the propositions supposed to have been made by me. I declare, moreover, that no name or sum was mentioned to me; that Mr. Randolph never received, either directly or indirectly, by himself or by another for his use, one shilling from myself, by my order, or according to my knowledge from any other public officer of France. I declare that he never made to me in this respect a single overture."[56]

Fauchet's successor, Pierre Auguste Adet, having examined Fauchet's papers, publicly certified "that whensoever Citizen Fauchet has had occasion to speak of Mr. Randolph in respect to his morality, he always describes him as an honest and upright man."[57]

Randolph now started making a series of errors that sealed his doom. First of all, he attacked Washington publicly in a letter on October 8, and even gave the press a copy of the letter before sending it to Washington. In his attack, Randolph mentioned the letter of July 25 that Pickering had refused to give him.

Washington coolly replied that Randolph could have copies of any and all letters that Randolph had written to him, plus his replies. As for the vindication of his conduct that Randolph was writing, Washington said that he had no desire to receive it except through the press!

Abandoning his sound reasoning and his fair mind, Randolph now sounded like the most rabid of the pro-Republican attacks that Washington had endured from the Freneau press. In a letter to Madison on November 1, Randolph wrote that "among the objects which the President and his party have in view, one is to destroy the republican force in the U.S. I feel happy at my emancipation from an attachment to a man who has practiced upon me the profound hypocrisy of a Tiberius and the injustice of an assassin."[58]

Randolph then published a pamphlet vindicating himself from any charge of misconduct. Point by point he went over the disputed dispatches, showing how their information contained nothing that was not available in newspapers. He then showed that there were many secret pieces of information worth French gold which Fauchet knew nothing about. In a dispatch from Fauchet to his government on January 26, 1795, Fauchet had admitted that Randolph gave him no information of any kind, secret or not, that had been useful either in fighting off the consequences of Jay's Treaty or for any other French purpose.

This factual refutation of any dishonor attached to his name Randolph was certainly entitled to make, but the angry conclusion addressed to Washington was, however, unreasonable, ill-advised and counterproductive: "To yourself, sir, I can never appeal. Your conduct on August 19, your letter of the 20th, and the declaration of those who felt a persuasion that they were fighting under your banners have long ago proclaimed that you had been in an instant transformed into my enemy."[59]

Washington's handwritten comments on this pamphlet were two: "What controversy between us?" and "His declaration at all times on these subjects have accorded with my opinions." Madison said of Randolph that "his greatest enemies will not easily persuade themselves that he was under a corrupt influence of France." Jefferson added that "even those who did not know him will acquit him of the charge of bribery. Those who know him had done it from the first." General Horatio Gates agreed that "he had the most degrading and undeserved treatment."[60]

Historians George Bancroft and William Henry Trescot agreed that Randolph had been above bribery and had been poorly treated by Washington. Chief Justice Roger Taney was of the same opinion, as was Irving Brant, who said that Pickering and Wolcott were gullible tools of Hammond in Britain's effort to get Randolph fired.[61]

Not all reaction to Randolph's pamphlet was favorable. John Quincy Adams, a close friend of Randolph, was amazed at the pamphlet's indiscretions. Madison in public said that nothing of moment seemed to have been said concerning the president, and very little concerning parties in general. Randolph could not possibly have been corrupt, Madison added, but his own words condemned his political career. John Adams sent Abigail a copy of the pamphlet, calling it "a very weak thing, a piece of revenge against the President."[62]

As a secretary of state Randolph had shown a number of strengths. He was calm and unpartisan when Washington and the nation badly needed someone of such a temperament. He knew international law well, and brought this knowledge to bear on a number of touchy issues. He played no favorites between France and England, but sincerely sought to steer a neutral course, carrying out the policy of his president. His restraint helped keep Washington from making errors that Hamilton's rashness helped manufacture.

Randolph's chief weakness was an indecision that kept his actions from being firm and forceful. Lacking a theoretical base, his diplomatic point of view was somewhat shallow. For example, when Britain made mockery of American neutrality, he opposed it but had no notion of how to counterattack.

Nevertheless up to this point Randolph's career had been a record of unbroken successes. Never beaten in an election, he had filled the highest public offices with honor. Caught in a crossfire between Jacobins and Tories, between lovers of France and lovers of England, he had to be sacrificed in order to relieve some of the pressure caused by fanatics on both sides. It was little consolation to him that his adversary, the British Minister George Hammond, had been caught in the same crossfire and been similarly dismissed from his post.

Final Years

Randolph now returned to his private law practice. He found himself in constant demand because of his extensive knowledge of the law.

In November 1795 he gave his servants their free papers. All of them accepted them except the cook, who put them into the fireplace, saying, "I ain't agoin to do noffin of the kind. Ise goin to live and die with master."[63] She died in his service. Several of the old negroes, including a blind one, were cared for by Randolph's children.

It was hard for Randolph to refrain from efforts to vindicate his name and his honor. He returned to the topic in a pamphlet called *Political-Truth* in 1796. In it Randolph said that the United States tried to start anew, free from old world vice and corruption. But she needed friends in order to gain her liberty from England, and reliance upon France kept her free from complete freedom.

Some framers of the Constitution, Randolph said, kept it deliberately vague so that they could work their unrepublican principles into the government: "The funding system, the irredeemable quality of the debt, the national bank, are features borrowed from the British system."[64] These people, he said, seek to preserve the defects of the Constitution — its least republican features. Repeating his defense as stated in his previous pamphlet, Randolph defied any accusers to name any secret he had ever given to Fauchet.

Had Randolph been a demagogue, he would have supported Jefferson and Madison as they wrote the Kentucky and Virginia Resolutions in reaction to the Alien and Sedition Acts. But by 1798 he had recovered his composure. One set of unconstitutional acts was no way to protest another set of them, he told Madison. In another national crisis, he returned to conduct by principles.

Madison's Resolutions as originally passed by the Virginia legislature said that a federal law could be nullified if, upon protest of the state legislatures, people in three-fourths of the states agreed that the law was a faulty one. "To afford an opportunity for a clamor throughout the United States will be a dreadful catastrophe," said Randolph. Madison then withdrew the nullification authority from his statement.

A new plague descended upon Randolph. Pickering, his successor, charged him with a debt of over $49,000 "for moneys placed in his hands to defray the expenses of foreign intercourse." Jefferson's grandson, Thomas Jefferson Randolph, said that Jefferson "was perfectly satisfied that Randolph had been robbed by his clerks."[65] Nevertheless Randolph was billed by the government for the amount.

Wilson Nicholas, to whom Randolph transferred all of his estate, paid off the debt in four equal installments. But government clerks kept sending bills to the estate of Nicholas. In 1825 Secretary of the Treasury Richard Rush gave "full discharge" of the entire debt, since over $60,000 in cash had been paid to meet the debt. This did not slow down government clerks, who by 1887 showed that Randolph still owed a balance of over $61,000.

Two trials had been run concerning the debts, but jurors could never reach a verdict. So Randolph had told Albert Gallatin, secretary of the treasury under Jefferson, to choose two impartial arbiters. Gallatin chose Comptroller of the Treasury Gabriel Duvall, who had arrived at a figure of $53,000, including interest. Duvall's report contained not the slightest hint of embezzlement, but simply tabulated arrearages after all receipts and expenditures had been recorded. "Never," says John J. Reardon, "had the government shown such aggressiveness in settling the accounts of one of its former officials."[66]

In later years Randolph was active in community affairs. His main interests involved proposals to improve public safety or to expand educational opportunities. He remained active as a lawyer. In 1808 he handled nearly half of all cases that appeared before the Virginia Court of Appeals. The following year his total fell to 19 of the 62 cases.

His wife's health improved after he left political life. When she died in 1810, he was grief stricken. He said that she had anticipated his every need and met it. Afflicted with hemiplegia, he walked daily on his crutch to her grave. He found some comfort and consolation in the sermons of John Wesley.

His daughter Lucy married Peter Daniel, his former law student, who later became a justice of the Supreme Court. His son Peyton Randolph wrote a six-volume study, *Reports of Virginia Appeals Courts*.

Randolph now lived first with one daughter, then another, to fight off attacks of depression. Active in Masonic affairs, he served as grand master of the Virginia Lodge.

To earn some needed money, he applied for the job as clerk of the Virginia Court of Appeals in October 1810, but he was turned down because of his poor health. A court judgment of $4500 against him in 1812 led to the sale of his remaining slaves to pay the bill. He died on September 12, 1813, at the age of 60.

During his final years he worked on a six-volume history of Virginia, but only fragments of his manuscript survive. Of special interest is his tender treatment of Washington. No one else, said Randolph, could have led the expedition to defend the British forts in the West as well as he. His bravery and patriotism were unequalled. "In no adversity," Randolph now said, "had his honor as a soldier or a man ever been stained. He was himself a pattern of subordination."[67]

Like the hero in a Shakespearian tragedy, Randolph's catharsis was seen in the return of a man of high principle, honor, and integrity. Gone was the rancor toward the man he had most admired, the man whose gravest error had ruined the late stage of a sterling career in the service of his nation. Once again Randolph was the friend, the colleague, the admirer of the one indispensable patriot.

In 1810 Randolph wrote to Judge Bushrod Washington, "My life will, I hope, be sufficiently extended for the recording of my sincere opinion of his [George Washington's] virtues and merit, in a style which is not the result of a mind debilitated by misfortune, but of that Christian philosophy on which alone I depend for inward tranquillity."[68]

12. John Rutledge: The Benevolent Dictator

In 1780 South Carolina was ruled by a man entrusted with more power than George III or any British king ever wielded there. He could have men put to death without a trial, confiscate property by his proclamation, and decide who was eligible to vote and who was not.[1] Why was one man given such absolute authority? When trusted with it, did he use it for personal glory or for the good of the citizens? This is the story of John Rutledge.

When eight British lords got the South Carolina grant from Charles II in 1660, their agents attracted settlers by saying they would be governed by the same authentic nobility as in England. When none of the Lords Proprietors came over, the agents invented a set of spurious titles, such as cacique and landgrave, which could be purchased and used, but fooled no one.

The settlers of South Carolina were thrifty and hard working immigrants from England, France, Germany, Belgium, and Switzerland. The land was free, because the proprietors did not build forts or roads, supply soldiers, suppress pirates, or protect against Indians. People learned to be resourceful, and to band together for mutual protection.

The father of John Rutledge was Dr. John Rutledge, a ship's surgeon in the East India Company's merchant service. Hearing from his brother Andrew that the beautiful Sarah Hext was the richest heiress in the colony, he came at once to Charlestown. Shortly thereafter, on Christmas Day, 1738, he married Sarah, and never practiced medicine again. Their first child, John, was born the following year.

South Carolina law made a husband the automatic owner of his wife's estate. But Dr. John wanted no plantation. He sold it so that they could live in a mansion in Charlestown. Sarah ultimately bore seven children. Dr. John's only occupation, other than tutoring the children, was learning how to mix exotic drinks.

As a young child, John Rutledge one day was found imitating his Uncle Andrew, an attorney. Using his siblings as jurors, John argued first one side, then the other, of a case against a preacher who had used wicked words in a sermon. Uncle Andrew, who had defended the Rev. George Whitefield in a similar case, prophesied that John would make a good lawyer, for he could argue either side of a case at will.

When Dr. John proved to know little Latin and Greek, Dr. David Rhind, the most popular tutor in the colony, was employed.[2] Young John, however, resented learning and refused to study, except for mathematics. Soon he became very proficient at mathematics.

A diet of little besides alcohol proved destructive and so Dr. John died in 1750 at the age of 37. John, now 11, became the male head of the family. People started calling him "Mr. Rutledge."

Uncle Andrew became the paternal substitute. John told his uncle that he would not read literature, for it was debilitating. So he began to pore through his uncle's law books: *Britton*, Edward Coke, *Fleta*, Ranulf de Glanville, and the laws of South Carolina.

Charlestown had an early theater. John loved to go there to watch the plays of Shakespeare, Addison, Congreve, Farquhar, and Lillo. His vocabulary grew at each theatrical performance.

In 1751 Uncle Andrew became the speaker of the House. John attended nearly every session, learning much about parliamentary procedure. Between his 12th and 16th birthdays the House debated issues illustrating the entire British constitutional system. John paid close attention, especially to debates on tax bills.

He liked Uncle Andrew's motto: "Care not who reigns; think only of who rules."[3] The phrase typified uncle and nephew. When John was 16, Uncle Andrew died, but the die was cast: John must become a lawyer, and some day be speaker of the House, like Uncle Andrew.

Since money was no problem, John studied law at the Middle Temple in London. He also found time to watch David Garrick play Lear, and to hear William Pitt give speeches in the House of Commons. In 1760 he was admitted to the English bar, and he won his first two cases.[4]

The Lawyer

On December 24, 1760, John landed back in Charlestown, dressed in black, for he was mourning his monarch's death. In a sense, two young men were inheriting their kingdoms: George III at 22 was taking over the British empire, and John Rutledge at 21 was preparing to rule South Carolina.

Early on Christmas morning John took the canoe, made of three huge cypress logs, upstream, with the tide, 12 miles to the Rutledge plantation. The welcoming party of blacks was lined up in order. In the forefront were the white-haired butler, the housekeeper, and the game cook. Next came the meat and vegetable cook, the coachman, the poultry man, the dairy man, the farrier, the wagon wright, the fisherman, and the preacher. Then came the houseboys, room servants, and stable boys. In the rear were field hands, mechanics, and lesser domestics.

Aside, in a separate group, were the personal servants, headed by portly Mauma, at whose breast all the Rutledge children had nursed. John embraced Mauma, and shook hands with her son Pompey, who was his personal servant and closest companion.

As soon as he was unpacked, John distributed kerchiefs to the women, sashes to the men, and toys that he had brought from London for the children.

Fully grown, John was not tall but was well built. He had an impressive voice and a dignified mien. His grey eyes darted rapidly under a broad forehead. He had reddish brown hair and highly arched nostrils. His cheerful disposition made him well liked. Often impatient, however, he would sometimes interrupt a person's speech. "His practicality was the source of his strength and also the mark of his limitations."[5]

Rutledge found that his mother had been a poor manager of the plantation in his absence. Debts were owed and details needed to be organized. Moreover, she insisted that the other children also be given a good education.

Rutledge agreed, but only on one condition — that he be completely in charge. He then set to work immediately to reduce their debts.

Within a few weeks, he invited his neighbors to a big feast, and announced his candidacy for the legislature. He visited every plantation on horseback, and won a three-year term at the age of 21. Then he told his mother that as an assemblyman he could not be jailed, so he had a three-year respite from debtors' prison. He assured her that all bills would be paid within that period.

Much as they needed money, Rutledge got his mother to cede two farms to John and Benjamin Chaplin, because they said they had bought them from Dr. John. Despite the lack of written proof, a man's word had to be honored, Rutledge felt.

A chivalric code underlay life among South Carolina aristocrats. For example, one kept between ten and twenty house slaves. More than twenty indicated one was ostentatious, less than ten that one was poor — both conditions were unforgivable.

Folk phrases governed conduct: "A man's word must be better than his bond, because unguaranteed. If he wrongs any man he must offer his life in expiation. He must always be ready to fight for his state or his lady."[6]

For avocations Rutledge preferred the theater and canoe racing. His crew of black rowers were always in top shape. He never played cards, cared little for dancing, and owned no race horse until he was 32, despite the fact that in his milieu horse racing was the favorite pastime.

The only case he ever lost in court was an early one. He defended Daniel Horry, charged with trespass by Richard Moncrieff. Colonel Charles Pinckney (father of the framer Charles Pinckney) won the conviction for Moncrieff in a jury trial. Rutledge was choosy about selecting clients. A case had to be right morally and politically, that is, it must conform to proper social standards.

Rutledge won what may have been America's first "breach of promise" suit. By cross-examining William Lennox, Rutledge got him to admit that he had promised to marry Mary Cooke but then had married someone else. When the jury awarded Mary £2,500, she gave Rutledge 100 guineas as his fee. The case attracted considerable attention, and made him in demand as a lawyer.

Rutledge's success in court derived from several factors. His emotional appeal swayed a judge or jury, yet beneath was a logical framework of law. The prominent merchant Henry Laurens gave his important cases to this young lawyer, saying that "he fronts a fact more quickly than anyone I ever knew."[7] When his chief rival Egerton Leigh betrayed a friend, it was considered to be a violation of the South Carolina code of conduct, and from then on Rutledge got most of his best clients.

Beginning in 1761 a triumvirate virtually ruled that state. James Parsons was 44, Charles Pinckney (father of Charles Cotesworth Pinckney) was 37, and Rutledge was 22. They handled all the important law suits, directed the Assembly, dominated the courts, and made most of the governmental decisions. An effective team, they rarely opposed one another in court. Although he was the youngest of the trio, Rutledge soon became their spokesman, largely because of his courtroom oratory.

When Governor Thomas Boone refused to seat Christopher Gadsden in the Assembly, alleging that his election was illegal, Rutledge protested on the grounds of the British constitution: only a legislative body can rule upon the legality of the election of its members.[8]

True to his promise to his mother, Rutledge gave his brothers either an education or a role in managing the family affairs. Out of debt, the Rutledge name was again respected, and his sisters were courted as desirable mates.

A friend of Rutledge at the Middle Temple had been James Grimké, of well-to-do Huguenot background. On May 1, 1763, Rutledge married Grimké's sister, Elizabeth, who was 19 years old. Mrs. Rutledge felt that John should have listened to her advice and marry within the aristocratic circle. "John is a law unto himself," she said. "I wonder sometimes if he is my own flesh and blood."[9]

As his wealth grew, Rutledge did not invest in more slaves or in western land. Instead he kept buying lots in Charlestown. The design of his mansion at 116 Broad Street betrays its intended use. It had only two bedrooms but a huge dining room, a large drawing room, and an ample wine cellar. Business would often be conducted in comfortable surroundings, with plenty to eat and drink. He himself consumed two bottles of Madeira each day.

In an effort to wean him away from the triumvirate and make him "a King's man," Governor Boone in 1764 appointed him attorney-general. At 25 he was 11 years younger than any previous attorney-general. Rutledge played his cards discreetly. After beating Parsons in a law suit he would invite him to dinner. Or he would best Colonel Charles Pinckney and then send him a case of cognac. It was hard to figure out what went on beneath the surface of the inscrutable Rutledge.

Jared Mangin, an overseer, tried to seduce a slave, Deborah. When she resisted, he beat her to death. As crown prosecutor, Rutledge got Mangin sentenced to be hanged. Charles Shinner, chief justice of South Carolina, who delivered the sentence, was not only an alcoholic but to everyone's knowledge had an octoroon mistress. Whatever their feelings about the justice of the case, people lost respect for a royal government that had such a disreputable chief magistrate.

Governor Boone sent his wife and children to England, and started living with a Mrs. Worthington. Even divorce would have been unacceptable in a governor, but cohabitation was unthinkable. Everyone accordingly ostracized the governor and his companion. For revenge, Boone dismissed the Assembly and called for a new election.

The triumvirs told the old Assembly to continue to meet, and so it did. Now Boone declared Gadsden ineligible to serve in the Assembly, because of a voting technicality. The triumvirs said that only the Assembly could rule on the ineligibility of its members, and so the Assembly voted 29–7 to seat Gadsden. Boone then refused to swear in Sir John Colleton as an Assemblyman, as was his right, but Colleton took part in the Assembly as a full member. Frantic, Boone appealed for help to the Board of Trade and Plantations, which told Boone that if he desired, he could come to London to plead his case in person. The trip was such an inconvenience that Boone stayed home. Having effectively countermanded the governor, the triumvirate in effect ruled the state.

To Britain, South Carolina was an ideal colony, for, unlike New England, it sent raw materials to England and purchased manufactured goods from the mother country. England paid a bounty of sixpence per pound on South Carolina's indigo, and lifted the Navigation Act on rice, increasing the profit to South Carolina planters. No other colony had such preferential treatment because no other one had such crucial exports for Britain.

The Patriot

After only ten months as attorney-general, Rutledge resigned in order to represent South Carolina at the Stamp Act Congress, which met in New York in 1765. He wrote to his mother: "This is my first trip to a foreign country."[10]

He could not help making comparisons between New York and Charlestown. Both had 14,000 inhabitants, but of these 2,000 were slaves in the northern city and 8,000 were slaves in Charlestown. Although shipping had been greater in Charlestown, Rutledge could see that the wider, deeper harbor in New York would make it eventually a much better port.

Most slaves in New York had Dutch masters. To avoid the New York transfer fee, slaves were smuggled across from Newark at night. He had never seen any smuggling of slaves, nor free slaves begging on the streets. In South Carolina it would have been unthinkable for the owner not to care for old or incapacitated slaves.

The cultural shock amazed Rutledge. Here most men chewed tobacco and spat everywhere. In South Carolina the only chewers were field hands. Lower Broadway and the Battery had many prostitutes—one never saw a prostitute on the streets of Charlestown. To walk on the docks of the East River was to risk one's life. The waterfront on the Ashley River was as safe as a churchyard. Rutledge saw graffiti on Trinity Church in New York City: "Rag of the whore of Babylon." If anyone felt that way about the Anglican church in Charlestown, it certainly was never expressed publicly.

Here Rutledge greeted his old friend David Douglass, manager of the Hallam theatrical company. Douglass could hardly wait to leave New York City for the South. Eggs were thrown nightly at the actors at the Chapel Street Theater, not as an expression of dramatic criticism but because "it is highly improper that play actors should appear when great numbers of poor people are starving."[11] A reviewer in the New York *Weekly Post Boy* concurred with these sentiments!

Sir William Johnson, high commissioner of his majesty to the Six Nations, made his annual purchases for over 30 trading posts while Rutledge was in New York. Since he bought more merchandise than any other six persons in America combined, his visit was given far more attention than that of the 23 strangers who had come to protest the Stamp Tax.

Rutledge asked Johnson how the Hodenosenee, the parliament of the Six Nations, operated. Each nation was sovereign internally, Johnson explained, but externally and especially in wartime the council of sachems was supreme. "If England is ever to become a great nation," said

Johnson, "she must go to school to the Iroquois. The Six Nations control this continent, not by accident, but through the triumph of their science of government."[12] Impressed, Rutledge traveled many times to Indian camps to study their lifestyle firsthand.

At the Stamp Act Congress, Rutledge and James Otis wrote a memorial to the House of Lords, asking the king to hear the colonies' petition protesting the Stamp Act. John Dickinson wrote a more pointed complaint to the House of Commons, arguing that the Stamp Act was a violation of the colonists' rights. The more cautiously worded memorial influenced George III to get Commons to repeal the objectionable law. The memorial recognized the king's sovereignty and quoted Blackstone, the one legal authority familiar to the king. Within three days after George III read this memorial, the Stamp Act was repealed.

Rutledge got Gadsden, chairman of the Committee on Justice in the South Carolina Assembly, to draw up a bill of complaints against Chief Justice Shinner that was approved 36–0 in the Assembly. The vote of no confidence was sustained by the House of Lords, and Shinner was removed. Having blocked the chief executive of the state, the triumvirate (particularly Rutledge) had now shown itself to be stronger than the chief magistrate.

By now the Rutledges were a legal dynasty. John's brother Hugh returned from London, married well, and built a bigger house than John's on the lot next door to him. Then brother Edward returned from London, married better, and built a larger mansion than Hugh's, across the street from his brothers. All three had successful law practices, but Mr. Rutledge (that is, John) always commanded the highest fees. Edward early became a Son of Liberty, while John and Hugh remained politically quiescent.

Growth of the population in rural South Carolina meant that courts had to be established in six country towns. Riding circuit, Rutledge would work his way down a line of clients, often outside, write a brief decision, and take his fee. One morning in Orangeburg he took in, before breakfast, over 100 guineas in fees. His law income tripled, largely because of rural fees.

Dr. John Haley, a Son of Liberty, killed Peter Delancey, a loyalist, in a drunken duel. Rutledge, co-counsel with Charles Cotesworth Pinckney for Haley, proved that Haley had given Delancey the first shot, by digging a bullet out of a wall. The loyalist jury acquitted Haley, since he had acted according to the accepted code.

In its own mild tea party, Charlestown reacted to Boston's in an orderly fashion. Directed by Rutledge, a group of Liberty Boys, unmasked and in broad daylight, rowed out to the British ship while the whole town watched in a holiday mood. They took the tea to an obscure warehouse, where it finally molded and was forgotten.

When the governor dismissed the Assembly in retaliation, Rutledge assembled them in the town square and organized them as the Committee on Public Safety. Everything was done in an orderly fashion.

The Legislator

At the First Continental Congress in 1774, however, Rutledge and Samuel Adams were such forceful leaders that Gouverneur Morris called them "a lot of rascals." Joseph Galloway of Pennsylvania moved for an administrative separation of England and America in which the colonies would have full authority to levy taxes but with trade administered by a joint commission under the crown. A majority of the delegates, including Washington and Rutledge, voted for the plan. But Gadsden had pushed through a procedural motion in which votes would be by states rather than by delegates. Galloway's plan was defeated, 7–6, and perhaps the last opportunity to avert war was lost.

At an impasse over what action to take, Rutledge asked fellow committee member John Adams to draw up a compromise plan. Adams's Act of Union was a watered down Galloway plan, which reserved taxation to the colonies but implied that the mother country might control trade. Adams thus drew up America's first act of union at the instigation of Rutledge.[13]

Samuel Adams then asked the Congress for a boycott on only a few items. Rutledge shocked everyone by asking for a total boycott on all trade with England, which was voted down 12–1. Rutledge pointed out that on the list of Samuel Adams only 5 percent of Massachusetts trade was affected, but 65 percent of South Carolina's rice and 100 percent of her indigo. "If we are to bear burdens in the cause of America," Rutledge reasoned, "they should be as equal as possible."[14] He then moved to exempt rice and indigo from the list. After a roar of protests, he relented and agreed to exempt rice. Although Congress approved this boycott, it never went into effect because subsequent events nullified it.

Asked who was the greatest man in the First Continental Congress, Patrick Henry replied, "If you speak of eloquence, Mr. John Rutledge of South Carolina is by far the greatest orator."[15]

Returning home, Rutledge met great opposition; South Carolinians heard that he had first suggested a total boycott that included rice and indigo, and then had accepted the boycott on indigo. To silence the indigo planters, Rutledge pointed out that his own plantation grew little rice but much indigo, so he would suffer as much as anyone. At this time the exports of South Carolina (including those from North Carolina through South Carolina ports) to Great Britain far exceeded the total exports to Britain of all colonies north of Maryland combined.[16]

Rutledge was now caught in the middle of the rising tide of nationalism. The Committee on Public Safety wanted to permit a shipment of horses to land, in violation of the national boycott. Rutledge supported this decision. The Liberty Boys demanded a new vote in the Committee and this time overruled Rutledge's position, 35-34. This landmark vote was seen as a sign that the rule of the triumvirate was ended. But it by no means meant that Rutledge had lost his leadership in the state.

In 1775 his cash income from earned legal fees was over £9,000, the highest in the colonies. He owned five plantations.[17] At this rate he would be one of America's richest men in another 15 years. Like Washington, he had everything to lose by siding with the patriot cause.

Rutledge's leadership was seen in his ability to convert the potential destructiveness of up-country mobs or Sons of Liberty into a positive stress towards justice and law. He succeeded because of the virtually complete support of his associates. They knew his values, his goals, and his techniques of operation. Trusting him, they willingly followed where he led. He maintained his leadership because he never purposely led them astray.

In the Second Continental Congress in 1775 Samuel Adams got Rutledge appointed chairman of the committee on government. This committee recommended that each state select a council of outstanding citizens to take over the state government until the king's representative governed according to the respective charters. Rutledge was also very active as co-chairman of the committee on trade.

His most important assignment, however, was to review, with Samuel Adams, the possible appointees for commander-in-chief of the Continental Army. His military experience, plus his many other attributes, made Washington their clear choice.

In June 1775 Rutledge's committee on government reported the offices of governor and lieutenant-governor of Massachusetts vacant, for the failure of the incumbents to observe the Massachusetts charter. The citizens of the state were empowered to elect their own government.

While Rutledge was in Philadelphia, William Henry Drayton took over as head of the Committee on Public Safety in South Carolina. Drayton threatened to use violence against loyalists in the up-country. To help restore order in South Carolina, Rutledge got Congress in November 1775 to approve a resolution permitting the state Convention (the interim governing body) to set up a civil government representing the people's interests "during the continuance of the present dispute between Great Britain and the colonies."[18]

In February 1776 Gadsden, fired up from reading Thomas Paine's *Common Sense*, started a movement calling for a complete break with England. Not yet ready to make the move, Rutledge said he was willing to ride night and day to Philadelphia to assist in reuniting Great Britain and America. His indecision was "a manifestation of his moderation of character and his philosophical habit of mind, which viewed the contest for American rights from a broader standpoint than that of local or even American patriotism."[19]

The Ruler

On March 21, 1776, a British vessel arrived at Charlestown authorized to seize South Carolina property and ships, describing the state as in a condition of rebellion. The response was rapid. On March 24 Rutledge presented a committee report, with a long preamble listing the grievances against the royal government, declaring "this Congress a full and free representation of the people of this colony, henceforth to be called the General Assembly of South Carolina."[20]

Adoption of this report by the elected representatives of the people made it the first independent legal definition of government in America, a forerunner of the United States Constitution. It had the traditional three branches of government. The General Assembly was to be elected biennially by the people, and was to choose a Legislative Council from its own members. Rutledge said that this government was to be temporary, until the differences with England were reconciled. He was elected president of the Republic of South Carolina on March 26. South Carolina had thus declared its independence well before July 4.

President Rutledge and General John Armstrong of the Continental Army prepared the defenses around Charlestown for a British naval attack in early June. The appearance of the British fleet united the hitherto split people. Lead weights were taken from windows to be cast into musket balls. Street barricades were erected. Public records and printing presses were moved into safer positions.

General Sir Henry Clinton, after warning the Americans to surrender, landed 3,000 men on Long Island, adjacent to Fort Sullivan. Knowing he needed help, Rutledge asked Washington for reinforcements. Washington sent troops under the command of Major-General Charles Lee.

Since the South Carolina militia had not yet been incorporated into the Continental Army, Rutledge was still their commander. He thus ignored Lee's order to pull Colonel William Moultrie's forces out of Fort Sullivan.

The British ships fired for hours at Fort Sullivan, but the stockade, built of palmetto trees, absorbed the balls, and held. Hence, South Carolina has since been called the Palmetto State. Three British ships got hung up on sandbars, and were easy targets for Moultrie's crack artillery. Although the British fleet fired seven times as much ammunition, it had received six times as many casualties as the Americans.[21] The civilian president had had more to do with the victory than had General Lee.

When Rutledge presented the national Declaration of Independence to the state Assembly on September 17, 1776, he said: "May the happiest consequences be derived to the United States from the independence of America, who could not obtain even peace, liberty, and safety by any other means."[22] Later, in December, in an address requesting continued support for the militia, he pointed out that the up-country districts now had representation that had been denied them under the crown.

The British organized and equipped the Cherokees to fight against the patriots. Rutledge chose Andrew Williamson, a seasoned Indian fighter, to command the defense. Williamson was tough and effective, and soon the Cherokees were routed. When Williamson ruled that 13 white men, painted as Indians, were to be tortured and killed as an example, Rutledge overruled him on the grounds of humanity. Rabid patriots accused their president of being soft on loyalists.

In January 1778 Rutledge presented the Articles of Confederation to the Assembly for its consideration. He said that the requisition of $500,000 from the Continental Congress might seem like a large amount, but it really was not when one asks what price can be placed upon freedom.

A power struggle between Rutledge and William Henry Drayton came to a head that spring. Drayton, as Chief Justice, resented the power granted to Rutledge, so he got a Presbyterian minister, William Tennant, to attack Rutledge as an atheist. Privately Rutledge was a deist but publicly he was an Anglican. The state constitution, which Rutledge supported, had carried over the Anglican church as the established church.

Tennant now added a new dimension to his attack, alleging that Rutledge did not believe in the people. The Assembly had passed a bill setting up a Senate elected by the people to replace the Legislative Council, which was elected by the Assembly. Rutledge said that although democracy looks good on paper, in practice "its effects have been found arbitrary, severe, and destructive."[23]

Other provisions of the bill were that South Carolina should be a state, not a republic, with a governor, not a president. The governor's veto could be overridden by a two-thirds vote in the Assembly. Finally, the Anglican church would be disestablished.

Realizing that he had been outmaneuvered by Drayton and seeing that he could scarcely veto such a large number of items objectionable to him, he gave a long address to the Assembly. We should be adhering to the new constitution, he said, but instead this law breaks it. If the Assembly can break the constitution, what protection do we have? If people want to change the constitution, there are prescribed ways to do so. But since this bill apparently meets with the approval of the people, and since as president I cannot break the constitution, I hereby resign. The Assembly sent him a resolution of thanks for his "vigilant and faithful discharge of duties" as president.

Bad luck now dogged him. He had asked General Robert Howe of the Continental Army for help in ridding the coast of British vessels. Howe had sent a contingent of 150 marines, and three British ships left the area. But in early April the American ship *Randolph* exploded while exchanging fire with a British ship, and virtually the whole crew was lost. Howe reminded the public that the expedition had been undertaken against his better judgment.

The Dictator

Starting at the bottom, Rutledge began his rise back to power. In April he was elected as a member of the Assembly. He was re-elected in November, this time under the provisions of the law he had refused to sign. By January 1779 he was back at the top, this time as governor and commander of the South Carolina military forces.

His speedy return was precipitated by the advance of British troops under General Augustine Prévost from the south. People recalled Rutledge's stellar role in the defense of Charlestown in 1776, and they wanted him in charge again as the British neared the city.

Under wartime conditions, the Assembly granted Rutledge and his council the power "to do everything that appeared to him and to them necessary for the public good."[24] Rutledge immediately assembled all the state militia available, and erected a permanent camp at Orangeburg, a central point between Charlestown and Augusta.

Once, securing enlistments, he lost his temper and hit a recruit with a riding whip. The next morning, in front of all the troops, he apologized to the lad and promised that no such thing would happen again.

In March 1779 Governor Rutledge issued a proclamation declaring that Americans going over to the British side would be summarily executed for treason and have their property confiscated.

Unknown was the size of the British army. General Moultrie, perhaps underestimating it, wanted to fight on, as General Prévost advanced. Rutledge, probably overestimating Prévost's forces, discussed capitulation terms with him. While Rutledge delayed a decision, discussing it with military commanders, Prévost intercepted a message from General Benjamin Lincoln, whose troops were coming to the rescue of Charlestown. Fearing the sort of entrapment that Burgoyne had suffered at Saratoga, Prévost withdrew his forces, and the siege of Charlestown was temporarily at an end.

The loyalists now went to work on Rutledge. John Wells, signing himself "Agricola," attacked him not only for striking a recruit but also for having three men executed without a trial. As a matter of fact, the execution of citizens without a trial was a power explicitly denied Rutledge. But the men involved were not citizens but slaves, and it is assumed that the infraction was a military one.[25] It is not unusual under wartime conditions or martial law for legal processes to be brief and decisive.

Was Rutledge a "dictator," as Wells alleged? David D. Wallace points out the care that the Assembly took in granting him this power. In the renewed grant of power contained in an ordinance in February 1780 a long preamble describes the historical precedent for such power, saying that "in times of danger and invasion, it has always been the policy of republics to concenter the power of the government in the hands of the supreme magistracy, for a limited time," in order to strengthen the defense.

Wallace shows that Rutledge was directed to submit his decisions to whichever members of his council were conveniently available, and that he could call out only one-third of the militia, except within an 80-mile radius of the invasion. Moreover, he could not subject the militia to the articles of war used for the Continental troops. Finally, says Wallace, the governors who succeeded Rutledge were granted similar powers until the War ended.[26]

Knowing that the British would return the following year, Rutledge tried to get special assistance. He sent an emissary to Havana, promising Spain help in rewinning St. Augustine in exchange for support in South Carolina, but Spain was deaf. He wrote to the Count d'Estaing, asking him to leave the West Indies during the hurricane season and join General Lincoln in freeing Georgia. D'Estaing laid a siege on Savannah but the British turned him back.

Rutledge issued a proclamation demanding that all men join the American forces or suffer confiscation of their property. There was little response to his call for troops, and it was apparent that the British forces would capture Charlestown this time.

To carry on the state government, Rutledge followed Lincoln's advice and left Charlestown on April 13, accompanied by three council members. He tried to set up training camps for recruits on the Santee River, but few recruits enlisted. By June he was forced to do his recruiting and training in North Carolina.

Assisted by naval forces under Admiral Arbuthnot, Clinton captured Charlestown on May 12. He took all valuable property, including slaves, to the West Indies, where he and his men sold the property and distributed the proceeds as war booty.

At first Clinton seemed to offer lenient surrender terms, with pardons to all who submitted and with no taxes except those passed by the Assembly. But in June he abolished the status of paroled prisoners, except for those in the Charlestown area, and demanded that they declare British allegiance or be treated as enemies. Even prisoners of war were told that they would have to fight against America, in violation of international law.

British soldiers robbed civilians in Charlestown. Court rights were given only to those declaring British allegiance. Property was seized without compensation. "To the poor it was submit or starve; to the rich, submit or lose estates."[27] Americans found armed were hanged as traitors; the British army turned out into the woods women and children whose homes had been burned.

Rutledge now wondered why he had worked so long for reconciliation with Britain. "The enemy seems determined to break every man's spirit," he said, "and if they can't, to ruin him."[28] He spoke from personal experience, for the British had confiscated all of his estates.[29]

Rutledge traveled north to Baltimore, then the national capitol, to request help. Washington gave him Baron de Kalb, and on their way south they recruited troops in Virginia and North Carolina. Some Congressmen, impatient with Washington's lack of victories, wanted to try out Horatio Gates, victor at Saratoga, as the southern commander and as a possible successor to Washington.

But at Camden, South Carolina, on August 16 Cornwallis surprised Gates and routed his army. De Kalb was killed, and Gates was soon replaced by Nathaniel Greene.

Rutledge continued to govern South Carolina from afar. He kept recruiting and building morale, living in Hillsboro, North Carolina, but riding into South Carolina to coordinate raids by his guerrilla leaders: William Davie, Francis Marion, and Thomas Sumter. These men organized partisan bands which harassed British outposts and harried their convoys. It is hard to overestimate their importance. Edward McCrady flatly states that "without the partisan leaders of South Carolina and their followers, the independence of America would never have been achieved."[30]

Rutledge was on the scene of at least fifty skirmishes against the British. By being lenient with captives, he switched many of them to the American side.

Bothered by the harassment, Cornwallis sent out a unit under

Colonel Patrick Ferguson to clean out the guerrilla pockets. At Kings Mountain near the border between the Carolinas, Ferguson and 1100 British and loyalist troops were surrounded on a hilltop. Sharpshooting American riflemen prevailed over the bayonet attacks of the British. Ferguson was killed, and the entire British contingent was either killed or captured.

When Rutledge's last council member, John Gervais, went up into Virginia, Rutledge was indeed a one-man ruler of South Carolina. The loyalists continued their charge that he was a dictator. One said of him that the people of South Carolina "vested more power in the breast of one man than is possessed by the most despotic power in Europe."[31] Why fight a war for liberty if you are willing to surrender your liberties, they asked.

Rutledge eventually got Greene to approve of a guerrilla war. In the late spring of 1781 Cornwallis moved his army of 4,000 men north towards Virginia. Greene's troops continued the partisan attacks upon the British supply wagons.

Rutledge persuaded Greene not to follow Cornwallis northward, but to come to the rescue of beleagured Charlestown. One by one Greene captured British posts until by December 1781 only Charlestown remained in British hands. It took another year before the British finally evacuated Charlestown.

When Rutledge returned to South Carolina in August 1781, his first official act was to issue a proclamation against plundering. He then suspended the use of state and Continental currency as legal tender because of their worthlessness. Needing currency, people for a while used ammunition and even indigo cubes as a means of exchange. Rutledge also appointed magistrates and probate judges, thus restoring the beginnings of civil government under American auspices.

Two of his measures drew criticism from loyalists. In September 1781 he pardoned all those who had taken British protection, provided they serve six months in the state militia. Confiscation of their property, plus banishment from the state, faced those who refused to return to American allegiance. In response, several hundred persons left British-held territory to serve in the American forces.

His second sweeping measure affected qualifications for voters. In December 1781 he instructed election managers not to accept ballots from anyone who had not left British protection for state allegiance by September 27, 1781.

When the Assembly met early in 1782 his unilateral authority was dissolved, but many of the first acts of the Assembly were in line with steps he had taken during the emergency. By its action, the Assembly in effect showed that Rutledge's behavior had not been dictatorial, or if so under military duress had been temporary, and in the best interests of the people. There is no evidence that he abused his unusual authority so as to bolster his or his friends' coffers.

Judge Aedanus Burke dissented from this interpretation of Rutledge's conduct. Under the pseudonym "Cassius," Burke said that his actions were unconstitutional, since the Assembly had no stated power to cede so much authority to one man. Burke also charged that Rutledge's motive in the election law was to concentrate the powers of the government in the hands of a few families by disfranchising the lower and middle classes of people.

Robert W. Barnwell, Jr., after a careful study of Rutledge's actions, found little substance in Burke's position.[32] Nor did the people of South Carolina, for they kept electing him to the highest offices. If Rutledge had exercised his authority severely on occasion, there had been a justifiable reason. He practically always showed discretion, humanity, and sound judgment. In addition, some of his measures hastened the economic recovery of the state. Scarcely any dictator ever was as unselfish as he, as genuinely concerned about the people's welfare, and as ready to relinquish the authority when the military emergency had passed.

The Judge

Rutledge served as a delegate to the Continental Congress in 1782–83, and as governor of South Carolina from 1782–84. Beginning in 1784, when he was appointed a judge of the South Carolina Court of Chancery, the rest of his career was in the judiciary, except for the Constitutional Convention and one term in the state legislature. No other framer had such extensive experience in all three branches of government.

He had not practiced law since 1776. His salary as chancellor (because of Chancery Court) was only $2500 a year, a sum easily exceeded by brothers Edward and Hugh as lawyers. He was now the leading jurist in the state. In one two-year period his docket was never held over for a single night. He listened to counsel courteously but was noted for his rapid decisions. Because he explained the reasons for his decisions, there was generally little complaint about them.

The shortlived state of Franklin (mostly in present-day east Tennessee) gave him 25,000 acres of land on the Elk River for his leadership during the War, but the land was a tax burden. From time to time he sold property, including city lots in Charleston. His social life was now greatly reduced.

Evenings he would go to the Exchange, where ship captains boarded.

He heard their problems—how they chose ports carefully, to avoid duties, to get best prices, to avoid payment in paper currency.

The British ships were making a killing. Smuggling was commonplace. American ship captains learned to buy goods through English agents in the West Indies and bring them in to a duty-free port as Americans. Rutledge never defended a smuggler, but he could see how laxity on the part of the federal government was leading to severe economic problems.

No one spoke much about the federal government now, since it seemed to be doing very little. When his seventh child, a son, was born, he named him States Rutledge, to show his continued interest in the Union.

The Framer

At the Constitutional Convention, Rutledge was named as head of a delegation that included Pierce Butler, Charles Pinckney, and Charles Cotesworth Pinckney. William Pierce called Rutledge "a man of abilities and distinction," who had achieved fame as an orator despite the fact that he spoke too rapidly.[33]

Arriving early in Philadelphia, Rutledge went to live at the home of his friend James Wilson. He stayed there three weeks, until his wife arrived in town. This time was well spent in discussing Convention strategy.

They made an interesting pair, complementing each other. Once Rutledge had been America's leading lawyer—now it was Wilson. While Rutledge practiced law, Wilson was his correspondent in Philadelphia. Unlikes attracted: Rutledge disliked books, Wilson read all the time. Wilson lacked practical political instinct—Rutledge's inspiration struck like lightning. Rutledge was relatively weak in written expression, whereas Wilson excelled at it.

They made an excellent team. Rutledge would leap at an instant decision, then turn to Wilson for details on how to carry it out. The conservative Rutledge balanced the liberal Wilson. Probably the big point was that "neither was an extremist nor irreconcilable."[34]

As they looked forward to the Convention, Rutledge said that the main problem would be to avoid internal dissension. From the start they realized they would have to do more than they were authorized to do—revise the Articles of Confederation.

Rutledge's wisdom led him past Jefferson on one score—open meetings were out of the question, for "the proposed Constitution could be an open covenant only if it was not arrived at openly."[35] Rutledge said that the delegates must agree in advance that not a word discussed inside the Convention should be repeated outside.

He knew that he had been called a "dictator" in South Carolina, so he asked Wilson to consult Franklin about him. Franklin respected Wilson highly, and had worked effectively with Rutledge in the first two Continental Congresses, when Rutledge had been Franklin's vice-chairman of the committee on trade.

Rutledge and Wilson asked Washington for his reaction to the proposed secrecy rule. Typically, Washington consulted the Virginia delegation and two days later that group agreed to it. Later, during the Convention, delegates agreed that during their lifetimes they would not reveal the details of what happened there. Their goal was to put principle above personality and purpose ahead of prejudice. They sincerely wanted the new Constitution to be given every possible chance to succeed as the foundation and skeleton for the erection of a just government for a great republic.

Rutledge was a practical man—he got things done. With no military training, he had outwitted the British in a way that would have done justice to military men like Washington or C.C. Pinckney. There is reason to believe that he had the best brain at the Convention.

He instantly sensed that there was no dearth of ideals, or of ideas about political systems, at the meeting. The problem was how to salvage high ideals and great ideas from ideologues. Rutledge was born for the occasion. There was no idea he had not heard before, and no ideal that he had not tested, or seen tested, on the anvil of political reality. Unselfish for personal gain or prestige, he would see that the new nation got every measure of practical excellence it deserved. He had not won virtually every one of his law suits by being stupid.

When patience ran low and tempers ran high over Sherman's proposal that states have equal votes in the Senate, Rutledge took over. On June 30 he had Sherman as his guest to dinner at the Indian Queen, where he now had his rooms. There was no smoking or drinking—Rutledge knew a Puritan when he saw one. He asked Sherman to say grace. Sherman prayed for ten minutes.

Then came the Little Compromise. Rutledge said that South Carolina, North Carolina, and Georgia would give up the required two-thirds vote in the navigation clause if Connecticut and Massachusetts would give up the effort for an immediate ban on slave importation. Five states in agreement, Rutledge pointed out, could carry the vote.

Since there already was a 13-year extension on slave importation, Sherman consented to extend the period to 21 years. But Sherman had one fear. Would North Carolina go along with this agreement, for here delegates had recently been aligning themselves with large states like

Virginia and Pennsylvania? Rutledge assured Sherman that he had received concurrence from Hugh Williamson, head of the North Carolina delegation. And so the deal was consummated.[36]

The larger issue, concerning the states having equal votes in the Senate, must also have been discussed at this meeting. Sherman had not been elected to the committee to work on the Great Compromise, possibly because it was his proposal under debate. Ellsworth carried Sherman's viewpoint, and Rutledge was also working on the committee involved in the Great Compromise at the same time.

The Union hung on the narrowest of margins. The vote on the Great Compromise was 5-4, as was the vote to extend the date for slave importation and the vote against the two-thirds majority required to pass navigation acts. The astounding fact is that in a Convention so evenly divided on so many crucial issues, there was somehow a unity of purpose based upon mutual respect that carried past the constant difference of opinion on specific issues.

The Committee of Detail, called the Drafting Committee, had Rutledge as chairman. He was the strong chairman of a strong committee, the other members being Ellsworth, Gorham, Randolph, and Wilson. The committee's job was prodigious—to collate and organize everything that the Convention had agreed upon up to July 26, with permission to draw upon everything that had been written on government since Magna Carta. Ralph Waldo Emerson said that Rutledge "was selected by the Convention as the lens through which it would read its own mind."[37]

The committee started with the Virginia Plan as it had been modified, and then considered primarily the Articles of Confederation, the New Jersey Plan, the Pinckney Plan, and the various state constitutions, especially that of New York.

At the outset Rutledge read to the committee an excerpt from the beginning of the Iroquois constitution of the Treaty of the Five Nations of 1520: "We, the people, to form a union, to establish peace, equity, and order...."[38] Where Madison, William Paterson, and Charles Pinckney had gone back through England to Greece, Rutledge found his basic ideas for government among native Americans.

Later another Indian idea was important. Rutledge knew that the Iroquois gave final power to the elder sachems. Thus, although all three branches of government are subject to checks and balances, the judiciary are the final source of authority. Now a judge, Rutledge found the means of getting his way.

Rutledge's views on other topics are insightful. At least seven years of residence in a state should be required before a person could represent that state in the House, he felt, and an even longer period of time for the

Senate. He favored property qualifications for federal officeholders, pointing out that the Committee of Detail had not been specific on this matter, since it did not want to displease the people by making the qualifications too high, nor render them meaningless by setting them too low.[39]

Like the other delegates, Rutledge drew upon his experience to support positions he took. Recalling his hectic days in trying to drive the British out of South Carolina, he insisted that the chief executive have complete military authority in wartime. He attacked the idea that all money bills should originate in the House, calling it a slavish copy of the British practice. Moreover, he added, this system had not worked at all in South Carolina, for it led to either connivance or avoidance, and thus served no useful purpose.

He recommended that a committee work out the details on how the federal government would assume the states' War debts. Assumption was a necessity, he argued on August 18, now that import taxes were to be reserved to the federal government.

His legal reasoning was nowhere better shown than in his adherence to his promise to Sherman to kill the two-thirds vote required in Congress to pass navigation acts. Disagreeing with Madison and Mason, he said that it does not follow that a grant to regulate trade would necessarily be abused. At worst, he said, it would be only a temporary inconvenience to the South. "As we are laying the foundation for a great empire, he continued, "we ought to take a permanent view of the subject and not look at the present moment only."[40] It was necessary to the commerce of the entire Union that trade be restored to the West Indies, he stated, and only a navigation act could secure that trade for America. Though this argument would still not have convinced the South, it was sufficient to defeat this crucial motion in the Convention.

Like Charles Cotesworth Pinckney, the only unforgivable flaw in the stance of Rutledge at the Convention was his position on slavery. Here he sturdily represented his constituents by saying there could be no compromise, either to outlaw slavery or to immediately stop slave importation. Like Pinckney, he insisted that if slavery were to be abolished by this Convention, there would be no Union. There is no question but that two countries (or three if the Middle States went half-way) would have resulted had the abolitionists refused to compromise. Hardheaded New Englanders, not the compromising type like Ellsworth and Sherman, would have preferred a smaller but better nation.

It is interesting to observe Rutledge's own practice concerning slavery. In 1760, when he took over his mother's plantation, he had 200. In 1775 he owned 60 and in 1787 he had 28. At his death in 1800 he had only one body servant, and this may have been because he did not want to break fully the South Carolina code of conduct. Like Jefferson, Madison, and Washington, all of whom owned fewer slaves as time passed, the combination of conscience plus the cost of keeping slaves made the institution virtually untenable to them.[41]

Not to be overlooked is the influence of his wife Elizabeth upon Rutledge. As Huguenots, the Grimkés stubbornly opposed oppression. Before she died, Elizabeth gave up all of her slaves. Her brother-in-law, John Grimké, was the south's first abolitionist. His daughters, Angelina and Sarah Grimké, became vigorous abolitionist crusaders in the troubled period preceding the Civil War.

At the South Carolina ratification convention, Rutledge's legal rhetoric was convincing. How could Rawlins Lowndes praise the feeble Articles of Confederation, he asked. And if Lowndes really wanted to give power to the people, why would he not support the Constitution, which did precisely that? There was no doubt in his mind, said Rutledge, that the South gained far more than it had given up. Moreover, as the population in the larger southern states grew faster than in the smaller northern ones, the South's advantage would continue to increase.

The Justice

As president, Washington asked John Adams who would make the best first chief justice of the United States. Adams replied that "if ability is to decide, take Rutledge—if politics, Jay."[42] John Jay, then governor of New York, had never tried an important case, but he had served in a number of diplomatic assignments, and he was selected.

The other members of the five-man Supreme Court were Rutledge, James Wilson, John Blair of Virginia, and Richard Henry Harrison of Maryland. New England was conspicuously lacking in representation.

Since the position was at first not a full-time one, Rutledge continued as a judge on the South Carolina Court of Chancery. He never attended a Supreme Court Session, but he sat with other Justices several times on circuit. In 1791 he resigned from the United States Supreme Court to become the Chief Justice of the South Carolina Supreme Court.

His health started to fail him. He had a very painful kidney stone, and he suffered from Bright's disease. He took very hard the death of Elizabeth in 1793. She had borne their ten children, and had been his constant companion and confidante through decades of turmoil.

Some said the severe depression now affected his sanity. "William Read described how John Rutledge tried to commit suicide in the Ashley River but was dragged out against his will by several Negroes and John

Blake."[43] Hamilton alleged that Rutledge had lost his mind, but based his conclusion on the mere fact that he talked too fast—a lifelong trait of his. But much as South Carolina loved and respected Rutledge, it is doubtful that he would have been elected to the state legislature, as he was in 1798, unless he had full command of his faculties.

In June 1795 Jay resigned as chief justice in order to negotiate a treaty with England. Rutledge, like James Wilson, wrote to Washington asking for the position. Washington appointed Rutledge as "Chief Justice, ad interim."

In 1795 Rutledge wanted to show that he did indeed place national service ahead of service to his state. Umbreit says that "at this time his reputation was probably equal to that of Jefferson—who had still some distance to cover before becoming president—or Jay. He was admired and trusted in his own state to an extent to which no other American, except Washington, was admired and trusted by his native section. There have been few Chief Justices whose previous judicial experience equaled his."[44]

Jay's Treaty was attacked throughout the nation, but especially in the South. Jefferson and Madison were active in alleging that it was virtually blackmail in submission to the British. South Carolina was particularly dissatisfied with Jay, not only because he had won the chief justice's appointment over Rutledge but also because he had replaced Tom Pinckney as minister to France.

Rutledge's big error at this time was not that he, like so many others, attacked the treaty, but that as chief justice he made his attack a public one. Washington was shocked to think that a high government official would publicly oppose what he felt was an important part of his foreign policy.

There was a lack of communication on both sides. Had Rutledge been in the national capitol and heard Washington's view of the treaty, it is unlikely that he would have been so visibly opposed to it. Had Washington known of Rutledge's deep depression over the deaths of his wife and his mother, he might have been less critical of Rutledge's stand against the treaty.

Prompted by Washington, the Senate refused to confirm Rutledge's appointment as chief justice. He had served in the ad interim role for four and a half months. Jefferson baldly called the non-confirmation "a declaration that they [the Federalists] will receive none but Tories hereafter into any department of the government."[45]

These were days in which bad debts kept catching up with distinguished people. In 1796 Rutledge and James Wilson visited General William Moultrie in the debtors' prison in Charleston. Wilson, an associate justice of the Supreme Court, was a fugitive from the law

John Rutledge 291

because of unpaid bills. Rutledge was behind in his payments too, but no one would dare serve a summons on him, especially in South Carolina.

One evening Moultrie was released to the custody of Rutledge and Wilson, so that the three distinguished debtors could attend the theater together. Moultrie saw the first two acts with his friends, but then his parole hour arrived and he had to return to prison. The next day Wilson and Rutledge visited the jailhouse to tell Moultrie how the final two acts of the play turned out.[46]

Rutledge died on July 18, 1800, at the age of 61. His early opponent Joseph Galloway, a Tory, had accurately stated that Rutledge had "looked into the arguments of both sides more fully than any I have ever met."[47]

What is the place of John Rutledge in American history? After studying the sources available to him, Alexis de Tocqueville said that "the authorship of the Constitution is quite clear—a man named John Rutledge wrote it. Who is he?"[48]

History has not a great deal to say about Rutledge, for he craved anonymity. Of course he did not write the Constitution, any more than did any one framer. But, as we have seen, he not only made crucial contributions to its final form but he was also one of the most active and effective leaders in the United States during the formative years of the republic.

People granted him power because he wielded it impersonally and for their welfare. He was a benevolent dictator.

His first step in life was to assume absolute control of his family's affairs, on his terms but for the family's good. Progressively he did the same thing for Charlestown, for South Carolina, and for the United States, except that in the last instance he had to learn to share power with others. He did this as naturally as if he had worked in a shared capacity all of his life.

This seemed to bother him not at all, for his eye was focused steadily on results. How could one govern for the benefit of all concerned—this was his constant goal. Unlike many leaders, he was intelligent enough to realize that when one does not aspire to personal fame and glory, that when one cares not who gets the credit as long as the job is well done, one's ego does not get in the way of doing those things for society that merit its lasting fame and glory.

13. Roger Sherman: The Awkward Clear-Headed Yankee

William Pierce of Georgia, who described most of his fellow delegates at the Constitutional Convention, called Roger Sherman "the oddest shaped character" he had ever seen. "He is awkward and unaccountably strange in his manner," Pierce said, "but in his train of thinking there is something deep and comprehensive. The oddity of his address, the vulgarisms that accompany his public speaking, and that strange New England cant makes everything that is connected with him gross and laughable, and yet he deserves infinite praise — no man has a better heart nor a clearer head. He is extremely artful in accomplishing any object — it is remarked that he seldom fails."[1]

Writing to Abigail, John Adams described Sherman as "an old Puritan, as honest as an angel and as firm in the cause of American independence as Mount Atlas."[2]

Who was this awkward country lawyer whose wisdom helped save the Constitution? How did his strength of mind and character compensate for his lack of sophistication and gracefulness?

Firmness ran in Sherman's blood. He was distantly related to General William Tecumseh Sherman and his brother, Secretary of State John Sherman. Sherman's great-grandfather came from England in 1636. At the age of 55 he became schoolmaster. "When two years later the selectmen of Watertown, Massachusetts, notified him that he had been superseded by another, he refused to surrender the key of the schoolhouse and was allowed to hold his post for three more years."[3]

Roger, the third child of William and Mehetabel Sherman, was born on April 9, 1721. William was industrious, loved books, and left a comfortable estate when he died. In older age, when Sherman lightly boxed the ears of an unruly child during family prayers, Mehetabel promptly boxed Roger's ears, saying, "You strike your child and I strike mine."[4] Quiet reigned during the rest of the worship.

In 1721 the Board of Trade and Publications, the overseer of the colonies, recommended that the crown resume the charters of all the proprietary colonies in America, and Connecticut and Rhode Island were asked to surrender theirs voluntarily. They refused. Their agent in England, Jeremiah Drummer, in his *Defence of the New England Charters*, declared that a liberal policy toward the colonies would be much more expedient than a forcible union, which they would naturally resent.

In 1723 William Sherman moved his family to Stoughton. In 1725 he and John Wentworth bought a tract of 270 acres from the Indians at a price of £160. Roger learned to work hard doing farm chores.

During the Shermans' Sabbath, which began at sunset on Saturday, everything was religion. There were church services morning and afternoon. Mother could neither make beds nor prepare food; children could neither work nor play. Roger could read the Bible and the catechism, or a Christian children's book. Finally, at sunset, he was free to play with the other children.

The school curriculum began with the *New England Primer*, with the upper grades studying the *Westminster Catechism*. English grammar, writing, and arithmetic were also stressed. Few girls attended school. Roger's sisters, when adult, signed legal documents with an "X." School met only in winter—in summer Roger did farm work or learned shoe repairing from his father.

Between school and private reading, Roger learned a lot about history, economics, logic, mathematics, physics, philosophy, and theology. He read poetry and knew a little Latin. An extant copy of a set of maxims he copied as a boy shows how serious-minded he already was.

In the War of the Austrian Succession in 1740 Roger did not enlist but many colonists did. At the disastrous Cartagena expedition only 1100 of the 3700 colonists' troops survived. Word came that better care had been taken of the English than the American troops. England gained new commercial advantages concerning the Spanish colonies but suffered some loss of respect in her own colonies.

As an adult Sherman was tall, unusually erect, with blue eyes and a fair complexion. His dress was plain but neat. His close-cropped brown hair, which he kept through his old age, contrasted strongly with the powdered wigs of the sophisticated gentlemen in New York and Philadelphia.

Religion to Sherman was more a guide to conduct than an exercise in spiritual exploration. He copied out a resolution of Connecticut churches condemning the fanaticism of the Great Awakening. A big impression upon him was *Doctrine of the Passions* by the hymn writer Isaac Watts. Among the rules of Watts that Sherman liked were: "Subdue pride—accustom yourself to candor. Suffer not your thoughts to dwell on the injuries you have received. Command your tongue to silence, if you cannot presently command your spirit."[5] Here Watts mentioned the practice of Julius Caesar, who when angered would not speak before reciting the Roman alphabet.

Sherman's self-love had an altruistic dimension, for it meant "the individual's interests so tied into the well-being of society that selfishness would be willingly subordinated to the needs of society."[6]

The Versatile Tradesman

In 1741 William Sherman died. His estate of £688 was left to Roger, with the provision that one-third would go to his mother, and Roger would have to support his brothers and sisters. Since he could sell his father's estate at only one-fourth of its appraised value, he was burdened with financial responsibilities for years.

Two years later Sherman moved the family 150 miles to New Milford, Connecticut, where his elder brother William lived. Life here was primitive. The shortage of currency made it a barter economy. Each man built his own home and barn. There were no stoves, carpets, or table forks. Self-reliance was needed, as there was little community spirit. With little or no tax funds, roads and bridges were neglected. Roger paid ten shillings in 1743 so that his family could use the bridge across the Housatonic River.

Sherman tried his hand at many occupations. He was at times a farmer, a shoemaker, and a surveyor. Since there were few newspapers, almanacs were very popular in the colonies. First Sherman contributed to almanacs published by Nathaniel Ames, and then from 1749 to 1760 he published his own almanacs. During the war against France the almanacs contained patriotic references to British victories.

In November 1749 Sherman married Elizabeth Hartwell of Stoughton. They had seven children, of whom three died in infancy.

The following year he became an assessor, and he and his brother William also bought a general store in New Milford. Eventually they opened other stores in New Haven and in Wallingford.

In 1751 he was elected leather-sealer, meaning that he checked on the accuracy of weights and measures. He became treasurer to handle the levy for the new meeting-house in 1752, and he was also appointed fence-viewer. These positions testify to two of his traits: a knowledge of mathematics and a reputation for honesty.

The British view was that the colonies were an economic asset whose trade was to be manipulated to benefit the mother country. The Hat Act of 1732 prohibited shipment of hats from one colony to another. The Molasses Act of 1733 put a high tax on rum, sugar, and molasses from non-British ports in the West Indies.

In 1740 the Massachusetts Land Bank issued excessive paper money, thus causing inflation. Connecticut did likewise, and soon the store owned by the Sherman brothers was receiving payment for goods in depreciated currency. In 1752 Sherman wrote a pamphlet asking the Connecticut General Assembly to outlaw depreciated currency from New Hampshire and Rhode Island. He also called for an import duty on rum, because of the social evil it spread.

Sherman often served as a church officer. In 1752 he became treasurer of the church building fund. He was also a deacon, and clerk of the church society, which appointed the town school committee, on which he served. He gave aid to neighboring towns and churches, and he helped introduce inoculation for smallpox into New Milford.

Sherman made a good living as surveyor for Litchfield County. Three of the early writers of surveying textbooks were young men tutored in surveying by Sherman. "It appears that he can claim to have inspired its formal teaching in America."[7]

The Public Official

In 1754 Sherman was named a selectman for New Milford. After having studied law in his spare time, he was admitted to the bar in Litchfield County. His rural appearance and style made him a favorite with farmers, who traditionally distrust lawyers. A Connecticut law of 1697 legislated against drunkards and lawyers. In the year 1755 Sherman handled 125 cases, and was now often called "Squire Sherman."

In May 1755 he became justice of the peace for Litchfield County, a position he held until he moved to New Haven. The same month he was elected to the Connecticut General Assembly. Except for the year 1756, he was elected to the Assembly each year until 1761.

Between 1759 and 1761 he was justice of the quorum, a position the equivalent of county judge. In one case he fined Samuel Peet three shillings for not having attended a church service for a month.

Sherman helped his brothers get a college education. Nathaniel and Josiah Sherman, aided by Roger, both graduated from the College of New Jersey (Princeton) and became ministers. When his brother William died in 1756, Roger received £243 from the estate for having served as administrator of William's affairs. Anthony Carpenter replaced William as Roger's business partner.

In 1760 Sherman's wife Elizabeth died. The following year he moved his family to New Haven, where he immediately became active in the White Haven Church. In 1761 the church society appointed him to the town school committee, and in 1763 and 1764 he was chosen moderator of the annual meeting of the church.

In May 1763 Roger married Rebecca Prescott in Salem. He was 41 and she was 20. They ultimately had eight children, one of whom died in infancy. Apparently Rebecca was a beautiful woman. Years later at a state dinner President Washington escorted her in to dinner, and seated her at his right. When John Hancock's wife complained that she should have been given this honor, Washington replied that it was his privilege to give his arm to the prettiest lady in the room.

Sherman continued to be popular with the electorate. He was elected deputy from New Haven to the colonial Assembly from 1764 to 1766. In May 1765 he was appointed justice of the peace from New Haven County, and that October he was selected as justice of the county quorum. In May 1766 the General Court chose him as judge of the superior court.

Under its charter, Connecticut elected all of its officers, and its laws were not subject to British veto, as long as they did not violate British law. "In no other colony was there a stronger passion for noninterference from without than in Connecticut. In none other was the population more homogeneous — it was almost entirely Anglo-Saxon."[8]

In the state government the upper house, called the Council of Assistants, had veto power over both the governor and the lower house, which was sometimes called the General Assembly but more properly called the House of Representatives.

Sherman had a reputation as a man of few words but much action. Once, when he was asked to speak at the dedication of a new bridge, he walked out on it, came back, and gave his total speech: "I don't see but that it stands steady."[9] A Dr. Jedediah Strong invented a vehicle run by machinery "small and enclosed in a cage." Asked his opinion of it, Sherman commented that "the machine will be a success if it will go."[10] He was right — the machine did not go, and was no success.

Often he performed his charity unobtrusively. When his wife rebuked him for paying too much for a piece of land, he replied that when he saw the seller's threadbare coat, he decided to help him by giving him more than the land was worth.

The Patriot

Diligent application to his various enterprises made Sherman a reasonably wealthy man. Living in New Haven, he contributed liberally to the Yale building fund. He served as treasurer of Yale from 1765 to 1776. For several years he and Acting President Naphtali Daggett were the only regular officers of the college.

The college treasurer received no salary but the job was easy. There were virtually no endowed funds to invest. Income depended upon tuition and grants from the colonial legislature. Tuition had recently been raised from 26 to 30 shillings annually. Sometimes when finances were low, Sherman would loan Yale money, and the trustees would ask for larger grants from the legislature. As Assemblyman, Sherman sat on the committee that recommended one grant of £160.

In 1768 Sherman received an honorary M.A. from Yale. President Ezra Stiles of Yale said that Sherman was "ever a friend to its interests," and wanted it kept in the hands of the clergy, those most appropriate to supervise "a religious as well as a scientific college."[11]

Sherman was a member of the state Council of Assistants from 1766 until 1784. He served as judge of the superior court of Connecticut from 1766 until 1789, when he resigned to be in the first United States Congress. He left the Council in 1785, when a new state law prevented a person from being a judge and a Councilman at the same time. Since these were annual appointments, Sherman must have possessed the confidence of the electorate to a remarkable degree.

Benedict Arnold ran an apothecary shop in New Haven, and also had a mercantile business in Newfoundland and the West Indies. When a disgruntled employee, Peter Boles, threatened to expose Arnold as a smuggler, Arnold and his followers whipped Boles on the town green. As judge, Sherman issued the warrant for Arnold's arrest. The 50-shilling fine was given to Boles as payment for "damages."[12] In later years Sherman was reluctant to support Arnold's frequent requests for military promotion.

The Sugar Act, the Quartering Act, and the Stamp Act led to general outbreaks of protest against Britain. Stamp agents were forced to resign their positions, including Jared Ingersoll, stamp agent for Connecticut.

Although Sherman opposed the Stamp Act, he expressed concern over the growing mob action. In a letter in 1766 he said that disrespect for law and authority "may lead to such disorders and confusions as will not be easily supressed. Is there not danger of proceeding too far in such measures, so as to involve the people in divisions and animosities among themselves, and endanger our charter privileges?"[13]

In 1767 the Townshend Act taxed imports of glass, lead, paper, painters' colors, and tea. Sherman served on a Council committee to determine how Connecticut should seek redress of grievance against the act. Throughout the colonies there was a spreading desire to boycott British goods.

The following year Sherman wrote a letter to William Samuel Johnson, the Connecticut agent in London, opposing the appointment of an Anglican bishop for Connecticut. If one were to come, Sherman said, he must expect no tax support, such as he would get in England. Nor should he expect a monopoly on the performance of marriage and other church rites. His position, said Sherman, would be the same as all other clergy.

When Lord North's government repealed the Townshend Act in 1770 but kept the tax on tea, a group of merchants in New Haven appointed Sherman chairman of a committee to protest the tea tax. The committee wrote that "the time is now come for us to determine whether we will be freemen or slaves. It is the cause of our country, of liberty, of all."[14] The statement not only supported the boycott on tea but also promised to cease trade with all colonies that observed the tea law.

Sherman was also gradually becoming interested in investing some of his money in western lands. The Susquehannah Company, owned chiefly by Connecticut investors, maintained that it had the original claim to land in western Pennsylvania. As a lawyer, Sherman at first seemed neutral in this land dispute, but in 1774 he wrote an article supporting the Susquehannah claim to the land.

Sherman pointed out that the Wyoming district of Pennsylvania, a strip of land 70 miles wide and 250 miles long, had originally been settled by the Susquehannah Company. Connecticut alleged that Charles II, in a charter given to that colony in 1662, defined the western border of the grant as extending to the South Sea (the Pacific Ocean). Since the main body of settlers were from Connecticut, the few Pennsylvania settlers did not contest the Susquehannah title claims at this time.

The problem arose in 1681 when Charles II gave the same land in his grant to William Penn. As attorney for the Susquehannah Company, Sherman argued that the second grant was illegal, for the title to the land had already passed away from the king. There began to be bloodshed between the two groups of settlers, and in 1774 the crown was in no position to adjudicate the dispute.

Sherman represented Connecticut in the First Continental Congress that year. Woodrow Wilson later said that Sherman, as chief spokesman for his state, was "rough as a peasant without, but in counsel very like a statesman, and in all things a hard-headed man of affairs."[15]

Sherman and John Adams became close friends in the Congress. Like many others, Adams distinguished between Sherman's appearance and his actions. "Hogarth's genius could not have invented a motion more opposite to grace," said Adams, describing Sherman's manner. "It is stiffness and awkwardness itself, rigid as starched linen or buckram." But Adams had nothing but praise for Sherman's "clear head and sound judgment."[16] Jefferson agreed, stating that Sherman "never said a foolish thing in his life."[17]

John Adams quoted Sherman as saying that he believed that Parliament had no authority to make laws for America. Sherman told another Massachusetts delegate to Congress, Thomas Cushing, that "no laws bind the people but such as they consent to be governed by. Have not each colony complete powers of legislation for all purposes of government, and are they in any sense subordinate to the legislature of Great Britain, though subject to the same King?"[18]

At this Congress Sherman signed the first of his important national documents, the Association agreement forbidding trade with Britain. In November 1774 at a New Haven town meeting Sherman was elected chairman of a committee of 31 persons authorized to see that the Association was enforced in town.

Unlike many of the colonial governors, Governor Jonathan Trumbull of Connecticut was thoroughly dedicated to the patriots' cause. In February 1775 Sherman informed the state treasurer that he had bought powder, lead, and flints (at a cost of £577) in New York City, to be stockpiled in his store and in the store of D. Austin.

News of the battles of Lexington and Concord reached New Haven on April 21. A town meeting was called, and Sherman was elected moderator. The conservatives advocated no immediate action beyond determining the plans of General Thomas Gage.

Fiery Benedict Arnold, a captain of militia, called out fifty men, seized ammunition from the powder house, and marched to Massachusetts, where he secured a commission and joined Ethan Allen to capture Crown Point from the British on May 10, 1775 — the day the Second Continental Congress convened.

The Legislator

Sherman served in the Continental Congress from 1774 to 1781 and again in 1783-84. He was, in one opinion, "perhaps the most influential figure in Congress toward the end of the Revolution."[19]

In Congress he was placed on several military committees. One was to purchase clothing for the soldiers, and another was to investigate fraud in army contracts. He had one important difference of opinion with Washington. To give him a stable army, Washington wanted enlistments to be for the duration of the War. But Congress feared a standing army. Sherman said that "enlistment for a long period is a state of slavery,"[20] and John Adams and others agreed.

In other committee work, Sherman joined fellow delegates in

advising New Hampshire to form its own government, and in working on a treaty with the Iroquois Indians. Sherman had a very humane approach to the Indians and their problems. Since he felt that the states might mistreat them, he favored giving the federal government jurisdiction over matters concerning the Indians. Like Jefferson, he believed that only Congress should have the authority to purchase land from the Indians.

In an effort to woo Canada into joining the insurrection, a committee of Sherman, John Adams, and George Wythe drew up a statement in March 1776 that promised Canada whatever form of government it preferred but Canada opted for loyalty to the crown.

The chores of a farm boy prepared Sherman for his arduous day as a legislator. Up at 5 a.m., he had early committee work, the Congressional session from 10 a.m. to 4 p.m., and then again committee work until 10 p.m. "Men who knew him said this arduous work took a toll of eight years from his life,"[21] said Roger Sherman Baldwin.

On June 11 Congress appointed a committee to draft a Declaration of Independence. Committee members were John Adams, Franklin, Jefferson, Robert Livingston, and Sherman. Relying heavily upon George Mason's Virginia Declaration of Rights and John Locke's second essay *Of Civil Government*, Jefferson basically drafted the document. Adams and Franklin made a few contributions but Livingston and Sherman seem to have contributed relatively little.[22]

On July 2 the Congress approved 12-0 (with New York abstaining) the resolution of Richard Henry Lee that "these colonies are, and of right ought to be, free and independent states." By the same vote on July 4 Congress adopted the Declaration of Independence. Later New York also instructed its delegates to support the declaration.

Sherman's third son, Isaac, a Yale graduate, enlisted in the army after the battle of Lexington. Isaac called his father "a kind of indulgent parent, who always consults the good of his children." Sherman commended Isaac to Washington, who in October 1776 found Major Sherman to be "an active and valuable officer."[23] Isaac served in numerous battles and ended up as a lieutenant colonel.

Washington's early setbacks scared the people of Connecticut. When the British overran southern New York and New Jersey in late 1776, the Connecticut General Court repealed an act requiring an oath of allegiance to the Revolutionary government. Tories began to be re-elected to office. Yale deserted New Haven and held classes in Farmington, Glastonbury, and Wethersfield.

In the Congress, the disunited states, fighting to gain their freedom from British domination, were in no mood to surrender their sovereignty to some superstate in America. From the start, the Congress was weak.

Sometimes a state would have no delegates representing it in the Congress.

Sherman now served on the Board of War and the Board of Treasury. He was also a member of committees on the post office and on foreign affairs. In 1777 he had a hand in replacing General Philip Schuyler with the British-born Horatio Gates. This action angered Hamilton, who was to marry Elizabeth Schuyler in 1780.

Sherman spearheaded the drive for statehood for the Vermont part of New York. In 1777, as General Burgoyne moved toward Fort Ticonderoga, Sherman introduced the Vermont petition for statehood into Congress. New Yorkers, especially James Duane, fought Sherman's resolution. Sherman's position was made more precarious by the division among Vermonters between those supporting and those opposing Ethan Allen.

After the humiliating defeat of General Gates at Camden, Vermonters threatened to make a separate peace with England unless they were recognized as a state. Congress, worried, appointed a committee that included Sherman to find a solution.

The committee recommended that New Hampshire and New York do what Massachusetts had already done—relinquish claims to the region. But southern states did not want an additional northern state, and New York and Pennsylvania felt that it was a bad precedent to dismember existing states. So, like the Wyoming controversy, this one was postponed until after the Constitutional Convention.[24] When Vermont was admitted as a state in 1791, it could say that one of its best friends had been Roger Sherman.

What plan of government was the new nation to adopt? The new Congress was powerless until it had a constitution that had been approved by the states. Sherman and Franklin both drew up plans of confederation for Congress. John Adams liked Sherman's plan better, but neither was adopted. Sherman's plan suggested two types of representation: "Call the colonies and call the individuals, and have a majority of both."[25] This was a preview of the Great Compromise of the Constitutional Convention.

John Dickinson of Pennsylvania finally drafted the Articles of Confederation. After months of debate they were adopted by Congress in November 1777. Sherman worked hard to strengthen the Confederation by trying to get the states to ratify these articles.

In 1778 President Stiles of Yale hired a French professor who was a Roman Catholic. Many persons in New Haven opposed having a Catholic professor, but Sherman warmly welcomed Monseigneur Martel to New Haven and the Yale campus.

In addition to his work in Congress, Sherman was on the Governor's

Council in Connecticut throughout the War. From 1777 to 1779 and again in 1782 he was a member of the state Council of Safety, which kept a watchful eye for suspected loyalists and also supervised the procurement of troops for the Continental Army.

Sherman's advice on how to fight inflation was to avoid printing paper money, but instead, insofar as possible, tax. If additional funds are needed, get them through domestic loans. Annual conventions of the confederated states suggested this action from 1776 through 1780, but the government lacked the power to tax, and so no action was taken. At the 1778 convention in New Haven, Sherman was the chairman and prepared the report. Rhode Island, and later New York, by their single votes kept Congress from getting the power to tax.

Sherman was the chief influence in getting Connecticut to stop issuing paper money but instead relying upon taxes to raise revenues. In 1779 Washington said that Connecticut was the only state to live up to its obligation of raising funds without debasing its currency.[26]

By the end of 1779 Congress had issued $241,000,000 of paper currency, to vie with $209,000,000 that had been issued by the states. Counterfeit money put out by the British and by unscrupulous Americans aggravated the problem. In 1780 Congress redeemed $40 of the old currency for $1 of currency backed by silver. But even the new money sank quickly in value. Before long it was being used for dog blankets and wall paper, because it was "not worth a Continental!"[27]

For his work in trying to get Congress to face up to fiscal responsibility, "to Roger Sherman is due the credit for an important step toward the organization of the Treasury Department,"[28] in the opinion of Forrest Morgan.

Sherman kept after the economic problems of the new nation. To fight inflation, he now recommended price-fixing, but Congress demurred. In an effort to reduce military costs, he suggested that families clothe their own soldiers, and that other supplies be sold to soldiers by sutlers at army camps.

In 1780 a Congressional committee on which Sherman served tried to get each state to support its troops. Washington said that the system would not work. General Nathaniel Greene, the quartermaster-general, charged that Sherman's object was "to keep the army as weak as possible. I believe him to be the worst politician that ever disgraced the American councils." Later that year, when Congress tried to dismiss Greene not only from his post but from the service altogether, Greene confessed, "Can you believe it that Mr. Sherman was my fast friend in all this affair? I have this from the best authority."[29]

Sherman suggested in a Congressional report in 1780 that states carved out of the public domain enter the Union on equal terms with original members. He repeated this stand in 1784. Thus he was "one of the prime movers of the anti-imperial commitment of the Founding Fathers. Sherman operated in the larger — even the largest — interest." His greatness lay in his capacity to compromise, "and his uncanny ability to mold the contending forces around him into a solid, cohesive, functioning unit."[30]

There were several explanations of Sherman's success as a legislator. Sherman said it in his own way: "Minorities talk, majorities vote." Jefferson said that Sherman was "a very able and logical debater. Steady in the principles of the Revolution, he was always at the post of duty. I had very great respect for him."[31] Silas Deane said that Sherman was as poorly calculated to appear in polite society, "as a chestnut-burr is for an eyestone,"[32] but in conversation with him one found him to be not only profound but clever.

In May 1783 Sherman and Richard Law were appointed by the Connecticut General Assembly to codify state laws. Their work, published under the title of *Acts and Laws of the State of Connecticut*, was adopted by the Assembly as the definitive law of the state in 1784.

That year Sherman held four public offices at once. He was in the Continental Congress, was mayor of New Haven, and was on the Governor's Council and the state superior court. The following year he served on the committee to revise the bylaws of New Haven.

In 1786, when Connecticut ceded her western lands to the Continental Congress, the state reserved a 120-mile strip along Lake Erie, then in the Northwest Territory, known as the Western Reserve. Sherman had a large part in securing this land for Connecticut. By 1800 the state had sold this land for $2,000,000 and used the proceeds as the nucleus for a state school fund.

For many years Sherman and Oliver Ellsworth formed an effective leadership team for their state. They served together on the Governor's Council, on the state superior court, and in the Continental Congress. They later worked together in the Constitutional Convention and the United States Senate. Ellsworth told John Adams that in his youth he had made Sherman his life model. Adams said, "Indeed, I never knew two men more alike, except that the Chief Justice had the advantage of a liberal education and somewhat more extensive reading."[33]

The Framer

Perhaps to reflect the views of their constituents, Sherman and Ellsworth began the Constitutional Convention as firm advocates of states' rights. The daily discussions persuaded them, however, that many of the nation's problems were national in scope, and could thus be handled effectively only by the central government. As fair-minded and conscientious delegates like Sherman and Ellsworth were convinced that they should adopt a more national perspective on many issues, they brought with them a number of less prominent delegates who had looked to them to articulate the position of protection of the rights of states.

At 66, Sherman was the oldest delegate except for Franklin. But his 138 speeches at the Convention made him the fourth most active delegate, behind Gouverneur Morris, Wilson, and Madison.

The historian George Bancroft said that "Roger Sherman was a unique man. No one in the Convention had had so large experience in legislating for the United States."[34] Bancroft praised Sherman for his candor, industry, insight, judgment, patriotism, and self-control.

On May 31 Sherman warned against errors made by the uninformed public, and recommended the election of one member per state to the Senate by state legislatures. There must have been a great difference between the Connecticut and Massachusetts legislatures, for the Connecticut delegates tended to consider state legislatures competent to make binding decisions while the Massachusetts delegates often derided the foolish or corrupt decisions made by state legislatures.[35]

Sherman wanted annual elections to the lower house, so that representatives would "return home and mix with the people." On similar grounds he wanted five-year terms for Senators, since "frequent elections are necessary to preserve the good behavior of rulers."[36] He feared that Congressional salaries might be set so low as to exclude the poor from serving, so on August 14 he recommended that they be set at $5 per day from the national treasury, with the states free to augment the amount if they wished.[37]

On June 11 Sherman moved that the lower house be apportioned according to population but that in the Senate each state have just one vote. Although his motion was defeated 6-5, he was here suggesting the ground on which the Great Compromise was finally reached. The Great Compromise was sometimes called the Sherman Compromise or the Connecticut Compromise. Sherman said that he wanted to see equality of votes in the Senate "not so much as a security for the small states as for the state governments, which could not be preserved unless they were represented and had a negative in the general government."[38]

Sherman's philosophy of government came out on June 28 when he spoke on what compromise meant: "The question is, not what rights naturally belong to man, but how they may be most equally guarded in society. If some give up more than others to obtain this end, there can be no reason for complaint. The rich man who enters into society along with the poor man gives up more than the poor man, yet with an equal vote he is equally safe. Were he to have more votes than the poor man, the rights of the poor man would immediately cease to be secure."[39]

Because it most directly represented the people, Sherman wanted to give the legislature the supreme power. He thought that the executive should be the arm of the legislature and subordinate to it, an idea he got from Rousseau. Like many other delegates still shuddering from their experience with George III, he wished to restrict the authority of the executive. The president, he felt, should be subject to a restricting council, just as the British prime minister is subordinate to Parliament. The president should not be able to veto laws of Congress, nor should he have much appointive power, in Sherman's view.

Forgetting some of the blunders of the Continental Congress during the Revolution, he believed that the legislature should control the military. He was particularly fearful of the danger of a standing army in peacetime, and on September 5 he expressed a wish for legislation restricting a standing army.[40]

Sherman wanted the national judiciary appointed by the legislature rather than by the executive. Gorham said the method used in Massachusetts was the best — appointed by the executive with the advice and consent of the Senate.[41] Gorham's method was preferred over Sherman's in the Convention.

Sherman was liberal in his treatment of new states, feeling that they should have every power that existing states had. He also suggested the method of deciding presidential elections that we still use today. In the absence of a majority in the electoral college, Sherman said that the House of Representatives should decide the election, with each state having one vote, to keep a few populous states from controlling the result.

The framers were vague about what to do with the office of vice president. Gerry and Williamson said that there was no need for such a position. Mason warned that if the vice president presided over the Senate, it would be a dangerous encroachment of the executive into the legislative branch. Sherman believed that unless the vice president presided over the Senate, he would have no job. Further, were the Senate to elect one of their members, that person would be deprived of a vote except in cases of a trial.[42] Sherman's views prevailed.

Because they are appointed rather than elected, judges should not have the power to veto laws, Sherman reasoned, lest they negate the wishes of the people. Also, the Supreme Court should not try presidential impeachments, since the judges had been appointed by the executive. The jurisdiction of the national courts, he felt, should be extended to cases beyond the scope of other courts. These would be cases between citizens and foreigners, between citizens and states other than their own, and between citizens from different states.[43]

There was a solidness in Sherman's character that, in time, became very fetching. Towards the end of the Convention he was three times selected by ballot to serve on committees dealing with knotty problems. On August 18 he was elected to the committee to work on federal assumption of state war debts. On August 25 he was placed on the committee defining the role of Congress in regulating commerce. And on August 31 he was elected to the Committee on Unfinished Business.[44]

There was a tendency in the Committee on Unfinished Business for members to insert pet clauses or concepts which they had not been able to get accepted in the regular course of business. Sherman thus moved to add on to the statement concerning the power of Congress to levy taxes and duties a description of the war debts and the phrase "for the payment of said debts and for defraying the expenses that shall be incurred for the common defense and general welfare."[45] Madison noted that only Connecticut voted for Sherman's motion.

Sherman's conversion to the federalist position was never as strong as was that of Ellsworth. Sherman realized that only the national government should perform certain functions, such as conduct foreign affairs, make war, and resolve conflicts between states. He also favored granting the national government the authority to regulate commerce, including taxation, reduction of the national debt, and control of the currency. He preferred to specify the purpose of taxation, and he did not want Congress to have the power to tax exports, since this, he felt, would be prejudicial to noncommercial states.

Even at the end of the Convention, Sherman favored reserving certain powers to the states. First would be no police power, and control of the militia except during wartime. He did not think that the national government should build canals or run a university. He believed that each state should decide on the method of ratification it would use. In his opinion there needed to be unanimous (not three-fourths) agreement by the states on amendments to the Constitution, lest the majority usurp the rights of the minority.

In the opinion of Roger Sherman Boardman, there are 11 features of the Constitution in which Sherman's influence, either individually or in conjunction with others, can be traced[46]:

1. States should not be allowed to issue paper money.
2. Senators should be chosen by state legislatures.
3. The president should command the militia in wartime.
4. National courts should have jurisdiction "between citizens of the same state claiming lands under grants of different states."
5. The national government should be impartial toward the commercial status of state ports.
6. State export or import duties should be for the use of the Union.

7. Although Congressmen should not be barred from holding state office, they should be ineligible to hold offices they created or in which they increased the salary.
8. In the event of no electoral majority, the president should be elected by the House of Representatives, with each state having one vote.
9. Congress may propose amendments to the states for their approval.
10. The federal government should pay the war debts of the states.
11. "No state, without its consent, shall be deprived of its equal suffrage in the Senate." Also, the internal police of each state shall not, without its consent, be affected by the national government.

Between November 14 and December 20, 1787, Sherman wrote five letters to the *New Haven Gazette* supporting ratification. He pointed out that the people of Connecticut were losing no sovereignty, but rather transferring some of it from the state to the federal government, so as to better protect the interests of all. Borrowing from Franklin, he said that small states would benefit from the Union just as Scotland had gained from union with England.

Sherman spoke effectively for the Constitution at the state ratification convention in Hartford on January 3, 1788. He stressed the protective checks and balances found in the new document. The legislature was checked by specific articles in the Constitution, by the modes of representation, and by the powers reserved to the states. Also, the powers of Congress are limited to those necessary to national survival and the general welfare. The president cannot be a tyrant, Sherman said, because of his short term of office. Federal courts are limited in jurisdiction, so that, Sherman believed, not one citizen in a hundred would have cause to appear before them. Since revenue will come from the sale of western lands and from import duties, there should be little occasion for a high rise in taxes. One witness said that Connecticut's convincing vote, 128-40, in favor of the Constitution was "owing in a considerable degree to the influence and arguments of Mr. Sherman."[47]

Final Years

Sherman's long career in public service was not good for the family coffers. In October 1789 he wrote to Governor Samuel Huntington, saying that Connecticut owed him £775 for his services in the Continental Congress. His daughters, he said, were making and selling gloves to help out. Connecticut finally paid him $7700 in 1792, the year before he died.

Nor was he the only Sherman to have financial problems. His two eldest sons, John and William, were business failures. His son Isaac, unpaid for his faithful service in the Continental Army, borrowed money from his father and $150 from Alexander Hamilton, which it took him three years to repay. Sherman's brother Nathaniel had invested £600 in national bonds, but could not redeem these. Eventually Sherman persuaded the Connecticut legislature to help Nathaniel get back £400 of his investment.

As a member of the first House of Representatives under the new Constitution, Sherman differed with his old friend, Vice President John Adams. For the president to be independent of the legislature, Adams argued, he should have the absolute right to veto a law. Sherman felt that this would give the president too much power. If the veto can be overruled by a two-thirds vote in Congress, Sherman said, it would better carry out the will of the people.

Pressure from the state ratifying conventions meant that the new Congress would have to consider adopting a Bill of Rights. During the Constitutional Convention Sherman had opposed such a bill, feeling that if anywhere it belonged in state constitutions, where there might otherwise be an infringement upon human rights. He further felt that since the federal government had not been empowered to act in a specific area, there would be no need to restrict that power. Finally, he said, there was the fear that the people would think that the stated rights were the only protected rights. For example, need there be one law stating that Congress cannot quarter troops in private homes, and another for each specific right?

Madison, of course, was not to be denied, and so the only question in the new Congress was what form should the Bill of Rights take? In Amendment 10 Sherman added the crucial words "to the United States" after the word "delegated," thereby stressing that an individual has certain rights which no government, whether local, state, or federal may properly abrogate.[48]

Ironically, Sherman saved Madison from a major error in getting the Bill of Rights adopted. Madison wanted to add this material to the Preamble. No, said Sherman, the people adopted the Constitution as it was presented to them, and we have no right to alter what the people have approved. Use the machinery for amendment as prescribed in the Constitution, said Sherman. "Madison's efforts to alter the basic document in 1789 would have undermined the nationalist foundations that he had worked so hard to establish in 1787, while Sherman, the archfederalist of the earlier period, became in 1789 the bulwark of a nationally founded Constitution."[49]

To raise revenue, Sherman supported in the Congress taxes on brandy, rum, and tobacco. He also stood behind Hamilton's national bank, and became a stockholder in it. He agreed with Hamilton that it would be in the national interest to protect home industries. Having 100 cents to the dollar made more sense to him than having 90 cents, as it had been. He opposed, however, the import duty of $10 per slave, for "he could not reconcile himself to the insertion of human beings as an article of duty among goods and merchandise."[50]

Sherman also supported Hamilton's position that not only should the federal government assume the war debts of the states but in doing so should not attempt to differentiate between original holders and more recent purchasers.

When Madison adamantly opposed the lack of differentiation, Sherman once more came up with a compromise: the federal government would not only assume the states' war debts, but it would also reimburse the states for their war contributions. Madison was thus appeased, and when Hamilton and Jefferson worked out their bargain on the location of the national capitol, the issue was resolved.[51]

Sherman believed that the president should not have the absolute power to remove persons appointed with the consent of the Senate, but that the Senate should also be involved in the removal. Here, of course, his viewpoint lost.

He recommended that America proceed cautiously on immigration, for too much of it would make it hard to retain a harmonious society. On the sale of western lands, he favored such sale to settlers but not to speculators or absentee landlords.

Evaluating Sherman's services in the First Congress, G.H. Hollister in his *History of Connecticut* said that "he appears to have known the science of government from childhood—he needed no teaching because he saw the moral, ethical, and political truths in all their relations, better than they could be interpreted to him by others. He looked not only at the present but at future generations."[52]

Sherman was re-elected to the House of Representatives in the Second Congress, but when William Samuel Johnson, president of Columbia College, had to stay in New York and resign his seat in the Senate, Sherman was elected by the Connecticut legislature to fill Johnson's unexpired term, which ran until March 1795. In the Senate he continued to support Hamilton's effort to put the federal treasury on a sound footing.

In 1792 Sherman voted against confirmation of Gouverneur Morris as minister to France, because "he makes religion the subject of ridicule and is profane in his conversation."[53] Sherman agreed that Morris had never betrayed a trust, but he felt that Morris might do so because of the lack of religious principles at the core of his character. Morris, nevertheless, with Ellsworth voting for his approval, was confirmed by a vote of 16-11.

As usual, Sherman served on a number of Senate committees. Boardman, including "only the more important committees on which Sherman was placed," came up with the staggering career total of 171, broken down as follows[54]:

Continental Congresses, 1774-80	91
Confederation Congresses, 1781 & 1784	44
First Congress (1789-91) as representative	23
Second Congress (1791-93) as senator	13

Excluded from the above totals are the many Connecticut state committees on which Sherman served, as well as the ones in the Constitutional Convention.

At the age of 70 Sherman could still ride a horse thirty or forty miles without fatigue. At 72 he had 10 living children and 11 grandchildren, and 36 more grandchildren were born after his death. His last public act was to participate in laying the cornerstone for South College at Yale on April 15, 1793. He died of typhoid fever on July 23, 1793. A large funeral in New Haven honored him on July 25.

President Stiles of Yale said that Sherman had "that dignity which arises from doing everything perfectly right. He was an extraordinary man — a venerable uncorrupted patriot."[55] Jonathan Edwards, Jr., said that Sherman's success in politics resulted from "acute discernment, sound judgment, and knowledge of human nature." He knew what was feasible and what was not, Edwards said — what people would bear in government and what they would not bear. "He had a rare talent of prudence or of time, adapting his measures to the attainment of his end."[56]

At New Haven's bicentennial in 1838 Professsor James Kingsley said that "no man in Connecticut ever enjoyed the confidence of the people of the state more entirely, or for a longer period, than Roger Sherman." In his public life, said Kingsley, he left the impression of deep sagacity and stern integrity, and his gift to the present is "the character of a great, and what is much more rare, of an honest, politician."[57]

His grandson, Senator George F. Hoar, summarized his career in a tribute to him: "He had a large share in the public events that led to the Revolution, in the conduct of the War, in the proceedings of the Continental Congress, in the framing of the Constitution, in securing its adoption by Connecticut, and in the action of the House and the Senate in Washington's administration. He was also for many years judge of the highest court in the state.

"He had a most affectionate and tender heart. He was very fond of his family and friends. Although reserved and silent in ordinary company, he was very agreeable in conversation, and had a delightful wit. Patrick Henry said that Roger Sherman and George Mason were the greatest statesmen he ever knew."[58]

Thus had this awkward but clear-headed Yankee helped to found a great nation. He was the only patriot to sign the four most important documents signalling America's break with England: the Association of the First Continental Congress, the Declaration of Independence, the Articles of Confederation, and the Constitution. As Christopher Collier properly concludes, "No one can gainsay his position as a major participant in the national politics that founded the American nation."[59]

14. George Washington: The One Indispensable Man

In a conclave of giants, there was one person who towered over all the rest. It may have been difficult, but the new nation could have spared John Adams, Franklin, Hamilton, Jefferson, or Madison, but without George Washington there would have been no United States of America as we know it today. How could one man be so indispensable, especially since nature or nature's God had been so lavish in providing a cornucopia of leaders of talent and distinction?

Clinton Rossiter said that "we cannot begin to understand the mind of a man like Washington unless we recognize his consuming belief in the existence of a common enduring interest of the whole community that rose above all private interests, that held out the hand of peace, order, and welfare to all men of all classes, and that provided the grand context of liberty, stability, and progress within which each man could pursue his own version of happiness."[1]

Abigail Adams visited Washington's camp near Boston in 1775. She was not given to flattery, and could on occasion be sharp-tongued. Yet she candidly confessed that on meeting Washington, she thought instantly of Dryden's high-flown lines:

> Mark his majestic fabric; he's a temple
> Sacred by birth, and built by hands divine.
> His soul's the deity that lodges there,
> Nor is the pile unworthy of the God.[2]

Robert Morris told a friend that Washington was "the only man in whose presence he felt any awe." A recent biographer calls Washington "a great man, a majestic figure, unquestionably the principal, the essential founder and champion of the American republic — the one man essential to the triumph of the Patriots in the War of Independence, to the creation of the American union, and perhaps even to the success of the democratic revolution throughout the world."[3]

Washington was not a great intellectual. He had not read much of law or government, and he was neither a military genius nor an inspired administrator. He had the personality flaws common to mankind, including a temper that could get him into trouble. If there was any one quality of his which was superlative it would be his character. In his maturity he bore countless unnecessary attacks, in the interest of a strong nation, and he never took the time to seek personal recrimination. Here at last, then, as Jefferson said, was a great man who was a truly good man.

Washington's father Augustine was a planter and businessman who had been educated in England. His first wife, Jane Butler, died in 1730 after bearing four children. Augustine married Mary Ball on March 6, 1731. George was born to them in Westmoreland County, Virginia, on February 11, 1732 (changed to February 22 in 1752 when the Gregorian calendar was adopted). George had a younger sister and three younger brothers. Seven of Augustine's nine children lived beyond infancy, an unusually high percentage at the time.

When George was three, Augustine built a farmhouse where Little Henry Creek runs into the Potomac, the site of present Mount Vernon. Later the family settled at Ferry Farm on the north bank of the Rappahannock River, opposite Fredericksburg. There Augustine died in 1743 at the age of 50. George inherited Ferry Farm, other lands, and ten slaves. His mother became his legal guardian.

George was a dutiful rather than an affectionate son. His mother had reared a brood of children and felt that her sacrifices were unrecognized. "In youth insecure, aggressive, striving, goaded by a sense of the inferiority of his station, Washington was headstrong, uninhibited, and quite self-centered. In short, he was not too lovable."[4]

He had only brief schooling, perhaps less than had Abraham Lincoln. His spelling was always poor but he had good handwriting and was an excellent draftsman. His favorite subject was mathematics. Most of his reading in his library of 900 volumes was utilitarian, in military and agricultural books. He did, however, read *Don Quixote* and *Tristram Shandy*, and he loved drama and history. His manners improved greatly as he pored over *Rules of Civility and Decent Behavior*.

George was fascinated by his half-brother Lawrence, who had served as a captain in an ill-fated effort by the British to invade New Grenada (modern Colombia) under Admiral Edward Vernon. Although Lawrence criticized the poor leadership of the British generals, he admired Vernon so much that he named his estate after him.

Should George become a sailor, as Lawrence suggested to Mary Washington? By no means, advised Joseph Ball, Mary's half-brother. It is much better to be a master of 300 acres of land, Joseph said, than to be master of a ship at sea.

As a young man, George became friendly with the Fairfax family. Colonel William Fairfax, who served on the Virginia governor's council, was a distant cousin to Lord Fairfax, who owned over 5,000,000 acres of land in the Northern Neck, the area between the Potomac and the Rappahannock Rivers. George became a close friend of George William Fairfax, the son of the colonel.

In 1748 George and George William Fairfax went on a surveying party across the Blue Ridge Mountains into the Shenandoah Valley. Meeting a party of Indians coming home from war, they gave the Indians some liquor, stimulating them to do a war dance over the one scalp they had collected.

George liked order and precision. His account books were accurate and neat. In his diary he conscientiously recorded planting dates, weather data, crop prices, and other items.[5] In 1749 he became surveyor of Culpeper County. He was so successful at surveying that in several years he owned 1400 acres of land.

He spent a lot of time on the frontier, where punishment for crime was severe. In 1751 Mary McDaniel, for stealing George's clothes while he was bathing in a river, received 15 whip lashes upon her bare back.

In the fall of 1751 George and Lawrence went to the Barbados, to try to help Lawrence recover from tuberculosis. It was George's only trip off the American continent. At home, he attended the theater and enjoyed many pastimes — billiards, cards, dancing, and riding. In November he spent three weeks in bed, suffering from smallpox. Although the illness left pockmarks on his face for life, it also left him immune to the disease in the course of his many military campaigns.

The Young Military Leader

In the spring of 1752 Washington again surveyed the Shenandoah Valley. He joined the Masonic order at Fredericksburg, but seldom attended lodge meetings. Lawrence died in July, granting Mount Vernon to George upon the death of his own wife and daughter. George succeeded Lawrence as one of Virginia's four adjutants, so now he was training militia.

The best horseman in the state, George was now 6'3" tall, with broad shoulders, a narrow waist, and sinewy limbs. He had a graceful carriage, and blue eyes and reddish brown hair.

He was always attracted to and by pretty women. As a young man he tried writing an acrostic verse to a Frances Alexandra but his muse expired at Frances Alexa. In 1752 he proposed twice to Betsy Fauntleroy, 15-year-old daughter of a prosperous merchant and planter, but Betsy would not have him. He remained single for six more years.

France had a large settlement in Quebec, a small one in New Orleans, and trappers and traders in between. The French built forts along the Ohio River valley in lands that they claimed. The Ohio Company, formed by Virginia residents, grew alarmed at the French demands. The Ohio Company claimed 500,000 acres on the upper Ohio River, and was planning to build a fort at the junction of the Allegheny and Monongahela Rivers.

In October 1753 Governor Robert Dinwiddie of Virginia appointed Washington to head a seven-man delegation to ask the French commander to withdraw from British territory. The return journey was perilous. Their Indian guides deserted them, and their horses were weak and overburdened, so they walked through the snow. Portaging rivers, they drew Indian fire. Washington fell off a raft into the icy Allegheny River, and nearly died from exposure to the cold. He wrote a journal of his trip, and included a good map of the Ohio country. Copies of his journal appeared in colonial newspapers and in the popular *London Magazine*. By the time he was 23, England had heard of his name.

In April 1753 Washington was made lieutenant-colonel under Colonel Joshua Fry, who commanded a regiment of Virginia militia. Their mission was to build a fort at the head of the Ohio River, and if anyone interfered, "to make prisoners of or kill and destroy them."[6] Dinwiddie announced that 200,000 acres of land in the Ohio Valley would be distributed among the volunteers.

The French moved in with 1,000 men and 18 cannons and pushed Ensign Edward Ward and his 40 men out of the site at the head of the Ohio River. The French built Fort Duquesne at this location. Since Colonel Fry had died in a fall from a horse, Washington was now in command. When he met Ward's retreating men he knew that his force was too small to fight the French, so he built a base forty miles south of Fort Duquesne, and waited for reinforcements from Virginia.

In the first outbreak of shooting in the French and Indian War, Washington's men defeated a contingent of French troops under the Sieur de Jumonville, who was killed in the battle. Hearing bullets whistle nearby, Washington said, "Believe me, there is something charming in the sound."[7]

The French retaliated with a force of 400 soldiers plus some Indians and defeated Washington's contingent of 300 troops at Fort Necessity on July 3, 1754. In the capitulation agreement, Washington was criticized for having admitted to the "assassination" of Jumonville. The fault may not have been his, for he knew little French and the translator may not have warned him about what he was signing. Back in Williamsburg, Dinwiddie dissolved the regiment and offered Washington a captaincy. He resigned from the militia in the fall of 1754.

In December 1754 Washington leased Mount Vernon, with its 2,000 acres and 18 slaves, from Lawrence's widow, in return for the annual payment of 15,000 pounds of tobacco. Since his mother was living at Ferry Farm, Washington was finally master of his household.

The following year he got into a fight over politics. While campaigning for George William Fairfax, he said something objectionable to William Payne, who was campaigning for William Ellzey. In the struggle, Payne knocked down Washington, whose troops had to be restrained from beating up Payne. There was talk of a duel. The next day Washington apologized for what he had said, and the matter was dropped.[8]

Washington now courted the beautiful Mary Eliza Philipse, heiress to a great estate. Tongues wagged, but Washington did not propose to her, perhaps because of her imperious manner. His head had also been turned towards pretty Sally Fairfax, the wife of his good friend George William Fairfax. His letters of admiration to her became so indiscreet that Sally had to ask him to stop writing to her.[9]

The French and the British began building forces for a major conflict. Major General Edward Braddock, commander of British troops in the colonies, was being sent with a force to capture Fort Duquesne and march to Niagara to meet other British forces there. Washington placed his brother John Augustine in charge of Mount Vernon, and joined Braddock. Since he would not pay for a commission in the customary manner, he had to go as a volunteer.

Braddock criticized colonial officials for not providing him with supplies. Washington defended them, saying that most had responded. He was already resentful over the fact that British regulars were reluctant to serve under a Virginia colonel. Benjamin Franklin helped Braddock get the necessary wagons and supplies.

Bogged down by the large supply wagon, the pace was slow, crawling forward at two miles per day. Having contracted malaria, Washington rode in a covered wagon. But on June 16, 1755, he suggested to Braddock that the forces be split, with the soldiers riding faster toward the French, and the supply wagons carrying up the rear. Braddock agreed.

Captain Beaujeu had about 250 French troops and 600 Indians at Fort Necessity. With the Indians shouting war whoops, Beaujeu ambushed the British advance unit from both sides. The columns of redcoats made excellent targets. British cannon was ineffective in the wooded gulches. In ranks ten or twelve deep, the British often fired into their own men.

Although his advice to divide the forces may have been questionable, Washington showed great bravery in the battle. With two other aides wounded, Washington carried messages back and forth, a constant target. Four bullets went through his coat, two horses were shot out from under him, but he stayed at his post. With two-thirds of the first unit killed or wounded, Braddock ordered a general retreat. He died of wounds on July 13.

In the fall of 1755 Dinwiddie made Washington a colonel in charge of all Virginia forces. Washington had been critical of both the bravery and the tactics of the British troops, but he was proud of the Virginia militia in their battle against the French.

Dinwiddie was unpopular with Virginia leaders, for he carried out orders from the crown, oversaw tax collections, and was getting wealthy through his commercial transactions. Increasingly, Washington attracted the attention of the Burgesses. One of them, Landon Carter, told him to "tread the same path that you first cut out, that your country may in the end feel the good effects that she promises herself from your singular virtues."[10]

In February 1756 Washington rode to Boston to try to get a regular British army commission from General William Shirley, who was also governor of Massachusetts. For the first time he saw the cities of Philadelphia, New York, and Boston. The Boston *Gazette* greeted "the Honorable Colonel Washington, a gentleman who has deservedly a high reputation for military skill and valor, though success has not always attended his undertakings."[11] He bought some new clothes, visited the fort in Boston harbor, and lost a little money playing whist and loo.

Although Shirley was not authorized to grant regular army commissions, he gave Washington a letter to Governor Sharpe of Maryland, telling Sharpe to rein in Captain John Dagworthy of Maryland, a former regular officer who refused to take orders from Washington.

Discipline was one of his chief problems. In one frontier skirmish against Indians, Washington lost 17 men, which he attributed to lack of discipline. He contemplated leaving the army because of this problem.

Eventually the Virginia Assembly gave Washington increased authority to handle discipline matters. Flogging was permitted as punishment, and the death penalty was approved for deserters. One man who deserted twice was indeed executed. Discipline now improved, so that when a Williamsburg newspaper called the Virginia regiment "dastardly debauchers," Washington defended his men and threatened to resign unless there was a public apology. Always patriotic, Washington exhorted his troops "to show our willing obedience to the best of kings."[12]

In 1757 Washington consulted with the Earl of Loudon, the new British commander. Washington attacked Dinwiddie for not giving better support to Virginia's soldiers in the field. Loudon, a friend of Dinwiddie, turned down Washington's request to incorporate Virginia's forces into the regular British army. Washington said that "we can't conceive that being Americans should deprive us of the benefits of British subjects."[13] He was already thinking of himself and his men as being not so much Virginians or Englishmen as Americans. Dinwiddie responded with an attack upon Washington, but hearing that Washington suffered from a severe attack of dysentery, Dinwiddie forgave him, and before long returned to England.

At the end of the 1757 campaign Washington continued to suffer from malaria, dysentery, and pyorrhea. To cure pyorrhea, teeth would be extracted, and soon he needed dentures. Dysentery was treated with a vegetarian diet, but there was no cure for malaria.

While her husband was in England, Sally Fairfax helped Washington with his diet. They maintained a continuous flirtation. But he now noticed Martha Dandridge Custis, a plump widow and heiress to an estate of £23,000. In the summer of 1758 he bought a ring for Martha. On the military trail he conducted the courtship largely by mail.

When William Pitt took over the leadership of the British cabinet, the war situation changed immediately. Pitt got Frederick of Prussia to fight off England's European enemies, and Pitt concentrated upon America. He soon had naval superiority over the French, and sent reinforcements to capture Fort Duquesne.

Washington commanded the Virginia troops, under the overall command of General John Forbes. As the British forces approached, the French, badly outnumbered, burned Fort Duquesne and fled. In November 1757 the fort was renamed Fort Pitt.

The army disbanded and went home. As Washington left the service, his officers paid him a great tribute as a leader. Undisciplined troops considered him a stern taskmaster, but loyal and conscientious ones found him to be both gracious and solicitous of their needs.

Failure to take Washington into their regular army was to cost the British a great deal. Is it possible that he might have been the British commander during the Revolutionary War? Probably not, but this kind of error, repeated constantly through the decades, made the coming cleavage inevitable.

The Country Squire

Washington was not always popular with the electorate. In 1755 and 1757 he was defeated as a candidate for the House of Burgesses. In 1758, unlike Madison, he supplied the voters with plenty of drinks. He was elected this time, and represented Frederick County for the next seven years.

On September 12, 1758, he sent Sally Fairfax a "guarded" love letter.

Sally replied, pretending not to catch on. On September 25 he wrote her, "Do we still misunderstand the true meaning of each other's letters?"[14] He said he wanted to play the role of Juba to her Marcia in Addison's *Cato*. Juba and Marcia were lovers.

Soon after, realizing that the affair with Sally was hopeless, he proceeded with Martha Custis. They were married on January 6, 1759. Martha, short and plump, had married Daniel Parke Custis, a wealthy planter who had died young, leaving her with two children, John (Jack) and Martha (Patsy). Two other children had died in infancy.

Not only was she one of Virginia's richest women, but her children had also inherited some valuable properties. When her estate passed into Washington's hands, he became one of the leading planters in Virginia.

She proved to be an excellent hostess, and he was always faithful to her. He treated her children with great affection, but he and Martha had no children of their own. Thus, the father of his country was the sire of no offspring!

Matrimony took some of the frontier crudeness off his manners. He rarely lost his temper now, and seldom used military language around the house. He became the typical country squire. He took lessons in fencing, went to the theater, danced, played cards, and became known for his courtesy and hospitality. The strain of his having to prove himself had been relieved.

In the summer of 1761 he rode to the spa at Berkeley Springs to get relief from malaria and dysentery. The cure seems to have worked, for he never suffered major attacks of either malady after that.

Washington was a good businessman and plantation manager. When he saw that tobacco depleted the soil, he turned to wheat. He also grew many other grains and fruits. He kept farm animals, ran two flour mills, made whiskey, and had a herring fishery on the Potomac. He operated a dairy and interbred animals, but "I make a miserable hand at breeding mules,"[15] he said.

In addition to his holdings in the Ohio Company, Washington got title to 30,000 acres of choice river lowlands that Dinwiddie had promised to Virginia veterans in 1754. Washington also asked Governor Dunmore for a colonel's share of another 5,000 acres, although technically he had resigned his commission before the regiment was disbanded. He also bought up the land rights of other soldiers and officers.

When the Treaty of Paris was signed in 1763, Washington and other Virginia planters petitioned the crown for a 12-year option on 2.5 million acres of royal land in the Ohio River valley.

The Royal Proclamation of 1763 temporarily reserved the land west of the Alleghenies for the Indians. Washington nevertheless told his surveyor to stake out claims in this area, feeling that the temporary order would some day be lifted. He was not the largest land speculator in his day, but he was one of the most successful ones.

As a stepfather, he took Jack Custis to King's College in New York when Jack was 18. But Jack was spoiled, with a servant, a horse, a three-room suite, and the privilege of dining with the professors. Jack lasted only a few months in college, and then returned home to marry Eleanor Calvert, granddaughter of the fifth Lord Baltimore. Learning from his own problems, Washington had Jack inoculated to save him from smallpox disfigurement.

Patsy contracted epilepsy at the age of 12. Various cures were tried but none worked. She died in an epileptic seizure in June 1773.

Along with George Mason, Washington was frequently asked to arbitrate local disputes. "It is a tribute to his integrity, knowledge, and fair-mindedness that he was often asked to manage the affairs of friends and to render an impartial opinion regarding conflicting claims to property."[16]

The Patriot

As a planter Washington wished to sell his produce free from British restraints. He thus opposed the tax and trade measures of the Grenville ministry. After passage of the Stamp Act he favored economic measures by the colonists, such as the nonimportation agreement of the Association. He would not go so far as to condone nonpayment of private debts to English merchants. But in 1769 he declared that it was time for action "to maintain the liberty which we have derived from our ancestors."[17]

His call for an economic boycott, joined to that of other colonial leaders, led to an announcement by Parliament that it would pass no more taxes for the purpose of raising revenue. The Townshend duties were repealed except for the tea tax. Now tea was the only item boycotted. Most American colonists turned to cheaper Dutch tea which was smuggled in from abroad. Like Franklin, Washington felt that British merchants should be reimbursed for tea that had been destroyed, but when Britain passed further restrictive acts, he bristled.

Bryan Fairfax, brother-in-law of Sally, urged Washington in the summer of 1774 to avoid extreme action. Washington replied, "I think the Parliament of Great Britain hath no more right to put their hands in my pocket, without my consent, than I have to put my hands into yours for money." Such taxation, he continued, was "not only repugnant to natural right, but subversive of the laws and constitution of Great Britain itself." His former friend, the British General Thomas Gage, had given, in

Washington's view, "an unexampled testimony of the most despotic system of tyranny that was ever practiced in a free government. Shall we supinely sit and see one province after another fall prey to despotism?"[18]

Washington joined George Mason in the Fairfax Resolves in denying that Parliament had the supreme legislative authority in the colonies. On July 18, 1774, Washington presided at the meeting in Alexandria in which the Fairfax Resolves were approved.

Washington was elected a delegate to the First Continental Congress in September 1774. He seems not to have contributed a great deal to the sessions. But when Captain Robert Mackenzie, who had served under him in the Virginia regiment, tried to wean him back to the British cause, Washington had a ready reply: "Permit me with the freedom of a friend to express my sorrow that fortune should place you in a service that must fix curses upon the contrivers." Why wonder that the Massachusetts people, "who are every day receiving fresh proofs of a systematic assertion of an arbitrary power, deeply planned to overturn the laws and constitution of their country and to violate the most essential rights of mankind, are being irritated, and with difficulty restrained from acts of the greatest violence and intemperance?"[19]

The General

The Second Continental Congress unanimously selected Washington as the commander-in-chief of Continental forces on June 15, 1775. His only possible rivals were Horatio Gates, a former major in the British army and now a Virginia planter but lacking in military field experience, and Colonel Charles Lee, who had excellent field experience but had just come over from England in 1773. New England leaders were not seriously considered because of the distrust of Yankees by delegates from the middle and southern colonies.

"There was about him," said John R. Alden recently, "an aura of power, determination, dignity, and probity that impressed everyone."[20] Accepting, Washington declared himself unworthy of the command and said that he would take no salary but only expense money.

What were his leadership qualities? His very size was commanding, although unlike many large persons, he was graceful in his carriage. His charisma derived from a combination of outward modesty and inward confidence — he seemed to know what he was doing. His integrity, dignity, and belief in his country's cause made him a reassuring choice during a time of confusion and stress. He used a teamwork approach, being willing to abide by decisions of the Congress, and by Councils of War in the field.

The confidence of Congress was not misplaced. He not only refused to use his office for personal gain but he was vigilant against any suggestion of officers using their positions to siphon off supplies or to accept bribes in requisitioning stores and munitions.

Charles Beard had the view that Washington and the other framers fought the Revolution in order to further their economic interest, especially their land holdings. As a matter of fact, "his huge stake in the Mississippi and Grand Ohio companies vanished into thin air with the coming of the Revolution, his settlement on the Great Kanawha was destroyed, his mill at Perryopolis went to rack, while squatters occupied the choicest sites of his western holdings."[21] In addition, as leader of the armed forces against the mother country, his life hung in balance. He would certainly have been put to death had the American cause failed.

Unlike many of the framers, Washington was not a brilliant speaker or writer. His mind was clear and logical but not rapid. "He developed a cool and discriminating judgment and with it a remarkable ability to take advantage of the insights of other men."[22]

His style of writing gradually improved until the power of his personality shone through his not very graceful composition. His mature style reflected the revolutionary rhetoric to which he was exposed, "a moral fervor which expressed his special religiosity," and occasional use of apt biblical metaphor.

Though his style was stiff, he was no stuffed shirt. He drank, gambled, attended cockfights, and wrote bantering letters to his brother-in-law Colonel Burwell Bassett. He loved to fish. Knowing no Latin or Greek, he recommended that his stepson Jack study French, mathematics, and surveying rather than the classics.

Travel broadened him. As indisputably the foremost traveler in America among the Founding Fathers, he abandoned any provinciality he might have had, and early developed a continental outlook.

Realizing he faced a long campaign, he put his affairs in order at Mount Vernon. He asked Jack Custis, Burwell Bassett, and his brother John Augustine to look after Martha. He wrote to John Augustine: "I am embarked on a wide ocean, boundless in its prospect, and from whence perhaps, no safe harbor is to be found."[23] He would not see Mount Vernon again for over six years. His cousin Lund Washington attended to his land interests during his absence.

His complement of general officers included, in order of seniority, Major General Artemas Ward, Charles Lee, Philip Schuyler, and Israel Putnam, with Brigadier General Horatio Gates as adjutant. When he, Lee, and Schuyler arrived in New York City on June 24, 1775, they were given a warm welcome, as was royal Governor William Tryon, just returning from England. About 20 to 25 percent of Americans were loyalists and a few were neutral but the majority were patriots.

The royal proclamation of August 23, 1775, withdrew the protection of the crown from all American rebels. When Governor Dunmore in November 1775 declared as free all indentured servants and slaves willing to bear arms, Washington responded by approving their service in the Continental Army. He wanted to make sure that slaves who enlisted under a promise of freedom were not returned to their masters. He favored the gradual emancipation of slaves by legislative authority. By his will he freed all slaves he held by his own right upon his wife's death. He also enjoined his heirs to provide for the children, the infirm, and the aged among the blacks.

In 1776 the British had certain advantages over the American colonists. Their population was four times as large, and their navy was equal to that of France and Spain combined. Their army of 50,000 troops, mostly veterans and well trained, was augmented by 30,000 Hessians and a number of loyalists, Indians, and blacks. British muskets used larger bullets and unlike American rifles could mount bayonets. Above all, the British knew that the colonies had a poor record of working together.

But in time the British disadvantages loomed ever larger. The war they were fighting was unpopular at home, especially among the common people. Slow transporatation and communication across the Atlantic produced extremely long supply lines. A tradition of military corruption, in which everyone involved took his cut, made for a costly and inefficient war.

The patriots, defending their homeland, could build a larger army than the British could send overseas. But most important of all, the patriots had suffered callous mismanagement and violation of their rights, and were willing to stake their lives on what they felt was a just cause.

When Washington arrived in Boston to assume command, there was insufficient powder for a gun salute. The capture of Ticonderoga on May 10, 1775, gave the patriots many cannon. Henry Knox, chief of the American artillery, moved the cannon into position on Dorchester Heights overlooking Boston. On March 5, 1776, General William Howe withdrew British forces from Boston.

To secure help from Britain's traditional rivals France and Spain, a formal declaration of independence was needed. North Carolina instructed its delegates to the Continental Congress on April 13 to vote for such a declaration; Virginia followed suit on May 15. By the end of June 1776 the British had been forced to leave all 13 colonies.

Washington knew from the beginning that his army was untrained and poorly equipped. They had short enlistment terms, and did not want to fight out of state. From his experience he knew that he would have a certain percentage of drifters, plunderers, and fair-weather soldiers. He early recommended more thorough training, better pay, longer enlistment terms, and a standing army rather than use of a militia.

On August 22, 1776, his headquarters banned bathing at Cambridge bridge: "Many men, lost to all sense of decency and common modesty, are running about naked upon the bridge whilst passengers, and even ladies of the first fashion, are passing over it, as if they meant to glory in their shame."[24]

As in his previous commands, Washington found that discipline had to be tightened before results could be expected. The penalty for disobedience or for double enlistment for money was discharge, plus thirty lashes. One captain was cashiered for cowardice at Bunker Hill and another for defrauding privates of their pay. Washington wrote to Lund Washington that Yankee officers were nearly as stupid as Yankee privates.

The initial conflicts did more to build British confidence than American. Putnam, who commanded the patriots on Long Island, did not guard his flank from Jamaica Pass, nor did Washington, on his inspection, notice the error. British forces under Henry Clinton broke the gap. Had General William Howe proceeded, he might have captured all of the patriots on Long Island.

While Howe dallied, Washington, aided brilliantly by Colonel John Glover of Marblehead, led a masterful retreat of the army across the East River on the night of August 29. Though urged to leave Manhattan by Charles Lee, Washington preferred to stay and fight. Fortunately, Howe ignored Clinton's advice to land troops at the north end of Manhattan, which would have cut off Washington's best escape route.

General Nathaniel Greene made the mistake of trying to hold Fort Washington against superior British forces and was overrun. Critics blamed Washington for not overruling Greene's decision. Escaping from Cornwallis at Fort Lee, Washington took 3,000 dispirited troops southwest across the Delaware River. He expected Charles Lee to join him with 4,000 men. As the Hessians plundered and raped, hundreds of New Jersey inhabitants switched to the British side. John Dickinson advised his brother to exchange Continental currency for pounds sterling. Since Congress expected the British to take Philadelphia, they moved to Baltimore.

When Charles Lee carelessly spent the night of December 12 in a tavern more than a mile from his troops, he was captured by the British and made a prisoner of war for many months. Facing Christmas, patriot morale hit rock bottom.

Reporting to Congress on December 18, Washington said that unless the Continental Army troops were vastly increased, "the game is pretty near up." Two days later he confessed to the President of Congress: "I have learned, ever since I have been in the service, to discourage all kinds of local attachments, denominating the whole by the greater name of American, but I have found it impossible to overcome prejudices."[25]

He then made one of the master strokes of the War. Knowing that many enlistments ended on December 31, he decided to piece together the various army remnants and attack. He secured a number of boats, 40 to 60 feet long and 8 feet wide, large enough to carry cannons as well as many men.

At dawn on December 26 he surprised the Hessians at Trenton. Covered by artillery support, one unit of Continentals attacked from the north and another from the east. The Hessians had 22 killed, 84 wounded, and 1,000 taken prisoner. The Americans had only four wounded men.

On December 30 he again crossed the Delaware with his troops. This time Cornwallis had 6,000 men awaiting him. Escaping by night, Washington headed for Princeton. When his troops were getting beat there, he personally led an attack within 30 yards of the British line. With artillery, Alexander Hamilton captured Nassau Hall at Princeton College. The victories at Trenton and Princeton not only greatly boosted American morale but also virtually regained New Jersey for the patriot cause.

With his men tired and with many enlistments running out, Washington could not attack the British supply base at New Brunswick, so he had his men retreat northeast to Morristown, where they spent the winter. Learning from his early mistakes, Washington had a good location for his winter camp. If Howe moved toward Philadelphia, he could hit Howe's forces from the north while other patriot forces held the Delaware River. If Howe moved north to try to meet British forces coming down from Canada, Washington could move to the Hudson River and block him.

Congress now authorized a Continental Army of 75,000 men, with each soldier to receive an enlistment bonus of $20, pay of 40 shillings a month, plus 100 acres of land at the end of the War. The army at Morristown began to grow. French help started arriving. Shiploads of ammunition and supplies procured by Beaumarchais began landing in March 1777 and continued. European officers appeared—Lafayette, DeKalb, Von Steuben, and others.

But there were still many setbacks. To block the British path toward Philadelphia, Washington met Cornwallis and Howe at Brandywine. Nearly entrapped, Washington managed to retreat with losses of 1,000 compared to British casualties of 500. Howe took Philadelphia without opposition on September 26, 1777.

Unwilling to always be on the defensive, Washington attacked at Germantown on October 4. Again American casualties doubled those of the British, and Washington had to retreat. His aggressiveness won him support both among the colonists and in Europe, where his campaigns were being carefully watched, especially in France.

After clearing the Delaware, Howe went into winter quarters in Philadelphia, where his troops could comfortably prepare for the spring campaign. Washington meanwhile took encampment 25 miles away at Valley Forge, about to experience one of its worst winters in years.

John Adams, now offended by "the superstitious veneration that is sometimes paid to General Washington," wondered how long the Continental Army was going to while away in idleness, instead of "destroying an enemy completely in our power."[26] Most of those who served under him, however, had complete confidence in Washington, because of his dignity, his calmness in adversity, and his bravery in battle.

Attacking from the north with a force of 8,000 redcoats and Hessians in midsummer 1777, General John Burgoyne captured Fort Ticonderoga without a battle. Angry Congress replaced General Philip Schuyler with General Horatio Gates. Before Gates could take over, the patriots won battles at Bennington and at Fort Schuyler. Gates then barred the advance of Burgoyne down the west bank of the Hudson.

Burgoyne wanted Gates to attack, but he wisely held back. In forested country crackshot patriot riflemen selected British officers as special targets. His Indians deserted Burgoyne, whose only hope now was for help from Clinton. When Clinton tried to come north, he was blocked. The patriots now outnumbered the British three to one, and had him nearly surrounded.

On October 17, 1777, Burgoyne surrendered to Gates at Saratoga. All royal troops had to return to England and stay out of the War. When Burgoyne violated this agreement, his army was sent off to prison camps. Although there had been many heroes in this campaign, Gates got chief credit for the victory and was now the choice among many Congressmen to replace Washington as commander-in-chief.

General Thomas Conway, a French officer serving with the patriots, charged in a letter to Gates that Washington was incompetent. Furious, Washington bawled out Gates, who had also been critical of him. One of Washington's generals, John Cadwalader, challenged Conway to a duel and gravely wounded him. After Conway recovered he returned to France and sent a letter of apology to "the great and good man," Washington.[27] The New England clique that had been using Conway as a front in their effort to remove Washington from command was now silenced.

Following the British defeat at Saratoga, the French entered the

War on America's side. Lord North's ministry got the repeal of the punitive laws that had led to the rebellion, and sent a commission headed by the Earl of Carlisle to offer the patriots complete amnesty and considerable freedom under the crown. Congress rejected the offer even before the British commissioners arrived. Washington agreed, saying that "the injuries we have received from the British nation are so many that they can never be forgotten."[28]

Clinton, who had replaced Howe as the British commander, abandoned Philadelphia on June 18, 1778. Chasing the redcoats, patriots under Charles Lee met them at the Monmouth courthouse on June 28. As a prisoner of war, Lee had been exchanged for British Major General Richard Prescott.

A determined thrust by the British forced Lee and his men to retreat. Washington brought up replacements, had words with Lee, and took the command away from him. Later Washington had Lee court-martialed on three charges: disobedience, unnecessary retreat, and disrespect toward a commanding officer. Lee was found guilty on all three charges, and Congress confirmed the action. John Laurens, an aide to Washington, challenged Lee to a duel and wounded him. Helpful early, Lee was now a hindrance to Washington. He was removed from the army, and died in 1782.

In 1778 Washington planned several joint land-sea operations with French Admiral Charles d'Estaing but none worked out. Washington chose Middlebrook for his winter quarters in 1778.

In the spring of 1779 George Rogers Clark recaptured Vincennes, thus freeing the frontier from Indian raids. Depressed by the lack of support from Congress, Washington in March 1779 wrote to George Mason that "I have beheld no day since the commencement of hostilities that I have thought America's liberties in such imminent danger as at the present. Friends and foes seem now to combine to pull down the goodly fabric we have been raising at the expense of so much time, blood, and treasure. Unless the bodies politic will exert themselves to bring things back to first principles, correct abuses, and punish our internal foes, inevitable ruin must follow."[29]

The summer brought better news. Anthony Wayne captured the British garrison at Stony Point, and John Sullivan won several convincing victories over tribes of the Six Nations that had sided with the British.

The year 1780 was the last good one for the British. Apparently aware of Washington's feeling of depression, Franklin wrote him from Paris that he should visit Europe after the War to enjoy his great reputation there, "free from the jealousy and envy of a man's countrymen. Here you would know and enjoy what posterity will say of Washington, for a thousand leagues have nearly the same effect as a thousand years."[30]

But at home Washington's headaches continued. In May Benjamin Lincoln surrendered his 5500 men at Charlestown. In August Gates advanced boldly on Cornwallis at Camden and was soundly beaten. Benedict Arnold, one of Washington's best commanders, tried to sell out West Point in September for $6,000 plus an English general's commission. Only the triumph of Nathaniel Greene at King's Mountain in October kept the year from being a complete disaster.

On January 1, 1781, some Pennsylvania troops mutinied and marched toward Philadelphia to demand back pay from Congress. Their commander, Anthony Wayne, got them to stop at Princeton. When Sir Henry Clinton sent two agents to try to lead the disgruntled soldiers into the British lines, the soldiers recovered their patriotism and hanged the agents.

The year 1781 marked the turning point of the War. On January 17 General Daniel Morgan defeated the British Banastre Tarleton at Cowpens, South Carolina. On March 1 Maryland ratified the Articles of Confederation, and now the previously disunited states had a governing document. Throughout the summer Greene, aided brilliantly by the guerrilla leaders Francis Marion and Thomas Sumter, drove the redcoats back to the sea coast in Georgia and South Carolina. The Spanish captured Mobile and Pensacola from the British.

The only British success led ultimately to their demise. For a time the turncoat Benedict Arnold led damaging raids in Virginia. When a British sea captain threatened to burn Mount Vernon, Lund Washington gave him the supplies he requested. Hearing of this, George Washington said he would rather have his home destroyed than give assistance to the enemy.

Tarleton then penetrated to Charlottesville and forced Governor Thomas Jefferson to flee Monticello. Cornwallis now had 8,000 troops to the 6,000 men of the Continental Army but, ignoring Clinton's advice to build his base at Old Point Comfort, he chose the inferior location at Yorktown, near the end of the peninsula between the James and York Rivers. If the British navy lost control of Chesapeake Bay, Cornwallis and his forces would be trapped.

Sensing a knockout blow, the French sent a fleet under Admiral Comte de Grasse to the area. Gleeful Washington said that "it is in our power to bring the war to a happy conclusion."[31] He persuaded Comte de Barras to take his squadron from Rhode Island to join de Grasse.

Washington ordered Lafayette to keep Cornwallis trapped on the peninsula, then feigned an attack at Clinton in New York, and marched south. Clinton awoke to the trap and wanted to head south to help Cornwallis, but he was blocked both by land and by sea.

On September 2 de Grasse landed 3,000 French troops at Jamestown.

On September 5 he defeated the British vessels under Admiral Thomas Graves. Cut off by land and sea, Cornwallis surrendered 7,000 troops on October 17, exactly four years to a day after the great victory at Saratoga. For all practical purposes, the War was over.

Washington's triumphal homecoming to Mount Vernon was marred by the death of Jack Custis from camp fever. Martha and her heroic husband traveled to Philadelphia, where they were feted during the winter months as he planned the next campaign. Martha, who had visited him often during the War, accompanied him to his new headquarters at Newburgh, New York. Washington's goal now was to contain Clinton's forces in the New York City area.

In the spring of 1782 Colonel Lewis Nicola tried to use the army to set up Washington as a king. Washington vigorously blasted the scheme.

In August Sir Guy Carleton told Washington that Great Britain would acknowledge American independence if the patriots would agree to deal mercifully with loyalists. Washington referred Carleton to Congress for a reply. Washington then refused to have Captain Charles Asgill executed in revenge for the loyalist execution of Joshua Huddy, a New Jersey captain who had killed a loyalist in New York City.

Late in 1782 at Newburgh, when the army threatened to use force to ensure getting their pensions, Washington came down hard on the leaders. Whoever favors this move is an enemy of our country, Washington said, for there is no quicker way to ruin a country than to have it split between the civil and the military authorities. Jefferson now said of Washington that "the moderation and virtue of a single character has probably prevented this revolution from being closed as most others have been by a subversion of that liberty it was intended to establish."[32]

In June of 1783 Washington wrote a letter to the state governors in which he described America's problems and opportunities as he saw them. Its vast lands and free institutions give America "a fairer opportunity for political happiness than any other nation has been favored with. This is the time of their political probation." Will we give our federal government the tone it needs, or relax it, "exposing us to become the sport of European politics? It is yet to be decided whether the Revolution must ultimately be considered as a blessing or a curse, not to the present age alone, for with our fate will the destiny of unborn millions be involved."[33]

How could Americans safeguard their splendid inheritance? By creating an indissoluble union under one federal head, he answered. By paying our obligations, and building adequate defenses. Among the people there needed to prevail "that friendly disposition which will influence them to forget their local prejudices and policies, to make those mutual concessions which are requisite to the general prosperity, and in some instances to sacrifice their individual advantages to the interest of the community."[34]

The Treaty of Paris was signed on September 3, 1783. On November 25 the British troops left New York City. In the triumphant procession Washington rode behind Governor George Clinton, showing that in his opinion the military should always be under civilian authority.

He submitted a bill of $450,000 to Congress to cover his expenses for the past eight years. The bill was precise on small items but vague on large ones. It included reimbursement for Martha's many visits to his headquarters. The Confederation Congress accepted it with no question.

At noon on December 4 he said farewell to his officers at Fraunces' Tavern. On December 23 he resigned his commission to Congress meeting at Annapolis with only seven states represented. He offered his "sincere congratulations to Congress," and thanked the officers and men who had served under him. He concluded: "I close this last solemn act of my official life by commending the interests of our dearest country to the protection of Almighty God, and those who have the superintendence of them, to His holy keeping."[35]

The Planter

Judging by the number of guests they had at Mount Vernon, he and Martha must have liked to entertain. From the time he returned home in December 1783, it was one and a half years before he dined alone with Martha. In one year he had eight tons of pork sent to the smoke houses. When Houdon came to take his measurements and plaster casts for his statue, Houdon and his four assistants were accommodated at Mount Vernon, along with two clergymen and several other guests who were already there.

Washington believed that Americans should honor debts to British merchants, as called for in the peace treaty. He saw the need for a national authority to bolster the treaty provisions. Seeing that many states passed laws saying that Americans need not honor English debts, the British refused to abandon their western forts. Washington himself paid the principal on his British loans, but not the interest, saying that British aggression had kept him from paying off his debts on time.

He now resigned from the vestry at church. Although he sometimes went to church he never took communion. His faith in God had been amply demonstrated during the dark days of the Revolution. He may have been influenced by the rising tides of deism and Unitarianism, and by the Masonic concept of a ruling Providence. Unlike Jefferson and Madison, he believed in an established church, where all would pay taxes to the church of their choice: Protestant, Catholic, Jewish, or Moslem. Nonbelievers could choose their favorite charities as beneficiaries.

He did not overeat. For dinner, which was in mid-afternoon, he would have a single dish and a half-pint to a pint of Madeira wine. His guests would be served an ample supper in the evening but all he would have would be "one small glass of punch, a draught of beer, and two dishes of tea."[36]

For amusement he had an excellent bowling green. He went to Annapolis horse races and permitted his slaves to also attend. His favorite sport was fox hunting. Von Steuben's young aide resented the lack of the usual contact between the mansion and the slave quarters; he had expected a midnight visit from a mulatto girl, but had none.

Washington had a sense of humor. When his large jackass, a gift from Charles III of Spain, showed no interest in mares, he said it was "too full of royalty to have anything to do with a plebeian race." When the animal "becomes better acquainted with republican enjoyments, he will amend his manners and fall into our custom of doing business."[37]

To attract his attention, tiny Martha would pull at his buttons until he smiled down upon her. He threatened to withdraw the financing of the education of two nephews when he discovered that after six or seven years of classical education, they could not write legibly or keep accurate acounts.

His mother had been so uncomplimentary of him during the War that many thought her a Tory. When people praised him, she said that he was off doing things that were none of his business, meanwhile letting her starve. Nevertheless when she died in 1789 she left most of her estate to him.

As a planter, he would often make a circuit of all five of his farms, riding about twenty miles before returning to dress for dinner. Handy mechanically, he made some minor inventions and supervised the erection of his farm buildings. He experimented with new planting methods, especially concerning himself with increasing soil fertility, and interbreeding animals to improve the strain.

He was a conscientious correspondent, insisting on answering every letter sent to him. He tried to sell his 30,000 acres on the Ohio and Great Kanawha Rivers, in what is now West Virginia, in small tracts, preferably to settlement societies or religious communities. On a creek called Miller's Run he had to sue to remove squatters; some of the squatters stayed on as tenants. In 1796 he sold these 2813 acres for $12,000.

He was magnanimous in his personal life. "Even when he himself had to borrow to pay his bills, he ordered an agent to collect no debts that would make 'the widow and the fatherless' suffer."[38] In 1785 the Virginia Assembly gave him a gift of 50 shares of stock in the Potomac River Company and 100 shares of stock in the James River Company. He did not want to accept these gifts but he also did not want to offend the Assembly. So he compromised and accepted the stock for support of "objects of a public nature," and everyone seemed pleased.[39]

Freeman says that "he had not a single degree of enthusiasm for the Society of the Cincinnati,"[40] and he would have wanted it disbanded except for two of its features: it was a bond to European officers who had helped America during the War, and it served as a charitable organization for needy veterans. He used his influence to somewhat reform the Society. He insisted that it be apolitical, that hereditary memberships be discontinued, and that no honorary memberships be awarded.

One of the reasons Washington wanted to link the Potomac with the Ohio River was to provide eastern access to western settlers who might otherwise sell their wheat and furs to England and Spain. "The western settlers," he said, "stand upon a pivot. The touch of a feather would turn them any way."[41] Pennsylvania, Maryland, and Virginia were all involved in the Potomac project. He could see that ground rules for control of interstate commerce were going to have to be established. But he was patient. "Democratical states," he wrote to Lafayette, "must always feel before they can see; it is this that makes their governments slow, but the people will be right at last."[42]

In 1785 he was elected president of the Potomac River Company, and declined the presidency of the James River Company. He was also working on a project to drain the Dismal Swamp and turn it into farmland. His income from rent on western lands was scarcely worth entering in his books, and he was receiving no profit at all from his Pennsylvania mill.

In 1786 he hired as secretary Tobias Lear, a Harvard graduate who spoke French and who was his most intimate associate for the next eight years. Lear was an excellent aide, for he had brains, discretion, a pleasing personality, and a capacity for hard work. He could "effect a good bargain or have repairs executed quickly; he could write an excellent letter or manage a pleasant dinner."[43]

Washington's old friend Henry Knox sent him a harrowing description of how insurgents, led by former captain Daniel Shays, were impeding law in Massachusetts. Had anyone told him three years ago, as he was retiring from the army, he said, "that at this day I should see such a formidable rebellion against the laws and constitutions of our own making, I should have thought him a bedlamite." Is the conclusion "that mankind when left to themselves are unfit for their own government — a melancholy proof of what our transatlantic foe has predicted?"[44]

Washington recommended that government officials listen to complaints and amend errors, but beyond that, be firm with insurgents: "Let the reins of government be held with a steady hand, and every violation of the constitution be reprehended; if defective let it be amended but not suffered to be trampled upon whilst it has an existence."[45] He did, however, urge leniency for the insurgents once the rebellion had been quelled.

Shays' Rebellion was not the only factor shaking Washington's faith in democracy. The states would not give Congress the taxing power it needed. The total income of the national government in 1786 was less than one-third of the annual interest on the national debt. The state of New York held its own conference with the Six Nations. Weak Congress permitted the states to squabble over western land claims.

On August 1, 1786, Washington said that "we have probably had too good an opinion of human nature in framing our confederation. Experience has taught us that men will not adopt measures best calculated for their own good, without the intervention of a coercive power. I do not conceive we can long exist as a nation without a power that will pervade the whole Union."[46]

Would the United States break down into several nations? It was already as large as the combined total of Britain, France, Ireland, Italy, and Spain. "European politicians were sure that this huge area could not be governed from any center but would become, like Germany or Italy, a grouping of petty sovereignties."[47]

One of Washington's dreams was for America to become economically self-sufficient. He wanted the United States to process its own raw materials. He encouraged American women not to slavishly follow European styles, and he urged the building of an American merchant marine, to carry American goods in peacetime and to assist the navy in wartime.

In early 1787 Washington had many problems. His brother John died in January, and his nephew George Augustine, who lived at Mount Vernon, lost a baby. Washington suffered from rheumatism, and was short on finances. "My estate for the last eleven years," he said, "has not been able to make both ends meet."[48]

Edmund Randolph finally persuaded him to attend the Constitutional Convention. He was embarrassed to have told the Cincinnati that he could not attend their meeting. He told Madison privately that he was boycotting their meeting because he disliked some of their anti-republican tendencies. "However great the danger seemed to be from the radical side, Washington was not going to countenance any faction of conservatives."[49]

He drew praise for agreeing to attend the Constitutional Convention. Madison said that "to forsake the honorable retreat to which he had retired and to risk the reputation he had so deservedly acquired, manifested a zeal for the public interest." Henry Knox believed that "nothing but the critical situation of his country would have induced him to so hazardous a conduct."[50] This was true. Washington wrote to Madison that "thirteen sovereignties pulling against each other and all tugging at the federal head will soon bring ruin on the whole, whereas a liberal and energetic constitution, well guarded, might restore us to respectability."[51]

The Framer

Washington was one of the first to arrive at the Convention. "It is not sufficient," he said, "for a man to be a passive friend and well wisher to the cause."[52] The Convention, he believed, should "adopt no temporizing expedient, but probe the defects of the constitution to the bottom and provide radical cures, whether they are agreed to [by the states] or not."[53]

Many of the delegates had served in the army or in the Congress with Washington. Many newspaper editorials based their hope for an optimistic outcome on the influence of Washington. Gouverneur Morris said that whenever Washington discussed the need for a strong union, "his eye was fixed and seemed to look into futurity."[54]

After being elected unanimously as president of the Convention, Washington asked indulgence for any unintentional errors he might make. The position as presiding officer helped get him ready for the United States presidency. Usually there were only about 30 delegates present, so clad in his military uniform and up on the dais, his presence was commanding. There are many stories of how his facial expressions influenced the debate: "anxious solicitude at acrimony changing to delight at fruitful compromise."[55]

States'-righters must have had conscience qualms to look at the brave man who had pled continually for support to save the lives and fortunes of his soldiers to a Congress that was weak and ineffectual. He was a living symbol of the need to build a stronger union than the existing one.

His influence can be overemphasized. No one at the Convention really wished to dissolve the Union—the question was over means, not ends. He made few specific proposals in the Convention. But his service here formed an integral bridge between being commander of the Continental Army and being the first president.

"His fine manners, together with his refusal to try to inflict his ideas upon the delegates, enabled him to perform superbly. He did not serve on committees, and he seldom spoke to issues. He maintained good order; others had to solve the many thorny questions that arose."[56]

Since much of the preliminary discussion on each issue took place in the Committee of the Whole, presided over by Nathaniel Gorham, Washington would sit and vote with the Virginia delegation. Typical of his voting was his vote to have money bills originate in the House of Representatives. Madison said that Washington opposed the measure but voted for it: "He gave up his judgment because it was not of very material weight with him and was made an essential point with others, who if disappointed, might be less cordial in other points of real weight."[57]

When a delegate moved to limit the size of a peacetime standing army to 3,000 men, Washington said he would support the motion if there was a companion one limiting the size of a potential aggressor's army to the same size. In one discussion he expressed the wish that America's ports would always be open as an asylum to "the oppressed and needy of the world."

When slavery was discussed, he said that no one wanted to see it ended more than he, and that he would vote for any effective measure to end slavery. Toward the end of the Convention he was so eager to get the new Constitution ratified that he favored a mere majority of seven states as sufficient to approve ratification.

When the convention adjourned, the records were put in his care. He was asked to hold them "subject to the order of Congress," if such a body should be "formed under the Constitution."

He realized that time would show the defects of the new plan, but that then the Constitution could be amended. "If evil is to come therefrom," he told his nephew Bushrod, "the remedy must come hereafter. I do not think we are more inspired, have more wisdom, or possess more virtue than those who will come after us."[58]

In his talks favoring ratification he pointed out the improvements over the Articles of Confederation. He questioned whether another convention could produce a better document, and he described the chaos that would follow nonratification.

He said that his "long and laborious investment resulted in a fixed belief that this Constitution is really a government of the people, that is to say, a government in which all power is derived from, and at stated periods, reverts to them; and that it is purely a government of laws, made and executed by the fair substitutes of the people alone."[59]

It had the power needed for its purposes, and no more, he said. Even the opposition to it had been valuable, for it had "called forth in its defense, abilities which have thrown new light upon the science of government. They have given the rights of man a full and fair discussion, in so clear and forcible a manner as cannot fail to make a lasting impression."[60] He wrote to Lafayette that if the Constitution were to be approved, "it will be so much beyond anything we had a right to expect eighteen months ago that it will demonstrate visibly the finger of Providence."[61]

Speaking of Washington, James Monroe wrote to Jefferson: "Be assured, his influence carried this government."[62] In all colonies the man on the street voiced the view expressed in the *Pennsylvania Herald*: "If the plan is not a good one, it is impossible that either General Washington or Doctor Franklin would have recommended it." Gouverneur Morris told Washington that "I have observed that your name to the new Constitution has been of infinite service. If you had not attended the Convention, the same paper would have met with a colder reception, with fewer and weaker advocates, and with more and more strenuous opponents."[63]

In 1787 Washington put the final touch to his mansion at Mount Vernon. It was a weathervane in the shape of a Dove of Peace, an ideal he sought all of his life and rarely found.

The President's First Term

In 1788 Washington said, "I never felt the want of money so sensibly since I was a boy fifteen years old."[64] Three times he had to put off paying the sheriff of Fairfax County when he came to collect money due on Mount Vernon. His lands in Greenbrier County were to be sold unless he paid his taxes. He was behind in his pew rent at church, and he could not pay his bill to Dr. James Craik.

He was not ambitious for the presidency. In October 1788 he said that accepting the position "would be attended with more diffidence and reluctance than I ever experienced before in my life."[65] Realizing that public figures are targets of fierce vilification in a republic, he later told Henry Knox, "My movements to the chair of government will be accompanied by feelings not unlike those of a culprit who is going to the place of execution."[66]

His personal wish would have been to retire to Mount Vernon. He wondered whether he could do as well as someone else in a new and untried position. But he was reluctant to refuse to answer his country's call. Was it not cowardly to fail to risk one's reputation merely to protect one's name? One of his thoughts was to accept the position briefly until the new government was off to a good start, and then resign.

When Jefferson returned from France in 1789, he was amazed to find that "the opposition to our new Constitution has almost totally disappeared. If the President can be preserved a few more years, till habits of authority and obedience can be established generally, we have nothing to fear."[67]

On March 7, 1789, Washington paid his final visit to his mother. Dying of breast cancer at the age of 80, she still lived alone, near her daughter Betty Lewis. Washington had not recommended that she live at Mount Vernon, for she would have no privacy, he said, at a house "to be compared with a well resorted tavern, as scarcely any strangers who are going from North to South, or from South to North, do not spend a day or two at it." As Freeman observed, "he owed her more, perhaps, than he had realized—his physical endurance, his resolution, his ambition to make his own way."[68]

He formulated seven rules as guidelines in making federal appointments[69]:
1. He would make no advance commitments.
2. His public affairs would not be affected by his private inclinations.
3. Friends and relatives must not "have the least sway" on public decisions.
4. Due regard should be paid to a person's fitness, qualifications, "and so far as is proper, to political considerations."
5. It is hard to remove a person once he is chosen.
6. As far as possible, appointments should be distributed among the various states.
7. Army veterans should be eligible to serve, if qualified.

On April 14, 1789, Charles Thomson, secretary of Congress, arrived at Mount Vernon with the fateful news: he had been unanimously elected president of the United States. Having given instructions to his nephew, George Augustine Washington, to manage Mount Vernon while he was gone, on April 16 Washington set out for New York City. At each town there was a triumphant welcome. Often bridges and roadways were festooned with flowers and leaves.

The gala welcome to New York City on April 23 included a 13-gun salute from a British packet. When Chancellor Robert R. Livingston of New York administered the oath of office, asking if he would defend, to the best of his ability, the Constitution of the United States, he must have realized how superfluous the oath was, for this man had given his life to preparing for and achieving this Constitution.

More than one-third of his Inaugural Address was given to religious matters. Perhaps now that he had no superior to turn to except God, he wanted to assure people that he felt responsible to an ultimate moral authority for his conduct. His only specific recommendation to Congress was that it should consider to what extent it would advocate Constitutional amendments, in reply to public interest in the matter. In closing he prayed to "the benign Parent of the human race that His divine blessing may be conspicuous in the enlarged views, the temperate consultations, and the wise measures on which the success of this government must depend."[70]

For all of his talk about needing money, he lived well as president. He had 14 white servants and seven slaves, plus a coach with six horses. To get access to the public and their views, since he decided not to accept invitations to homes, he had two levees or public socials each week. Occasionally he would visit the theater. Senator William Maclay, a chronic complainer, was horrified that he would expose "ladies of character and virtue" to such an "independent representation" as Sheridan's play *The School for Scandal*.

Two early problems faced the new president: what was the Senate's precise function, and how was one to balance the executive departments between the president and Congress? On May 21, 1789, the House of Representatives passed bills authorizing the creation of the executive departments of Foreign Affairs, Treasury, and War. At first, Washington had these departments report directly to Congress; as time permitted, he read their reports.

The first bill passed by Congress prescribed how oaths of office were to be administered. Washington signed it on June 1.

He was warmly welcomed on a trip through New England in the fall of 1789. A bit irked at the Connecticut blue law forbidding Sabbath travel, he found the tavern at Ashford "not a good one," and the parson's sermons "very lame discourses."

Washington gave his first Annual Address to Congress on January 8, 1790. He spoke on the organization of the militia, on the census, on a system of uniform weights and measures, and of the needs for post offices and better roads. He encouraged American factories, especially in defense industries. Education was, he said, "the security of a free Constitution." To assist education he recommended either a national university or aid to schools already established. Education would teach people "to know and to value their own rights, to distinguish between oppression and the necessary exercise of lawful authority, and to discriminate the spirit of liberty from that of licentiousness."[71]

In May 1790 Washington contracted pneumonia. On May 15 Dr. Charles McKnight said he had every reason to expect the President to die. There was widespread gloom. Abigail Adams said that no one else could set up the new government properly. "Most assuredly I do not wish for the highest post,"[72] she said. But by May 20 he was better. Doctors told him to work less and exercise more, something hard to do in his position.

At a levee an aide, David Humphreys, kept Washington outside the assembly room and then entered shouting, "The President of the United States!" Washington never regained his composure again that evening. Angry at Humphreys, he told him never to give him a formal introduction again.

Although he was criticized for social stiffness, Washington blamed it on his physical condition. Again Abigail Adams defended him: "He is polite with dignity, affable without familiarity, distant without haughtiness, grave without austerity, modest, wise, and good."[73]

When his nephew, Bushrod Washington, applied for appointment as United States district attorney for Virginia, Uncle George replied that "however, deserving you may be, your standing at the bar would not justify my nomination of you in preference of some of the oldest and most esteemed General Court lawyers in your state."[74]

Jefferson wanted the permanent national capitol on the Potomac. Robert Morris wanted the temporary capitol moved to Philadelphia. Hamilton wanted federal assumption of the states' wartime debts. So in the summer of 1790 supporters of all three worked out an omnibus compromise, and by August 4 all three requests had been approved by Congress.

Major Pierre Charles L'Enfant, who had served in Washington's army, was selected as the architect to build the federal city. Washington selected the 100 square-mile site. He got landowners to donate every other lot to the federal government, on the assumption that the retained lots would more than double in value. The national government had appropriated no money for the federal district, and Maryland and Virginia very little. Naming the city after Washington was the decision of the three federal commissioners, after consultation with Jefferson and Madison.

L'Enfant proved to be very contentious. Jefferson felt that his grandiose design for the district was inappropriate, but time has shown it to be both workable and esthetic. Washington chose as the design for the White House a plan submitted by an Irish architect, James Hoban. The Capitol was a composite of ideas from Jefferson, French architect Stephen Hallet, and English architect William Thornton.

While the federal government was being formed, the Georgia legislature had sold 15.5 million acres of land claimed jointly by Georgia and Spain. The land lay between the Mississippi and Yazoo Rivers. In August 1790 Washington announced that, by treaty, these lands belonged to the Choctaw and Chickasaw nations. That month Washington signed a treaty with the agent for the Indians, granting Georgia much of the disputed land. Even Spain seemed satisfied, for she was involved in the Nootka Sound dispute with Britain, and wanted no war over the disputed land. Even critics of Washington agreed that he had handled the dispute well.

He traveled so much that nearly every town had an inn that alleged that "George Washington slept here." It apparently was not always an enjoyable honor to have him, however. In Bladensburg, Maryland, he boarded one night with "an old black woman. Jealous of this preference shown such a lowly person, irate townspeople had the next day torn down her outhouse."[75] In 1790, after Rhode Island had ratified the Constitution, Washington traveled there to assure residents that the federal government had no hard feeling toward the state despite its non-cooperative attitude.

In New York City dentist John Greenwood made Washington a set of dentures. The uppers were carved from hippopotamus tusk; the lowers had a base of the same material, but attached to it by gold pivots were human teeth. Not very comfortable, these dentures did not last long.

Early in 1791 came the beginning of what was to develop into a vendetta. Madison had originally recommended Hamilton as secretary of the treasury. Later Hamilton said he would never have accepted the post had he known how bitterly Madison would oppose him.

Hamilton's plan for a national bank had been approved by Congress. Washington looked to his cabinet for advice on whether to sign the bill. Jefferson, Randolph, and Madison agreed that the bill would be unconstitutional, since the Constitution did not specifically empower Congress to create a bank. Hamilton and Henry Knox insisted that such a power was implied in the Constitution.

The three Virginians then attacked the concept of implied powers, although Jefferson had previously supported it and according to Dumas Malone, "the doctrine of implied powers really originated with Madison."[76] Madison had defended the doctrine in *The Federalist*.

Although it is true that Hamilton's policies were benefiting the North more than the South, the Virginians seemed to be using a smoke screen to cover their real goal: check Hamilton's rising influence upon Washington on governmental matters. In later years, President Madison fought hard to get a national bank approved.

In February 1791 Hamilton wrote a masterly refutation of the Virginians' attack, showing that in time a strict interpretation of the Constitution would undermine the central authority. At this time Hamilton could not know what a great job President Jefferson would do in buying the Louisiana territory under the doctrine of implied powers.

In the late spring of 1791 Washington toured the southern colonies. He received a warm welcome everywhere, especially in Charleston where he was impressed by the large number of beautiful women. In covering the 1887-mile trip without accident or illness, he found the people satisfied with the new government.

Although he had earlier called them "butchering monsters" full of "savage fury," as president in 1791 Washington felt sorry for the Indians, "poor wretches" who were victims of "diabolical" white men. Why is it not the same crime to kill an Indian as a white person, he asked. He believed that the government should keep its treaties with the Indians, and be careful in land purchases to safeguard their rights.

To get advice and consent on a treaty with the Creek Indians, he accompanied Knox to the floor of the Senate. When he saw all the fusses and delays, even though the treaty was finally approved, he was heard to say, as he departed, that he would "be damned if he ever went there again."[77] From that time on, presidents have not taken part in Congressional floor debates.

Because the British, from their western posts, encouraged Indians to resist American settlements, Washington sent General Arthur St. Clair to establish a permanent post at the main Miami village (now Fort Wayne, Indiana). St. Clair was ambushed, losing 950 men killed and wounded. A congressional investigation finally authorized a uniform federally supervised militia, a goal that Washington had long sought.

He appointed Anthony Wayne to organize an army along the Indian frontier, and "undertook what was probably the most extensive effort to conciliate hostile tribes ever engaged in by any United States government."[78] The policy succeeded with the Six Nations but not with northern tribes organized by the British along the Canadian border to resist American settlement there.

Washington had hoped for teamwork in his cabinet, but it was not to be. In February 1792 Jefferson said he planned to resign at the end of the term because he opposed Hamilton's policies, which he considered to be favorable to the business interests at the expense of the rest of the public. Hamilton then played into Jefferson's hand by conducting secret meetings with the British minister, George Hammond, telling him to ignore Jefferson's warnings to England to abandon their western posts.

Hamilton did a better job in replying to Jefferson's specific complaints. Most of the public debt, Hamilton pointed out, came not from current overspending but from Revolutionary War expenses. Also, funding the national debt brought foreign capital to the United States. The debt did not reduce purchasing power; where there were the greatest number of debt certificates, there was also the most circulating capital. Further, to discriminate among the holders of federal securities would have been not only unwise but impossible. The quickest way to build a monarchy, Hamilton concluded, is to undermine public credit and prepare the way for demagogues.

The first presidential veto occurred on April 5, 1792, when Washington, following the recommendations of Jefferson, Randolph, and Madison, vetoed a bill to alter the method of computing House membership. Congress did not attempt to override the veto.

A newspaper war raged between Federalists and Republicans. Philip Freneau, for the Republicans, printed in his *National Gazette* for July 4, 1792, the statement that "since the glorious peace of 1783, artifice and deception" have wrought "one revolution in favor of the few. Another must and will be brought about in favor of the people." John Fenno replied in the *Gazette of the United States* on July 7 that Freneau's paper was the tool of a junto of politicians whose goal was "to oust from the government almost every man now in the administration."[79]

Disturbed by the party rancor, Washington said that the papers "are surcharged and some of them indecently communicative of charges that stand in need of evidence for their support."[80] Knowing that Jefferson was behind Freneau's paper, Washington said that it, by sowing opposition to the government, was tending to disunite the nation and encourage anarchy, the quickest route toward monarchy.

Jefferson had said that the nation was being taken over by speculators and would-be monarchists. But he favored another term for Washington, since "North and South will hang together if they have you to hang on,"[81] he told Washington.

Washington stated that in his visits around the country he did not find the discontent that Freneau and others were finding. Jefferson answered that the federal assumption of state war debts had increased the federal debt unnecessarily and had corrupted both branches of the legislature. Although Jefferson seemed to be saying that only Washington could keep the fires of patriotism aglow, "his plea much resembled an invitation for the General to keep his camp fire burning in a powder magazine, while the kegs were being opened."[82]

Washington told Madison that he would not seek a second term, because he felt unqualified to handle the business, legal, and constitutional problems that came up, and because he felt he had failed to provide the harmony that would keep party spirit from working against the national interest. Madison agreed that party spirit was rising, but that was all the more reason to stay on as president, since only he could help the nation achieve unity.

Here Madison, a chief cause of the problem of a split nation, spoke as if he were opposed to the split. Madison saw the nation divided between a party trying to set up a mixed monarchy, and a weak minority that might want to overthrow the government to prevent the monarchy. Another four years of Washington's "temperate and wise administration," said Madison, and perhaps both types of enemies of the government would fade away. Undecided as to whether to run again, Washington asked Madison's help in drafting a farewell address.

Washington continued to seek for peace within the cabinet. In August 1792 he wrote Jefferson: "How unfortunate that whilst we are encompassed on all sides with avowed enemies and insidious friends, that internal dissensions should be harrowing and tearing our vitals. Without more charity toward opposing opinion, I believe it will be difficult to manage the reins of government or to keep the parts of it together. My earnest wish is that there may be liberal allowances and mutual forbearances on all sides."[83] He sent a similar letter to Hamilton.

Hamilton's response to Washington was that Jefferson had persistently opposed his policies and that he had only struck back in defense. He promised to support Washington's plan for a more cooperative administrative team.

Jefferson's reply charged that Hamilton's system "flowed from principles adverse to liberty, and was calculated to demolish the Republic by creating an influence of his department over the members of the legislature." Jefferson properly accused Hamilton of intruding into his area of foreign affairs. After leaving the administration, Jefferson said, he would defend his honor as a private person from the "slanders of a man whose history is a tissue of machinations against the liberty of a country which has heaped honors on his head."[84]

Lacking a navy, the United States could not protect American shipping in the Mediterranean. Jefferson and Washington discussed the annual bribe paid to Algerian pirates to keep them from attacking American shipping. Jefferson said that the House of Representatives might not appropriate the bribe money. Then, according to Jefferson, Washington said that "he did not like throwing too much into democratic hands." If the House "would not do what the Constitution called on them to do, the government would be at an end and must then assume another form." Jefferson said that he was thus petrified with the thought—this man wants to be a king![85]

Can the president fire a cabinet member without Senate approval, since the appointment requires that approval? Madison worked hard in the House of Representatives to give the president sole dismissal power, but in the Senate the vote was a tie. Vice President Adams voted for the bill, breaking the tie. Madison and other students of government rejoiced that Congress could not now take over control of the cabinet, and the president would have more independence in carrying out his responsibilities.

As he neared the end of his first term, Washington could see that many of his goals had been achieved. Bills had been passed revising the excise tax, apportioning the House, establishing a mint, improving the postal service, and creating a uniform federal militia. Two other issues had been postponed but not voted down: a uniform system of weights and measures, and settlement of western land disputes.

The first term was almost as important as the Constitutional Convention, since now specific decisions were being made that had been postponed at the Convention. Fleshing out the government over the skeleton of Constitutional articles required constant decision making. Precedents were being established, and since they might last for a long time, they carried much weight. Sensing this, Washington was cautious and discreet whenever a new step was being tried.

Perhaps because John Adams had given Washington a lot of trouble when he had been commander of the Continental Army, Washington did not make Vice President Adams his executive officer. As a result, to this day the position is largely an honorary and a standby post.

On a rare vacation at Mount Vernon, Washington no longer hunted. The fence of his deer park had broken, and the deer now grazed in his woods. Rather than have them destroyed by his hounds, he got rid of the dogs, of which he had been very proud. Now, instead of fox-hunting, he sat on his porch and watched the gentle forest creatures browse.

The President's Second Term

Washington was re-elected by unanimous vote of the electors. His two elections were the only unanimous ones in American history.

The Reign of Terror during the French Revolution brought out differing reactions from Jefferson and Washington. Jefferson's friend, William Short, was an American attaché in Holland. Having witnessed the Terror, Short told Jefferson that he had seen "the most mad, wicked, and atrocious assembly that was ever collected." Jefferson chastised Short for his lack of faith in democracy. It was necessary, Jefferson said, that "many guilty people fell without the forms of trial and with them some innocent." Rather than see the cause of liberty fail, Jefferson continued, "I would have seen half the world desolate."[86]

Despite all the bloodshed that Washington had witnessed in battle, he detested violence. He protected Tories from persecution. "He believed that extralegal violence, whether initiated by aristocrats or republicans, followed the same road."[87] But Jefferson was glad to see Washington tell Short to stop criticizing the French, "the sheet anchor of this country."

Jefferson knew that the Republican newspaper attack upon his administration was causing Washington great anguish. Jefferson told Madison that Washington was "extremely affected by the attacks made and kept up on him in the public papers. I think he feels those things more than any person I ever yet met." Flexner says that "Jefferson stated that he was 'sincerely sorry' to see Washington so hurt, but he made no effort to still or abate the attacks made by his partisans and his employee on his aging chief."[88] Despite Jefferson's opposition, Washington sought no recrimination. He said, "I have never discovered anything in the conduct of Mr. Jefferson to raise suspicions in my mind of his insincerity."[89]

Years later, after Washington was dead, Jefferson admitted that Washington had, in "scrupulously obeying the laws through the whole of his career, civil and military," behaved in a manner "of which the history of the world furnishes no other example."[90] Alas, a candid statement of this sort over Jefferson's name in Freneau's paper in the 1790s could have kept that great man from many a headache!

Madison, after breaking with Washington, criticized him for listening to the people. He said that Washington had been "cool, considerate, and cautious, ever scrutinizing into public opinion, ready to follow where he could not lead."[91] This scarcely sounds like Jefferson's "monarchist"!

Washington wanted to see Americans settle the Northwest Territory, as a protection against Canadian settlement there. Unruly Indians disturbed American settlers, so Washington sent Anthony Wayne to subdue them. Although he wanted Americans to observe the land rights of the Indians, he believed in firmness in repelling their invasion into non-Indian lands.

The main principles of Washington's foreign policy were to avoid foreign wars, to pursue America's interests concerning Europe, and to accord equal treatment to England, France, and Spain.

The Whiskey Rebellion again brought out differences among American leaders. Hamilton advocated killing the ringleaders: "Without rigor everywhere, our tranquillity is likely to be of very short duration, and the next storm will be infinitely worse."[92] Washington said that since the rebellion had ceased, federal laws were again being observed, and so he pardoned the leaders. Madison praised Washington for acting with wisdom and tact.

After Washington signed Jay's Treaty on June 25, 1795, a torrent of criticism engulfed him, saying that he had been duped by Hamilton into becoming England's lackey. When the House of Representatives asked to review the instructions and correspondence relating to the treaty, Washington adamantly refused, on the ground of separation of powers between the executive and legislative branches. Subsequent presidents have tended to follow this precedent.

Typical of the Republican attack upon him at this time was the vilification by Franklin's grandson, Benjamin Franklin Bache. Writing in his newspaper *Aurora*, Bache said that Washington had been carried by "false ambition" to the "precipice of destruction." He had become "the omnipotent director of a seraglio instead of the first magistrate of a free people."[93] Washington was depicted as a person of small ability, with insufficient education, taking part in the Revolution not out of patriotism but for personal fame and profit from land speculation.

In 1796 Washington received a birthday present in the form of a treaty with Spain concluded on February 22 by envoy Thomas Pinckney. Spain accepted the American version of the Florida boundary, and promised not to stir up southern Indians against the United States, which now had free passage on the lower Mississippi.

That year Washington sent to the Senate for ratification a treaty with Tripoli that offended some Christians by its opening words: "As the government of the United States of America is not in any sense founded on the Christian religion, as it has in itself no character of enmity against the laws, religion, or tranquillity of Moslems, and as the said states have never entered into any war or act of hostility against any Mohammedan nation, it is declared by the parties that no pretext arising from religious opinions shall ever produce an interruption of the harmony existing between the two countries."[94]

The Republican attack upon Washington continued when James Monroe was replaced as minister to France. Monroe wrote a long "View of the Conduct of the Executive," in which Washington was described as hostile to France. His patience wearing thin, Washington answered with a 44-page rebuttal in which he said that "to state facts for the information of Congress and not to write eulogisms on the French nation or conduct was the object of the then President. If Mr. Monroe ever fills the chair of government, he may let the French minister frame his speeches."[95]

In his Farewell Address, given on September 19, 1796, Washington used material Madison had given him earlier and Hamilton had provided more recently. He advised the nation to avoid internal strife through party factions and unnecessary involvement in European power struggles.

In May 1797 a number of American newspapers printed translations of Jefferson's letter to Philip Mazzei in which Jefferson accused Washington of monarchical ambitions. Relations between the two great Americans were cool after that time. As would be expected, Washington vigorously opposed the anti-Federalist stance of the Kentucky and Virginia Resolutions of Jefferson and Madison. "Opposers of the government," he said, "will stick at nothing to injure it."[96]

On July 4, 1798, he once again accepted the position as commander of the American army, as President Adams prepared the nation for war against France. He was not to take the field unless invasion was imminent, and since that time never came, his army turned out to be one largely on paper.

Washington could not legally free Martha's slaves in her lifetime, but in his will he arranged for both their slaves to be freed upon her death, which took place in 1802. The will provided for security for aged slaves, and education for the younger ones. It also provided for shares of stock to be used to finance public schools and a national university. The largest part of his estate consisted of western land holdings totaling over 49,000 acres.

He who had been first in war was now recognized as first in peace. He wrote to Lafayette: "I wish to see the sons and daughters of the world in peace and busily employed in the more agreeable amusement: increase and multiply, as an encouragement to which we have opened the fertile plains of the Ohio to the poor, the needy, and the oppressed of the earth."[97]

On December 12, 1799, he caught cold riding in the snow. His condition worsened into a severe throat infection. He said finally, "I feel myself going. I thank you for your attention, but I pray you to take no more trouble about me. Let me go off quietly. I cannot last long." His death on December 14 sent the entire nation into mourning. When the news reached Europe the armies of Napoleon and the British channel fleet saluted his memory.

Significant throughout his post-War life were the tributes paid him by his former adversaries, the British. From 1783 onward, British officers had called at Mount Vernon to pay their respect to him as a military leader and as a man. Upon his inauguration as at his death, British naval salvos saluted their erstwhile opponent. Surely part of Washington's greatness was due to his nurture in the traditions of a great nation whose political mistakes had cost her dearly. William IV, the son of George III, later declared that Washington was "the greatest man who ever lived."[98]

Brooks Adams, calling Washington the greatest man of the eighteenth century, said that "his greatness consists chiefly in that balance of mind which enabled him to recognize when an old order had passed away. He prevailed not only because of an intelligence and elevation of character which enabled him to comprehend and persuade others, but also because he was supported by a body of the most remarkable men whom America has ever produced."[99]

Writing with typical magnanimity in *The American Commonwealth*, James Bryce said that "Washington stands alone and unapproachable, like a snow-peak rising above its fellows into the clear air of morning, with a dignity, constancy, and purity which have made him the ideal type of civic virtue to succeeding generations. No greater benefit could have fallen the Republic than to have such a type set from the first before the eye and mind of the people."[100]

15. James Wilson: The Capitalist and World Citizen

Which framer came up with a philosophy of government, based upon the law of nations, that saw the American experiment as the first step in a world order based upon adherence to God's law? Which framer, although an associate justice of the United States Supreme Court at that time, died a fugitive from justice for not having paid his debts? The two questions have but one answer—James Wilson.

James Wilson was born in 1742 in the village of Caskardy, six miles west of St. Andrews, in the county of Fife, said to be the most democratic shire in Scotland. His father, a shrewd and industrious farmer, was an elder of the Church of Scotland. Like many Fifers, he was noted for his dry wit. Wilson's mother, Alisan Lansdale Wilson, was a tall, strong, and pious woman. Wilson had three older sisters and three younger brothers.

The family was of moderate means. Their diet was simple: oatmeal porridge for breakfast, barley broth with cabbage for lunch, and potatoes and milk for supper.

A tall, nearsighted lad, Wilson at 14 graduated from grammar school and walked to St. Andrews to take an examination for a scholarship at the university. Tuition was £10 per year, so the scholarship meant a big saving to the family. His siblings resented the fact that they had to sacrifice so that James could get a university education and become a clergyman in the Calvinist Church of Scotland.

The university at St. Andrews was the region's boast. It had been started in 1410 by a group of masters who were former students at the University of Paris. The area was populated by Scottish Covenanters, who had a tradition of rebellion against civil authority.

Nearby Edinburgh University was the seat of the Scottish Renaissance, which had been begun by David Hume and Francis Hutcheson, and continued by George Berkeley, Hugh Blair, Thomas Reid, William Robertson, and Adam Smith. The mutual stimulation among these economists, historians, and philosophers made "Edinburgh, for a generation or more, the greatest university in Christendom."[1]

The University of St. Andrews had a classical curriculum. Wilson spent four years at Saint Salvator College of the university, studying ethics, Greek, history, Latin, logic, mathematics, philosophy, and science. In vogue among Wilson's professors were Newton's physics, Locke's psychology, and the philosophies of Berkeley, Hume, Hutcheson, and the third Earl of Shaftesbury.

Wilson spent one year studying divinity at St. Mary's College of the university. Then, however, his father died and his formal education ceased. A good student, Wilson became a tutor, working until his sisters had marriage prospects and his brothers could help support his mother. In 1765 he studied bookkeeping in Edinburgh from Thomas Young, who admitted that young Wilson beat him at the national pastime of golf even though Wilson had never before played the game.

Wishing to free himself from family responsibilities, and sensing a better future in the new world, Wilson arrived in New York City in 1765, to find a seething cauldron of colonial dissent. The writings of James Otis were popular. Citing James Harrington, Otis declared that government is founded on God's irrefutable law. When this law is violated, Otis said, it is up to the King's Bench to declare acts of Parliament unconstitutional. Otis cited cases from English constitutional law to buttress his position. Otis called the Sugar Act of 1764 "taxation without representation."

In 1766 Wilson moved to Philadelphia, where he received a position as an instructor in Latin at the College of Philadelphia. This college granted him an honorary M.A. degree on May 20, 1766, "in consideration of his merit and his having had a regular education in the universities of Scotland."[2] In Philadelphia Wilson read the series of letters by John Dickinson under the pen name of "A Pennsylvania Farmer," in which Dickinson defended the position that Parliament had no right to tax the colonies for revenue purposes.

Wilson's cousin Robert Annan loaned Wilson money so that he could study law under Dickinson. An avid law student, Wilson now read such authorities as Blackstone, Burlamaqui, Richard Hooker, Lord Kames, Locke, Montesquieu, Pufendorf, and Algernon Sidney. In his notebook was a definition from Cicero: "A lawyer is a man who knows how to give advice and apply in the most cautious manner those laws and that constitution that private men are directed by in a state."[3]

Wilson's best friend, Billy White, was preparing for the Anglican ministry. During their long conversations about religion, Wilson abandoned his Calvinism for a more liberal theology.

After less than a year's apprenticeship to Dickinson, Wilson began a law practice in Reading in 1767. Land disputes made up most of the cases at the time. In August 1767 Wilson received permission to practice not only in Berks County but also in Chester, Cumberland, and Lancaster counties. This was important, since land title cases typically spread from one jurisdiction to another.

In 1768 Benjamin Franklin's wife Deborah gave Wilson her power-of-attorney to recover a debt from a Reading innkeeper named Drury. Drury was so impressed with Wilson's skill and tact that he immediately made Wilson his attorney.

Wilson was also trying his hand at writing. In 1768 he and Billy White wrote a column for the *Pennsylvania Chronicle* under the name of "The Visitant." In the manner of Addison, The Visitant discussed moral virtue, dress, manners, philosophy, and current affairs. There was much speculation over who The Visitant was, and Wilson and White were flattered that "some suspected Joseph Galloway, famous for his wit and learning."[4]

Wilson now wrote a pamphlet, *Considerations on the Nature and Extent of the Legislative Authority of the British Parliament*. Billy White showed the essay to Dr. Francis Alison, vice-provost of the College of Philadelphia. Alison liked it, but wanted to suggest some revisions before it was printed. The pamphlet did not get recognition until it was published in 1774, by which time its ideas were much more common.

John Armstrong, a lawyer in Carlisle, invited Wilson into his law practice, and so Wilson moved there in 1770. Near the frontier, Carlisle had endless land title cases to settle. Wilson was kept busy here and in neighboring counties. Robert Morris chose Wilson to represent him in an important land case. Land acquisition now began to become an obsession with Wilson.

A beautiful heiress entered the stage of his life. Rachel Bird was stepdaughter to the eminent Colonel John Patton of nearby Birdsboro. Wilson taught Rachel to play piquet and she beat him. Soon he longed for another defeat! He professed love but she professed celibacy. He was pleased when she allowed him to write to her. He was amazed at how "a thousand little trifles which are wholly indifferent to others become so many sources of delight to those who love."[5]

He proposed marriage—she gave him her friendship. Billy White finally came to Wilson's aid. White's fiancée, Mary Harrison, was a close friend of Rachel's. White got Mary to have Rachel disclose her true intention, which was that Wilson should not give up the suit.

On November 5, 1771, they were wed at St. Gabriel's Episcopal Church, across the river from the Birdsboro estate. The heiress and her new husband had a reception amid peacocks, deer, and the boxwood hedges of Birdsboro.

Rachel's brother Mark became Wilson's partner in a number of business ventures. Recognized as a shrewd lawyer in land litigation, Wilson was now employed to defend Pennsylvania's right to land along the Virginia border.

The Wilsons' first child, Mary (called Polly), was born in September 1772. Wilson's mother kept writing from Scotland, asking him for letters and money. Wilson gave little of either, although he occasionally did send her some money. He did not yet repay the money he had borrowed for his trip to America, however, and his brother William asked him to repay it as soon as he could.

The Patriot

On July 12, 1774, a meeting in Carlisle called for a Congress of deputies from all of the colonies to consider reaction to Britain's presence in Boston, and to establish a policy of nonimportation from England. After helping draw up the agenda, Wilson was appointed to be on a committee of correspondence. Then he was selected to be one of the three deputies from the county to a meeting in Philadelphia of "the General Congress." This meeting of Pennsylvania deputies was held on July 15. After affirming loyalty to George III, the meeting resolved that a colony-wide Congress should be assembled to redress grievances and restore harmony with England.

Wilson now resurrected his 1768 pamphlet and brought it up to date. He omitted mention of the benefits the colonies received from their relationship to England. He traced the history of Parliament, showing the ascendancy of the power of the people. Parliament, he said, by violating the rights of Englishmen in America, was violating the British constitution and had thus forfeited its authority. The only remaining allegiance of Americans was to the crown. This was one of the earliest coherent statements of reasons for the American opposition to Parliament.

Wilson attended a state convention in Philadelphia in January 1775 that approved the work of the First Continental Congress. It resolved that America should set up its own manufactures so as not to have to buy English goods. Wilson told the convention that Americans were now merely exerting traditional British liberties. The House of Commons represents the English people, he said, but it no longer represents Englishmen in America. In his talk Wilson now denied that even the king should have a hand in framing colonial policy.

On January 29 Wilson hurried back to Carlisle to help organize the militia of Cumberland County. By the end of April he was commissioned as "colonel of the 4th Battalion of Associators" in the county. The next month he was elected as a delegate to the Second Continental Congress.

The Association seemed not to be working. It was simply making Parliament more angry. The Coercive Acts remained in force, and General Gage had instituted martial law in place of the Massachusetts government. Because of the outbreak of hostilities at Lexington and Concord, the radicals were more numerous in the Second Congress. Now there were firebrands like John Adams, Samuel Adams, John Hancock, and Patrick Henry, as well as the more moderate Franklin, Jay, Washington, and Wilson.

Wilson was placed on the committee to advise Massachusetts on what to do. The committee's advice was that the Massachusetts Assembly should continue to function "until a Governor, of His Majesty's Appointment, will consent to govern the colony according to its charter."[6]

John Adams and Wilson served on a committee to print $2,000,000 in paper currency. Adams wrote to Abigail that Wilson's "fortitude, rectitude, and abilities greatly outshine his master's."[7] John Dickinson was far too cautious to please Adams at this time.

Wilson was also on the committee on Indian affairs. One of the problems concerned intertribal rivalries. An aggressive group of Delawares led by White Eyes were used to keep the Iroquois neutral and to fend off the Iroquois should they side with the British. Wilson became one of the most influential members of Congress in dealing with the border tribes.

Some of his committee work involved land transactions. At Fort Pitt, he helped achieve a settlement favorable to Pennsylvania in a land dispute with Virginia. He tried to persuade Congress to forbid further immigration from Connecticut into the Wyoming valley. He made an effort to get Congress to have his friend, Arthur St. Clair, lead an attack upon Detroit, where he had land holdings. He was disappointed when Congress decided on a different plan for the conquest of Canada.[8]

In 1776 Wilson stated that whoever refused to sign the Association should be disarmed. But he vacillated on relationship to the crown. In May 1776 he opposed a recommendation that the colonies assume all the powers of their government. "Why pull down the old house before you have the new one built?"[9] he asked. In addition to Wilson, the main opponents to a declaration of independence in Congress were John Dickinson, Robert Livingston, and Edward Rutledge.

A great change occurred in Congress in the month of June. One of the factors responsible for the change was the failure of the military campaign in Canada. Wilson, like other speculators in western land, feared that their holdings might be at the mercy of a hostile Britain. Wilson's earlier writings show that ideologically he was also quite ready for the separation, and so he supported the Declaration of Independence. Even with his vote, however, Pennsylvania would have voted 4–3 against separation, had not both John Dickinson and Robert Morris been absent from the vote.

In his maturity Wilson was tall, inclined to be stout, with a ruddy face, a white wig, and thick glasses. His manners were stiff. "Shyness cloaked itself under an aloofness that was attributed by his enemies to arrogance."[10] Chivalrous, he was more at home with women than with men. Since their wives were old friends, he was a good friend of Robert Morris. Other close friends were William Bingham, Francis Hopkinson, and Dr. Benjamin Rush.

As his fortunes improved, Wilson became philanthropic, frequently contributing to educational and charitable organizations. He was always more at home among books and ideas than at social gatherings. His fame as a lawyer was so widespread that when he was bested on an obscure point about the constitution of Iceland, his adversary William Findley chortled for weeks about having beaten James Wilson.

Wilson's faith in democracy, Geoffrey Seed believes, exceeded that of all other Founding Fathers.[11] To Wilson, government was a pyramid in which the people were the base. He was the main proponent of the idea of one man, one vote. Suffrage, he said, would build patriotism and social cohesion. The voter exceeds a prince, he felt, for the prince's sovereignty was derivative but the voter's was original.

James Bryce said that Wilson's works "display a profundity of view in matters of constitutional theory which place him in the front rank of the political thinkers of his age."[12] "Morality," Wilson said, "has its intuitive truths."[13] Most people, he felt, have this God-given instinct toward morality. Since it is common to all, what is good for one person is good for another. The wider the franchise, the better the government, for each individual can make a unique contribution.

Wilson knew that without responsibility, liberty degenerates into license. People must obey the laws they helped make, he said, and follow the officials they helped elect. Under good government, a person gains more than he loses, for "he will gain more by the limitation of other men's freedom than he can lose by the diminution of his own."[14]

Since Wilson had been somewhat tentative about supporting the break with England, his opponents attacked him as not being a true patriot. Finally a "Defense of Wilson" was drawn up and signed by all of his colleagues in the Continental Congress, to show that his views were respected even by radicals who always favored immediate separation.

In Congress in 1776 Wilson said that Virginia's claim of land stretching to the Pacific Ocean was based on the mistaken notion that the Pacific was not more than 100 miles from the Atlantic. When Virginia would not cede its claims, Wilson threatened that Pennsylvania would stay out of the Confederation.

Wilson also attacked what he felt was inconsistent in the southern view that slaves could be counted as a basis for proportional representation but not as a basis for taxation. Not to tax slaves would be to encourage slave-holding, and Wilson was deeply opposed to slavery.

Wilson left Congress to be with Rachel when their son Bird was born in January 1777. While at Carlisle, he checked up on the possibility of locating a supply depot there.

During this winter federal funds were so low that Congress sent the frostbitten soldiers some kersey cloth, with needles and thread, so that they could sew their own coats.

Wilson was placed on a committee to decide what to do with maritime prizes seized from neutral countries. Thus began two American institutions: the United States Navy and admiralty courts.

Wilson was asked to write an address to the American people, explaining the reason for the actions of Congress. John Dickinson toned down some of Wilson's statements. "Our purpose," Wilson said, "is not to establish an independent empire, but to defend and re-establish the constitutional rights of the colonies."[15] By the time the people read these words, they were made obsolete by the bad turn of military events and the inflamed rhetoric of Thomas Paine arousing Americans to action.

Because he had a cool nature, Wilson had relatively few friends. His astute mind caused people to mistrust him, feeling that he had an unstated motive behind his words and deeds.

In February 1777 he led the opposition to a statement in the Articles of Confederation that all sovereign power rested in the separate states. Wilson believed that the Confederation derived its power from the states acting collectively. For revenue, Wilson advocated that Congress pass a land tax, a salt tax, and a poll tax.

Wilson served on a number of Congressional committees. He asked Robert Morris to nominate him as the chief law officer of the new nation. Perhaps because he felt that Wilson was being too forward, Morris never brought up the matter. Wilson was, however, seriously considered for appointment on the three-man commission to France.

Wilson's career in 1777 was hectic. Because he, along with George Clymer and Benjamin Rush, refused to support the new Pennsylvania state constitution, all three were not selected by the Assembly as delegates to the Continental Congress. Wilson believed that Philadelphia had granted too many concessions to western settlers in framing the new document. When, however, William Moore declined to serve in the Congress, Wilson was appointed as his replacement.

Early in September 1777 Wilson was once again removed from Congress by the Assembly. Instead, he was made a delegate to the Pennsylvania constitutional convention, which was also meeting in the state house in Philadelphia, across the hall from the Continental Congress. It was a simple matter for Wilson to keep abreast of the actions of Congress.[16]

The Entrepreneur

Because of his opposition to the state constitution, Wilson was now out of favor with the electorate. His law practice and his business interests engaged his time for the next few years.

In the opinion of Charles P. Smith, "Wilson did more than any other man of his generation to give shape to the concept of a federal judiciary with appellate jurisdiction over the state courts."[17] In a key case, Wilson represented Gideon Olmstead, an American seaman who had led a successful attempt to seize the British sloop *Active* in late 1777. Dissatisfied with the admiralty court's award of one-fourth of the ship's value to Olmstead, Wilson appealed the case to the Court of Commissioners set up by Congress to hear appeals from state courts. They awarded Olmstead a higher percentage of the prize money.

States were so reluctant to accept federal authority that Pennsylvania refused to pay Olmstead as directed by the Court of Commissioners. Years later, in 1809, the District Court of Pennsylvania finally observed the federal ruling and granted the money to Olmstead. Supreme Court Justice Bushrod Washington gave fines and prison terms to members of the Pennsylvania militia for resisting federal authority. Had he still been alive, the action would have been sweet revenge for the federal-minded Wilson.

In June 1778, when General Clinton and the British troops evacuated Philadelphia, Wilson moved there from Carlisle, and from then on Philadelphia was his home. A harrowing event occurred there in early 1779. Wilson, pleased that the Assembly had authorized a public vote to determine whether there was support for the new state constitution, took the opportunity to speak widely against it.

Defenders of the constitution, led by the artist Charles Willson Peale, accused Wilson, Robert Morris, and other opponents of the constitution of being greedy, trying to make money by disobeying the price controls authorized by the document. Mobs began to seize stores of crops owned by Morris and others. A ragged group of militia, led by a mob, shouted "Get Wilson!"

In his defense Wilson turned his home into a fortress. About twenty of his friends, led by General Thomas Mifflin, fought off the mob's attack. Shots were fired and men were bayonetted. By the time President Joseph Reed of Pennsylvania arrived and restored order, six men had been killed (only one on Wilson's side) and 17 had been wounded. Wilson fled to the country home of Robert Morris for safety. Tempers gradually subsided, and in March 1780 the executive council of the state granted general clemency to all participants.[18]

Wilson now turned his attention to banking. On July 7, 1780, the Bank of Pennsylvania opened, organized by Robert Morris and his partner Thomas Willing, with Wilson's help. All bank funds were to be used to buy food and munitions for the army. Bank officers were to receive reasonable salaries, but bank subscribers were to receive no profits. The bank could issue bank notes bearing 6 percent interest. At first the bank was a success, but the inflationary rate of both state and Continental currency caused the demise of the bank in September 1780.

What Wilson had in mind was that the Bank of Pennsylvania should be converted into a national bank. He advanced several ways in which this would benefit the nation. The bank would provide both currency and credit facilities, he said, and thus expand domestic and foreign commerce. It would not only help stabilize foreign exchange rates, he felt, but it would also assist in preventing an adverse balance of trade.[19] Wilson got many of his ideas about finance from Adam Smith, David Hume, and Sir James Stewart, all of whom believed that adequate credit facilities were the key to rapid economic expansion.

Undaunted by the failure of the Bank of Pennsylvania, Wilson and Robert Morris started a drive to get approval for a national bank. They were motivated by a need to help the nation's crippled economy as well as to get more capital for their various business enterprises.

Superintendent of Continental Finances in 1781, Robert Morris proposed the bank to the insolvent Continental Congress. Congress reluctantly agreed, and the Bank of North America was chartered on December 31, 1781, with Thomas Willing as president. Within a few weeks the bank could lend Congress $100,000.

By 1783 a rival bank tried to set up, but Gouverneur Morris and Wilson were able to keep it from getting a charter. Old foes of Wilson and Robert Morris, those who had supported the state constitution, now attacked the Bank of North America, saying it was shipping available specie overseas in order to import luxury items for the wealthy. Wilson himself owed the bank large sums of money, forcing President Willing to threaten Wilson with legal action in order to get him to repay his loans. Wilson defended the bank before Congress, but the antibank forces prevailed and the charter was revoked.

Wilson was the foremost land speculator among the Founding Fathers. During the War Wilson bought land in the holdings of the Illinois-Wabash Company, one of America's largest land enterprises. In 1780 he was elected president of the company, which owned over 60 million acres of land divided into 84 shares. Ten shares had been put aside to give to influential men who would give aid to the company. The company's title to the land was based upon vague terms of Indian purchases which it hoped to get Congress to recognize.

As company lawyer, Wilson received one-half share (400,000 acres), and he had purchased another share. In addition, he held proxies for the estate of George Ross (former company president) and for four Maryland men who owned a share among them. In company votes Wilson thus exercised control over 3½ votes.

Wilson also entered into a partnership with William Bingham, Mark Bird, and Robert Hooper. Bingham was an agent for Congress in the West Indies. The partnership formed the Canaan Company, which held land on the Susquehanna River in southern New York. Ultimately the only partner to benefit was Bingham, who maintained control of his share of the holdings and gave his name to the town of Binghamton.

As a private land speculator, Wilson had his problems. He would make a small down payment and get a preliminary warrant from the land office. This authorized him to run surveys, a costly process. Sometimes the land ended up being in rocky, swampy, or inaccessible country. His greed led him to buy up larger tracts that he could process. Sometimes squatters were on the land, or there were rival claims to the land. Often Wilson could not get clear title fast enough to sell the land at a profit, and he would have to forfeit his claim because of being behind in his payments.

Wilson did much better as an attorney for land companies or for the state of Pennsylvania. In November 1782 he represented Pennsylvania at Trenton in the Wyoming land controversy with Connecticut. Wilson alleged that Pennsylvania settlers preceded Connecticut ones in the territory, and produced 39 Indians deeds and papers compared to 2 for Connecticut. The commissioners, who were approved by the Confederation Congress, ruled unanimously in favor of Pennsylvania.

Rebuffed by this decision, Connecticut argued that it granted only the jurisdiction over the land to Pennsylvania, but that individual land titles remained in the hands of the Connecticut settlers. Wilson represented Pennsylvania in working out a compromise in which Connecticut ceded the Wyoming territory to New York, Pennsylvania, and the United States, in exchange for which Connecticut got title to the land (but not the jurisdiction) of the Western Reserve. Wilson was pleased that an instrumentality of the federal government was working effectively to arbitrate disputes between states. This experience prepared Wilson for his role in helping get a federal judicial system established in the federal Constitution.

The Legislator

After an absence of over four years, Wilson took a seat in Congress on January 2, 1783. Wilson formed an immediate alliance with Madison, and the two worked together to help strengthen the Confederation. Although the big problem was how to reimburse soldiers for back pay, Wilson pointed out other fiscal needs, such as the interest and the principal on domestic and foreign loans, and current operating expenses. To pay off the soldiers, Wilson recommended a tax system on both the land values and the number of the population.

He knew that there was a general American dislike of taxes, partly because of having had to pay what they considered to be unjust British taxes. But he urged Congress to face fiscal responsibility, something that was getting increasingly difficult for him to do in his personal life.

Of the $3,000,000 required by Congress to meet annual operating expenses, Wilson recommended that equal amounts come from three sources: a salt tax, a land tax, and an impost on trade. Congress discarded the salt tax, but set up a method of evaluating real estate for the land tax. With the income to be used solely to pay war debts, Congress adopted a 25-year 5 percent ad valorem tax on all imports. It was never collected because New York refused to grant approval to the needed amendment to the Articles of Confederation.

Wilson served on a Congressional committee that concluded that a peacetime standing army was needed to discourage possible foreign aggressors. The committee recommended a small contingent of four infantry regiments, one artillery regiment, and a corps of engineers.

In 1785 Wilson led a drive to get permission for Congress to regulate commerce, but Richard Henry Lee successfully blocked the effort. Attendance in Congress was now lackadaisical. There were 14 times during the session when no quorum was reached. Usually only nine states or fewer were represented. The President of Congress, David Ramsay, wrote to Benjamin Rush in 1785 that "the present Congress for want of more states has not power to coin a copper. In 1775 there was more patriotism in a village than there is now in the thirteen states."[20]

By 1786 the Wilsons had two daughters and four sons. Wilson maintained occasional contact with his family back in Scotland. The Wilson country home was at Somerset on the Delaware River near the iron works owned by Wilson and Mark Bird.

The Wilsons entertained on a lavish scale. The Marquis de Chastellux, invited to dinner at the Wilsons, praised the charm and hospitality of his hosts. After a rich dinner came port, tobacco, songs, and gay conversation. "One cannot lose a kingdom more gaily," wrote the Marquis, "but it is impossible to be more gay in forming a republic."[21]

Wilson's joy turned suddenly to sorrow on April 14, 1786, when Rachel died, at the age of 39. While attending young James, 7, in his illness, she contracted his malady and succumbed.

Along with Robert Morris, Benjamin Rush, and Thomas Paine, Wilson attended the informal sessions of the Society for Political Inquiries that met at Franklin's home. Wilson was elected to membership in the American Philosophical Society in 1786. He served as president of the St. Andrews Society from 1786 to 1789, and became an honorary member of the Society of the Cincinnati in 1789.

When the charter of the Bank of North America had been revoked, confidence of European investors in the bank had been shaken, and cash resources shrank from a high of nearly $60 million to $37 million early in 1786. The bank received a charter from Delaware in January 1786. In February Paine began writing pamphlets defending the bank. Franklin came out in support of renewing its charter. With the bank capital limited to $2,000,000, Congress finally renewed the charter for a period of 13 years in the spring of 1787.

The Framer

No doubt Wilson's greatest contribution to the new nation came from his services at the Constitutional Convention. James Bryce called him "one of the deepest thinkers and most exact reasoners"[22] at the Convention, and Max Farrand said that only Madison surpassed him in the importance of their Convention work.[23] Farrand found him to be in some respects Madison's intellectual superior, although he was less practical and less flexible than Madison.

William Pierce admired the "legal and political knowledge" of Wilson, saying that "government seems to have been his peculiar study, all the political institutions of the world he knows in detail, and can trace the causes and effects of every revolution from the earliest stages of the Greek commonwealth down to the present time."[24]

In the opinion of Charles P. Smith, "Wilson espoused more of those principles which have since become prominent features of American democracy than any other delegate," for "his ideas were more in harmony with what would be the future pattern of American social and political development."[25]

Some of Wilson's best speeches in the Convention concerned the executive. He favored a single executive elected directly by the people. His colleagues were not in favor of that much democracy, so he worked out the electoral college plan in which the people still had the determining vote.

The trouble with the plural executive, he said, was that it prevented the pinpointing of responsibility. He cited history to show that the worst tyrants were plural executives: the 30 tyrants of Athens, the Decemvirs of Rome, and Parliament, which he called a worse tyrant than the king. Wilson saw a similarity between the presidency and the Anglo-Saxon kingship, which was a limited monarchy. He realized, however, that to be effective the president needed to be independent of the legislature and the judiciary.

On June 11 Wilson received a favorable vote, 6–5, that representation in the Senate would be like that in the House, on the basis of population. But the small states hacked at this method until they finally got it overruled in the Great Compromise. Meanwhile, when William Davie of North Carolina pointed out, on June 30, that proportional representation would make the Senate so large and unwieldy that it could not serve its function as a wise reflective body, Wilson said that he was embarrassed to admit his error, and he now conceded that the Senate would have to remain relatively small. This was the beginning of the end of the large states—they never again made a good case for proportional representation in the Senate.

What Madison did not destroy in William Paterson's New Jersey Plan, Wilson did. Admittedly this Convention is not empowered to make final decisions, Wilson said, but that should not prevent it from making the best possible recommendations. "Will a citizen of Delaware be downgraded by becoming a citizen of the United States?" he asked. He showed that unicameral legislatures have often become tyrannical, lacking an inner check upon themselves. He showed why a single executive is better than a plural one: "To control the legislature, you divide it; to control the executive, you unite it."[26]

Should members of the House of Representatives be elected by the people? No, said Gerry. The Massachusetts legislature, elected by the people, has demagogues who can be elected but are ignorant, lazy, or criminals. Wilson's faith in the people was undaunted. Government must flow from its true source, the people, he said. "The legislature ought to be the most exact transcript of the whole society."[27] Madison and Mason concurred with Wilson, and soon the Convention voted to approve Wilson's stand.

Should wealth be a criterion for apportionment in the House of Representatives? Robert Morris and other members of Wilson's clique thought so. Wilson broke with his fellow capitalists. "The majority of people ought to govern the minority," he said. "If numbers be not a proper rule, why is not some better rule pointed out? In 1783," Wilson said, "after elaborate discussion of a measure of wealth, Congress was satisfied that the rule of numbers does not differ much from the combined rule of numbers and wealth." He could not agree that property was the primary object of government. "The cultivation and improvement of the human mind was the most noble object."[28]

Wealth was dropped as a determiner, from that point forward. In the words of Charles P. Smith, "almost alone among his contemporaries Wilson foresaw that America's commercial spirit was not the exclusive possession of a caste, but the most emphatic expression of a national psyche."[29]

That day, July 13, Wilson gave another speech in favor of majority rule. Gouverneur Morris was fearful that new states would some day wrest control away from the original 13. We must avoid the error England made, Wilson replied, of being jealous over the growing colonies. When interior states grow large enough, they should be admitted on equal status with coastal states, he said. If they grow to be more than the seaboard states, they as the majority should govern. Numbers, he concluded, are "surely the natural and precise measure of representation."[30]

On that very day the Confederation Congress adopted the Ordinance of 1787 for the government of the Northwest Territory, which provided for the eventual admission of Ohio, Michigan, Indiana, Illinois, and Wisconsin on an equal status with the 13 original states.

Should naturalized citizens be eligible to serve in Congress? Gerry thought not, lest "persons having foreign attachments be sent among us and insinuated into our councils, in order to be made instruments for their purposes."[31] Wilson disagreed. Pennsylvania, he said, was a good example of a large and prosperous state settled recently by immigrants. Most of their Revolutionary War generals had been "foreigners," as were three of the delegates to this Convention (Thomas Fitzsimmons, Robert Morris, and himself). The Convention established residence requirements of seven years for the House of Representatives and nine years for the Senate.

Wilson's unsuccessful fight to have Senators directly elected by the people brought out one important point — sovereignty can be divided between state and federal governments. States'-rights advocates seemed to Wilson to assume that state sovereignty was somehow better than federal sovereignty. Wilson said that they were basically the same: "Both state and federal government receive their authority directly from the people and owed responsibility immediately to them. A general government was no monster set in motion by a few master brains, but a living instrument of the popular will, amenable to it."[32]

A similar point came up in the administration of how to fill vacancies in the Senate. Wilson preferred that the state legislature, rather than the governor, make the choice, since generally the legislature was elected directly by the people, and the governor (at that time) was usually selected by the state legislature.[33]

Wilson saw the limitations of his argument, however, and opposed having Congress appoint the national judiciary, lest there be too much "concealment, intrigue, and partiality." With Madison, he fought a losing battle for a council of revision, in which a combination of the executive and judges could absolutely overrule Congress. Wilson believed that this council would help buttress the independence of the judiciary, and at the same time help prevent encroachments by the legislature upon the people's rights.

Wilson explained that federal inferior courts were needed, since there were overlapping jurisdictions among the states, for example, on such a thing as admiralty law. Seeing that states were fearful of federal intrusion, Wilson and Madison wisely settled for the phrase: "the national legislature be empowered to institute inferior tribunals."[34] They knew that one Convention could handle only a limited number of hot issues, and that many details could be worked out at a later date.

The judiciary can declare an act of the legislature unconstitutional, Wilson said, thereby preventing "legislative despotism." He believed that the legislature needed to operate within an agreed-upon framework. "The power of the Constitution," he explained, "is paramount to the power of the legislature acting under that Constitution."[35] The actions of the legislature must therefore be subject to judicial review, not as to their wisdom, but as to their constitutionality.

Wilson served on two of the most important committees of the Convention. On the Committee of Detail, he seems to have been the one who molded the disjointed parts into a single harmonious document.[36] In the Committee of Style chief credit for the final phrasing of most of the Constitution goes to Gouverneur Morris. However, delegate Abraham Baldwin told President Stiles of Yale that "the work of this committee was done by Morris and Wilson."[37] There seems little doubt that Wilson was one of the chief framers of the Constitution.

Near the close of the Convention, Hamilton moved that the new Constitution first be submitted to Congress for approval, and then be referred to state conventions for ratification. Wilson vehemently opposed asking for the approval of Congress. It would, he said, "be worse than folly to rely on the concurrence of the Rhode Island members of Congress in the plan. After spending four or five months in the laborious task of forming a government for our country, we are ourselves at the close throwing insuperable obstacles in the way of its success."[38] Others agreed with Wilson, and Hamilton's motion was defeated.

Wilson knew that Americans would have to grow into an "expanded patriotism" in order to serve as responsible citizens of a great nation.

Provincialism would not get the work done. "To embrace the whole," he said, "requires an expansion of mind, of talents, and of temper. Some will be indolent," he predicted, "and some disguise their refusal to grow by calling it moderation or prudence. By these means," he concluded, "the patriotic emanations of the soul which would otherwise be diffused over the whole Union, will be converged to a very narrow part of it."[39]

For a lawyer, Wilson showed remarkable adaptability to change. Despite his concern for the formal aspects of law, Wilson had, in the view of Charles P. Smith, "an extraordinary awareness of the unrealized potentialities that lie always outside them. Wilson's concept of government was a dynamic one. Wilson wished to maintain as much flexibility as possible, and he rarely failed to show a tender solicitude for the unfolding of the new and unanticipated. He perceived the secret of the highest politics — to create such forms as give the greatest range to the viability of society without being tempted to impose arbitrary patterns on the flow of history."[40]

At the end of the Convention, Wilson described what had been accomplished. "After the lapse of six thousand years since the creation of the world," he said, "America now presents the first instance of a people assembled to weigh deliberately and calmly, and to decide leisurely and peaceably, upon the form of government by which they will bind themselves and their posterity."[41] A feeling of historical awareness in their perspective was one of the remarkable qualities present in most of the framers.

The Ratifier

James Wilson deserves special recognition as a ratifier not only because of his important role in getting Pennsylvania to ratify the Constitution but also because of the quality of his talks during the ratifying period.

Wilson's first important speech favoring ratification took place in the State House Yard in Philadelphia on October 6, 1787. This talk was influential not only in Pennsylvania, but throughout the colonies. Like the good lawyer that he was, Wilson took the chief arguments against the Constitution and answered each in turn.

First was the charge that the Constitution should have had a Bill of Rights. Wilson's rebuttal was that "it would have been superfluous to have stipulated with a federal body of our own creation that we should enjoy those privileges of which we are not divested."[42] Wilson pointed out that in civil cases, such as those handled by admiralty courts and courts of equity, trial by jury was not pertinent.

Next came the charge that states were losing their sovereignty. Here Wilson showed that the only sovereignty surrendered was that necessary for national union, and that without the union, states could not long remain sovereign. State politicians might complain about losing their jobs, he said, but that would be no loss to the state. Wilson cited that state legislatures determined the method of selecting presidential electors, and elected two senators to Congress. Also, to be eligible to vote for the House of Representatives a person had to be qualified to vote for his state's lower house.

The final charge was that the Senate would be a "baneful aristocracy." Wilson replied that it was checked by the House of Representatives, and both were checked by the executive and the judiciary.

His conclusion contained his climax: "I will confess that I am not a blind admirer of this plan of government, and there are some parts which, if my wish had prevailed, would certainly have been altered. But when I reflect how widely men differ in their opinions, I am satisfied that anything nearer to perfection could not have been accomplished. It is the best form of government which has ever been offered to the world."[43]

The Pennsylvania ratification convention in December 1787 was important for several reasons. As the first large state to consider ratification, Pennsylvania might determine how other large states would respond. Many Pennsylvanians were proud of their state constitution of 1776, which had been built upon entirely different principles. Finally, it gave Wilson a chance to defend a Constitution, after his earlier attacks upon the state constitution. Wilson was the leading speaker among those supporting the new document.

Wilson stressed the uniqueness of the occasion. The size of the country, both now and in the future, made its form of government a topic of importance to the world, he said. This form of government, based on the people's consent, was unique. It was a "confederate republic," which Montesquieu said had "all the internal advantages of a republic, together with the external force of a monarchical government."[44]

Wilson used the figure of a pyramid to illustrate the structure of the government. This figure he had found in Sir William Temple and Sir James Stewart. A free government, Wilson stated, is built upon the broad base of the people. Its power rises, being confined to the legislature, the judiciary, and finally the executive, but it is only as strong as its base, not its upper rungs.

His opponents still called him an aristocrat, working for the benefit of Robert Morris and his other wealthy friends. Since the proceedings of the Constitutional Convention had been kept secret, he could not point out how many times he had spoken for the people's power there.

If this experiment in government fails, Wilson predicted, it will indicate that people cannot govern themselves. He then showed how the Constitution remedied the weaknesses of the Articles of Confederation. In society, he said, we surrender something in order to gain something. In this structure of government, he insisted, the individual would surrender the least and get the most in return.

Again the lawyer had carefully prepared his brief. Congress would not abuse the taxing privilege, in his opinion. In fact, direct taxes would probably go down, since most funds would come from imposts, which would largely be paid by foreigners. A peacetime standing army would be the best safeguard against internal or external dangers. Concerning a Bill of Rights, he showed that in the seven states whose constitutions had no such bill, civil rights were just as secure as elsewhere. He declared that it would be impossible to list all of the rights of the people.

Would the states lose their sovereignty? The sovereign power has never been grounded in the states, he asserted — it resides in the people. They willingly surrender as much or as little as they deem prudent to the state and federal governments. This Constitution, he repeated, is framed not merely for the states but more especially for the people who dwell in the states.[45]

Wilson had expected to hear complaints that the presidency was too powerful, but instead he was confronted with the charge that it was too weak, a mere tool of the Senate. Wilson retorted that when the two branches act together, the Senate can do nothing without the president. "Clearly he holds the helm," said Wilson, "and the vessel can proceed neither in one direction nor another without his concurrence."[46]

Wilson was particularly explicit in explaining the need for a federal judiciary. What state court could fairly arbitrate cases involving citizens of different states, he asked. Imagine the feelings of a merchant whose property was at the mercy of the laws of Rhode Island! Only federal courts could adjudicate cases between states, or between a state and a foreign nation. Federal courts might help maintain the peace, he reasoned, for if foreign merchants could not collect legitimate debts, they might ask their governments to intervene with force.

Someone asked about the treason clause in the Constitution. Since Wilson had worked on it in the Committee of Detail, he explained that treason was defined narrowly, with safeguards for the accused, lest there be conviction on inadequate evidence during times of high emotion. Wilson quoted Montesquieu that "if the crime of treason be indeterminate, this alone is sufficient to make any government degenerate into arbitrary power."[47]

Towards the end of his speech at the ratification convention Wilson turned loose the oratorical power that led Francis Hopkinson to say that he combined the talents of a Cicero with those of a Demosthenes. Wilson stressed responsibility to not only the 13 colonies but to "innumerable states yet unformed, and to myriads of citizens who in future ages shall inhabit the vast uncultivated" regions of the continent. The Constitutional Convention, he said, had formed a plan "commensurate with a great and valuable portion of the globe."[48] Only a federal republic was appropriate for such a vast terrain, he stated, because it provided both stability and flexibility.

The principle of federalism as developed here, he averred, brought fruition at last to the dream of Henry IV of France and the Duc de Sully, who envisioned "a system of government, for large and respectable dominions, united and bound together in peace, under a superintending head, by which all their differences may be accommodated, without the destruction of the human race."[49]

Wilson predicted a glorious future for America. "There are not on any part of the globe finer qualities for forming a national character than those possessed by the children of America,"[50] he declared. He then listed those qualities: industry, perseverance, docility in acquiring information, firmness in adversity, and patience and magnanimity under the greatest hardships.

America was destined to lead the world in the science of government, he said. "By adopting this system, we shall probably lay a foundation for erecting temples of liberty in every part of the earth." Many nations will benefit from this new government, he predicted. In Europe, people will emigrate here, and princes will restore their liberties in order to keep them there. This government, Wilson said, "will be subservient to the great designs of Providence with regard to this globe: the multiplication of mankind, their improvement in knowledge, and their advancement in happiness."[51] Thus had the best orator among the framers affirmed the motif of all revolutions, that this action is being taken in the name of mankind in order to produce a better world.

The ratification vote carried, 46–23, on December 12. The next day a large group celebrated at Epple's Tavern on Race Street in Philadelphia. The first of 13 toasts was "to the people of the United States." The last was "to peace and free governments to all the nations in the world."[52]

A celebration in Carlisle on December 27 was less felicitous. Held outdoors, the party was interrupted by a mob that opposed the Constitution. They attacked Wilson with clubs, knocked him down, and beat him. He might have been killed had not an old soldier jumped over him, receiving blows intended for Wilson.[53]

At the great Federal Procession in Philadelphia on July 4, 1788, ten men walked arm in arm, symbolizing the ten states that had ratified the Constitution. Wilson, representing Pennsylvania, gave the oration for the occasion. His main point was that now the success of the government lay in the hands of the people of America — liberty could be secured only by responsible citizenship on the part of all Americans.

The World Citizen

In April 1789 Wilson wrote a letter to President Washington, asking to be appointed chief justice of the United States. Washington would have preferred greater modesty. For a number of reasons, Washington chose John Jay as America's first chief justice. Jay had Hamilton's support and came from New York, a state lukewarm toward the federal system. As secretary of foreign affairs in the Confederation Congress, Jay had demonstrated great tact and diplomacy. Moreover, Wilson's widespread land speculation, plus his unpaid debts, was already widely known.

Wilson was the chief architect of the new Pennsylvania state constitution which was adopted in 1790. Although it served as a model for other state constitutions and was widely admired in Europe, it once more got Wilson into controversy. Adherents of the 1776 constitution, which prescribed a unicameral legislature, felt that the old constitution provided for government by the people, the essence of democratic government. But the unicameral legislature had long been criticized for lacking checks and balances. Reflecting Wilson's view, the *Pennsylvania Gazette* said that "all single governments are tyrannies — whether they be lodged in one man, a few men, or a large body of the people."[54]

Motions by Wilson which were adopted by the Pennsylvania constitution convention included[55]: (1) the legislature should have more than one branch, (2) the supreme executive power should be vested in a single person, (3) the executive should have a qualified veto on legislative acts, and (4) Supreme Court judges should have life tenure during good behavior and be independent as to salaries.

Having been an active participant in both the federal and the state constitutional conventions, Wilson could make comparisons between the two results. He felt that the state constitution excelled the federal one on the following matters[56]: (1) the executive and the Senate were elected directly by the people, (2) appointments by the executive needed no Senate confirmation, and (3) proceedings of both legislative houses were by open public discussion.

Lectures that Wilson delivered as a professor of law at the College of Philadelphia from 1789 to 1792 mark him as a prophet of a new age of international cooperation. Wilson felt that he was founding a new school of American jurisprudence. What would make America's high mark in the world? It would be her love of liberty and law, he replied.

"Without liberty, law becomes oppression. Without law, liberty becomes licentiousness. Property, highly deserving security, is not an end but a means. How contemptible is that man who inverts the order of nature, and makes his property not a means but an end."[57] After this talk, given on December 15, 1789, Wilson received a doctor of laws degree from the college.

Because of the care he took in assembling his material and because his views combined the Scottish scholastic jurisprudence with the Anglican common law tradition, his lectures are probably "the best statement we have of the considered legal theories of a Founding Father. In Wilson the Calvinist doctrines of his father, with their almost overwhelming sense of individual responsibility, fused with the Anglican view of an ordered, structured society to create a view of life in which the free-moving, responsible individual was confronted by definite moral choices, and liberty was secured through law."[58]

Wilson believed that all mankind constituted a universal society under God. Civil law is based on natural law, which is grounded in God's nature. God Himself works by law, Wilson said. He quoted Richard Hooker on the universality of law: "Her seat is the bosom of God; her voice, the harmony of the world."[59] Civil law begins in custom which has the consent of society.

In Wilson the theology student underlay the law student. In his lectures he said that "far from being rivals, religion and law are twin sisters. Indeed, the two sciences run into each other. The divine law, as discovered by reason and moral sense, forms an essential part of both. The supreme law is the will of God. Morality, like mathematics, has its intuitive truths. We discover the will of God by our conscience, by our reason, and by the Holy Scriptures. Our instincts are the oracles of eternal wisdom; our conscience, in particular, is the voice of God within us."[60] Thus, concludes Charles P. Smith, "every man who will listen to this inner voice may play a creative role in a democracy."[61]

By basing itself on the sovereignty of the people rather than upon the sovereignty of the crown, American common law would exceed that of Great Britain, Wilson said. God, as the author of the moral and social nature of man, would be the ultimate authority. American law, Wilson predicted, would reflect Saxon law before it was corrupted by the Norman influence, which brought in feudal serfdom and restrictions on land tenure. British law had been so much based on custom that it could not change with the times. American law, as founded on the Constitution, had the flexibility to endure in a changing world.[62]

America was indeed, for Wilson, a city set upon a hill. Through the example of her government, America would make it possible to create a better world order. To Wilson, all civilized nations formed a single community, governed by a moral law based upon universal human nature. The law of nations, of divine origin, was simply the law of nature. To neglect the law of nations would be to neglect God's law, which would be especially deplorable in America, where the people possessed the ultimate sovereign power.[63]

In criminal law, Wilson sought three goals: protection of society, reformation of the criminal, and crime prevention. To achieve these ends he recommended three aspects of punishment — moderation, speediness, and certainty. Severe sentences make juries wary of awarding them, and engender general disrespect for the law, he felt. "A nation broke to cruel punishments becomes dastardly and contemptible," in his opinion. Speedy trial and punishment he believed would help deter crime. More than anything else as a deterrent was the certainty of punishment. "The strict execution of every criminal law," he said, "is the dictate of humanity as well as of wisdom."[64] He also recommended a return to the Anglo-Saxon practice of having the criminal make reparation to the victim for the inflicted damage.[65]

As he looked at the law of nations, Wilson envisioned an application of universal law that would guarantee justice, peace, and harmony among the nations. Just as an individual, in his own best interest, recognized the authority of a court system, so nations, in their own best interests, would sooner or later submit themselves to the operation of a legal system, especially since universal law made what was right for one right for all. He asked, "Are states too proud to receive a lesson from individuals? Is the idea of a common judge between nations less admissible than that of a common judge between men?"[66]

"Wilson insisted on his vision of a larger citizenship of men who are not only loyal citizens of a nation but of the world. We can win our way into this great commonwealth through the 'power of moral abstraction,' which will enable individuals 'so distant as to elude our benevolence' to become 'known to the heart as well as to the understanding.'"[67]

Wilson praised Henry IV of France for having the vision of a united European confederacy. To Wilson this was, like the federated American republic, a forerunner of the coming commonwealth of nations, a confederation of united nations. America, said Wilson, was Henry IV's dream come true.

The unifying document in Wilson's conception was the United States Constitution. Just as Americans had learned, the hard way, to trust the adjudication of their disputes to an impartial, professional Supreme Court, so would the nations of the world learn, probably the hard way, that it was in their best interests to settle disputes amicably by law, rather than by military might.

Wilson felt that the Supreme Court incorporated the law of nations into American municipal law. Thus, matters of international law involving chiefly merchant and mercantile law and the law of contracts were being integrated into the fundamental bases of American law. The crucible of American experience was therefore to produce the foundation for an international order which would bring peace, harmony, and prosperity to the nations.[68]

Wilson saw beyond the mere fulfillment of obligations between nations. "At last it is acknowledged," he said, "that mankind are all brothers," and that "the duties of humanity are incumbent upon nations as well as upon individuals. The law of that great and universal society requires that each nation should contribute to the perfection and happiness of the others," Wilson said. By creating a climate of opinion in which people identified their primary allegiance to mankind as a whole, Wilson felt that he was preparing nations for the next natural step — the formation of an international court of justice, modeled on the United States Supreme Court, whose decisions would be accepted as a part of international law and order.[69]

Clearly, Wilson's lectures were a landmark in the development of American jurisprudence. An outstanding trial attorney, he had no match as a legal theorist in his time. Ellsworth, Jay, Jefferson, Mason, Randolph, and George Wythe were all keen legal students. "But Wilson alone of the great political figures of his day spelled out in detail his view of the nature of law, a view so broad that it encompassed philosophy, psychology, and political theory. Nor is Wilson's jurisprudence obsolete. The rise of the modern philosophic schools of realism, existentialism, and personalism — all of which have something in common with Wilson's own metaphysic — may bring students of jurisprudence to reexamine the legal theories of James Wilson with fresh understanding and sympathy."[70]

The Supreme Court Justice

As a member of the first Supreme Court, Wilson, along with Ellsworth, carried out the intent of the framers that the Supreme Court would be the final authority not only in appellate jurisdiction but also in adjudicating disputes between states and in determining the constitutionality of legislative acts.

In the case of *Chisholm v. Georgia*, Wilson made a landmark ruling, namely that the Supreme Court had jurisdiction over a state which was a party to a suit. When the Court concurred, chaos ensued. All states feared suits which would be determined beyond their jurisdictions. In Georgia the lower house passed a bill saying that any agent of the national government who tried to execute the process served by the

Supreme Court would be "declared guilty of felony and shall suffer death, without benefit of clergy, by being hanged."[71]

The day after the Supreme Court decision an amendment to the Constitution was introduced into Congress, making states immune to suits by individuals. Modified, this was ratified as Amendment No. 11 in 1798.

Congress in 1792 asked Supreme Court justices to hear appeals of cases concerning veterans' pensions. Wilson refused to sit, saying that this was an executive, not a judicial, matter. He said that if a higher executive or legislative body reviewed the decision, it would be an infringement upon the prerogative of the judiciary. Attorney General Randolph tried to get the Supreme Court to hear a class-action suit on the case, but the Court refused. Congress reconsidered, and took this assignment away from the Supreme Court.

Ambitious Wilson laid before Washington a plan to codify all of the laws of the United States. Washington turned down the offer, after hearing Randolph's views that no one person could do such a mammoth task, that political bias would be inescapable, and that more pressing issues lay before the country.

In September 1793 Wilson married Hannah Gray in Boston. He was 51 years old and she was 19. Wilson's children, two of whom were older than Hannah, accepted her warmly. Perhaps under Hannah's prodding, Wilson gave his personal slave Thomas Purcell his freedom as a New Year's gift that year. In May 1796 Hannah's first child, Henry, was born. Henry was Wilson's seventh child.

In 1794, when whiskey rebels intimidated excise officers, robbed the mail, and threatened to attack Pittsburgh, Wilson notified Washington that in Allegheny and Washington counties federal law was being opposed by forces too strong to be handled by local law enforcement officers, so Washington called out the militia to quell the rebellion.

Even as a Supreme Court Justice, Wilson had many business interests. When the iron works and sawmill that he owned with Mark Bird failed, Wilson built an industrial center, Wilsonville, on the Wallenpaupack River, consisting of a large cloth mill, two sawmills, and 22 houses and shops. He was also a member of a company for manufacturing maple sugar, and he was part-owner of two vessels, one in the West Indian and the other in the China trade.

With Silas Deane, Wilson planned to supply the French navy with masts. With Deane and Robert Morris, he wanted to establish a trade agency in Nantes. He refinanced his debt of $71,000 due to the Bank of North America in July 1794. He tried to interest English speculators in investing in lands in western Pennsylvania.

Unfortunately, credit was easily extended to Wilson. He had once been a wealthy man, and he was known to be a close friend of Robert Morris and other tycoons. Since he held high governmental positions, everyone felt that he was a good financial risk.

Wilson wrote a tract in the 1790s in which he explained his philosophy as a land speculator. Europe had surplus capital that needed to be invested — America had surplus land that needed capital for improvements. Hence the two should get together, to the advantage of each. He called for safe passage on clean ships of European immigrants to the open lands, with a line of inns ready to accommodate the newcomers on their way west. At the land site, the settlers should find farm animals and farm utensils available at reasonable prices. Wilson never found investors to underwrite his scheme. Robert Morris did secure investors for his Holland Company, which failed shortly thereafter.

Wilson's technique of borrowing money to pay for a tract of land, then selling the tract to make a down payment on a larger tract, and so on up the line, began to fail in the 1790s. As long as his credit was good, he could keep pyramiding his investments. General depression in 1794–95 proved his undoing, for the upward spiral of inflation ceased, and he could no longer meet his creditors' demands. Had he been able to hold out until the upturn in the business cycle, he probably would have survived, since his holdings ultimately produced considerable wealth for his heirs.

In the winter of 1796–97 financial panic hit Philadelphia. In six weeks 150 businesses failed, and 64 people were sent to debtors' prison, including many of the leading citizens such as Robert Morris.

Wilson and Hannah hid out from creditors in the dirty Morris Tavern in Bethlehem. They moved to New Jersey, where a creditor caught up with Wilson in Burlington and had him jailed. His son brought money to bail him out.

There were now a number of states which Associate Justice Wilson could not enter, because of warrants out for his arrest. He could no longer return to Philadelphia. In July 1798 Governor Samuel Johnston of Pennsylvania feared that Wilson would have to be impeached because of his debts.

A fugitive from justice, Wilson traveled south, hoping to straighten out his land holdings there. He went to Edenton, North Carolina, the home of his good friend and colleague, Associate Supreme Court Justice James Iredell.

When Wilson failed to pay Pierce Butler, a delegate to the Constitutional Convention, any of the $197,000 he owed him, he was once again jailed. To try to borrow funds involved paying from 24–30 percent on a loan. To make matters worse, Wilson's agent Joseph Thomas was stealing money from him.

Wilson was released from Edenton jail in time to greet Hannah, who came south to visit him. She could not take a walk, for her shoes had no soles. Even in such dire straits, Wilson would not sell his lands to pay creditors. In July 1798 he caught malaria. He then had a stroke, and died on August 21, 1798, at the Horniblow Tavern in Edenton. He was buried on the estate of Mrs. Iredell's father. In 1811 Benjamin Rush sadly observed to John Adams that "there was scarcely a single deceased person that was active in our Revolution that has not died poor in Pennsylvania."[72]

During the Constitutional Convention Washington had said that Wilson was "as able, candid, and honest a member as any one in the Convention."[73] James Bryce summarized Wilson's importance to America: "The services which such a mind as Wilson's—broad, penetrating, exact, and luminous—can render to a nation can hardly be overestimated. Whoever gives to a nation at the outset of its career, sound, just principles for the conduct of its government, principles which are in harmony with its character and are capable of progressive expansion as it expands, is a true benefactor to that nation. Such a one was James Wilson."[74]

R.G. McCloskey felt that Wilson somehow saw more clearly America's future than did any of his distinguished colleagues: "It is not too much to say that the ideas of James Wilson more nearly foreshadowed the national future than those of any of his well-remembered contemporaries. No one of them—not Hamilton, or Jefferson, or Madison, or Adams, or Marshall—came so close to representing in his views what the United States was to become."[75]

16.
The Founding Fathers Today

On September 17, 1987, the United States of America celebrates the bicentennial of the signing of its federal Constitution. Chief Justice Warren E. Burger, who celebrates his 80th birthday that day, is chairman of the Bicentennial Commission. The entire year Burger sees as a time for re-examining how well modern Americans follow the letter and spirit of the Constitution, "the most utterly unique experiment in government in the history of the world."[1]

One fascinating way to enter the subject is to ask, how would the Founding Fathers react to the problems of modern America? Although we can never be sure how they would face the changed conditions, we can be reasonably sure, based on their life records, that certain characteristic traits would emerge.

For example, Oliver Ellsworth would probably be able to enlarge his patriotism to include a larger political entity, without surrendering an iota of his love for his native Connecticut. In an international forum like the United Nations, Benjamin Franklin would be the ever resourceful peacemaker, as he was at the Constitutional Convention. Nathaniel Gorham's experience as chairman of the Committee of the Whole might recommend him as the presiding officer of a national or international assembly. That astute and ambitious business manager, Alexander Hamilton, would volunteer to tackle ways to reduce the national debt.

The genteel student of government, James Madison, would be well versed on governmental structures that the nation might wish to explore. He would be helped by the open and honest contributions of another deep student of political structures, George Mason. Quick, intuitive insights would be provided by aristocratic Gouverneur Morris. Duty, honor, and service could be counted upon from Charles Cotesworth Pinckney. Utter integrity, albeit coupled with a lack of common sense, would be the likely contribution of Edmund Randolph.

The person who would see quickly to the heart of any problem would be John Rutledge. Roger Sherman would be notable for his honesty, clear head, and good heart. In a gathering of giants of virtue,

George Washington would be outstanding for his magnanimity. An antidote to terrorism would be the international court set up by James Wilson in his search for international law and order. Our problems are scarcely more massive than theirs, and yet these delegates and their companions were able to frame a structure of government that has well stood the tests of time and change.

Our heritage from the framers includes a lesson in the dynamics of effective group processes. Modern political bodies can learn from the experience of the Constitutional Convention. In his transmittal letter to Congress, Washington spoke of "a spirit of amity" that bred "mutual concession" on "points of inferior magnitude." This atmosphere "encouraged frankness, dampened suspicion, soothed hurt feelings, and made compromise a virtue rather than a weakness."[2]

Since they had a consensus of purpose there was a minimum of posing and pouting. Free from television cameras, they need not be photogenic but they needed wisdom and probity. Despite their self-assurance, their innate modesty meant that they could learn from their fellows. When they reached an impasse, they made effective use of representative study committees, and mutual respect led them to accept most committee recommendations. Few political assemblies have ever developed such a constructive dynamic or accomplished so much in so short a time.

C.J. Antieau, professor of constitutional law, says that "the best of the Founders knew well that the broad concepts they used would have to be construed by later generations with reference to the imperative values and social interests of a developing morality and culture."[3] Nathaniel Gorham said that the vagueness of key terms made them appropriate in a document that would have to be re-interpreted in the light of changing values and conditions. James Wilson believed that the weakness of British common law, its too great reliance on custom and precedent, would be avoided in America, where the law could be molded in accordance with the public will.

The Intent of the Framers

In summer 1985 the United States Attorney General said that the current administration would press for "a jurisprudence of original intention," and thus deplores a recent Supreme Court ruling that the framers intended for the government to maintain "a strict neutrality" towards religion.

Supreme Court Justices John Paul Stevens and William J. Brennan, Jr., feel that the original intent of the framers cannot be discovered.

Even to make such a search, says Brennan, is "little more than arrogance cloaked as humility." To woodenly restate views of the framers from an entirely different historical era would be to turn "a blind eye to social progress," Brennan avers. "The ultimate question must be," he feels, "what do the words of the text mean in our time? For the genius of the Constitution rests not in any static meaning it might have had in a world dead and gone, but in the adaptability of its great principles to cope with current problems and current needs."[4]

Judge Irving R. Kaufman of the United States Second Circuit Court of Appeals says that determining the framers' intent would be not only difficult but dangerous. For example, if the intent were to be in conflict with subsequent amendments (such as the Bill of Rights or Amendment No. 14 guaranteeing due process and equal protection under law), which should have the preference, the intent or the written Constitution as amended?

Kaufman quotes Madison in *The Federalist* No. 14: "Is it not the glory of the people of America that they have not suffered a blind veneration for antiquity to overrule the suggestions of their own good sense?"[5] Also, on the floor of Congress in 1796 Madison said that "whatever veneration might be entertained for the body of men who formed our Constitution, the sense of that body could never be regarded as the oracular guide in expounding the Constitution."[6] "Through a written constitution and judicial enforcement," says Kaufman, "the framers intended to preserve the inchoate rights they had lost as Englishmen."[7]

Judge Kaufman points out the need for judicial restraint, lest the federal courts, consisting of appointed judges, overrule the wishes of the people as expressed through the elected legislative and executive branches. Judicial restraint exists in the legal processes themselves, he feels, since judges must observe prescribed rules in interpreting the Constitution. "Lacking the power of the purse or the sword," Kaufman states, "the courts must rely on the elected branches to enforce their decisions. The Constitution balances the danger of judicial abuse against the threat of a temporary majority trampling individual rights."[8] Thus, America's fundamental political ideals, given expression in a written Constitution, depict the endless struggle in a free society to achieve a balance between the wishes of the people and individual rights protected by law.

Most delegates agreed with Mason's statement that, insofar as possible, the three branches of government should be independent of one another, and that there should be frequent elections of the executive and legislative branches, to see if the people's will is being carried out. Madison clearly stated that the Constitution must show how the people are to be protected from the government itself, not only through checks and balances among the three branches but also by limiting the powers of federal and state governments and by protecting individual rights from encroachment by any level of government whatsoever.

Most of the Founding Fathers showed not only faith in America's future but a sense of responsibility towards posterity. Once he gained a federal perspective, Ellsworth never wavered in his faith in his country's destiny. Hamilton accurately predicted that one day the United States would be an industrial giant. At the Convention on June 26 Madison said that "it was more than probable we were now digesting a plan which in its operation would decide forever the fate of republican government."[9]

Madison saw responsible freedom as America's, and the world's, last best hope. In his final year he envisioned the ark of the Union as bearing "the hope of the world." When confused by intergovernmental strife, he said, Americans should always resort to help from "a Higher Power." Thus, he said, "our country, if it does justice to itself, will be the workshop of liberty to the civilized world, and do more than any other for the uncivilized."[10]

Showing his faith in America's future, Gouverneur Morris said that "the proudest empire in Europe is but a bubble compared to what America will be in the course of two centuries."[11] All the world looked to the United States for light, he believed. "The whole human race," he said, "will be affected by the proceedings of this Convention."[12] We must take care, said Rutledge, for we are laying the foundation for a great empire. In all of his legislation, Sherman kept in mind the welfare of future generations.

Washington felt that the Constitution evinced the finger of Providence. Its vast lands and free institutions gave America a better chance for political happiness for its citizens than any other country had. But would the people overcome local prejudices and build the strong government required by its circumstances? Washington interpreted the Constitution as the first proper step in that direction.

Wilson believed that America's size made its form of government a matter of importance to the whole world. He said that a federal republic was needed, out of responsibility for myriads of unborn citizens. He predicted a bright future for the nation, because Americans had unsurpassed stores of industry, patience, perseverance, and magnanimity. America would lead the world in the science of government, he felt. By adopting the Constitution, he said, "we shall probably lay a foundation for erecting temples of liberty in every part of the earth."[13]

Wilson's philosophy of law synthesized psychology, religion, and political theory, and is thus as up-to-date as modern schools of existentialism and transcendentalism. America's unique contribution, he believed, would be its combined love of liberty and love of law. "Without liberty, law becomes oppression," he said, and "without law, liberty becomes licentiousness."[14] This remains as good a summary of American political ideals as has ever been penned.

Democracy

The Founding Fathers were ambivalent in their feelings about democracy. On the one hand, they felt that they were innovating in creating a government built upon the consent of the people. Franklin, a walking witness to the idea that the common people could produce a giant, persistently pled for equal votes and equal opportunities for the poor. Mason said that since all power is derived from the people, the only laws they must obey are those to which they have given their consent. Mason struck hard for the poor: since the Senate is the few representing the few, he said, purse strings must be controlled by the House, lest the rich represent merely their own interests.

Aristocratic Gouverneur Morris stated that in the eyes of their Creator, all men are equal. Sherman desired frequent elections so that the people's voice would be continually respected. Washington boycotted meetings of the Cincinnati because he disliked their antirepublican tendencies. This government, he said, is really a government of the people, since all power comes from them. Government in a democracy may be slow, he confessed to Lafayette, "but the people will be right at last."[15] Because he believed the people to be the base of the pyramid of government, Wilson favored direct popular election of the president and the Congress. He was the originator of the concept of one man, one vote.

Gouverneur Morris expressed the widely held view that the United States should be an asylum for the poor and the oppressed of every nation. Sherman did not want governmental salaries set so low as to exclude the poor, and he stated that if the rich are given more representation than the poor, the rights of the poor are lost. At the Convention Washington expressed the wish that the ports of America would always be open as a refuge to "the needy and the oppressed of the world." He wrote to the Marquis de Chastellux that "the philosophers and virtuous men in all nations look upon our rising republics as a kind of asylum for mankind. God grant that we may not disappoint their honest expectations by our folly or perverseness."[16]

On the other hand, many framers had serious doubts about the ability of the people to govern themselves. Hamilton quoted David Hume to the effect that since every man is a knave, government must protect us from our evil passions. The people, said Hamilton, seldom judge right. Society, he believed, was tired of the excesses caused by democracy and now willingly permitted the rich to restrain its imprudence and errors. One reason that Hamilton favored the Supreme Court as the ultimate arbiter was that, unlike the executive and the legislature, it lacked direct access to power.

Madison realized that the United States was too large to be a democracy but would have to use the representative government of a republic. He told Jefferson that since the majority had the control of government in America, the danger of misused power would come when the majority invaded the private rights of the individual. Witnessing the Jacksonian revolution, Madison could only feel that the democratic republic had degenerated into mobocracy.

Mason pointed to good monarchies, like those of Solomon, Hadrian, and Henry of Navarre, and to bad democracies, that is, those manipulated by demagogues to become mobs or ignorant enough to elect legislators who engage in bribe and corruption. Since the form of government seemed to provide no guarantee of liberty, Mason put his faith in a Bill of Rights which protected the individual from any depredation, governmental or otherwise.

Gouverneur Morris doubted that the common man could govern himself well. People, he feared, were ignorant enough to barter away their liberty for security. As for himself, he said, he clearly preferred liberty over democracy.

Charles Cotesworth Pinckney felt that Congress should be elected by the state legislatures, since the people are too easily swayed by demagogues into making unwise choices. Randolph opposed both monarchy and "democratic licentiousness." Democracy looks good on paper, said Rutledge, but in practice its effects are "arbitrary, severe, and destructive." He could point to his own one-man rule in South Carolina as having had largely the contrary of these effects.

In summary, the framers wanted a republic with democratic aspects incorporated into it, but above all, protection of the rights of the individual from even the government iself.

Civil Rights

Many of the framers had a deep concern for civil liberties. Hamilton said that the first goal of all law is to maintain the absolute rights of individuals. Since these rights are God-given, he added, no human can lawfully curtail them. Madison inverted John Locke's statement that the goal of government is to protect property. Instead, said Madison, a man has a property in his rights. Government thus exists not only to protect one's real estate but more importantly one's freedom of expression, liberty of conscience, and safety of person. Madison has to his credit the fact that, unlike most Presidents, he did not seek to curtail civil liberties even in wartime, when leaders are wont to cite national security reasons for measures limiting liberties.

Mason said that by nature all men are free and have such inherent rights as suffrage, freedom of press and religion, and due process of law. To prevent abuse of power by the government, a constitution needs to contain a Bill of Rights, he felt, specifying which rights are to be protected. Sherman agreed with Mason that an individual has basic rights which no government—local, state, or national—can abrogate.

Wilson argued that Parliament, by violating the colonists' rights as Englishmen, forfeited its authority as a lawmaking body for the colonies. Like Franklin, Jefferson, and Paine, Wilson moved readily from the rights of Englishmen to the natural rights of all mankind. Men are not equal in talents or virtue, Wilson said, but in rights and obligations: "The natural rights and duties of man belong equally to all."[17]

Did Indians too have rights that should be observed? Most framers thought so. Franklin opposed harsh treatment of Indians. As governor, Randolph went out of his way to be fair to them. Rutledge was so impressed with the Iroquois government that he used their constitution as a model in the Committee of Detail at the Convention. Sherman favored humane treatment of Indians. Feeling sorry for them because of mistreatment by white people, Washington insisted that Indian treaties be faithfully observed. His administration made perhaps the most determined effort of all to conciliate hostile tribes.

The Framers on Business

What was the attitude of the framers toward business? The lawyers tended to be more favorable than the planters. Gorham, Hamilton, and Gouverneur Morris all spoke frequently in favor of protecting business interests. Charles Cotesworth Pinckney felt that wealth should be a partial basis for apportioning the House of Representatives.

Capitalism was just in its infancy. Adam Smith's daring book, *The Wealth of Nations*, had just been published in 1776. Smith bravely asserted that perhaps mercantilism, the reigning economic doctrine, was less beneficial than a free enterprise system. Under mercantilism a government controlled its commerce so as to have more exports than imports, with the resulting favorable balance of trade bringing gold bullion into the national coffers in payment of the excessive exports. As in medieval times, the government reserved the right to regulate industry, control wages and prices, and aid or deter business companies in line with predetermined national goals.

Because of their mercantilist backgrounds, most Founding Fathers would be incensed at the huge trade deficit that the United States incurs each year, and would look to the federal government for prompt action to reverse the excess of imports over exports.

Even Hamilton was more of a mercantilist than a capitalist. He believed that the rich should pay taxes on their luxuries, and that their private credit should support the government's public credit. By precept and example he opposed those who made big profits out of their governmental connections. He favored high wages for labor, seeing labor as more crucial, in America, to the productive processes than capital.

As Charles Beard stated, "the myth of rugged American individualism" ended in 1791, when Hamilton's Report on Manufactures asked Congress to aid infant industries through bounties, tariffs, and other supports. Assumption of the War debt, establishment of a national bank, and expansion of the credit system were all designed to help business and thereby aid the nation. Even the construction of ports, canals, roads, bridges, and post offices—all of which Hamilton favored—were beneficial to business first and the rest of America second. Beard shows that American businessmen have never really wanted to keep government out of business. They wanted protection from foreign competition through tariffs, protection from unfair competition through anti-trust laws, and protection from labor organizations through antiunion laws. Only in more recent times have they learned that with protection comes regulation in some form or other.

Sherman favored wage-and-price controls during an economic recession. Most framers recommended control of the issuance of paper currency, in order to fight inflation. Parliament had passed every manner of law regulating commerce, many of which had led to the break with England. But aside from the debate over the navigation act, which the South considered to be favorable to the North, there was relatively little quarrel over the clause giving Congress the power to regulate commerce. It was assumed that was a natural function of government.

Since the rapid expansion of American industry brought a high standard of living and other benefits (as well as problems), many people link free enterprise to the Constitutional freedoms. For example, after confessing that "we exported our finest people to America, lost them, and have to begin again," Margaret Thatcher said that her goal for Britain is "to have anchored this country as a free-enterprise society under a rule of law, with the government serving the people, and not dominating them. In other words, if we in practice had a constitution similar to yours—that the aim of government is the pursuit of life, liberty, and the happiness of the people."[18]

The Beard Thesis

In 1913 Charles Beard, in *An Economic Interpretation of the Constitution*, levied two charges at the framers: that they were investors in land, securities, currency, and commerce who fostered the Constitution for pecuniary gain, and that they got an undemocratic document ratified in an undemocratic manner. Merrill Jensen concurred, stating that the Articles of Confederation embodied the doctrines of the Declaration of Independence but that conservative property owners in the Constitutional Convention "engineered a conservative counter-revolution and erected a nationalistic government whose purpose in part was to thwart the will of 'the people' in whose name they acted."[19]

After a careful study, Robert E. Brown concluded that Beard mishandled his historical evidence. Persons who benefited from the new Constitution included those from all economic levels, not just the rich, Brown found. Small property holders were as much interested in protecting property as large ones. The fact that three-fourths of the adult free males did not vote for ratification delegates indicates indifference, not disfranchisement. Brown's two conclusions were that the processes engendering the Constitution were basically democratic ones, and that "it was adopted by a people who were primarily middle-class property owners, especially farmers who owned realty."[20]

Forrest McDonald made a detailed analysis of the economic interests of the 55 framers and the 1111 delegates to state ratification conventions. He found that a significant number of these people had important economic interests that were adversely affected by the new Constitution. Their most significant property holdings were in farm land, not in securities, bills of credits, or mercantile interests. There was no sign in the Constitutional Convention of a consolidated group working to achieve its special interests, he said.[21]

Others who debunked "the Beard thesis" included E. James Ferguson, Richard Hofstadter, and Jackson Turner Main. Ralph Ketcham calls it "a gross perversion to picture Madison's work and that of his fellow delegates as a sinister plot to feather their own nests. The most thorough comparison of interests with votes indicates almost no significant correlation along lines of economic self-interest. Those with wealth in land and slaves and those with wealth in commerce and securities did not form separate blocs. The clauses against paper money and repudiation of contracts received mixed backing. Public creditors among the delegates failed to act together. Many members were heavily in debt, and many had voted for debtor relief laws in their states," but none did here. "Two of the non-signers, Gerry and Mason, were respectively the largest holder of public securities and the wealthiest creditor and landowner."[22]

Beard himself changed his position. In *The Republic* in 1943 he said that the Founding Fathers had built the Constitution in order to preserve "the sacred fire of liberty and the destiny of the republican model of government." The following year in his *Basic History of the United States* Beard praised the checks-and-balances system of government for its ability to block the accumulation of despotic power in any hands, including those of democratic majorities.

The National Debt

How would the framers react to a national debt of over two trillion dollars? Ellsworth, "the Cerberus of the Treasury," might suffer apoplexy. Although he called the national debt ("provided it was not excessive") a national blessing, Hamilton worked hard to reduce it, lest the interest payments become intolerable. Hamilton insisted that "the creation of debt should always be accompanied with the means of extinguishment."[23] Leaving government service, he gave Washington a debt-reduction plan, to prevent "that progressive accumulation of debt which must ultimately endanger all government."[24]

Madison declared that each generation should be required to pay for the cost of its wars, thus discouraging both wars and huge national debts. Gouverneur Morris, Charles Cotesworth Pinckney, and Roger Sherman all recommended that the government raise taxes in order to meet operating deficits. Taxation reduced inflation, they said, but the issuance of paper money increased it. Among others, Washington insisted that Americans should honor debts to English merchants, despite the outcome of the War.

The Framers on Education

Most of the framers realized that whether the new system of government would succeed depended on the support of its citizens. "To embrace the whole requires an expansion of mind, of talents, and of temper," said Wilson, lest "the patriotic emanations of the soul which would otherwise be diffused over the whole Union, be converged to a very narrow part of it."[25] Charles Cotesworth Pinckney called it "political heresy" for a state to consider itself to be an entity separate from the Union.

A modern observer, Paul Eidelberg, says that "the paramount failure of the Founding Fathers is the Constitution does not provide for the education of the rulers."[26] Eidelberg believes that a national university should have been established at that time. Many framers and all early Presidents were in agreement on this issue. Farrand says that "power to establish a national university free from religious distinctions was considered to be included in the power over the seat of government, it being assumed that that was where it would be located."[27] Washington favored both a national university and federal aid to education.

Ralph Ketcham thinks that education should be our highest current priority. "Cherishing the values of freedom in every facet of our public life, from the training of citizens to the corridors of the highest legislative and executive offices," he declares, "is our most important task. A bill of rights can often protect us from over-zealous and tyranny-tending public officials," but how can we "for very long be guarded against our own apathy, folly, or mean-spiritedness? It would be reckless to place too much confidence in our paper barriers to protect rights when we have not as well undertaken to calm the torrents of prejudice, bigotry, and uncharitableness among ourselves, the ultimate rulers in a self-governing community."[28]

Many Americans are more loyal to their political party than to the national interest. They could benefit from reading Madison's warning against factions in *The Federalist* No. 10, and Washington's caution against party involvement contained in his Farewell Address.

Realizing how hard the framers worked to develop a formula for representation in the House of Representatives, John P. Roche believes it is ludicrous that modern Americans do not rectify the imbalances contained in the current electoral college. "If one were to indulge in counter-fantasy," Roche says, "he would be tempted to suggest that the Fathers would be startled to find the College still in operation — and perhaps even dismayed at their descendants' lack of judgment or inventiveness."[29]

Terrorism

Terrorism in its modern form was quite unknown to the framers, but based upon their reactions in crises, one might expect them to be firm but humane. Randolph wanted the rioters in the Whiskey Rebellion pardoned, and that was what Washington did. Rutledge refused to execute white men painted as Indians who attacked patriot lines, but he seemed fully capable of standing up to a military threat or emergency. Although he risked his life more than once fighting Indians, Washington had a sympathetic understanding of their plight, and forgiveness was an important part of his makeup.

The framers were capable of firm, stouthearted, and at times imaginative reaction to violence used against them, but they seemed to be in such excellent command of their common humanity as not to stoop to the low level of those who would employ dirty or inhumane tactics against them.

Nuclear War

In a world living under the cloud of possible nuclear annihilation, what wisdom do the Founders furnish us? They could scarcely be expected to conceive of the monstrous problems of survival caused by the misuse of our knowledge in the vast oversupply of nuclear destructive weapons. Once again we shall have to be content with general principles.

First of all, every framer was patriotic to the extent of being willing to risk his life in defense of his country. An overpowering factor was what they considered to be the justice of their cause—the defense of liberty in the nation, and perhaps throughout the world.

But they were also humane, and knowing how many innocent people would die in a modern nuclear exchange, they would no doubt expend every iota of their prodigious efforts to avert it.

A peace commissioner at the Treaty of Paris, Franklin hoped to never see another war. He told Josiah Quincy that "there was never a good war or a bad peace."[30] He described war as a combination of theft and murder, saying that "a nation that makes an unjust war is only a great gang."[31] In a letter to Edmund Burke he called warmakers ignorant people unable to settle differences amicably, and said that the wiser part of the people, if unable to prevent wars, should "alleviate as much as possible the calamities attending them."[32]

Gouverneur Morris was greatly influenced by the writings of Samuel Pufendorf, who taught that the natural condition of mankind is universal peace. Pufendorf synthesized religion and law in a universal moral order. Even military-minded framers like Hamilton and Charles Cotesworth Pinckney were humane in their approaches to methods of conducting war and holding prisoners of war. Washington wrote to Lafayette: "I wish to see the sons and daughters of the world in peace," and described how western lands in America were being opened to "the poor, the needy, and the oppressed of the earth."[33]

The Global Village

The global village, a world community brought about by the modern revolutions in transportation, communication, commerce, and weaponry, would not be foreign to a number of the Founding Fathers. John Adams said that in France there was "scarcely a peasant or footman" who did not know Franklin's name and face, "and who did not consider him a friend to humankind."[34] Adams said that they believed that Franklin would set aside monarchy and special privilege throughout the world, and restore the golden age. Hearing of the French Revolution, Franklin said, "God grant that not only the love of liberty, but a thorough knowledge of the rights of man, may pervade all the nations of the earth, so that a philosopher may set his foot anywhere on its surface and say, 'This is my country.'"[35] By himself becoming such a citizen of the world, Franklin, despite his humble origin, showed others the way to membership in the family of mankind.

Gouverneur Morris believed in the brotherhood of man under the Fatherhood of God. Like John Adams and Hamilton, both of whom defended British loyalists when attacked by mobs, Morris decried unnecessary American raids across the Canadian border. "I plead the cause of humanity to a gentleman,"[36] he stated. In the Convention on July 2 he reminded his colleagues that they were "representatives of the whole human race."[37] Later, as he witnessed the cruelty of the Reign of Terror in Paris, he wondered how humanity could sink so low.

Like the early Puritans, Wilson envisioned the United States as a city set upon a hill, shedding its light for the world to follow. By her example America would make it possible to create a better world order, he felt. "Wilson regarded all civilized nations as forming a single natural society, governed, as with a single community, by a moral law based on human nature."[38]

The Law of Nations

Their experience, both at the Convention and in the federal service, made many framers familiar with international law. Those who served in the diplomatic corps, like Ellsworth, Franklin, Gouverneur Morris, and Charles Cotesworth Pinckney, could see that nations needed common assumptions and values in order to benefit from international relations. "Franklin, arguing that Americans were capable of the self-government which they claimed as their natural right, had extended his argument to include mankind. The rights of Americans were the rights of men."[39]

Hamilton, writing as "Camillus," quoted the law of nations frequently as he defended Jay's Treaty in 1795. One instance was to verify that there is recovery of private debts on both sides when a war ceases. Also, "nations acknowledging no common judge on earth must of necessity constitute a special tribunal for the purpose. The mode of commissioners has been repeatedly adopted."[40]

Does the law of nations bind the United States? Yes, answered Hamilton, showing that it had done so when the colonies were under Britain, and no subsequent action had ever been taken to deny it. American common law assumed it, as did the practice of the American government in the executive, legislative, and judicial branches. Hamilton derived this concurrence not only from the European practice but "from a higher source, the eternal principles of morality and good faith."[41] No one nation can establish or alter the law of nations: "An established rule of the law of nations can only be altered by agreements between all the civilized powers, or a new usage generally adopted and sanctioned by time."[42]

As secretary of state, Madison quoted international law to protest British seizure of American ships. Mason believed that the world was governed by natural law, and that obedience to that law brings liberty. At the Convention on September 14 Gouverneur Morris argued that Congress should have the right "to define and punish offenses against the law of nations."[43] Charles Cotesworth Pinckney cited examples from international law to show the origin of articles in the Constitution dealing with foreign affairs. Rutledge charged Sir Henry Clinton with a violation of international law in ruling that American prisoners of war would have to bear arms against the United States.

James Wilson was the framers' expert on the law of nations. From James Harrington he derived the concept that all government is based on God's irrefutable law. Civil law is based on natural law, Wilson said, which in turn is based upon God's law. God Himself works by universal law. To violate civil law is thus to violate God's law, a very serious offense. The supreme law of the universe is the will of God, said Wilson, which is discoverable through one's reason and conscience, as well as by reading the Scriptures.

American citizens, Wilson averred, needed to obey not only their civil laws but also the law of nations, which is God's law. With nations as with individuals, "integrity and sound policy go hand in hand," and so promises must be kept and treaties honored so as not to destroy the international moral order. As individuals unite in society, they agree to refer their disputes to neutral arbiters, and accept the resulting decisions. "Is the idea of a common judge between nations less admirable than that of a common judge between men?"[44] Wilson asked.

Wilson saw two ways of extending the law of nations into more universal realms. "What was immediately attainable was the extension to the federal courts of the United States of a vast volume of jurisdiction involving the law of nations—matters of private international law concerning, in the main, merchant and mercantile law and the laws regarding contracts."[45] England had already done this, and Wilson found authorization for this action in Article III, Section 2, of the Constitution.

The other method of extension also grew out of his law lectures at the College of Philadelphia. As he discussed man as a member of the commonwealth of nations, Wilson developed a plan for an international court of justice modelled on the United States Supreme Court. It would be to the advantage to both nations in a controversy, he said, to have an impartial judge weigh equities and come up with a compromise solution. Citizens of each nation then need not criticize their leaders as being weak for having conceded some points, and the citizens could well be spared the tragedy of war as a supposed solution.

Spurred by his idealism to ever greater heights, Wilson said that adherence to law was only part of the required conduct between nations. Since "the duties of humanity are incumbent upon nations as well as individuals, the law of that great and universal society requires that each nation should contribute to the perfection and happiness of the others. Nations," he dared to say, "ought to love one another."[46]

International Cooperation

The framers were, above all, practical men. Faced with a difficult political situation, they combined their talents to produce a solution in the form of the world's best constitution. A thinker like Rutledge could see at a glance the problem of the modern world: there is no sovereignty with sufficient authority to outlaw international terrorism, nuclear experimentation in earth's atmosphere, and nuclear war itself. When they were faced with a similar problem under the Articles of Confederation, they created a larger sovereignty sufficient to get the job done, but limited in stated ways so as to prevent an abuse of power. The world needs a new set of Founding Fathers with something like the wisdom, humanity, and willingness to compromise that characterized the American leaders in 1787.

Without world law, there will be world lawlessness. World lawlessness in the nuclear age can lead not only to atomic terrorism but even to a nuclear holocaust. Multinational corporations account for an ever greater percentage of international trade. Radio waves, television beams, and supersonic jetliners refuse to confine themselves within national borders. As J. Bryan Hehir says, "The challenge today is to move from the fact of interdependence to the formulation of rules and institutions for the management of interdependence."[47] Wendell Willkie's phrase is more true today than in his day: "One world or none."

In *The Federalist* No. 15 Hamilton wrote that "there is nothing absurd or impracticable in the idea of a league or alliance between independent nations for certain defined purposes precisely stated in a treaty regulating all the details of time, place, and circumstance."[48] Madison was never an isolationist, for he knew that the United States would need allies in war and in peace. When Harriet Martineau interviewed Madison in 1834, she found a man who believed that the concept of a government of federated states could be expanded indefinitely: "He observed that kings, lords, and commons might constitute a government which would work a long while in a kingdom no bigger than Great Britain, but that it would soon become an absolute government in a country as large as Russia, from the magnitude of its executive powers. It was a common but serious mistake to suppose that a country must be small to be a republic, since a republican form with a federal head can be extended almost without losing its proportions, becoming all the while less, instead of more, subject to change."[49]

Roger Sherman in 1775 was properly wary of surrendering Connecticut's sovereignty to a superstate, since the experience of government under Britain had been so distasteful. But as he saw the chaos existing among the disunited states, Sherman became a strong supporter of the federal Union, albeit still insisting on underwriting guarantees to protect individual and state rights.

In his Farewell Address, Washington warned against unnecessary involvement in Europe's constant quarrels, but he did not reject allied help, such as France provided in the War against England. In his opening charge to the Constitutional Convention, Washington advised the delegates to "adopt no temporizing expedient, but probe the defects of the constitution to the bottom and provide radical cures, whether they are agreed to or not."[50] Ostensibly Washington would recommend similar radical probing into causes and cures of current problems.

Like Madison, Wilson saw the American federation as a prototype of a world federation. The dreams of Henry IV and his minister Sully were being realized in the United States, Wilson felt. It is not a matter of losing sovereignty, he said. By transferring sovereignty to the higher body, the lesser body guaranteed its safety and survival. Moreover, at the present time, no nation has sovereignty over the control of international war. What is needed is the creation of a sovereignty that does not now exist. This is precisely what the framers did in building a Constitution that superseded the Articles of Confederation. Necessity was the father of imagination. Wilson was careful to point out that when the larger sovereignty was created, it was carefully defined so as not to include unnecessary elements, which were reserved for the lesser sovereignties.

Civilized nations are finally recognizing that all mankind are brothers, Wilson said. Harming one's neighbor ultimately ends in harming oneself. A common judge administering universal law would, he felt, provide justice, peace, and harmony in the international community. Distant people become known to our hearts and our understanding, he explained, through the unifying cement of a universal moral code. Law and order will reign in the family of mankind as soon as the peace-keeping authority is established through an international federation of nations.

Their experience under the Articles of Confederation taught the framers several lessons on how to strengthen a federation. It cannot operate effectively under a single-vote veto system. It needs to be supported by a compulsory funding formula rather than by donations. It needs to have police power adequate to enforce its laws. The entire concept of the federation needs support from the people it serves. This support comes only after comprehensive dialogue (and sometimes suffering from the weakness of the federation) concerning the needs, purposes, alternatives, and safeguards against the abuse of power of the larger sovereignty.

Opponents to the Constitution in 1787 said that the United States, ten times larger in size than any previous federation, was too huge to be held together by a common government. The three natural sections of the nation — northern, middle, and southern — could each be a federation, it was alleged. It was also predicted that smaller states would be swallowed up by larger ones. "Those antagonists were precisely like the enemies of world federation now," said Carl Van Doren, "when it is obvious that no difficulty in the way of a world government can match the danger of a world without it."[51]

The Constitution of the United States has served nobly as a charter through the growth from a nation of 13 to one of 50 states, and from an economy 90 percent agricultural to one only 5 percent agricultural. Enormous social, economic, and political changes have scarcely affected the efficacy of the document — a great tribute to the wisdom and foresight of the Founding Fathers.

The Framers on Religion

Religion seems capable of dividing any group of people, including the framers of the Constitution. Should there be an established church, that is, one supported by tax funds? Ellsworth and Washington believed there should be, although Washington added that the taxpayer's funds should go to the church or the charity of his choice.

Madison, Mason, Gouverneur Morris, Charles Cotesworth Pinckney, Randolph, and Rutledge all opposed an established church. Most of these men had deep religious convictions, but they felt that to give one church access to tax funds was to interfere with the freedom of conscience of those attending other churches, or no church at all. Jean de Crèvecoeur believed that one of America's greatest strengths was its religious tolerance. Supreme Court Justice John Paul Stevens, noting the wide divergence of viewpoint among the framers on religion, said "I am not at all sure that men like Madison, Jefferson, Franklin, or Paine would have regarded strict neutrality on the part of religion as 'bizarre'."[52]

Franklin, a deist, modestly gave God credit for his own inventiveness. He contributed funds to Catholic, Jewish, and Protestant churches, and said he would be prepared to give to the first Moslem mosque in Philadelphia. Ellsworth, Hamilton, C.C. Pinckney, and Sherman were orthodox Christians who regularly attended church and contributed funds for religious purposes.

Madison's deep faith told him that all persons are God's children, with a dignity and an importance resulting from this spiritual origin. This view of course had political implications in terms of an individual's rights and responsibilities.

Although Mason stressed freedom of religious worship, he felt that a republican form of government could not be maintained without justice, frugality, and virtue, and he said that it was the mutual duty of all citizens to practice Christian love, charity, and forbearance towards one another. Gouverneur Morris advocated religious freedom for everyone, including Catholics. Candid Randolph was more likely to let the public see his deism than would the more cautious Rutledge expose his brand of deism.

Washington had deep religious convictions. He often gave God credit for divine intervention, as at the Constitutional Convention and during trying times in the Revolutionary War. He consistently asked for God's blessing and guidance in his public undertakings. He devoted a great deal of his First Inaugural Address to religion, as if to assure citizens that he felt responsible not only to them in a political context but to God in a spiritual one.

Washington was influenced by Masonic ideas concerning Providence and by deistic thought in which God is conceived of as a Prime Mover. His most controversial statement on religion occurred in the treaty with Tripoli in 1796 when he said that "the government of the United States is not in any sense founded on the Christian religion,"[53] and that therefore religious differences should never interrupt the harmony between the United States and Moslem nations. Since this is a delicate area of current American foreign policy, one is tempted to wonder how Washington's approach would work in the Middle East today.

James Wilson called religion and law "twin sisters," saying that "divine law" forms an essential part of both disciplines. Man's conscience and reason, helped by the Holy Scriptures, enable him to discover the supreme law, which is the will of God. God, as the author of the moral and social nature of man, is the ultimate authority on all human matters, including legal ones. The conscience, or God's voice within man, brings out the eternal wisdom of the Creator. "Every man who will listen to this inner voice," Wilson said, "may play a creative role in a democracy."[54]

Ralph Ketcham feels that nearly all the Founding Fathers were committed to the same moral standards. "To them all," Ketcham says, "the Ten Commandments, the Sermon on the Mount, and the twelfth chapter of Romans were canonical."[55] Key phrases from that chapter of Romans include: "We belong to each other, and each needs all the others. Love each other with brotherly affection. Be at peace with everyone. Conquer evil by doing good."

Conclusion

It may be going too far to say that the Founding Fathers, having deposed George III, installed in his stead God as king. But at least a deep religious current that expressed itself in the highest moral standards characterized nearly every one of the framers.

"The Framers insisted in 1787, and their document insists today," says Clinton Rossiter, "that order is the price of liberty, duty of happiness, deliberation of wise decision, and constitutionalism of democracy. Who can deny that the Constitution, conceived in this tough-minded philosophy, has made it possible for a restless race to have its stability and its progress too?"[56]

Perhaps the unsung heroes of the American Constitution are the American people. As outstanding as were the Founding Fathers, "even more remarkable was the behavior of the American people as a whole." Since politics is controversial, there must have been some cuss words and a few black eyes over the documents. "But most of them accepted the outcome with good grace and learned to be satisfied with the new system." As Franklin said at the Convention's end, all works of human hands are flawed, but if we are determined to give this form of government our support, it has a good chance to serve well as the framework of an admirable government. And so the American people, wisely led by perhaps the outstanding political assemblage in human history, "executed a basic reform in their governmental system in a truly republican contest, without convulsion, even without the loss of a single life."[57]

No one of the framers got every one of his wishes, one sign of the greatness of the document. Better to improve on what we have today, they reasoned, rather than to wait to achieve a perfect Constitution. But they achieved what they set out to do, and then some. Inspired by their superlative send-off, subsequent generations of Americans can fashion the structure to serve an ever growing, ever changing society. As they headed homeward from Philadelphia in 1787, the framers could feel that "it might be possible to give the future world a safe foundation for its house, and leave it to posterity, if it would, to model that house with justice and adorn it with wisdom and goodness."[58]

References

1. The Miracle at Philadelphia

1. Carl Van Doren, *Benjamin Franklin* (Viking, 1938), pp. 747–8.
2. Clinton Rossiter, *1787: The Grand Convention* (Macmillan, 1966), p. 41.
3. John R. Alden, *George Washington* (Louisiana State University Press, 1984), p. 226.
4. Rossiter, p. 11.
5. James Morton Smith, ed., *The Constitution* (Harper & Row, 1971), p. 25.
6. Burton J. Hendrick, *Bulwark of the Republic* (Little, Brown, 1937), pp. ix–x.
7. Rossiter, p. 12.
8. Douglas Southall Freeman, *George Washington*, vol. 6 (Scribners, 1954), p. 116.
9. Catherine Drinker Bowen, *Miracle at Philadelphia* (Little, Brown, 1966), p. 83.
10. James Morton Smith, p. 39.
11. Ibid., p. 14.
12. Max Farrand, *The Framing of the Constitution of the United States* (Yale University Press, 1913), p. 7.
13. Max M. Mintz, *Gouverneur Morris and the American Revolution* (University of Oklahoma Press, 1970), p. 150.
14. David Little, *Arizona Republic*, September 28, 1985, p. D4.
15. Rossiter, p. 36.
16. Ibid., pp. 48–9.
17. Ibid., p. 50.
18. Freeman, p. 48.
19. Rossiter, p. 45.
20. Farrand, *Framing*, pp. 9–10.
21. Hendrick, p. 64.
22. Bowen, p. 45.
23. Carl Van Doren, *The Great Rehearsal* (Time-Life Books, 1965), p. 27.
24. Bowen, p. 89.
25. *New York Times*, November 3, 1985, section 4, p. 4.
26. Van Doren, *Great Rehearsal*, p. 104.
27. Rossiter, p. 152.
28. Ibid., p. 153.
29. See *American Historical Review* (1914) 19: 282–98.
30. Bowen, p. 45.
31. Howard Swiggett, *The Extraordinary Mr. Morris* (Doubleday, 1952), p. 119.
32. James Morton Smith, p. 121.
33. Ibid., p. 177.
34. Paul Eidelberg, *The Philosophy of the American Constitution* (The Free Press, 1968), pp. 233–4.
35. Ralph Ketcham, *James Madison* (Macmillan, 1971), p. 190.
36. Bowen, p. 88.
37. Rossiter, p. 19.
38. Swiggett, p. 147.
39. Rossiter, p. 138.
40. Van Doren, *Great Rehearsal*, p. 19.
41. Bowen, p. 13.
42. Van Doren, *Great Rehearsal*, p. 36.
43. Ibid., p. 37.
44. Bowen, p. 108.
45. Van Doren, *Great Rehearsal*, p. 114.

2. The Great Compromise

1. Ketcham, p. 215.
2. Ibid.
3. Bowen, p. 72.
4. Arthur T. Prescott, *Drafting the Federal Constitution* (Greenwood Press, 1968), p. 697. Reprint of 1941 edition by Louisiana State Univ. Press
5. Ibid.
6. Ibid., pp. 698-9.
7. Ibid., p. 699.
8. Ibid., p. 522.
9. John P. Roche, in James Morton Smith, p. 162.
10. Bowen, p. 57.
11. Arthur T. Prescott, pp. 594-6.
12. Ibid., p. 597.
13. Eidelberg, pp. 189-90.
14. James Morton Smith, p. 17.
15. Robert R. Palmer, in James Morton Smith, p. 84.
16. Bowen, p. 242.
17. Ibid.
18. Ibid., p. 229.
19. Van Doren, *Great Rehearsal*, p. 192.
20. Arthur T. Prescott, pp. 791-2.
21. Josephine F. Pacheco, ed., *The Legacy of George Mason* (George Mason University Press, 1983), p. 39.
22. Ibid., p. 36.
23. Farrand, *Framing*, p. 208.
24. Alexander Hamilton, John Jay, and James Madison, *The Federalist* (Modern Library, 1937), p. 337.
25. Van Doren, *Great Rehearsal*, p. 235.
26. Bowen, p. 272.
27. Swiggett, p. 133.
28. Arthur T. Prescott, p. 90.
29. Rossiter, p. 253.
30. Ibid., p. 261.
31. Ibid., pp. 180-1.
32. Ibid., p. 239.
33. *New York Times*, November 3, 1985, section 4, p. 4.

3. Oliver Ellsworth: The Education of a Connecticut Yankee

1. James Grant Wilson and John Fiske, eds., *Appleton's Cyclopaedia of American Biography* (D. Appleton & Co., 1888), p. 336.
2. Kenneth B. Umbreit, *Our Eleven Chief Justices* (Harper, 1938), p. 86.
3. William G. Brown, *The Life of Oliver Ellsworth* (Macmillan, 1905), p. 16 (hereinafter called Brown).
4. Ibid., p. 17.
5. Ibid., p. 24.
6. Ibid., p. 28.
7. Umbreit, p. 91.
8. Brown, p. 36.
9. Ibid., p. 41.
10. Ibid., pp. 41-2.
11. Umbreit, p. 94.
12. William G. Brown, "A Continental Congressman: Oliver Ellsworth, 1777-1783," *American Historical Review* (July, 1905) 10:763 (hereinafter called Brown, *AHR*).
13. Christopher Collier, *Roger Sherman's Connecticut: Yankee Politics and the American Revolution* (Wesleyan University Press, 1971), pp. 169-70.
14. Brown, *AHR*, p. 766.
15. Ibid., p. 770.
16. Brown, p. 101.
17. Ibid., pp. 103-4.
18. Umbreit, p. 82.
19. Arthur T. Prescott, p. 26.
20. Daniel J. Boorstin, *The Americans: The National Experience* (Vintage Books, 1965), p. 403.
21. Brown, p. 140.
22. Ibid., p. 133.
23. Ibid., pp. 158, 168.
24. Rossiter, p. 250.
25. Brown, p. 165.
26. Roger Sherman Boardman, *Roger Sherman: Signer and Statesman* (Da Capo Press, 1971), p. 273. Reprint of 1938 edition by University of Pennsylvania Press.
27. Collier, p. 275.
28. Van Doren, *Great Rehearsal*, p. 232.

29. Brown, p. 175.
30. Hendrick, p. 371.
31. Umbreit, p. 99.
32. Ibid., p. 83.
33. Wilson and Fiske, p. 336.
34. Umbreit, pp. 106-7.
35. Brown, p. 260.
36. Ibid., pp. 246-7.
37. Ibid., p. 253.
38. Ibid., p. 256.
39. Ibid., p. 284.
40. Samuel Edwards, *Rebel! A Biography of Tom Paine* (Praeger, 1974), p. 234.
41. Ibid., p. 235.
42. Brown, p. 285.
43. Ibid., p. 290.
44. Ibid., p. 305.
45. Umbreit, p. 108.
46. Brown, p. 301.
47. Ibid., p. 304.
48. Ibid., p. 325.
49. Edwards, p. 254.
50. Brown, pp. 330-1.
51. Ibid., pp. 344-5.

4. Benjamin Franklin: The World Recognizes An American

1. Alice J. Hall, "Philosopher of Dissent: Benjamin Franklin," *National Geographic* (July 1975), 148:95.
2. Richard B. Morris, *Seven Who Shaped Our Destiny* (Harper & Row, 1973), p. 9.
3. Van Doren, *Franklin*, p. 44.
4. Frank L. Mott and Chester E. Jorgenson, *Benjamin Franklin* (American Book Company, 1936), p. cvi.
5. Morris, *Seven*, p. 21.
6. Van Doren, *Franklin*, p. 104.
7. Mott and Jorgenson, p. xciii.
8. Charles W. Meister, "Franklin as a Proverb Stylist," *American Literature* (May 1952) 24:158-9.
9. Mott and Jorgenson, p. lviii.
10. Van Doren, *Franklin*, pp. 128-9.
11. Ibid., p. 173.
12. Ronald W. Clark, *Benjamin Franklin: A Biography* (Random House, 1983), p. 96.
13. Van Doren, *Franklin*, p. 215.
14. Ibid., p. 217.
15. Morris, *Seven*, p. 23.
16. Van Doren, *Franklin*, p. 213.
17. Ibid., p. 223.
18. Ibid., p. 225.
19. Ibid., p. 240.
20. Clark, p. 138.
21. Van Doren, *Franklin*, p. 282.
22. Ibid., p. 290.
23. Morris, *Seven*, pp. 21-2.
24. Van Doren, *Franklin*, p. 352.
25. Ibid., p. 369.
26. Ibid., p. 372.
27. Ibid., p. 376.
28. Ibid., p. 378.
29. Clark, p. 216.
30. Ibid., p. 246.
31. Ibid., p. 245.
32. Van Doren, *Franklin*, p. 519.
33. Mott and Jorgenson, p. xcviii.
34. Clark, pp. 272-3.
35. Van Doren, *Franklin*, p. 529.
36. Ibid., p. 550.
37. Morris, *Seven*, p. 37.
38. Van Doren, *Franklin*, p. 632.
39. Ibid., p. 572.
40. Clark, p. 331.
41. Ibid., p. 328.
42. Van Doren, *Franklin*, p. 606.
43. Ibid., p. 600.
44. Ibid.
45. Ibid., p. 639.
46. Morris, *Seven*, p. 17.
47. Alice J. Hall, p. 116.
48. Van Doren, *Franklin*, p. 627.
49. Ibid., p. 698.
50. Clark, p. 384.
51. Van Doren, *Franklin*, p. 713.
52. Ibid., p. 722.
53. Clark, pp. 412-3.
54. Morris, *Seven*, p. 20.
55. Van Doren, *Franklin*, p. 764.
56. Ibid., p. 782.

5. Nathaniel Gorham: The Voice of Business

1. David C. Whitney, *Founders of Freedom in America* (J.C. Ferguson, 1965), p. 103.

2. Van Beck Hall, *Politics without Parties: Massachusetts, 1780–1791* (University of Pittsburgh Press, 1972), p. 264.
3. Ibid., p. 189.
4. Edmund C. Burnett, ed., *Letters of Members of the Continental Congress* vol. 8 (Peter Smith, 1963), p. 863.
5. Ibid., p. 318.
6. Edmund C. Burnett, *The Continental Congress* (Macmillan, 1941), p. 646.
7. Burnett, *Letters*, p. 337.
8. Ibid., p. 395.
9. Van Beck Hall, p. 221.
10. Burnett, *Letters*, p. 490.
11. James T. Flexner, *George Washington and the New Nation (1783–1793)* (Little, Brown, 1969), p. 103.
12. Richard Krauel, "Prince Henry of Prussia and the Regency of the United States, 1786," *American Historical Review* (October 1911) 17:46.
13. Ibid., p. 51.
14. Arthur T. Prescott, p. 24.
15. Burnett, *Letters*, p. 611.
16. Van Beck Hall, p. 265.
17. Ibid.
18. Ibid., p. 269.
19. Farrand, *Framing*, p. 100.
20. Bowen, p. 128,
21. Theodore C. Pease, "The Ordinance of 1787," *Mississippi Valley Historical Review* (September 1938) 25:171.
22. Farrand, *Framing*, p. 110.
23. Max Farrand, ed., *The Records of the Federal Convention of 1787*, vol. 2 (Yale University Press, 1937), p. 17.
24. Ibid., pp. 41–3.
25. Ibid., p. 46.
26. Ibid., p. 48.
27. Ibid., pp. 73, 79.
28. Umbreit, p. 73.
29. Farrand, *Records*, p. 270.
30. Ibid., p. 499.
31. Whitney, p. 104.
32. Arthur T. Prescott, p. 389.
33. Farrand, *Records*, p. 293.
34. Ibid., p. 439.
35. Farrand, *Framing*, p. 188.
36. Van Beck Hall, p. 266.
37. Farrand, *Records*, p. 540.
38. Ibid., p. 420.
39. Ibid., p. 491.
40. Van Beck Hall, p. 272.
41. Ibid., p. 249.
42. Ibid., p. 285.
43. Bowen, p. 289.
44. Ibid., pp. 285–6.
45. Jonathan Elliot, ed., *The Debates in the Several State Conventions on the Adoption of the Federal Constitution*, vol. 2 (Lippincott, 1861) p. 52.
46. Ibid., p. 106.
47. Bowen, pp. 287–8.
48. Rossiter, p. 289.
49. Freeman, p. 145.
50. *Mississippi Valley Historical Review* (September 1953) 40:259.

6. Alexander Hamilton: A Portrait in Paradox

1. Dorothie Bobbe, "A Reappraisal of Alexander Hamilton," *New York Times Magazine*, January 6, 1957, p. 15.
2. Bower Aly, ed., *Alexander Hamilton: Selections* (Liberal Arts Press, 1957), pp. 23–4.
3. Ibid., p. 25.
4. Ibid., p. 26.
5. Ibid.
6. Ibid., p. 28.
7. Marie B. Hecht, *Odd Destiny: The Life of Alexander Hamilton* (Macmillan, 1982), p. 34.
8. Richard B. Morris, ed., *Alexander Hamilton and the Founding of the Nation* (Dial Press, 1957), p. 78.
9. Hecht, p. 56.
10. Morris, *Hamilton*, p. 81.
11. Morris, *Seven*, p. 248.
12. Ibid., p. 257.
13. Ibid., p. 249.
14. Aly, pp. 71, 77.
15. Morris, *Hamilton*, pp. 84–5.
16. Hecht, p. 82.
17. Ibid., p. 81.
18. Frederick C. Prescott, *Alexander Hamilton and Thomas Jefferson*

(American Book Company, 1934), p. xxiii.
19. Hecht, p. 99.
20. Ibid., p. 104.
21. Frederick C. Prescott, p. 26.
22. Hecht, p. 123.
23. Farrand, *Framing*, p. 89.
24. Whitney, p. 109.
25. Van Doren, *Great Rehearsal*, p. 117.
26. Arthur T. Prescott, p. 787.
27. Hamilton et al, p. 90.
28. Ibid., p. 142.
29. Ibid., p. 213.
30. Frederick C. Prescott, p. xxvi.
31. Hamilton et al, p. 495.
32. Ibid., p. 506.
33. Eidelberg, p. 243.
34. Ibid., p. 225.
35. Hecht, p. 144.
36. Aly, p. 100.
37. Van Doren, *Great Rehearsal*, p. 286.
38. *New York Times Book Review*, August 1, 1982, p. 11.
39. Rossiter, pp. 307–8.
40. Aly, p. xiii.
41. Morris, *Hamilton*, p. 242.
42. Ibid., p. 270.
43. Hecht, p. 215.
44. Flexner, p. 354.
45. Aly, p. 147.
46. Ibid., pp. 151–2.
47. Ibid., p. 154.
48. Virginia Moore, *The Madisons: A Biography* (McGraw-Hill, 1979), p. 183.
49. Ketcham, p. 312.
50. Morris, *Hamilton*, p. 317.
51. Ibid.
52. Ibid., p. 286.
53. Hecht, p. 234.
54. Morris, *Hamilton*, p. 412.
55. Ibid., p. 392.
56. Aly, p. 160.
57. Morris, *Seven*, p. 253.
58. Hecht, p. 287.
59. Ibid., p. 292.
60. Ibid., p. 322.
61. Ibid., p. 323.
62. Ibid., p. 325.
63. Ibid., p. 343.
64. Morris, *Hamilton*, p. 437.
65. Ibid., pp. 282–3.
66. Hecht, p. 380.
67. Ibid., p. 379.
68. Ibid., p. 386.
69. Aly, p. 144.
70. Ibid., p. 169.
71. Ibid., p. 174.
72. Ibid., p. 235.
73. Ibid., p. 166.
74. Ibid., pp. 170–3.
75. Hecht, p. 411.
76. Aly, pp. 176–7.
77. Hecht, p. 416.
78. Ibid., p. 419.
79. Ibid., p. 422.
80. Aly, p. 197.
81. Ibid., p. 191.
82. Ibid., p. 212.

7. James Madison: Political Theorist Turned Patriot

1. Morris, *Seven*, p. 192.
2. Hendrick, p. 40.
3. Moore, p. 42.
4. Ibid., p. 43.
5. Ketcham, p. 47.
6. Ibid., p. 48.
7. Morris, *Seven*, p. 199.
8. Ketcham, p. 142.
9. Ibid., p. 112.
10. Ibid., p. 114.
11. Morris, *Seven*, p. 211.
12. Harold S. Schultz, *James Madison* (Twayne, 1970), p. 44.
13. James Morton Smith, p. 129.
14. Ketcham, p. 187.
15. Schultz, p. 57.
16. Ketcham, p. 208.
17. Schultz, p. 76.
18. Ketcham, p. 303.
19. Ibid., p. 77.
20. Morris, *Seven*, p. 206.
21. Hamilton et al, p. 337.
22. James Morton Smith, p. 167.
23. Van Doren, *Great Rehearsal*, p. 279.
24. Ketcham, p. 300.
25. Hamilton et al, p. 294.
26. Schultz, p. 95.
27. Ketcham, p. 330.

28. Schultz, p. 109.
29. Ibid., p. 117.
30. Moore, p. 10.
31. Ibid., p. 11.
32. Ketcham, p. 311.
33. Schultz, pp. 131-2.
34. Ibid., p. 135.
35. Ibid.
36. Ibid., p. 141.
37. Ketcham, p. 439.
38. Ibid.
39. Ibid., p. 447.
40. Ibid., p. 455.
41. Moore, p. 212.
42. Schultz, p. 8.
43. Ketcham, p. 466.
44. Ibid., p. 465.
45. Ibid., p. 499.
46. Schultz, p. 149.
47. Ketcham, p. 551.
48. Ibid., p. 532.
49. Ibid., p. 536.
50. Ibid., p. 537.
51. Whitney, p. 146.
52. Ketcham, p. 579.
53. Moore, p. 325.
54. Schultz, p. 192.
55. Ketcham, pp. 608-9.
56. Ibid., p. 655.
57. Ibid., p. 646.
58. Moore, p. 446.
59. Ketcham, p. 671.
60. Moore, p. 472.
61. Morris, *Seven*, p. 220.
62. Moore, pp. 476-8.
63. Schultz, p. 5.

8. George Mason: Champion of Human Rights

1. Robert A. Rutland, *George Mason: Reluctant Statesman* (Colonial Williamsburg, 1961), p. 110.
2. Ketcham, p. 71.
3. Rutland, p. 10.
4. Ibid., p. 24.
5. Helen Hill, *George Mason, Constitutionalist* (Harvard University Press, 1938), p. 50.
6. Rutland, p. 22.
7. Hill, p. 32.
8. Rutland, p. 34.
9. Pacheco, p. 11.
10. Hill, p. 104.
11. Ibid., p. 105.
12. Pacheco, p. 13.
13. Hill, pp. 113-4.
14. Pacheco, p. 15.
15. Hill, p. 115.
16. Ibid., p. 114.
17. Ibid., p. 118.
18. Ibid., p. 119.
19. Ibid.
20. Pacheco, p. 61.
21. Rutland, p. 57.
22. Ibid., p. 111-4.
23. Pacheco, p. 19.
24. Rutland, p. 65.
25. Pacheco, p. 19.
26. Rutland, p. 68.
27. Ibid., p. 69.
28. Ibid., p. 75.
29. Farrand, *Framing*, p. 74.
30. Eidelberg, p. 55.
31. Arthur T. Prescott, p. 348.
32. Ibid., p. 439.
33. Farrand, *Framing*, p. 168.
34. Van Doren, *Great Rehearsal*, p. 186.
35. Hill, p. 128.
36. Farrand, *Records*, pp. 587-8.
37. Farrand, *Framing*, p. 186.
38. Farrand, *Records*, pp. 618-9.
39. Rutland, p. 94.
40. Van Doren, *Great Rehearsal*, p. 276.
41. Rutland, p. 106.
42. Hill, p. 249.
43. Rutland, p. xii.

9. Gouverneur Morris: Witty and Aristocratic Lothario

1. Bowen, p. 42.
2. Mintz, p. 15.
3. Ibid., p. 30.
4. Ibid., p. 41.
5. Swiggett, p. 6.
6. Ibid., p. 27.
7. Ibid., p. 43.
8. Mintz, p. 76.
9. Ibid., pp. 75-6.
10. Whitney, p. 158.

11. Mintz, p. 77.
12. Ibid., pp. 112–3.
13. Swiggett, p. 57.
14. Ibid., p. 55.
15. Ibid., p. 52.
16. Rossiter, p. 109.
17. Swiggett, pp. 67–8.
18. Ibid., p. 77.
19. Ibid., p. 81.
20. Mintz, p. 160.
21. Ibid., p. 146.
22. Swiggett, p. 114.
23. Arthur T. Prescott, p. 29.
24. Farrand, *Framing*, p. 62.
25. Mintz, p. 189.
26. Swiggett, p. 121.
27. Farrand, *Records*, p. 104.
28. Ibid., p. 254.
29. Farrand, *Framing*, p. 201.
30. Ibid., p. 181.
31. Swiggett, p. 137.
32. Mintz, p. 209.
33. Swiggett, p. 169.
34. Ibid., p. 168.
35. Ibid., pp. 170–3.
36. Ibid., p. 191.
37. Ibid., p. 226.
38. Ibid., p. 221.
39. Ibid., p. 263.
40. *Concise Dictionary of American Biography* (Scribners, 1964), p. 702.
41. Swiggett, p. 260.
42. Edwards, p. 206.
43. Swiggett, p. 333.
44. Ibid., p. 342.
45. Ibid., p. 352.
46. Ibid., p. 347.
47. Frederick C. Prescott, p. 412.
48. Swiggett, p. 368.
49. Farrand, *Framing*, p. 144.
50. Swiggett, p. 348.
51. Ibid., p. 399.
52. Ibid., p. 403.
53. Ibid., p. 408.
54. Mintz, pp. 239–40.
55. Ibid., p. 240.

10. Charles Cotesworth Pinckney: The Soldier and Patriot

1. Marvin R. Zahniser, *Charles Cotesworth Pinckney: Founding Father* (University of North Carolina Press, 1967), p. 11.
2. Ibid., p. 13.
3. Ibid., pp. 18–9.
4. David Duncan Wallace, *South Carolina: A Short History* (University of North Carolina Press, 1951), p. 245.
5. Francis Leigh Williams, *A Founding Family: The Pinckneys of South Carolina* (Harcourt Brace Jovanovich, 1978), p. 54.
6. Zahniser, p. 44.
7. Ibid., p. 46.
8. Williams, p. 147.
9. Edward McCrady, *The History of South Carolina in the Revolution, 1775–1780* (Russell & Russell, 1969), p. 476.
10. Williams, p. 172.
11. Ibid., p. 173.
12. Ibid., p. 175.
13. Zahniser, p. 79.
14. Williams, p. 199.
15. Zahniser, p. 88.
16. Farrand, *Framing*, p. 31.
17. Arthur T. Prescott, p. 359.
18. Farrand, *Records*, p. 371.
19. Ibid., p. 373.
20. Farrand, *Framing*, p. 151.
21. Van Doren, *Great Rehearsal*, pp. 190–1.
22. Zahniser, p. 97.
23. Ibid., p. 99.
24. Ibid., p. 71.
25. Ibid., p. 106.
26. Ibid., p. 112.
27. Ibid., p. 115.
28. Ibid., p. 133.
29. Ibid., p. 137.
30. Ibid., p. 143.
31. Ibid., p. 154.
32. Edwards, p. 221.
33. Zahniser, p. 158.
34. Ibid., p. 164.
35. Ibid., p. 169.
36. Henry W. Bragdon and Samuel P. McCutchen, *History of a Free People* (Macmillan, 1960), p. 173.
37. Zahniser, p. 175.
38. Ibid., p. 184.
39. Ibid., p. 204.
40. Williams, p. 319.
41. Zahniser, p. 214.

42. Ibid., p. 217.
43. Ibid., p. 221.
44. Ibid., p. 231.
45. Williams, p. 330.
46. Whitney, p. 177.

11. Edmund Randolph: The Conscientious Moderate

1. Moncure D. Conway, *Omitted Chapters of History Disclosed in the Life and Papers of Edmund Randolph* (G.P. Putnam's Sons, 1888), p. 11.
2. John J. Reardon, *Edmund Randolph: A Biography* (Macmillan, 1974), p. 45.
3. Ibid., p. 70.
4. Conway, p. 157.
5. Ibid.
6. Ibid., p. 58.
7. Reardon, p. 85.
8. Conway, p. 59.
9. Reardon, p. 88.
10. Conway, p. 68.
11. Ibid., pp. 69–70.
12. Ibid., p. 62.
13. Ibid., p. 63.
14. Ibid., pp. 64–5.
15. Ibid., p. 66.
16. Ibid., p. 67.
17. Reardon, p. 97.
18. Ibid., p. 100.
19. Farrand, *Framing*, p. 77.
20. Arthur T. Prescott, p. 333.
21. Farrand, *Records*, pp. 17–8.
22. Ibid., p. 89.
23. Farrand, *Framing*, p. 125.
24. Conway, p. 167.
25. Farrand, *Records*, p. 374.
26. Arthur T. Prescott, p. 155.
27. Bowen, p. 232.
28. Conway, pp. 96–7.
29. Ibid., p. 99.
30. Ibid., pp. 165–6.
31. Reardon, p. 142.
32. Conway, p. 108.
33. Ibid.
34. Reardon, p. 143.
35. Van Doren, *Great Rehearsal*, p. 273.
36. Conway, p. 108.
37. Reardon, p. 167.
38. Conway, pp. 129–30.
39. Ibid., p. 140.
40. Ibid., pp. 168–70.
41. Ibid., p. 173.
42. Ibid.
43. Ibid., p. 151.
44. Ibid., p. 153.
45. Ibid., pp. 190–1.
46. Ibid., p. 207.
47. Ibid., p. 219.
48. Ibid., p. 231.
49. Ibid., p. 266.
50. Ibid., pp. 291–2.
51. Ibid., pp. 317–8.
52. Ibid., p. 287.
53. Zahniser, p. 128.
54. Reardon, p. 320.
55. Conway, p. 250.
56. Ibid., p. 320.
57. Ibid.
58. Ibid., pp. 358–9.
59. Reardon, p. 331.
60. Ibid., pp. 346–9.
61. Irving Brant, "Edmund Randolph, Not Guilty," *William and Mary Quarterly*, 3rd series (April 1950) 7:179–98.
62. Reardon, p. 332.
63. Conway, p. 361.
64. Ibid., p. 364.
65. Ibid., pp. 370–1.
66. Reardon, p. 355.
67. Conway, pp. 380–1.
68. Ibid., p. 380.

12. John Rutledge: The Benevolent Dictator

1. Robert W. Barnwell, Jr., "Rutledge, 'The Dictator,'" *The Journal of Southern History* (May 1941) 7:218–22.
2. Rossiter, p. 130.
3. Richard Barry, *Mr. Rutledge of South Carolina* (Duell, Sloan & Pearce, 1942), p. 14.
4. Rossiter, p. 131.
5. Umbreit, p. 56.
6. Barry, p. 24.
7. Ibid., p. 63.

8. Wallace, p. 217.
9. Barry, p. 72.
10. Ibid., p. 103.
11. Ibid., p. 104.
12. Ibid., p. 108.
13. Whitney, p. 190.
14. Barry, p. 166.
15. Ibid., p. 168.
16. Wallace, p. 257.
17. Rossiter, p. 131.
18. McCrady, p. 107.
19. Wallace, p. 282.
20. McCrady, p. 113.
21. Ibid., p. 159.
22. Ibid., p. 181.
23. Ibid., p. 239.
24. Ibid., p. 319.
25. Barnwell, p. 218.
26. Wallace, pp. 292-3.
27. Ibid., p. 297.
28. Ibid., p. 299.
29. Rossiter, p. 131.
30. McCrady, p. 564.
31. Barnwell, p. 219.
32. Ibid., p. 224.
33. Arthur T. Prescott, pp. 331-2.
34. Barry, p. 317.
35. Ibid., p. 321.
36. Ibid., pp. 331-2.
37. Ibid., p. 340.
38. Ibid., p. 339.
39. Farrand, *Records*, p. 249.
40. Ibid., p. 452.
41. Barry, pp. 328-9.
42. Ibid., p. 352.
43. Zahniser, p. 127.
44. Umbreit, pp. 54-5.
45. Ibid., p. 77.
46. Barry, pp. 357-8.
47. Umbreit, p. 67.
48. Barry, p. 365.

13. Roger Sherman: The Awkward Clear-Headed Yankee

1. Van Doren, *Great Rehearsal*, p. 49.
2. Boardman, p. 175.
3. Ibid., p. 5.
4. Ibid., p. 8.
5. Ibid., pp. 25-6.
6. Collier, p. 12.
7. Ibid., p. 8.
8. Boardman, p. 65.
9. Bowen, p. 93.
10. Collier, p. 331.
11. Boardman, pp. 99-100.
12. Collier, p. 54.
13. Boardman, pp. 91-2.
14. Ibid., p. 108.
15. Ibid., p. 116.
16. Ibid., p. 123.
17. Bowen, p. 93.
18. Boardman, p. 117.
19. *Concise Dictionary of American Biography*, p. 950.
20. Boardman, p. 140.
21. Ibid., p. 167.
22. Van Doren, *Franklin*, p. 549.
23. Boardman, pp. 137-8.
24. Collier, pp. 150-5.
25. Boardman, p. 171.
26. Collier, p. 169.
27. Boardman, pp. 185-6.
28. Ibid., p. 185.
29. Ibid., pp. 184-5.
30. Collier, p. 148.
31. Ibid., pp. 193, 316.
32. Boardman, p. 115.
33. Ibid., p. 230.
34. Ibid.
35. Farrand, *Framing*, p. 80.
36. Boardman, p. 260.
37. Farrand, *Records*, pp. 291-2.
38. Ibid., p. 5.
39. Whitney, p. 197.
40. Farrand, *Records*, p. 509.
41. Collier, p. 252.
42. Farrand, *Records*, p. 537.
43. Collier, p. 253.
44. Farrand, *Records*, pp. 329, 419, 481.
45. Farrand, *Framing*, pp. 176-7.
46. Boardman, pp. 254-7.
47. Ibid., p. 276.
48. Ibid., p. 295.
49. Collier, p. 301.
50. *Annals*, First Congress, quoted in Boardman, p. 291.
51. Collier, pp. 293, 295.
52. Quoted in Boardman, pp. 284-5.
53. Collier, p. 12.
54. Boardman, pp. 348-56.
55. Collier, p. 332.
56. Ibid.

57. Quoted in Boardman, pp. 336–7.
58. Ibid., p. 2.
59. Collier, p. 100.

14. George Washington: The One Indispensable Man

1. Quoted in Flexner, p. 133.
2. Bowen, p. 194.
3. Alden, pp. xi, 1.
4. Morris, *Seven*, p. 33.
5. Hendrick, p. 13.
6. Alden, p. 24.
7. Ibid., p. 27.
8. Hill, p. 48.
9. Morris, *Seven*, pp. 51–2.
10. Alden, p. 46.
11. Ibid., p. 51.
12. Morris, *Seven*, p. 63.
13. Ibid., p. 47.
14. Alden, p. 78.
15. Ibid., p. 92.
16. Ibid., p. 94.
17. Morris, *Seven*, p. 64.
18. Alden, p. 101.
19. Whitney, p. 213.
20. Alden, p. 112.
21. Morris, *Seven*, p. 62.
22. Alden, p. 83.
23. Ibid., pp. 113–4.
24. Ibid., p. 118.
25. Hendrick, p. 15.
26. Alden, p. 149.
27. Ibid., p. 163.
28. Ibid., p. 169.
29. Hill, p. 169.
30. Van Doren, *Franklin*, p. 611.
31. Alden, p. 198.
32. Morris, *Seven*, p. 71.
33. Hendrick, p. 19.
34. Ibid., p. 20.
35. Alden, p. 210.
36. Flexner, p. 23.
37. Alden, p. 214.
38. Flexner, p. 422.
39. Freeman, p. 29.
40. Ibid., p. 45.
41. Hendrick, p. 26.
42. Bowen, p. 243.
43. Freeman, p. 203.
44. Flexner, p. 99.
45. Freeman, p. 72.
46. Flexner, p. 91.
47. Ibid., p. 105.
48. Freeman, p. 79.
49. Flexner, p. 101.
50. Ibid., p. 111.
51. Ibid., p. 101.
52. Bowen, p. 195.
53. Flexner, p. 106.
54. Freeman, pp. 95, 98.
55. Flexner, p. 123.
56. Alden, p. 225.
57. Farrand, *Framing*, p. 139.
58. Hendrick, p. 99.
59. Flexner, p. 143.
60. Ibid.
61. Freeman, p. 165.
62. Flexner, p. 139.
63. Freeman, pp. 119–20.
64. Ibid., p. 144.
65. Alden, p. 234.
66. Morris, *Hamilton*, p. vii.
67. Flexner, p. 226.
68. Freeman, pp. 159–60.
69. Ibid., pp. 161–2.
70. Ibid., p. 195.
71. Flexner, p. 239.
72. Freeman, p. 260.
73. Flexner, p. 200.
74. Freeman, p. 220.
75. Ketcham, p. 318.
76. Quoted in Flexner, p. 280.
77. Ibid., p. 217.
78. Ibid., p. 304.
79. Freeman, pp. 361–2.
80. Flexner, p. 360.
81. Freeman, p. 359.
82. Ibid., p. 360.
83. Ibid., p. 368.
84. Ibid., pp. 369–70.
85. Flexner, pp. 357–8.
86. Ibid., p. 389.
87. Ibid.
88. Ibid., pp. 392–3.
89. Alden, p. 296.
90. Flexner, p. 423.
91. Ibid., p. 420.
92. Moore, p. 49.
93. Alden, p. 280.
94. Conway, p. 156.
95. Swiggett, p. 335.
96. Alden, p. 298.
97. Flexner, p. 72.
98. Alden, p. 304.

99. Swiggett, pp. 146-7.
100. Aly, pp. 189-90.

15. James Wilson: The Capitalist and World Citizen

1. Charles Page Smith, *James Wilson, Founding Father* (University of North Carolina Press, 1956), p. 5.
2. Geoffrey Seed, *James Wilson* (KTO Press, Millwood, NJ, 1978), p. 4.
3. Charles P. Smith, p. 25.
4. Ibid., p. 35.
5. Ibid., p. 39.
6. Ibid., p. 65.
7. Ibid., p. 67.
8. Seed, pp. 10-1.
9. Ibid., p. 13.
10. Charles P. Smith, p. 202.
11. Seed, p. 21.
12. *Concise Dictionary of American Biography*, p. 1221.
13. Seed, p. 17.
14. Ibid., p. 20.
15. Charles P. Smith, pp. 75-6.
16. Ibid., pp. 102, 107.
17. Ibid., p. 127.
18. Ibid., pp. 129-39.
19. Seed, p. 38.
20. Charles P. Smith, p. 199.
21. Ibid., p. 210.
22. *Concise Dictionary of American Biography*, p. 1221.
23. Farrand, *Framing*, pp. 197-8.
24. Van Doren, *Great Rehearsal*, p. 49.
25. Charles P. Smith, p. 256.
26. Ibid., pp. 232-3.
27. Ibid., pp. 225-6.
28. Whitney, pp. 235-6.
29. Charles P. Smith, p. 257.
30. Van Doren, *Great Rehearsal*, p. 147.
31. Farrand, *Records*, p. 268.
32. Charles P. Smith, pp. 236-7.
33. Farrand, *Records*, p. 231.
34. Seed, p. 72.
35. Ibid., p. 111.
36. Farrand, *Framing*, p. 126.
37. Ibid., p. 181.
38. Charles P. Smith, p. 251.
39. Seed, pp. 80-1.
40. Charles P. Smith, pp. 260-1.
41. Farrand, *Framing*, p. 62.
42. Seed, p. 88.
43. Ibid., pp. 91-2.
44. Ibid., pp. 94-5.
45. Van Doren, *Great Rehearsal*, pp. 225-6.
46. Seed, p. 110.
47. Ibid., p. 187.
48. Charles P. Smith, p. 269.
49. Ibid., p. 277.
50. Seed, p. 119.
51. Charles P. Smith, p. 277.
52. Van Doren, *Great Rehearsal*, p. 228.
53. Bowen, p. 277.
54. Seed, p. 123.
55. Ibid., pp. 128-9.
56. Ibid., pp. 129-39.
57. Charles P. Smith, pp. 311, 313.
58. Ibid., p. 319.
59. Ibid., p. 326.
60. Ibid., pp. 330-2.
61. Ibid., p. 333.
62. Seed, pp. 151-2.
63. Ibid., p. 154.
64. Ibid., p. 157.
65. Ibid., pp. 156-7.
66. Ibid., p. 156.
67. Charles P. Smith, p. 339.
68. Seed, p. 156.
69. Ibid., p. 154.
70. Charles P. Smith, p. 341.
71. Ibid., p. 359.
72. Seed, p. 177.
73. Ibid., p. 178.
74. Ibid., p. 179.
75. Ibid., p. 182.

16. The Founding Fathers Today

1. Jane Nevis, "The Constitution Chronicles," *New York Times Magazine*, September 22, 1985, p. 114.
2. Rossiter, pp. 180-1.
3. *New York Times*, October 27, 1985, section 4, p. 22.

4. *Arizona Republic*, October 13, 1985, p. A5.
5. Irving R. Kaufman, "What Did the Founding Fathers Intend?" *New York Times Magazine*, February 23, 1986, p. 59.
6. Ibid., p. 60.
7. Ibid., p. 67.
8. Ibid., p. 69.
9. Rossiter, p. 239.
10. Morris, *Seven*, p. 220.
11. Swiggett, p. 348.
12. Farrand, *Framing*, p. 62.
13. Seed, p. 119.
14. Charles P. Smith, p. 311.
15. Bowen, p. 243.
16. Van Doren, *Great Rehearsal*, p. 292.
17. Charles P. Smith, p. 334.
18. John Newhouse, *New Yorker* (February 10, 1986), 61:88.
19. Quoted in James Morton Smith, p. 2.
20. Robert E. Brown, *Charles Beard and the Constitution* (Princeton University Press, 1956), p. 200.
21. Forrest McDonald, *We the People: The Economic Origins of the Constitution* (University of Chicago Press, 1958), pp. 349–50.
22. Ketcham, pp. 229–30.
23. Morris, *Hamilton*, p. 286.
24. Hecht, p. 287.
25. Seed, pp. 80–1.
26. Eidelberg, p. 248.
27. Farrand, *Framing*, p. 189.
28. Quoted in Pacheco, p. 58.
29. Quoted in James Morton Smith, p. 163.
30. Van Doren, *Franklin*, p. 698.
31. Ibid., p. 712.
32. Clark, p. 328.
33. Flexner, p. 72.
34. Van Doren, *Franklin*, p. 292.
35. Van Doren, *Great Rehearsal*, p. 292.
36. Swiggett, p. 27.
37. Rossiter, p. 205.
38. Seed, p. 154.
39. Van Doren, *Great Rehearsal*, p. 6.
40. Morris, *Hamilton*, p. 393.
41. Ibid., p. 394.
42. Ibid., p. 413.
43. Arthur T. Prescott, p. 532.
44. Seed, pp. 154, 156.
45. Ibid., p. 156.
46. Ibid., p. 154.
47. *New Yorker* (February 24, 1986) 62:105.
48. Hamilton et al, p. 90.
49. Moore, pp. 467–8.
50. Flexner, p. 106.
51. Van Doren, *Great Rehearsal*, pp. xxi–xxii.
52. *New York Times*, October 27, 1985, section 4, p. 1.
53. Conway, p. 156.
54. Charles P. Smith, p. 333.
55. Ketcham, p. 48.
56. Rossiter, pp. 272–3.
57. Alden, p. 233.
58. Van Doren, *Great Rehearsal*, p. 192.

Bibliography

Alden, John R. *George Washington: A Biography*. Baton Rouge: Louisiana State Univ Pr, 1984.
Aly, Bower, ed. *Alexander Hamilton: Selections*. New York: Liberal Arts Pr, 1957.
American Historical Review (1914) 19:282-98.
Antieau, C.J. *New York Times*, 27 Oct 1985, 4:22.
Appleton's Cyclopaedia of American Biography. New York: D. Appleton, 1888.
Barnwell, Robert W. Jr. *The Journal of Southern History* (May 1941) 7:218-22.
Barry, Richard. *Mr. Rutledge of South Carolina*. New York: Duell, Sloan, & Pearce, 1942.
Boardman, Roger Sherman. *Roger Sherman: Signer and Statesman*. New York: DaCapo Press, 1971. Reprint of 1938 ed.
Bobbe, Dorothie. *New York Times Magazine*, 6 Jan 1957, p. 15.
Boorstin, Daniel J. *The Americans: The National Experience*. New York: Vintage, 1965.
Bowen, Catherine Drinker. *Miracle at Philadelphia*. Boston: Little, Brown, 1966.
Bragdon, Henry W. & Samuel P. McCutchen. *History of a Free People*. New York: Macmillan, 1960.
Brant, Irving. *William & Mary Quarterly*, 3rd series (April 1950) 7:179-98.
Brennan, William J. Jr. *Arizona Republic*, 13 Oct 1985, p. A5.
Brown, Robert E. *Charles Beard and the Constitution*. Princeton: Princeton Univ Pr, 1956.
Brown, William G. *American Historical Review* (July 1905) 10:763.
_____. *The Life of Oliver Ellsworth*. New York: Macmillan, 1905.
Burnett, Edmund C. *The Continental Congress*. New York: Macmillan, 1941.
_____, ed. *Letters of Members of the Continental Congress*, vol. 8. Gloucester, MA: Peter Smith, 1963. Reprint of 1936 ed.
Clark, Ronald W. *Benjamin Franklin: A Biography*. New York: Random House, 1983.
Collier, Christopher. *Roger Sherman's Connecticut*. Middletown, CN: Wesleyan Univ Pr, 1971.
Concise Dictionary of American Biography. New York: Scribners, 1964.
Conway, Moncure D. *Omitted Chapters of History Disclosed in the Life and Papers of Edmund Randolph*. New York: G.P. Putnam's Sons, 1888.
Edwards, Samuel. *Rebel!: A Biography of Tom Paine*. New York: Praeger, 1974.
Eidelberg, Paul. *The Philosophy of the American Constitution*. New York: Free Press, 1968.
Elliot, Jonathan, ed. *The Debates in the Several State Conventions on the Adoption of the Federal Constitution*, vol. 2. New York: Lippincott, 1861.
Farrand, Max. *The Framing of the Constitution of the United States*. New Haven: Yale Univ Pr, 1913.

―――――, ed. *The Records of the Federal Convention of 1787*, vol. 2. New Haven: Yale Univ Pr, 1937.
Flexner, James Thomas. *George Washington and the New Nation (1783–1793)*. Boston: Little, Brown, 1969.
Freeman, Douglas Southall. *George Washington: A Biography*, vol. 6. New York: Scribner's, 1954.
Hall, Alice J. *National Geographic* (July 1975) 148:92–123.
Hall, Van Beck. *Politics Without Parties: Massachusetts, 1780–1791*. Pittsburgh: Univ of Pittsburgh Pr, 1972.
Hamilton, Alexander, John Jay, & James Madison. *The Federalist*. New York: Modern Library, 1937.
Hecht, Marie B. *Odd Destiny: The Life of Alexander Hamilton*. New York: Macmillan, 1982.
Hehir, J. Bryan. *New Yorker* (24 Feb 1986) 62:105.
Hendrick, Burton J. *Bulwark of the Republic*. Boston: Little, Brown, 1937.
Hill, Helen. *George Mason, Constitutionalist*. Cambridge: Harvard Univ Pr, 1938.
Kaufman, Irving R. *New York Times Magazine*, 23 Feb 1986, pp. 42 ff.
Ketcham, Ralph. *James Madison*. New York: Macmillan, 1971.
Krauel, Richard. *American Historical Review* (Oct 1911) 17:46–51.
Little, David. *Arizona Republic*, 28 Sep 1985, p. D4.
McCrady, Edward. *The History of South Carolina in the Revolution, 1775–1780*. New York: Russell & Russell, 1969. Reprint of 1901 ed.
McDonald, Forrest. *We the People: The Economic Origins of the Constitution*. Chicago: Univ of Chicago Pr, 1958.
Meister, Charles W. *American Literature* (May 1952) 24:158–9.
Mintz, Max M. *Gouverneur Morris and the American Revolution*. Norman: Univ of Oklahoma Pr, 1970.
Mississippi Valley Historical Review (Sep 1953) 40:259.
Moore, Virginia. *The Madisons: A Biography*. New York: McGraw-Hill, 1979.
Morris, Richard B., ed. *Alexander Hamilton and the Founding of the Nation*. New York: Dial Pr, 1957.
―――――. *Seven Who Shaped Our Destiny*. New York: Harper & Row, 1973.
Mott, Frank Luther & Chester E. Jorgenson. *Benjamin Franklin*. New York: American Book Company, 1936.
Nevins, Jane. *New York Times Magazine*, 22 Sep 1985, pp. 106 ff.
Newhouse, John. *New Yorker* (10 Feb 1986) 61:88.
New York Times, 3 Nov 1985, 4:4.
Pacheco, Josephine F., ed. *The Legacy of George Mason*. Fairfax, VA: George Mason Univ Pr, 1983.
Pease, Theodore C. *Mississippi Valley Historical Review* (Sep 1938) 25: 171.
Prescott, Arthur Taylor. *Drafting the Federal Constitution*. New York: Greenwood Pr, 1968. Reprint of 1941 ed.
Prescott, Frederick C., ed. *Alexander Hamilton and Thomas Jefferson*. New York: American Book Company, 1934.
Reardon, John J. *Edmund Randolph: A Biography*. New York: Macmillan, 1974.
Rossiter, Clinton. *1787: The Grand Convention*. New York: Macmillan, 1966.
Rutland, Robert Allen. *George Mason: Reluctant Statesman*. Williamsburg, VA: Colonial Williamsburg, 1961.
Schultz, Harold S. *James Madison*. Boston: Twayne, 1970.
Seed, Geoffrey. *James Wilson*. Millwood, NY: KTO Press, 1978.

Smith, Charles Page. *James Wilson, Founding Father, 1742–1798*. Chapel Hill: Univ of North Carolina Pr, 1956.
Smith, James Morton, ed. *The Constitution*. New York: Harper & Row, 1971.
Stevens, John Paul. *New York Times*, 27 Oct 1985, 4:1.
Swiggett, Howard. *The Extraordinary Mr. Morris*. Garden City, New York: Doubleday, 1952.
Umbreit, Kenneth B. *Our Eleven Chief Justices*. New York: Harper, 1938.
Van Doren, Carl. *Benjamin Franklin*. New York: Viking Press, 1938.
―――――. *The Great Rehearsal*. New York: Time-Life Books, 1965.
Wallace, David Duncan. *South Carolina: A Short History*. Chapel Hill: Univ of North Carolina Pr, 1951.
Ward, Geoffrey C. *New York Times Book Review*, 1 Aug 1982, p. 11.
Whitney, David C. *Founders of Freedom in America*. Chicago: J.G. Ferguson, 1965.
Williams, Frances Leigh. *A Founding Family: The Pinckneys of South Carolina*. New York: Harcourt Brace Jovanovich, 1978.
Zahniser, Marvin R. *Charles Cotesworth Pinckney: Founding Father*. Chapel Hill: Univ of North Carolina Pr, 1967.

Index

Adams, Abigail 90, 265, 292, 312, 338-9, 352
Adams, Brooks 347
Adams, John 51, 67, 172, 194, 259, 292, 300, 303, 312, 373, 386; congressman 87, 89, 91, 276, 298-301, 326, 344, 352; Constitution v, 2, 4, 11-2, 37, 39, 122; diplomat 54, 87; president 63-5, 134-7, 158, 160, 168, 207-8, 228-37, 346; vice president 47, 158, 227, 265, 289, 308, 343
Adams, John Quincy 159, 170, 172, 265
Adams, Samuel 12, 45, 51, 84, 96, 108, 181, 276-7, 352
Addison, Joseph 142, 270, 319, 350
Adet, Pierre 228, 264
Administration of Justice Act 6
Albany Plan of Union 38, 79
Alden, John R. 321
Algerian pirates 343
Alien & Sedition Acts 158, 234-5, 267
Alison, Francis 350
Allen, Ethan 299, 301
amendments (to Constitution) 39, 42, 44, 103, 105, 108, 151-2, 154, 184, 186-8, 210, 237, 250, 252-3, 255, 306-8, 338, 371, 376
American Bible Society 238
American Colonization Society 169
American Philosophical Society 12, 72, 78, 87, 147, 359
Ames, Nathaniel 294
Andre, John 118
Annan, Robert 349
Annapolis Convention 11, 122, 148, 184, 246
Antieau, C.J. 375
Antigua 213

Arabia 247
Arbuthnot, *Admiral* 282
Aristotle 142, 153-4
Armstrong, John 350
Armstrong, John, *General* 165, 278
Arnold, Benedict 52, 118, 189, 199, 242-3, 297, 299, 328
Articles of Confederation 2-3, 6-10, 13, 18-9, 22-3, 25, 28, 38, 41-3, 52, 54, 56, 99, 107-9, 119-23, 148-50, 190, 222, 225, 243, 247-8, 279, 285, 287, 289, 301, 311, 328, 335, 354, 358, 365, 382, 388, 390
Asgill, Charles 118, 329
Association 6, 114, 177, 299, 311, 320, 351-2
Australia 3
Austria 205-6, 231, 293

Bache, Benjamin Franklin 345
Bacon, Francis 142
Bacon, Matthew 49, 193
Bagehot, Walter 3
balance of powers 16, 26, 36-7, 108, 152, 180, 187, 287, 307, 345, 364, 371, 376, 383
Baldwin, Abraham 13, 14, 26, 362
Baldwin, Roger Sherman 300
Baltimore, Lord 320
Bancroft, Edward 88
Bancroft, George 29, 265, 304
Bank of North America 8, 92, 200, 244, 356, 359, 371
Bank of Pennsylvania 356
Bank of the United States 163, 168
Barbados 314
Barber, Francis 114
Barlow, Joel 63

411

Barnwell, Robert W., Jr. 284
Barras, *Comte de* 328
Bassett, Burwell 322
Bassett, Richard 13, 27
Bayard, James 137-8
Beard, Charles 15, 83, 322, 381-3
Beaujeu, *Captain* 316
Beaumarchais, Pierre Caron de 88, 232, 325
Bedford, Gunning 13, 26, 28, 35, 48, 142, 205
Beethoven, Ludwig van 84
Belgium 3, 269
Bellamy, Joseph 47
Bellamy, Mr. (XYZ Affair) 232
Berkeley, George 348-9
Bible 48, 238, 293, 368, 387, 392
bicameral legislature 3, 19-20, 24, 36, 149, 248
Bicentennial Commission 374
bill of rights 40, 42, 44, 107, 126, 151, 179, 181, 186-8, 225, 252-3, 308, 363, 365, 376, 379-80, 384
Bingham, William 199, 353, 357
Bird, Mark 350, 357-8, 371
Blackstone, William 49, 114-5, 193, 213, 275, 349
Blair, Hugh 348
Blair, John 14, 289
Blake, John 289-90
Blount, William 13
Boardman, Roger Sherman 306, 310
Boles, Peter 297
Boone, Thomas 272-3
Bos, *Abbé du* 161
Bossuet, Jacques 193
Boston Massacre 194
Boston Port Bill 6
Boston Tea Party 6, 84-5, 143, 177, 275
Botetourt, Norborne 176
Boudinot, Elias 114
Bowdoin, James 97-9, 101
boycott 5-6, 82-3, 114, 161, 176-8, 214, 276-7, 297-9, 320, 333, 351
Brackenridge, Hugh Henry 48, 142
Braddock, Edward 79, 316-7
Bradford, Andrew 69-71, 74
Bradford, William 142-3, 262-3
Bradhurst, Samuel 139
Brant, Irving 265

Brazil 3
Brearley, David 13, 22
Brennan, William J., Jr. 375-6
Brillon, Madame 90
Broglie, Prince de 200
Broom, Jacob 13
Brown, Robert E. 382
Brown, William G. 57, 67
Bryce, James 3, 347, 353, 359, 373
Bunyan, John 69
Burger, Warren E. 374
Burgoyne, John 8, 89, 196, 220, 281, 301, 326
Burke, Aedanus 221, 284
Burke, Edmund 82, 86, 89, 151, 385
Burlamaqui, Jean Jacques 15, 36, 114, 142, 349
Burnett, William 70
Burr, Aaron 48, 121, 132, 136, 138-40, 142, 157, 205, 208, 235, 237, 261
Bute, *Lord* 23, 81
Butler, Nicholas Murray 140
Butler, Pierce 13, 22, 29-33, 102, 285, 372
Byron, *Lord* 143

Cadwalader, John 326
Caesar, Julius 113, 132, 294
Calhoun, John C. 57-8
Callender, James 137
Calvert, Eleanor 320
Campbell, William 216
Canaan Company 357
Canada 3, 6, 50, 80-1, 83, 91, 109, 116, 165-7, 194, 198, 208, 210, 244, 297, 300, 315, 341, 345, 352, 386
Carleton, Guy 329
Carlisle, Lord 197, 327
Carmichael, William 204
Carpenter, Anthony 295
Carroll, Daniel 13
Carter, Landon 317
Catherine the Great 9, 199
Cervantes, Miguel de 313
Charles I 37
Charles II 269, 298

Chase, Samuel 61, 117
Chastellux, *Marquis de* 359, 378
check and balance system *see* balance of powers
Chesterfield, *Lord* 203
Chief Justice 60–3, 256, 260, 289–90, 303, 367
China 45, 371
Chisholm v. Georgia 256, 370
Church, John B. 121, 139
Cicero 15, 349, 366
Cincinnati, Society of the 12, 122, 139, 238, 245, 247, 332–3, 359, 378
civil rights 36, 115, 152, 155, 168, 181, 187, 195, 235, 256, 308, 321, 323, 362–3, 365, 376–7, 379–80
Claiborne, William 163
Clap, Thomas 47
Clark, Abraham 13
Clark, George Rogers 146, 183, 247, 260, 327
Clarke, Alured 86
Clay, Henry 170, 172
Clinton, DeWitt 165
Clinton, George 45, 117–8, 121, 132, 198, 210, 254, 330
Clinton, Henry 219–20, 278, 282, 324, 326–9, 355, 387
Clymer, George 13, 354
Cockburn, George 166
Coercive Acts 352
Cogswell, William 151
Coke, Edward 173, 270
Coles, Edward 163–4
Coles, Isaac 163
Colleton, John 273
Collinson, Peter 76
Columbia College (King's College) 55, 114–5, 139, 192–3, 209, 309, 320
committee of correspondence 5, 84, 194, 214, 351
Committee of Detail 37–8, 57, 95, 104, 223, 250, 287–8, 362, 365, 380
Committee of Style and Arrangement 38–9, 186, 202, 362
Committee of the Whole 18, 20–1, 95, 100–1, 104, 249, 335, 374
Committee on Postponed Matters 38, 202, 306
common law 49, 61, 133, 368, 375, 387
Condorcet, *Marquis de* 90
Congreve, William 270
Connecticut 4, 7, 13, 19–20, 25, 28–9, 43, 45, 47, 49–53, 55–8, 61, 66–7, 92, 97, 101, 110, 165, 191, 286, 293–304, 307–10, 338, 352, 357, 374, 389
Connecticut's Fundamental Orders 38
consent of the governed 16, 214, 217, 299, 364, 368, 378, 382
Constable, William 199, 203, 205
Constitution v, vi, 1–47, 56–60, 62, 66, 92, 101, 103–5, 107–8, 112, 122–6, 129, 133, 136–7, 140, 150–3, 155, 158–9, 162–3, 165, 167–8, 170–2, 181–2, 184, 187–8, 190, 195, 200, 204, 208, 210–1, 225, 239–40, 247, 250–4, 256, 259, 266, 278, 286, 289, 291–2, 306–8, 310–1, 333–8, 340, 343, 357, 362–6, 368–9, 371, 374–7, 380–4, 387–93
Constitutional Convention v, 1–46, 48, 55–8, 68, 92, 95, 100–9, 114, 122–4, 141–2, 148–52, 184–6, 189, 201–4, 210, 222–5, 228, 247–51, 254, 258, 284–9, 292, 301, 303–8, 310, 333–6, 344, 359–64, 366–7, 372–5, 377–8, 380, 382, 386–7, 389, 391–2
Continental Association *see* Association
Continental Congress 6–9, 13–4, 25, 29, 48, 51–5, 58, 86–9, 93, 95, 97–100, 109–10, 114–5, 117–8, 120–2, 144–50, 177, 179, 182, 194, 196–200, 215, 240–4, 276–9, 282, 286, 298–303, 305, 307, 310–1, 321–30, 333–5, 337, 351–62, 367, 375
Convention *see* Constitutional Convention
Conway, Thomas 326
Cooke, Mary 272
Cooper, Charles 138
Cooper, Myles 115
Cornwallis, *Lord* 9, 116, 119, 183, 219, 242–3, 282–3, 324–5, 328–9

Cosby, William 191
council of revision 19, 103, 151, 195, 362
Coxe, Tench 235, 237
Craik, James 336
Crèvecoeur, Jean de 8, 44, 391
Croswell, Harry 137-8
Cruger, Nicholas 113
Cuba 281
Cushing, Thomas 84, 107, 299
Cushing, William 61, 256
Custis, Daniel 319
Custis, John 319-20, 322, 339
Custis, Martha (Patsy) 319-20
Cutler, Manasseh 102

Daggett, Naphtali 297
Dagworthy, John 317
Dana, Francis 13, 100
Daniel, Peter 268
Danton, Georges 90, 159
Dartmouth College 63
Davie, William 13, 25-6, 63, 282, 360
Deane, Silas 87-9, 145, 198, 303, 371
Declaration of Independence 6-7, 13, 87, 142, 144, 146, 152, 169, 179, 181, 190, 195, 217, 225, 279, 300, 311, 323, 352, 382
Declaratory Act 5
Defoe, Daniel 69, 73
deism 15, 71, 245, 279, 331, 391
DeKalb, *Baron* Johann 217, 282, 325
DeLancey, Peter 214, 275
DeLaumoy, *Colonel* 219
Delaware 8, 11-3, 15, 20, 23-4, 26, 28-9, 38, 43, 52, 74, 97, 101, 150, 181, 246, 359-60
democracy 15, 21, 36-7, 41, 92, 123, 125-6, 137, 139, 148, 152, 171, 187, 203, 208, 249, 279, 333, 335, 343-5, 353, 359-60, 364, 367-8, 378-9, 382-3, 392
Demosthenes 51, 366
Denham, Thomas 70
DeSaussure, Henry 236
d'Estaing, *Count* Charles 281, 327

Diamond, Martin 15
Dickinson, John 12-4, 20-1, 30, 38, 81, 105, 146, 275, 301, 324, 349, 352-4
Dinwiddie, Robert 315, 317-9
District of Columbia 59, 128, 163, 166, 188-9, 309, 339
Douglass, David 274
Drayton, Charles 215
Drayton, William Henry 216, 277, 279
Drummer, Jeremiah 293
Dryden, John 312
Duane, James 6, 118, 301
Dunmore, John 144, 178, 241, 319, 323
Duvall, Gabriel 267
Dwight, Timothy 50, 51

Edinburgh University 348-9
education (views of framers) 383-4
Edwards, Jonathan 47, 73, 140
Edwards, Jonathan, Jr. 310
Eidelberg, Paul 384
electoral college 33-4, 38, 44, 56, 104, 136, 158, 165, 185, 305, 344, 359, 364, 384
Elliot, Jonathan 171
Ellsworth, Abigail 49, 52
Ellsworth, Oliver 47-67, 235, 303, 374, 377, 391; chief justice 60-3; congressman 51-5, 120; diplomat 63-6, 386; final years 66-7; framer 13, 21, 25-6, 28, 30-2, 37, 55-7, 104-5, 287-8, 303, 306, 391; lawyer 49-51, 370; ratifier 57-8; senator 58-60, 310, 370, 383; youth 47-9
Ellzey, William 316
Ely, Samuel 96, 97
embargo 156, 161-2
Emerson, Ralph Waldo 140, 287
England *see* Great Britain
Erie Canal 163, 210
established church 4, 8, 67, 143-5, 147, 151, 179, 182, 217, 245, 331, 390-1
Europe 29, 39, 53, 58, 76, 88, 91, 129, 147, 163, 191, 194, 207, 209,

230, 233, 329, 332-3, 345-7, 359, 366-7, 372, 387, 389
executive branch 32-5, 43, 102, 106, 123, 125, 137, 149-50, 156, 187, 202, 248-50, 288, 305, 338, 346, 359-60, 362, 364, 371, 376, 379, 387

Fairfax, Bryan 320
Fairfax, George William 314, 316, 318
Fairfax, *Lord* 246, 314
Fairfax, Sally 316, 318-9
Fairfax, William 313
Fairfax County militia 178-9
Fairfax Resolves 177-9
Fallon, James 220
Farquhar, George 270
Farrand, Max 359, 384
Fauchet, Joseph 260, 262-6
Fauchet Affair 262-6
Fauntleroy, Betsy 314
The Federalist 36, 39, 42-3, 124-5, 127, 148, 152, 155-6, 169, 340, 376, 384, 389
Fenno, John 130, 155, 258, 342
Fenwick, Joseph 189
Ferguson, E. James 382
Ferguson, Patrick 283
Few, William 13
Findley, William 353
Fitzsimons, Thomas 13, 361
Flahaut, Adelaide de 204-5, 208
Flahaut, *Count* de 204, 208
Flexner, James T. 345
Florida 53, 159, 163, 260, 346
Forbes, John 318
Fox, Charles James 86, 140
France 5, 8-9, 23, 60-1, 63-5, 75-6, 78, 80, 82, 87-93, 130, 132-3, 135, 145, 147, 154, 156, 158-61, 163-5, 167, 175, 181, 183, 196, 198-9, 203-8, 228-35, 242-4, 256-66, 269, 315-8, 323, 325-8, 330, 333, 336, 339, 344, 345-6, 369, 371, 386, 389
Franklin (state) 284
Franklin, Benjamin 68-94, 134, 177, 312, 316, 345, 350, 359, 374, 378, 380, 386, 391; civic improver 72-3; colonial agent 80-6; final years 93-4; framer v, 1, 6, 12-4, 16-7, 20, 22, 25-7, 29, 31, 33-4, 38, 40-1, 54, 92, 108, 143, 170, 202, 223-4, 286, 304, 336, 392; patriot & diplomat 54, 86-92, 145, 198, 300, 320, 327, 352, 385-6; printer 69-72; publisher 73-5; scientist 76-7; statesman 77-80, 301; youth 49, 68-9
Franklin, Deborah 72, 82, 86, 350
Franklin, James 68-9, 75
Franklin, William 72, 78-81, 83, 86
Franklin, William Temple 80, 88
Free Masons 73, 78, 90, 241, 268, 314, 331, 391
freedom of the press 107, 158, 180, 191, 230, 258, 342, 380
Freeman, Douglas Southall 3, 332, 337
French & Indian War 315-9
French Revolution 93, 130, 135, 154, 159, 189, 194, 203-8, 227-8, 344, 386
Freneau, Philip 48, 130, 142, 155, 258, 264, 342, 345
Fry, Joshua 315
Furman, Richard 238
Furman University 238
Furneaux, Philip 144

Gadsden, Christopher 216, 218, 239, 272-3, 275, 278
Gage, Thomas 299, 320, 352
Gallatin, Albert 136, 162-3, 169, 267
Galloway, Joseph 276, 291, 350
Garrick, David 270
Gates, Horatio 117, 196-7, 265, 282, 301, 321-2, 326, 328
Gênet, Edmond 64, 207, 227-8, 256-8, 260
George II 212
George III 5, 6, 44, 81-2, 84-5, 87, 89, 162, 196, 213-4, 269-70, 275, 305, 347, 351, 392
Georgia 3, 7-8, 12-3, 22, 24-6, 28, 43, 56-7, 75, 82, 97, 153, 188,

216, 234, 250, 256, 286, 292, 328, 339, 370
Gérard, Conrad 197
Germany 269, 333
Gerry, Elbridge 57, 108, 259; diplomat 229-33; framer 13, 15, 20-2, 25-6, 30-2, 34, 41, 100-2, 107, 149, 186, 223-4, 305, 360-1, 383; legislator 51, 97, 110
Gervais, John 283
Giles, W.B. 258
Gilman, Nicholas 13
Gimat, John Joseph 119
Gladstone, William 2
Glanville, Ranulf de 270
Glen, James 212
global village 386, 388-90
Glover, John 117, 324
Gordon, William 118
Gorham, Nathaniel 95-111, 120, 186, 374-5; congressman 96-7; framer 13-4, 18, 22, 25, 27, 30-1, 35, 37, 40, 57, 100-9, 249, 305, 335, 380; land speculator 109-11; president of Congress 97-100
Gorham, Rebecca 95
Grand Company of Pennsylvania 177
Grasse, *Comte* de 328
Graves, Thomas 329
Grayson, William 97-8, 153, 189
Great Awakening 293
Great Britain 4-6, 9, 14, 23, 25, 30, 37, 42, 48, 53-4, 60, 62-5, 76, 78-87, 89, 91, 115-20, 122, 128, 130-5, 146-7, 154, 156, 159-68, 174-9, 182, 189, 193-200, 204-5, 207-8, 210, 212-21, 227-9, 231, 236, 240-5, 256-7, 260-6, 269-70, 272-83, 285-6, 288, 290, 293-302, 305, 307, 311, 313, 315-30, 337, 339, 341, 345, 347-52, 355, 360-1, 368, 371, 380-1, 387-9
Great Compromise 22, 27-46, 56, 92, 101-2, 150, 201, 223, 249-50, 287, 301, 304, 360
Greece 287
Greene, Nathaniel 200, 220-1, 282-3, 302, 324, 328
Greenwood, John 340
Grenville, *Lord* 133, 262-3, 320
Grimké, James 272

Grimké, John 289
Griswold, Roger 48
Grotius, Hugo 114, 133, 192
Guizot, François 140

habeas corpus 38, 96, 126, 168, 179
Hadrian 187, 379
Haley, John 214, 275
Hall, Van Beck 96
Hallet, Stephen 339
Hamilton, Alexander 65, 110, 112-40, 146, 148, 150-7, 163, 168-9, 189, 290, 308, 312, 373-4, 377, 381, 383, 386-7, 389, 391; final years 138-40, 208-9, 237-8; framer v, 1, 2, 10-1, 13-5, 21, 23-5, 33, 36, 38, 42-3, 57, 100, 104, 122-4, 201, 203, 254, 362, 378-80; lawyer 120-1, 137-8; legislator 54, 120-2, 196; politician 61, 63, 134-7, 194, 228, 235-7; ratifier 124-6; secretary of treasury 59, 60, 110, 126-34, 227, 255-61, 263, 266, 309, 339-41, 343, 345-6, 367, 383; soldier 116-20, 233-4, 301, 325, 385; youth 112-6
Hamilton, Betsey Schuyler 117, 121, 135, 137-9, 208, 301
Hammond, George 131, 133, 262, 265-6, 341
Hancock, John v, 12, 96, 98, 101, 108, 296, 352
Harper, Robert G. 231
Harrington, James 349, 387
Harrison, Benjamin 44
Harrison, Mary 350
Harrison, Richard Henry 289
Hartford Convention 167, 210
Harvard College 77, 237, 332
Hat Act 294
Hauteval, Lucien 231
Hayne, Robert 170
Hehir, J. Bryan 389
Helvetius, Madame 90
Henry, Patrick 61, 63, 242, 261, 311; Constitution v, 12, 13, 45; legislator 145, 184, 240, 245, 276, 352; patriot 144, 176, 179, 182;

ratification 39, 44, 152-3, 187-8, 251-3
Henry, Prince of Prussia 99-100, 102
Henry IV of France (Henry of Navarre) 187, 366, 369, 379, 389
Hessians 323, 325-6
Hite, Isaac 246
Hoar, George F. 310
Hoban, James 339
Hobbes, Thomas 114, 142, 154
Hofstadter, Richard 382
Hogendorp, Gijsbert van 200
Holland (Netherlands) 2, 9, 54, 229-30, 257, 344
Holland Company 372
Hollister, G.H. 51, 309
Hooker, Richard 349, 368
Hooper, Robert 357
Hopkinson, Francis 12, 353, 365
Horry, Daniel 219, 272
Hottinguer, Jean 230-2
Houdon, Jean 89, 191, 204, 330
House of Representatives 15, 19, 21-2, 25-7, 34, 36-8, 56, 60, 92, 102, 105, 107, 110, 123, 128-9, 136-7, 149, 152-6, 185, 201-2, 208, 210, 223, 233, 248-50, 255-6, 287-8, 304-5, 307-10, 335, 338, 342-3, 345, 360-1, 364, 378, 380, 384
Houston, John 218
Houston, William 13, 142
Howe, Richard 85, 87
Howe, Robert 55, 218, 220, 280
Howe, William 87, 323-5, 327
Huddy, Joshua 118, 329
Huger, Daniel 238
human rights *see* civil rights; natural rights
Hume, David 81, 114-5, 149, 154, 348-9, 356, 378
Humphreys, David 2, 339
Hunt, Samuel 138
Hutcheson, Francis 348-9
Hutchinson, Thomas 5, 84-5, 143

Iceland 353
Illinois 361

Illinois-Wabash Company 356-7
impeachment 34, 202, 250, 305
India 45
Indiana 361
Indians 5, 12, 78-9, 81-3, 110, 145, 147, 169, 175, 177, 181, 215, 218, 240, 247, 253, 262, 269, 274-5, 279, 287, 293, 300, 314-7, 319, 323, 326-7, 333, 339, 341, 345-6, 352, 357, 380, 384
Ingersoll, Charles Jared 162
Ingersoll, Jared 13, 61, 297
international court 370, 375, 388, 390
international law 61-2, 121, 133, 160, 225, 227-8, 257, 265, 282, 348, 369-70, 375, 385-90
Iredell, James 372-3
Ireland 83, 211, 333
Italy 91, 333

Jackson, Andrew 3, 167, 170-1, 379
Jackson, Francis 162
Jackson, John 163
Jackson, William 17
James I 37
Jay, John 2, 6, 12, 43, 114, 124, 191, 200, 227, 259, 289, 370; chief justice 256, 258, 260, 289-90, 367; diplomat 60, 64-5, 98, 133, 146, 160; legislator 51, 115-7, 195, 352
Jay's Treaty 60, 64-5, 133, 160, 207, 227-9, 261-2, 264-5, 290, 345, 387
Jefferson, Thomas 125-6, 133, 140, 143-4, 148, 189, 240, 245, 265, 289-90, 312-3, 329, 331, 336, 344-5, 370, 373, 379-80, 391; congressman 182, 299, 300, 303; Constitution v, 12, 18, 42-5, 149, 151-2, 187-8, 252, 285; Declaration of Independence 181, 300; diplomat 91, 183, 203-4, 243, 336; final years 169-70, 172; governor 36, 145, 147, 242-3, 245, 328; Kentucky Resolutions 136, 158, 165, 171, 234, 267, 346; patriot 29, 173, 182, 240; president

63, 66-7, 134, 136-7, 158-62, 168, 208, 236-8, 267, 340; secretary of state 59, 60, 65, 112, 128, 130-2, 156, 164, 205, 227, 255-9, 309, 339-44; state legislator 86-7, 144, 182, 240; vice president 100, 135, 158, 228-30, 233-4, 267, 346; Virginia Statute for Religious Freedom 147, 181, 183, 245
Jeffries, John 91
Jenifer, Daniel of St. Thomas 13, 16
Jensen, Merrill 382
Jesus Christ 71, 213, 268, 293, 346, 391
Jews 44, 71, 145, 199, 331, 391
Johnson, Andrew 35
Johnson Thomas 257
Johnson William 274
Johnson, William Samuel 13-4, 18, 21, 25, 28, 38, 55, 58, 107, 123, 298, 309
Johnston, Samuel 372
Jones, John Paul 206
Jones, Joseph 146
judicial branch 35-6, 43-4, 47, 53, 59, 102-3, 125, 149-50, 187, 249, 255, 287, 305-7, 354-5, 357, 360, 362, 364-5, 376, 387
Judiciary Act of 1789 53, 58-9, 62, 255
Jumonville, *Sieur* de 315
Junto 70, 72-3
jury trial 38, 107, 126, 178, 180, 186, 363, 369

Kalm, Peter 74
Kames, *Lord* 80, 349
Kant, Immanuel 76
Kaufman, Irving R. 376
Keats, John 143
Keimer, Samuel 70, 71
Keith, William 70
Kent, James 137
Kentucky 15, 147, 156, 234, 247, 261
Kentucky Resolutions 136, 158, 165, 171, 234, 267, 346
Kenyon, Lord 65
Ketcham, Ralph 131, 143, 171, 382, 384, 392

King, Rufus 63, 65-6, 99, 108, 209, 233, 237, 258; framer 13, 21, 24, 26, 28-9, 31, 39, 100-2, 106-7
Kingsley, James 310
Knox, Henry 2, 9, 12, 110, 200, 233-4, 253, 257, 260-1, 323, 332, 334, 336, 340-1
Knox, Hugh 113
Krauel, Richard 100

Lafayette, *Marquis* de 119, 181, 196, 203-5, 217, 238, 243, 325, 328, 332, 336, 347, 378, 385
land speculation 14-5, 83, 109-11, 134, 146-7, 175, 207, 254, 298, 309, 319-20, 322, 332, 336, 344, 346-7, 350, 352, 356-7, 367, 371-3, 382
Langdon, John 13, 32
Lansing, John 13, 24, 122
Laurens, Henry 9, 13, 51, 117, 119, 214, 272
Laurens, John 327
Law, Richard 303
Lear, Tobias 332
Lee, Arthur 88-9, 146
Lee, Charles 50, 117, 217, 278-9, 321-2, 324, 327
Lee, Henry 48, 142, 188, 219
Lee, Richard 128
Lee, Richard Henry 9, 12-3, 44-5, 51, 144-6, 153, 176, 300, 358
Leibnitz, Gottfried von 90
Leigh, Egerton 272
Leigh, Peter 212
Leland, John 151
L'Enfant, Pierre Charles 339
Lennox, William 272
Lewis, Betty 337
Lewis, Morgan 138, 142
Liberia 169
Lillo, George 270
Lincoln, Abraham 3, 168, 201, 313
Lincoln, Benjamin 218-20, 281, 328
Little Compromise 286
Littleton, Thomas 173
Livingston, Catherine 193
Livingston, Gilbert 126
Livingston, Henry W. 208

Livingston, Robert R. 192, 194–5, 199, 208, 259, 300, 337, 352
Livingston, William 13–4, 114, 192–3
Locke, John 15, 37, 45, 114, 142, 155, 169, 179, 192, 300, 349, 379
Loudon, *Earl of* 317
Louis XVI 91, 156, 203, 205–6, 256
Louisiana 208, 260
Louisiana Purchase 159, 208, 237, 340
Lowell, John 165
Lowndes, Rawlins 225, 289
Luzerne, *Chevalier de la* 146

McCloskey, R.G. 373
McClurg, James 14
McCrady, Edward 282
McDaniel, Mary 314
McDonald, Forrest 382
McDougall, Alexander 114
McHenry, James 13, 135–6, 187, 234–5
McKenney, Thomas 171
Mackenzie, Robert 321
McKnight, Charles 338
Maclay, William 338
Macon, Nathaniel 163
Madison, Dolley 157, 159, 162–4, 166–71
Madison, James 100, 103–5, 112, 120, 124, 134, 141–73, 183, 185, 187–9, 289, 312, 318, 331, 339, 373–4, 376, 389, 391; Continental Congress 54, 86, 145–8; final years 168–72; framer 2, 3, 7, 11–2, 14–22, 24–9, 31–2, 34–40, 42–3, 46, 123, 148–51, 201–2, 223, 249, 287–8, 304, 306, 308–9, 333–5, 359–60, 362, 377, 379, 382; president 161–8, 210, 238, 340; ratifier 124, 151–3, 251–2, 254, 376, 384; Republican opposition leader 60, 93, 127–33, 153–8, 230, 234, 255–6, 258–9, 264–5, 267, 290, 340, 342–6, 376; secretary of state 59, 159–61, 387; youth 48, 141–3
Magna Carta 42, 179, 287

Main, Jackson Turner 382
Maine 69, 101, 108
Malone, Dumas 131, 340
Mangin, Jared 273
Marbury, John 59
Marie Antoinette 90
Marion, Francis 220, 282, 328
Markham, William 213
Marshall, John 12, 52, 59, 171, 228–33, 246, 373
Martin, Alexander 13, 142
Martin, Luther 1, 13, 24, 26, 30, 41, 48, 58
Martineau, Harriet 171, 389
Maryland 8, 10–1, 13, 15, 28, 32, 43, 52, 74, 117, 136, 166, 173–4, 176, 181, 187, 225, 258, 261, 277, 289, 317, 324, 328, 332, 339, 357
Mason, Ann 174
Mason, George 173–90, 311, 370, 374, 378, 380, 387, 391; Fairfax Resolves 177–9, 321; final years 188–90; framer 14, 16, 18, 20–1, 24, 26–7, 30–6, 38–40, 46, 100, 184–6, 224, 248–9, 288, 305, 360, 376, 379, 383; legislator 146, 182–4; patriot 176–7, 327; planter 173–6, 320; Virginia Declaration of Rights 144, 179–82, 300; Virginia Ratification Convention 57, 151, 153, 186–8, 251
Mason, John 114
Mason, Sarah 183
Massachusetts 3–8, 11, 13, 20, 27–9, 35, 37, 41, 43, 45, 58, 79, 82, 84, 86, 95–102, 104, 106–7, 109–11, 148, 155, 165, 178, 222, 252, 276–7, 286, 292, 295, 299, 301, 304–5, 317, 321, 323–4, 332, 352, 360, 371
Mather, Cotton 69–70
Mather, Increase 73
Mazzei, Philip 185, 346
Mellimelli 160–1
Mercer, George 176
Mercer, John 173, 175
Mercer, John Francis 13, 32, 146
Mercier, James 247
Meredith, Gertrude 209
Meredith, Hugh 70
mesmerism 91

Michigan 361
Middleton, Arthur 216, 219
Middleton, Henry 215, 219, 221
Mifflin, Thomas 355
militia 32, 47, 50, 56, 78, 97, 99, 101, 123, 161, 165-6, 175, 178, 180, 224, 247, 278-81, 299, 306, 338, 341, 344, 351, 355, 371
Miranda, Francisco de 135
Molasses Act 295
Moncrieff, Richard 272
Monroe, James 44, 147, 164, 167, 172, 258; Constitution 12, 336; diplomat 64, 159-60, 207, 228, 261, 346; legislator 135, 153, 205; president 99, 100
Montague, Charles 215
Montaigne, Michel de 142
Montesquieu, *Baron de* 16, 36, 114, 142, 349, 364-5
Moore, Benjamin 139
Moore, William 354
Morgan, Daniel 328
Morgan, Forrest 302
Morier, John 164
Morris, Anne Randolph 209-11
Morris, Gouverneur 121, 137, 140, 191-211, 374, 377-8, 383, 385-6, 391; diplomat 63, 133, 203-7, 256-7, 260-1, 309, 386; final years 207-11; framer 1, 6, 13-5, 19, 26-9, 31, 34, 36, 38, 39, 103, 105, 184, 201-3, 304, 334, 336, 361-2, 379-80, 387; legislator 51, 193-8, 208, 276, 356; youth 191-3
Morris, Lewis (grandfather of Gouverneur) 191
Morris, Lewis (half-brother of Gouverneur) 195
Morris, Robert 121, 206, 312, 339, 353, 355-6, 359, 371-2; financier 53-4, 120, 127, 199, 205, 207, 244, 356, 364, 372; framer 8, 13-4, 17, 27, 360-1; land speculator 110, 203, 350; legislator 51-2, 353-4
Morris, Staats Long 195, 200
Morse, Jedidiah 169
Moslems 44, 71, 160, 331, 346, 391-2
Motte, Rebecca 219
Moultrie, William 216, 218, 220, 278-80

Mount Vernon 10, 12, 153, 175, 184, 224, 246, 263, 313-4, 316, 322, 328-30, 333, 336-7, 344, 347
Mozart, Wolfgang 84
Münchhausen, *Baron* Karl von 82
Murat, Joachim 159
Murray, William Vans 63, 234

Napoleon Bonaparte 63-5, 140, 159-60, 164, 167, 208, 210, 230, 233-4, 347
national bank 60, 118, 121, 128-9, 155, 159-60, 171, 255, 266, 309, 340, 356, 381
national debt 60, 127-9, 132, 134, 154-5, 186, 200, 306, 333, 341-2, 374, 381, 383
national university 163, 306, 338, 347, 384
natural law 15-6, 115, 179, 192-3, 320, 349, 368-9, 385-8, 392
natural rights 4, 10, 15-6, 304, 379-80, 386
navigation act 31, 57, 106, 148, 168, 176, 186, 224, 250, 273, 286-8, 381
Nelson, Thomas 13
Nelson, William 176
Netherlands *see* Holland
neutrality 54, 60, 62, 64, 257, 260, 266
New England 4, 32, 37, 63, 67, 106, 162, 165-7, 224, 233, 237, 273, 288-9, 292, 321, 326, 338
New England Confederation 5
New England Primer 293
New Grenada 313
New Hampshire 13, 24, 29, 32, 43, 188, 252, 295, 300-1
New Jersey 4, 7, 9, 11-3, 15, 20, 22-4, 26, 28, 43, 50, 52, 57, 70, 74, 81-2, 86, 97-8, 101, 142, 246, 300, 324-5, 329, 372
New Jersey Plan 23-4, 38, 123, 150, 287, 360
Newton, Isaac 90, 349
New York 7, 11-4, 21, 24, 28-9, 38, 43-4, 50, 58, 79, 97-8, 101, 104, 110, 113-7, 120-4, 126, 132, 134,

138-40, 142, 148, 191-6, 198-201, 207, 209-11, 254-5, 274, 287, 293, 299-302, 309, 320, 322, 324, 328-30, 333, 337, 357-8, 367
Niagara Falls 74
Nicholas, Robert Carter 242
Nicholas, Wilson Cary 158, 259, 267
Nicola, Lewis 329
North, *Lord* 9, 143, 327
North Carolina 8, 12-3, 25, 27-8, 43-4, 62, 171, 181, 216, 234, 276, 281-2, 286-7, 323, 360, 372-3
Northwest Territory 10, 15, 146, 183, 303, 345, 361

Ogden, Aaron 142
Ogden, David B. 210
Ogden, Samuel 195
Ohio 361
Ohio Company 83, 175, 177, 315, 319, 322
Oliver, Andrew 84, 85
Olmstead, Gideon 52, 355
Orders in Council 162, 164
Ordinance of 1787 10, 361
Otis, James 275, 349
Otto, G.W. 17
Oxford University 81, 192, 213

Paca, William 261
Pacheco, Josephine F. 181
Paine, Thomas v, 10, 63-4, 66, 173, 198, 207, 229-30, 255, 278, 354, 359, 380, 391
Parliament 5, 6, 9, 25, 42, 78-80, 82-5, 115, 164, 177, 182, 193, 212, 214, 270, 275, 299, 305, 320-1, 349-52, 360, 380-1
Parsons, James 272-3
Parsons, Theophilus 101
party politics 44, 156, 171, 204, 228-9, 236-7, 239, 256-7, 260, 346, 384
Paterson, William 13, 15, 22-3, 26, 28, 48, 57, 257, 287, 360
Patton, John 350
Paxton Boys 81

Payne, William 316
peace (views of framers) 385, 388-90
Peale, Charles Willson 355
Pendleton, Edmund 144
Pendleton, Nathaniel 13
Penn, Thomas 80, 81
Penn, William 298
Pennsylvania 4, 11-3, 20, 22, 28-9, 43, 45, 52, 55, 68, 70-1, 74, 78, 81-2, 86-7, 92, 97, 101, 132, 171, 175, 179, 181-2, 194, 199-202, 243, 255, 276, 287, 298, 301, 324, 327-9, 332, 349-59, 363-7, 371-3, 393
Phelps, Oliver 110
Philipse, Mary Eliza 316
Pickens, Andrews 234
Pickering, John 13
Pickering, Timothy 63-5, 136, 138, 165, 167, 229-30, 235, 259, 262-5, 267
Pierce, William 13, 25, 56, 100, 122, 149, 201, 285, 292, 359
Pinckney, Charles (cousin of Charles Cotesworth Pinckney) 219, 235; framer 13, 20-1, 27, 30, 32, 34, 38, 57, 100, 222-4, 249, 285, 287; legislator 97-8, 236; opponent of C.C. Pinckney 234, 236-8
Pinckney, Charles (father of Charles Cotesworth Pinckney) 212, 272
Pinckney, Charles Cotesworth 212-39, 263, 374, 383, 391; diplomat 63, 226-33, 386; framer 13-4, 20-1, 23, 26, 30-2, 57, 149, 222-4, 228, 285, 288, 379-80, 383, 387; lawyer 214, 220-2; legislator 214-5, 217, 222, 226, 237; presidential candidate 136, 235-8; ratifier 224-6; soldier 215-20, 227-8, 233-5, 286, 385; XYZ Affair 229-33; youth 212-4
Pinckney, Elizabeth 212-3, 221, 227, 239
Pinckney, Mary Stead 222, 229, 232-3, 237
Pinckney, Sarah Middleton 215, 221
Pinckney, Thomas 12, 134, 213, 216-20, 222, 227-9, 235-6, 238, 256, 260, 290, 346
Pinkney, William 160

Pitt, William 270, 318
Plater, Eliza 191
Plater, George 191
Plutarch 69, 113
Poland 199
"Poor Richard" 74, 76
The Pope 44, 108
Pope, Alexander 73, 113, 143
Portugal 83
prayer 1, 67, 144, 286
Preamble to Constitution 39, 202, 287, 308
Prescott, Arthur T. 44
Prescott, Richard 327
president 37-8, 42, 44, 56, 60, 103-4, 108, 132, 154, 202, 251, 288, 305-9, 360, 365, 378
Prévost, Augustine 218, 280-1
Prevost, George 166
Priestley, Joseph 144
Princeton College 13, 48, 55, 63, 114, 142, 295, 325
Pringle, John 89
Privy Council 4, 80, 84
property 29, 51, 92, 98, 115-6, 120, 155, 180-1, 193, 195, 201, 282, 288, 361, 365, 368, 379, 382
Prussia 85, 318
Publius Valerius 124
Pufendorf, Samuel von 114, 142, 192-3, 349, 385
Purcell, Thomas 371
Putnam, Israel 322, 324

Quartering Act 6, 83, 297
Quebec Act 6, 116, 177
Quesnay, François 82
Quincy, Josiah 91, 215, 385

Ramsay, David 358
Randolph, Betsy 242-3, 245-6, 254-5, 262, 267
Randolph, Edmund 147, 177, 240-68, 374, 391; attorney general 155, 254-9, 340, 342, 371, 384; Fauchet Affair 262-5; final years 266-8; framer 12, 14-5, 18-9, 21, 23, 33, 35, 37-8, 40, 57, 107, 149, 151, 186, 249-51, 258, 287, 333, 379; governor 246-8, 253-4, 380; lawyer 241-2, 255, 259, 262, 266-7, 370; legislator 146, 242-6, 254; ratifier 189, 251-3, 258; secretary of state 133, 227, 240, 259-66; youth 240-1
Randolph, John 240-1, 244-5
Randolph, John (of Roanoke) 161, 209, 255
Randolph, Peyton 240-1, 245
Randolph, Richard 209
ratification 40-4, 56-8, 60, 104, 107-8, 124-6, 150-3, 155, 171, 186-8, 203, 224-6, 250-3, 258, 289, 306-8, 335, 340, 363-7, 382
Read, George 13, 38
Read, Jacob 97
Read, William 289
Reardon, John J. 267
Reed, Joseph 198, 355
Regulators 99, 101
Reid, Thomas 348
religion 67-8, 70-1, 76, 83, 104, 108, 113-4, 135, 137, 139, 143-4, 147, 152, 154, 157, 169, 175, 181-4, 191-5, 197, 203, 210, 212-5, 217, 224, 230, 239, 243, 245, 249-50, 252, 268, 292-3, 295-8, 301, 309, 330-1, 336-8, 346, 348-9, 366, 368, 375, 377-80, 385-6, 390-2
"Report on Manufactures" 130, 381
Republic of South Carolina 278
Revolutionary War v, 7-9, 11, 16, 30, 45, 52, 54, 91, 116-21, 127-8, 130, 145, 147, 168-9, 182-3, 194-200, 204, 210, 215-21, 226-7, 231, 242, 244, 277-84, 288, 299-302, 305, 308, 310, 312, 321-30, 332, 341, 344, 346, 356, 361, 373, 383, 389, 391
Reynolds, Maria 135
Rhind, David 270
Rhode Island 4, 7, 8, 11-2, 17, 44, 50-1, 54, 58, 60, 75, 97, 104, 120, 152, 293, 295, 302, 328, 340, 362, 365
Richardson, Samuel 73, 74
Rivington, James 115, 194

Robertson, Donald 141
Robertson, William 348
Robespierre, Maximilien 260
Roche, John P. 34, 153, 384
Rodgers, John 114
Roosevelt, Franklin D. 168
Root, Jesse 48
Ross, George 357
Ross, Robert 166
Rossiter, Clinton 3, 16, 45-6, 57, 127, 312, 392
Rousseau, Jean Jacques 37, 88, 305
Rules Committee 17
Rush, Benjamin 11, 15, 48, 353-4, 358-9, 373
Rush, Richard 267
Russia 3, 9, 389
Rutledge, Andrew 269-70
Rutledge, Edward 12, 87, 215, 219-22, 226-8, 234-5, 237, 275, 284, 352
Rutledge, Elizabeth Grimké 272, 289
Rutledge, John 269-91, 374, 388, 391; dictator 280-4, 286, 384; framer 4, 13-4, 16-7, 21-2, 27, 29-30, 33, 37-8, 57, 100, 102, 104, 107, 149, 250, 285-9, 377, 379-80; judge 284-5, 289; lawyer 270-3, 275, 277, 284-6; legislator 54, 120, 216-7, 271, 276-8, 280, 284, 286; ruler 218, 278-80, 284, 286, 387; Supreme Court justice 60, 226-7, 289-90

St. Clair, Arthur 341, 352
Sainte-Beuve, Charles 90
Salomon, Haym 145, 199
Santo Domingo 234
Schuyler, Philip 50, 117, 119, 135, 138, 196, 301, 322, 326
Scudder, Nathaniel 197
Seabury, Samuel 114-5
secrecy, rule of 18, 46, 149, 151, 285-6, 364
Sedgwick, Theodore 158
Seed, Geoffrey 353
Senate 21-9, 34, 36-8, 56, 58-61, 101-3, 105-6, 123, 126-9, 137, 140, 150, 152-3, 156, 185, 187, 201-2, 205, 208, 210, 223, 248-50, 255, 258, 260, 262, 286-8, 290, 304-7, 309-10, 338, 341, 343, 346, 360-1, 364-5, 378
Shaftesbury, *Earl of* 349
Shakespeare, William 192, 203, 268, 270
Sharpe, Horatio 317
Shays, Daniel 11-2, 98-9, 148, 332-3
Sheridan, Richard Brinsley 338
Sherman, Elizabeth 294-5
Sherman, Isaac 300, 308
Sherman, John 292
Sherman, Rebecca 296
Sherman, Roger 292-311, 374, 381, 383, 389, 391; final years 307-11; framer 13-5, 20-2, 25, 30, 32, 35-6, 57, 149, 286-8, 303-7, 378, 380; judge 295-7, 310; lawyer 295, 298; legislator 51-2, 205, 295-303, 309-10, 377; public official 55, 295-7, 302-3, 311; tradesman 294-5
Sherman, William 292-4
Sherman, William Tecumseh 292
Shinner, Charles 273, 275
Shirley, William 79, 317
Short, William 344
Sidney, Algernon 37, 169, 179, 349
Silence Dogood 69
Skipworth, Fulwar 63
slavery 22, 29-31, 57, 93, 110, 121-2, 130, 146-7, 153, 163-4, 169-70, 174, 181, 185, 188, 195, 200-1, 212, 215, 221-5, 238, 244-5, 250, 252, 255-6, 266, 268, 271, 274, 281-2, 286-7, 309, 323, 331, 335, 347, 354, 371, 382
Smalley, John 48
Smith, Adam 15, 129, 348, 356, 380
Smith, Charles P. 355, 359, 361, 363, 368
Smith, Jonathan 109
Smith, Robert 162, 164
Smith, Samuel Stanhope 48, 142
Smith, Thomas 193
Smith, William 192-4
social compact 4, 15, 115, 192
Socrates 71, 89

Solomon 187, 379
Solon 89
South Carolina 3, 4, 8, 9, 12–3, 20, 22, 28–30, 43, 45, 54, 57, 97, 136, 153, 155, 162, 170, 188, 212–27, 234–8, 250, 256, 269–91, 328, 340, 379
Spaight, Richard 13
Spain 9, 12, 53, 63, 135, 146–7, 152, 159–60, 163, 198, 204–5, 228, 247, 257, 260–1, 281, 293, 323, 328, 331–3, 339, 345–6
Sparks, Jared 202
Stamp Act 5, 48, 81–4, 176, 213, 240, 274–5, 297, 320
Stamp Act Congress 5, 14, 274–5
state sovereignty 24, 56, 224–6, 249, 256, 300, 304, 306–7, 361, 364–5, 383, 389
states' rights 9, 21, 39, 56, 101, 169, 181, 253, 303–4, 334, 361, 389
Sterne, Laurence 203, 313
Steuben, Friedrich von 325, 331
Stevens, John Paul 375, 391
Stewart, James 356, 364
Stiles, Ezra 297, 301, 310, 362
Stoddert, Benjamin 236
Strong, Caleb 13, 27, 39, 100, 102, 107
Strong, Jedediah 296
Sugar Act 297, 349
Sullivan, John 120, 217, 327
Sully, *Duc de* 366
Sumter, Thomas 220, 282, 328
Supreme Court 4, 34–8, 47, 51–2, 59–63, 102–3, 125, 134, 170, 212, 226, 248, 255–7, 289, 305, 348, 355, 367, 369–72, 375, 379, 388
Susquehannah Company 298
Swain, Benjamin 109
Swift, Jonathan 143, 203
Swiggett, Howard 16
Switzerland 2, 269

Talleyrand, Charles de 64, 140, 204–5, 230–2
Taney, Roger 265
Tarleton, Banastre 220, 328
Tazewell, Henry 245

tea tax 5, 6, 298, 320
Temple, William 364
Tennant, William 279
Tennessee 234
terrorism (views of framers) 384–5, 388
Thatcher, Margaret 381–2
Thomas, Joseph 372
Thomson, Charles 97, 337
Thomson, James 73
Thornton, William 339
Tocqueville, Alexis de 3, 46, 291
Todd, Payne 157, 169
Tories 52, 54, 86, 115, 120–2, 144, 194–6, 198, 215, 221, 242, 245, 266, 279–80, 290–1, 300, 302, 331, 344, 386
Townshend Acts 83, 297–8, 320
treason 365
Trescot, William Henry 265
Tripoli 346, 391
Troup, Robert 114–5, 134
Trumbull, Jonathan 50, 52–5, 299
Trumbull, Jonathan, Jr. 66
Tryon, William 195, 322
Tucker, George 172
Tunis 160
Turgot, Robert Jacques 89
Tyler, John 11

Umbreit, Kenneth 59
unicameral legislature 20, 23, 367
United Nations 181, 369, 374, 388–90
Universal Declaration of Human Rights 181
University of Pennsylvania 73
University of Virginia v, 169

Van Buren, Martin 28
Van Doren, Carl 41, 79, 90, 94, 126, 390
Van Schaack, Peter 194
Venezuela 135
Vermont 136, 198, 301
Vernon, Edward 313
vice president 60, 104, 237, 305, 344

Villette, Madame de 232, 234
Virginia 3, 8–14, 18, 22, 25, 28, 30, 36, 39, 42–5, 52, 86, 97, 108, 124, 128, 141, 144–55, 169–70, 173–90, 203, 234, 243–9, 251–5, 257–8, 262, 267–8, 282–3, 286–7, 289, 313–23, 328–33, 335–7, 339–40, 344, 347, 351–3
Virginia Declaration of Rights 144–5, 179–82, 187–8, 190, 300
Virginia Plan 12, 17–20, 23–4, 27, 35, 38, 123, 149–51, 240, 248–50, 287
Virginia Resolutions 136, 158, 165, 167, 169–70, 234, 267, 346
Virginia Statute for Religious Freedom 147, 181, 183, 245
Volney, *Comte* de 64
Voltaire 88–90, 184, 232

Wallace, David D. 281
Walpole, Horace 85
Walpole, Thomas 86
Walton, George 13
War of the Austrian Succession 293
War of 1812 164–8, 210, 238
Ward, Artemas 96, 322
Ward, Edward 315
Warville, Brissot de 90
Washington, Augustine 313
Washington, Bushrod 268, 335, 339, 355
Washington, D.C. *see* District of Columbia
Washington, George 77, 112, 121, 157, 166, 189, 225, 289, 312–47, 375, 384–5, 389; final years 135, 137, 230, 233–6, 346–7; framer v, vi, 1–4, 7, 12, 14, 17–8, 27, 32, 37, 41, 45, 92, 100–1, 107, 109, 149, 152, 203, 222, 224, 247–8, 252, 286, 334–6, 373, 377, 391; general 50, 52, 54–5, 116–20, 182, 195–7, 210, 216–7, 220, 233–6, 241, 277–8, 282, 299–300, 302, 321–30, 334, 344, 346; legislator 318, 321; patriot 86–7, 176–8, 276–7, 320–1, 346, 352, 378; planter 174–5, 184, 245–6, 318–20, 330–4; president, first term 47, 59, 127, 130–2, 141, 153, 156, 191, 204–7, 226–7, 236, 254–9, 289, 296, 334, 336–44, 367, 371, 380, 391; president, second term 60, 99, 133–4, 168–9, 207, 227–8, 240, 259–66, 344–6, 383–4, 389; unique leadership 51, 126, 154, 158, 171–2, 178, 196, 207–8, 239, 268, 290, 312, 321, 327, 329, 345, 347; young military leader 314–8, 384–5; youth 313–4
Washington, George Augustine 333, 337
Washington, George Steptoe 157
Washington, John Augustine 316, 322, 333
Washington, Lawrence (half-brother of George) 175, 313–4
Washington, Lawrence (nephew of George) 255
Washington, Lund 322, 324, 328
Washington, Martha 157, 318–9, 322, 329–31, 347
Washington, Mary Ball 313, 316, 331, 337
Watson, James 208
Watts, Isaac 73, 293–4
Wayne, Anthony 260, 327–8, 341, 345
Webster, Daniel 58, 170, 172
Webster, Noah 9, 10, 50
Webster, Pelatiah 10
Wedderburn, Alexander 84, 143
Wellington, *Duke of* 167
Wells, John 281
Wemyss, James 220
Wentworth, John 293
Wentworth, Paul 88
Wesley, John 268
West, Benjamin 13
Western Reserve 303, 357
West Indies 7, 9, 80, 112–3, 116, 130, 147, 160, 262, 282, 285, 288, 297, 357, 371
Westminster Catechism 293
West Point 118, 328
West Virginia 15, 331
Whately, Richard 251
Whately, William 84–6
Whipple, William 197

Whiskey Rebellion 133, 156, 261, 345, 371, 384
White, Alexander 128
White, Billy 349-50
Whitefield, George 73, 75, 83, 270
Whitehead, Alfred North 189
Wickes, Lambert 88
Wilkes, John 214
William IV 347
William and Mary College 77, 142, 145, 241-2, 254
Williamson, Andrew 279
Williamson, Hugh 13-4, 21, 27, 287, 305
Willing, Thomas 356
Willis, Nelly 172
Wilson, Hannah 371-3
Wilson, James 348-73, 375, 377-8, 392; entrepreneur 290, 351, 355-8, 361, 371-2; final years 290-1, 372-3; framer 13-4, 16, 20-5, 27, 30-1, 33, 37-8, 42, 46, 56-7, 103-4, 107, 149-50, 223-4, 250, 285-7, 304, 359-63, 380, 383; lawyer 285, 349-51, 353, 355, 357, 363, 365, 368, 370; legislator 54, 120, 351-4, 358-9; ratifier 363-7; Supreme Court justice 61-2, 256, 259, 289-90, 370-3; world citizen 367-70, 386-90; youth 348-9

Wilson, Rachel 350, 354, 359
Wilson, Woodrow 168, 298
Winder, William 166
Wisconsin 361
Witherspoon, John 114, 142, 153
Wolcott, Oliver 63, 65, 262-3, 265
Wood, Thomas 193
world community 348, 367-70, 386, 388-90
world federation 390
Wyoming district land 92, 298, 301, 352, 357
Wythe, George 14, 17, 145, 182, 245, 253, 300, 370

XYZ Affair 229-33

Yale College 47-8, 63, 67, 77, 192, 297, 300-1, 310, 362
Yates, Robert 13, 14, 26, 122
Yazoo Case 160, 339

Zenger, John Peter 191

www.ingramcontent.com/pod-product-compliance
Lightning Source LLC
Chambersburg PA
CBHW051203300426
44116CB00006B/418